Torrents of Spring

SOVIET AND POST-SOVIET POLITICS

Torrents of Spring

SOVIET AND POST-SOVIET POLITICS

Jonathan R. Adelman
University of Denver

McGRAW-HILL, INC.

New York St. Louis San Francisco Auckland Bogotá
Caracas Lisbon London Madrid Mexico City Milan
Montreal New Delhi San Juan Singapore Sydney Tokyo Toronto

This book was set in New Century Schoolbook by ComCom, Inc.
The editors were Peter Labella and Fred H. Burns;
the production supervisor was Paula Keller.
The cover was designed by John Hite.
R. R. Donnelley & Sons Company was printer and binder.

TORRENTS OF SPRING
Soviet and Post-Soviet Politics

 This book is printed on recycled, acid-free paper containing 10%
postconsumer waste.

1 2 3 4 5 6 7 8 9 0 DOC DOC 9 0 9 8 7 6 5 4

ISBN 0-07-000359-9

Library of Congress Cataloging-in-Publication Data

Adelman, Jonathan R.
    Torrents of spring: Soviet and post-Soviet politics / Jonathan R.
    Adelman.
        p.   cm.
    Includes bibliographical references and index.
    ISBN 0-07-000359-9
    1. Soviet Union—History.   2. Former Soviet republics.   I. Title.
DK266.A475   1995
947—dc20   94-16403

About the Author

JONATHAN R. ADELMAN is professor in the Graduate School of International Studies at the University of Denver. He received his B.A. from Columbia College in 1969 and his Ph.D. in Soviet politics from Columbia University in 1976. Since then he has authored *The Revolutionary Armies* (1980), *Revolution, Armies and War* (1985), and *Prelude to the Cold War* (1988), and has coauthored *The Dynamics of Soviet Foreign Policy* (1988) and *Symbolic War: The Chinese Way of War, 1840–1980* (1993). Professor Adelman has also edited *Communist Armies in Politics* (1982), *Terror and Communist Politics* (1984), and *Superpowers and Revolution* (1986) and coedited *Contemporary Soviet Military Affairs: The Legacy of World War II.* His articles have appeared in a number of academic journals, including *Studies in Comparative Communism, Armed Forces and Society, Survey, International Journal of Public Administration,* and *Crossroads.*

Professor Adelman has been Lady Davis Visiting Associate Professor at the Hebrew University of Jerusalem (1986) and Visiting Professor at the University of Haifa (1990), both in Israel. He has also been Visiting Professor at Janus Pannonius University in Hungary (1991). In the last few years he has several times been visiting scholar at the Russian Academy of Sciences in Moscow and at Beijing University and People's University in Beijing. He has made five United States Information Agency speaking tours of countries ranging from Spain, Yugoslavia, and Germany to India, Hong Kong, and Japan. Currently he is on the Executive Committee of the Section on International Security and Arms Control of the American Political Science Association.

To My Father,
Benjamin Adelman,
A True Scientist.

Contents

Preface

Trotsky relates that shortly after the October Revolution, Lenin turned to him and in German proclaimed, "My head is swimming." So we too, specialists and students of the former Soviet Union, may wish to exclaim that our heads are swimming in the wake of the dizzying revolutionary events of the last decade. In the last eleven years the central regime in Moscow has had five leaders (Brezhnev, Andropov, Chernenko, Gorbachev, Yeltsin). Fifteen independent states, many of them quite unfamiliar to us (who can say anything about Kyrgyzstan or Turkmenistan?), have replaced one unified central state. The Soviet Union is gone, the Cold War is over, the once powerful Soviet military has fallen apart and splintered, and Russia and Ukraine are even quasi-allies of the United States. These revolutionary changes have destroyed our familiar postwar world and planted us firmly in *terra incognita*.

These revolutionary events demand a new kind of textbook to examine the swiftly changing realities of the former Soviet Union. We must find anchors for ourselves that will not be swiftly swept away by the continuing pace of revolutionary events. This will not be easy, given the rapid changes often induced by revolution. In the French Revolution the twelve years from 1792 to 1804 brought Monarchy, Convention, Directorate, Consulate, and Empire. And this was not the end. In 1814 there was restoration of the Bourbon monarchy, in 1815 a failed Bonapartist return, in 1830 revolution and the establishment of the Orleans monarchy, in 1848 revolution and the creation of the Second Republic, in 1851 the establishment of a new Bonapartist monarchy, in 1870 revolution, in 1871 the creation and failure of the Paris Commune, and soon thereafter the establishment of the Third Republic (which mercifully lasted until 1940).

We obviously need firm anchors in revolutionary times. In this volume, we suggest four major anchors, two of which are not usually found in other books (emphasis on fourteen non-Russian new states and the future directions of capitalism, democracy, and nation building), a third (history of the former Soviet Union) seldom provided in any depth, and a fourth that is a more traditional anchor (physical, social, and demographic realities, ideology, and organization). In Part One we begin in a traditional way, by providing a six-chapter overview of current developments. We review the physical, social, and demographic realities and the legacies of the old order (ideology, organization, planned economy). Then we place the former Soviet Union in a comparative framework with other Communist and revolutionary regimes.

In Part Two we devote seven chapters to a history of Tsarist Russia (one chapter) and the Soviet Union (six chapters). College students generally have a weak understanding of Soviet or Tsarist history. Yet history is not the account of a vanished past but a powerful force molding the former Soviet Union today. The old is still much with us, whether in restoring prerevolutionary names to Soviet cities (Saint Petersburg and Ekaterinoslav) and flying prerevolutionary flags or in recognizing the strong impact of Soviet authoritarianism, socialism, and imperialism on the popular consciousness. Students need to understand the past before they can grasp the present. This volume, by providing significantly more historical coverage than is common in such volumes, can give students a good basis on which to judge the present.

In Part Three we devote six chapters to the current Time of Troubles. The first two chapters update our understanding of the last eleven years in Soviet and post-Soviet history. Then in the next four chapters we turn to the histories of and current developments in all fifteen emerging states, ranging from Slavic Russia, Ukraine and Belarus (Chapter 16), Transcaucasus (Chapter 17), Central Asia and Kazakhstan (Chapter 18) to Moldova and the Baltics (Chapter 19). Few students know anything of these non-Russian states, and other books provide little coverage in this area. Yet these states have over 145 million people. Ukraine, Belarus, and Kazakhstan have nuclear weapons, and Central Asia has strategic significance. Civil wars have recently been fought, or are still being fought, in four of the new states (Azerbaijan, Moldova, Georgia, Tajikistan), and a major war is being waged between Armenia and Azerbaijan over Nagorno-Karabakh.

I spent seven happy years as a graduate student at Columbia University learning almost nothing about the fourteen non-Russian republics before receiving my Ph.D. in Soviet politics in 1976. I suspect my experience was not unique in the Moscow-centered world of the Sovietologist. The only book I remember reading on other republics was one on Ukraine by John Armstrong. In the past this might have been excusable, but today we need a detailed understanding of these vital emerging states, an understanding not provided in other books on the subject. In short, we need to retool.

Finally, in Part Four we provide three chapters on the future of democracy, capitalism, and nation building in the former Soviet Union. Again, this is new and we draw heavily on the academic literature on these subjects and on the numerous historical cases of successful and failed attempts to create democracy, capitalism, and a new nation.

In the final chapter we provide a brief epilogue reviewing some major themes in the book and considering possible future events.

In this volume we inevitably have not been able to cover everything. We have scouted institutions in the belief that they are changing so rapidly that only modest coverage is necessary or useful. We have downplayed traditional ideology (Marxism-Leninism), limiting ourselves to a discussion of its legacy and impact on the former Soviet Union. We believe this will not detract from the value of the book for these are not the needed foci in the 1990s.

In the face of ongoing revolutionary change in the former Soviet Union, the book will obviously need revision on a frequent schedule. But its stress on the fifteen emerging nations, the future of democracy, capitalism, and nationhood, and history, together with some traditional review of basic realities will, we hope, stand the test of time and respond to the revolutionary changes sweeping the former Soviet Union today.

ACKNOWLEDGMENTS

It is always a pleasure to acknowledge those who made the current volume possible. My earliest intellectual debts are to Seweryn Bialer. The following readers for McGraw-Hill have been uniformly most helpful: Linda J. Cook, Brown University; Evelyn Davidheiser, University of Minnesota–Minneapolis; Larry Elowitz, Georgia College; Roger Kanet, University of Illinois; Thomas Magstadt; Joseph Nyomarkay, University of Southern California; Donald Pienkos, University of Wisconsin–Milwaukee; Jane Rainey, Eastern Kentucky University; Leonas Sabaliunas, East Michigan University; Richard Siegel, University of Nevada–Reno; and Vladimir Wozniuk, Lafayette College. The editors at McGraw-Hill, first Bertrand Lummus and now Peter Labella, have always been thorough professionals in helping to shepherd this project from first to last.

As ever, the home front is very important. I wish to thank my father for his ever-present help in times of need. My wife, Dora, and my son, David, have been extremely important parts of my life in making all this possible.

Jonathan R. Adelman

Torrents of Spring

SOVIET AND POST-SOVIET POLITICS

PART ONE

Overview of Current Developments

How can we understand a part of the world that encompasses 8.5 million square miles (almost three times the size of the United States) and eleven time zones and has suddenly produced fifteen new states? This is a daunting task for students, and in the first six chapters we provide an overview of developments in the former Soviet Union (FSU). We sketch out in the early chapters the physical, social, and demographic realities often unfamiliar to students. Then we look at the legacy of the seventy-four years of Soviet rule, a legacy of planned economy, Marxist ideology, and highly centralized and bureaucratized organization of society. In the final chapter we turn to a comparison of the Soviet experience with that of other states and a study of post-Soviet politics. The student is then prepared for the lengthy historical section in Part Two.

1

Introduction

In December 1991 the Soviet Union, a superpower bristling with 1000 ICBMs, 27,000 nuclear weapons, 6000 jet fighters, 45,000 tanks, 4 million troops, and 500,000 KGB troops, simply and peacefully dissolved.[1] This stunning event ended the Cold War and transformed international politics.

How are we to understand the fifteen successor states (here called the FSU, or Former Soviet Union) to a country so vast that it encompassed almost half of two continents but belonged fully to neither Europe nor Asia? Even more important, why should we care? If history is made by the winners and we Americans admire success, why should we study the tattered remnants of a failed ideology and nations with poor chance of making the transition to democracy, capitalism and nation building? Yet this is an area that has had a powerful impact on the rest of the world, particularly in the twentieth century, and its impact is likely to continue, for better or for worse.

ROLE IN TWENTIETH CENTURY

Tsarist Russia and the Soviet Union played a powerful role in determining the fate of European and world politics in the twentieth century. Even weak Tsarist Russia helped the Triple Entente that defeated the Triple Alliance in World War I. The Russian withdrawal from the war after the October Revolution opened the door for the five great German offensives that brought the Germans perilously close to victory in the spring and early summer of 1918. The October

---

[1]This peculiarly peaceful implosion will need to be explained in the light of totalitarian theories. The comparison of the Soviet Union with Nazi Germany would lead one to expect the end to come not in a whimper but in an Armageddon, in a Germanic Götterdämmerung, like Hitler's final stand in the Berlin bunker.

Revolution introduced the revolutionary socialism that was to challenge the international order after World War II.

During the 1920s the weak Soviet Union had little impact in world affairs. But in the early 1930s Soviet failure to push the Communists to unify with the Socialists in Germany helped the Fascists to gain power in 1933. The short-lived Ribbentrop-Molotov Pact in August 1939, which divided Eastern Europe between Russia and Germany, sealed the doom of Poland and launched World War II. At a cost of 27 million Russian deaths, the Red Army ultimately drove the invading German Wehrmacht out of Soviet territory and eliminated over 2 million men permanently from the German army by June 1944. In the final year of the war, the Soviet drive to Berlin, together with the Anglo-American advance in the west, sealed the fate of the Third Reich and laid the base for the Cold War.[2]

The Cold War from 1947 to 1989 pitted the Soviet Union and its allies in Eastern Europe and Asia against the United States and the West. This titanic struggle, ultimately won by the United States and the West, was the central axis of international politics for most of the second half of the twentieth century.

FUTURE ROLE

Despite significant current problems with pay, personnel, redeployment from Eastern Europe, morale, and transition to a volunteer army, Russia will likely in a few years merit Boris Yeltsin's recent boast that the Russian army is "powerful, organized and disciplined."[3] Today, it has 18,000 nuclear weapons, over 40,000 tanks, and nearly 2 million troops. Even after deep cuts, Russia will retain a formidable force and powerful military-industrial complex.[4] In the nuclear arena, a Russia with even 5000 nuclear weapons would still be the number two nuclear power in the world. Other nuclear powers, such as China, India, France, and Israel, have only a few hundred nuclear weapons and limited delivery systems. Only China has intercontinental ballistic missiles, and none of them have developed nuclear submarines capable of delivering MIRVd weapons. Russia's huge land mass (6 million square miles) in the center of Eurasia—bordering on Eastern Europe in the west, Iran and Afghanistan in the south, and China in the east—gives it a major strategic advantage over the West. The Middle East, 5600 miles from Washington, is only 300 to 400 miles from Russia.

The non-Russian states of the FSU will also have military and political

---

[2]See Jonathan Adelman, *Prelude to the Cold War*, Lynne Rienner Publications, Boulder, Colorado, 1988.

[3]See Gabriel Schoenfeld, "Troops or Consequences," *Post-Soviet Prospects*, no. 21, September 1993.

[4]The vast and powerful research complex of the Soviet Union included 1.5 million scientists and engineers, largely in military research. After the collapse of the Soviet Union, 95 percent of them remained in Russia, creating a strong base for future growth, despite currently desperate economic circumstances and emigration abroad. See Tim Beardsley, "Selling to Survive," *Scientific American*, February 1993.

significance. The struggle among Russia, Turkey, and Iran for influence over the nearly 50 million Moslems in Kazakhstan and Central Asia reflects their importance. Belarus, Ukraine, and Kazakhstan have retained nuclear weapons, although they are now committed to eventually eliminating them. Yet if it succeeds in its efforts to hold onto some of its Black Sea Fleet and nuclear weapons and build a 400,000-man army, Ukraine may develop into a major regional actor.

This military power in the region of the FSU will be enhanced by the disarmament of much of the rest of the world. In addition to halving its troop strength in Europe to 150,000 men, the United States is committed to major reductions in its overall military strength (perhaps down to a 560,000-man army). NATO is forgoing nuclear theater modernization, and Germany, the once-feared power, will reduce in its armed forces to 370,000 troops, 4000 tanks, and no nuclear weapons. In Asia Japan, with only 250,000 troops and no nuclear weapons, devotes only 1 percent of its GNP to the military. The United States is closing down much of its operation in South Korea and the Philippines. Only China is pursuing a limited buildup. With the two great military powers of World War II (Germany and Japan) militarily emasculated and the United States sharply reducing its military spending, even a diminished Russian and Ukrainian military power will be potent.

On the economic front, any possible success, however unlikely, would transform Russia or a Slavic bloc with Ukraine and Belarus into a renewed economic giant. Russia retains enormous assets—the best array of natural resources in the world, the second best scientific establishment, the second largest number of college-educated people, the fourth largest population, the fourth largest economy.[5] A prosperous and democratic series of states would form a major pole in international politics and economics, together with North America, Western Europe, and Japan.

The other likely possibilities—a civil war within Russia or Ukraine, war among key republics, or contribution to nuclear proliferation—would have devastating consequences for the rest of the world. In the last Russian civil war (1918–1920), 11 million people died—of disease or from secret police killings, battlefield slaughter, and pogroms. Reds, Whites, Greens, and Blacks, with troops from twenty-six foreign nations mixed in, battled for two and a half years until the fabric of society came apart. Today, the horror of civil war seems too awesome to contemplate in a world of advanced conventional and nuclear capabilities and delivery systems.[6] But it remains a possibility.

Another possibility would be war among the larger successor states. Already, Azerbaijan is fighting Armenia over Nagorno-Karabakh, and there have been civil wars within Georgia and Tajikistan. If Russia and Ukraine fail

[5]The scientific establishment was able to keep the Soviet Union on a par militarily with the United States. Today, the United States employs over 3000 Russian scientists. See Tim Beardsley, "Selling to Survive," *Scientific American,* February 1993, p. 95.
[6]See Jonathan Adelman, *The Revolutionary Armies,* Greenwood Press, Westport, Connecticut, 1980, on the Russian and Chinese civil wars.

to make the transition to capitalism, democracy, and nation building, a battle between them would be possible. Russians, including Yeltsin, do not genuinely support Ukrainian independence and view the Crimea and perhaps Eastern Ukraine as part of their territory.[7] Ukrainians, remembering the Tsarist past, Stalin's murder of 5 to 7 million peasants in the 1932–1933 Ukrainian famine, the millions of victims of collectivization and Great Purges, and Soviet attempts to repress Ukrainian independence, have their own strong grievances. History has shown that newly emerging nations and strong minority groups with ties to external powers have not mixed well—and there are 11 million Russians in Ukraine.

In a world with many nations (such as Iran, Iraq, and Libya) eager for nuclear technology, how long will Russian (and Ukrainian) nuclear technology and their 15,000 tactical nuclear weapons remain locked up within the FSU? Especially when Russian nuclear scientists are making less than $30 a month?[8]

Any move by the Central Asian republics and Kazakhstan, which will have over 100 million people before the year 2040, towards Islamic fundamentalism would have significant impact beyond their borders and would transform Iran from an international outcast to a major player in the region.

Finally, there remain the muddling down or muddling through options. Currently, Russia and Ukraine have been muddling down, with massive economic and political problems, but little violence. This is likely to continue in the short run but is unlikely in the long run, especially given the violent past of the FSU. Even a lengthy continuation of this option would seriously impact Western Europe and Asia, for the FSU occupies 40 percent of Asia and 40 percent of Europe. Uncertainty and disorder in an area this size makes the rest of the world uneasy.

VALUE OF PREDICTIONS

Past predictions about Russia and the Soviet Union have been notoriously wrong, and we should be wary about making any now.[9] In 1914 the Anglo-French forces eagerly awaited the arrival of the Russian steamroller into Berlin; it was delayed by only thirty-one years! In October 1917 the West was stunned by the Bolshevik seizure of power, and during the Russian civil war the West expected that the Whites, with Western support, money, and arms, would rout the Bolsheviks; the Whites were destroyed. Few believed in the 1930s that Stalin

[7]At a Washington conference with the Russian Foreign Ministry attended by the author in April 1993, a Russian speaker related how the Russian Embassy in Warsaw warned the Poles not to get too close to the new Ukrainian state since "soon there won't be a Ukrainian state any more."

[8]The 1992 Bush program to employ Russian nuclear scientists on American payrolls was only a small start in preventing a possible nightmare.

[9]The remoteness of the Soviet Union, veil of secrecy, rigid Soviet authoritarianism, and the lack of information have made the art of prediction extremely chancy. For ideas about improving post-Sovietology, see Frederic Fleron, Erik Hoffman, Edward Walker, "Whither Post-Sovietology?" *Harriman Institute Forum,* vol. 6, nos 6–7, February–March 1993.

could turn a backward Soviet Union into a powerful country; he did. No one bothered to invite the Soviet Union to the Munich conference that settled the fate of Czechoslovakia; shortly thereafter the Russian-German pact settled the fate of Poland. In June 1941 the official estimate on the desks of President Roosevelt and other Western leaders was that the Germans would smash into the Soviet Union in the summer and take Moscow; stubborn resistance and the Russian winter destroyed the invaders. Similarly, in 1945, after the dropping of two atomic bombs on Japan, General Lesley Groves, the head of the Manhattan project, declared that it would take the Soviet Union at least twenty years to build a bomb; in 1949 the Soviet Union exploded an atomic bomb. The West was surprised in the Khrushchev era both by the space and military spectaculars of 1957 and 1959 and by the 1956 denunciation of Stalin. The 1964 coup against Khrushchev was unexpected. In 1985 the selection of Mikhail Gorbachev as the new leader of the party led most to conclude that little major change was in the offing. In 1991 the ineptitude of the August military-security coup, which arrested Raisa Gorbachev but not Boris Yeltsin and controlled the Baltics but not Leningrad, shocked many foreign observers. This record leads us to proceed with caution when predicting the future.

DISTINCTIVE RUSSIAN PATH

Behind this abysmal record of prediction is the difficulty of understanding a country and regime very different from the United States and the West in terms of history, geography, politics, and culture. While the West for centuries was moving toward capitalism, democracy, and nation building, Moscow was moving towards state-run development, autocracy, and empire. Tsarist Russia was the "third Rome" (after the fall of Rome and Constantinople) for international Orthodox Christianity, and Soviet Russia became the "socialist fatherland" for international socialism. This divergence from Western trends lasted for over 600 years for Russia, until 1989.

Tsarist Russia continued serfdom until the 1860s, centuries after it had disappeared from Western Europe. While Western governments were extending the democratic franchise in the nineteenth century, the Tsarist regime was rejecting even a parliament until the 1905 Revolution and then trying to emasculate the four Dumas that met before 1917. With democracy advancing rapidly in the West, Tsar Nicholas II in the 1890s proclaimed his allegiance to medieval Muscovy, absolute monarchy, and the trinity of autocracy, orthodoxy, and Russia. The Provisional Government's semi-democratic interlude after the February Revolution lasted but eight months until ended by the October Revolution.

The Bolshevik seizure of power set Russia on an authoritarian, socialist course strikingly different from that of the West. The 1920s gave some brief hope of a move toward the Western route, but the 1930s, with Stalin's massive state-directed industrialization and modernization and centrally planned economy, turned the Soviet Union in a different direction. So too did the massive state-sponsored terrorism, culminating in the Great Purges, the erection of a large-scale forced-labor empire, the forcible deportation of millions of *kulaks*, and the state's connivance in a famine that killed millions of Ukrainians in the early 1930s. During the war the Soviet Union, after a short dalliance with Nazi Germany, did ally with the West but they remained strange bedfellows. The postwar Stalin era, with its renewal of purges, cultural orthodoxy, secrecy, and isolation, again widened the gap with the West. Although Khrushchev and Brezhnev did modernize the regime, stop the terror, and introduce certain reforms, the Soviet Union continued to battle the West in the Cold War. Only during the Gorbachev era (1985–1991) did this conflict begin to ease off. Still, there remains significant popular support in Russia for many aspects of the old regime, although not for the party and its privileges.

Authoritarian in politics, socialist in economy, enormous and largely cold in climate and geography, the FSU was far from the West in theory and practice. The notions of state ideology, ruling party, and officially sanctioned elite have had no real parallel in the West for hundreds of years, save during the brief Fascist era. Now, as we begin to enter the twenty-first century, the question is how far the gap will close now that the old Communist authoritarian mold has been broken and the party has been liquidated.

A major problem for Western observers is the enormous gap between various sectors of the society. The military of the Soviet Union in the 1980s was a First World military, but its consumer sector a veritable Third World sector with dreadful housing, inadequate food, and terrible services. The combination of 19 million university-educated citizens and the world's second best scientific establishment with 24 million peasants working largely by hand in the fields is mind-boggling. Very little was mediocre. Things were either very good (science, culture, military, education) or very bad (services, consumer goods, housing). Conceptually, this has been very difficult for Western observers.

MODELING THE FUTURE

In this context, traditional Western models have only limited applicability. Where should we start?

First, there is the muse of history. In this book we give serious weight to the history of the Soviet Union and its Tsarist legacy. Only through understanding the very different history of this country, from Lenin to Gorbachev and Yeltsin, can we hope to understand current developments. The book covers Soviet history from Lenin to Gorbachev and developments in the FSU since the dissolution of the Soviet Union in December 1991.

We need to give serious attention to the physical and demographic constraints on the area. In the West, state and society are in balance, with society often more important than the state. Traditionally, Russia has had a powerful state and a weak society.

We need to see the Soviet Union as a revolutionary state, from the February and October 1917 revolutions to Stalin's "revolution from above" in the 1930s and the 1991 Second Russian Revolution that dissolved the Soviet Union. The 1917 revolutions created a powerful state; the 1991 revolution has yet to bear serious fruit. There are parallels with revolutionary France (the 1789, 1830, 1848, and 1871 revolutions) and China (the 1911, 1949, and attempted 1989 revolutions), where revolutions have lasted for generations rather than a decade or two.

We need to look at the Third World for models. Most Russians and non-Russians are either peasants or the children of peasants. This has contributed deeply to the passivity, fatalism, and respect for authority that are so pervasive in their political culture. The poor standard of urban living, the harsh life, the political authoritarianism, the power of the military and secret police, elite privileges, ethnic strife, external invasions, and military coup attempts that seem natural in the Third World seem equally natural to many in the FSU.

TOWARDS DEMOCRACY, CAPITALISM AND NATIONHOOD

The economic, political, and cultural institutions that have historically been the prerequisites for democracy, capitalism, and nation building are largely lacking in the FSU.

Economically, the system in the FSU was authoritarian socialism—huge enterprises were expected to respond to the will of the central planners. There was no cult of the entrepreneur, little private property, no concept of prices or profits and minimal market. Marketing and advertising were irrelevant and consumer preferences largely ignored. Quantity, not quality, heavy industry, not consumer industry, were the order of the day.

For the FSU the capitalist path is strewn with obstacles. Any rapid transition to a market economy will probably lead to massive unemployment, high inflation, and substantial dislocation. In 1993 the alternative to a 2000 percent inflation rate in Russia seemed to be a possible leap in the unemployment rate from 1 percent to 20 percent or even 30 percent. Given the huge size of the economy and population, foreign assistance can be helpful but of only limited impact. Retraining the population to work hard and the managers to respond to market forces will be a lengthy and difficult process. There are only twenty to twenty-five First World countries in the world, located largely in Western Europe and North America. Recent success stories—notably the Four Tigers of Asia—were smallish countries in the Western orbit, former Western or Japanese colonies with strong Confucian influence, trade-driven economies with a strong commercial drive. None of this applies to the FSU.

There is no real model for change out there. The earlier Soviet attempts at reform—NEP, the 1965 Kosygin reform, the Gorbachev reforms—were failures. The Eastern European models, from East Germany to Hungary and Yugoslavia, were discredited by the events of 1989 and their inability to create modern, sophisticated economies. Western and Japanese models contain so many elements that are foreign to the FSU that they will be of limited utility.

The path to democracy seems equally strewn with obstacles. Only twenty-five countries have been long-term democracies—and they too have been largely concentrated in North America and Western Europe. A strong middle class, a civic political culture, durable legal norms and values, public commitment to democracy, a multi-party system, and an independent judiciary are common to democratic societies. And the FSU? A history of ruthless authoritarianism and absolutism—Tsarist or Communist, a weak middle class, terror and secret police rule, no commitment to democracy, no free press, and a one-party system have been the norm. The authoritarianism of Leonid Kravchuk in Ukraine and the despotism in many republics in Transcaucasus and Central Asia come as no surprise. In Russia democracy is very tenuous, a brief flower of three or four years' growth under another authoritarian, Yeltsin.

Finally, there is nation building, a rather dismal topic in the Third World in the 1960s and 1970s. Tsarist Russia, followed by the Soviet Union, was an empire, and never a nation, for over 600 years. For most of the fourteen non-Russian successor states to the FSU, the situation is even worse. Ukraine, Belarus, Central Asia, Transcaucasus, and Moldova all lack any real national past or even many of the prerequisites for nationhood. Only the Baltics had some, if limited, experience as independent nations in the interwar period.

The FSU must find its own way, incorporating elements of foreign models into a distinctive product. It is too early to pronounce the success or failure of such an effort. Two things are certain: The birth will be long and difficult, if it succeeds at all, and whatever happens will have real impact on the rest of the world.

2

FSU: The Physical Realities

For American students to understand the FSU takes a leap of imagination.[1] During the Cold War, relatively few American students visited the Soviet Union. Now, unstable conditions in the fifteen successor states have discouraged travel there. Russian and Soviet history are known to only a small number of American students. Geography and climate have seemed unimportant to Americans, a dull subject safely relegated to junior high school.

However, geography and climate have been vitally important to the United States and the FSU. With three thousand miles of ocean to the east and over five thousand miles of ocean to the west, coupled with relatively weak neighbors in Canada and Mexico, the United States has not been invaded since the War of 1812. In two world wars the United States could remain aloof from the conflict for over two years before entering the war (1917, 1941). Even in World War II neither Germany nor Japan was able to mount any attack on the American mainland. In the postwar era the United States fought wars in Korea, Vietnam, and the Persian Gulf, many thousands of miles away from American shores.

Climate and land have been beneficial, not problematic, factors for the United States. It enjoys a relatively temperate climate which promotes the large food surpluses of the Middle West. The bulk of the country is relatively flat, with the Appalachians and Rocky Mountains obstructing neither transportation nor communication. The long coastlines have created a strong natural setting for dynamic growth on the East Coast and West Coast.

---

[1]Obviously, to use CIS (Commonwealth of Independent States) would be aesthetically more pleasing and optimistic than FSU (former Soviet Union). Yet with the Baltics and several other republics, including Azerbaijan, opting out of the CIS, and with other states only on its periphery, for now we must stay with FSU to be accurate.

By contrast, in the territory of the FSU the lack of a flourishing natural environment and defensible frontiers has placed great strains on the state to provide the basic needs of the population for food, clothing, shelter, and defense. These physical realities have promoted the power of the state and the weakness of society. While a flourishing natural environment and temperate climate promoted strong civil society and weak state in the United States, in Tsarist Russia and the Soviet Union only state mobilization of all resources has provided defense against natural and human threats to security and existence.[2] The harshness of the climate, physical separation from the West, and lack of warm-water ports have limited Western influence in offsetting these intense physical problems. Geography and climate have not predetermined political and economic outcomes, but they have placed major obstacles in the path of a Russian and Soviet development along more familiar Western lines.

GEOGRAPHIC OVERVIEW

The broad geographic features of the FSU have only slight resemblance to those of the United States. There is the same vast size of continental proportion with large internal distances. However, the FSU, with its 8.6 million square miles making up one-sixth of the earth's surface, is nearly three times the size of the United States. The FSU is 3700 miles north to south, and it measures a staggering 6000 miles east to west. With eleven time zones, the sun is coming up at 8:00 a.m. on the Russo-Polish border in the west when it is already set in the Bering straits in the east at 7:00 p.m. The FSU stretches from Arctic icy wastes and tundras in the north to deserts and the subtropics in the south.[3]

The bulk of the vast territory, over 70 percent, is occupied by the Russian Republic, with 6.5 million square miles. Kazakhstan occupies over 1 million square miles, Ukraine 240,000 square miles, and then there is a series of twelve smaller states with less than 1 million square miles all together. (See Table 2.1.) By contrast, the United States and China have roughly 3.6 million square miles each, France 211,000 square miles, and Germany 134,000 square miles.

Much of the territory of the FSU consists of icy and relatively worthless real estate. No less than 40 percent (or 3.5 million square miles) of the FSU—an area larger than the territory of the United States—consists of permanently frozen subsoil in areas with temperatures below freezing for most of the year. The surface thaws in summer, but the subsoil remains frozen from a depth of 60 to 670 feet. There are an additional 2 million square miles of desert and semidesert. Only a third of the territory is reasonably temperate. The United States has

---

[2]By civil society we mean here a situation where the power of the society exceeds that of the state, where the rights of the individual and the power of intermediate structures (interest groups, corporations, religious bodies, etc.) exceed and limit those of the state.

[3]For this section, see James Gregory, *Russian Land, Soviet People*, Pegasus, New York, 1968, chapter 1; and Georges Jorre, *The Soviet Union: Its Land and Its People*, John Wiley and Sons, New York, 1967, chapter 7.

**TABLE 2.1. Land Mass of
the Fifteen Successor States
to the Soviet Union**

(millions of square miles)	
Russia	6.56
Kazakhstan	1.06
Ukraine	.24
Turkmenistan	.18
Uzbekistan	.15
Belarus	.08
Kyrgyzstan	.07
Tajikistan	.06
Georgia	.03
Azerbaijan	.03
Lithuania	.02
Latvia	.02
Estonia	.02
Moldova	.01
Armenia	.01
	8.64

Source: Michael Florinsky, editor, *Encyclopedia of Russia and the Soviet Union,* McGraw-Hill, New York, 1961.

twice as much arable territory (24 percent:11 percent) and permanent pastures and meadows (33 percent:16 percent) as the FSU. Only in wastelands and urban cities does the FSU have the lead (36 percent:10 percent).

The FSU is located north of the bulk of the United States. Most of its territory is on the same latitudes as Canada with its Great Plains north of our Great Lakes. Moscow is 250 miles north of London, at the latitude of Glasgow, and Saint Petersburg, 500 miles north of London, is at the latitude of southern Greenland. Arkhangel, an important port, is but 120 miles from the Arctic Circle. In the far south, Volgograd (former Stalingrad) is at the latitude of Paris and Yalta at the latitude of Bordeaux. The most southerly point in Kazakhstan is at the latitude of Gibraltar, on the southern coast of Spain. During winter snow spreads over all the FSU except a small part of the Crimean coast. There is almost no easy access to warm water ports with much of the coast icebound throughout the year. The FSU is almost landlocked, occupying a vast plain. The Volga River functions as an inland sea.

Population density varies enormously, ranging from 600 people per square mile in the Moscow region to 25 to 40 in nonindustrial Siberia to near zero in the Aralo-Caspian desert, the northern tundra, the Caspian steppe and the Russian-Siberian forests. The Russians occupy a vast Great Plain that straddles two continents without significant frontiers. In the west the Swedes, Lithuanians, Poles, and Germans, in the east the Chinese and Japanese, and in the south the various Asian nations have been enemies. There are no natural defense zones, such as oceans or mountains, to divide the FSU from many of its fourteen neighbors.

CLIMATE AND TERRAIN

Great differences in climate and terrain have impacted the development of the state. Although they have not determined the nature of the state, they have set great obstacles on its development in a manner more familiar to Western students. As James Gregory has observed,

> climate influences the evolution of people as well as soils, and not only the climate of today but that of preceding centuries. During successive generations the Russians have struggled with the forces of nature in the Plains and there can be little doubt that a process of selection has taken place which has given the people their characteristic toughness and strongly influenced their attitude to life. Driven from the more clement climate of the wooded steppe to the harsher environment of the Oka-Volga region, they came to terms with nature through a long period of hardship. . . . Later in their history the Russians had to try to come to terms with another type of climatic environment, that of the steppe, where the severe winter, lack of deep snow, and drought are problems which have to be overcome even today.[4]

The general severity of weather is well known. The bulk of the territory is at a high latitude with no mountains to break Arctic winds and no barriers to Asian winds. The moderating influence of the Mediterranean is diminished by the Carpathian, Caucasus, and Balkan mountain ranges; the influence of the Atlantic, by the mountains of Scandinavia. With a weak sea impact (unlike the situation for the United States and Great Britain), the continental aspect is dominant. This means little rain, strong winds, marked temperature variations, and a short spring and fall. The small exceptions to this are in a part of the Far East with significant moisture and monsoon climate, the subtropical Transcaucasus with hot summers and mild winters and the southern coast of the Crimea with a Mediterranean climate. The rest of the FSU knows the harshness of an icy winter and the dry heat of summer. The east, south, and center are routinely invaded by Siberian high pressure fronts in the winter. Long and hard winters mean that the far north averages below freezing temperatures seven months of the year. Saint Petersburg knows frost for five to six months, Moscow for four to five months and Kiev for three to four months.[5]

There are four distinctive regions. The most famous, the Arctic region, encompasses Eastern Siberia, the polar zone, the Bering Sea, and the Barents coast. Here in winter average days in Eastern Siberia can be 22 to 40 degrees below zero, North Polar days 40 degrees below zero, and Pacific days 13 degrees below zero. Summers can reach a balmy 40 degrees. This severe climate obviously prevents any serious human activity. The second zone, the sub-Arc-

[4]Gregory, *Russian Land, Soviet People*, p. 230.
[5]Jorre, *The Soviet Union: Its Land and Its People*, chapter 3.

tic zone, is a little more bearable, but at times not much. In Central Siberia in January the temperature can reach 40 degrees below zero, in Eastern Siberia 58 degrees below zero. Summer days can be in the 50s and 60s. But winter blizzards and frozen ground can yield three months of night.

The third zone, the Temperate Zone, encompasses the Atlantic-Arctic Forest. In January in the west the average is 5 degrees above zero, in the east 13 degrees below zero. Summer days can be in the 50s and 60s. The final zone, the Subtropics, sees January days with an average of 25 to 45 degrees and hot summer days in the high 70s and 80s.

The bulk of the FSU, and especially Russia, is subject to severe climate with hard and long winters, quick spring thaws that turn the roads to mud, and early autumn frost. Spring in April and May brings massive breakups of ice on rivers with large scale floods and enormous quantities of mud. Summer in the north means white nights (virtually no darkness) in Saint Petersburg with wondrous sunsets. In January the mean temperature ranges from 46 degrees below zero in Yakutsk and 59 degrees below zero in Verkhoyansk and 4 degrees below zero in Vladivostok and Irkutsk to over 32 degrees in the Southern Crimea and Central Asia. Snow remains on the ground in Eastern Siberia for up to eight months a year, compared to two or three months in Ukraine and almost never in Central Asia and the South Caucasus.

Life in Siberia is especially difficult. In winter there is nothing to stop the chilly blasts from the Arctic while the Atlantic and Pacific are prevented from moderating the Arctic winds. The winters are very long but without deep snow, and the summers are very hot but short. In the worst place, like Verkhoyansk, winters can reach 95 degrees below zero while hot summers exceed 100 degrees, a world record annual swing of 140 to 160 degrees. Northern Siberia experiences frost nine or ten months a year. Winter ends only in April with mass flooding in a very short spring followed by a short hot summer. Thunder, whirling dust, hail, and hordes of mosquitos mark this short summer, followed by frosts in August, ice in the river by September, and real winter in October. Within Siberia there is marked variation, from eighty-seven days of snow in Yeniseisk in Central Siberia to only twenty-seven days of snow in Irkutsk and nine days of snow in Blagoveshchensk in Eastern Siberia.

Summers are also variable, with mean temperatures on the East Siberian coast and in northern Russia in the 40s, in Kiev and Kazan around 65 degrees, and in Central Asia around 86 degrees. Rainfall varies enormously, from an arid six to eight inches in the Aralo-Caspian Sea area in the south to sixteen inches in Central and Eastern Siberia and twenty to twenty-four inches in the west of Russia. The relatively modest rainfall reflects the remoteness of the Atlantic, the shallowness of the Baltic, the inaccessibility of the Indian Ocean, and the size and location of the lakes.[6]

For Moscow the impact is relatively severe by American standards. The average temperature stays below freezing from late October until the middle of April, for almost six months. In December, January, and February the mean

---

[6]Gregory, *Russian Land, Soviet People*, chapters 3–4; Jorre, *The Soviet Union: Its Land and Its People*, chapter 3.

temperature is a trying 12 to 17 degrees. Spring comes late in April and then is rapidly followed by summer with three months in the 60s.[7]

REGIONS OF FSU

We could compare the Center and Donets-Dnieper region with older Western European industrial regions and Belarus, Ukraine, and Central Black Earth regions with rural Western Europe. Siberia is similar to Canada and Central Asia, and Azerbaijan to Southwest Asia. Almost half of Russian territory, in Eastern Siberia and the Far East, has but 6 percent of the population and only one major city (Krasnoyarsk).[8]

There are four major climatic zones. The most famous is the massive tundra zone of the far north comprising 15 percent of Russian territory, or more than 1.2 million square miles (an area equal to 40 percent of the United States). The tundra occupies a zone 70 to 150 miles wide in European Russia and 300 to 400 miles wide in Western Siberia. Here severe winters, violent winds, short growing season, dry climate (6 to 7 inches of precipitation a year), frozen and poor soil and shallow roots have deprived the terrain of any trees. Long, cold, and dark winters can easily reach 40 degrees below zero and the short summers are in the 50s. The flat glacial surface is broken by bogs and marshy soil without vegetation. The tundra is famous for its reindeer and the 100,000 native people who herd them. Each of the 2 million reindeer can migrate 100 to 500 miles and roam an average of one square mile. The small native populations lead a harsh life, hunting, fishing, and breeding reindeer over difficult terrain.[9]

The second major climatic zone is that of the great Russian-Siberian forest that stretches over almost 50 percent of the terrain of the FSU, or a territory greater than that of the United States. The taiga zone includes massive damp and spongy forests with peat bogs and marshes that inhibit travel. This enormous forest belt extends from the Baltic to the Pacific, from the White Sea to the Black Earth steppes (see below). It includes such famous areas as Saint Petersburg, Moscow, and the Urals. Moscow itself was originally a town in an open space in the forest. The Ural mountains, isolated in the middle of the Great Plains, are 110 miles wide and 1500 miles long. The quality of the grayish soil is poor and dry. The texture resembles plastic clay. The winters are long and hard, and the summers moist and moderately warm. Bears, wolves, foxes, and fish are numerous in the Siberian sector of the forest. For Russians today this vast forest helps to define not only the geography and space of the country but its very being.[10]

---

[7]Gregory, *Russian Land, Soviet People,* chapter 4.
[8]*Soviet Geography,* vol. 31, no. 3, March 1991.
[9]Gregory, *Russian Land, Soviet People,* chapter 5; Jorre, *The Soviet Union: Its Land and Its People,* chapter 5.
[10]For Russians a dacha in the forest continues to represent a highly desired part of life. While in Moscow in 1990 I was struck by the value that many Russians placed on owning such a dacha outside of Moscow. When I protested that life in such a place must be rather dull, I was abruptly upbraided for not understanding the wonders of such a place.

The third major zone is that of the endless steppe, that vast expanse of territory covering 21 percent of the FSU and extending from Ukraine to Siberia, including Western and Central Ukraine, Central Black Earth Zone, Moldova, Middle Volga, and Western Siberia. This area of 1.7 million square miles is more than 50 percent of the size of the United States. It represents the rest of the FSU save for the deserts in the south. The traditional path of invaders, the steppe provides a monotonous and immense horizon that has defined the country for centuries. The black soil of the steppe, which takes up 12 percent of the country, supports the best agricultural areas of the former Soviet Union. This black earth region has a temperate climate blessed with frequent rains and blackish soil similar to loess. A second zone of steppe, from the Crimea to Lower Volga and Kazakhstan, has chestnut and brown soil and a continental climate that lacks moisture. The soil is alkaline and inferior to the Black Earth region, especially because of its soluble salts.

Finally, there is the desert region of the south in Central Asia, which accounts for less than 20 percent of the FSU. The Aralo-Caspian Desert alone takes up almost 50 percent of Central Asia. The grey soils of the desert face high temperatures, low and irregular rainfall, and recurrent drought.[11]

RIVERS AND COASTS

Unlike the United States, the FSU has been singularly unblessed in regard to rivers and coasts. It has a short coastline, much of it near cold, poor, and sparse territory. The coasts, save in the Far East and Kamchatka peninsula, are largely a series of nearly straight lines with minimal inlets and peninsulas that do not jut out far. There are few and small islands near the coasts, which tend to be flat, low, and marshy areas with few good anchorages or safe harbors.

Ice, bitter winters, and poor local conditions denude the bulk of the coasts and seas of much value. In the west the short Baltic coast borders on a Baltic Sea that is unusable 160 days a year. The waters are very shallow, with numerous reefs and shoals, made even more treacherous by recurrent fog. The Arctic coast, except for Murmansk, is beset by ice for five to twelve months a year. The White Sea knows ice from October until April, and the Kara Sea has ice most of the year. In the west the Bering and Okhotsk seas are polar in character, while the Bering Straits are recurrently visited by fog. The ports of Nikolyaevsk and Vladivostok are closed six and three and a half months a year by ice. Georges Jorre analyzes this dismal picture:

> To sum up, the coasts of the Soviet Union are nearly everywhere badly endowed by Nature, and the seas, which are generally cold, scarcely penetrate the land. This has serious effects on the climate, which is, moreover, greatly influenced by the arrangement of surface relief.[12]

[11]Jorre, *The Soviet Union: Its Land and Its People,* chapters 6, 16–17.
[12]Jorre, *The Soviet Union: Its Land and Its People,* chapter 2, especially p. 15.

Russia and to a lesser extent Ukraine possess mighty raging rivers. Nine of its rivers are over 1000 miles in length. The longest (Ob-Irtysh, Amur, Lena, Yenisei, Volga) exceed 2000 miles in length. The basins of the largest eleven rivers each drains an area greater than the territory of Great Britain. These rivers have provided the base for most important cities from Kiev (Dnieper), Novosibirsk (Ob), Yaroslavl, Astrakhan, Kazan (Volga) to Moscow (Moscow) and Saint Petersburg (Neva). The eastern conquest of Russian Siberia came heavily along the major rivers.

The problems come with their very low volume, enormous meltdowns, and wrong direction. The Yenisei and Lena rivers are frozen ten months a year at the mouth, other Siberian rivers an average of seven months, and even the Volga and Dnieper three months. They have very slow currents and gentle gradients. In the springtime the floods provide roughly 60 to 75 percent of the entire year's discharge. The roaring torrents of spring can be awesome and extremely dangerous. In May the enormous meltdown of the Volga River can raise its level over 52 feet.[13]

NATURAL RESOURCES

The greatest benefit from such vast territory, apart from providing defensive depth, is the vast natural resources under the soil. Into the late 1980s the former Soviet Union was producing 12 million barrels of oil, far more than Saudi Arabia or Iraq. Before the recent downturn, it provided 20 percent of the oil, 40 percent of the gas and 15 percent of the coal produced in the world. The bulk of the oil and gas is found in the forbidding wastes of Western Siberia, which supplies 67 percent of the oil and 69 percent of the natural gas produced in the FSU. Russia supplies 90 percent of the oil (largely from Western Siberia) and the majority of the coal and electricity produced in the FSU. Natural resources, together with arms sales, have provided the great bulk of exports to the world. The majority of the 2 billion dollars of foreign investment in Russia in 1992 went into oil and natural gas.[14]

By 1994 oil production had slumped to 70 percent of its 1988 levels. Factors including a lag in developing new fields, no new investment, logistics problems, antiquated equipment, decay of capital stock, exhaustion of cheaper and more accessible fields, labor and organization chaos, disruption of ties with other republics, disintegration of the Soviet Union, and a collapsed ruble have harmed production. Reserves were plundered at a rate three to five times higher than in Saudi Arabia. The future is grim, unless there is massive (and

---

[13]Jorre, *The Soviet Union: Its Land and Its People,* chapter 6.
[14]Arild Moe, "The Future of Soviet Oil Supplies to the West," *Soviet Geography*, vol. 32, no. 3, March 1991, pp. 137–167; and World Bank, OECD, IMF and European Bank of Reconstruction and Development, *A Study of the Soviet Economy*, OECD, Washington, Washington, D.C., vol. 3, chapter V.7. For the United States, massive oil imports are responsible for close to 50 percent of the large trade deficit.

unlikely) foreign investment. Western Siberia is well past its prime, and European Russia is largely played out. Even massive drilling, by government estimates, will not stem the decline that seems likely to drop oil production a further 20 percent by the year 2000. At that point, thanks to some conservation (induced by closing many aged factories), Russia would have a surplus only 50 percent of that in 1991.

In contrast, gas production has barely declined and coal production has only moderately declined, much of that induced by strikes in the mines. With the world's greatest reserves of gas (40 percent of the total), gas, despite the expense of conversion from coal and oil, would seem the likely choice of fuel for the future. By 1990 the majority of all domestic energy was provided by gas, which also provides major export earnings. Although there are vast coal reserves (third largest reserves in the world), the health problems of miners, the major environmental degradation, and cost of mining in more remote and inaccessible locations make this a less likely choice. Coal production declined 20 percent in the late 1980s. Nuclear plants, once the wave of the future, are now producing less than 50 percent of planned output and future construction has all but halted in the wake of Chernobyl. Hydroelectric power, potentially plentiful, does massive environmental damage and comes at a high cost.[15]

The FSU was the world's number one producer of iron ore, zinc, and nickel, number two in gold and aluminum, and number three in copper. Its uranium reserves are the largest in the world. Serious problems, from obsolete and poorly maintained equipment to excessive exploitation of deposits to heavy pollution, hinder future development.[16]

The only major hope was for major conservation to ease the energy problem. By various estimates energy use could be cut 30 to 40 percent, through better insulation and higher pricing, without impacting production.[17]

ENVIRONMENT

Massive environmental degradation prompted a strong environmental movement and formation of an Environmental Protection Agency in the late 1980s in the Soviet Union.[18] Yet severe economic difficulties and other higher priorities have left environmentalism lagging far behind Western standards. Only 12

[15]Leslie Dienes, "Prospects for Russian Oil in the 1990s: Reserves and Costs," *Post-Soviet Geography*, vol. 34, no. 2, February 1993; Matthew Sagers, "Review of Energy Industries in the Former USSR in 1991," *Post-Soviet Geography*, vol. 33, no. 4, April 1992; *Post-Soviet Geography*, vol. 33, no. 6, June 1992, p. 405; and Murray Feshbach and Alfred Friendly, Jr., *Ecocide in the USSR*, Basic Books, New York, 1992, chapter 7.

[16]World Bank, OECD, IMF, European Bank of Reconstruction and Development, *A Study of the Soviet Economy*, OECD, Washington, D.C., 1991, vol. 3, chapter V.6.

[17]Murray Feshbach and Alfred Friendly, Jr., *Ecocide in the USSR*, Basic Books, New York, 1992, chapter 7.

[18]For a new and disturbing study of the depth of environmental problems in the FSU, see Feshbach and Friendly, *Ecocide in the USSR*.

percent of the water is clean and 56 percent is heavily polluted. No less than 15 percent of the land has been severely damaged by development. At least 60 million citizens of the FSU live in environmental disaster areas. Fully 26 percent of the population lives in 123 cities where the pollution level is a startling ten times greater than the legal limit. Among major countries, only China, India, and Iran have worse air. There are hundreds of toxic waste sites around the country.[19]

The names Chernobyl, Aral Sea, and Baikal symbolize the massive problems. The explosion of Reactor Number 4 at Chernobyl in Ukraine in 1986 killed perhaps several hundred people, forced 100,000 people to evacuate a 20-mile zone, left 250,000 people inhabiting a zone of uncertain safety, and affected another 2 million people. The total cost of cleanup and rebuilding for Chernobyl is estimated at 38 billion rubles. Massive irrigation and contamination of cotton fields has destroyed the Aral Sea, the world's fourth largest lake, which has lost 67 percent of its water and dropped 47 feet in recent years. It may simply vanish within a decade. Nearby the rate of infant mortality, 110 per 1000, is greater than even in Africa. Runoff of chemicals and dessication of the lake bottom are the sources of the problem. Lake Baikal, the world's largest fresh water lake, is suffering from industrial pollution dumped into the lake on a large scale.[20]

Some progress has been made in improving the environment. Work has been stopped on almost a dozen nuclear reactors and standards have been tightened. Massive programs to redirect rivers to Central Asia have been canceled. Many heavily polluting factories and military plants have closed in the early 1990s. Economic problems, caused by closing many factories, have actually helped the environment.

The national takeover of local factories and severe economic difficulties have slowed this process. With the total environmental cleanup bill estimated to be at least 1.5 trillion dollars and the cost of economic damage at 15 percent of GNP annually, the few billions of dollars that will likely be available in coming years will not even provide a bandaid for a severe problem. Meanwhile, the dark clouds of industrial pollution continue to scar over a hundred cities, toxic agricultural chemicals seep into the water supply, the salt and sand from the Aral Sea blow up violent dust storms in Central Asia, fish-killing worms infest the Volga and Don, and badly maintained oil and gas pipelines are leaking across the vast landscape.[21]

[19]See Michael Smith, "A Tale of Death and Destruction," *The Geographical Magazine*, vol. 26, no. 3, March 1990, pp. 10–14; Joan DeBardeleben, "Economic Reform and Environmental Protection in the Soviet Union," *Soviet Geography*, vol. 31, no. 4, April 1990, pp. 237–256; and Marshall Goldman, "Pollution in the Soviet Union: The Growth of Environmentalism and Its Consequences," in Anthony Jones, Walter Connor, and David Powell, editors, *Soviet Social Problems*, Westview Press, Boulder, 1991, chapter 3. The economic costs of cleanup would be huge, as seen in Eastern Europe. Generally, a country needs to spend at least 2 percent of GNP to keep from sinking and 5 percent of GNP for improvement. In the former Soviet Union the sums would have to be much higher.
[20]See the special issue on the Aral Sea disaster in *Post-Soviet Geography*, vol. 33, no. 5, May 1992.
[21]Feshbach and Friendly, *Ecocide in the USSR*, pp. 252–258.

TRANSPORTATION

The transportation network in the FSU is underdeveloped, at the level of the 1920s in the United States. Enormous distances and the harsh climatic conditions are major impediments. Violent frosts, protracted cold weather, sudden rainstorms, spring mud, and the absence of metal in many areas hinder development. They make it enormously costly to create and maintain the kind of first-rate road networks so familiar in the West and so important to the development of a modern economy and polity. The modern road network (18,000 miles) is 1 percent of the density of Western Europe. There are large unpopulated areas that lie between major population centers.

There is no unified national highway system. The 600,000 miles of public roads represent a density only 7 percent of that of the United States. Quality is so poor that trucks weighing over six tons can use only 10 percent of all roads. Parts of Russia, like the Far North, lack any hard surface roads. A lack of concrete and asphalt means that only 19 percent of the roads are open all year around. Roads are plagued by massive cracking and poor drainage. Vast stretches of dirt and gravel access roads are frequently impassable. Over 60 percent of all Russian villages lack any hard surfaced roads to connect them to each other. As a result, 40 percent of the cost of agriculture is transportation. A weak service station infrastructure, poor road equipment (average age of over twenty years), and a terrible repair record compound the situation. In 1991 a government plan called for massive repair work and construction of 170,000 miles of new roads, but this project has been shelved for lack of money.

With a shortage of trucks (only 15 percent of the American number), poor quality of existing trucks, bad roads, weak service infrastructure, and lack of spare parts, it is a miracle that there is any trucking industry. The average truck speed is an appalling 12 miles an hour, 20 to 27 miles an hour on the best highways (compared to 50 miles an hour in Western Europe). Little wonder that trucks carried less than 2 percent of freight in 1992.[22]

Rivers, the natural alternative, stubbornly flow south to north in Siberia and north to south in European Russia into the Black Sea and Caspian Sea, rather than east to west. Many rivers are frozen over for as much as five months a year. When they unfreeze in the early spring or begin to freeze in the early fall, they become extremely treacherous and dangerous. The average river is navigable only 150 to 200 days a year. Rapids on many rivers pose additional dangers. Most oceans are frozen or inaccessible most of the year.

The railroads, then, have naturally emerged as the engine of transportation development. They are used six times more intensively than in the United States and account for over 50 percent of passenger traffic and 75 percent of nonpipeline freight traffic. There are no fewer than 200 passenger trains a day between Moscow and Saint Petersburg. They carry 25 percent of the world's

---

[22]Denis Shaw, "Road Building in the Russian Federation," *Post-Soviet Geography*, vol. 33, no. 10, October 1992; David Zaslow, "Trucking in the Soviet Economy," *Soviet Geography*, vol. 31, no. 4, April 1990, pp. 173–194.

passenger traffic and over 50 percent of the world's freight traffic. Their condition is poor, yet there is little alternative. The average citizen takes twenty trips on the trains every year. Conditions for freight are so difficult that freight trains average 20 miles an hour.[23]

Americans are used to a car culture in which the average family has two cars. However, in the FSU only one family in six has a car, and almost no one has two cars. Only in the Brezhnev era did the Soviet Union begin to produce more than 1 million cars a year, compared to over 10 million produced for the American market. The quality gap is possibly even greater than the quantity gap. Moskvichs, Zhigulis (Ladas for export) and Okas are pathetic. They are small in size, poorly built, and fall apart easily. More people die on Soviet roads (59,000) than on American roads (40,000) each year despite the fact that the United States has six times more all-weather roads and almost ten times more cars.[24]

There is a fairly large-scale airline industry in the wake of the liquidation of the Aeroflot monopoly in November 1991. Before the breakup Aeroflot was the world's number one airline, with 2500 planes carrying 400,000 people a day over routes that cover 700,000 miles. Several national airlines, including Air Ukraine, have emerged in 1992 and 1993, but old planes, lack of jet fuel, aged flight control equipment, poor maintenance, rudimentary cabins, and dreadfully maintained airports plague the airline industry. Fully 30 percent of all requests for tickets are denied.[25]

The physical realities of the FSU are sobering. One-third of the FSU consists of tundra waste or deserts and nearly half is a vast expanse of forests. Almost half of the territory has few inhabitants. The often harsh climate and northern latitude pose basic problems for survival and development. The lack of warm water ports or east-west ice-free rivers further restricts transportation across this vast Eurasian territory. Only a small fraction of the FSU possesses good agricultural land. A vast supply of natural resources only partially offsets these problems. These enormous problems, which in the past have promoted bureaucratic centralism and a strong state and weak society, continue to negatively impact all attempts to move toward the familiar Western institutions of capitalism and democracy.

---

[23]Jorre, *The Soviet Union, Its Land and Its People,* chapter 14; John Cole, "The Soviet Railroad System: Some Comments on Traffic and Lengths of Haul, 1928–1988," *Soviet Geography,* vol. 32, no. 2, February 1991, pp. 106–118; and World Bank, vol. 3, chapter V.3.

[24]*Soviet Geography,* vol. 32, no. 1, January 1991, pp. 62–67. In 1970 the Brezhnev government opened the Volga Automobile Plant with the help of Fiat in Togliatti. By 1988 there were 11 million cars on the road. However, the quality remains execrable. While in Moscow last year, I had to help push a one-year-old Zhiguli down the street because its carburator system had broken down in its first 10,000 miles.

[25]World Bank, vol. 3, chapter V.3.

3

FSU: The Social and Demographic Realities

The FSU is a paradox in terms of social and demographic realities. In science, education, and culture, despite significant erosion in the last several years, it ranks among the world's leaders. The Soviet Union itself conducted a protracted arms race with the West. American universities have hired 3000 senior Russian scientists. In ballet, classical music, and chess the Soviet Union has produced world-class artists, from Mikhail Baryshnikov and Rudolf Nureyev to Gary Kasparov and David Oistrakh. The Soviet Union regularly bested the United States at the Olympics. Furthermore, it provided free and excellent education and universal health care and a secure existence before the West.

However, the Soviet Union lagged far behind the West in standard of living. Poor food supplies, minimal and shoddy consumer goods, and a lack of cars, basic hotels, and restaurants marked it as an "Upper Volta with nuclear weapons."

Yet a large-scale study of Soviet emigrés found that even this dissatisfied group found much good in the Soviet experience. No fewer than 59 percent found the Soviet standard of living somewhat or very satisfying, compared to only 14 percent who were very dissatisfied. Only with regard to the supply of goods were the majority (53 percent) dissatisfied. A majority found housing (67 percent), jobs (63 percent), and medical care (59 percent) satisfactory. Overall, 66 percent endorsed socialized medicine (52 percent strongly), and 49 percent endorsed state ownership of heavy industry (38 percent strongly). However, the great majority rejected collectivized agriculture (only 13 percent supported it) and residence permits to control population (11 percent favored them). Low Soviet expectations, reinforced by generations of isolation from the world, the peasant origins of the majority of the urban dwellers, and traditional Soviet socialization and propaganda had their impact on the way Soviet citizens viewed the world.[1]

A survey of Soviet citizens in the late 1980s found that the majority viewed poor quality and quantity of food and consumer goods as major problems. Close to a majority worried about unequal distribution of goods, high prices, low incomes, and environmental pollution. Housing and medical care were concerns of one-third of the population. Housing (17 percent), low incomes and high prices (16 percent), environmental pollution (14 percent), gangsterism (12 percent), and quantity and quality of food (11 percent) headed the list of urgent concerns.[2]

POPULATION AMONG THE NATIONS

The 1989 census found 286 million Soviet citizens, including 145 million Russians, to be the most numerous nationality in Europe, trailed next by the 80 million Germans in a unified Germany. Apart from the Russians, the 44 million Ukrainians, 17 million Uzbeks, and 10 million Belorussians made up the only nations with more than 10 million people. There are two principal non-Slavic groups in the FSU—15 million Transcaucasians (Armenians, Georgians, and Azeris) and 35 million Central Asians (Tajiks, Turkmen, Uzbeks, Kyrgyzs, and Kazakhs). There are 3.4 million Moldovans and 25 million nationality minorities (such as Jews, Germans, Poles). The Slavs made up 66 percent of the FSU, the Moslems 15 percent, and the Transcaucasians almost 6 percent.[3]

During the 1979–1989 decade the Slavs grew only 5 percent while the Tajiks increased 45 percent, the Uzbeks and Turkmen grew 34 percent, the Kyrgyzs 33 percent, and the Kazakhs 24 percent. Although in 1979 fewer than 1 percent of all Slavs had five or more children, 29 to 38 percent of all Central Asian families had five or more children.[4]

There was also growing fluency in Russian among non-Russians. This was especially true among the Slavs where 19 percent of Ukrainians and 29 percent of Belorussians did not report Ukrainian or Belorussian as their native language and presumably considered Russian to be their native language. A majority of Ukrainians (56 percent) and Belorussians (55 percent) reported fluency in Russian. In Central Asia half of the Kazakhs reported fluency in Russian as a second tongue, while only one-fourth of the Tajiks, Kyrgyzs, and Turkmen did.[5]

---

[1]James Millar, editor, *Politics, Work and Daily Life in the USSR,* Cambridge University Press, Cambridge, 1987, chapter 2. These low expectations may help explain how former Soviet citizens have weathered a 50 percent drop in their standard of living by 1994 without resorting to violence or mass protest. As was seen in World War II, they are inured to a harsh life.

[2]A. Sogomonov and A. Tolstykh, "About Our Concerns," *Soviet Sociology,* vol. 29, no. 3, May–June 1990.

[3]For this demographic data see *Population Today,* vol. 18, no. 3, March 1990, p. 6.

[4]Michael Ryan and Richard Prentice, *Social Trends in the Soviet Union From 1950,* St. Martin's Press, New York, 1987, p. 41.

[5]*Population Today,* vol. 18, no. 3, March 1990, p. 7.

There were over 12 million mixed marriages in the FSU, especially in urban areas, where they formed 18 percent of the population. This was especially true among those minorities who lacked a separate autonomous region within the FSU (Germans and Poles) or who rejected the one given them (Jews). A majority of Jews (53 percent) and Germans (65 percent) entered into mixed marriages. Fully 38 percent of all Belorussians, 33 percent of all Ukrainians, and 16 percent of all Russians married outside their ethnic group. In Central Asia the rate was much lower, below 10 percent for all the major nationality groups. In the Transcaucasus the rates for Azeris (8 percent), Armenians (12 percent), and Georgians (14 percent) were also low.[6]

In terms of the new republics, Russia with 148 million people and Ukraine with 52 million people dwarfed the rest. The other large republics are Uzbekistan (20 million), Kazakhstan (17 million), Belarus (10 million), and Azerbaijan (7 million). In the 3.5 to 5.5 million range are Georgia, Tajikistan, Kyrgyzstan, Moldova, Lithuania, and Turkmenistan. The smallest new states are Armenia (3 million), Latvia (3 million), and Estonia (1.6 million).[7]

While 1 million people (especially Jews, Poles, and Germans) left from 1987 to 1990, a survey estimated that 7 million people, including 1 million professionals, would emigrate in the 1990s. In a 1991 survey, one-third of the adult urban population would like to leave, at least temporarily. Ethnic battles, national disasters, unemployment, and revival of ethnic awareness have pushed as many as 2 million Russians and over 500,000 Armenians and Azeris to return to their native nation-states.[8] Continued emigration from the Baltics and Central Asia by nonnatives will likely continue in the 1990s.

There are 54 million people living outside their nation-states, including 25 million Russians, concentrated in Ukraine (11 million) and Kazakhstan (6 million). According to surveys, most Russians wish to stay and most natives are not yet particularly hostile. Russians form 38 percent of the population of Kazakhstan, 34 percent of Latvia, 30 percent of Estonia, 22 percent of Ukraine, and 21 percent of Kyrgyzstan. They are over 20 percent of the population of the capitals of eleven of the fourteen other states, and a majority or near majority in Alma Ata (Kazakhstan), Bishkek (Kyrgyzstan), and Riga (Latvia).[9]

RELIGIONS

All of the major Western religions—Christianity, Islam, and Judaism—are represented in the FSU and usually are strongly tied to a given nationality. Thus, Russians have tended to be Russian Orthodox, Central Asians Moslems, Lithuanians Roman Catholics, Latvians and Estonians Lutheran Protestants,

[6]*Journal of Soviet Nationalities,* vol. 1, no. 2, Summer 1990, pp. 164, 171.
[7]Murray Feshbach and Alfred Friendly, Jr., *Ecocide in the USSR,* Basic Books, New York, 1992, p. 272.
[8]Vladimir Rukavishnikov *et al.,* "Social Tension: Diagnosis and Prognosis," and G.F. Morozova, "Current Migratory Phenomena," *Sociological Research,* vol. 32, no. 2, March–April 1993, pp. 41, 93.
[9]Chauncy Harris, "The New Russian Minorities: A Statistical Overview," *Sociological Research,* vol. 34, no. 1, January–February 1993.

and so on. For some groups, like Jews, there has been an identity between religion and nationality.

The Russian Orthodox Church, a branch of Eastern Christian Orthodoxy with its own separate rituals and beliefs, has been predominant in Russia since the tenth century when Kievan Prince Vladimir accepted Christianity. In the seventeenth century it underwent a split in which those who refused to accept the new ritual (Old Believers) were persecuted and forced to the periphery of the empire. The Bolsheviks largely persecuted the church, except during World War II and recently under the Gorbachev regime. Under Yeltsin religion has been largely, but not totally, freed from state repression. Overall, the support for Russian Orthodoxy comes from the Slavs, plus the Moldavians, Karelians, Chuvash, Georgians, and Abkhazians.

The western borderlands, under the influence of the Polish-Lithuanian state for centuries, tended to be independent of the Russian Orthodox Church. The Roman Catholic Church is strong in Lithuania, western Belarus, and western Ukraine, which were part of Poland or Lithuania during the interwar period. Lutheran Protestantism is strong in Latvia and Estonia.

In the south, the Armenians, with an ancient Christianity dating to the fourth century and their own quarter in the Old City of Jerusalem, have their own independent Armenian Christian Church. Their autonomous development of Christianity, predating Russian Orthodoxy by six centuries, has given them a distinctive orientation apart from the predominant trends in Russian Orthodoxy.

Islam is also widespread as a result of Russian conquest of Central Asia and the Transcaucasus. Sunni Islam was spread by the Arab conquest of East and Central Asia in the eleventh century and later reinforced by the Mongol and Turkish conquests. Sunni Islam predominates in Central Asia, North Caucasus, Dagestan, and among Turkish speakers. By contrast, the Azeris and Kurds support the Shiite sect, which predominates in Iran and is strong in Iraq.

Judaism is also a significant factor in the Soviet Union. In 1897 there were 5 million Russian Jews, before the massive emigration of 1.5 million Russian Jews to the United States by 1924. From 1990 to 1994 more than 500,000 Jews emigrated, primarily to Israel but also to the United States. The remaining 1 to 2 million Jews have traditionally played a major role in science and the economy.

URBANIZATION

With massive programs of industrialization and modernization and an ideology favoring their extensive development, the Soviet Union witnessed some of the most rapid urbanization in the twentieth century. In 1920 only 15 percent of the population lived in cities, but by the early 1990s 66 percent were urban dwellers. This represents an increase of 169 million people in cities and a decline of 18 million people in rural areas. The 1930s saw a doubling of the urban population, and in the 1980s Soviet cities grew by 25 million people.[10]

---

[10]John Cole, "Changes in Population of Larger Cities of the USSR, 1979–1989," *Soviet Geography,* vol. 30, no. 3, March 1990, pp. 160–162.

The growth rate was highly uneven across the Soviet Union. Bratsk, which did not exist before 1956, now has 255,000 people. There were 700 cities in Tsarist Russia; there are over 2000 cities in the FSU, 400 of them new. In 1989 roughly 80 percent of the population in North and Central Russia lived in cities, while only 54 percent of the Azerbaijanis and only 40 percent of Central Asians lived in cities.[11]

There were twenty-three cities in the FSU with a population of over 1 million people and fifty-seven cities with over 500,000 people. This made the FSU number one in the world in megacities. The top twenty-three cities have 40 million people and the next fifty-seven cities another 21 million people. This represents a massive change from 1900, when only Moscow and then Saint Petersburg had more than 1 million people, and even from 1959, when there were only three cities with a population of more than 1 million. Table 3.1 lists the top ten cities by population in the FSU and their population growth in the most recent decade.

Moscow and Saint Petersburg have been the twin Russian capitals for over 500 years. The decisive events in the August 1991 coup occurred in these two cities, as they have repeatedly in Russian and Soviet history. The coup failed in Saint Petersburg thanks to strong opposition of the mayor, the population, and the regional military commander. In Moscow it took three days to fail, but the opposition of Boris Yeltsin, the population, and a significant part of the KGB and military was decisive.

Moscow has symbolized Russia ever since the end of the Mongol period in Russian history. It had no strong defenses or great waterway to justify its existence, but the tremendous expansion of the Russian empire after the fifteenth century came out of Moscow. It is located in a transitional zone with more rain and less extreme temperatures than areas further north. It is formed

---

[11]Cole, pp. 162–163; Moshe Lewin, *The Gorbachev Phenomenon*, University of California Press, Berkeley, 1989, chapters 1–2.

TABLE 3.1. Population and Growth Rate in Ten FSU Cities, 1979–1989

City	Population (1989) (million)	Growth Rate (1979–1989)
Moscow	9.0	10%
St. Petersburg	5.0	9%
Kiev	2.6	21%
Tashkent	2.1	16%
Baku	1.8	13%
Minsk	1.6	26%
Kharkov	1.6	12%
Gorkii	1.4	7%
Novosibirsk	1.4	9%
Ekaterinburg	1.4	13%

Source: Paul Lydolph, "Recent Population Characteristics and Growth in the USSR," *Soviet Geography*, vol. 30, no. 10, December 1989, p.724.

around a river, some hills, and a central core with concentric zones separated by boulevards. There are many famous buildings, including the Kremlin, forts, palaces, convents, churches, and cathedrals. In 1750 it had 150,000 people; by 1897, over 1 million people; and in 1914, 2 million people. By 1939 the population had reached 4 million; in 1965, 6.4 million; and today, 9 million people.[12]

Politically, Moscow was the capital of Tsarist Russia (and center of the Russian Orthodox Church) for almost three centuries before 1703, of the Soviet Union since March 1918, and of Russia since December 1991. Under a highly centralized and authoritarian regime, enormous power was centered in Moscow. The first victory of World War II for the Red Army came in front of Moscow in the winter of 1941, when it held and hurled back the German army. Moscow has Russia's number one university (Moscow State University), number one research center (Russian Academy of Sciences since 1934), numerous educational and scientific institutions and museums, and 1500 research, planning, design, and testing institutes. These institutions employ 28 percent of the scientific doctorates and 25 percent of the scientific workers in Russia. Over 700,000 students study in eighty-five higher educational institutions.[13]

Commercially Moscow has been a natural marketplace for trade on the Moscow-Volga Canal and in the capital region of 18 million people. Its role as the national railroad and air hub and as the center for economic planning and budgetary distributions reinforced its role as the leading economic center. Every day 1 to 2 million shoppers pour into Moscow from outside the city. Industrially, it has emerged as a strong textile, food, and electric producer.

Saint Petersburg was an artificial city built by Peter the Great on the Baltic Sea in the far west of Tsarist Russia at the beginning of the eighteenth century. Peter the Great meant it to be a new capital which would serve as the Europeanized capital of the country, opening it to Western influences. It remained so until 1918 when the advance of the German army forced the return of the capital to Moscow, where it has remained ever since. After Lenin's death in 1924, the city was renamed for the founder of the Soviet state. After the dissolution of the Soviet Union, the name reverted to its original form.[14]

Apart from its western site, Saint Petersburg has few advantages. Located so far north, the climate is harsh and difficult and the terrain poor. The surrounding land is filled with bare hillocks, sandy plains, marshes, and pine forests. Thousands may have died during the construction of the new capital. It remains probably the most beautiful city in Russia with huge avenues, beautiful bridges, and such famous buildings as the Winter Palace, the Hermitage museum palace, and Preobrazhensky and Saint Isaac Cathedrals. Saint Petersburg has famous and scenic suburbs associated with the Tsars in Tsar-

---

[12]Georges Jorre, *The Soviet Union: Its Land and Its People*, John Wiley and Sons, New York, 1967, pp. 257–260.

[13]Andrew Bond, "Moscow Under Restructuring: Introduction to Special Issue," *Soviet Geography*, vol. 29, no. 1, January 1988, pp. 1–15. This massive centralization of universities and research institutions is sharply divergent from the American practice of spreading such institutions all over the United States, from California to Chicago to New York to Boston and elsewhere.

[14]Jorre, *The Soviet Union: Its Land and Its People*, pp. 260–265.

skoe Selo, Peterhof, and Gatchina. It contains many important institutions, schools, and libraries. During the mass transformation of the country beginning in the 1930s, its strong industrial base allowed it to become an even greater metallurgical and ship-building center.

The October Revolution took place in Saint Petersburg (then Petrograd) in October 1917 (Julian calendar). After the move of the capital to Moscow in March 1918, it remained an important city, but its political leaders, from Grigorii Zinoviev (1927) and Sergei Kirov (1934) to Andrei Zhdanov (1948) and Grigorii Romanov (1985) all lost their bids for the top leadership of the party. During World War II the city was encircled by German troops for 800 days. No fewer than 500,000 to 800,000 civilians died of starvation, perhaps more than twice as many as the total number of American soldiers who died on both fronts of the war.[15] Today Saint Petersburg remains an important city with past Tsarist and Soviet glories.

EDUCATION

One of the proudest achievements of Soviet society was to conduct a veritable educational revolution that took Soviet rockets into space and to the moon in 1957 and 1959 and brought strategic parity with the United States in the 1970s. In 1913 roughly 60 to 70 percent of the population was illiterate and the average person dropped out of school after two to four years. By 1990 illiteracy was a legacy of the past, the average Soviet citizen had gone to high school, and free education had produced a well-educated society. At the elite level there is the Russian Academy of Sciences, with 30,000 staff members doing research, and first-rate schools such as Moscow State University and Saint Petersburg State University. Nineteen million people have graduated from university. Today there are more than 5 million students in FSU higher educational establishments. Another 75 percent of the population has gone to high school. Long school years, six days a week for school, a strong emphasis on science, and special schools for both the gifted and the backward have produced a well-educated population. Even in Central Asia the number of university- and high-school-trained workers in the economy is close to the level in Russia. There is an extensive network of technical schools and evening and correspondence schools.

With the average family in 1988 owning a television set and receiving two to three newspapers and three to four magazines a week, the educational base of Soviet society was strong. Knowledge of foreign languages is far more widespread than in the United States and approximates the European standard. A survey in Taganrog found that 94 percent of the population knew the leading American politicians and 78 percent knew key foreign scientific and technical discoveries.[16] However, problems since the dissolution of the Soviet Union,

---

[15]See Harrison Salisbury, *The 900 Days: The Siege of Leningrad,* Harper and Row, New York, 1969.
[16]Vladimir Shlapentokh, *Public and Private Life of the Soviet People,* Oxford University Press, New York, 1989, chapter 4.

such as the rising cost of newspapers and magazines and the rising preference of young people for making money rather than staying in school, have depressed the picture.

There are, also, significant problems even with FSU education. As in most societies, the university students are drawn disproportionately from the better-educated strata of society. The 3 million school teachers with 105 million students no longer know what values and socialization they are expected to provide in a rapidly changing and chaotic society. Already in 1988 a poll found that 33 percent of the parents and 90 percent of the teachers were unhappy with the rigid and traditional educational system that stressed rote learning over analysis and discussion.

Problems are more serious in rural schools, which in 1986 accounted for 75 percent of all schools, 54 percent of all teachers, and 42 percent of all students. Yet 76 percent of these schools had no running water or sewerage and 57 percent lacked central heating in a country with a long and hard winter. The majority of schools lacked indoor toilets or indoor gyms.[17]

HEALTH

For decades free medical care for all (in the United States 37 million people have no health insurance), twice as many doctors per capita as in the United States, extensive preventive care, and almost three times more hospital beds than in the United States seemed to symbolize the superiority of socialism over capitalism.[18] However, the depressing realities led Soviet Health Minister Evgenii Chazov to bemoan the "sad state" of Soviet medicine in 1987. The health system reflected the hierarchical, conservative, and authoritarian tendencies of Soviet society. The system is stratified with elite elements enjoying a markedly higher standard of care with special hospitals and pharmacies. The system is vastly underfunded, with the United States spending three times more of its GNP (12 percent) on health than the former Soviet Union (4 percent). This put the Soviet Union seventy-fifth in the world in percentage of GNP spent on health.[19]

There is a major shortage of basic medicines and disposable syringes,

---

[17]Anthony Jones, "Problems in Schools," in Anthony Jones, Walter Connor, David Powell, editors, *Soviet Social Problems,* Westview Press, Boulder, Colorado, 1991, chapter 12; Michael Ryan and Richard Prentice, *Social Trends in the Soviet Union From 1950,* St. Martin's Press, New York, 1987, chapter 7; and Shlapentokh, *Public and Private Life of the Soviet People,* p. 63.

[18]Obviously, the ultimate passage of President Clinton's universal health care program would significantly alter the American medical situation. While the states of the FSU are predominantly European and Central Asian, the overall comparison with the United States is logical both in terms of size and in terms of their past rivalry in the Cold War. This data is, undeniably, somewhat more favorable to the FSU than similar European data would provide.

[19]For this section, see David Powell, "Aging and the Elderly," and Mark Field, "Soviet Health Problems and Convergence Hypotheses," in Jones et al., *Soviet Social Problems,* chapters 5, 10; Ryan and Prentice, *Social Trends in the Soviet Union From 1950,* chapter 8.

which leads to syringes regularly being reused. Doctors are massively indifferent to their patients, as they have an average of two minutes to talk to them after filling out three basic forms. Medical personnel are poorly trained and often indifferent to their patients. Low pay, poor facilities, and a large bureaucracy promote corruption and bribery in the system. Elderly, nonproductive patients often receive short shrift. Patients are given no choice within the system. Medical equipment is often seriously outdated and poorly maintained. There is a shortage of operating tables, surgical lamps, and bactericidal lamps. Food service in hospitals could border on the criminally inadequate. The situation is horrible in rural areas. Two-thirds of rural hospitals have no hot water, 50 percent have no running water, and 25 percent have no sewage system. In Central Asia almost half of the hospitals do not meet local sanitation and hygiene standards.

With an infant mortality rate of 25 per 1000, the Soviet Union ranked fiftieth in the world, after Barbados and the United Arab Emirates, and at the level of East Harlem. This level of infant mortality is three times that in the United States and six times that in Japan. In Central Asia the rate is 46 to 56 per 1000, a level worse than that in many Third World countries. Life expectancy for men (59) is thirteen years less than in the United States (72) and for women (74) four years less. Life expectancy, which declined in the last years of Brezhnev to 62 years for men, ranked thirty-second in the world, at the level of Paraguay. A 1988 survey found 53 percent of all children in poor health and 40 percent of draftees unfit for service.[20]

All of these problems have intensified with the breakup of the Soviet Union. The successor states, struggling with enormous problems, have not been able to maintain health spending, much less increase it to the necessary level.

HOUSING

For most Americans, housing issues seem confined to the homeless or the poor or which neighborhood one can afford. In the FSU, over 50 percent of the population sees housing as a major problem. The quantity and quality of housing is the worst in the industrialized world. Apartments are raw, poorly constructed, ugly. Houses are rare. Citizens have been entitled to 100 square feet per person, a space little bigger than the norm for prisoners in American jails. The average housing space per person is 160 square feet, with wide regional variations, barely 30 percent of the American norm.[21]

The majority of apartments (50 to 70 percent) are shared with parents, grandparents, and other relatives. Only one-third of all newlyweds are able to find their own apartment, and many wait ten or twenty years. Fully 14 million families are now waiting on an enormous list for new or better housing. One

[20]Feshbach and Friendly, *Ecocide in the USSR*, pp. 271–283.
[21]Andrew Bond, Misha Bekindas, and A.J. Treyvish, "Economic Development Trends in the USSR, 1970–1988," *Soviet Geography*, vol. 32, no. 1, January 1991, pp. 12–15.

citizen in eight has no separate apartment and lives in rented space in an apartment, a communal apartment, or a hostel. Millions of desperate people live in dormitories, rented rooms, and trailers.[22]

The quality of apartments is poor, with many apartments falling apart almost as soon as they are completed. There are few modern appliances and no decent common areas. The earthquake that killed over 30,000 Armenians in 1988 would have killed fewer than twelve people in a modern city like San Francisco. Very low rents, below the cost of maintenance, ensure that apartments will age quickly.

Homes and private apartments are beyond the financial reach of the population, 80 percent of whom received free apartments. There are differences in the climate, food, access to consumer goods, price of food, quality of services, and housing conditions within the FSU. Cities are better off than rural areas, west and south better than east and north, Moscow and Saint Petersburg better than all the rest.[23]

The housing situation is in transition, with the whole system of ownership and allocation now in flux. In general, there is a strong movement towards private ownership and creation of an active housing market, which has long-range potential to alleviate the depressing picture painted above.

Igor Birman found that the American standard of living is almost four times higher than that in the former Soviet Union. In consumer durables and household services, the gap was roughly 8:1, in food 2.5:1, in medicine 2:1 and in education 1:1.[24] This gap has increased recently. However, active progress towards capitalism and a free market system offers some hope for the future in the FSU.

---

[22]Shlapentokh, *Public and Private Life of the Soviet People,* chapter 2.

[23]Shlapentokh, *Public and Private Life of the Soviet People,* chapter 2.

[24]Igor Birman, *Personal Consumption in the USSR and the USA,* St. Martin's Press, New York, 1989, p. 157. Another study put the Soviet standard of living somewhere between number fifty and number sixty in the world. See *Current Digest of Soviet Press,* vol. 40, no. 39, October 26, 1987.

4

The Legacy of the Old Order: Organization and Ideology

As the fifteen successor states strive toward some form of capitalism, democracy, and nation building, they do not start with a clean slate. Rather they must operate in an environment deeply penetrated by the legacy of Tsarist Russia and seventy-four years (forty-six years for the Baltics) of the Soviet Union. The institutions with which they must work, the economy which they must transform, and the values and ideology which they must change were all formed, shaped, and conceived during the lengthy Communist era. The forms and shapes of capitalism, democracy, and nationhood are all familiar to American students.[1] What is less familiar is the legacy of socialism and empire.

In the Soviet Union the government accounted for over 90 percent of the GNP. The private sector, save for private plots and small entrepreneurs, was abolished by the middle 1930s. The tradition of great central authoritarian power and the establishment of an authoritarian socialist state without serious private power endowed key institutions with enormous power over the lives of individuals.

OLD BUREAUCRATIC STRUCTURES: BREZHNEV REVISITED

The Brezhnev era was the golden era of institutional domination of Soviet politics. Brezhnev realized that Stalin's terror and Khrushchev's constant ex-

---

[1]While capitalism and democracy are familiar to students, nationhood may not be. There are 2000 to 5000 nations in the world, defined by criteria such as common language, history, religion, and experience on a common soil, yet only 200 nation states are organized as sovereign states. The unique aspect here was that the Soviet Union contained over a hundred nations but formed the world's last great multinational state until its end in 1991.

periments were counterproductive. He implemented a policy of consensual bureaucratic pluralism which gave leading bureaucratic organizations lifetime tenure for their officials, real budget increases yearly and significant autonomy over their own affairs. Policy then revolved not around a powerful leader but around negotiation and compromise by leading bureaucratic actors (army, secret police, party, government, and others) over critical policy decisions. This policy showed results in its first twelve years, but then diminishing returns in its final six years.[2] By 1973, the most powerful institutional actors—the military (Andrei Grechko), secret police (Yuri Andropov), government (Alexei Kosygin), and foreign ministry (Andrei Gromyko) and party (Leonid Brezhnev)— were represented by full members of the Politburo.

Except during the latter Stalin era, the party was the leading institution in Soviet politics. Nearly all key political players were Communists. In the late Brezhnev era one-third of the voting members of the Politburo were members of the Council of Ministers, and nearly all the ministers were members or candidate members of the party Central Committee.

The highest organ in the party was the Politburo, with ten to fifteen members, voting and nonvoting. An inner body within the Politburo often functioned as the supreme policy-making body within Soviet politics. Theoretically (and actually in 1957) it was selected from the Central Committee, often of over 300 members, which represented a vast cross section of the party elite. The Central Committee Secretariat consisted of ten to fifteen secretaries who met weekly to discuss the work of the staff and were responsible for the economy, the party, the military, culture, and foreign policy. There were over twenty Central Committee departments, containing thousands of officials, with broad authority over society and the economy.

The party's youth wing, or Komsomol, was a mass organization serving to promote party values and interests. Emulating the party, there were primary organizations in the work place and then above them the typical district, city, regional, republic, and central organizations. District first secretaries and higher had to be Communists. Komsomol possessed its own newspaper and tasks, such as tourism and school excursions.

The Constitution made the USSR Supreme Soviet the highest body of governmental authority. Traditionally, it was divided into two chambers, the Council of the Union and the Council of Nationalities, each with 750 members. There were no multicandidate elections but only one candidate approved by the party for each position. The Council of Nationalities provided nationality representation and the Council of the Union was composed of deputies, largely people with full-time jobs, elected from districts with equal numbers of inhabitants. Nearly all the top party leaders were deputies. The Supreme Soviet met rarely (one or two times a year) and only for a few days. It functioned as a rubber stamp and legitimating device, with little impact on policy making.

---

[2]There are numerous works on Soviet institutions. One of the best for traditional Soviet structures is Jerry Hough and Merle Fainsod, *How the Soviet Union is Governed*, Harvard University Press, Cambridge, 1979, chapters 8–13.

The Presidium of the Supreme Soviet, meeting between the infrequent sessions of the body, exercised significant power, at least on paper. Including most key Communists, it met every two months and performed a number of important ritual functions. Brezhnev, Andropov, Chernenko, and Gorbachev all headed it, thereby functioning as head of state as well as head of the party.

A more important governmental body was the Council of Ministers, responsible for much legislation. Including around a hundred members, it convened every several months to consider key issues. Its Presidium contained the elite of the governmental structure who made significant decisions, supervised the executive branch, and ran the ministries and state committees. These ministries, numbering from fifty to one hundred, often had staffs that exceeded 1000 officials organized into a number of specialized administrations and departments. Most ministers were specialists with strong experience in their particular ministries. A parallel body was the Defense Council, which dealt with important security issues.

Another powerful body was the State Planning Committee (Gosplan). Its power was great in an economy where the state controlled the means of production. Gosplan reconciled various ministerial requests within the context of regime priorities and scarce resources. Gosplan supervised overall economic balances and helped run individual sectors of the economy.

The Soviet military, with 4 million soldiers and officers, was a vast, closed institution. Its main political administration was responsible for political activities and supervision of cultural, sport, Komsomol, and trade union activities. Most officers and administrators were party or Komsomol members. Tight control over military information and close ties to the heavy industrial complex reinforced its influence.

The secret police, or KGB, was a powerful actor with upwards of 500,000 employees and troops. Its tentacles reached into every part of the Soviet Union. Its head from 1967 to 1982, Yuri Andropov, even managed to succeed Leonid Brezhnev after his death in 1982—although Andropov first had to disassociate himself from the KGB by becoming a party secretary in 1982. The KGB conducted massive espionage abroad, protected Soviet secrets at home, provided valuable intelligence data on all dissent within the country, and helped gather statistics on and attempt to curb corruption in the state-run economy. It also actively combatted all dissident movements at home and checked on possible security leaks in embassies and missions abroad.

The Academy of Sciences was a vast and elite organization with more than 40,000 scientific personnel and over 600 academicians. The academy participated in decisions on research, education, and the planning process. Some of its institutes were involved in foreign policy issues, with Yevgenii Primakov sitting in the Gorbachev Politburo.

The trade union had more than 120 million members, nearly all those gainfully employed in the civilian sector. Over thirty branches of the trade union served to organize the sector. Trade union officials participated in problem solving on all levels of society. Largely they were a "company union," representing the establishment rather than the masses. They were supposed to promote productivity and were forbidden to strike. They did espouse the usual worker concerns in policy arenas, such as better wages, working conditions, and safety conditions.

REFORMING BUREAUCRATIC STRUCTURES: GORBACHEV ERA

Mikhail Gorbachev, after his first two years in office, came to realize that this immense bureaucratic structure of 17 million people was both his political base and one of the main obstacles to real progress. In his remaining four years (1987 to 1991) he made significant, but not radical, changes in the institutional structure. Always he was limited by the bureaucratic conservatives on his right (such as Yegor Ligachev) and the radical reformers on his left (such as Boris Yeltsin), both of whom wanted to overthrow him. In the end he chose the bureaucracy, as witnessed by his strong swing to the right in the winter and spring of 1991 and the leadership of the August 1991 coup by his senior security-military bureaucrats (Vladimir Kryuchkov, Boris Pugo, Dmitrii Yazov).

Gorbachev was unable, and perhaps unwilling, to alter the fundamental stranglehold of the center over the economy, the high priority for defense and security, the dominance of the core over the periphery. By the summer of 1991, after six years in office, Gorbachev had cut the military by roughly 10 percent, the government bureaucracy by some higher but less than awesome figure, and security and internal police almost not at all. The vast bureaucratic phalanx of 17 million administrators in Moscow and the provinces remained solidly in place. So, too, did the party, with its 500,000 apparatchiki and 19 (by then 15) million members.

Yet Gorbachev had also made some serious changes, enough to undermine the massive structures but not topple them. His greatest move in 1989 and 1990 was to create a system of democratically elected parliaments which increasingly showed the power of the reformers. The parliaments began to develop some real power of their own and sharply undermined the legitimacy of the old bureaucratic structure and the Communist Party monopoly on power. Although Gorbachev had only been indirectly elected by the people (and hence was fatally flawed), charismatic leaders such as Boris Yeltsin in Moscow and numerous republican and aspirant non-Russian national leaders used the process to demonstrate their power. By the summer of 1991 over 4 million Communists had left the party, and it was rapidly losing its dominance over society.

The failure of the military-security coup in August 1991 accelerated this process. The leading role of top party leaders in the coup and the failure of the party's central bodies to denounce the coup lost it most of its remaining credibility. Gorbachev himself resigned as General Secretary of the Communist Party and helped dissolve the party. His attack on the KGB, his call for transferring all its armed units to the military, and his desire to try its top leaders showed how far the secret police had fallen. The appointment of reformers at the head of the military (Shaposhnikov) and KGB (Bakatin) demonstrated how rapidly the old institutions were losing their power. The traditional respect for and fear of the power and authority of the military and secret police was already in sharp decline even before the abortive security-military coup dealt it a fatal blow. Glasnost undermined respect for the system, and the secret police in particular.

Thus, Gorbachev accelerated the process of disintegrating the old structure. However, he was too associated with it himself to long survive, and in December 1991 his power, and that of the Soviet Union, came to an abrupt end.

POST-COMMUNIST BUREAUCRACY: FSU REVISITED

In the post-Communist successor states, much of the old bureaucracy has remained. In the Transcaucasus, Central Asia, and Kazakhstan very little has changed, except for some of the personnel. In those states which have been at war, such as Armenia, Azerbaijan and Georgia, features of the old system have even been reinforced, given its value in wartime. The army and secret police have been created or strengthened in those states. In Ukraine the attempt to build a new large-scale conventional army, heavily modeled on its illustrious Soviet predecessor, and Kravchuk's bid for near-absolute power in the spring and fall of 1993 showed the power of the past.

In Russia itself the ongoing battle between Yeltsin and the Parliament showed that much has not changed. The Party and Gosplan are gone, but no new multiparty system has arisen in its place. In September 1993 Yeltsin successfully called for new elections for Parliament in December 1993 and for the presidency in June 1996, a proposal that would finally move in that direction. The army and secret police are changed, but not transformed. The bulk of the government bureaucrats have remained in their posts, presidential power often being brought to the localities not by democratic means but by presidential appointees in the old manner. The power of the president remains vast. Yeltsin's new elite consists heavily of Westernized cosmopolitanized intellectuals, as opposed to the party bureaucrats who ruled for seventy years.[3] The final veto power remains, as ever, the military and security forces, now chastened by their 1991 failure and headed by nominal reformers.

And yet the old bureaucratic base, especially in view of widespread public indifference or hostility to capitalism and democracy (see last section in this chapter), has remained an important asset for former Communist apparatchiki turned reformers like Yeltsin. In truly reformed post-Soviet regimes, who will need 17 million bureaucrats to administer every phase of life? What role would 2.5 million agricultural bureaucrats play if private farmers were to make their

---

[3]See Ovsei Shkaratan, "The Old and New Masters of Russia," *Sociological Research,* vol. 31, no. 5, September–October 1992. The majority of the Yeltsin cabinet ministers have doctoral degrees and are fluent in English.

own decisions about their own land? What would happen to the hundreds of thousands of minions of the KGB if a truly democratic state found little to forbid and much to admire in the alien West? Does Russia need to allocate 20 to 25 percent of its GNP and over 60 percent of its scientific manpower to the military in a more peaceful world? While the phalanxes of the Party and Gosplan and part of the military-industrial complex have been dismantled, the bulk of the old edifice has remained intact.

IDEOLOGY: OLD-TIME RELIGION

In the Soviet and Tsarist Russian experience, ideology has played a major role in political life. Indeed, ideology has suffused Soviet and Tsarist Russian culture to an extent that would be amazing to most Americans, unused to official texts, authoritative institutions, and suppression of deviation. Ideology became institutionalized in the dominant Party bureaucracy and its supremacy over society. As Zbigniew Brzezinski wrote in the 1960s in his work on ideology and power,

> The Soviet political system thus involves one-party dictatorship, with its outstanding character being the indoctrination of society in Party ideology and the shaping of all social relations according to that ideology.[4]

The Soviet Union had an official ideology, an authoritatively approved set of policies that citizens were supposed to support and follow.[5] Providing a critique of prior social organization, the ideology set forth a vision of a future ideal society, deprecated moral and traditional restraints in achieving these goals, and demanded action in their achievement. Ideology provided a framework for current policies and future developments. This belief system provided a guide for action legitimizing the sole allowable political authority. The state formally and informally socialized its citizens thoroughly in this official belief system. Especially after the demise of terror in the Khrushchev era, ideology replaced terror as a powerful prod to sanctioned action.[6]

Ideology, then, was not simply a theoretical guide to action divorced from reality but, in the Soviet Union, an integral part of power. Chief ideologues, such as Nikolai Bukharin in the Leninist era and Mikhail Suslov in the

---

[4]Zbigniew Brzezinski, *Ideology and Power in Soviet Politics*, Praeger, New York, 1962, p. 88

[5]Indeed, authoritarian political cultures have traditionally been strong in Eastern Europe as well as in the Soviet Union. During the interwar period all of the Eastern European countries, except Czechoslovakia, had authoritarian, nondemocratic regimes. At the beginning of the war protofascist regimes emerged in countries like Rumania and Hungary. Even now, in 1991, these authoritarian tendencies remain strong. In June 1991 the entire Rumanian parliament stood for a minute of silence in honor of its World War II protofascist dictator, Ian Antonescu, who was later executed by the Allies for atrocities. In 1992 and 1993 Slobodan Milosevic ran a hard-line, highly authoritarian regime in Serbia that ruthlessly crushed the Moslems and Croats elsewhere in the former Yugoslavia.

[6]Donald Barry and Carol Barner-Barry, *Contemporary Soviet Politics*, Prentice-Hall, New York, 1987, chapter 3.

Brezhnev era, wielded considerable power. All the leaders, from Lenin to Brezhnev, were expected to show some prowess in the ideological arena. There were clear limits on the impact of ideology on power and strong flexibility in manipulating the ideology to justify political decisions. Ideology helped provide an action program usable for mass consumption and an apocalyptic and utopian image of the future. Ideology provided a consciousness of purpose and history in order to be a guide for action. The regime constantly resorted to this body of symbols in order to rationalize and legitimize one-party rule. With the Party theoretically tied to the masses, the ideology extolled the Party, justified the policy line, and provided an important instrument of political control. Ideology set a framework for political action, limited acceptable options, defined priorities, and shaped the methods used in the system.[7]

Soviet ideology stressed rejection of capitalism, private property, a multiparty system, private agriculture, high salaries, and liberalism, and the promotion of collective agriculture, forced industrialization, and atheism. Certain truths were variable; others became dogmas. The leading role of the Party, the evils of capitalism, socialist ownership of the means of production, the superiority of the collective over the individual, atheism, and the triumph of socialism were integral to the faith.

The ideology, then, served a set of definable functions. Its political function was important as it put Party policy above criticism, eliminated any competing private sector of society, and placed great power in the hands of the state through collectivism. The anti-Western orientation excluded alien ideas while the antireligious concept removed possible competing faiths. Ideology provided a language for discourse and the possibility of expressing differences within an overall acceptable framework. Ideology legitimized the state and the Party by showing their dedication to higher goals and emphasizing their need to set goals and allowed the Party to be the sole interpreter of the doctrine. Soviet Marxism contributed to social integration and unification by transcending classes, religions, and nationalities with a unified universalist doctrine of shared beliefs that all could internalize. Ideology set societal goals, such as the building of communism, that justified sacrifices by the population. Finally, it served an innovative function by insisting that change was necessary in order to keep up with history, make societal changes apace with technological changes, and limit possible alternative developments.[8]

Ideology had some advantages for policy makers. By stressing long-term trends it could alert decision makers to important changes that must be made in the system. Ideology pushed Soviet military mobilization in the 1930s against the Nazi threat and in the 1950s as an opening to the Third World with anticolonialism. Its mobilization capabilities in World War II were impressive.[9]

---

[7]Brzezinski, *Ideology and Power in Soviet Politics.*
[8]Barry and Barner-Barry, *Contemporary Soviet Politics,* chapter 3.
[9]See Jonathan R. Adelman, *Prelude to the Cold War,* Lynne Rienner Publications, Boulder, Colorado, 1988, for a comparative analysis of the capabilities of the Soviet and American armies in World War II.

Ideology functioned as a surrogate religion. Secular redemption replaced religious salvation. Lenin was made a demigod, with the obligatory visit to his mausoleum. The doctrine demanded great sacrifices from the population. It set goals, gave meaning to life, and inspired action. In the absence of scientific validation, the doctrine had to be taken on faith as an article of belief. There was a secular priesthood (Party ideologues), doctrine (Marxism-Leninism), original sin (division of labor), catechism (*Short Course* of Stalin for many years), punishment of deviants (purges), good (socialism) versus evil (capitalism), and redemption (membership in the Party).[10]

THE IMPACT OF IDEOLOGY AT THE END OF THE SOVIET UNION

Soviet-style Communism historically stood for a "hard" version of revolutionary socialism, while social democrats have stood for a soft, reformist socialism. Soviet Marxism-Leninism demanded nationalization of the economy, denigration of civil liberties, rule by an elitist party with no rivals, and willingness to use violence and coercion. The end usually justified the means.

With the demise of Soviet Marxism and the Soviet Union, alternative ideologies, such as fascism, liberalism, nationalism, or authoritarian conservatism, should have great appeal. Only nationalism has shown much power to mobilize the masses. Religion has revived but is still quite tentative in much of the country. Neofascism, as reflected by Pamyat (a strongly anti-Semitic, rabidly nationalist organization), remains a fringe phenomenon. Liberalism, a powerful creed in the West, has had little echo in such a traditionally authoritarian state. Authoritarian conservatism seems to have little mass support. Only a tepid reformist democratic socialism seems to have strong popular appeal.

Much of the population still accepts large aspects of the old-time ideology, or at least those appealing policies which were consistent with Marxism-Leninism. Studies of Soviet emigrés in the 1980s showed 66 percent supported socialized medicine, 49 percent backed state ownership of heavy industry, and 39 percent were opposed to the rights of the accused versus the rights of the state.[11] In February 1989 only 46 percent of Muscovites supported a multiparty system and 41 percent said they would vote for the Communist Party in an election. Fully 32 percent said it would play a more important role and another 33 percent said the same role. After the first session of the Congress of People's Deputies in June 1989, only 42 percent opposed a one-party system.[12]

Ideology, without the party, remains a potent factor. A Soviet sociologist wrote early in 1991 that

[10]Barry and Barner-Barry, *Contemporary Soviet Politics*, chapter 3.
[11]Brian Silver, "Political Beliefs of Soviet Citizens," in James Millar, editor, *Politics, Work and Daily Life in the USSR,* Cambridge University Press, Cambridge, 1987, chapter 4.
[12]L.G. Bykov, L.A. Gordon and I.E. Mintusov, "Reflections of Sociologists on the Political Reforms," *Soviet Sociology,* vol. 30, no. 1, January–February 1991, pp. 30–34.

in our country only the CPSU (Communist Party of the Soviet Union) has legitimacy of authority by dint of tradition. Despite current widespread mistrust of the party, society continues to relate to it precisely as to an authority which to a considerable extent is keeping the country from falling into chaos.[13]

A 1990 study of sophisticated Muscovites found 40 percent of scientific workers, 55 percent of high school students, and 64 percent of those training to be school teachers opposed democracy. Fully 64 to 79 percent of the members of all three groups had no interest in participating in societal change despite the fact that over 80 percent were unhappy with the developments in their country. Fear of authority still gripped roughly 80 to 90 percent of all respondents. Only the clergy and writers gave low ratings to the police and Komsomol. Less than 1 percent of the scientific workers or future teachers belonged to any informal organization. Authoritarian tendencies were especially strong among the future teachers. Only 16 percent of them felt it was all right to speak negatively of the country with foreigners, and only another 16 percent approved of spontaneous demonstrations. A meager 23 percent agreed that "those who are not with us are not against us." And less than half (41 percent) felt that individual rights and freedom were of any importance.[14]

Marxist-Leninist ideology had a strong impact on the development of Soviet society. Even economically irrational programs, such as state farms in the countryside or abolition of private property in the cities, continued under the imprimatur of the ideology that proclaimed them innately superior. Despite the end of Soviet Marxism, Marxism still influences a significant portion of the populace and the key societal institutions. The key leaders in Soviet politics—Mikhail Gorbachev, Boris Yeltsin, Anatoly Sobchak, Eduard Shevarnadze—were all Communists, usually apparatchiki for decades. A traditionally ideologically oriented society was in search of an acceptable ideology, or at least a well-articulated and plausible political belief, to lead it into the new post-Marxist-Leninist world.

AFTER THE FALL: IMPACT OF MARXIST IDEOLOGY AFTER 1991

Marxism may be long gone, but its impact has lingered. Democracy has been unpopular even in the former twin capitals. In November 1991 only 11 percent of Muscovites favored an American political system and 23 percent a Swedish one. In February 1992 in Saint Petersburg people preferred a firm hand (43 percent) to a democratic system (only 28 percent).[15] In October 1992, 64 percent

[13]M.I. Urnov, "How Ready Are We For Democracy?" *Soviet Sociology,* vol. 30, no. 2, March–April 1991, p. 23. Urnov also found that even among scientific workers only 43 percent chose freedom over material well-being if there was a choice.

[14]Urnov, pp. 6–25.

[15]See Vladimir Iadov, et al., "The Sociopolitical Situation in Russia in Mid-February, 1992," *Sociological Research,* vol. 32, no. 2, March–April 1993. The famed sociologist Tatyana Zaslavskaia

of Russians preferred greater security for society (a socialist value) compared to 19 percent who preferred greater individual freedom (a democratic value). A mere 19 percent agreed that "only capitalism can save our country" (a capitalist value), while 44-percent disagreed (a socialist value). In November 1992, 51 percent of Russians favored a strong leader over democracy while only 31 percent favored democracy. However, they did not want the old-time religion reinstated, for by a 46 percent to 11 percent margin they thought Marxism was bankrupt. Only 28 percent thought it was all right to privatize state-run enterprises while 40 percent disagreed. In March 1993 Russians by a large margin (72 to 21 percent) thought that the state should provide everyone with a job (a socialist value). And 63 percent thought that state control over prices was useful while 59 percent thought state control over private businesses was useful (socialist values). This suspicion of democracy was seen in the weakness of parties and in the increasing identification of democracy and capitalism with corruption, economic misery, and foreign domination. The limits on Yeltsin's ability to move rapidly to capitalism and democracy seemed clear.[16] In more conservative Belarus or Central Asia, poll results would be more hostile to capitalism and democracy.

There was no foreign occupation, as in Germany and Japan in 1945, to destroy the old and proclaim the new. There was no Western occupation regime to reform the old structures and try to implant a new ideology. The peaceful implosion of the old Soviet Union, and the difficulties of the transition to democracy, capitalism, and nation building, have complicated the task of reformers. It helps explain the ongoing power of traditional Communists in new countries in Ukraine, Central Asia, and Transcaucasus.

Former Communists have played a dominant leadership role in the great bulk of the new states, from Russia and Ukraine to Central Asia and the Transcaucasus. In 1993 former Communists came to the fore in Lithuania (Brzauskas), Georgia (Shevardnadze) and Azerbaijan (Aliyev), as in much of Eastern Europe. Although not necessarily Marxists, they do represent the past.

The destruction of the old order and creation of a new, more democratic, capitalist, and nationalist order will be a long and difficult process. The great difficulties in making the transition only enhance the lingering impact of the old ideology and the old institutions. A successful new order will have to be a blend of old and new thinking and institutions, just as Bonapartism in France and Stalinism in Russia integrated diverse elements of the old and the new. In the end much will have changed, but much of the old will yet have endured. In this context, it is important that we understand the old ideology, the old institutions, and the old economy (see next chapter) as significant elements of the past that will survive into the twenty-first century.

---

found in a 1990 survey that 52 percent of Russians supported the Bolshevik seizure of power in the October Revolution, 40 percent would have supported the Bolsheviks had they been alive in 1917, and 39 percent thought that the October Revolution reflected the will of the people. See Tatyana Zaslavskaia, "Socialism, Perestroika and Public Opinion," *Sociological Research*, vol. 31, no. 4, July–August 1992.

[16]*The New York Times*, April 18, 1993, pp. E1, 5.

5

The Legacy of the Old Order: Planned Economy

In this chapter we review the planned economy that was a distinctive feature of the Soviet Union from its inception in 1929 until the demise of the regime in 1991. Although many think of the economy in the most negative terms, the system had many successes and positive features, and it is with these that we begin.

ECONOMIC SUCCESS

For a number of decades the general reviews for the Soviet economy were quite positive. As Morris Bernstein put it in an introduction to his 1981 edited volume on the Soviet economy:

> For several reasons the institutions, policies, accomplishments and problems of the Soviet economy are important and interesting to a wide audience of policy makers, business executives, scholars, students and citizens. First, the USSR is a political, military and economic superpower. Second, the USSR created a distinctive economic system—now commonly called a socialist, planned economy—that subsequently was adopted, with modifications, by other countries in Eastern Europe, Asia and Latin America. Finally, the USSR offers its economic system and economic development strategy as a model to Third World nations seeking rapid economic development and social change.[1]

Despite great waste, the Soviet economy generated major gains for the system for over forty years, from 1930 until the middle 1970s. During the 1930s the Stalinist system created a powerful heavy industrial base and modern-

---

[1]Morris Bernstein, "Introduction," *The Soviet Economy: Continuity and Change*, Westview Press, Boulder, Colorado, 1981, p.xi.

ization campaign that provided a strong base for the ultimate defeat of Nazi Germany in World War II. In the postwar period the economy staged an impressive recovery from the massive destruction wrought by the Nazis. From 1950 to 1985 Ed Hewett has calculated that Soviet economic growth (4.5 percent a year) substantially outpaced American economic growth (2.7 percent a year) and was competitive with three leading Western European countries (4.5 percent a year). In the 1980s the economy generated weak growth until falling into recession in the late 1980s and depression in the early 1990s.[2] By 1990 the Soviet Union led the world in production of steel, pig iron, iron ore, crude oil, gas, and fertilizers.

The rapidly growing economy provided fruits not only for the state but also for society. The economy guaranteed full employment and job security, cheap necessities (housing, transport, recreation), and reasonable equality of income for most people. Education was free and food was massively subsidized and cheap. During its first decade, the Brezhnev regime met the modest consumer expectations of the bulk of the population. As Seweryn Bialer observed, by 1977 the standard of living had doubled.[3] The low expectations of Soviet consumers, most of whom were either peasants or only one generation removed from the dismal countryside, could be met by the system. In 1960 over 90 percent of the population lacked televisions or refrigerators, 67 percent had no sewing machines, and over 50 percent had no radio. By 1984 refrigerators, radios, and televisions were universal and 67 percent had sewing machines.[4]

From this economy skewed towards heavy industry and the military, the Soviet Union achieved superpower status in the military arena, allowing it to compete with the United States in the Cold War and control Eastern Europe. Having defeated Nazi Germany in World War II, the Soviet Union stressed a defense posture that competed well against the West and provided massive exports to the Third World. The space program was first rate, from hitting the moon with an unmanned probe in 1959 to building space stations in the 1980s. The Soviet Union was the world leader in the production of steel, concrete, and cement. The Soviet Union constructed a good natural gas system and drilled the world's deepest oil wells. Its long distance high voltage transmission lines and hydroelectric turbines were of high quality. The Soviet economy produced more oil than Saudi Arabia and more gold than anyone save South Africa. Its subway system was first-rate.

The massive investments and sacrifice in stressing producer goods and technology transformed a country with 3 million industrial workers in 1928 to one with 35 million in 1980. Illiteracy was 67 percent in 1928, nil in 1980. In 1928 a paltry 5 percent of the work force had professional or semiprofessional education; in 1980, 24 percent. In 1928, 15 percent of the people lived in cities; by 1990, over 67 percent.[5]

[2]Ed Hewett, *Reforming the Soviet Economy*, Brookings Institute Press, Washington, D.C., 1989, p. 38.
[3]Seweryn Bialer, *Stalin's Successors*, Cambridge University Press, Cambridge, 1980, pp. 150–154.
[4]Hewett, *Reforming the Soviet Economy*, p. 39.
[5]R.W. Davies, "Economic Planning in the USSR," in Morris Bernstein, editor, *The Soviet Economy: Continuity and Change*, Westview Press, Boulder, Colorado, 1981, chapter 1.

ECONOMIC FAILINGS

This economic system, though with tremendous waste, made the Soviet Union industrially competitive through massive investments in industry, education, and defense. The emerging postindustrial society, with stress on computers, telecommunications, miniaturization, and services, rendered the old Stalinist industrial model obsolete. The high growth rates of the 1930s and 1950s declined markedly to 6 percent a year in the 1960s, 4 percent in the 1970s, and 1 to 3 percent a year in the 1980s. The CIA has estimated that the economy grew an average of 1.8 percent a year in the first half of the 1980s and 1.6 percent a year in the late 1980s. Many critics, including Gorbachev, said that real growth was zero if vodka and oil were excluded from the equation.[6] By 1990 the economy, already in deep trouble in the 1980s, began to slide into deep recession and then depression in the early 1990s with the start of the transition to capitalism.

The technological gap between the Soviet Union and the West widened in the postindustrial era. The Soviet Union was left with a vast and increasingly obsolete industrial economy, matched with a pathetic agricultural sector, alienated labor force, and ill-fed and ill-clothed population.[7] Although the Soviet Union produced more machines a year than the United States, only 16 percent of them were at the world standard—by 1989 the country was importing 1 billion dollars a year of machine tools. Labor productivity, despite a well-educated labor force, was one-third the level of the West. The system relied on manual labor for 40 percent of industrial output, 60 percent of construction work, and 70 percent of agricultural output.[8] Defense was absorbing 15 to 25 percent of GNP, compared to 5 percent in the United States. Military industry utilized the majority of the vast scientific manpower.

The consumer goods sector was a disaster. Quality was virtually nonexistent. Only 8 to 17 percent of Soviet goods were at world standard, making even Eastern European goods as desirable. Soviet consumer and manufactured goods were so poor that they constituted less than 10 percent of Soviet exports to Western Europe. Zhiguli cars were built with 1960s technology. Many goods, scorned by even a desperate public, piled up in the warehouse. Repairs were scarce; taxis and buses were jammed. Good telephones, radios, and washing machines were often nonexistent. In 1988 the United States had 120 times more computers than the Soviet Union.[9]

[6]Anders Aslund, "Gorbachev, Perestroyka and Economic Crisis," *Problems of Communism*, vol. 40, nos. 1–2, January–April 1991, p.29; and Stanislaw Shatalin, "Social Development and Economic Growth," in Anthony Jones and William Markoff, editors, *Perestroika and the Economy: New Thinking in Soviet Economics*, M.E. Sharpe, Armonk, New York, 1989, p. 196.
[7]Nicholas Spulber, *Restructuring the Soviet Economy,* University of Michigan Press, Ann Arbor, 1991.
[8]Boris Kurashvili, "Restructuring and the Enterprise," in Anthony Jones and William Moskoff, editors, *Perestroika and the Economy, New Thinking in Soviet Economics,* M.E. Sharpe, Armonk, New York, 1989, pp. 25–26; Nicholas Spulber, *Restructuring the Soviet Economy,* University of Michigan Press, Ann Arbor, 1991, chapter 4; and Ed Hewett, *Reforming the Soviet Economy,* chapter 2.
[9]Anders Aslund, *Gorbachev's Struggle for Economic Reform,* Cornell University Press, Ithaca, New York, 1989, chapter 1.

The level of waste in the system was often staggering. Nikolai Shmelev calculated that 20 to 25 percent of the work force was superfluous. In agriculture 20 percent of all grain, 10 percent of meat, and 60 percent of fruits and vegetables were ruined, spoiled, lost, or stolen before they reached the market. The country produced 800 million pairs of shoes and imported another 100 million pairs, yet was poorly shod. It produced twice as much mineral fertilizer and fourteen times more combines than the United States yet was lacking in agricultural technology. The system maintained three times more inventories per unit than the United States yet had serious shortages of goods. Plants that took an average of two years to build in the West took an average of eleven years in the Soviet Union.[10]

The system could not cope with an economy that produced millions of products. Declining financial discipline, increased hoarding and imbalances, an ever more complex economy, and more discriminating consumers fostered increasing shortages. Barter, rationing, and private enterprise began to replace the formal plan, which was supposed to order all aspects of the economy. Corruption, localism, overcentralization, waste, and late orders pervaded the economy. With the beginnings of reform in the late 1980s, many enterprises used their autonomy to stop producing many unprofitable goods, no matter how much in demand. Gigantomania reined ever more as a single vast factory was often the sole producer of a product for the entire economy. By contrast, in the West the massive use of subcontractors traditionally cut costs and improved flexibility. With more money to spend and less to buy, savings soared from 19 billion rubles in 1965 to 220 billion rubles in 1986 and over 330 billion rubles in 1991. Areas neglected by large-scale production became the zone of the private entrepreneurs.[11]

Imbalances were everywhere. The system produced a surplus of poor quality consumer goods and shortage of high quality goods. Investment spending was concentrated in enormous projects, often unfinished, while smaller projects were neglected. Labor demand was excessive in European Russia and the reverse elsewhere.[12]

ECONOMIC PRIORITIES

Historically, the priorities of the Soviet economy were geared to security and defense considerations. The first three five-year plans starting in 1929 laid a strong base for heavy industry and the military. Ever since then the great majority of investment has gone into industry, with great stress on heavy

[10]Nikolai Shmelev, "Economics and Common Sense," in Jones and Moskoff, *Perestroika and the Economy, New Thinking in Soviet Economics*, pp. 268–272.
[11]V.A. Korostelev, "The Rebirth of Small Scale Commodity Production," in Jones and Moskoff, *Perestroika and the Economy, New Thinking in Soviet Economics*, pp. 45–58.
[12]Hewett, *Reforming the Soviet Economy*, chapter 2.

industry (in 1986, 89 percent of industrial stock was in heavy industry).[13] This enabled the Soviet Union to become an industrial superpower, the fourth largest industrial producer in the world. In the 1980s industry continued to receive priority and the military sector absorbed 15 to 25 percent of the GNP, compared to 5 percent in the United States.

Agriculture was sadly neglected during the Stalin era, receiving 10 percent of investment. Only under Khrushchev (20 percent) and Brezhnev (25 to 30 percent) did it receive massive investment. Housing and social services were neglected for decades. In the late 1980s spending on health (4 percent of national income) and education (6 percent of national income) was half the level in the West. The economy was more labor intensive in agriculture (19 percent of workers) and industry and construction (38 percent) than in the United States (3 percent and 28 percent respectively). Trade, food, and services in the Soviet Union (34 percent of workers) were smaller sectors than in the United States (62 percent).[14]

ECONOMIC STRUCTURE (TRADITIONAL MODEL)

Modelled on the German war economy of World War I, the centrally planned economy made its appearance during the "war communism" era of the civil war (1918–1920). After the NEP interlude (1921–1928), Stalin recreated the system with the advent of rapid industrialization, collectivization, and modernization in the 1930s. The system affirmed the dominance of politics over economics with rapid and abrupt changes instituted by the political leadership.[15] Key decision makers were the party elite, the Politburo, the Central Committee, and their staff. The governmental actors were the Council of Ministers with a hundred ministries and committees, a system going back to the late 1930s. Their control of the nationalized means of production and their stress on production goods and capital goods were the core of the system for sixty years.

The key to the system was the economic center in Moscow and its planning process. The plan directed the state enterprises, collective and state farms, and households. The plan specified production targets for key goods and products and relied on a series of material and physical balances. The center set the priorities for the economy, created a yearly and a five-year operational plan, and set industrial policy. It provided ministries, departments, and agencies with a physical input-output plan. The plan decided payments to the budgets,

---

[13]Spulber, *Restructuring the Soviet Economy*, chapter 3.

[14]*Soviet Geography*, vol. 31, no. 1, January 1990, p. 5; Padma Desai, *The Soviet Economy: Problems and Prospects*, Basil Blackwell, Oxford, 1987, chapter 1; and Anders Aslund, *Gorbachev's Struggle for Economic Reform*, Cornell University Press, Ithaca, New York, 1989, chapter 4.

[15]This, of course, is ironic since it was the Marxists who asserted that the economic base drove political, social, and cultural superstructure.

the size of wage funds, and new construction. Even in the early 1990s the center still allocated parts of investment, the movement of labor, the scope and structure of production units, and the relationship between suppliers and buyers.[16]

The massive economic bureaucracy centered in Moscow implemented the plan and directed every phase of the economy. The entire country was run as one centralized, multibranch and multiplant corporation with state ownership of the great majority of the means of production. Seventeen million administrators (12 percent of the labor force) ran the economy with 130 million workers, peasants, and employees. The elite consisted of 3 million top managers, who were chief engineers, managers, and key accountants, and 14 million members of the managerial-technical staffs of enterprises and association. The top 2 million people belonged to the *nomenklatura,* the party-appointed ruling apparat, which was run by less than 1000 people. They were the directors of the top hundred enterprises, presidents of republics, chairmen of regional and city executive bodies, members of the Supreme Soviet, Council of Ministers, and Central Committee, and first party secretaries of provinces and regions. This elite ran over 1.3 million production units including 43,000 state industrial enterprises, 26,000 construction enterprises, 47,000 farm units, 260,000 service establishments, and more than 1 million retail trade outlets. They performed this staggering task through 400 organizations, each with its own bureaucratic staff of departments, offices, and main administration. These included state committees, all-union ministries, union-republic ministries, and regional ministries.[17]

The elite was stratified with ten echelons of managers, ten echelons of specialists with university degrees, and ten echelons of technicians, accountants, and dispatchers. This hugely complex economic bureaucracy ran a vast economy without private property, market forces, or profits and losses. The bureaucracy rewarded and punished its subordinates while lacking formal rules.[18]

The Politburo made broad decisions in conjunction with the Council of Ministers. The council, headed by the Soviet Prime Minister, functioned as the board of directors of the system, as an executive arm of the political leadership. It set general supervision, coordination, and strategy for the economy.

The next layer was Gosplan (the state planning commission). Gosplan, as the executive agent of the Council of Ministers, translated its broad directives to input/output plans and supply/demand balances. Gosplan sent its directives to the industrial ministries, which worked with input/output plans. They had operational responsibility for enterprise output. Next came the functional state committees with specific responsibility for advice and feasibility studies

---

[16]Spulber, *Restructuring the Soviet Economy,* chapter 1.

[17]Paul Gregory, *Restructuring the Soviet Economic Bureaucracy,* Cambridge University Press, Cambridge, 1990, chapter 1.

[18]Gregory, *Restructuring the Soviet Economic Bureaucracy,* chapter 1; and Spulber, *Restructuring the Soviet Economy,* chapter 1.

in prices, investment, and technology. Then planning reached the enterprises that carried out the directives and met the goals.[19]

Frequently plans were changed because of weaknesses in planning for regions, shocks to the system, and problems of making plans fit for all subunits. The system promoted massive bargaining for input and output plans. The massive flow of directives from the top down was countered by a massive amount of bargaining, negotiating, and political deal-making rising up from the bottom. It was the whole process of informal deals and bargains that actually transformed the paper plan into reality, if one quite different from that which appeared on paper. Gossnab (the state supply committee) and the ministries tended to predominate at the operational level. The players in the system saw the plan as a bid in resolving resource allocation problems. Each ministry and enterprise sought general and favorable plans that made minimum demands on their capabilities. Numerous problems, including difficulties in determining plan fulfillment, concern over ruining relations with suppliers, and the need to formulate supply needs before output plans were known, hampered the formulation of supply plans. Ministries and enterprises entered into informal and often covert agreements to arrange supplies to fulfil plans. This promoted ministerial autarchy.[20]

The Party played a major and powerful role in economic affairs. While the central Party organs directed from above, the local Party organs attempted to implement central wishes tempered by their own localist desires. Central bureaucratic institutions responded only to the Party center and not to local Party organizations. Local Party organizations often lobbied the center for more supplies, wages, and plan changes. Local Party officials had a significant role in representing the local enterprises, influencing resource allocation decisions and promoting money and wage funds. Local Party organizations often were in conflict with the Party center in their attempts to protect local enterprises and withhold key information. They also helped the center by making assignments that were in their interest but not in that of the local enterprises. Party organizations at all levels were deeply involved in the economic planning and implementation.[21]

The budget was developed in accord with the financial plan drawn up by the Ministry of Finance and Gosplan. The budget accounted for 75 percent of all resources with even division between all union and regional spending. The budget showed how the center managed the economy, reallocated resources, absorbed the nation's wealth, and redistributed it. There was tremendous regional variation. The 1989 budget spent 1125 rubles per capita in Estonia and 380 rubles per capita in Tajikistan.[22]

There were three systems of distributing resources and inputs. Gossnab distributed material inputs among production enterprises. The State Commit-

[19]Gregory, *Restructuring the Soviet Economic Bureaucracy,* chapter 1.

[20]Gregory, *Restructuring the Soviet Economic Bureaucracy,* p. 103.

[21]Gregory, *Restructuring the Soviet Economic Bureaucracy,* pp. 143–145.

[22]Spulber, *Restructuring the Soviet Economy,* chapter 6.

tee for Foodstuffs and Supplies bought food products from the agricultural sector. The Ministry of Trade distributed consumer goods and services to the population. The retail and trade sector employed 10 million people. In 1988 the state ran 71 percent of retail trade; cooperatives, 26 percent; and the private sector, 3 percent.

This system of distribution eliminated marketing, advertising, financing, responsiveness to consumer wishes, and informal deals. With shortages of goods and few resources, supermarkets, or department stores, the retail sector lagged behind that of the West. Inventories were high relative to sales and markup much smaller than in the West.[23]

The planning process had numerous problems. It worked best for weapons, electric energy, oil, and gas, where it could give priority, meet definable needs, and do quantifiable tasks. In other areas the lack of a balanced, checked, and aggregated plan led to serious problems. There was massive hoarding and understating of production capabilities in order to meet contingencies and quantitative output goals and win bonuses for the managers. Risk taking went unrewarded and materials and investment were controlled from above. The plan tried to generate billions of decisions for hundreds of thousands of enterprises for labor, wages, costs, profits, investment, and materials for 20 to 30 million products. Invariably it failed, and often by a wide margin. Localism and departmentalism defeated central intent. The quantity and quality of production was unrelated to market demands and public desires. Perennial shortages, staggering waste, imbalances, stagnation, corruption, and declining growth rates were the result. The plan tried to plan the unplannable, an entire vast economy, and failed.[24]

The system created massive imbalances within the economy. Heavy industry was favored over light industry, industry over agriculture, production over services, and proven technologies over new but untried technologies.

The marketing and retail system was very backward. The system thrived on perennial shortages and habitually ignored the needs of the consumers for the satisfaction of the plan. With only 20 percent the number of the retail outlets of the United States, the economy offered few quality goods and even fewer places to buy them. These features accentuated that familiar feature of Soviet society—long lines outside of relatively empty stores.

Prices remained a serious problem in the system. Historically prices were fixed for long periods of time at levels unrelated to patterns of scarcities and need. Without a market, arbitrary prices sent distorted signals within the economy. Minimal prices for apartments, which rented for 2 percent or 3 percent of wages, favored those with better apartments, promoted poor maintenance, and hindered labor migration.[25] Food, until the spring of 1991, was

---

[23]International Monetary Fund, World Bank, OECD, European Bank for Reconstruction and Development, *A Study of the Soviet Economy,* OECD, Washington, D.C., 1991, vol. 3, chapter V.2.

[24]Alec Nove, "An Economy in Transition," in Abraham Brumberg, editor, *Chronicle of a Revolution,* Pantheon, New York, 1990, pp. 50–71.

[25]The sad state of rent-controlled housing in New York City, which favored a privileged few at a high cost to the housing supply, has shown that this phenomenon was not limited to socialist states.

sold for far less than cost, promoting overconsumption and inadequate production. In 1991, prices varied wildly, with steel and oil going for 15 to 30 percent of the world market price while color televisions went for three times and personal computers over sixty times the world market price.

The banking system, until near the end, was a vast monopoly run by a single enormous bank. In 1988 the State Bank had 4500 branches, 200,000 employees, and an incredible 178 million savings accounts. The bank controlled money and credit in the economy. Since 1970 the money supply has grown at almost twice the rate of real output, thereby creating a rapid growth in savings. Large budget deficits, autonomous enterprises, consumer fears about the future, and rising prices have pushed inflationary trends in the Soviet economy. Even in 1990 the old system provided 98 percent of all loans to state enterprises.[26]

Until the late 1980s foreign trade was a monopoly of the Ministry of Foreign Trade. The economy worked to protect domestic industries and promote relative autarchy. The government determined the volume, price, structure, direction, and even transportation of foreign goods. The Ministry of Foreign Trade planned all transactions, prepared and participated in negotiations, ran foreign trade corporations, and drafted trade plans. The ministry worked through foreign trade commissioners, trade delegations, and monopolies to promote its goals. In 1988 more than half of all trade was within the framework of the Council of Mutual Economics Assistance, which mainly encompassed Eastern Europe. An additional 20 to 25 percent was with the West and 10 to 15 percent with Third World countries.

With the Gorbachev reforms, this began to change. Since 1987 many enterprises, ministries, and associations have been allowed to deal directly with foreign corporations. However, even at the end in 1991 there were significant limitations on the hard currency they could retain and other details of trade deals. The lack of a convertible ruble, an unworkable infrastructure, and a massive bureaucracy hampered foreign trade[27]

The ultimate symbol of the failure of the system to provide goods and services to the population was the vast increase in savings and monetary overhang in the economy. Savings increased rapidly to over 300 billion rubles, or over 50 percent of the GNP. Combined with underground and enterprise free money, there were over 500 billion rubles in search of goods by 1991.[28]

INDUSTRY

The state owned and operated nearly all industry. In the name of economies of scale and specialization, it favored enormous monopolistic enterprises. Nearly 87 percent of the 6000 products in machine building were manufactured by one single plant each. The largest single enterprise produced 75 percent of all

---

[26]Spulber, *Restructuring the Soviet Economy*, chapter 7.
[27]Spulber, *Restructuring the Soviet Economy*, chapter 12.
[28]International Monetary Fund, et al., *A Study of the Soviet Economy*, vol. 1, chapter III.3.

production for the top 38 industrial products. Nearly 46,000 industrial enterprises, with assets of 800 billion rubles, employed 35 million people.[29]

Centralized planning eliminated the link between producers and consumers that ensures responsiveness to market demands. Under this system there was no feedback. No new firms with new ideas were allowed to enter the market. The system received very poor information on markets and competition. It stressed autarchy and vertical integration without competition to root out ineffective firms. Infrastructure support tended to be poor as it did not contribute directly to plan fulfillment. The rigidities of the system promoted a technological lag of ten to fifteen years behind the West. No less than 90 percent of all capital went for delayed projects. The low retirement rate of assets (1 percent a year) and slowness in completing new projects left the average industrial asset an amazing twenty-seven years old. Soviet industrial products were, not surprisingly, uncompetitive with the West. Only 2 percent of industrial products were sold abroad while 40 percent of imports from the West were manufactured goods. Soviet products could be sold mainly in the Third World.[30]

Industrial productivity was perhaps 40 percent of the American level. Overstaffing, the lack of incentives to do a good job, poor training and work plans, weak inputs and tools, and failure to deliver goods on time were common. Quality was especially poor in shoes, trucks, textiles, and computers.[31]

The industrial purchasing system was extraordinarily cumbersome. Three huge organizations, Gosplan, Gossnab, and Gosbank (State Bank) controlled a vast network of enterprises and tried to match producers with users. With no market system to indicate how to distribute produce, this system worked through suppliers functioning as monopolistic producers using central control of the vast industrial production network. The producers had the power to dictate price, terms, and quality. Buyers tried to evaluate brands, quality, and price; sellers estimated the demand for these goods. The system worked through gross material balances set from above for raw materials, fuel, machinery, and equipment.[32]

Under Gorbachev there was some increase in enterprise autonomy and increased leasing of plants to cooperatives. Prices were no longer rigid but began to float. Some military industries began conversion to civilian products. Many ministries sharply reduced their superfluous staff. Small businesses and joint stock companies were now officially a part of the system. There was increasing recognition that the informal bargaining and politicking from the bottom up, which was such an integral part of the system, should be recognized and partially legitimized (and in some ways decriminalized).

[29]International Monetary Fund, *et al., A Study of the Soviet Economy,* vol. 2, chapter IV.2, vol. 3, chapter V.8.

[30]International Monetary Fund, *et al., A Study of the Soviet Economy,* vol. 3, chapter V.8; and Spulber, *Restructuring the Soviet Economy,* chapter 4.

[31]International Monetary Fund, *et al., A Study of the Soviet Economy,* vol. 3, chapter V.8.

[32]Spulber, *Restructuring the Soviet Economy,* chapter 11.

The Soviet industrial system was concentrated in Russia (60 percent) and Ukraine and Belarus (20 percent). The rest of the country accounted for only 20 percent of industrial output.

AGRICULTURE

Agriculture was a recurrent and never solved Soviet problem. Failures in the agricultural sector required massive food imports under Brezhnev and Gorbachev and the imposition of rationing in many parts of the country in 1988. The system could meet only the most basic needs of the population.

Chapter 2 showed that the Soviet Union lacked the excellent climate and terrain of the United States. Cold temperatures, poor soil, short growing seasons, and irregular and inadequate rainfall prevailed throughout much of the country. Central Asia resembles New Mexico and Arizona; Siberia, Saskatchewan and Manitoba; and only part of Ukraine resembles the American Middle West.

Soviet agriculture, which accounted for 20 percent of investment and had 27 million people working on collective farms and state farms, cultivated more land than any other country.[33] In the United States, agriculture absorbs 5 percent of investment and employs 3 percent of the work force. One-third less of the land is cultivated than in the former Soviet Union. Yet in the FSU low labor productivity required annual imports of 20 billion dollars a year in food, equal to the 20 to 30 percent of food lost in the system each year.

Agriculture had long been the Achilles' heel of the regime. Stalin's decision in 1929 to forcibly collectivize agriculture, deport the richest peasants (kulaks), and eliminate private farming established a system that remained in force until the late 1980s. In 1953 agricultural output, devastated by low yields, poor pay, confiscatory pricing, underinvestment, and World War II, was no greater than in 1928. The cost of this neglect has been enormous. In 1990 subsidies for agriculture exceeded 115 billion rubles, or 12 percent of the GNP and 30 percent of farm income. In 1990 investment in agriculture required 50 billion rubles, 23 percent of all state investment, and the writing off of 70 billion rubles in farm loans. Investment went mainly for tractors, trucks, farm machinery, livestock premises, irrigation, and drainage. Objective conditions were bad, but deeper problems lay in institutional arrangements, labor problems, and a past history of neglect.[34] As James Millar concluded, "A comparison of Soviet and United States agriculture, then, reveals what appears to be an inordinate absorption of current resources in Soviet agriculture to produce a still inadequate and highly costly output."[35]

The levels of capital and manpower remained serious problems. Despite

---

[33]Spulber, *Restructuring the Soviet Economy*, chapter 10.
[34]International Monetary Fund, *et al.*, *A Study of the Soviet Economy*, vol. 3, chapter V.5.
[35]James Millar, "The Prospects for Soviet Agriculture," in Bernstein, editor, *The Soviet Economy: Continuity and Change*, chapter 13, and particularly p. 282.

enormous investment during the Khrushchev, Brezhnev, and Gorbachev eras, Soviet rural infrastructure was very weak. Rural roads were in terrible shape, machinery often neglected, and retail trade poorly organized. Spare parts were in short supply, machinery was of poor quality and hard to find at the right time, and manual labor often predominated over the use of machines. Rural construction was often a disaster area, millions of tons of collected grain lay out in the open fields, and transportation, storage, and packaging were disastrous. The labor pool, 65 percent female and quite old and unskilled, remained poor and unmotivated. During the harvest at least 15 million workers had to be mobilized for an average of one month to bring in the crops. After six decades of collectivization of agriculture, the peasants had lost their love of the land and took no pride in their work. There was no real relation between their effort and their reward. Farm prices remained low, and rural incomes lagged substantially behind those of the urban sector.[36]

The bureaucratic structure remained firmly in place as a major obstacle to progress. Two and a half million bureaucrats administered the rural sector. Overcentralized decision making was incompatible with the flexibility required at the rural level. Targets were too high and too short term to adequately develop the agricultural sector. Production was inefficient and the distribution process sadly defective. A monopolistic sector had little incentive to respond to market demand. Even in 1991 state orders and state procurement prices still dominated the rural sector. The problems of pricing, transportation, storage, processing, and distribution plagued the system. Equipment often stood idle for lack of spare parts and trained operators. Poor packaging, lack of suitable facilities for storing chemicals and equipment, weak quality control, and untimely delivery of fertilizers and chemicals haunted the system. The stress on very large farms, overly detailed supervision, and too many specialized products strangled initiative and production.[37]

Agriculture did make some progress after the end of the Stalinist era. From 1955 to 1980 agricultural production grew at 3.4 percent a year, more than twice the population increase. The Russian diet almost doubled in quality by 1980 and was substantially better than that in the bulk of the Third World. Only a few First World countries (United States, Canada, Argentina, and Australia) have been able to develop low-cost agriculture. However, the agricultural growth rate fell from 5 percent a year in the 1950s to 3 percent a year in the 1960s and 1 percent a year in the early 1970s. The late 1970s saw an average of 205 million tons of grain produced a year, but the figure for the late 1980s was 200 million tons of grain.[38]

The rural exodus continued to depopulate the countryside. Low wages, few

[36]Alec Nove, "Soviet Agriculture—the Brezhnev Legacy and the Gorbachev Cure," in Ferenc Feher and Andrew Arato, editors, *Gorbachev: The Debate,* Humanities Press, Atlantic Highland, New Jersey, 1989, chapter 7.
[37]Millar, "The Prospects for Soviet Agriculture," in Bernstein, editor, *The Soviet Economy: Continuity and Change,* chapter 13.
[38]Millar, "The Prospects for Soviet Agriculture," in Bernstein, editor, *The Soviet Economy: Continuity and Change,* chapter 13; and Spulber, *Restructuring the Soviet Economy,* chapter 10.

amenities, frequent lack of water or gas, terrible housing, poor consumer goods, and weak medical care pushed the best and the brightest off the farm. The poor quality of rural education—small schools (often one room schoolhouses) in disrepair, poor teachers, and the lack of a well-rounded education—intensified this trend. So too did the bright lights of the city with better amenities and opportunities for advancement. Overall, 2 to 3 million rural inhabitants, overwhelmingly between fifteen and thirty-five years of age, moved to the city every year. A 1970 survey of Novosibirsk province found that only 12 percent of the children of farmers wanted to be farmers and almost 90 percent wanted to be industrial workers.[39]

The predominant forms of agriculture were state farms, with 76 percent of all land, and collective farms with the other 23 percent. Private farms accounted for less than 1 percent of the land. State farms, historically favored by the regime, were run on the industrial model by a director with a number of production units (brigades) similar to shops. State farms meant that the state owned the land and had a right to the output; the men and women working on the farm were only workers with no rights to the land or output. Working from plans sent down from above, these state farms tried to meet targets for sales, costs, capital, and profit. They predominated where vast scale seemed likely to provide economy of scale, as in Central Asian cotton fields, Black Earth grain areas, and Siberian and Kazakhstan virgin lands. State farms did have small private plots available for the workers to do with as they wished.

Collective farms, originally the predominant form, were in decline, but still accounted for 12 million households. Collective farmers did not own the land, which belonged to the collective. Each household was allowed a small private plot of less than one acre. The collective farm was required to meet plans established by state orders with compulsory deliveries to the state at fixed prices.[40]

Gorbachev, who received his correspondence degree in agronomy and who was responsible for agriculture in the Politburo from 1978 to 1985, moved cautiously in this area. After the failure of supercentralization of agroindustry in 1985, he moved towards Chinese-style reforms, allowing more capitalism in the countryside. He stressed the need for more agricultural machinery and contracts with small autonomous work units. In 1988 he called for the leasing of land to peasants. The response of the peasants was weak. In 1990 the Soviet government approved the creation of private farms, as did the Russian republic. This position was controversial because the population opposed (by a 46-42 margin) turning over the land to private farmers. At the end in 1991 the old structure remained solidly in place in the countryside.[41]

A real cure for all these woes will be very expensive. Massive spending is

[39]David Powell, "The Rural Exodus," in Bernstein, editor, *The Soviet Economy: Continuity and Change.*

[40]Spulber, *Restructuring the Soviet Economy*, chapter 10.

[41]Anders Aslund, "Gorbachev, Perestroyka and Economic Crisis," *Problems of Communism*, vol. 40, nos. 1–2, January–April 1991, pp. 39–40.

needed to provide a good rural infrastructure to bring the produce to market. A decent quality of life is a necessity if the rural exodus of the best and the brightest is to slow. Bureaucratic interference in peasant decisions must be sharply reduced. The modern use of fertilizers will require a motivated farming population, good storage space, and spreading machinery. The peasants must be able to buy decent consumer goods in order to motivate them to take risk to earn money. To overcome the strong habits of six decades, massive inertia, and the bureaucratic stranglehold will require enormous effort, lasting at least one generation, before private farming becomes a profitable reality.[42]

TELECOMMUNICATIONS

Advances in telecommunications—from satellites and fax machines to optical imaging and interactive computers—have epitomized the new advanced postindustrial order in the West. The isolated Soviet system, geared to the world of smokestack industries and military orders, performed very poorly in adapting the Soviet economy to this new order. Even telephones, such an integral part of the old order, remained a weak sector despite almost 2 million employees in the Ministry of Post and Telecommunication. Telephones were poorly made and the lines were badly maintained. Only 25 percent of all households had telephones, compared to nearly everyone in the United States and Western Europe. The waiting list for telephones was a staggering 15 million people, including 120,000 people in Moscow. Over 100,000 villages lacked even a single telephone. In 1991 there were only 2000 to 3000 international lines to Moscow. Telex was popular, with almost 3000 international subscribers.[43]

The system was outdated, with antiquated switching equipment. There were 600 lines between Moscow and Leningrad. Local calls were free and long-distance calls were subsidized. Only the use of nineteen satellites and installation of fax machines offered hope by 1991.

LABOR FORCE

The revolution from above initiated by Stalin in the 1930s and continued by his successors wrought enormous changes in the size, distribution, skills, and education of the Soviet labor force. Even after the massive industrialization of the 1930s, in 1940 there were still 32 million people engaged in agriculture compared to only 13 million workers in industry. But by 1985 there were only 25 million people in agriculture and 38 million workers in industry. Wages were differentiated on the basis of sex, training, branch of industry, sectors, enterprises, skills, and hardship. High output targets, taut allocation of scarce

[42]Nove, "Soviet Agriculture—the Brezhnev Legacy and Gorbachev Cure," in Feher and Arato, editors, *Gorbachev: The Debate,* chapter 7.
[43]International Monetary Fund, et al., *A Study of the Soviet Economy,* vol. 3, chapter V.4.

resources, and aging and obsolete equipment produced an alleged labor short-age. Members of the working class received higher wages than those in trade or education.[44]

The elite party apparatchiki *(nomenklatura)* gained great privileges, ranging from luxury housing, summer homes, and visits to resorts to low-priced goods, foreign travel, and entertainment. At the bottom there were over 35 million poor people and almost 60 million pensioners, living in dire straits. While 5 percent of Russians lived below the poverty line, 51 percent of Tajiks did so.[45]

The education level of the population has improved dramatically in the last fifty years. During World War II the typical soldier had four years of education. By 1990, 60 percent of the population had graduated from an academic high school and 6 percent (almost 19 million people) had graduated from univer-sity.[46]

There was a sharp drop in the growth rate of the population. During the 1980s the labor force grew by less than 1 percent a year, and the growth came mainly in Central Asia and the Transcaucasus. Formerly one of the major factors in growth, labor inputs became a neutral factor rather than a force for growth. Labor productivity, which grew more than 6 percent a year in the 1960s, dropped to less than 4 percent a year in the 1970s and 3 percent a year in the 1980s. Yet there was a labor surplus. Featherbedding, or superfluous overmanning, accounted for 10 to 20 percent of the work force, or 13 to 26 million people. The lack of an intensive work routine, the need to storm (work furiously) at the end of the quarter or do crash work to meet the plan quota, and the poor product quality promoted the need for enterprises to keep surplus laborers. Much of the work was done "for the warehouse" rather than for sale to the public. This was even more true in agriculture, where upwards of 70 percent of the labor force does mainly manual labor.[47] There was a high rate of female participation in the work force, higher even than in the West. Retirement was relatively early, at 55 for women and 60 for men. In 1990, 2 million people were officially unemployed, but the reality was probably closer to 4 million people, mainly in Kazakhstan, Central Asia and the Transcaucasus. Labor turnover was relatively high at 20 percent a year, but lower than in the United States.[48]

TECHNOLOGICAL PROGRESS

One of the major reasons for the Gorbachev reform efforts was that Soviet technology was lagging behind that of the West. At first blush, this may seem odd. If the state was allocating most investment into research and development

[44]Spulber, *Restructuring the Soviet Economy,* chapter 5.

[45]*Restructuring the Soviet Economy,* chapter 5; and International Monetary Fund, et al., *A Study of the Soviet Economy,* vol. 2, chapter IV.6.

[46]International Monetary Fund, et al., *A Study of the Soviet Economy,* vol. 2, chapter IV.6.

[47]Vladimir Kostakov, "Employment: Scarcity or Surplus?," in Anthony Jones and William Moskoff, editors, *Perestroika and the Economy: New Thinking in Soviet Economics,* M.E. Sharpe, Armonk, New York, 1989, pp. 158–175.

[48]International Monetary Fund, et al., *A Study of the Soviet Economy,* vol. 2, chapter IV.6.

and the country had the world's second largest and best scientific establishment, then why did this problem develop? Especially why given the
technocratic bent of the Brezhnev administration, dominated by engineers, and
its strong positive view of science?

The system had a series of structural impediments to innovations. Science
thrives on the rapid and unimpeded flow of information, but Soviet science was
cut off from the rest of the world. Party controls played havoc with the scientific
establishment, especially in the late Stalinist era. Most talented scientists,
technicians, and engineers worked for the military-industrial complex, which
was separated from the civilian sector.

The planning process slowed down the rate of technological progress. The
system, based on the Marxist theory of value, priced new products often very
cheaply. This deterred risk taking if the rewards were to be modest. The
incentive structure for managers was built around bonuses which relied on
meeting quantitative quotas for output. Using a new product always incurred
risk because it could slow the current rate of production, require retraining of
the labor force, increase spoilage and down time, and bring problems in
smoothing out the production line and arranging a good supply of materials.
With little positive return and great risk, managers preferred to avoid innovation. Change always entailed unanticipated risks which could be avoided if the
enterprise continued to produce the same product.

Thus the structure of the research and development system served to retard
technological innovation. There was no good connection between research and
development institutes and the enterprises that could use them. The planning
process tended to penalize innovative, but risky, enterprises. These problems
accelerated as the rate of technological innovation increased in the 1970s and
1980s.[49]

SECOND ECONOMY

Historically, the failings of the centrally planned "first economy" led to the
existence of an unofficial "second economy." Parts of the second economy were
legal—private plots that produced 25 percent of agricultural output on 3
percent of the land (but with 25 percent of all labor inputs), private housing for
30 percent of the population, and the private activities of professionals. The
legal private sector generated perhaps 10 percent of the GNP, and 75 percent
of this was in agriculture. Then there was the vast arena of semilegal and illegal
private enterprise. With 500 billion rubles in search of goods, there was
tremendous demand for goods and services not provided in decent quality or
quantity by the state. An increasingly alienated population frequently transformed public property into private property.

Employees often stole state property and took it home, for personal use or

---

[49]Joseph Berliner, "The Prospects for Technological Progress," in Bernstein, editor, *The Soviet
Economy: Continuity and Change,* chapter 14.

trade. They diverted freight to the black market. They used state resources to build private houses. Soviet employees rerouted finished goods from their final destinations. In stores clerks set aside quality goods for their own use or that of their friends. They speculated in goods, dealt illegally in foreign currencies, and traded with foreigners. There was an almost endless number of ways to steal from the state, from bribing the police and giving gifts to supervisors to selling official positions and padding reports and obtaining unwarranted bonuses. On collective farms it was even easier to carry out these measures. Corruption flourished especially in ports—such as Leningrad, Riga, and Odessa—and in the south of the country—the Transcaucasus and Central Asia. Increasing output of private cars, enhanced exposure to foreign travel, and accelerating savings intensified this trend.[50] However, the fact that this second economy was illegal and that people could be sent to jail for economic crimes naturally limited public enthusiasm for it, as did the fact that many people lacked access that would allow them to commit such crimes.

Gorbachev sought to legalize much of the second economy and use this private initiative in a legal manner to bolster the economy. The 1986 Law of Industrial Enterprise, the 1988 Law of Cooperatives, and the 1990 Law of Enterprises sought to promote cooperatives and individuals working for private gain. By 1991 the fledgling movement faced significant public opposition, but it did provide a base for the future radical transition to capitalism.

AT THE FALL: SOVIET ECONOMY 1991

The state of the Soviet economy at the end of the Soviet Union was deplorable. Despite all of Gorbachev's reforms, the fundamental core of the centrally planned economy, although crippled and increasingly marginalized, was still intact. Gorbachev tried to pull the party out of the economy, push leasing of land to the peasants, promote private and cooperative ownership of production, and increase enterprise autonomy. Nonetheless, the economy was in recession, poised for depression.

The center still disposed of great resources and directed the economy. Although in 1990 the state was supposed to be reduced to commanding only 40 percent of all capital equipment, it still controlled 96 percent. Private and cooperative enterprises, although growing, remained peripheral. In October 1990 cooperatives and private enterprise accounted for only 6 to 11 percent of all production. In 1990 state orders accounted for 75 percent of production and the state employed 84 percent of all workers, generated 87 percent of national income, and provided 89 percent of all capital.[51] As Nicholas Spulber concluded:

---

[50]Spulber, *Restructuring the Soviet Economy*, chapter 11; and Gregory Grossman, "The 'Second Economy' of the USSR," in Bernstein, editor, *The Soviet Economy: Continuity and Change*, chapter 4.
[51]International Monetary Fund, et al., *A Study of the Soviet Economy*, vol. 2, chapter IV.2.

In fact, throughout the 1980s, perestroika did not revolutionize the scope of ownership rights, the established patterns of business organization and motivation, the traditional labor and industrial relations, nor the key economic functions of government in any significant way. Progress toward even centrally regulated markets was consequently limited mostly to a slow and as yet marginal development of cooperatives. This less than revolutionary beginning . . . [implies that] development under perestroika of private, individual and cooperative production and small-scale trade has been far less impetuous through the 1980s than through the first years of the NEP.[52]

The reasons for the failure of the reforms are numerous. Transforming a centrally planned socialist economy into a market-driven semicapitalist economy is enormously difficult. The various decrees and directives of the Gorbachev regime were often ambiguous and inconsistent. Popular support for the changes remained relatively weak while the vested bureaucratic interests fought hard against their implementation.

The legacy of the old economic order is a heavy burden for Yeltsin and other FSU reformers. Capitalism, as the final chapters show, is very difficult to create in the absence of critical values, norms, structures, and attitudes. The old system, for all its failings, provided basic goods and security for all, if at a low level. There is no recipe for the transition from socialism to capitalism. Not surprisingly, in Russia much of the old economy remains—huge nonproductive state plants, state-run agriculture, enormous government bureaucracies, state commitment to avoiding unemployment and starvation. Only in 1992 and 1993 has there been much of an effort to break decisively with the past. Naturally, without state planning and a party to direct it, the old system has run worse than ever. And a number of republics, seeing the chaos in Russia, have tried to move even more slowly. In the coming chapters we discuss Soviet history and then turn to the reform efforts now under way, with varying success, in the new states to create a modern capitalist system.

---

[52]Spulber, *Restructuring the Soviet Economy*, p. 268. NEP is the New Economic Program of liberalization, which was instituted in 1921 after the end of the civil war and lasted until 1928, when Stalin introduced a massive program of economic transformation and central planning.

6

Soviet and Post-Soviet Politics: A Comparative Perspective

To understand the Soviet Union from 1917 until its demise in 1991 takes a leap of imagination for American students. To understand the bewildering changes in the fifteen successor states of the FSU challenges even the specialist in the region.

SOVIET POLITICS: A COMPARATIVE PERSPECTIVE

In addition to the usual foreign policy issues and unique features (size, multiethnic empire, special mission), there are special problems for those studying the FSU. Tsarist Russia and the Soviet Union repeatedly faced serious threats—both external and internal—in this century. Two million Russians were killed in World War I; the figure reached 27 million killed and 25 million homeless in World War II. Then for over forty years the Soviet Union fought the Cold War. It faced serious economic development problems as well.

As a revolutionary power similar to England after 1649, France after 1789, and China after 1949, the Soviet Union fought foreign intervention and the Whites in the Civil War (1918–1920). As the heir to Tsarist Russia (after the brief interlude of the Provisional Government), the Soviet Union inherited the authoritarian Tsarist political culture, a multiethnic empire, and a weak economic and technological infrastructure. Seeking to create a Marxist-inspired utopia, the regime pursued radical change. In its use of mass terror in the 1930s under Stalin, the Soviet Union has been compared to Nazi Germany.

We can draw on several models to help us understand the Soviet Union in its turbulent history (see Table 6.1). These models involve simplifications of

TABLE 6.1. Comparative Framework for Understanding the Soviet Union

Theories	Model	Nature*	
		Strength	Weakness
Political			
Tsarist continuity	Tsarist Russia	Political culture	Radical change
Revolutionary	France 1789–	Dictator culture	Socialism Military
Marxist	Socialist utopia	Radical change	State terror
Totalitarian	Nazi Germany	Terror	Social support
		Rapid change	
Economic			
Industrial development	Western Europe/U.S.	Industrial focus	Terror
Post-industrial development	Japan	Perestroika	Isolation from World
Military			
Military competition	Prewar Germany	Industrial emphasis	Great Purges
Psychological			
Psychological	Freudian	Great Purges	Economic changes

*Strengths and weaknesses refer to the strengths and weaknesses of the model in understanding Soviet realities.

reality in order to point out key features that help explain Soviet political developments. However, we lack the space to discuss other models developed in the 1950s and 1960s, such as "interest group" and "Kremlinology."[1]

MILITARY MODEL

Our first model deals with military competition, which has been such a critical feature of Soviet politics. It argues that all nations exist in a Hobbesian world of anarchic competition in which only the strong survive. While today brutal competition for survival is most evident in the Yugoslav civil war and the repeated Arab-Israeli wars, historically it was the main feature of European politics. Unbridled and bloody warfare reduced Europe from 300 states in 1600 to roughly 25 states by 1900—and eliminated large states such as Poland.[2]

For Russia, military competition was always a major feature of existence. Its open frontiers led to four invasions of Russia from 1709 (Charles X of Sweden), to 1812 (Napoleonic France), to the German invasions of World War I

[1]Kremlinology as it developed in the 1950s in an era of very restricted access to any information about the Soviet Union focused on the relative power of elite members of the government in an attempt to understand events cloaked in secrecy.

[2]See Charles Tilly, *The Formation of the Modern European State System*, Princeton University Press, Princeton, 1975.

(1915) and World War II (1941).[3] As a revolutionary power it faced, in its view, the undying enmity of the traditional European powers trying to destroy it. Counterrevolutionary forces destroyed revolutionary regimes in France (1814, 1871), Europe (1848), Taiping China (1850s), and Hungary (1849, 1919). Between 1918 and 1920 the Western allies and Japan provided troops and arms in an effort to destroy the Soviet regime.

During the 1930s the threat to the Soviet Union markedly increased. The rise of Nazi Germany in the west and Imperial Japan in the east boded ill for the Soviet Union. So, too, did the appeasement policy of the Western powers and the military unpreparedness of the United States in the 1930s. All this intensified the Soviet interest in modernization and industrialization in the 1930s.

The experiences of the Civil War and World War II reinforced Soviet emphasis on the military factor. The cost of failure was enormous and the payoff from military preparedness great. The "lessons" of war promoted war preparedness, massive overinsurance, economic modernization and industrialization, and central control of resources.[4] Military competition took a new form after victories in World War II made the Soviet Union a superpower. Lacking economic, political, or cultural superpower capabilities, the Soviet Union could be a superpower only in the military realm.[5]

This forced the Soviet Union, which lagged behind Europe economically, to adapt its domestic politics to military mobilization. As early as Peter the Great, Russian domestic modernization was driven by the needs of military competition. During the eighteenth and most of the nineteenth century at least 40 percent of the annual budget was devoted to the military.[6] As Leon Trotsky observed,

> The history of Russia's state economy is an unbroken chain of efforts—heroic efforts in a certain sense—aimed at providing the military organization with the means necessary for its continuing existence. The entire government apparatus was built and constantly rebuilt in the interests of the treasury. Its function consisted in snatching every particle of the accumulated labor of the people and utilizing it for its own ends.[7]

German victories from Tannenberg in 1914 to Riga in 1917 made clear the great gap that separated Germany from Russia in 1918. The more sophisticated the weapon, the greater the gap, as shown in Table 6.2.

For Stalin, these facts demanded the creation of a wartime economy in

---

[3]This is not to ignore Russian expansion east, west and south. Rather it is to stress the Russian perception of threat.
[4]For these lessons for the Great Patriotic War, see Jonathan Adelman and Cristann Gibson, editors, *Contemporary Soviet Military Affairs: The Legacy of World War II,* Unwin, Hyman, Boston, 1989.
[5]Its Marxist appeal to Western Europe in the 1930s and 1940s and Third World in the 1950s and 1960s rapidly faded by the 1970s and 1980s.
[6]For more about the Imperial Russian Army and Tsarist Russia, see John Curtis, *The Russian Army Under Nicholas I, 1825–1855,* Duke University Press, Durham, North Carolina, 1965; and Bernard Pares, *A History of Russia,* Alfred Knopf, New York, 1947.
[7]Leon Trotsky, *1905,* translated by Anya Bostock, Random House, New York, 1971, p. 5.

TABLE 6.2.   German and Russian Weapons Production, World War I

Weapons (thousands)	Germany	Russia	German Advantage
Airplanes	47.3	3.5	13.5:1
Machine Guns	280.0	28.0	10.0:1
Cannons	64.0	11.7	5.5:1
Shells	306.0	67.0	4.6:1
Rifles	8,547.0	3,300.0	2.6:1
Bullets	8,200,000.0	13,500,000.0	1:1.7

Source: *Sovetskaya voennaya entsiklopedia*, Voenizdat, Moscow, 1978, vol. 6, p. 275.

peacetime in the 1930s to close the gap between a weak Russia and a powerful Germany. As Stalin said in 1931, "We lag behind the advanced countries by 50 to 100 years. We must make up this distance in 10 years. Either we do this or they crush us"[8] Only in the Gorbachev and Yeltsin era did this thinking become outmoded.

ECONOMIC MODEL

The economic dimension provides a second way in which to view the Soviet Union. During the period from 1920 to 1985, the principal issue was industrial modernization; in the 1990s the issue was the postindustrial transformation of the economy. The key problem is that the vast majority of over 150 Third World countries seeking to industrialize have failed—only a handful (Japan, the Four Tigers of Asia, Israel, Spain) have succeeded. The Four Tigers of Asia are small, formerly Japanese or British colonies, under a Western defense umbrella with neo-Confucian culture and trade-driven economies. Israel is a small country with massive immigration, high levels of educational attainment, and strong American financial support. Spanish peripheral capitalist development occurred on the fringe of Europe and benefitted from massive integration into the European Community. Japan has a massive trade-driven economy, with large-scale government interference, a high savings rate, and a disciplined work force. None of these countries was an obvious model for Soviet development.

The Soviet Union has been the only large, nontrade-driven economy to successfully industrialize in this century. But rapid economic development demands certain prerequisites noticeable in these successful economies:

1. Strong authoritarian political leadership with one-party rule
2. Suppression of domestic demand and consumption in favor of governmentally mandated long range goals
3. Suppression of powerful trade unions
4. High savings rates

[8]Joseph Stalin, *Works*, Foreign Languages Publishing House, Moscow, 1955, vol. 13, p. 41.

5. Strong sense of communal identity with government or society
6. Significant emphasis on societal values over individual values
7. Weak emphasis on civil liberties
8. Powerful governmental role in running economy with long-range planning[9]

All of these are found in the Soviet Union during the developmental period. There were also some distinctive Soviet factors, such as maintenance of a strong defense posture (shared only with Israel, Taiwan, and South Korea) and isolation from the world economy. On the other hand, the Soviet Union had the great advantage of possessing the world's greatest supply of natural resources and a large labor force to develop these resources.

However, by the 1980s the neo-Stalinist command economy began to falter seriously as the world economy changed and the massive aggregation of new natural resources, capital, and manpower slowly dissolved in the Soviet Union. This was a significant factor in its demise.

POLITICAL

There are at least four competing political models: revolutionary, continuity, totalitarian, and Marxist (including neo-Marxist). Each one has different premises, actors, and implications.

Revolutionary

The revolutionary model compared revolutionary Russia with revolutionary England (1644–1660), revolutionary France (1789–1814), and revolutionary China (1949–1978).[10] This model, developed especially by Crane Brinton, Barrington Moore, and Theda Skocpol, found numerous similarities in the development of these societies. Revolutionary Russia after the October Revolution faced problems common to other agro-bureaucratic empires, like France and China. Militarily, it found itself under attack from domestic counterrevolution aided by foreign intervention. Russia had to fight a civil war, just like the civil wars in England in the 1640s, the civil war in China from 1946 to 1949, and the Vendée insurrection in France. Foreign powers were hostile and repeatedly attacked revolutionary France, destroying it in 1814. Revolutionary China saw itself forced into the Korean War to protect its borders from the advancing Americans in November 1950.

At home, there was a period of violence, followed by a Thermidorian reaction (occurring in Russia in the 1920s) and a period of revolutionary consolidation of power (as under Stalin and Bonaparte). The successful dicta-

[9]See Charles Lindblom, *Planning and Markets,* Yale University Press, New Haven, 1982.
[10]For classic works in this genre making these comparisons, see Crane Brinton, *Anatomy of a Revolution,* Random House, New York, 1938; Theda Skocpol, *States and Social Revolution,* Cambridge University Press, Cambridge, 1979; and Barrington Moore, *Social Origins of Dictatorship and Democracy,* Beacon Press, Boston, 1965.

tors integrated the old high elite culture with the new low mass culture of the peasants, while destroying their enemies. In the process the rights of women and minorities were often the price paid for this consolidation.[11] There was a massive opening of government careers to men of talent from the lower classes.

The military machine was built up and became powerful through the elimination of the feudal encumbrances of the old regime, mass mobilization of a newly politically conscious populace, and the opening of the office corps to men of talent from all classes. The new, vastly enhanced governmental machine could now provide adequate resources to support a much more powerful military machine. In France, the new army dominated Europe by 1807, and in Russia the new Red Army occupied half of Europe by 1945. Finally, after the waning of the revolutionary phase, a postrevolutionary decline set in, epitomized in Russia by the Brezhnev era. This would lead to a major systemic crisis and the ultimate demise of the postrevolutionary regime (1660 English restoration, 1814 French restoration).

This model, obviously, has its virtues. But its limits are clear too. There was no equivalent to the Great Purges, the elimination of the kulaks, and the Ukrainian famine in other countries to account for the massive killings, starvation, and imprisonment that were such prominent features of the Stalinist regime. Nor was there an emphasis on economic development in France, England, or even China, where the Cultural Revolution and Great Leap Forward were economically irrational and counterproductive. The great enhancement of technological capabilities impacted the actions of Russia in the 1930s. In 1993 the new postrevolutionary FSU hardly resembled Bourbon France in 1815 or Stuart England of 1660.

Continuity

The continuity model borrows from the French aphorism, "The more things change, the more they stay the same." George Kennan in his review of a work on Russia written in 1839 by a French aristocrat, Marquis de Custine, has asserted:

> Here, as though the book had been written yesterday . . . appear all the familiar features of Stalinism: the absolute power of a single man; his power over thoughts as well as actions; the impermanence and unsubstantiality of all subordinate distinctions of rank and dignity—the instantaneous transition from lofty station to disgrace and oblivion; the indecent association of sycophancy upwards with brutality downwards; the utter disenfranchisement and helplessness of the popular masses; the nervous punishment of innocent people for the offenses they might be considered capable of committing rather than ones they had committed; the neurotic relationship to the West; the frantic fear of foreign observation; the obsession with espionage; the secrecy; the systematic mystification; the general silence of intimidation; the preoccupation

---

[11]For this point, I am indebted to our former colleague, Dr. Glenn Fieldman.

with appearances at the expense of reality; the systematic cultivation of falsehood as a weapon of policy; the tendency to rewrite the past.[12]

This theory made the indisputable point that the Soviet Union occupied most of the territory of Tsarist Russia (minus Poland and Finland) and inherited much from its Tsarist ancestors. There was a powerful leader and highly authoritarian, centralized political culture, with no tradition of democracy or mass participation. Dissent was viewed as treasonous. There was a xenophobic distrust of foreigners and desire for isolation from the world. There was the Russian sense of superiority and semireligious messianism, the Russian belief in the universal validity of an official creed, whether reflected in the Tsarist concept of a "Third Rome" or the Soviet "leader of international socialism." There was ever the debate between Westernizers and Slavophiles, between those who insisted on Russia's special mission and uniqueness and those who wished to see it integrated in the world. There was the problem of a multi-ethnic empire, which left the Soviet Union as the world's sole remainder of an era that had vanished in Europe in 1918. The 1991 Russian Revolution dissolving the Soviet Union echoed the 1917 February Revolution dissolving Tsarist Russia.

There are limitations to this argument. Tsarist Russia was a backward agro-bureaucratic empire with a population consisting largely of illiterate or semiliterate peasants with low levels of political consciousness. Two-thirds of the population was urban and highly literate, living in an industrial super-power. The power and influence of the Russian Orthodox Church faded. Rather than being a weak and peripheral power on the fringe of Europe after 1860, the Soviet Union became a superpower. The post-Soviet move towards capitalism, democracy, and nationhood reflects a radical break with this autocratic, repressive Russian past. Nonetheless, in the new political setting that began in December 1991, some of the old—the pre-1917 Russian flag, anti-Semitism, authoritarianism, pogroms (of Armenians)—is resurfacing.

Totalitarianism

A third model was that of totalitarianism, elaborated by Hannah Arendt, Zbigniew Brzezinski, and Carl Friedrich in the late 1940s and early 1950s.[13] This theory, developed during the beginning of the Cold War, equated the Soviet Union with Nazi Germany as a new "totalitarian" state. Such a state had six features: official ideology, a single party led by one man, terroristic secret police, communications monopoly, weapons monopoly, and a centrally directed economy. These states atomized the population, relentlessly drove

[12]George Kennan, *The Marquis de Custine and His Russia in 1839*, Princeton University Press, Princeton, 1971, pp. 124–125.

[13]See Hannah Arendt, *The Origins of Totalitarianism*, Harcourt, Brace, Jovanovich, New York, 1973; and Carl Friedrich and Zbigniew Brzezinski, *Totalitarian Dictatorship and Autocracy*, Praeger, New York, 1956.

towards perfection, and passionately extolled the virtues of the leader and the party.

The analysis was best for the 1930s, when a powerful secret police at Stalin's behest executed over 750,000 people and sentenced 3.8 million people to labor camps or other punishment.[14] The theory accentuated the centralist nature of the regime, its drive for change and demands for ritualist purity.

But the totalitarian model leaves much unexplained. It could not explain more "ordinary" periods before 1930 and afterwards, nor does it have any relevance to the Gorbachev era of free emigration, *glasnost, perestroika,* and openness to the West. Even within the Stalinist era it does not explain the social bases of support for the regime, the great victory in World War II, or the broad uncoerced support for many policies within the party and population. Finally, by equating the Soviet Union with Nazi Germany, it leaves no room for the positive accomplishments of the Soviet regime, from achieving a high level of growth and modernity to winning World War II. Today, this model can provide no clue to the peaceful implosion of the Soviet Union or to its hesitant moves towards capitalism, democracy, and nationhood.

Marxism-Leninism

With Marxism-Leninism as the official creed of the Soviet Union from 1917 to 1991, Marxism in its Leninist variant had an impact on policy. Marxism served as an ideological filter of what was and was not acceptable and desirable. For over seventy years Marxism promoted nationalized property over private property, centralized planning over the marketplace, collective and state farms over more efficient private farming. It supported a one-party dictatorship in the name of the workers and peasants over a competitive multiparty system. Marxism defined national interest in terms of an ideological state mission to achieve socialism and communism. Certain classes (aristocrats, capitalists, kulaks, and rich farmers) were seen as hostile while other classes (workers, the poor, and peasants) were seen as friendly. The reshaping of society in the interests of the ideology and friendly classes was the state goal, with terror and repression considered acceptable tools to achieve this end.

Marxism did have its limits. The violent debates within the Soviet leadership, the wide policy swings between different eras, and the need to adapt policies to changes in environments all vitiated its role. Soviet leaders interpreted Marxism to fit their needs. Thus, the Marxism of Gorbachev or Khrushchev had little in common with that of Stalin or Brezhnev.

Although Marxism-Leninism remained the official ideology of the Soviet Union, a variety of neo-Marxist critiques, from those of Leon Trotsky and Milovan Djilas to various Eurocommunists in the 1970s, provided views critical of the developments in the Soviet Union. They focused on the development of

---

[14]See *New York Times,* February 14, 1990 for the official Soviet count on the Stalinist period from 1930–1953 alone.

a powerful bureaucracy, emergence of a new ruling class, and the deformation of the worker's state. Their influence was minimal within the Soviet Union, but they showed the creativity of Marxist thought outside of official shackles.

Psychological

Psychological theories, developed by Nathan Leites, Alexander George, and Robert Tucker, emphasized the need to step down from the level of systems to that of the individual.[15] Leites suggested a changeless Bolshevik personality under Lenin as the father figure, who reacted to the degenerate behavior of the nineteenth century intelligentsia, but Tucker advanced a more sophisticated theory about Stalin. These theorists argued that individuals do not react solely to systemic needs but also have been deeply impacted by their psychological needs and aspirations.

These theorists were the most convincing about the Stalin era. Who else beyond Stalin would have ordered massive Great Purges that destroyed tens of thousands of high party leaders, all of Lenin's former close lieutenants, and millions of hapless Soviet citizens? In times of crisis there is little doubt that the idiosyncratic behavior of the leader can come to the fore. The repudiation of Stalin in the Khrushchev and Gorbachev era illustrated the depth of the revulsion felt at such policies.

The problem is that psychology does not play a significant role in ordinary times when bureaucratic needs and the pressures of the domestic and international environment make themselves strongly felt. Its explanatory power outside of the Stalin era is limited. Even the Stalin era was shaped by numerous nonpsychological factors—menacing external threat, historical tradition of crushing real and imagined opposition, serious economic and political backwardness, and the strong support of many elements in the party and populace for a rapid transformation of the Soviet Union. Thus it is hard to explain industrialization or modernization policies in terms of psychology. Today, in post-Soviet politics, psychology seems to have relatively little to offer.

We can analyze Soviet reality on different levels—the individual level of the psychology of the leader or the masses, the state and societal level (macroeconomic variables or macropolitical variables), and the international level. For each period in Soviet politics, different models seem applicable. For the Lenin era, revolutionary and Marxist theories are appropriate as the nascent Soviet regime fought for its very survival in the Civil War. For the Stalin era, the totalitarian and continuity theories provide clues as Stalin integrated elements of traditional Russian culture into a program of radical political change. The psychological theories can provide insight into the Great Purges, and the

[15]See Nathan Leites, *The Operational Code of the Politburo,* McGraw-Hill, New York, 1951; Alexander George, "The 'Operational Code': A Neglected Approach to the Study of Political Leaders and Decision-Making," *International Studies Quarterly,* no. 8, 1969; and Robert Tucker, *Stalin As Revolutionary, 1879–1929: A Study in History and Personality,* W.W. Norton, New York, 1973.

industrial development model and military competition model can show the rationale behind the massive Stalinist programs of industrialization, modernization, and collectivization. For the Khrushchev and Brezhnev era, these same models continue to provide insight, while the psychological model can help us to understand the complex reaction to the Stalin era. For the Gorbachev and Yeltsin eras of radical change, the models of postindustrial economic development, a changing military competitive context, and revolution can be useful. Gorbachev's attempt to find the center, even as it was evaporating between a rising reactionary threat on the right and revolutionary reformism on the left, showed the futility of moderates in revolution.

Finally, we must ultimately make judgments for ourselves as to the relevance of each of the models. Each model provides some insights but at the price of obscuring other key elements. In the final analysis only the well-informed student can develop a properly informed and balanced view of Soviet politics.

POST-SOVIET POLITICS: A COMPARATIVE PERSPECTIVE

Here let us suggest a few relevant models for post-Soviet development. The successor states are undergoing an attempted triple revolution—trying to achieve capitalism, democracy, and nationhood—in a short period, an attempt with few precedents in recent history. This is an incredibly difficult, if not impossible, task. We discuss each of these issues in three chapters at the end of the book. Here we will mention some of the relevant models for each.

For nationhood we have witnessed the breakup of the world's last great multinational empire. The relevant models would be the three multinational empires that disintegrated in 1917 (Tsarist Russia) and 1918 (Austro-Hungarian, Ottoman Turkish) and the travails that followed each disintegration. For nation building, as opposed to empire destroying, we could look both at the early Western experiences (Western Europe, United States) in the sixteenth to eighteenth centuries and, perhaps more relevantly, the large-scale attempts at nation building in the Third World in the 1950s and 1960s. We can also look at the late nation building cases in Europe in the 1860s (Italy, Germany) and the consequences for the international system. These naturally are sobering examples, given the enormous difficulties for both the putative states and the regional and international systems.

For democracy we can look at the transition from authoritarian regimes to democratic regimes. We can examine cases of democratic failure in the interwar era (Germany, Spain, Portugal, Italy) and of success in the postwar era (Germany, Japan, Italy). We can look at democratic successes and failures in Third World countries, especially Latin America. We can also review the prerequisites for democracy derived from the successful cases of the United States and Western Europe.

For capitalism we can look at the cases of transition from noncapitalist regimes to capitalist regimes. We can look at problems in the transition to capitalism in Europe, Asia, and Latin America. We can focus on the prerequisites for successful capitalist development as seen in the United States, Western Europe, Japan, and the Four Tigers of Asia.

By looking at the existing literature and cases of success and failure in capitalism, democracy and nation building, the student can develop a strong historical and comparative framework for analyzing the likelihood of success or failure in these areas for the fifteen successor states to the former Soviet Union.

PART TWO

Soviet History from Lenin to Brezhnev

Current developments in the former Soviet Union cannot be understood without a solid understanding of the Soviet past. These seven chapters take us from the legacy of the Tsarist past through the end of the Brezhnev era in 1982. They show how and why the Soviet Union traveled a distinctly different path from the one taken by Western countries, and why the path of authoritarianism, socialism, and imperialism prevailed. The chapters also show that, far from being frozen in a single mode, the Soviet Union underwent dynamic political and economic developments that transformed the former Tsarist empire into something strikingly different, a quasi-modern and powerful state with a well-educated and largely urbanized population. Dramatic events of enormous power crowd the coming pages—from the great cataclysms of World War I and World War II to the horrors of the Great Purges and Ukrainian famine to the political and economic transformation of the country. These events continue to have a great impact on the FSU today. Understanding the past is thus essential to making sense out of a chaotic present.

7

The Legacy of Tsarist Russia

The world of Tsarist Russia seems far removed from that of the Soviet Union in 1991 or the FSU in 1994. However, the flying of the Russian flag over the parliament building, the renaming of Leningrad as Saint Petersburg, the flourishing of national passions and religiosity, pogroms (against Armenians), and the emigration of the Jews fearful of persecution are redolent of the Tsarist period.

The country that the Bolsheviks inherited from Tsarist Russia (after the eight-month interlude of the Provisional Government) was a welter of contradictions. Tsarist Russia, so vast and mysterious, was both powerful and weak, both First World and Third World. A hybrid country, Russia encompassed more than 40 percent of Europe but also over 40 percent of Asia. How can we explain the contradictions between its enormous size (one-sixth of the earth's surface) and its limited power, between its indisputable poverty and backwardness and its great flowering of culture and civilization? How could a country so weak in Europe that it never won a campaign against a major enemy (Austria-Hungary excluded) after 1814, yet expanded to become the largest country in the world? How could such a beclouded Russia in the nineteenth century produce such geniuses as the poets Alexander Pushkin and Mikhail Lermontov, such novelists as Leo Tolstoy, Feodor Dostoyevsky, and Ivan Turgenev, and such composers as Peter Ilyich Tchaikovsky? How could a country disintegrating and falling apart in World War I still produce such ballet geniuses as Igor Stravinsky, Serge Diaghilev, Vaslav Nijinsky, and Anna Pavlova, such composers as Serge Prokofiev, such directors as Konstantin Stanislavsky, and such poets as Anna Akhmatova, Osip Mandelshtam, and Nikolai Gumilov?[1]

---

[1]This depiction of the greatness of Russian culture shows the complexity of Tsarist Russia. Its economy was similar to that of a Third World country, but its culture rivaled that of any First World country. These contradictions remain today with a Russia high in culture and science but very low in consumer goods.

Side by side with this flowering of culture and enlightenment existed the bleak Russian countryside, where 75 percent of the population, largely illiterate, dwelled. Anton Chekhov, with literary license, wrote about the peasants in 1897:

> these people lived worse than cattle and it was terrible to be with them; they were coarse, dishonest, dirty and drunken. . . . Who keeps the tavern and encourages drunkenness? The peasant. Who embezzles and drinks up the funds that belong to the community, the schools, the church? The peasant. Who steals from his neighbors, sets fire to their property, bears false witness at court for a bottle of vodka? The peasant. . . . Crushing labor that made the whole body ache at night, cruel winters, scanty crops, overcrowding; and no help and nowhere to look for help. Those who were stronger and better off could give no assistance, as they were themselves coarse, dishonest, drunken, and swore just as foully. The most insignificant little clerk or official treated the peasants as though they were tramps, and addressed even the village elders and church wardens as inferiors, and as though he had a right to do so.[2]

Imperial Russia, which lasted a millennium from the founding of Kievan Rus in the tenth century to the overthrow of Tsar Nicholas II in February 1917, left an indelible imprint on the Soviet Union.[3] The Bolsheviks, who occupied largely the same territory as the tsars, inherited a country with enormous gaps in its political and social structure, with a strong, centralist, authoritarian political culture, with a vast empire but poor land. They inherited an economically backward state, which yet competed with more advanced European states. The Bolsheviks inherited a country that had mounted an impressive drive for economic development in the last several decades before the war, yet failed to close the gap with Western Europe. They found a country where the majority of the people were illiterate, yet literacy was gaining rapidly and a modern industrial sector, though small, had been created.

HISTORICAL FRAMEWORK BEFORE 1825

The Russian state developed from the small principalities that first emerged around Kiev in the tenth century. The drive towards a larger unified state and ties with Western Europe were decisively smashed by the arrival of the Mongols in 1240. Only between 1380 and 1450 did the Muscovy prince achieve independence, at the same time as the Turks were destroying the last bastion of Byzantine Christianity in Constantinople in 1453. And only in 1480 were the Mongols finally removed from Russia. Their legacy of 240 years of barbarizing Russia and separating it from Europe was felt for centuries. Moscow, then, emerged as the capital of the fledgling state in the fifteenth century, a status

---

[2]Theodore Von Laue, *Why Lenin? Why Stalin?*, J.B. Lippincott, Philadelphia, 1974, p. 27.
[3]Technically, Tsarist Russia or Imperial Russia only lasted from the time Ivan IV took the title of tsar in 1547 until the overthrow of Nicholas II in 1917. Here we use the word in its broader, pre-Soviet sense.

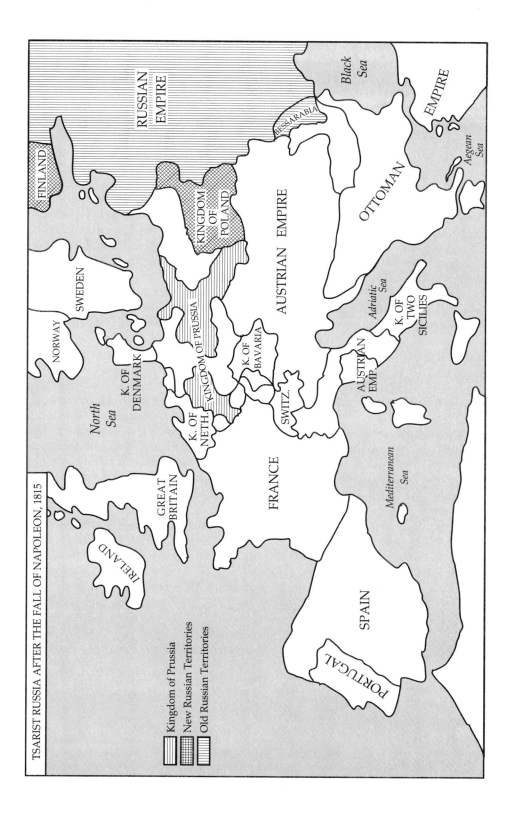

TSARIST RUSSIA AFTER THE FALL OF NAPOLEON, 1815

Kingdom of Prussia
New Russian Territories
Old Russian Territories

RUSSIAN EMPIRE

FINLAND

BESSARABIA

Black Sea

Aegean Sea

OTTOMAN EMPIRE

KINGDOM OF POLAND

AUSTRIAN EMPIRE

KINGDOM OF PRUSSIA

SWEDEN

NORWAY

K. OF DENMARK

North Sea

K. OF NETH.

K. OF BAVARIA

SWITZ.

Adriatic Sea

K. OF TWO SICILIES

AUSTRIAN EMP.

FRANCE

GREAT BRITAIN

IRELAND

Mediterranean Sea

SPAIN

PORTUGAL

which it would yield early in the eighteenth century to Saint Petersburg. Moscow found itself relatively isolated on the vast expanses of the flat and frozen Eurasian plains and forests, with few resources, markets, or ports except in remote and peripheral areas.[4] From this modest beginning, the state continually aggrandized itself. By 1600 it had grown twelve times to become the largest state in Europe. And with the acquisition of Siberia, it again tripled in size by 1650. Then expansion to the west absorbed much of Poland by the late 1790s. By 1800 Russia had taken the Crimea and during the Napoleonic Wars seized the Baltics, Finland, and Bessarabia. Russia took Vladivostok by 1860 and much of Central Asia by 1885. Thus, in 1917 the Bolsheviks inherited the world's largest land mass from the tsars.

Four points about this inheritance are important. First, Tsarist Russia, despite its serious problems, had been an enormously successful enterprise in acquiring that most basic commodity, land. From a small state of 170,000 square miles in 1460, it had expanded to 6 million square miles by 1650 and over 8 million square miles by 1900. The Tsarist empire has been rated as the third most successful ever in the history of the world. Stalin in 1940 and 1945 pursued still more land with his acquisition of the Baltics, Bessarabia, Western Ukraine, and Belorussia lost in the Civil War.[5] In this recovering of the lost patrimony he was faithful to the Tsarist tradition.

Second, this legacy was a vast but poor empire, heavily populated by non-Russians. Had Russia been content to remain within its ethnic framework, this would not have occurred. But Russian expansionism into the Baltics, Ukraine, Central Asia, and Transcaucasus, in the best imperialist tradition, had left the new regime saddled with a major nationality problem. Unlike ethnic groups in the United States, these non-Russian groups were largely small nations, with their own territory, language, culture, and history. In 1917, Russians were only 47 percent of the population of the Russian empire. The loss of Poland, Finland, the Baltics, and Bessarabia in the Russian Civil War eased this problem, but it recurred with the new territorial gains in 1940 and 1945. For seventy-four years the Bolsheviks controlled the world's last great multiethnic empire. Only in 1991 did fourteen non-Russian nations secede and declare independence.

The regime had coupled territorial growth with population growth. In 1550 Austria (20 million people) and France (19 million people) dwarfed Russia (10 million people). By 1850 Russian population had grown to 68 million and then exploded to 170 million by 1914. Together with huge territory, a large population, the greatest in Europe, would be seen as a major asset. But the low level of economic development vitiated the advantage.[6]

Third was the legacy of Peter the Great, the first truly modernizing tsar and an obvious hero for the new regime in 1917. Ruling Tsarist Russia from 1689 to

---

[4]See William Blackwell, "Introduction," in his edited volume, *Russian Economic Development From Peter the Great to Stalin*, Franklin Watts, New York, 1974, p. xix.
[5]Richard Pipes, *Russia Under the Old Regime*, Charles Scribner's Sons, New York, 1974, p. 13.
[6]Pipes, *Russia Under the Old Regime*, p. 13.

1725, Peter the Great sought to forcibly transform Russia into a modern state by dint of central command. Peter was not a revolutionary but a military reformer, who sought to use Western technology in order that Russia might compete effectively in European politics. He sought to modernize the economy, state, and society through a policy of enforced Westernization. He built a new capital, Saint Petersburg, on the western approaches of the empire to symbolize the changes. He abolished the Patriarchate and forcibly subordinated the church to the state, promoted industrialization and educational reforms, created a bureaucracy open to talent, and established Russia's first newspaper and the Academy of Sciences. He ordered urban Russians to shave off their beards and replace their caftans with Western clothes. While many of his ideas were later muted, these twin heritages, of rapid change on the Western model and brutal coercive state means to achieve them, were a significant legacy to the new regime. By 1725 the main features of Tsarist Russia—autocracy, serfdom, bureaucracy, militarism, and state-run religion—were well in place.[7]

Finally, there was the legacy of an authoritarian, and often cruel, state dominating a weak civil society. Western notions of a civil society, with strong protection for the rights of individuals, with popular elections, powerful interest groups, and intermediate groups between the individuals and the government, were largely unknown in Russia. Foreign expansionism went hand in hand with a powerful state extracting extensive resources from a poor society. The most famous tsars, from Ivan the Terrible to Peter the Great, also exhibited streaks of cruelty that became proverbial in Russian history.

HISTORY FROM 1825 to 1914

The Decembrist Revolt of 1825 ushered in the modern era in Russia. Tsar Alexander I (1801–1825) had died childless in 1825 and most Russians presumed the new Tsar would be his younger brother, Konstantin. But Konstantin in 1822 had made a secret pact transferring his right to the throne to his younger brother Nicholas. During a three-week period of mass confusion after Alexander's death in 1825, insurgents tried to seize control of the government.

The insurgents in December 1825 were largely aristocrats deeply influenced by their exposure to France during the Russian occupation in 1814. In 1816 the dissidents had formed a Union of Welfare. The northern branch, under Prince Trubetskoi, advocated classical liberal beliefs such as freedom of the press and religion, social justice, an end to serfdom, and representative government. The southern branch in the Ukraine, under Colonel Pavel Pestel, took on a more authoritarian hue, demanding expropriation of the landlords, an eight-year military dictatorship, forced Russification of minorities, expulsion of the Jews, and creation of a unified, democratic, and centralized republic. This split foreshadowed later divisions in the Russian body politic.

The coup attempt in December 1825 was a dismal failure. Soldiers milled

[7]Blackwell, *Russian Economic Development From Peter the Great to Stalin*, p. xx.

around in Saint Petersburg and were easily dispersed. The government preempted the coup attempt in the south. Afterwards 121 rebels were tried, a few executed, and most exiled to Siberia. On the surface, this was not an event of great importance.[8]

Yet it had profound impact on Russian history. For future revolutionaries, appalled at the brutality of Tsarism, the young aristocrats in exile in Siberia became the symbol of their cause. For the new Tsar Nicholas I, they demonstrated the unreliability of the old aristocracy, many of whom had led or sympathized with the Decembrists. The reactionary reign of Tsar Nicholas I (1825–1855) rigorously shut the door on European influence on Russia by forbidding travel to Europe, severely limiting European travel to Russia, tightening censorship, and suspending the teaching of philosophy, metaphysics, and law in the universities. The government placed severe limitations on the universities by restricting entry to them, censoring professors, and transforming them into preparatory centers for government service. Economically, the government resisted industrialization and relied on the conservative peasant communes.

During the reign of Tsar Nicholas I, debate flourished between the Slavophiles and Westernizers.[9] The Slavophiles, supporting the Tsar's policy, believed in a romantic Russian nationalism that repressed non-Russians and Jews. They believed that Russia was a superior country, a country for the future. The Slavophiles attacked the decadence, rationalism, and the West and Peter the Great. They hailed the mysticism of Russian Orthodoxy as the unique true religion of the Third Rome.[10] They opposed constitutional government and praised autocracy and the peasant commune as the true Russian alternative to the West.

The Westernizers believed that Russia was not unique but was only falling further behind the Western countries. They called for modernity, science, and rationality, embodied in education, a free press, and free thought. The only true standard for Russia was the Western one. Naturally, their hero was Peter the Great.

The death of Tsar Nicholas I in 1855 and the stunning Russian defeat at the hands of England, France, Ottoman Turkey, and Piedmont in the Crimean War (1853–1856) brought rapid change. The defeat shattered the myth of great Russian power so lovingly nurtured by the regime after the defeat of Napoleon and the Russian march into Paris in 1814. Under the new Tsar Alexander II (1855–1881), Russia reluctantly embarked on the Era of Great Reforms (1861–1874), designed to end Russia's fatal lag behind Western Europe in economic development, literacy, and industrialization.

---

[8]See Anatole Mazour, *The First Russian Revolution, 1825,* Stanford University Press, Stanford, 1944.
[9]This debate continues today. The cosmopolitan Westernizers strongly endorse Yeltsin's attempt to transform Russia into a Western country with capitalism, democracy, and nationhood; the Slavophiles denounce this and support the creation of a separate line of development.
[10]Here Moscow was seen as the Third Rome, succeeding the first Rome (Imperial Rome) and the second Rome (Eastern Orthodoxy), which had fallen in, respectively, the fifth and fifteenth centuries.

The most important reform was the 1861 Emancipation Statute ending serfdom in Russia. While most serfs had been freed three or four hundred years earlier in Europe, the institution of serfdom had become widespread in Russia in the seventeenth century. There were still 22 million serfs in Russia (44 percent of the population) in 1860.[11] Under the onerous terms of liberation, the peasants were saddled with redemption payments for forty-nine years and remained tied to the commune (the local village, which periodically redistributed the land and ruled village affairs) while the nobles retained substantial land. The average peasant, often illiterate and lacking capital, modern methods of farming, and storage facilities, was left with only six acres of land (to be reduced to three and a half acres by 1900) and heavy debts. Peasant land hunger was not satisfied by this arrangement. Nonetheless, the emancipation undercut the nobles, who, losing much land and free labor, went into an irreversible decline.

Tsar Alexander II reformed antiquated institutions and broadened the political franchise. He granted autonomy to high schools and universities, separated the courts from the legislative and executive branches, restricted censorship, and backed the autonomy of rural *(zemstvo)* and urban *(duma)* assemblies. He modernized the army, ending the requirement of service for twenty-six years and replacing it with universal military training for a six-year period. The Tsar also promoted an independent judiciary with his 1864 reform, introducing irremovable judges, court trials, public trials, and trial by jury. Although he did not industrialize Russia or lessen his autocratic power, Alexander II did reduce the gap between Russia and Europe.[12]

But the gap remained wide. After the failure of revolutionary attempts to go to the people in the early 1870s, pre-Marxist populist revolutionaries increasingly turned to terrorism. In 1881 they succeeded in assassinating the "Liberator Tsar," Alexander II.

Once again, the cycle of revolution-repression repeated itself, echoing 1825. The new Tsar Alexander III (1881–1894), like Tsar Nicholas I, saw the need for stringent repression. He greatly enhanced the power of the secret police *(Okhrana)*. In August 1881 the Tsar signed laws allowing him to temporarily or permanently suspend all laws whenever he chose. By a March 1882 decree any citizen could be subjected to police surveillance without cause. Thousands were exiled or sentenced to hard labor for membership in revolutionary groups.

Politics was again declared the exclusive province of the government and any other political activity declared a crime. A reinforced Department of Police and Corps of Gendarmes ensured the implementation of this law. The secret police had vast powers to search, arrest, interrogate, imprison, exile, and blackball any Russian citizen. Operating without judicial oversight, they could censor all activity, enforce martial law, and supervise labor camps and places of exile in Siberia. In order to distract the public, Jews in European Asia and

[11]Serfdom had persisted in parts of Europe until the Napoleonic wars.
[12]Basil Dmytryshyn, *USSR: A Concise History,* Charles Scribner's Sons, New York, 1971.

Armenians in the Transcaucasus were singled out for especial discrimination, repression, and pogroms.[13]

The death of Alexander III in 1894 and anointing of Tsar Nicholas II marked a new era in Tsarist politics. Nicholas II was a remarkably poor choice to lead Russia into the twentieth century. A relatively unintelligent and narrow-minded man, Tsar Nicholas II looked backward to medieval Muscovy for his inspiration. He was a conservative and reactionary autocrat who felt that he deserved unlimited power by dint of his royal birth. He believed that his absolute power was the will of God and that he was not accountable to his subjects. But he lacked the ruthlessness of a Nicholas I, which might have prolonged his rule. A devoted family man, he let his love for his wife and his son, the hemophiliac Tsarevich Alexis, influence his public policy. By the end of his rule the illiterate Siberian monk, Grigorii Rasputin, had significant influence at court solely because Rasputin could lessen the Tsarevich's seizures. In September 1915 the Tsar abandoned Petrograd (currently Saint Petersburg) for the front and left power in the incompetent hands of his wife and Rasputin (who was assassinated in December 1916).

His extreme Russian nationalism and anti-Semitism alienated the national minorities (who formed a majority of the population) and the Jews and deeply harmed the Russian image in foreign affairs. Many nationality minorities, such as the Poles, were incensed at the virulent Russification of their homelands, at the attempt to eliminate the national characteristics of the local area in favor of a completely Russian identity. The Tsar's opposition to a real parliamentary system before 1905 also alienated key elements in the population. His lack of understanding of the nature of the revolutionaries led him to repress them without dealing with the reasons for their popularity.[14]

Yet the rapid pace of industrialization, pursued to make Russia militarily competitive in Europe, and the Japanese victory in the Russo-Japanese War in 1904–1905 created an explosive environment. The sudden attack by the Japanese on Port Arthur in January 1904, their victories at Liaoyang and Sha river, their successful defeat of the Russian Far Eastern fleet in the summer of 1904 and sinking of the Baltic Fleet in the straits of Tsushima in May 1905 were sharp blows to the monarchy. The wave of strikes in 1895–1897 had shown the dissatisfaction of the workers with their poor living conditions and the lack of legal trade unions to represent them. Frequent peasant violence reflected peasant discontent with their poverty and lack of land. The university students had been rebellious ever since the great strikes of 1899. The discontent of the nationalities with forced Russification was equally intense. A wave of assassinations of top leaders, most notably the Minister of the Interior von Plehve (1904), preceded the revolution. In November 1904 a *zemstvo* conference in Saint

---

[13]Pipes, *Russia Under the Old Regime,* pp. 300–314. This marked the beginning of a massive Jewish movement to the United States, with 1.5 million Russian Jews emigrating by 1924. An additional 1 million Eastern European Jews also emigrated, creating the modern American Jewish community.
[14]Theofanis Stavrou, editor, *Russia Under the Last Tsar,* University of Minnesota Press, Minneapolis, 1969.

Petersburg set the tone for future events by calling for basic civil liberties, an elective assembly, and amnesty for criminals.

In January 1905 Father Gapon, a priest associated with the failed attempt of Zubatov to organize police-run trade unions, led a gathering of workers to the Winter Palace to address the "Little Father," as the Tsar was called. They were met with a hail of police bullets to inaugurate Bloody Sunday, which ended the myth of a wonderful, remote tsar who cared about his people.[15] By summer the strike wave accelerated in the cities, and peasant attacks on the landlords multiplied in the countryside. In June sailors on the battleship *Potemkin* rebelled against its officers and took refuge in Rumania. In October a general strike paralyzed Saint Petersburg. The next week the new Saint Petersburg Soviet called for a constituent assembly, civil liberties, an eight-hour working day, arms for the working class, a political amnesty, and repeal of the state of emergency.

At that fateful moment, the Tsar issued the October Manifesto, the most important document since the 1861 Emancipation Decree. Written under the influence of the new Prime Minister, Count Sergei Witte, the manifesto guaranteed basic civil liberties by declaring citizens to be free and equal with rights to freedom of person, speech, and assembly. It provided a broadly elected Duma with real legal powers. Count Witte proceeded to smash the revolution in Saint Petersburg in November and in Moscow in December with the aid of a troubled, but still marginally loyal, peasant army. In 1906 and 1907 the government relied on the army and the police to repress the uprising, especially in the countryside.

Then the government began to whittle away at all the concessions made in October 1905. The government brutally repressed the revolution, issued repeated decrees of martial laws, and undermined the Dumas by restricting their electoral base and authority. The Tsar, in the 1906 Fundamental Laws, retained the title of Autocrat, exclusive power over foreign policy, and the right to negotiate treaties, declare war and peace, head the church, and convene and dissolve the Dumas. Tsar Nicholas II retained the right to hire and fire all top government officials, sign all laws, pardon convicts, revise judicial sentences, and declare a state of emergency which would void all legislation. He sent home three Dumas in less than ten years. In response, revolutionaries killed 4000 government officials in 1906 and 1907 before the government liquidated their movement.[16]

The major political response to the 1905 Revolution, besides repression, was to accelerate industrialization and attempt to resolve the agrarian problem. Massive peasant rioting in 1905 and 1906 showed that the peasant commune, to which all peasants were legally bound, was not only economically inefficient but politically unstable. From 1906 to 1911 the main figure was Prime Minister Peter Stolypin, who resolved to abolish the communes and create a conserva-

[15]See Walter Sablinsky, *The Road to Bloody Sunday,* Princeton University Press, Princeton, 1976.
[16]Donald Treadgold, *Twentieth Century Russia,* Rand McNally, Chicago, 1964; and Basil Dymytryshyn, *USSR: A Concise History,* Charles Scribner's Sons, New York, 1970.

tive and prosperous capitalist peasantry. In 1907 he canceled redemption payments and pushed aid to help peasants buy land. By 1914, 10 percent of all peasants were independent farmers and 70 percent had started the process of leaving the commune. The assassination of Stolypin in 1911 slowed this process and the coming of war in August 1914 halted it, well short of completion.

On the eve of World War I Russia had made great strides. The number of city dwellers had tripled to 26 million in fifty years, the peasants were increasingly claiming their land, and illiteracy was dropping rapidly. Yet 70 percent of the population remained peasants, the majority of the population was still illiterate, and the gap between Russia and Western Europe was growing.[17]

WORLD WAR I

Russia entered World War I together with the Western democracies—France and England—against Imperial Germany and the Austro-Hungarian Empire.[18] World War I began with a rapid German offensive into the Low Countries and France in an attempt to win a quick victory. The Russians, responding to Allied pressure to attack the Germans in the rear, launched a rapid and poorly prepared invasion of Eastern Germany that led to disaster at Tannenberg in August 1914. There the Second Army disintegrated, its commander General Samsonov committed suicide, and 130,000 Russians were killed, wounded, or taken captive. In the fall of 1914 repeated Russian attempts against the Germans ended in defeat, although the Russians did manage to stay in the war.

Limited successes against the weaker Austro-Hungarian armies softened the impact of these defeats. In August and September 1914 five Russian armies routed four Austro-Hungarian armies in Galicia. However, in 1915 the Germans mounted a major offensive with nearly forty divisions in the east. The result was disaster, as the numerically superior Russian armies were driven from Galicia, Poland, Lithuania, and much of Belorussia—an area with 25 million citizens. This disaster cost the Russian army another 2 million casualties, and over 1 million POWs were taken by the Germans and Austrians. In 1916 a counteroffensive led by General Brusilov made gains against the Austro-Hungarian army, but at the prohibitive cost of 1 million casualties. By February 1917 the Russian army had suffered 2 million dead, 5 million casualties, and had lost 2 or 3 million POWs, with few gains on the ground.

When a women's day demonstration in Petrograd merged with a bread riot to show dissatisfaction with the regime's performance in February 1917, the February Revolution began. The massive losses in the war and the failure to achieve any decisive victories were major causes of the revolution. So too was the government's failure to mobilize public sentiment for the war effort and the

[17]Dmytryshyn, *USSR: A Concise History.*
[18]For an analysis of the Tsarist army in World War I, see Jonathan Adelman, *Revolution, Armies and War*, Lynne Rienner Publications, Boulder, Colorado, 1985.

breakdown of the economy and transportation network in the face of enormous wartime pressure. By 1917 the Russian economy was producing at only 75 percent of the industrial level of 1913 and its railroads were running at less than 50 percent of peacetime capacity, despite heightened wartime needs. Only 30 percent of its industrial output went to the war.[19] The huge cost of the war, impossible for the weak Russian economy to support, spread chaos and devalued the ruble by 67 percent.[20] The mobilization of 15 million people into the army and the blockade of Russia by the Central Powers took a huge toll. The war brought down Imperial Russia.

TSARIST INHERITANCE

We look now at the Tsarist social structure, institutions, political culture, economy, and foreign and defense policy, which the Bolsheviks, after the eight-month interlude of the Provisional Government, inherited in October 1917.

Social Structure

The social structure of Russia in 1917 remained backward and underdeveloped. The social structure of a typical Western country—strong middle class, weak and dissolving peasantry, significant working class, strong capitalist (and perhaps aristocratic) elements—was unknown in Tsarist Russia. Tsarist Russia had a weak capitalist class, a failing aristocratic class, a small and rebellious working class, a tiny radical intelligentsia, and a vast peasant stratum.

In underdeveloped Russia, the peasants constituted 70 to 80 percent of the population, the largest but lowest stratum. Having largely emerged from serfdom only fifty years earlier, they still bore many of its marks. The peasants rose in rebellion in 1905 and 1917. Dissatisfied with their lives and poverty, the peasants farmed largely small plots with antiquated farm implements. By 1916 peasants controlled 67 percent of the cultivated land but made an average of only $80 a year, from farm and nonfarm labor.[21]

The peasants lived poor, harsh, and simple lives in log cabins *(izbas)*, decorated with icons on their rough walls. They practiced basic hygiene, wore simple clothes, and slept on primitive ceramic stoves. Possessed of a sense of fatalism, most peasants thought concretely and pragmatically, and had little interest in politics. The peasants were legally and socially segregated from the ruling educated minority. Separated by enormous distances, cut off from

---

[19]Peter Gatrell, *The Tsarist Economy, 1850–1917,* St. Martin's Press, New York, 1986, p. 185; and William Blackwell, editor, *Russian Economic Development From Peter the Great to Stalin,* Franklin Watts, New York, 1974, pp. 54–57.
[20]Blackwell, *Russian Economic Development From Peter the Great to Stalin,* pp. 60–62.
[21]The income figure is for 1900, but little had changed by 1916.

communications, isolated in their villages, the peasants were largely unsophisticated and apolitical. They rose up in the Razin (1670s) and Pugachev (1770s) revolts and in the 1905 and 1917 Revolutions with primal furor motivated by a desire for land and equality. Looting and smashing the landlord estates and property, they sought what they thought belonged to them. Although forming the great majority of the population, the peasants were largely atomized and cut off from the political currents that would determine Russia's future. The peasants were the objects of change, rather than its agents, except for the time of riots and rebellion. They could destroy, but they could not build.[22]

The next stratum in importance, and related to the peasantry, was the industrial working class. Although it numbered only 3.5 million workers, it achieved a powerful role in 1917 due to its strategic location in the main Russian cities. A new creation of the Russian industrialization drive in the last fifty years of Tsarism, the working class tended to be radicalized and alienated from Tsarism, which seemed largely indifferent to its concerns. The workers would provide the backbone for the October Revolution and the Red Army in the Russian Civil War (1918–1920). The workers had more political consciousness and education than the peasants, from whom they had sprung within the last generation. Perhaps 50 to 70 percent of them were literate.[23] Many workers retained close ties to the peasantry. By 1917 their low wages, poor working conditions, and long hours in the factories drove them to rebellion. During the Civil War 700,000 workers fought in the Red Army.[24]

The third stratum was the intelligentsia. In a Third World country like Russia in 1917, it included all those willing to dedicate their lives to the role of ideas and the concerns of society rather than narrow material pursuits. In Russia the intelligentsia included many of the 80,000 professionals as well as other well-educated members of society repulsed by the crude, reactionary, anti-intellectual and antimodern autocracy of Tsarist Russia. Given the dependence of many strata in society (especially merchants, clergy, and nobles) on the crown, the intelligentsia was one group independent and highly critical of Tsarism. Although their numbers were small, the members of the intelligentsia had great influence through their ideas, often radical. Their natural arenas were the intellectual salons, universities, fat journals (thick literary reviews covering intellectual topics), and the *zemstvo*. They provided many of the recruits for the revolutionary parties.

A fourth stratum was the capitalist class, usually the most powerful element in Western societies. But here it was largely missing. The general poverty of the state and remoteness from the main currents of European trade and development helped limit the size of the capitalist class. It was quite

[22]For an excellent analysis of the role that peasants play in revolution, see Barrington Moore, *Social Origins of Dictatorship and Democracy*, Beacon Press, Boston, 1965; and Theda Skocpol, *States and Social Revolutions*, Cambridge University Press, Cambridge, 1979. For more on Russian peasants, see Pipes, *Russia Under the Old Regime*.
[23]Peter Gatrell, *The Tsarist Economy, 1850–1917*, St. Martin's Press, New York, 1986, pp. 163–165.
[24]See David Mandel, *Petrograd Workers and the October Revolution*, St. Martin's Press, New York, 1981.

conservative and tied to the state, which traditionally had controlled all trade and industry as a royal monopoly and had not allowed independent capitalist development. The capitalists remained merchants without capitalist ethos. This "missing class," to borrow from Richard Pipes, was generally poorly educated, unenergetic, isolated, and cautious. Tied to the state, it did not actively promote the usual bourgeois agenda of civil liberties and democracy because it feared the vast mass of peasants and workers who were strongly anticapitalist. Its role was further diminished by the powerful role of foreign capital, which by 1917 furnished one-third of all industrial capital and one-half of bank capital for development. Dependent on the state and foreigners, fearful of the masses, small and inert, the Russian capitalists were largely monarchists and national-ists unable to leave their imprint on Russia's fate.[25]

Finally, there was the aristocracy, a stratum which traditionally had domi-nated most European societies for many centuries and left its mark well into the twentieth century. Again, the Russian pattern was different. Given the fact that the nobles were the strongest, richest, best-educated, and most conscious stratum in society, the Tsars were especially careful to control them. In Russia the monarchy traditionally had reduced the nobles to political impotence by making property conditional on service to the crown. The tsars deliberately created a service nobility in tying status and power to service to the crown. The crown scattered noble property over many provinces and promoted a rapid turnover in state property to avoid the formation of a powerful, landed aristocracy with strong local roots.

The tsars made sure that there were very few rich nobles. By 1860, 67 percent of all nobles had no serfs and 98 percent of the remainder had fewer than the hundred serfs necessary to maintain the life of a gentleman. Thus, apart from perhaps one or two thousand, the vast majority of the nobles were relatively impoverished and unable to mount any challenge to the regime. With over 90 percent of them dependent on the regime for their livelihood, the nobles could not pose a serious challenge. The Emancipation Decree of 1861 further impoverished them by depriving them of much of their land and free labor.[26] Already by 1905 the nobles had lost one-third of the land left them in 1861. Only three times in history did the nobles ever mount a challenge to the crown—the Times of Troubles (early 1600s), 1730, and 1825—and they failed every time. By 1917 they were a class in decline, unable to offer serious resistance to revolu-tionary change.[27]

Of course, class structure is not the only way to analyze groups in Tsarist society. Another, very important one is the division of Tsarist Russia into Russian and non-Russian elements, Slavs and non-Slavs. The great expansion of the Russian Empire to the south and east had absorbed so many non-Rus-sians and non-Slavs that by 1917, 53 percent of the population were not

---

[25]Pipes, *Russia Under the Old Regime.*
[26]However, from the peasant point of view, the decree was too fair to the nobles by paying them for their land and reserving for them the best available land.
[27]Pipes, *Russia Under the Old Regime,* chapter 7.

Russians and 35 percent were not Slavs. This conquest of native peoples had not been a gradual process but one accompanied with a great deal of brutality, pillage, and plunder. The resentment of the minorities, who had their own cultures, languages, and histories, was often passionate.

This was intensified by the Russification programs of Nicholas I and Nicholas II, which turned Russia into a "prison house of nationalities." The brutality that accompanied the destruction of the two great Polish revolts of the nineteenth century (1831, 1863) reinforced this animosity. Peoples such as the Poles, Finns, Balts, and Transcaucasians yearned for freedom and even independence. Instead, not only were they a part of a repressive empire, but they had to conduct public business in Russian, learn Russian in schools, and face discrimination as nationality minorities. The authorities also incited hatred against the Poles, Jews, Tartars, Armenians, and Caucasians.[28]

The last two tsars in particular made the 5 million Russian Jews living largely in the Pale of Settlement in the western provinces their special target of wrath.[29] Forbidden to reside in the major Russian cities, denied admittance to Russian schools under quotas, barred from owning land, and subjected to over 600 special laws against them, Jews were not allowed to become government bureaucrats or military officers. Recurrent pogroms after 1881 killed thousands of Jews and pushed over 1.5 million Russian Jews to emigrate to the United States. Although most Jewish radicals were Zionists, Bundists, or Mensheviks, some became leaders in the Bolshevik party (Trotsky, Zinoviev, Kamenev, Sverdlov, Radek).[30]

This social structure favored the victory of the Bolsheviks in the October Revolution. With a missing capitalist class and a weak and declining aristocracy, the Bolsheviks did not face strong and united opposition from the upper classes. The Bolsheviks could mobilize the strong but small working class and pacify the vast but atomized peasantry.

INSTITUTIONS

The Tsarist institutional legacy was important for the Bolsheviks, who lacked their own institutions before the October Revolution.[31] They inherited a large

[28]It should be noted that anti-Russian sentiment varied greatly among the different nationalities. Some of the smaller nationalities simply assimilated with the Russians, and some, such as the Armenians, saw the Russians as a bulwark against their Turkish enemy.

[29]Not allowed to reside in most of the Tsarist Empire except with special permission, the great majority of Russian Jews were forced to reside in the Pale of Settlement, a large territory in the western part of the empire annexed largely in the late eighteenth century.

[30]The differences among these various radical groups is discussed in detail in the next chapter. Zionists were those who wished to emigrate to Palestine to create a Jewish state (after 1948 Israel); Bundists were those who wanted to create a socialist autonomous Jewish entity in Eastern Europe or Russia.

[31]By contrast, the Chinese, Vietnamese, and Yugoslav Communists, who came to power through protracted rural insurrections, developed a powerful army and a capable government and party bureaucracy before the final seizure of power.

central government bureaucracy, a small but capable secret police, a huge but weak army, the creaking Russian Orthodox Church, a small but growing educational system, and a nascent parliament.

Most important was the central government bureaucracy, which held the country together. The bureaucracy, with several hundred thousand bureaucrats in the two capitals, was a relatively small force to rule the country. It was famous for its venality, sluggishness, inefficiency, and repressive political views. The etiquette of bribes, tips, and extortion was elaborate and well defined. The relatively well-educated bureaucrats often treated the citizens as aliens in their own country. They had an elaborate system of symbols, uniforms, and titles for their distinctive ranks. The elite civil service formed a conservative and self-perpetuating caste with strong emphasis on hierarchy. The premodern Tsarist bureaucracy, for all its flaws, held the far-flung empire together for the autocracy.[32] The Bolsheviks were forced to maintain much of the bureaucratic structure after their seizure of power, and it took two decades to thoroughly recreate it in their own image.

The Bolsheviks transformed the secret police and the army, reduced the power of the Russian Orthodox Church, and abolished the Duma. The secret police and army, as the key instruments of repression, were especially important institutional legacies. The Tsarist secret police (Okhrana), which originated after the failed Decembrist revolt in 1825, was a small but effective force in penetrating and destroying the revolutionary movement. An Okhrana agent, Roman Malinovsky, had headed the last Bolshevik faction in the Duma before 1914. As for the army, it was enormous, ponderous, and notoriously ineffective. Apart from victory over the Turks in 1878, its last great victories had come a century before in the Napoleonic Wars. A reactionary and monarchist officer corps, a mass of semiliterate peasants in the ranks and noncommissioned officer corps, and a tradition of brutality and repression meant that the Bolsheviks would have a gargantuan task in trying to create a modern and effective army after 1917.

Next came the Russian Orthodox Church. The last Eastern European nation to convert to Christianity, Russia had become Christian only during the reign of Prince Vladimir in 988. With the destruction of Byzantium by the Turks in 1453, Muscovy soon was the only major power still proclaiming Eastern Christianity. Forcibly absorbed as a department of the Russian state by Peter the Great, the Church was relatively weak politically. Proclaiming that the Moscow line of Tsars was the most ancient and prestigious line descended directly from the Roman Emperor Augustus, the Church argued that tsars had divine authority directly from God and were the earthly equivalent of God. It supported royal absolutism, proclaimed Imperial Russia as the best regime in the world, and maintained that after the fall of Rome to the barbarians and Constantinople to the infidel Turks, Muscovy represented the purest and most pious Christian kingdom in the world.

Its philosophical orientation—denouncing earthly existence as an abomina-

---

[32]Pipes, *Russia Under the Old Regime,* chapter 11.

tion and praising humility, silent suffering, and acceptance of one's fate—predisposed the Church to political passivity. The low level of learning in the Church, its stance against rationality and education, the lack of any international ties, and its stress on mysticism, ritual, and ecstacy weakened the role of the Church in the modern world. So too did its Great Schism in the 1660s, which pushed millions of its followers into the camp of the Old Believers. The failure of the Church to oppose serfdom, pogroms, or massacres and its indifference to social injustice deeply alienated much of the population. Thus, while the Church remained a significant actor as the official state religion in Tsarist Russia, it had no independent institutional base once Tsarism was overthrown in 1917. It remained the center for tens of millions of Russian Orthodox believers, but could not be the kind of strong political force that the Polish Catholic Church became.[33]

Unlike the legislatures in England or the United States, in Russia the Dumas were a relatively brief phenomenon, existing only from 1906 to 1917. Before that there had been urban (Duma) and rural *(zemstvo)* assemblies in the nineteenth century with limited franchise and minimal power. Despite the promises of the October Manifesto, the Tsar in 1906 moved to reduce any possible power for the first Duma. With four Dumas in eleven years, their power was relatively weak and limited. In the words of Thomas Riha, "The regime seemed unable to live with the legislature, which had any self-respect, even a legislature elected under a limited suffrage and hedged with all manners of restrictions."[34] The suppression of its successor, the Constituent Assembly, in January 1918 did not cause serious problems for the Bolsheviks.

The universities, built on the German model, were quite strong, with the Academy of Sciences formed in 1725 at the time of Tsar Peter the Great. Famous Russian scientists, such as Andrei Markov (mathematical chains), Dmitrii Mendeleev (periodic laws), Ivan Pavlov (psychological reflexes), and Ilya Mechnikov (biological immunology), reflected a strong scientific base. With 70,000 students in 1914, the universities increasingly became open to students from all classes, as the number of nobles dropped from 70 percent of all students in 1865 to 35 percent in 1915. However, repeated student strikes in the late 1890s, during the 1905 Revolution, and in 1911 led to great strain between the universities and the autocracy. The universities, as upholders of scientific rationality, inevitably fought with the Russian Orthodox Church and the mysticism, absolutism, and reactionary views of Tsarism.[35]

There was rapid progress in setting up elementary and secondary schools. By 1914 there were nearly 10 million elementary school students, more than

[33]The Polish experience was very different since the Polish church, after the liquidation of the Polish state by the 1790s, became the repository of Polish nationalism and thereby extremely popular for 125 years. Pipes, *Russia Under the Old Regime*, chapter 9.

[34]Thomas Riha, quoted in Theofanis Stavrou, editor, *Russia Under the Last Tsar*, University of Minnesota Press, Minneapolis, 1969, p. 111.

[35]Alexander Vucinich, "Politics, Universities and Science," in Stavrou, editor, *Russia Under the Last Tsar*, pp. 159–176.

four and a half times the number in 1885. Nearly 68 percent of the population were literate in 1913, compared to 32 percent in 1891.[36]

POLITICAL CULTURE

By 1917 there emerged a revolutionary counterculture based on the intelligentsia, workers, and peasants with institutional support among the revolutionary parties and universities. But official Tsarist culture, as it had for centuries, remained the predominant culture in Russia—authoritarian, repressive, and centralized. The center claimed a monopoly on politics, a monopoly it slowly and reluctantly yielded to a still weak Duma at the end of its reign.

The regime used force frequently, whether in pogroms against Jews, in violent suppression of Polish revolts, or in mass repression of the 1905–1907 revolution. The secret police searched out and repressed revolutionaries on a small scale while the army smashed any large-scale revolts. The powerful cult of the Tsar, supported by the authority of state and church, was the keystone of the system. The rights of the individual were considered relatively minor compared to the rights of the state and the Tsar, whose power was not officially limited throughout most of Russian history. For many centuries the various classes of society were rigorously and officially subordinated to the Tsar. Indeed the land and factories were his property, the throne his inheritance, and the serving class, including the civil servants, "his slaves."[37] Democracy was an abstract concept of little real value in a state where serfdom had been abolished less than sixty years before the revolution and where one-third of the population in 1913 was officially characterized as "aliens." A powerful Great Russian chauvinism suffused the official culture. While there were some progressive stirrings from below, the dominant belief of the culture was that politics belonged to the elite. The masses, with low political consciousness, remained purely the object of politics.

For Russian conservatives, then, the Tsar and the Church were sacred, the trinity of Orthodoxy, Autocracy, and Nationality (Russian, that is) was essential, and the supremacy of Russia to other nations assumed. Stability, force, and violence were intrinsic to the preservation of the social order. Education (beyond a brief stay in elementary school), rationality, and Western culture were evil. A superior Russia remained isolated, faithful to its traditional values. For the Russian conservatives, led by Konstantin Pobedonostsev (1827–1907), the Procurator of the Holy Synod, only these values could save Russia.

The many centuries of Tsarist absolutism and repressive official culture had a major impact on the revolutionary counterculture by preventing the development of any participant culture. The bulk of the population were

---

[36]Arcadius Kahan, *Russian Economic History: The Nineteenth Century,* University of Chicago Press, Chicago, 1989, pp. 173–186.
[37]For a good analysis of the patrimonial state, see Pipes, *Russia Under the Old Regime,* p. 83.

marginalized in an official culture that denied them participation. The Leninist argument—that a hardened core of professional revolutionaries must steer the unenlightened masses to victory and socialism—gained credence in a society where secret police repression made open political activity impossible and where the bulk of the people were illiterate or semiliterate with little political consciousness. The Marxist arguments about the ruling class brutally oppressing the workers and peasants for their own good made sense in a backward autocratic society where there was a vast gap between the official ruling Russia and a second Russia of lowly peasants and workers. The Marxist stress on the role of the small industrial proletariat gained support in a society where the working class was restive under its harsh conditions and the peasants had rebuffed the revolutionaries in the "going to the people" movement in the early 1870s. Thus, the elitist Bolsheviks with their strong leader (Lenin) and highly centralized structure ("democratic centralism") unconsciously mirrored the Tsarist society that they wished to destroy.

But the history of Russian revolutionaries is far greater than that of the Bolsheviks, founded only in 1903 and officially a separate party after 1912. The first real revolutionary groups had sprang up already in the early 1860s. The early period of revolutionary activity in the 1860s and 1870s is filled with important leaders such as Michael Bakunin, Sergei Nechaev, and Peter Tkachev. The failure of the "going to the people" campaign in 1874, when the peasant were cold to the thousands of enthusiasts who poured into the countryside, led to a search for a new way. In the late 1870s the wave of populist terror finally claimed the life of Tsar Alexander II in 1881.

The Russian Social Democrats emerged by the 1890s. Split into "soft" (Menshevik) and "hard" (Bolshevik) groups by 1903, the Social Democrats called for a revolutionary socialist transformation of Russia. While the Bolsheviks wanted a small elitist party that would skip over the capitalist phase and directly build socialism, the Mensheviks desired a broader, more open party that would be the "loyal opposition" during the lengthy capitalist phase in Russian development. The Mensheviks, led by Julius Martov and Pavel Axelrod, felt that Russia was ready not for socialism but for a liberal-democratic regime on the Western European model. This was staunchly rejected by the Bolsheviks, led by Vladimir Lenin. Before 1917, both factions were relatively small, persecuted groups with their leaders forced into exile abroad.[38] Their major base was among the workers and intelligentsia elements in the major cities.

The Socialist Revolutionary Party, heir of the early populists (*narodniki*), tried to represent the peasants. Originally formed in the 1880s with a terrorist wing, the party won a majority in the Constituent Assembly election in November 1917. It stood for a decentralized regime based on the peasantry, with loose party and government organization. The peasants would be given all land without compensation, agriculture would take priority over industry, and private property would be reinforced. The SRs backed the usual radical platform of universal suffrage, civil liberties, national self-determination, labor

[38]See Theodore Von Laue, *Why Lenin? Why Stalin?* J.B. Lippincott, Philadelphia, 1971, pp. 70–85.

legislation, and revolutionary socialism. They lacked a strong organization or a mechanism to translate their large, but isolated and atomized, peasant base into political activism.

Finally, there were the liberals (or Kadets, for Constitutional Democrats), representing the middle-class intelligentsia, bourgeoisie, and liberal landlords. Led by Paul Milyukov and Alexander Guchkov, they demanded moderate change and a liberal democratic regime supporting the sanctity of private property. They hoped to transform Russia on the Western European model. During World War I, although the Social Democrats largely opposed the war in theory, they supported it in practice in hopes of receiving aid from democratic France and Britain after the war. Always they feared that the revolution would go too far and drive them out of power. Isolated from the upper classes above them and the lower classes below them, they were a small but optimistic Westernized element.[39]

Overall, then, the revolutionary movement was split into four parties plus the nationalist parties. Under Tsarism they were largely neutralized by the Okhrana. But, repeatedly, whether in the worker strikes of 1895–1897 and 1903, the peasant riots after 1902, the student demonstrations after 1899, the 1905 Revolution, or the February Revolution of 1917, their ideas would have far more support than their small numbers warranted. For the enthusiasm with which the masses met World War I was short lived and soon replaced by a war weariness and defeatism that opened the door to the twin revolutions of 1917.

ECONOMY

Tsarist Russia left an ambiguous economic legacy to the Bolsheviks. On one hand, the regime had made impressive strides in industrializing and modernizing Russia in the period from 1880 to 1913. By 1913 Russia was the fifth greatest industrial power (and seventh greatest power in terms of GNP) in the world, and Russian industry was ten times greater in output than in 1861. On the other hand, the tsars had not closed the yawning gap which separated Russia from Western Europe and the United States. Indeed, in 1913 Russian industrial output was still only 50 percent of the value of agricultural output. In many ways, the gap had grown even larger.[40]

Russia lagged far behind Europe. Between 1907 and 1911, the infant mortality rate per 1000 was 245 in European Russia, 174 in Germany, 128 in France, and 116 in England and Wales. In 1900, 72 percent of all juveniles and adults in Russia were illiterate, compared to 56 percent in Spain, 23 percent in Austria, and 17 percent in France.[41] But, the most important statistics are contained in Table 7.1.

---

[39]Von Laue, *Why Lenin? Why Stalin?* pp. 80–85.

[40]William Blackwell, editor, *Russian Economic Development From Peter the Great to Stalin*, Franklin Watts, New York, 1974, p. 42.

[41]See Peter Gatrell, *The Tsarist Economy, 1850–1917*, St. Martin's Press, New York, 1986, pp. 33–34.

TABLE 7.1. National Income per Capita in Russia and the West, 1861, 1913

National Income (1913 rubles)

Countries	1861	1913
United States	450	1033
United Kingdom	323	580
Germany	175	374
France	150	303
Italy	183	261
Spain	—	199
Russia	71	119

Source: Paul Gregory, *Russian National Income, 1885–1913*, Columbia University Press, New York, 1982, pp. 155–157.

In 1913 the United States had over nine times the income per capita of Russia, England five times, Germany more than three times, and even Italy over two times. Every major country except Italy actually widened its lead over Russia after 1861. The gap between Russia and the United States grew from 369 rubles in 1861 to 914 rubles in 1913. Only by dint of its huge population did Russia have a national income in 1913 equal to that of England, which had roughly one-fifth of its population. Stanley Cohn has calculated that Russia grew a tolerable 1.0 percent a year per capita between 1860 and 1913, but the United States grew 2.2 percent, Germany 1.8 percent, and France 1.4 percent.[42]

Russia in 1914 was an underdeveloped country, with about $600 to $800 per capita income in current terms. Hampered by a poor environment, harsh climate, and inaccessible natural endowment, isolated from the main currents of European trade, and fettered by a thin population strewn across a huge land mass, Russia developed slowly. The long history of serfdom further slowed development. Driven by international security considerations, Russia strove to substitute its quantity for European quality. As late as 1800 Russian cities accounted for only 3.5 percent of its population (compared to 20 percent in England) and even in 1900 a mere 13 percent (compared to 70 percent in England).[43]

Rapid urbanization and industrialization came very late to Russia, only after 1885. From 1897 to 1917 Russian cities doubled in size, from 13 million to 26 million people.[44] This reflected the great leap forward of Russia especially under Finance Minister Count Sergei Witte (1892–1903). Witte sought capital from foreign capital inflows, extraction of agricultural surpluses by rigid

[42]Stanley Cohn, "The Soviet Economy: Performance and Growth," in William Blackwell, editor, *Russian Economic Development From Peter the Great to Stalin,* Franklin Watts, New York, 1974, p. 324.

[43]Alexander Baykov, "Economic Development of Russia," in Blackwell, editor, *Russian Economic Development From Peter the Great to Stalin,* pp. 6–8.

[44]Peter Gatrell, *The Tsarist Economy, 1850–1917,* St. Martin's Press, New York, 1986, p. 67.

controls, and a high rate of forced savings by consumption taxes. He stressed the need for extensive railroad building (including the Trans Siberian Railroad), rapid growth of heavy industry, introduction of the gold standard, and public education. This came at a high cost: severe taxes on the peasants, poor conditions for the workers, and rapid industrialization suborning the landlords. A weak capitalist class mandated a powerful state role in the economy. The program was unpopular but pursued by the government desperate to close the gap with Russia's European rivals.[45]

Tsarist Russia made an indelible imprint on the Bolsheviks. It left an economy in the early phases of industrialization, which still lagged far behind the West despite some impressive successes. The class structure of Tsarist Russia was that of a traditional agrarian-bureaucratic society, with a huge mass of peasants, small working class, impotent bourgeoisie, and declining aristocracy. Institutionally, the Bolsheviks inherited a strong but incompetent and reactionary bureaucracy, a massive but ineffective army, a small but effective secret police, and a large but isolated and politically impotent Russian Orthodox Church. Tsarist Russia also had a direct impact on the psychology of the Bolsheviks. For all the talk about revolutionary change and socialism, for the Bolsheviks in 1917, and for that matter in 1929, the predominant reality was that the world of Tsarist Russia was still very much with them.

[45]Theodore Von Laue, "The State and the Economy," in Blackwell, editor, *Russian Economic Development From Peter the Great to Stalin.*

8

Revolution and Civil War

The February and October Revolutions in 1917 and the Russian Civil War (1918–1920) formed a decisive chapter in Russian history. These revolutions rapidly and permanently altered the political and social structure of the country. The failure of the February Revolution to consolidate itself led to the subsequent October Revolution. While the timing of the February Revolution was unexpected, its final success did not seem striking given the disintegration of the Tsarist government. But the second, October, revolution took the West completely by surprise, as did the equally unexpected victory of the Bolsheviks in the Russian Civil War. They formed a backdrop for the 1991 Russian revolution that disintegrated the Soviet Union and created formally fifteen successor states. Given the importance of revolutions and civil wars in shaping the contours of new regimes, we need to spend significant space in understanding their nature.

FEBRUARY REVOLUTION

The events in Russia at the beginning of 1917 cannot be separated from their European context. In all the European states thirty months of devastating trench warfare and stalemate on the Western Front had produced millions of casualties, billions of dollars of expenditures, and little prospect of a resolution. In France there were serious army mutinies in 1916 and the first rumblings had been heard in the Imperial German Army. For Russia the situation was especially bitter as Russia had endured the greatest number of casualties (perhaps 7 million) and the least success of the major powers. From Tannenberg to Poland the German army had marched triumphantly against the Tsarist Army, with nary a defeat.

Wars are often the accelerator of radical change, and World War I, which would ultimately destroy no less than four empires, was to be no different. The devastating losses undermined the legitimacy of the Tsarist regime, which, given the German ancestry of the Tsarina, was falsely accused of pro-German sentiments.[1]

The real weakness came at the top. The weak Tsar Nicholas II, the mystic Tsarina Alexandra, and the illiterate Siberian wonder monk Grigorii Rasputin were all incapable of stopping the rot. Their top advisers, like the aged and senile Prime Minister Goremykin, were too often incompetent. No longer did the Tsar have advisers like Stolypin and Witte. By becoming commander-in-chief of the Tsarist army in the fall of 1915 and moving to the front at Mogilev, the Tsar directly tied his rule to success in the war. He left Rasputin and the Tsarina to run the government, a truly disastrous decision.

The major Tsarist institutions also cracked under the strain of war. The Tsarist army, despite mass recruitment of new officers and mass levy of peasants into the ranks, was unable to compete with armies of more advanced societies such as Germany. The Tsarist government, saddled with an ailing economy and creaking administrative apparatus, was unable to adequately mobilize the economy and population for war. By 1916 industrial output had actually declined significantly from 1913, rather than rising sharply, as in England, France, and Germany. The autocratic government refused the efforts of volunteer institutions to mobilize the population for war. The Church proved largely irrelevant, hampered by its identification with Tsarism. And the small but efficient secret police would soon find itself overwhelmed by the demands of February 1917.

The main social props of the regime were seriously weakened. The Tsarist officer corps, so devoted to the Tsar, had been demoralized and devastated by the early years of the war. By 1917 most officers were no longer aristocratic career officers but new recruits from the nascent middle classes, without strong loyalty to the Tsar. By 1917 the capitalists were angry at the Tsar for losing the war and increasingly bankrupt as production declined. The landlords, a declining force before the war, became impotent. The Tsar's close association with the Tsarina and Rasputin and the losing war effort further discredited the Tsar himself.

The first serious cracks in the Tsarist structure were seen in the assassination of the despised Siberian monk, Grigorii Rasputin (1872–1916), in December 1916. In January and early February dissatisfaction increased with strikes in the factories, food demonstrations, riots, and a breakdown in transportation. After several delays, the Fourth Duma opened in the middle of February 1917. Although most members of the Duma were loyal to the government, the government strengthened its forces in Petrograd and increased police searches

---

[1]For a further development of the connection between external losses and internal revolutions, see Theda Skocpol, *States and Social Revolution,* Cambridge University Press, Cambridge, 1979.

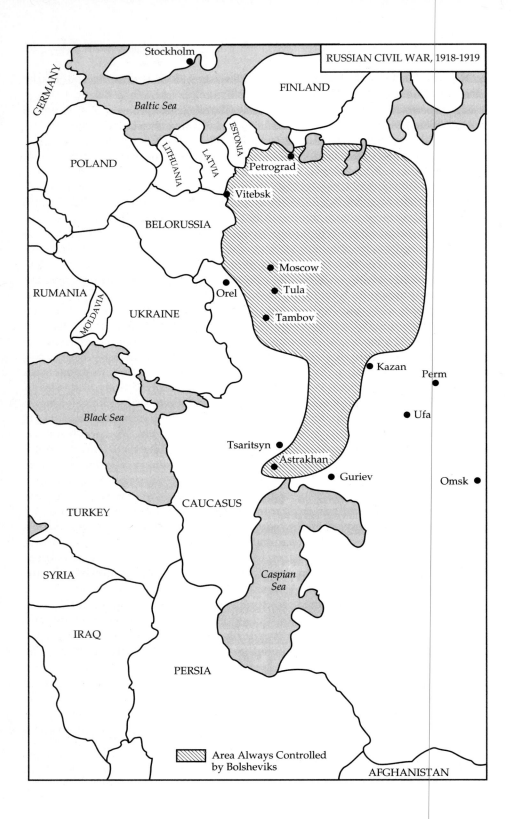

RUSSIAN CIVIL WAR, 1918-1919

Stockholm

FINLAND

GERMANY

Baltic Sea

POLAND

ESTONIA

LITHUANIA

LATVIA

Petrograd

Vitebsk

BELORUSSIA

Moscow

Tula

RUMANIA

Orel

UKRAINE

Tambov

MOLDAVIA

Kazan

Perm

Black Sea

Ufa

Tsaritsyn

Astrakhan

Guriev

Omsk

TURKEY

CAUCASUS

SYRIA

*Caspian
Sea*

IRAQ

PERSIA

Area Always Controlled
by Bolsheviks

AFGHANISTAN

and censorship to prevent any trouble. Less than a week later the Tsar returned to Army Headquarters in Mogilev. Behind in Petrograd he left an undated signed decree calling for the dissolution of the Duma.[2]

That same day there broke out a wave of strikes, led by the Putilov factory workers. Within two days these strikes swelled into a mounting tide of large-scale demonstrations in the capital. The next day from Mogilev, the Tsar, totally ignorant of the extent of the uprising, ordered the commander of the Petrograd garrison to crush the disorders. However, at this point the peasant recruits in the army, significantly influenced by the populace and leftist agitation, refused to fire on the crowds. The local police proved inadequate for this task. By the end of February the revolution had seized the streets of Petrograd. On February 26, the Tsar tried to play his last card by ordering in troops to crush the revolt and demanding the dissolution of the Duma. That night and the next day regular soldiers in Petrograd, led by an elite guards regiment, revolted and joined the demonstration. Soon the entire Petrograd garrison joined in and by the end of February the revolutionaries had seized most of the government buildings in Petrograd.

At this point on February 27, the more progressive members of the Duma met and declared themselves the legitimate power in Petrograd. At the same time in the same building another group, the more radical Petrograd Soviet of Workers' and Soldiers' Deputies, also came into being. Their struggle ultimately decided the fate of the revolution. But at this moment their dual appearance signalled the nearing of the end for Tsarism.

At this point Tsar Nicholas II, having lost his capital and government bureaucracy, remained in power. His attempt to send in military forces from outside failed when the units went over to the revolution. On March 1 the Tsar started for Petrograd but was forced to go instead to Pskov, the headquarters of the commander of the Northern Front. On March 3, responding to urgent pleas from all sides, the Tsar abdicated in favor of his brother Michael. But this maneuver failed to save the Romanov dynasty. For that same day the Grand Duke Michael kindly declined the proffered throne until such time as the democratically elected Russian people should offer it to him. This, of course, never happened. This marked the end of the Romanovs and triumph of the February Revolution.

The February Revolution was wildly popular throughout Russia, and spread like wildfire through the country. Everywhere the old government vanished, the army units joined the revolution, and soviets sprang up like mushrooms after a rain. The total cost of the revolution—less than 200 people killed and 1300 wounded—reflected its broad base of support.[3]

In February, and even more in October, there were really three revolutions in one. There was the peasant revolution in the countryside which was the real

[2]For the February Revolution, see William Chamberlin, *The Russian Revolution*, 2 volumes, Princeton University Press, Princeton, 1987; and Tsyoshi Hasegawa, *The February Revolution: Petrograd 1917*, University of Washington Press, Seattle, 1981.
[3]Basil Dmytryshyn, *USSR: A Concise History*, Charles Scribner's Sons, New York, 1974, p. 43.

dynamite for social change. Without the peasants there would be no soldiers for the army and no food for the city.[4] The peasants' demands were simple: They wanted the land of the state, Church, and landlords for themselves. Second, there was the urban revolution, which soon became the workers' revolution. They wanted socialism, not the bourgeois aspirations of the landlords; the factories, and not the land. Finally, there were the aspirations of the nationality minorities, which would lead to the independence of the Poles and Finns and temporary independence for the Azeris, Armenians, and Georgians until the end of the civil war.

FROM FEBRUARY TO JULY

The events from the February Revolution to the October Revolution are usually seen as a tragedy in the West. For the moderate leaders, first Prince Lvov and then Alexander Kerensky (a Socialist Revolutionary), were unable to ride the tiger of the February Revolution and eventually succumbed to the Bolsheviks.

From the beginning of these revolutions there was a dual governmental system in Russia that reflected the deep divisions between the two Russias. On one hand, there was the official government, the legitimate heir of the Tsarist system, the Provisional Government. It was "provisional" because it was felt that a legitimate government could only be founded on the results of the elections to the Constituent Assembly to be held in November. It was dedicated to carrying on the war, preparing the ground for the Constituent Assembly, and delaying serious actions until then. During this period it moved towards the left as the power of the upper-class liberals faded and that of the Socialist Revolutionaries and Mensheviks increased. From the beginning it was challenged by a more radical institution, the Soviet of Workers' Deputies. Initially under the control of the moderate Mensheviks and Socialist Revolutionaries, it represented increasingly the views of the workers, peasants and soldiers, the "second Russia."

Initially, in the period from March to May, there was a strong tendency in all quarters to give the Provisional Government a chance. Even among the Bolsheviks, as they returned from exile in Siberia or abroad, there was strong conciliationist sentiment. This was not shared by Lenin, however. When he returned from exile through Germany, he proclaimed his famous "April Theses." To a shocked party, he declared that there should be no compromise with the bourgeois or upper-class elements, no support for the Provisional Government, and support only for "All Power to the Soviets." Russia must leave the imperialist war, and the Bolsheviks must prepare to seize power. Although these thoughts seemed heretical at first, they soon gained acceptance in the party.

As the war dragged on, the economy disintegrated, and the peasants began

---

[4]For the best analysis of peasants in revolution, see the classic work by Barrington Moore, *Social Origins of Dictatorship and Democracy*, Beacon Press, Boston, 1964.

to seize the land of the landlords, support grew for a more radical government. This spontaneous rural revolution saw peasants killing their landlords and seizing the land after the Provisional Government refused to consider leaving the war, as this would mean a break with Russia's democratic allies, England, France and the United States. Giving factories to the workers, the government believed, was beyond the pale, and legitimizing land seizures must wait for the elections in the fall. Initially in March the Temporary Committee of the Duma dissolved itself and formed the Provisional Government. The government under Prince Georgii Lvov, a wealthy aristocrat, represented the "first Russia." Upper class Kadets and Octobrists, such as Foreign Minister Paul Milyukov, War Minister Alexander Guchkov, Agriculture Minister Andrei Shingarev, and Holy Synod Procurator Vladimir Lvov, dominated the Cabinet. Such a conservative group lacked legitimacy and legal authority in the eyes of the peasants and workers. A losing war, deteriorating economy, and rebellious population did not augur well for the future.

The Provisional Government confronted the representatives of the "second Russia," the Petrograd Soviet of Workers' and Soldiers' Deputies. In the early months, this body was unsure of its political power and functioned more as a loyal opposition than as a rival for power. Under "dual government" the Provisional Government had formal power but minimal authority and the Soviets had significant authority but no formal power.

The split between the two bodies had started in March. On March 2 the Petrograd Soviet issued the famous Order Number 1, declaring that soldier committees would control all weapons and would be the political arm of the Soviet in the army. The order prohibited officers from controlling weapons, acting harshly towards men, requiring saluting, or insisting on their traditional prerogatives. This seriously undermined both the power of the officers and army discipline. The Soviets now spoke vigorously for peace while the Provisional Government wanted to continue the war.

By the beginning of May this conflict and growing antiwar sentiment led to the resignation of the prowar Foreign Minister Milyukov and Defense Minister Guchkov from the Provisional Government. In the new government there was a distinct move to the left, with six of fifteen ministers in the Provisional Government representing the moderate socialists. This is not to ignore the real accomplishments of the first "bourgeois" government: amnesty for political prisoners, abolishment of capital punishment and exile, equality for all citizens, freedom of speech, press and assembly, reform of the government, an eight-hour workday, the right to strike, changes in the Church, and autonomy for Finland and semiautonomy for Poland. Yet the Provisional Government still lagged behind increasingly radical popular sentiment.

The continuation of the war, the growing disintegration of the country, and the return of thousands of political exiles fueled demands for peace, land for the peasants, factories for the workers, and autonomy or independence for the nationality minorities. Lenin's radical "April Theses" had not only denounced the imperialist war in Europe but called for the workers and poor peasants to rule Russia and demanded the end of the Provisional Government and transfer of power to the Soviets. Despite strong initial resistance, by May this was the line of the party.

FROM JULY TO OCTOBER: THE FINAL DENOUEMENT

By June the more leftist Provisional Government, now under the influence of the Socialist Revolutionary Alexander Kerensky (who formally became Prime Minister that month), made a last stab at victory in the war. An offensive by General Alexei Brusilov initially advanced in Galicia against the weaker Austro-Hungarian forces. But a German counteroffensive two weeks later routed the Russians and seized additional territory.

This final defeat of the Russian army had disastrous consequences. The defeat in Galicia triggered a strong revolutionary upsurge in Petrograd. During the "July Days" hundreds of thousands of demonstrators took to the streets to demand an end to the war and a transfer of all power to the Soviets. The demonstrators were joined by sailors from the Kronstadt naval base and some soldiers. The Bolsheviks, however, wavered, and eventually decided (apart from their military organization) to stand aside from these demonstrations. Eventually, Kerensky was able to crush the anarchic, leaderless revolt, scatter the demonstrators, arrest some Bolsheviks, and send the rest into hiding or exile (Lenin fled to Finland). Kerensky resurrected old charges that Lenin and the Bolsheviks were German agents for taking German money and passing through Germany on the way to Russia in a "sealed train." The Kerensky forces occupied the headquarters of the Bolshevik party and its newspaper *(Pravda)* and arrested some leaders.[5]

But this success was to be short lived. The right wing, seeing the demise of the radicals, searched for deliverance from that tepid socialist Alexander Kerensky (prime minister since July) and his reformist government, dominated by Socialist Revolutionaries and Mensheviks. General Lavr Kornilov, Commander-in-Chief of the Russian army, at an All-Russian State Conference in late August denounced anarchy and declared the socialists responsible for all of Russia's problems. Kerensky called on Kornilov to restore order after the failure of the Brusilov offensive. Soon Kornilov, seeing the ineptitude of the Kerensky regime, fancied that he would become the savior of Russia.

Using the pretext that the capital must be evacuated in the face of a German offensive that threatened Petrograd, Kornilov sent a cavalry corps towards Petrograd to crush both the government and the Soviets. There ensued a complex interaction between Kerensky and Kornilov. Finally it became clear that Kornilov was trying to stage a coup when he sent additional troops to move on Petrograd. Realizing the danger, the government and Soviet mobilized their forces against this imminent danger. The Petrograd garrison and Kronstadt sailors rallied to the regime, the workers under Bolshevik influence were armed, and the population mobilized. Spontaneous risings among the

[5]Alexander Rabinowitch, *Petrograd Bolsheviks and the July 1917 Uprising*, Indiana University Press, Bloomington, 1968.

troops, aided by the Bolsheviks, led to officers being shot and thousands of troops returning to the cities of Russia. The Kornilov forces were stopped short of Petrograd and refused to fight. In the aftermath Kornilov's allies were arrested, the military disintegrated, and the Bolsheviks now gained great credibility against both the threats of the military on the right and ineptitude of the socialist moderates. The weapons that were distributed to the workers to fight Kornilov would in just two months be turned against the government in the October Revolution.

This episode was the critical one before the October Revolution. Once the bankruptcy of the Kerensky regime was apparent by the fall of 1917, the main threat to a left-wing dictatorship of the Bolsheviks was a right-wing military dictatorship. The right in many countries has historically looked to a "man on horseback" to save the situation.[6] Why, then, could Kornilov be destroyed so easily?

The primary reason was that the army of 1917 had changed radically from the army of 1914. For the most part its officers were no longer career Tsarist officers but new recruits on temporary assignment to the army, and its soldiers were now peasants in uniform who had been strongly impacted by the war losses and the February Revolution. Between February and October over 1 million soldiers, largely peasants, simply deserted the front and went home. The army, then, was no longer isolated from society but rather had become an integral part of the revolution. It had ceased to be a loyal bulwark of reaction.[7]

Thus, the defeat of the Kornilov coup opened the door for the October Revolution. As a result of their strong role in defeating the rightist coup, the Bolsheviks gained legitimacy and support. In February they had been a small party of 23,500 members, with relatively little influence. By June, at the First All-Russian Congress of Soviets in Petrograd, the Bolsheviks had 105 delegates, significant but still far inferior to 248 Menshevik and 285 Socialist Revolutionary delegates. The failure of the "July Days" had been a major setback, but the Kornilov coup and continued drift towards the left soon revived Bolshevik fortunes. The Kornilov coup propelled the Bolsheviks to the center of political life and their 25,000 Red Guards to a significant role in the events of September. By September their ranks had swelled to 240,000 members, and they had gained a majority in the Petrograd and Moscow Soviets and significant support in as many as 250 Russian cities. After the destruction of the Kornilov coup, the Bolsheviks could easily dominate the executive committee of the Petrograd Soviet (fourteen Bolsheviks and eleven non-Bolsheviks).

By October Leon Trotsky was the head of the Petrograd Soviet.[8] At this

---

[6]The Russian military smashed the Hungarian revolution in 1849, the French army destroyed the Paris Commune in 1871, the Russian army liquidated the Russian revolution in 1905, and the Spanish army destroyed the Spanish revolution by 1939.

[7]See Allan Wildman, *The End of the Russian Imperial Army*, Princeton University Press, Princeton, 1980.

[8]Leon Trotsky, who had been the President of the Petrograd Soviet in 1905, was a co-leader of the October Revolution with Lenin, and later Foreign Commissar and War Commissar. After losing the Leninist succession struggle, he was exiled abroad and finally was murdered by Stalin's agent, Ramon Mercador, in Mexico City in 1940.

time Lenin, in hiding in Finland, called for an immediate seizure of power, based on strong Bolshevik support in the army and cities. The majority of Bolsheviks (now 400,000 members) initially supported Grigorii Zinoviev and Lev Kamenev in opposing any armed insurrection. They argued that the tide was turning in favor of the Bolsheviks, that the Bolsheviks and their allies would win a majority in the Constituent Assembly elections, and that the Bolsheviks should rule together with other socialist parties. In the end, though, most Bolsheviks rallied behind Lenin.

When Kerensky tried to suppress the Bolsheviks on October 24, the Bolsheviks under Lenin and Trotsky launched a counterstroke under the rubric of the Military Revolutionary Committee of the Executive Committee of the Petrograd Soviet. Their Red Guards achieved complete success the next day. After the Bolsheviks took the Winter Palace, Kerensky escaped from the city, only to find little support outside. Thus, without much fanfare, the Bolsheviks launched their October Revolution. The total cost in Petrograd: twenty killed and a few wounded. In Moscow, though, the fighting with the Junkers (officer cadets) was much bloodier but the results were the same.[9]

UNEXPECTED NATURE OF OCTOBER REVOLUTION AND CIVIL WAR

Since we know the outcome of the October Revolution, it is often hard to recapture the feelings of the time. But here we will try to find the answers to the most important questions: Why was it unexpected and indeed shocking at the time, and why did it succeed? Here we begin by looking at the totally unexpected nature of the October Revolution. After all, with the February Revolution in 1917 having deposed the Tsar and replaced him with a quasi-democratic system (with elections scheduled for November), why should there be a second revolution? Socialism had been much heralded in Europe ever since the publication of *The Communist Manifesto* by Karl Marx and Friedrich Engels in 1848. Communism had not really been "a specter haunting Europe" in 1848, but the proponents of socialism thrived and prospered during the second half of the nineteenth century. By the turn of the century the socialists formed the largest single party in Germany and were an increasingly significant element in many European countries. The poverty of the urban masses, the dislocations of early industrial development, the entry of the masses into politics, and the large gap between a small, wealthy elite and a more numerous, depressed, lower class fueled these developments. By 1914 the Second International (an alliance of European socialist parties) had seemed to be developing into a significant force in European politics.

Yet socialism (and even more so authoritarian socialism, or Communism) had by 1917 never been able to turn its attractions into real political power. The

[9]Alexander Rabinowitch, *The Bolsheviks Come to Power: The Revolution of 1917 in Petrograd*, W.W. Norton, New York, 1978.

most spectacular events in Europe from 1848 to 1917 had represented crushing defeats for socialism. The 1848 revolutions, some with socialist overtones, had been ruthlessly repressed, nowhere more dramatically than in the June Days in Paris. In 1870–1871 the formation of the Paris Commune, a political organization with strong socialist overtones, had been smashed by the guns of the counterrevolution. In 1914 the attempts of the Second International to prevent the mass slaughter of World War I had been destroyed by powerful popular nationalist feeling.

Nor were these defeats for socialism confined to the pre-1917 period. In 1919 the Hungarian Communists, having come to power in April under Bela Kun, lasted a mere 133 days in power before being crushed by the Rumanian army. In 1919, 1920, and 1923 attempts at revolution in Germany were all bloodily repressed. So too were nascent revolts elsewhere in Europe. Even after the horrendous devastation of World War I killed almost 10 million soldiers in a four-year bloodbath, the weakened European order still was strong enough to resist the socialist blandishments. Indeed, this would continue in the 1920s and even during the Great Depression of the 1930s, which logically should have propelled the Communists to power in Western Europe. Rather, in the 1930s fascism swept to power in Germany, Italy, and Spain and authoritarian, neofascist regimes predominated in Eastern Europe (except for Czechoslovakia).

Revolutionary successes are relatively rare; revolutionary failures are frequent. In French history we celebrate the 1789 revolution, but often forget the failures of the 1848 and 1871 revolutions (and perhaps 1968?). We remember the successful 1917 Russian Revolution, but forget the disasters of the 1825 and 1905 revolutions, and the Pugachev and Razin rebellions. In China we remember the successful 1911 and 1949 revolutions, but lose sight of the numerous disastrous attempts at revolution by Sun Yatsen before 1911 and the defeat of the Taiping Rebellion, Nian Rebellion, and White Lotus Uprising in the nineteenth century. Perhaps nothing should make us more aware of revolutionary failure than the abortive Chinese Revolution in the spring of 1989 that was crushed by the People's Liberation Army in Tienanmen Square. Thus, revolutionary attempts are numerous but revolutionary successes are rare—and this makes sense if we remember the great coercive power of the army and secret police that is usually at the disposal of the government.

Thus two questions are inevitable: How did the Bolsheviks manage to come to power in October 1917 and so easily extend their power through most of the country? How did they manage to hold onto the power they won in October 1917?

SOURCES OF BOLSHEVIK VICTORY IN THE OCTOBER REVOLUTION

How did the Bolsheviks, with less than 400,000 members and garnering support from at most 25 percent of the population, take and hold victory in the

October Revolution? The moderates, epitomized by the peasant moderates (Socialist Revolutionaries), working-class moderates (Mensheviks), and upper-class moderates (Kadets), all failed to respond to the imperatives of the Russian Revolution of 1917. Revolutionary momentum created demands that the Provisional Government moderates were either unable or unwilling to respond to effectively. The masses had now gained sharply heightened political consciousness and expectations. The peasants wanted their land, the workers their factories, and the soldiers peace—and they wanted it now, not at some far-off time. They had little faith in these moderate groups and demanded that government move to bridge the enormous gap between the two Russias, the "official Russia" of the old Tsarist upper classes and institutions and the "second Russia" of workers and peasants (who were most of the soldiers).

The Bolsheviks came closest to expressing the revolutionary sentiments of the lower classes. The majority of the Bolsheviks came from the lower classes and their leaders, espousing Marxism, focused their attention on mobilizing the workers and, somewhat, the peasants.[10] The Bolsheviks offered the desired land to the peasants, factories to the workers, and peace to the soldiers. They thus sought openly to mobilize the lower classes around important revolutionary positions. They followed through on these promises. Once in power they brought peace to Russia (Treaty of Brest-Litovsk in March 1918), gave land to the peasants (Decree on Land in October 1917), and greatly enhanced the rights of workers.

There was little confidence in 1917 in democratic institutions. The Bolsheviks easily dispersed the Constituent Assembly that met for the first and only time in January 1918. Limited democracy had only existed in Russia between 1906 and 1917, when there had been four Dumas with little result. The backbone of democracies, a strong middle class, was absent in Russia.

Other parties, both Marxist and non-Marxist, were weak in both ideology and organization. The Kadets and Octobrists were really only interest groups, representing a relatively thin middle- and upper-class stratum. Their Western-style appeals, their strong desire to hold on to private property, and their past association with Tsarism had little appeal to the Russian masses. The Mensheviks were more popular—indeed they were bigger than the Bolsheviks in February 1917. But their moderate ideology, opposition to an immediate transition to socialism, desire to be a loyal opposition to a modernizing bourgeois government, and weak organization all pushed them into a free fall from power even before October 1917. As for the Socialist Revolutionaries, they did represent the peasants and gained the majority of the votes in the Constituent Assembly elections of November 1917. But their leadership was uninspired and the party organization very weak, and the SRs fatalistically failed to develop an action program reaching beyond the numerous but isolated and atomized peasants.

The Bolsheviks, although far from the disciplined legions imagined by their

---

[10]The Marxism of the Bolsheviks, in its Leninist version, was much harder, more authoritarian and elitist than traditional Marxism in Western Europe.

enemies, were still a better-organized party with an attractive political program. The Bolshevik emphasis on the lower classes, especially the industrial workers, gave them a strong base in the cities. The Bolshevik program of building a socialist utopia in Russia gave hope to the lower classes and assigned them, for the first time, a predominant role in the creation of Russia's future. The Bolshevik slogan of national self-determination, and the freedom given to Poland, Finland, and the Baltics, seemed to hold a way out of the "prison house of nationalities."

Finally, their rivals were unable to call on their natural resources to offset these Bolshevik advantages. Normally, the upper classes and their allies would have launched a military coup to crush the Bolsheviks. But the bulk of the soldiers were at the front, and those in Petrograd (and to a lesser extent Moscow) were thoroughly politicized by the Bolsheviks. When Kornilov and other White leaders called on the army to move, it was immobilized by massive antiwar sentiment bred by fatigue and disgust with the army after three long years of war. The other logical allies for the anti-Bolshevik coalition, the foreign armies, were thoroughly occupied in October 1917 with major action on the Eastern front and had no troops to spare. Indeed, the German and Austro-Hungarian armies supported a Bolshevik victory in the hopes (later proved correct) that this would take Russia out of the war. And, finally, the normally passive peasants, who had given the Tsar the victory in December 1905, when the peasant army had crushed the revolution, were now unwilling to fight for the old order.

RUSSIAN CIVIL WAR

Here we will briefly sketch the main developments in the Russian Civil War. First, we must briefly review the period from the October Revolution until the outbreak of the Russian Civil War in May 1918. After seizing power in the October Revolution, the Bolsheviks immediately proceeded to implement their program. At the Second All-Russian Congress of Soviets in November the Bolsheviks had a majority—390 delegates to 240 from other socialist parties. The withdrawal of a number of the moderate socialists facilitated the Bolshevik's seizure of government power. This body approved a decree on peace, which called for immediate negotiations and a peace without annexations. Its land decree abolished land ownership without compensation and turned all the land of the landlords, churches, and monasteries over to the local land committees and Soviets. It abolished the private ownership of land. The Soviet also created the first Soviet government, in the form of a Council of People's Commissars headed by Lenin and including many other Bolshevik luminaries, Trotsky among them.

The Bolsheviks rapidly extended their power throughout the country. Within three months their writ extended through the bulk of Russia as the same factors that had brought them to power in Petrograd replicated themselves elsewhere. At times the fighting was heavy, as in Moscow, but the result was the same. In addition, they extended their control over the army, already in a state of disintegration, the major railroad lines, and the cities. Numerous decrees undertook major social and governmental reforms in the name of socialism. All Russians became citizens of the republic, worker control of the factories was established, the court system was abolished, the Kadets were declared counterrevolutionary, and a secret police (Cheka) was established.

The biggest problems were restoring order, determining how to deal with the elections for the Constituent Assembly in November 1917, and coping with nationality discontent. The final results of that election were not that bad for the Bolsheviks—10 million votes, 25 percent of the total—but it left them only the second largest party in Russia after the Socialist Revolutionaries, with 17 million votes. After one brief and stormy session of the Constituent Assembly in January, Lenin had it forcibly dissolved. This marked a key signpost in the development of the authoritarian and dictatorial nature of the party, one already seen in the forcible seizure of power in October. As for growing nationality discontent, the central regime lacked popular support in many areas for its own program of limited self-determination.

Military opposition to the Bolsheviks began in the south with the Don Cossack revolt in December 1917 and the creation of a volunteer army under General Kaledin and General Kornilov. By April 1918, after the suicide of Kaledin and death in battle of Kornilov, General Denikin emerged as the White leader. By the summer of 1918 he controlled the Don and North Caucasus. The Whites were an amorphous group opposed to the Bolsheviks. More major fighting began in May 1918 when 40,000 Czech Legion former prisoners of war, being shipped across Siberia to Vladivostok for ultimate transportation to the Western front to fight Germany, rebelled along the Trans-Siberian Railroad.[11] This forced the formation of a Red Army under Leon Trotsky, the War Commissar from March 1918 until 1925. In 1918 the Whites and their allies at one point controlled 75 percent of all Russian territory, and in 1919 they mounted an effective drive that took them in October to the very outskirts of Petrograd and near Moscow. But they were beaten back both times, and in 1920 the Red Army, after retreating from an advance on Warsaw, had cleared Russia of the bulk of all Whites. Final victory was achieved in November 1920.[12]

The Civil War was so complicated that it might be better to take it one region at a time. Throughout the Civil War the Bolsheviks held onto Moscow, Petrograd, and the thirty core Russian central provinces. The battle was over important points on the periphery. After the Treaty of Brest-Litovsk, Ukraine had nine governments in twenty-three months. The Bolsheviks seized Ukraine in February 1918 only to surrender it almost immediately to the Germans, who established the puppet regime of Hetman Skoropadsky in March. In November, after the defeat of Germany in the war, Ukrainian Socialists under Simon

---

[11]For overall histories of the Russian Civil War, see Evan Mawdsley, *The Russian Civil War,* Allen and Unwin, Boston, 1987; and W. Bruce Lincoln, *Red Victory,* Simon and Schuster, New York, 1989.
[12]A good short summary of the civil war is contained in Michael Florinsky, editor, *Encyclopedia of Russia and the Soviet Union,* McGraw-Hill, New York, 1961.

Petlyura took power from Skoropadsky. A second Bolshevik invasion in February 1919 took power for eight months until Denikin wrested it back in the fall of 1919. A third Bolshevik invasion in December 1919 was more successful, until a Polish invasion took much of Ukraine away in May 1920. The Bolsheviks finally settled the issue in December 1920. In some Ukrainian cities there were as many as a dozen regimes in a year.

In the Baltics German power, dominant in 1918, continued even after their defeat. General Yudenich used the Baltics as an unsuccessful launching point to try to seize Petrograd in October 1919. In 1920 the Bolsheviks recognized the independence of the Baltic states.

In the far north of Russia Allied troops landed in Arkhangel and Murmansk in the summer of 1918. After ineffectual activity and some fighting, the Allies withdrew in the fall of 1919, allowing the Bolsheviks to retake these two key ports.

In the Transcaucasus the three states—Armenia, Azerbaijan, and Georgia— declared their independence in April and May 1918. Denikin defeated a Red Army thrust into the region in January 1919. England landed troops in Batum and Baku, France in Odessa, but to little effect. Denikin's thrust north was fatally delayed by Red Army troops at Tsaritsyn (Stalingrad). After his defeat in the fall of 1919 in his drive on Moscow, Denikin fell back on the Black Sea coast. The Red Army swept into the area and forced his successor, Baron Wrangel, to evacuate the coast for Turkey in November 1920. This signalled the end of the civil war.

In the Far East, English, French, Japanese, and American troops landed at Vladivostok in August 1918. The Czech Legion and the Japanese successfully gained ground in this region. In November 1918 Admiral Kolchak proclaimed a White government at Omsk and invaded the Urals in January 1919. General Frunze, later War Commissar, led a successful Red Army counterattack, which took Omsk in November 1919 and later moved on Irkutsk. In February 1920 the Bolsheviks captured Kolchak and shot him.

This disaster prompted the withdrawal of all Allied forces in the Far East save 80,000 Japanese troops, who left under American pressure in October 1922. The French and English left Ukraine and Transcaucasus in the spring of 1919 and the north of Russia later in 1919. By 1920 the Bolsheviks were triumphant everywhere, save for the new nations (Finland, Baltics, Poland) that had gained their independence.

PROBLEMS FACED BY BOLSHEVIKS IN RUSSIAN CIVIL WAR

Even more surprising than the October Revolution was the success of the Bolsheviks during the Russian Civil War.[13] After their surprise seizure of power

---

[13]Much of the analysis of the Russian civil war is taken from Jonathan Adelman, *The Revolutionary Armies,* Greenwood Press, Westport, Connecticut, 1980.

in October 1917, the world confidently expected their early fall from power. Once the enemies of the Bolsheviks took the field in the Russian Civil War in May 1918, most observers expected the imminent demise of the regime. Never before had a socialist regime come to power in any country in the world—and now it defied all of the other European countries not only in taking power but in retaining it!

This is even more surprising if we consider the array of powers aligned against the Bolsheviks in the 1917–1920 period. First, there was the unanimous enmity of all of the world's major powers. To them the Bolsheviks, as atheist Communists, represented the darkest forces of the radical left. For the democratic countries in Europe and the United States, Bolshevik expropriation of private property, refusal to honor Tsarist debts, Red terror against enemies of the regime, and publication of Tsarist secret agreements with Western European countries represented a complete repudiation of everything that the democracies stood for. For the remaining autocratic powers in Japan and Eastern Europe, Communism represented a dire threat to their well being.

So it was hardly surprising that many countries landed troops in Russia and financed the enemies of the Reds to the tune of 1 billion dollars—a very considerable sum seventy years ago. By 1919 no fewer than 80,000 Japanese troops had landed in the Far East (where they would remain to 1922) and contingents of British, French, and American troops had landed on Soviet soil. Even more important was the occupation by Imperial Germany before November 1918 of the western third of the Soviet Union. Newly independent former Russian territories, such as Poland and Finland, were notably hostile to Russia and supported military action against her.[14]

Even worse, the Bolsheviks lacked any experience in government or the military. In revolutionary regimes like those in China and Vietnam, the new Communist leaders usually had experience in directing the government of millions of people and running a major army that had propelled them to power. But the Bolsheviks, when they seized power in a coup in October 1917, had no experience whatsoever in such areas. As recently as February 1917, they had been a small and dispersed party of 23,500 members, living in hiding in the underground in Russia, deported to exile in Siberia (Kamenev and Stalin), or living abroad in foreign exile (Lenin, Trotsky, Bukharin). Even in October 1917 there were only 400,000 Bolsheviks. Without government bureaucrats, secret police agents, or military officers in their ranks, how would they run the country?

They had to rule a country devastated by war. By 1917 Russia had suffered 7 million casualties in the war. In March 1918 the Bolsheviks ceded Ukraine, Belorussia, and the Baltics to Imperial Germany. In 1917 industrial production was down to 75 percent of the 1913 level; in 1920, 14 percent. In 1920 agricultural output was only 60 percent of the 1913 level.

---

[14]Of course, as in Vietnam, Western intervention could actually have positive aspects for the Communists, who could now become defenders of the Motherland against foreign aggressors. This added a nationalist tinge to the Bolshevik cause.

The Whites had much stronger military skills and abilities. The majority of Tsarist career officers, monarchist by orientation and aristocratic by birth or achievement, naturally favored the Whites. Officers were so numerous in the White ranks that there were even officer battalions. By contrast, the Bolsheviks had no military officers or even noncommissioned officers in their ranks and had to coerce over 70,000 Tsarist officers to fight for them.[15]

It was not easy to mobilize a populace that had rebelled in February and October against participation in one war to enter a second one willingly. It was even more problematic when the iron discipline of an army was often enforced by former Tsarist officers, the local representatives of a hated old order. Although both sides faced this problem, it was especially acute for the Bolsheviks given the enmity of the former Tsarist officers and passive indifference of the peasant soldiers. While the former Tsarist officers had little love for revolution, the peasants were ambivalent about the urban, Marxist Bolsheviks, who had many non-Russian leaders (Trotsky, Zinoviev, Kamenev, Sverdlov, Dzerzhinsky, Stalin) and who favored expropriating the land taken by the peasants in 1917. Nearly 3 million soldiers (mostly peasants) deserted the Red Army in 1918 and 1919 and hundreds of Tsarist officers committed treason.[16]

There were problems within the party itself. The vast and rapid expansion of the party, left it a vast and incoherent organization, whose ranks were filled with youthful enthusiasts, careerists, and even hostile elements. During the Civil War there was no way to unify the party and create the desired party monolith. Having achieved dizzying success in the October Revolution, many Bolsheviks believed in the immediate and radical transition to communism in a form of "great leap forward." They favored a radical "war communism" that created a nationalized socialized economy, bloody repression of all hostile White elements, a truly revolutionary army without any former Tsarist officers, and the active spread of international revolution abroad. This chiliastic spirit soared as the casualty toll mounted. It was only with great difficulty that Lenin and his followers managed to keep Tsarist officers in the army (facing down a 1919 challenge by the Military Opposition), restrain the greater excesses of the Cheka (secret police), and limit commitment to the international revolution, as embodied in the Comintern.

Finally, there were serious problems within the class structure and social structure of Russia. The great bulk of the old upper classes—aristocrats, capitalists, bureaucrats, landlords, and educated elements—were deeply hostile to the Bolsheviks. Many of the peasants were profoundly alienated by the atheism and Marxism of the Bolsheviks, its urban proletariat stress, internationalism, and heavy non-Russian presence in the leadership.[17] The international-

[15]For the Whites, see Richard Luckett, *The White Generals,* Viking Press, New York, 1971.

[16]For peasant problems, see Orlando Figes, *Peasant Russia, Civil Russia,* Clarendon Press, Oxford, 1989.

[17]Much of the population, especially in Ukraine, was strongly anti-Semitic and upset over the prominence in the party of such Jewish Bolsheviks as Leon Trotsky, Yakov Sverdlov, Grigorii Zinoviev, Lev Kamenev, and Karl Radek. Ironically, the Jewish community rejected them too as totally Russified elements.

ism of the Bolsheviks had limited appeal to the non-Russian minorities, many of whom preferred independence to a limited autonomy in the Soviet Union. The Civil War famine and disease shrank the working class and reduced the size of the population of Petrograd and Moscow by almost 40 percent.

REASONS FOR THE BOLSHEVIK VICTORY IN RUSSIAN CIVIL WAR

With this long litany of problems, it seems surprising that the Bolsheviks even bothered to take the field of battle, let alone that they prevailed. The creation of a strong army, party, government, and secret party would seem to be a task for decades, not for a year or two. The recruitment of expert and reliable personnel and institutionalization of new norms and standards in these bureaucracies was a task for a generation. What factors, then, allowed the Bolsheviks to prevail?

First, there was the question of political leadership and political will within the party. The quality of political leadership in the party—men such as Vladimir Lenin, Leon Trotsky, Grigorii Zinoviev, Lev Kamenev, Joseph Stalin, Felix Dzerzhinsky, Yakov Sverdlov—was quite high and markedly superior to that of the Whites. In all revolutions the quality of political leadership is usually the highest in the first generation as many men are drawn into politics who otherwise would not participate in the political arena. Who could compare these brilliant political revolutionaries with the narrow-minded White generals and admirals such as Anton Denikin, Nikolai Yudenich, Alexander Kolchak?[18]

As political radicals, they understood better than the White generals the political nature of the contest and the need to win the hearts and minds of the Russian people. While the Bolsheviks devised programs to attract the workers, peasants, and nationalities, the Whites never created a coherent program. The White association with Tsarism and tendency to use force against the peasants deeply harmed their cause.

The Bolsheviks, even if dispersed and fractious, were more unified around a single center (Moscow) than the Whites, strewn in all directions of the empire and often in conflict with each other. In Trotsky's phrase, the Bolsheviks constituted the "samurai of the revolution," for which no less than 300,000 gave their lives. They were the cement of the Red Army and cause; the Whites lacked such a cadre element.[19]

The Bolsheviks built nascent bureaucratic institutions during the Civil War, even if these worked poorly. In the Red Army they recruited 70,000 Tsarist officers, promoted tens of thousands of noncommissioned officers to the officer

[18]In the American Revolution the first generation—that of George Washington, Thomas Jefferson, Benjamin Franklin, John Adams, James Madison, James Monroe—was also the best.
[19]Russian White officers, like their South Vietnamese counterparts in 1975, often were corrupt and had one eye on emigrating abroad.

corps, installed commissars to watch over the Tsarist officers, and spread propaganda for their cause among the ranks. In the government they recruited many of the old civil servants *(chinovniki)* and limited persecution to a minimum. In the party Yakov Sverdlov and Joseph Stalin sought to regularize and institutionalize the organizational framework. In the Cheka Felix Dzerzhinsky tried to create a flexible yet decisive instrument of repression. With the resources and prestige of Moscow and Petrograd, they made some progress in all these areas. By contrast, the divided and dispersed Whites, without access to central resources and without a stable rear (the Bolsheviks always held onto the thirty Central Russian provinces), never were able to create even nascent bureaucratic structures.

The Bolsheviks could command the central resources to compensate for their other deficiencies. By controlling Moscow and Petrograd, they controlled the traditional symbols of authority and their considerable financial, personnel, and symbolic resources. They gained control of the large military reserves accumulated by the Tsarist regime to fight in World War I. They acquired some limited loyalty from the servants of the old regime in the various bureaucracies. They recruited an army of 5.5 million men by 1920, compared to less than 1 million men in the White armies. They could use their secure interior lines of supply and communications to divide and isolate their dispersed White armies.

The Bolsheviks also benefited from the historical accident of the developments in World War I. The major European countries despised Soviet Russia and, under certain circumstances, could have crushed it. Indeed, Lenin himself on one occasion noted that only a few Allied army corps could have seized Moscow. But the protracted and exhaustive nature of World War I greatly tired all of the participants and provoked revolution in the defeated Central Powers (Germany and Austro-Hungary) and their ally, Ottoman Turkey, at the end of the war. This removed the dire German threat to Soviet existence and forced the withdrawal in March 1918 of German armies from the one-third of Russia they had occupied. As for the victorious Allies, the Americans were eager to withdraw from the continent and the British and French were far too drained by massive war losses to support any major intervention in Russia.

The Bolsheviks created a more flexible nationalities policy and denounced the Great Russian chauvinism of their White enemies. The Poles in particular preferred a weak Bolshevik regime that at least pledged allegiance to self-determination to a strong Great Russian chauvinist regime under a General Denikin or Admiral Kolchak. For such a White regime, the first order of the day would be to attack its archenemy, Poland, and such an attack might be successful. Thus the Polish regime made only a small attack on Soviet Russia in 1919, when it was very weak, and reserved a greater attack for 1920, when the defeat of the Whites was ensured.

Even after victory, by 1921 the weak Soviet regime had lost a significant part of the Tsarist patrimony—Poland, Finland, Western Ukraine and Western Belorussia, Bessarabia—abroad and, at home, was forced to retreat to the New Economic Program.

IMPACT OF RUSSIAN CIVIL WAR ON SOVIET POLITICS

The Russian Civil War had a profound impact on Soviet politics. This was hardly surprising given its enormous cost (11 to 13 million deaths, including 300,000 Bolsheviks) and torturous path. For the great majority of the Bolsheviks, the war was their first real experience in the Party. For the older prerevolutionary Bolsheviks it was the first time they had ever had the heady experience of being in power or even working with the other members of the Party. For before 1917 the Party leaders had been scattered abroad, in jail in Russia, or in the secretive revolutionary underground inside the major cities of Russia.[20]

For the Bolsheviks the Civil War was, to borrow from Lev Kritsman, "the heroic period of the Russian Revolution."[21] It was a period of enormous *sturm and drang*, of tremendous sacrifice and great achievement, of the final conquest of the long held dream of a socialist Russia slaying all of the numerous domestic and foreign counterrevolutionary dragons. Victory in the Civil War ensured Bolshevik rule, albeit at high cost.

For the Party, the Civil War created an alternative policy culture to that of the pre-1917 period or the 1917 revolution. While the earlier periods had been noted for their antistate, anticentralist proclivities (manifested in Lenin's *State and Revolution*), the Civil War culture proclaimed the virtues and necessities of rule from Moscow and a powerful centralist state to destroy strong counterrevolutionary elements. Given the weak revolutionary impulse, especially in rural and nationality areas, only the power of the center could give the provincial Bolsheviks the force they needed for victory. The Civil War promoted a cult of violence and repression, reflected in the growing power of the Cheka. For without the Cheka and Red Terror, it was doubtful that the Bolsheviks could have remained in power against the Whites and their White Terror. Massive terror by the Whites and their allies—the shooting of the twenty-six Baku Commissars, the shooting of Lenin in August 1918, the assassinations of Volodarsky and Uritsky in 1918, the blowing up of Party headquarters in 1919, the killing of 50,000 Bolsheviks and sympathizers—contributed to a state of siege mentality in which brutal force seemed the only way.[22]

Together with this cult of violence and repression came a cult of Lenin and the leadership. As the Party composition changed drastically during the Civil War, there was a felt need in the lower ranks for a new religion and a new mythology to justify the suffering and to rally the masses. Although Lenin

---

[20]For a broad view of some of these issues, see Diane Koenker, William Rosenberg, and Ronald Suny, editors, *Party, State and Society in the Russian Civil War*, Indiana University Press, Bloomington, 1989.

[21]See Lev Kritsman, *Geroicheskii period russkoi revolutsii*, Gosizdat, Moscow, 1926.

[22]In August 1918 Fanya Kaplan shot Lenin three times at close range. Although Lenin did recover, the shooting evidently impaired his health and was a factor in subsequent strokes and his early death at 53 in 1924.

strongly resisted the role of a "new Tsar," he was venerated by many. The embalming of Lenin after his death in 1924 (again against Lenin's wishes) and the creation of the Lenin Mausoleum in Red Square laid the basis for the Stalinist cult of personality.

The Civil War transformed the Party. By 1921 the great majority of the members were Civil War or 1917 communists, for whom the lengthy pre-1917 history of the Party was something they had only heard about. For them the Party was the revolutionary party of 1917 or the party of state power in the Civil War. Perhaps half of the Old Bolsheviks were gone by 1921, having succumbed to disease, shooting and repression, the White army, exhaustion, or simple disgust at the evolution of the Party from one of idealism to ruthless pragmatism and repression. Despite their relative youth, many of the top Party leaders died before 1927. In the Civil War Yakov Sverdlov died of influenza; the twenty-six Baku Commissars were shot by the British. Lenin died in 1924, partly from his wounds. In 1925 Mikhail Frunze, new War Commissar, died on the operating table, and in 1926 Felix Dzerzhinsky, head of the Cheka, died prematurely.

In their place came a Civil War generation, quite different from the old elite of cosmopolitan revolutionary intellectuals of middle- and upper-class background (Lenin, Zinoviev, Kamenev, Bukharin, Trotsky). This new generation, epitomized by Stalin, was lower class in origin, never had gone to the universities, and trained in the rough and ready school of the underground before 1917 and of the Civil War from 1918 to 1920. Largely in the provinces during the Civil War, they found themselves face to face with White terror and the White armies. This new generation rapidly replaced the old revolutionary intelligentsia everywhere, except in the top ranks of the party, by 1927.

Other key institutions also were rapidly changing. The Cheka, founded only in December 1917, rapidly grew in prominence during the Civil War. Given the weakness of the Bolshevik base, the actions of counterrevolutionary groups in the major cities, the White terror, and rapid movement of the White armies, the Cheka soon found itself very busy. Not only did it shoot 50,000 to 100,000 people (many of them innocent) during the Red Terror, but it established the first concentration camps for Whites, took hostages of White officers, guarded the rear of the army, and took on a number of civilian tasks (even taking care of the 4 million orphans of the Civil War). By 1921 the secret police had emerged as a new, rough, and powerful institution under Felix Dzerzhinsky.

The Bolsheviks, without any experienced government bureaucrats and few university-educated professionals in their ranks, were forced to rely heavily on the traditional Tsarist bureaucracy. This institution underwent the least change of any institution during the Civil War. Although it remained corrupt, slow moving, and inefficient, the bureaucracy provided a way to extract revenue, raise troops, and mobilize resources. Not until the late 1930s would it become thoroughly Bolshevized.

This was true to a less degree of the army. Tsarist officers were 75 percent of the Red Army officer corps in 1918, 10 percent by 1921. But as late as 1929 they still wrote 90 percent of the field regulations for the army. The peasant soldiers remained restive, and many temporary Bolshevik officers were eager to return to civilian life. Only a massive restructuring and reduction in size could transform the Red Army into a modern institution capable of defending the Soviet Union from major foreign armies, not just the inept White forces.

Thus, by 1921 the Party and secret police were major political forces; the army and government, dominated by non-Bolsheviks in the lower and middle levels, needed massive transformation before they became legitimate and powerful actors. This augured well for the Stalinists who were strong in the lower and middle ranks of the party and in the secret police.

The new regime in 1921 looked out on a world greatly changed from the expectations of 1917. The domestic base of the urban proletariat and the worker-peasant alliance had been eroded by the Civil War. The industrial proletariat base had shrunk by half and the new recruits were indifferent to the Bolsheviks. The peasants had often been hostile and passively supported the Bolsheviks for fear of landlord return and Tsarist restoration. Abroad, dreams of an international proletariat revolution were smashed by the defeat of the German and Hungarian revolutions. The Bolsheviks seemed to have achieved the ultimate Pyrrhic victory, as they had triumphed in a world devoid of international or domestic allies.

9

The Fateful Interlude of the 1920s

The 1920s in the Soviet Union were a peaceful and tranquil interlude among the stormy events of the first half of the twentieth century. This interlude was preceded by World War I, the twin revolutions of 1917 and the Russian Civil War. By 1921, 10 to 14 million people had died, largely from famine and disease, agriculture was at 43 percent of the 1913 level, and industry a paltry 14 percent of the prewar year.[1] It was followed in the 1930s by dekulakization, the Ukrainian famine, and the Great Purges—all of which killed millions of people—and then the even worse atrocities of World War II. Sandwiched between these events, the 1920s often seem to have the warm glow of a peaceful, relatively tranquil era.

The turn away from the protracted violence of the 1914–1921 era was sudden and dramatic. At the beginning of 1921 economic failings, peasant revolts, and factory strikes posed a real threat to the Bolsheviks. In March 1921 the Kronstadt sailors, originally the most ardent Bolshevik supporters, rose in revolt. Demanding Soviets without Communists, the sailors denounced the rule of commissars, secret police repression, and Soviet bureaucracy. Lenin rallied hundreds of delegates to the Tenth Party Congress, Red Army cadets, and Chekists (secret police agents) to crush the revolt mercilessly.[2] The ever-pragmatic Lenin afterwards swiftly moved to create a more lenient and popular regime.

[1]See Alec Nove, *An Economic History of the USSR*, Penguin Books, Harmondsworth, England, 1969, pp. 83–94.
[2]See Paul Avrich, *Kronstadt 1921*, Princeton University Press, Princeton, 1970; and Israel Gentzler, *Kronstadt 1917–1921*, Cambridge University Press, New York, 1983.

NEW ECONOMIC PROGRAM

This new program, the New Economic Program (NEP), reversed war communism. At its heart were large-scale concessions to the peasants, or a "peasant Brest-Litovsk." There were to be no more forcible requisitions of peasant grain or attempts to push the peasants toward socialist property. Rather they needed only pay a tax in kind (later set at 10 percent) and could lease land, hire labor, and choose the kind of land tenure they desired. The peasants were to enjoy what they wanted most: private agriculture. The party also denationalized many small industries, leasing them for hire. It turned the majority of the retail trade over to the private NEP men, or small middlemen, and to cooperatives. Money was now reintroduced, as was a conventional market system. The Party did retain the "commanding heights" of industry, banking, mining, and foreign trade. Attempts (largely unsuccessful) were made to attract foreign capital. All of these economic concessions were accompanied by a tightening of political control of the country, with the elimination of all political opposition.[3]

As Table 9.1 shows, by 1926 industrial production exceeded the 1913 level and agricultural output was nearly at that level.

The 1920s were also noted for their relative freedom of expression and experimentation, expressed in the novels of Maxim Gorky, Ilya Ehrenburg, and Mikhail Sholokhov, the experimental theater of Vsevolod Meyerhold, and the movies of Sergei Eisenstein.

So, too, were there few restrictions on the family. The 1926 Family Code echoed the 1918 Family Code in liberating the family from the traditional conservatism of the Tsarist era. The government made divorce and abortion easy to find, civil marriages replaced church marriages, and the sexes were declared equal. The government declared adultery, bigamy, and incest non-punishable acts. All members of the family were declared independent of each

---

[3]Robert Daniels, *Conscience of the Revolution,* Simon and Schuster, New York, 1969, chapter 7; and Donald Treadgold, *Twentieth Century Russia,* Westview Press, Boulder, Colorado, 1989.

TABLE 9.1. Russian Economic Production, 1913, 1921, 1926*

| | Year | | |
Product	1913	1921	1926
Industrial Output	10.2	1.4	11.1
Coal	29.0	8.9	27.6
Electricity	1.9	.5	3.5
Steel	4.2	.2	3.1
Grain	80.1	37.6	76.8

*Industrial production is defined in terms of 1926 billions of rubles; coal, steel, and grain in terms of millions of tons; and electricity in terms of billions of kilowatts.
Source: Alec Nove, *An Economic History of the USSR,* Penguin Books, Harmondsworth, England, 1969, p. 94.

other with a sharp decline in the role of the patriarchal father. Overall, the 1920s represented considerable legal freedom and liberation for the family.[4]

On an institutional level, it was a period of consolidation and relaxation after the horrible strains of the four years following the February Revolution. Bourgeois specialists continued to play a key role in the army and government, but they were gradually being phased out in favor of newly recruited Communists. The secret police was small and effective, but far from the powerful entity it had been in the Civil War or became in the 1930s. Only the Party, which faced the dual problems of the Leninist succession struggle and political normalization, underwent great strains and repeated purges. There the power of the apparat and its permanent members, the apparatchiki, underwent great expansion.[5]

The power of these institutions was far from what it became in the 1930s, and for most Russians life returned to a pleasant calm after the horrors of the 1914–1920 period. Even in the area of religion, a concerted battle with the Russian Orthodox Church, which had included seizure of Church property and the arrest of the Metropolitan of the Church, ended in an entente by 1927. The Smolensk archives showed that religion remained strong despite the valiant efforts of Yemelian Yaroslavsky's League of the Militant Atheists. Smolensk province, with over 2 million people, had in the 1920s no fewer than 564 churches (with over 700 priests) and 30 synagogues for the faithful. The Party remained weak, with 5000 to 10,000 members in the province of over 2 million people, and the Young Communist League was equally weak. The Party organization was repeatedly racked by corruption, drunkenness, sexual degeneracy, and bribery. Even among workers, only 5 percent belonged to the Party. Thus, outside the major cities, among the bulk of the population, the Party was weak and life continued largely as it had been before the revolution—but not entirely, for the old ruling classes were gone, as were their institutions.[6]

Nor were the nationality minorities unduly disturbed, for in the early 1920s the party sought to at least go part way to meet their grievances, even if only symbolically. The 1922 formation of the USSR and the 1923 Soviet constitution provided cultural autonomy for the minorities, with the use of local languages, customs, and the creation of new alphabets. The national minorities now had their own republics or autonomous regions, federated in the USSR, and with the theoretical (but not to be exercised) right of secession. The new constitution created an elaborate system for the Russian, Belorussian, Ukrainian, and Transcaucasian Republics, with varying levels of official representation of the minorities. Too, there was formal equality for all citizens, something that had been denied to one-third of the population before 1917. Moscow was still powerful but not pushing the forcible Russification of the Tsarist era.[7]

---

[4]See Basil Dmytryshyn, *USSR: A Concise History*, Charles Scribner's Sons, New York, 1971.
[5]By 1922 there were already 15,000 apparatchiki and the power of the Party institutions, notably the Secretariat, Orgburo, and Politburo, grew apace. See Merle Fainsod and Jerry Hough, *How the Soviet Union Is Governed*, Harvard University Press, Cambridge, 1979, pp. 124–129.
[6]See Merle Fainsod, *Smolensk Under Soviet Rule*, Harvard University Press, Cambridge, 1958, chapters 18–22, pp. 44–49.
[7]Theodore Von Laue, *Why Lenin? Why Stalin?* J.B. Lippincott, Philadelphia, 1971, chapter 9.

SEEDS OF FUTURE PROBLEMS

Little wonder, then, that this period is considered the most peaceful of any of the three decades between 1914 and 1944. But even here there were the seeds of future violent events. It was during the 1920s that Lenin died and Stalin won a long and protracted five-year struggle for succession. That such an era should give rise to a Stalin, who would soon uproot the "civil peace" of the 1920s and turn the Soviet Union back on the path of "civil war" in the 1930s is one of the paradoxes of our time. If Nikolai Bukharin was truly the avatar of the 1920s, then why was he so easily defeated in 1929 and later summarily shot by Stalin?

The New Economic Program implemented by Lenin in 1921, in response to the chaos induced by the Civil War and the numerous scattered uprisings of 1920 and 1921, was not a Marxist program. Rather it represented a forced concession from the Bolsheviks, much like the Treaty of Brest-Litovsk, wrested from the reluctant Bolsheviks in March 1918. As pragmatists, the Leninist Bolsheviks were ever willing to take "one step forward, two steps backward" in order to save the revolution and live to fight another day. This was one of the aspects of the Bolsheviks that was to sharply separate them from the fascists, who, in World War II, were willing to risk everything, including their very survival, on one grand throw of the die.

But the civil peace of the 1920s, however necessary, was contrary to the very nature and being of the Bolsheviks, who were dedicated to radical social change and an apocalyptic vision of the ultimate victory of the international socialist revolution. The improbable victories in the October Revolution and Civil War, the disintegration of four great empires by 1918 (Tsarist Russia, Austro-Hungary, Ottoman Turkey, Imperial Germany), the incipient if failed revolutions in Germany, Austria, and Hungary after the war, and the shaking of the European order to its foundations by the World War, all convinced the Bolsheviks that the future lay with them. However, the civil peace of the 1920s would have suited the temperament of any democratic party in Western Europe, or even peasant parties in Eastern Europe, just fine.[8]

But acceptance of the status quo in the Soviet Union—as implied in Lenin's concept of the partnership between workers and peasants—would have dire consequences for the future. First, it would mean abandoning the radical program of socialist transformation, and nullifying the great sacrifices made in the name of socialism. Second, such acceptance would leave the Bolsheviks forever an alien authoritarian party in an essentially peasant Russia. As the party of urban Marxism relying first and foremost on the cities and then the industrial proletariat, the Bolsheviks would be doomed to irrelevance. For, as Teodor Shanin has shown in his study of the Russian peasants in 1920s, the peasants were essentially alien and indifferent to the Bolsheviks.[9] Rather, traditional peasant institutions and values had displaced the soviets and

---

[8]For a good description of the Bukharan advocates of "civil peace," see Stephen Cohen, *Bukharin and the Bolshevik Revolution*, W.W. Norton, New York, 1973.
[9]Teodor Shanin, *The Awkward Class*, Cambridge University Press, Cambridge, 1972.

Communist values in the countryside, where the Bolsheviks were seen as a small and largely irrelevant nuisance. Less than 1 in 300 peasants even belonged to the party, and most of them were simple opportunists with no commitment to the revolution or the Bolsheviks. In 1927, 98 percent of all sown area was in private hands in 25 million plots scatted across Russia, with over 90 percent in traditional Russian peasant communities (or *mir*).[10]

Third, the Bolsheviks would be left not only at the mercy of the peasants and with only a small industrial proletariat base, but also at the mercy of alien bureaucratic institutions. In the Civil War the Bolsheviks succeeded in gaining only the commanding heights of the government and army, which functioned but poorly and inefficiently. During the 1920s the Bolsheviks gained a greater foothold through purges and reformation of the structures. Still, even by the end of the 1920s neither of these two critical institutions had become modern implements of Bolshevik rule.

The Bolsheviks, with their proletariat base, simply lacked the well-educated, experienced professionals to run these organizations and infuse them with revolutionary ethos. The revolutionary experience of the Civil War had been too short to have a significant impact on these organizations. The Bolsheviks lacked the material and human resources to transform them.

Fourth, the Bolsheviks in the 1920s period of Thermidor had temporarily changed their political style. During the 1917–1920 period they had tried to eliminate the old traditional culture and impose radically new policies of war communism, atheism, radical social reform, and the like. The failure of this effort by 1921 led to a Thermidorian reaction of seeking accommodation with the underlying social realities of the 1920s: a largely peasant, traditional Russia; strong conservatism in many areas of life; resistance to many social reforms (such as to women's rights by patriarchal peasants); and anti-Semitism, xenophobia, and strong male chauvinism. During the 1920s the regime stopped trying to transform society and accommodated itself to these features, many of them hostile to radical social reform. Any reading of the material gathered in the Smolensk archives in the 1920s, as summarized by Merle Fainsod, will convince one instantly of the great gap between the "revolutionary Russia" of the Bolsheviks and the still powerful "traditional Russia" of the countryside and smaller cities. But, by doing this—as seen in Bukharin's famous call to peasants to "enrich themselves"—the Bolsheviks were also putting into question whether any real changes were possible and whether peasant numbers and conservatism and bureaucratic inertia would sink the original Bolshevik program.

Finally, the Bolsheviks were traumatized by the premature death of Vladimir Lenin in January 1924. Under normal circumstances Lenin, who was born in 1870, would probably have led the Bolsheviks through the 1920s and the 1930s. His death at age 53 was a deep shock to a profoundly Leninist party. At every turn it had been Lenin who had shown the way. In 1917 in April and September he had shown the way to the seizure of power in the October

---

[10]Nove, *An Economic History of the USSR*, p. 106.

Revolution. In March 1918 he had overturned a Party majority to gain approval for the Treaty of Brest-Litovsk. During the Civil War he had been the indispensable leader of the government and the Party. In March 1921 at the Tenth Party Congress Lenin had led the Party in the sharp reversal from war communism to NEP. At every stage he had always been there. Suddenly, after two years of illness, he was gone.[11]

The party was left leaderless. It was as if the Chinese Communists had lost Mao in 1952 or the Yugoslavs had lost Tito in 1947. Other top leaders, including War Commissar Mikhail Frunze (1925) and Cheka head Felix Dzerzhinsky (1926) were to die in the 1920s, on top of the serious losses during the Civil War. This created the crisis of the latter 1920s as the Party groped its way to the future without its familiar leader and some of his key associates.

LENINIST SUCCESSION STRUGGLE

The struggle to succeed Lenin, which had begun even before his death, took five long and harsh years of struggle to be resolved. Joseph Stalin finally subdued his rivals in 1929, marking a historic change in Soviet politics. And his almost quarter-century of rule in the Soviet Union created a Stalinist command polity that would leave indelible marks on the Soviet Union even forty years after his death in 1953.

The likelihood that Joseph Stalin (1879–1953) would ever become the supreme leader of the Soviet Union seemed very remote in 1918 or even 1922.[12] He had not been one of the prominent leaders of the party before 1917 or during 1917. He had not been in the limelight among Lenin's top lieutenants during the October Revolution but rather had labored in obscurity. During the Civil War his record could not compare to that of Trotsky, who molded the Red Army into a force to save the revolution, or Zinoviev, who ran the Communist International. For Trotsky, as for many in the party, Stalin was a "grey blur" before 1924, a man of bureaucracy and Party affairs, the Party General-Secretary since 1922. Even then, only the death of Yakov Sverdlov in 1919 had opened that door for him. And the General-Secretary of the Party at that time was seen as the top Party bureaucrat and not as the likely successor to Lenin. Only under Stalin in the 1930s would it become the most important post in the leadership.

Bolshevik leaders like Lenin, Trotsky, and Zinoviev, while definitely men of action, had been members of the revolutionary intelligentsia, at home in the world of ideas or on the speaker's podium, wooing the masses in print or in mass meetings. Stalin was not a theoretician with bold new ideas but a man of action. He would occasionally come up with ideas (as "socialism in one country") but these were not central to his political persona. Lenin in his fifty-three years filled fifty-six thick volumes with speeches and writings; Stalin

---

[11]Leonard Schapiro and Peter Reddaway, editors, *Lenin: The Man, The Theorist, The Leader*, Praeger, New York, 1967.
[12]For a psychobiography of Stalin's early years up to 1929, see Robert Tucker, *Stalin As a Revolutionary, 1879–1929*, W.W. Norton, New York, 1973.

in seventy-three years filled only twelve much thinner volumes with his works. Stalin had gone to high school and then Tiflis Theological Seminary to study for the priesthood. After that, rather than studying abroad, like members of the cosmopolitan revolutionary intelligentsia, he had been an undergrounder, repeatedly arrested and finally spending the years 1913 to 1917 in exile in Siberia. He lacked the university education, travel and years abroad, participation in vigorous debates abroad, and natural intellectual curiosity that so marked men like Lenin, Trotsky, and Bukharin. As a Georgian, his spoken Russian remained poor and thickly accented throughout his life. He was a poor public speaker without charisma. Short, with a pock-marked face and stiff left arm, Stalin was often rude and abrupt, even by Bolshevik standards.

How could he even be compared with Leon Trotsky (1879–1940), the other half of the Lenin-Trotsky leadership, the chairman of the Petrograd Soviet in 1905 and 1917, the first Foreign Commissar, and then the War Commissar who molded the Red Army and led it to victory? How could he compare with such a brilliant revolutionary leader, such a great speaker and organizer, a man whom Lenin himself called "undoubtedly the most able man in the leadership"? How could Stalin compare with Nikolai Bukharin, the youthful leader of the Moscow Bolsheviks, the leading theoretician of the party, the leader of the Comintern, a much-read author who had become a candidate member of the Politburo at age thirty-one, the man whom Lenin called "the darling of the party"? How could Stalin be compared with Grigorii Zinoviev and Lev Kamenev, two of Lenin's oldest and most trusted lieutenants, who now ran the powerful Petrograd and Moscow Party machines and the Comintern? How, even, could Stalin be compared to lesser lights, like Mikhail Tomsky (1880–1938), the head of the trade union movement, or Aleksei Rykov (1881–1938), the head of the government after 1924? For Stalin after the October Revolution had been first the Commissar of Nationalities and then the chairman of the Workers and Peasants Inspectorate, posts of limited importance compared to those of his illustrious rivals.

How could Stalin overcome the opprobrium cast on him by the immortal Lenin, who at the end of his life called Stalin "inexcusably rude" and power hungry and demanded his ouster from his current post as General Secretary of the Party? How could he overcome the fact that Lenin rejected him as a candidate for the top post and even wanted him kicked out of the leadership?

And, finally, if we gaze at the 1922 Politburo, Stalin's chances for success seemed dim indeed. Stalin was one of the seven full members of the Politburo. But apart from Lenin, who would soon die, all five of the other full members (Kamenev, Zinoviev, Trotsky, Rykov, and Tomsky) ultimately opposed him, as did one (Bukharin) of the three candidate members. Even as late as May 1924, after Lenin's death, Stalin stood alone in a Politburo dominated by six other luminaries, all ultimately hostile to him—Trotsky, Zinoviev, Bukharin, Rykov, Tomsky, and Bukharin.[13]

---

[13]For Bukharin, who has naturally become a hero for reformers in the Soviet Union of Gorbachev and Russia of Yeltsin, see Stephen Cohen, *Bukharin and the Bolshevik Revolution,* Oxford University Press, Oxford, 1980.

HOW DID STALIN WIN AGAINST GREAT ODDS?

Without excellent revolutionary background, intellectual qualities, charisma, Lenin's endorsement, or Russian ethnic origins, Stalin seemed an unlikely candidate to succeed Lenin in 1924. And yet he did within five years. How did he do it?[14]

First, we must look at the playing field on which the decision was made. The playing field had changed markedly from 1917 or even 1920. Otherwise, Stalin would have had no chance compared to Lenin's other lieutenants. The times had changed radically. By 1926 many of the leading Bolsheviks of 1918 (Lenin, Frunze, Sverdlov, Dzerzhinsky, Artem) were dead and at least half of the thin strata of Old Bolsheviks from before 1917 were gone. The Party elite was no longer a cosmopolitan revolutionary intelligentsia, centered in the twin capitals of 1917. Now the Party was a ruling party with national scope and responsibilities.

The new generation of former undergrounders and civil war veterans came to the fore. Not for them the endless hairsplitting or references to European revolution, the occupation of revolutionary ideologues and dilettantes. For them the real work was the tough, hard work of repressing the Whites, propagandizing an indifferent population, and building socialism. As a generation that rarely had left Russia, rarely had gone to university, and came heavily from the lower classes, its school of revolution was the harsh battles of the underground or Civil War, not the intellectual discourses held in various European capitals. For this rising generation of locals, Stalin, the tough, practical "man of steel," the party apparatchik, the man from the lower classes, was the ideal representative to lead them to power and to battle.[15] For they not only wanted power, they wanted a "third revolution" to transform Russia and build socialism. For them, NEP was a mere holding pattern until the revolution could start again.

Stalin's enemies made a classic mistake in misunderstanding the contest at hand. Zinoviev and Kamenev thought that holding onto Petrograd and Moscow was adequate for victory, as it would have been in 1917 but was no longer in 1924. Trotsky thought that his brilliant record, coleadership of the party with Lenin, and role as War Commissar were adequate, as they might once have been. And Bukharin, for several years in a duumvirate with Stalin, also overrated his power. None of them took Stalin seriously as a potential heir. Rather than uniting against Stalin, they divided among themselves. Zinoviev and Kamenev united with Stalin against Trotsky, and then Bukharin united with Stalin against Zinoviev, Kamenev, and Trotsky, until it was too late.

---

[14]There are several very good biographies of Stalin and his rise to power, including Robert Tucker, *Stalin As a Revolutionary, 1879–1929*, W.W. Norton, New York, 1973; Adam Ulam, *Stalin: the Man and His Era*, Viking, New York, 1973; and Isaac Deutscher, *Stalin*, Vintage, New York, 1967.

[15]Robert Merton has made a useful distinction between locals and cosmopolitans. In this context the Stalinists were the locals, the Russian-oriented element, with little interest in European or international socialist affairs.

This misunderstanding of the playing field and underestimating of the power of a rival is not uncommon. All the candidates could be excused for not really believing that Lenin would die, for he was still so young, the unquestioned leader of the Party, and the source of their authority. Without him, in many ways, they were lost, for they had learned to function only as his lieutenants. Of them, only Stalin really yearned for the leadership. They never understood until the end how ruthless Stalin was (in Bukharin's words, a "Genghis Khan"). They thought that if they were defeated, the results would be the same as in Lenin's day—rapid reinstatement to their posts. For how could the Party do without them?

Each of Stalin's opponents had serious problems of his own. Trotsky, while brilliant and charismatic, had no taste for or interest in factional politics and preferred to stay above the Party, as he had stood apart from both Mensheviks and Bolsheviks for many years before 1917. He refused to take up the cudgels against Stalin over the nationality question in 1923 and failed to return for Lenin's funeral in January 1924. Zinoviev was widely considered a mediocre blowhard, and Kamenev labored in his shadow. Bukharin was too "soft" for the battles ahead, preferring the gentler arts of chess and butterfly collecting to the bruising world of power politics.

There were the positive qualities of Stalin himself, an excellent politician. Stalin had some solid credentials, including the editorship of *Pravda* in 1912, membership in the elite group that made the October Revolution, full membership in the Politburo after 1919, and a close relationship with Lenin, from whom he had rarely, if ever, deviated. He was cautious and patient, willing to bide his time, to exploit the errors of his enemies, and identify with the new movements in the party and the country. He was one of the few leaders of the party who actually hailed from the lower classes. His background as an undergrounder who had grown up in Georgia and fought the Civil War in the provinces (Tsaritsyn) made him an ideal leader of the rising undergrounder and Civil War generation. His ruthlessness, pragmatism, and toughness suited him ideally for this role. Stalin used his position as General Secretary of the Party after 1922 to promote his allies and remove his enemies in the provinces. He was an excellent bureaucrat and first-rate politician, who knew how to make alliances. His alignments with first one faction and then another after 1924 showed him to be a very deft and capable politician, always keeping his goal in sight.

His choice of issues in the succession struggle was masterful. Even though the international climate remained peaceful and the Party became more chauvinist and less internationalist, his enemies often chose to fight old battles. Trotsky, Zinoviev, and Kamenev often spoke for "international revolutionary socialism." By contrast, Stalin's "socialism in one country," although at odds with traditional Party doctrine that the revolution could be achieved only on an international scale, had strong appeal within the Party ranks, among those who had seen the repeated failure of European socialism contrasted to their own success. Socialism in one country appealed strongly to Russian nationalism, political self-preservation (who needed a revolutionary party to run an NEP

Russia?), national traditions of radical centralist actions, and a response to the harsh realities of 1928 Russia.[16] As Stalin declared in 1925 that Russia alone could achieve victory with international revolution,

> According to Lenin the revolution draws its forces above all from among the workers and peasants of Russia itself. According to Trotsky, we have it that indispensable forces can be found only in the "arena of the world-wide proletarian revolution." And what if the world revolution is fated to come late? Is there a gleam of hope for our revolution? Comrade Trotsky gives us no hope at all. . . . According to this plan, our revolution has only one prospect: to vegetate in its own contradictions and have its roots rot while waiting for the world-wide revolution.[17]

As a thoroughly Russified Georgian, Stalin knew how to appeal to latent Russian nationalism and anti-internationalism within the Party. He understood that the new generation of party apparatchiki and Russian masses did not really care about the old debates but wanted a relatively simple dogma to fill their lives. And this Stalin gave them, with the elevation of Lenin to sainthood, the creation of the Lenin Mausoleum, and the famous oath that Stalin made at Lenin's funeral that, with regard to various items, "We vow to you, Comrade Lenin, that we will spare no effort to fulfill this bequest too with honor."[18]

He skillfully exploited the weakness of his enemies. Stalin instinctively recognized that each had an Achilles heel and moved to neutralize these dangerous enemies. Against Trotsky he could use the fact that he had become a Bolshevik only in 1917, that as War Commissar he was the most likely "Bonaparte" of the Russian Revolution, that he had alienated workers and trade unionists by his support for militarization of labor in 1920, and that he had frequently criticized Lenin before 1917. Furthermore, Stalin could use the fact that Trotsky's arrogant behavior as War Commissar—his support for the use of 75,000 Tsarist officers in the army, his stress on discipline, and his opposition to a special proletarian military doctrine—had alienated most army communists. Against Zinoviev and Kamenev Stalin could use their opposition to the October Revolution, Zinoviev's arrogant behavior as head of the Comintern, and their complacent behavior as "feudal barons" of the twin capitals. Against all three Stalin could subtly use the fact that they were Jews in a country that was notably anti-Semitic. Against Bukharin, Stalin could count on his opponent's placid character and lack of active mobilization of his forces against Stalin.

Furthermore, Stalin too could count on Lenin's final testament, in which Lenin declared Zinoviev and Kamenev the "strike breakers of the October Revolution," Bukharin as a man who never understood the dialectic (the key to Marxism), and Trotsky as a man too isolated and arrogant. In this, Lenin played into Stalin's hands for had he really wished to stop Stalin, he should have

---

[16]Nove, *An Economic History of the USSR*, p. 31.
[17]Daniels, *Conscience of the Revolution*, p. 251.
[18]Treadgold, *Twentieth Century Russia*, p. 214.

named a successor, and he didn't. The early death of Lenin in January 1924, before he acted to remove Stalin, gave Stalin a strong advantage. He could claim that Lenin's critical comments about him were said only in his last days and that he complained about everyone.

POLITICAL EVENTS OF THE 1920s

With the recovery of the economy under NEP after 1921, the emphasis shifted to the succession crisis and, by the latter 1920s, the viability of NEP itself. Lenin's two strokes in 1922 and his third stroke in March 1923 signalled the onset of the crisis. With Lenin already incapacitated at age fifty-two and the Party still reeling from the devastation of the Civil War, the battle was likely to be long and complex.[19] It lasted seven years, until the end of the decade, and only then did Stalin emerge totally victorious. Already in 1922 Lenin's actions foretold a difficult future. At that time he turned against Stalin because of Stalin's Russian chauvinism in treating the Georgians (the group from which, ironically, he came). In December 1922 in his last testament Lenin further muddied the waters by failing to name a successor and by making negative remarks about all the likely contenders. He deprecated Stalin for concentrating "enormous powers in his hands," but he also attacked Trotsky for his "too far reaching self-confidence."[20]

The next month Lenin called for Stalin's ouster as General Secretary because of his "rudeness" and asked Trotsky to lead a charge against the Stalinists on the Georgian question of nationality autonomy against Russian centralism. But Lenin failed to recover. Between 1922 and 1924 Stalin adroitly aligned himself with Zinoviev and Kamenev against Trotsky. At the Twelfth Party Congress in April 1923, the first ever without Lenin, the majority of delegates backed Stalin, and Trotsky stood apart from the debate. He neither led the charge nor used Lenin's Testament against Stalin. By the summer of 1923 the Stalinists were sufficiently ascendant that Zinoviev and Bukharin met a group of supporters in a cave in the north Caucasus to plot their next move. But when there developed the "scissors crisis" in the summer of 1923 (with peasants unable to afford increasingly expensive industrial goods) and a wave of strikes ensued in the cities, the non-Stalinists took heart and went on the offensive.

These crises coincided with the rising revolutionary tide in Germany. That October Trotsky and a group of forty-six oppositionists challenged the leadership—but at a crucial Central Committee meeting, Trotsky again was absent with a mysterious illness. By December, after a compromise was worked out, Trotsky withdrew without a fight. Already at this point the opposition to Stalin was weak, centered mainly in Moscow. When Bukharin and his followers

---

[19]By far the best treatment of the Lenin succession struggle is to be found in Daniels, *Conscience of the Revolution.*

[20]Daniels, *Conscience of the Revolution,* p. 179.

joined the Stalin camp in 1924, the left opposition was isolated. At the Thirteenth Party Conference in January 1924, Stalin pummelled the opposition, which won only 3 of 131 votes.[21]

After Lenin's death, Stalin further consolidated his position. At Lenin's funeral Stalin took the lead with his dramatic avowal of fealty to the departed leader. He built the Lenin Mausoleum, renamed Petrograd Leningrad, and soon published his work, *Foundations of Leninism,* as the basis of his legitimacy as the new leader. Stalin strengthened his hand with the Lenin enrollment of 200,000 new Party members, largely political neophytes. In the absence of Trotsky, Stalin moved actively towards the rightists, led by Bukharin, and against his former partners Zinoviev and Kamenev. This alliance was formalized in the summer of 1925.

At the Thirteenth Party Congress in May 1924, four months after Lenin's death, Zinoviev appeared as nominal leader and Stalin survived the reading of Lenin's Testament before the Congress. This was the first Congress after Lenin's death, and it signalled the beginning of the new Stalinist style of dull, monolithic, and monotonous congresses.

By the fall of 1924 Stalin had taken the Moscow Party organization away from Zinoviev, ousting the Zinovievite Zelensky and replacing him with Uglanov. But his efforts to seize Leningrad from Zinoviev were slowed by Zinoviev's determined resistance. At the same time Stalin continued to agree with Zinoviev in his drive against Trotsky. Trotsky's attack on Stalin and Zinoviev in October 1924 in his "Lessons of October" was a mistake that drew them temporarily together and allowed Zinoviev to appear as the nominal leader of the party. In January 1925 they united to oust Trotsky as War Commissar and in October 1925 from the Politburo.

But later in 1925 they formally split and Zinoviev attacked the Stalin-Bukharin rightist alliance. Trotsky stood apart from this battle. Zinoviev upheld the traditional idea of the importance of the international revolution; Stalin demanded socialism in one country. By December 1925 the Fourteenth Party Congress witnessed the battle of the Muscovite Stalinists against the Leningrad Zinovievites, with Stalin winning 559 to 65. The new Stalin-Bukharin alliance promoted three Stalinist allies (Kirov, Voroshilov, and Molotov) to the Politburo, and Voroshilov replaced Mikhail Frunze as War Commissar. The next month Stalin ousted Kamenev as Deputy Chairman of the Council of People's Commissars and Zinoviev as chairman of the Leningrad Soviet and soon installed Sergei Kirov, a loyal Stalinist, as Leningrad Party secretary.[22]

In 1926 Trotsky finally joined with the defeated Zinoviev and Kamenev in the United Opposition.[23] In April 1926 at a Central Committee plenum Kamenev declaimed, "It is enough for you [Trotsky] and Zinoviev to appear on the same platform and the party will find its true Central Committee."[24] Stalin

---

[21]Daniels, *Conscience of the Revolution,* chapter 9.
[22]Daniels, *Conscience of the Revolution,* chapter 12.
[23]Daniels, *Conscience of the Revolution,* chapter 12.
[24]Daniels, *Conscience of the Revolution,* p. 272.

responded by driving Zinoviev from the Politburo. In September 1926 Trotsky and Zinoviev even appeared defiantly in a rally at a Moscow factory. But their campaign fizzled against Stalin and the Party machine. In October 1926 the three leaders capitulated after Trotsky and Kamenev were driven from the Politburo and Zinoviev was ousted from his post as chairman of the Comintern. The following spring there was a revival of the opposition over Stalin's policies in China. By fall the oppositionists tried to lead demonstrations during the anniversary of the October Revolution in Moscow and Leningrad, but they were dispersed. At the climactic Fifteenth Party Congress in December 1927 Stalin successfully excluded any opposition delegates. Seventy-five oppositionists, including the three leaders, were ousted from the Party and Trotsky was sent into exile in Alma Alta. The other two leaders soon capitulated and were temporarily readmitted to the party. As for Trotsky, he wandered from Alma Alta to Prinkipo, Norway, France, and Mexico, where Stalin's agent, Ramon Mercader, assassinated him in 1940.

But now, at the moment of victory for the Stalin-Bukharin axis, Stalin decided to break with Bukharin.[25] During 1928 and 1929 Stalin, advocating a more radical line that would lead to the massive transformation of the Soviet Union in the 1930s, increasingly went on the offensive against Bukharin and his allies, Aleksei Rykov and Mikhail Tomsky.

The precipitating action was the grain crisis that arose early in 1928. The peasants, reacting to crop failures and low prices, began to market less grain than normal. The right argued that the problem was low prices and that the peasants, who formed seventy percent of the country, should be pacified. But Stalin and his followers demanded strong action and blamed the kulaks (rich peasants and small landlords). Stalin went to West Siberia, an area without drought, and used emergency coercive measures to seize available grain. This was followed up in May 1928 with the Shakhty trial of Donets engineers, in which bourgeois specialists were blamed for all the industrial problems. By July the Central Committee demanded the extension of emergency measures (the Urals-Siberian method) to the entire country. By 1929 it spoke for rapid industrialization, emergency measures against kulaks, mechanization and collectivization of private farming, forcibly bringing the peasants under control and using their surplus to finance industry.[26]

The horrified rightists opposed coercion of the peasants and demanded higher prices for agricultural produce. They argued that a strong peasantry was the basis for Soviet power and that kulaks should be squeezed only by taxation. They supported a slow industrialization, borne by the urban working class, and good relations with the peasant majority. They wanted to continue NEP into the 1930s.

On paper the Rightists seemed strong, with Bukharin heading the Comintern, Tomsky the trade unions, and Rykov running the government. In the

---

[25]Daniels, *Conscience of the Revolution,* chapter 13.

[26]For the best analysis of the debates, see Moshe Lewin, *Political Undercurrents in Soviet Economic Debates,* Princeton University Press, Princeton, 1974.

Politburo in 1928 they counted on a majority with the rightist Stalinists Voroshilov and Kalinin likely to join them. But they failed to win the Stalinists, and the Rightists, despite strong institutional and public support, went down quietly.

Although in 1925 Leningrad had been the center of opposition, in 1928 it was Moscow under Uglanov that led the anti-Stalinist group. In October 1928 Stalin openly attacked the rightist opposition and in November crushed the opposition, defeated Uglanov, and installed Molotov to run the Moscow organization. In April 1929 Stalin ousted Bukharin from the Comintern. Similarly, Stalin moved against Tomsky's trade union organization and gained control of it by June 1929. By the Sixteenth Party Conference in April 1929, the Party fully backed the Stalinist line of creating the radical First Five-Year Plan. By November 1929 Bukharin was ousted from the Politburo and he was followed by Tomsky and Rykov in 1930.

In crushing the rightist opposition, Stalin utilized more than simple organizational superiority. For the truth was that the Bukharinist rightist program had a fundamental weakness as serious as that of the advocates of "international proletarian revolution." Bukharin was undoubtedly right in warning of the dangers of declaring war on the peasantry and trying to accelerate the pace of industrialization, but his concept of NEP continuing for a generation seemed weak to many Bolsheviks. What kind of revolutionary party could continue indefinitely to rely on the backward peasants and the blackness of the countryside to propel the country forward? And how would Russia ever find the industrial power to combat rising enemies in the 1930s at the snail-like pace envisaged by Bukharin? For all of Stalin's proverbial greyness, his call for a "third revolution" of the 1930s, for a radical transformation of Russia into a powerful, modern, and literate industrial power, had great appeal in the Party ranks and among the masses for whom the October Revolution and Civil War had been but a beginning.

The 1920s began and ended with violent and swift turns in Soviet politics. In between, the 1920s provided an oasis of calm and tranquility, providing the seed bed for future radical change. This era of civil peace, international and domestic calm, mixed economy, and private ownership of land and retail trade naturally became the reference point for Gorbachev's reforms and Yeltsin's drive for capitalism and democracy. It also provided an important thrust to the future development of Stalinism.

10

Stalinist Transformation of the 1930s

The 1930s, in establishing the fundamental contours of the Stalinist command economy and polity, were the most dynamic and decisive decade in Soviet politics. That decade saw rapid industrialization and modernization, preparation of the Red Army for war (while Western nations were largely asleep), large-scale improvements in education and modernization. Yet it was a time of unnecessary horrors, of the deaths of millions of people in the collectivization drive, Ukrainian famine, and Great Purges. As a Russian story tells it, after the war two people meet. The Stalinist says, "If it hadn't been for Stalinist policies, we would never have stopped the Germans at Stalingrad." The anti-Stalinist replies, "If it hadn't been for Stalinist policies, the Germans would never have gotten to Stalingrad."

ALL STALIN'S MEN

Stalinism was a great deal more than just Stalin writ large. Here we look in depth at some of the leading men who made Stalinism work. Although he had his share of toadies (like Poskrebyshev, Vyshinsky, Mekhlis, Yezhov, and Shchadenko), Stalin had a strong group of intelligent and capable men around him. Vyacheslav Molotov, Georgii Orzhonikidze, Sergei Kirov, Lazar Kaganovich, Kliment Voroshilov, Georgii Malenkov, Lavrentii Beria, and Nikita Khrushchev were all "Stalin's men." Several, such as Kirov and Ordzhonikidze, died from unnatural causes in the 1930s but most flourished and survived Stalin after 1953.

They were tough, relatively young, shrewd, and vigorous men who had joined the party before 1917 but had not been prominent before the late 1920s. They owed their loyalty and rise to Stalin but also had their own independent thoughts. They were not intellectuals or "rootless cosmopolitans" but moderately educated generalists and pragmatists who knew how to get things done. Many were not Russians as the list included Armenians (Mikoyan), Georgians (Beria and Ordzhonikidze), Jews (Kaganovich). Here we profile several of them.

Vyecheslav Molotov. This tough, efficient, and diligent member of the Party from 1905 was related to the composer Scriabin. By 1928 he was a full member of the Politburo, and in 1930 he was named head of the government. He signed many lists of purge victims to be shot and emerged in 1939 as the new People's Commissar of Foreign Affairs. In 1940 he met with Hitler in Berlin and in 1941 it was Molotov, not Stalin, who informed the nation of the German attack. He took part in all wartime conferences and the "Molotov cocktail" was named for this colorless bureaucrat. After the war he lost favor and his Jewish wife was sent to the camps in 1949. At the nineteenth Party Congress in 1952 Stalin denounced him and only Stalin's death saved him. He emerged in 1953 as the new Foreign Minister and number three man in the government. The rise of Khrushchev doomed him, and in 1956 he was ousted from his position as Foreign Minister and in 1957 he participated in the ill-fated Anti-Party Group that wanted him as General Secretary of the Party. After a brief reprieve he was expelled from the party in 1961.

Lazar Kaganovich. The only Jewish member of Stalin's Politburo, he started work at age fourteen in a shoe factory and joined the Party in 1911. A tough and ruthless leader, he emerged in 1925 as the leader of the Ukrainian Communists and by 1930 the Moscow Communists. In the early 1930s he was a leader in collectivizing the Ukraine and Western Siberia and in building the Moscow subway (which bore his name for many years). He was Stalin's leading troubleshooter in heavy industry and ran the railroads during World War II as a member of the State Defense Committee. He fell out of favor with Stalin after the war during the wave of anti-Semitism and only Stalin's death saved him. He opposed the de-Stalinization campaign of Khrushchev and was ousted from the leadership for his role in the Anti-Party Group in 1957. Sent to run a potash works in the Urals, he was expelled from the Party in 1961.

Georgii Malenkov. A ruthless and intelligent bureaucrat who graduated from technical high school, he served as a political worker in the Red Army in the Civil War and joined the Party in 1920. By 1934 he headed the important personnel section of the Central Committee and in 1937 and 1938 was close with Nikolai Yezhov, the dreaded head of the NKVD, successor to the Cheka. By 1941 he was a candidate member of the Politburo and during the war was in charge of aircraft production as a member of the State Defense Commission. In 1949 he helped organize the purges known as the Leningrad Affair and was close to Beria. In 1952 he read the political report at the Nineteenth Party Congress and was seen as Stalin's likely heir. After Stalin's death, he became the head of the government and launched the relatively moderate "New Course." The fall of Beria hurt him and in February 1955 the rising Khrushchev ousted him as Prime Minister. In 1957 he was a member of the failed Anti-Party Group and was expelled from the Central Committee and Politburo. In 1961 he was expelled from the Party.

Anastas Mikoyan. The ultimate survivor who spent forty years in the Politburo, Mikoyan was the only Armenian in the leadership. A consummate politician, he went to Armenian Theological Seminary and avoided being shot in the execution of the twenty-six People's Commissars in Baku in 1918. At age 26 he was on the Central Committee in 1922 and a candidate member of the Politburo in 1930. An excellent administrator, he was repeatedly in charge of trade and foreign trade in the late 1920s and the 1930s. But he was also ruthless, and in February 1937 he ran the Central Committee plenum that condemned Bukharin and Rykov and also helped to purge Armenian Communists. During the war he was a member of the State Defense Committee and Deputy Prime Minister. Stalin turned against him in the early 1950s and he was saved by Stalin's death. He was the only leading old Stalinist to support Khrushchev's attack on Stalin in 1956 and his attack on the Anti-Party Group in 1957. He performed a number of key diplomatic roles. In 1964 he became President, but his luck finally ran out when he opposed the ouster of Khrushchev in 1964 and he was retired as the last of the Leninist old guard in 1965. But he was reelected to the Central Committee in 1971, a sign that he was not in disgrace like the other old Stalinists.

Kliment Voroshilov. Interestingly, Voroshilov was usually considered the stupidest man on the Politburo but also the most reliable Stalinist in the sensitive post of War Commissar from 1925 to 1940. A man of courage and modest intellect, he was devoted to Stalin. Already at age eight a herder of sheep, and at age ten a miner, he had little education but in 1898 was an early member of the socialist movement in Lugansk. During the Civil War he helped lead the vital First Cavalry Army, where he became close to Stalin. By 1921 he was a full member of the Central Committee and in 1924 commander of the vital Moscow military district. Although generally considered a moderate and an opponent of terror and collectivization, he followed Stalin and supervised the purges and executions of tens of thousands of officers during the Great Purges (1937–1941). In 1935 he was named one of five marshals of the army. His failure in the Winter War with Finland led to his firing as War Commissar. His glorification of cavalry, denigration of tanks, and promotion of the purges greatly harmed the army. His weak performance in the defense of Leningrad in 1941 led to his ouster, but he was allowed to run the partisan campaign during the war. By the early 1950s Stalin was calling him an English spy and he was kept away from Politburo meetings. After 1953 he was head of state and helped oust Beria. But in 1957 he supported the Anti-Party Group and then switched sides. This led to his ouster from public life but not his disgrace, and in 1966 he was elected to the Central Committee and in 1968 received awards.[1]

OVERVIEW OF STALINIST POLITICS

Having defeated the rightists in 1929, the Stalinists proceeded to implement a radical program of economic and political change. After the crisis of 1930, the Stalinists implemented massive programs of modernization, collectivization, and industrialization. In 1932 oppositionists put forth the Ryutin Program, calling for a revival of the rightist program, an economic retreat, decline in the growth rate of industrialization, and freeing the peasants from the collectives. The program called for purging Stalin, the "evil genius" who had "brought the Revolution to ruin." Although Stalin and Kaganovich wanted Ryutin shot, more moderate elements prevailed. Ryutin was expelled from the Party, and Zinoviev and Kamenev were shipped to the Urals. The following month Nadezhda Alliluyeva, Stalin's wife, committed suicide, at least partly in reaction to the negative reports about what was happening in the countryside. When a mournful Stalin offered to resign, no one took up the gauntlet.

In January 1934 the Stalinists convened the Seventeenth Party Congress, the "Congress of Victors." Former oppositionists such as Zinoviev, Kamenev, Bukharin, and Radek addressed the congress. A moderate line prevailed, although there is a vigorous dispute among specialists over whether this line was in opposition to Stalin (Conquest and Hough) or represented the Stalinist line (Getty).[2] This Great Retreat meant a more moderate tempo of growth in the Second Five Year Plan, reconciliation with the former oppositionists, a secret ballot in the Party, and the adoption of the line "cadres decide everything." Given the rising international danger from Nazi Germany and Imperial Japan, a reconciliation with the population seemed prudent. Similarly, in 1932 the peasant right to private plots was affirmed, and in 1933 there was an end to mass deportations in the countryside. Sergei Kirov, the Leningrad Party leader, was clearly one of the favorites of the congress.

But in December 1934 a deranged student, Leonid Nikolayev, evidently with official connivance, managed to assassinate Kirov in his Leningrad Party headquarters. Nevertheless, despite the frenzied reaction of deporting and shooting thousands of alleged accomplices of the murderer, there was no change in the political mood. Even in 1936, as the lull was broken by the beginning of the Great Purges (see section below), the Stalinist Constitution was proclaimed. With no mention of Marxism-Leninism and only two men-

[1]The best source for additional information on these men is Roy Medvedev, *All Stalin's Men*, translated by Harold Shukman, Anchor, Garden City, New York, 1985.
[2]Jerry Hough and Merle Fainsod, *How the Soviet Union Is Governed*, Harvard University Press, Cambridge, 1979, p. 156; Robert Conquest, *The Great Terror*, Macmillan, New York, 1968, p. 36; and J. Arch Getty, *The Origins of the Great Purges*, Cambridge University Press, Cambridge, 1985, chapter 4.

tions of the Party, the Constitution provided a series of democratic rights. With universal, direct suffrage, and a series of rights and duties for citizens, the constitution seemed a step forward. Unfortunately, it remained a paper document.

But the storm clouds were already gathering. In 1935 and 1936 there were two trials, of Zinoviev and Kamenev. The stage was set for the Great Purges and the mass liquidation of the bulk of the Party and government elite in the orgy of violence and repression. By 1939, at the Eighteenth Party Congress, the Stalinists would reign supreme over a desolate landscape.

INSTITUTIONAL CONTEXT

Having overcome the rightist opposition, the Stalinists radically altered the key institutions, which were expanded, bureaucratized, and empowered with great privileges in the 1930s. By 1939 millions of Soviet citizens belonged to the new elite of administrators, managers, chairmen of collective farms, professionals, military and secret police officers, technical personnel, and Party and government bureaucrats. These vast new bureaucracies had their own little Stalins, proliferating red tape and officials. The privileges of the bureaucrats, from *dachas* (country houses) and special pay envelopes to access to special stores and education, were numerous and hierarchically well developed.[3]

Spending on the army soared almost fifty times in the 1930s and its size increased seven times. By 1940 a much larger and more effective army, albeit one suffering from the Great Purges, had begun to emerge. And by 1937 the secret police had become the single greatest power, to be tamed somewhat only after the end of the Great Purges. Its vast economic empire, hundreds of thousands of troops, millions of informers, and networks abroad commanded great fear.

The Party in the 1930s was far from being a monolithic, efficient machine instantly responsive to Stalin. The great pressure from above for deeds was often resisted by a local privileged elite. Only after the Great Purges of 1937 was central authority firmly established. As Getty has concluded,

> The party in the thirties was neither monolithic nor disciplined, its upper ranks were divided and its lower organizations were disorganized, chaotic and undisciplined. Moscow leaders were divided on policy issues and central leaders were at odds with territorial secretaries whose organizations suffered from internal disorder and conflict. A bloated party membership containing political illiterates and apolitical opportunists plus a lazy and unresponsive regional leadership was hardly a formula for a Leninist party.[4]

[3]Moshe Lewin, "Society, State and Ideology During the First Five Year Plan," in Sheila Fitzpatrick, editor, *Cultural Revolution in Russia, 1928–1931*, Indiana University Press, Bloomington, 1978, pp. 66–77; and Donald Treadgold, *Twentieth Century Russia*, Rand McNally, Chicago, 1972, p. 294.
[4]Getty, *The Origins of the Great Purges*, chapter 1, p. 7; and Merle Fainsod, *Smolensk Under Soviet Rule*, Harvard University Press, Cambridge, 1958.

The massive enrollments of new members in the early 1930s inexorably led to massive purges in the later 1930s. In 1933 and 1934 alone over 1 million Communists were ousted from the Party. In 1935 almost 10 percent of the Party members were ousted and purges struck again in 1936. Only after the Great Purges of 1937–1941 did the Stalinists feel they had established their authority and begun to create the kind of Party organization they desired.[5]

STALINIST TRANSFORMATION OF SOCIETY

In 1928 and 1929 Stalin routed the leaders of the right opposition and decided to implement a radical program of change. Given the tranquillity at home and abroad, this was an extraordinary decision. The Stalinists, in carrying out this revolution from above, were motivated by a desire to industrialize and create a stronger state in a hostile world, Stalin's personal desire for greatness, the revolutionary traditions and the prerevolutionary heritage of state-run industrialization, and the ideological demands of centralized politics.[6] At the Sixteenth Party Congress in June 1930, Lazar Kaganovich declared the need for "Bolshevik tempo" and proclaimed that the Soviet Union would become the world's number one industrial power in ten years. Support for this program came from youth, workers, former leftist enemies of Stalin, lower ranks of the party and Komsomol, and a population eager for a brighter future.[7] Stalin pursued three major programs during the 1930s: collectivization, industrialization, and modernization. He launched a major offensive against all of the capitalist elements in the society and economy—kulaks in the countryside, private traders and old specialists in urban industry, and foreign investors in industry.[8]

The major innovation was to create the world's first planned economy directed totally by the state. The state, by eliminating the role of private capitalists and traders in industry and by collectivized agriculture, controlled all economic resources. Through the State Planning Commission, it imposed a high rate of savings (30 percent in 1932), directed investment to desired sectors, hired and fired planners and managers, and used plenipotentiaries and high levels of coercion to enforce the central will. The people's commissariats (later ministries) controlled the major enterprises and state plans, with indicators for quantities of output, prices, wages, and costs having binding power. The plan reigned supreme, with detailed production and delivery goals for every major item. The state instituted one-man management and gave great power to the

---

[5]Getty, *The Origins of the Great Purges,* chapter 2.
[6]For a good view of these massive programs and policies, see Robert Tucker, *Stalin in Power: The Revolution From Above, 1928–1941,* W.W. Norton, New York, 1990.
[7]R.W. Davies, *The Soviet Economy in Turmoil, 1929–1930,* Harvard University Press, Cambridge, 1989, chapter 8.
[8]Davies, *The Soviet Economy in Turmoil 1929–1930,* introduction.

central planners. The system worked on a grand scale but with much waste and inefficiency.[9] As Merle Fainsod has commented,

> The Plan opened up an exhilarating period of struggle and combat, a leap forward into the New Jerusalem . . . The air was electric with positions to be stormed, class enemies to be destroyed and fortresses to be built. . . . The last remnants of private capitalism and old "bourgeois culture" appeared to be headed for extinction.[10]

At a time of the Great Depression in the West, Stalinism seemed to offer the hope of a heroic new society, to be created through a curious mixture of sheer brutality and idealistic fervor.

INDUSTRIALIZATION AND MODERNIZATION

Rapid heavy industrialization created the modern Soviet industrial sector. Stalin realized that Russia's industrial lag could be fatal in wartime. In 1931, after depicting Russian history as a series of "continual beatings due to backwardness" by everyone from the Mongol khans and Swedish feudal lords to the Anglo-French capitalists, Japanese barons, and German Junkers, Stalin declared, "We lag fifty to one hundred years behind the advanced countries. We must cover this distance in ten years. Either we do this or they will crush us."[11] In a hostile international environment without friends, Western aid, or colonies, the Soviet Union stood alone. World War II proved the importance of his thinking.[12]

In 1927 Soviet national income stood at the level of the United States in 1880. With energy usage per capita at 13 percent of the American level, the Soviet factory worker produced 15 percent as much as the American factory worker.[13] The Red Army, unable to produce its own first-rate planes or tanks, was widely considered barely able to repel a Romanian or Polish attack.

The period from 1917 to 1929 had not lessened the gap between the Soviet Union and other countries. On the positive side, it had reduced the importation of luxury goods and the mass use of servants, so typical of an underdeveloped society like Russia in 1913. By unilaterally canceling Tsarist debts, it had wiped clean the slate from the past. By decreasing military spending through the reduction in the size of the army to only 560,000 men, the regime had slashed its expenditures. By promoting industrialization, the state had tried to modernize society.

[9]Alec Nove, *An Economic History of the USSR*, Penguin Books, Harmondsworth, England, 1982, pp. 263–267.
[10]Hough and Fainsod, *How the Soviet Union Is Governed*, p. 149.
[11]Quoted in Hiroaki Kuromiya, *Stalin's Industrial Revolution*, Cambridge University Press, Cambridge, 1988, p. xi.
[12]See Jonathan R. Adelman, *Prelude to the Cold War: The Tsarist, Soviet and United States Armies in Two World Wars*, Lynne Rienner Publications, Boulder, Colorado, 1988.
[13]R.W. Davies, *The Soviet Economy in Turmoil, 1929–1930*, chapter 1.

However, the chaos of the Civil War period and the early 1920s retarded Soviet growth. In the early 1920s the American Relief Administration under Herbert Hoover actually had fed millions of starving Russians. The implementation of an eight-hour workday lowered production. The favoring of industry over agriculture created poor terms of trade for the peasant majority and retarded agricultural production, so vital in a backward economy. The cancellation of foreign debts guaranteed that no few foreign investment would be made in the Soviet economy. Rapid growth in the German and American economies widened the gap in the 1920s.[14]

Industrialization offered more than a strong base for military power. With only 18 percent of the population living in cities in 1926, it offered a way out of the dilemma of a Party devoted to the workers ruling a country largely consisting of peasants. By 1939 the number of urban residents had doubled to 56 million while rural residents declined by 6 million. The Stalinists relied on their working-class base for the survival of the regime and to provide the social support for the transformation of the 1930s.[15] Industrialization offered the hope of creating a modern, socialist society with a decent standard of living and upward mobility for the masses.

Stalinist industrialization played a significant role in the Soviet victory in World War II. It provided a much stronger industrial base and military industry than Tsarist Russia had had. In 1940 Soviet steel production was over four times that of 1928, electric energy nine times, coal four times, and oil almost three times. By 1940 Soviet GNP per capita was eighty percent higher than it had been in 1928.[16]

The 1930s had a great impact on the workers and peasants. For the tens of millions of peasants flowing from the countryside to the city, the revolution meant an increased standard of living (though still at a low level by Western standards) and access to culture and education, but in a strictly regimented society. There were massive labor shortages and much changing of jobs. For peasants the revolution meant rampant discrimination and poverty under the direct control of the state. The only way out was through movement to the cities. For workers it often meant a high level of upward mobility as they filled hundreds of thousands of new positions in Soviet industry and government. The working class expanded from 3.7 million industrial and construction workers in 1928 to 10.1 million in 1940. Most were former peasants, and the overwhelming majority (92 percent) had only an elementary school education or less. The regime repeatedly mobilized workers into worker brigades, collectives, and communes to accomplish vital tasks. At the same time the regime tried to liquidate the "hostile" classes of kulaks, private capitalists, and NEP men.[17]

---

[14]Davies, *The Soviet Economy in Turmoil, 1929–1930,* chapter 13.
[15]See Kuromiya, *Stalin's Industrial Revolution,* p. x; and Nove, *An Economic History of the USSR,* p. 267.
[16]Hough and Fainsod, *How the Soviet Union Is Governed,* p. 153.
[17]Lewin, "Society, State and Ideology during the First Five Year Plan," in Fitzpatrick, *The Cultural Revolution in Russia, 1928–1931,* pp. 60–62.

During the First Five Year Plan (1929–1933), the Party pushed heavy industrialization at a breakneck pace. The goals for a 250 percent increase in industrial production, 330 percent increase in heavy industrial production, and quadrupling of electric power were totally unrealistic. They were predicated on blue-sky assumptions about good harvests, increased foreign trade, qualitative productivity increases, and declining defense spending. These predictions led to an industrial crisis in the summer of 1930. Yet major gains were made, enough for Stalin to declare victory in 1933. The costs—disorganized industry with bottlenecks and shortages, increased shortages of material and human resources, great waste, misallocation of resources, shoddy workmanship, poor safety standards, weak food supply, and terrible housing—were real and problematic. By 1937 steel production reached almost 18 million tons, more than four times the 1928 level, and electric power production skyrocketed from 2.0 billion kilowatts in 1913 to 48 billion by 1940.[18] The Great Leap Forward was successful, if at huge cost.

During the Second Five Year Plan, the Soviet economy performed better in the 1934–1936 period. Stalin at this time declared that "Life has become better, comrades, life has become more joyous." By 1936 the state completed a strong metallurgical base and made great progress in chemicals, steels, and metals. In 1935 the Donbass coal miner Alexei Stakhanov, in an achievement that was rigged from start to finish, produced fourteen times the work norms with the help of unskilled auxiliaries. This launched a Stakhanovite campaign for higher work norms and Stakhanovite imitators. Defense spending escalated from 3 percent of the budget in 1933 to 16 percent in 1938.[19]

These problems and advantages continued throughout the 1930s, but the Great Purges slowed down the system at the end of the 1930s. On one hand, the state could concentrate resources and set priorities without regard to profit, public desire, or private enterprise. It could enforce a war economy in peace-time, enforce a high rate of savings in a savings-poor country, squeeze the peasants and workers, and derive state revenues from manipulated prices. At the same time, there was much waste from ignoring economic costs, substantial bureaucratic deformation of the system, and much arbitrary interference in economic processes. The campaign syndrome would provoke major inconsistencies in the system.[20]

COLLECTIVIZATION

Although industrialization and modernization were programs pursued in both socialist and capitalist states, the same is not true of collectivization. Poland and Yugoslavia abandoned collectivization in the 1950s, China in the late 1970s, and the Soviet Union under Gorbachev after 1988.

What were the alternatives to collectivization? Basically two. In the final

---

[18]See Treadgold, *Twentieth Century Russia*, pp. 289–291.
[19]Nove, *An Economic History of the USSR*, chapter 9.
[20]Nove, *An Economic History of the USSR*, pp. 72–74.

years of the Tsar Nicholas II, Stolypin advocated a private, individualist capitalist system that would favor the rich peasants and the kulaks. Such a system was ideologically unacceptable to the Bolsheviks. Or, as Bukharin put it in the 1920s, the state could hope for a gradual "growing over" of the capitalist sector into a socialist sector. By calling on the peasants to "enrich themselves," by supporting a gradual voluntary collectivization and balanced growth of light and heavy industry, socialist interests could be served without alienating the peasants. But such a program was based on the unlikely trans- formation of peasants into socialists (less than 1 percent joined collective farms before 1928), put the state at the mercy of the peasants, and provided neither economic nor political control over the peasantry. To the centralist radicals in Moscow, imbued with the civil war psychology, this seemed to provide no answer to their problems of immediately modernizing and strengthening the Soviet Union in a socialist manner.[21]

Stalin pursued collectivization for a number of reasons. The Soviet Union was committed to building a socialist state and destroying rural capitalism. Given the unwillingness of the peasants to part with their land, only state coercion and terror could forcibly impose socialism on the peasantry. Other- wise, the bulk of the population (70 percent) would continue to represent a large capitalist sector in a socialist state. The Soviet regime was weak in the vast countryside. As the Smolensk archives showed, even the rural soviets were weak and inept, and rural Communists far from being in control. The 300,000 rural Communists represented less than one Communist per 3300 people in the rural areas. By creating collective farms and machine tractor stations, the regime could greatly enhance the control of the rural apparat over not 25 million private plots but 250,000 collectives.

There was much that was irrational in Russian agriculture in the 1920s. Like Polish agriculture, it was plagued by primitive equipment, backward peasant culture, poorly educated peasants, and irrational systems of land distribution into many small plots. Nearly half of all households had no draft animals, and poverty was widespread. Land was not held individually but communally, with strips of land assigned to households. The Bolsheviks thought that by unifying all peasant plots into large farms and providing modern machinery, they could rationalize the system and create a new, more advanced socialist system.

The regime wanted to smash its enemies in the countryside. In the rather pathetic kulaks it saw the potential leaders of a popular political opposition to the regime.[22] Although this might be tolerable in peacetime, it could be very dangerous in wartime. Therefore, far better for the state to strike at its enemies with full force in peacetime and deprive the enemies of their leaders, than to do it in wartime. This way, the regime could gain solid control of the countryside.

Finally, there was the broad question of providing grain for the rapidly

---

[21]Herbert Ellison, in William Blackwell, editor, *Russian Economic Development From Peter the Great to Stalin*, New Viewpoints, New York, 1974, chapter 10.
[22]Given the poverty of the Russian countryside, a kulak might own a couple of horses and cows and hire a few laborers, often on a seasonal basis.

growing cities and investment capital for the industrialization effort. This is a much disputed point, but our concern here is not reality but the thinking of the Stalinists. Thirty percent of all grain had been marketed in 1914, but this had dropped to 14 percent in 1927.[23] To the Stalinists it seemed necessary, as Evgenii Preobrazhensky (a Trotskyite in the 1920s) had suggested, to squeeze the peasants to provide the needed capital for industrialization. This would provide both capital and the migration of tens of millions of peasants to the cities where they would become workers. Too, the doubling of the Soviet urban population in the cities in the 1930s would require a doubling in the amount of grain requisitioned for the cities. This needed to be supplied in a reliable way at low prices. This could be achieved only by gaining direct control over the grain, rather than by leaving it in the hands of unreliable kulaks and peasants.

There was the psychology of the Civil War era, when the peasants had shown themselves to be an unreliable element. Three million largely peasant soldiers deserted the Red Army in 1918 and 1919. In 1920 and 1921 there were large-scale peasant revolts against the regime.[24] Only fear of landlord and Tsarist restoration and dislike of the Whites pushed the peasants sullenly into the Bolshevik camp. The simple questions then were: Was it safe to leave the fate of the state in the hands of such dubious elements? Would it not be better to solve the peasant problem by socializing them?

Of course, many of these ideas soon proved themselves false. The peasants strongly resisted collectivization. The creation of modern socialist agriculture proved a chimera. Agriculture became the Achilles heel of the regime for the next fifty years.[25] But the state did gain political control over the peasantry through the collectives and machine tractor stations and economic control over the supply of the grain to the city. It squeezed the peasants and doubled grain requisition for the expanding cities. Tens of millions of disgruntled peasants flocked to the cities.

The regime relentlessly created a new regime in the countryside. The peasants were organized largely into collective farms, which in theory were agricultural producer cooperatives jointly operated by its members. Each member shared in its output relative to the quantity and quality of labor days worked. Part of the output went to the state and capital and reserve funds while the remainder was distributed among the members, who could keep small private plots. The countryside was dotted with machine-tractor stations, which were state enterprises which, for a fixed sum paid in kind, carried out for the collective farms specific agricultural tasks that required the use of tractors, combines, and other machinery. This promoted efficiency and party control over the collective farms in theory, but often led to waste and inefficiency in practice.

During the Stalinist struggle with the rightist opposition, a sudden grain

---

[23]Basil Dmytryshyn, *USSR: A Concise History*, Charles Scribner, New York, 1986, p. 165.
[24]See Jonathan R. Adelman, *The Revolutionary Armies*, Greenwood Press, Westport, Connecticut, 1980.
[25]But, as one wit has pointed out, Achilles—like the former Soviet Union—did manage to walk on that heal.

crisis in 1928 confronted Stalin.[26] Faced by a reduction of one-third in grain collections, Stalin resorted to the forced requisition of grain in Siberia. The success of this operation reinforced the Stalinist belief that the kulaks were hoarding grain and should be summarily dealt with. After the defeat of the rightist opposition, who opposed this as "military-feudal exploitation of the peasantry," and a new grain crisis, Stalin in November 1929 announced a "great turn" in agriculture. He argued that the poor and middle peasants were willing to join the collectives. Stalin also called for the "liquidation of the kulaks" as a class. The January 1930 decree called for all haste, despite a lack of any preparation or knowledge of local conditions, and with strong peasant opposition to the loss of their land. Even who was a "kulak" was unclear. War communism and revolution from above, backed by the power of the state, returned full force. By January 1930, 50 percent of all households had joined the new collective farms, mostly under protest and only on paper.

The rural areas erupted into chaos. Looting, panic, suicides, confiscation of property, flight of richer peasants, and open violent resistance to the Bolsheviks were the order of the day. The number of animals shrank by half as the peasants declared, "Drink, eat—it's all ours now." Millions of kulaks were seized, deprived of property, and shipped in cattle cars to Siberia or simply killed. More than 1 million families were deported, with as many as one-third of the deportees dying on the way. In the east they had to build new homes without horses or ploughs. Twenty-five thousand workers were sent to the villages to reinforce the Party and secret police units. Stalin later told Churchill that this war with the peasantry was equal to the World War II.[27]

In March 1930 Stalin called a halt to forcible collectivization with his famous "Dizzy With Success" speech. Disingenuously blaming the excessive zeal of local cadres, he called for an end to excesses, coercion, and rapacious local cadres. He relented by allowing homes, little plots (one acre or less), small animals, and chickens to remain as the personal property of the collectives in the artel form. Now peasants could sell their surplus on the free market after making the required large grain deliveries at fixed low prices. Peasants could obtain income through their private plots, whose produce could be sold on an open market, and through pay for their work days on the collective farm from the surplus income left at the end of the year. By 1937 there were 240,000 collective farms and 4000 state farms. Within three months after Stalin's speech in March 1930, the number of collectivized households dropped from 55 percent to 24 percent.[28]

---

[26]The causes of this crisis were mainly economic—distorted prices, weak administration, lack of industrial goods, incorrect relationship between industrial and agricultural prices—rather than political. But the Stalinists, with their Civil War orientation, saw it as essentially politically and responded accordingly. See Robert Conquest, *The Harvest of Sorrow*, Oxford University Press, Oxford, 1986, chapter 5.

[27]See Nove, *An Economic History of the USSR*, chapter 7; and Merle Fainsod, *Smolensk under Soviet Rule*, Harvard University Press, Cambridge, 1958, chapter 12; and Alec Nove, *Stalinism and After*, Allen and Unwin, London, 1979, chapter 2.

[28]Nove, *An Economic History of the USSR*, pp. 172–176.

But this was only a temporary retreat. After June 1930 the state resorted to stringent taxation, force, persuasion, propaganda, and bureaucratic measures to gradually achieve the same goal. In December 1932 the peasants were tied to the land through introduction of internal passports needed for movement within the country. During the 1932–1933 Ukrainian famine (see below) the state relentlessly pressured the peasants into the collective farms. By 1934, 71 percent of all households were in collectives; in 1936, 90 percent. The state kept pushing for state farms, where farmers became state-paid agricultural workers with no ties to the land.

The state reinforced the collective farms with the creation of machine-tractor stations in 1929. Run and owned by the state, the MTS received payment in kind from the peasants for use of the machines. This further tightened the state grip on the countryside as well as provided needed technical assistance and education.

The results, of course, were terrible—poor harvests, demoralized peasantry, massive slaughter (roughly 50 percent) of farm animals, few and poorly kept tractors, disorganized distribution, and poor transportation. A sullen peasantry produced little and ate less—as much as 25 percent less than before collectivization. Hundreds of thousands of peasants resorted to terrorism, sabotage, and guerrilla activity or were sent to exile. But the state had the political and economic control it had long sought. In 1928 grain procurement had been 10.8 million tons; in 1931 it was 22.8 million tons; and in 1933, during a famine, 22.6 million tons. From 1930 to 1933 state exports of grain abroad averaged almost 3 million tons. The state had won, but at what a price![29]

The regime kept up the pressure even after the peasants had reluctantly and passively acquiesced in the new order. A 1939 Central Committee plenum reduced the size of private plots, increased discipline and livestock and crop quotas, and tightened controls over the peasants. The government introduced a war economy in peacetime.[30]

STALINIST CULTURE

Under Stalin the 1930s saw a major cultural change from the 1920s. Gone were the social experimentalism, the freedom from tradition, and centralist authoritarianism of the 1920s. Instead, Stalin reemphasized authority and prerevolutionary cultural traditions. At the end of the 1920s and beginning of the 1930s there was a genuine attempt at cultural revolution in Russia. During that time the stress was on purging the old bourgeois specialists, replacing them with promoted workers, attacking traditional institutions, and stressing the "proletarianization" of the state. Hundreds of employees of the Academy of Sciences and thousands of engineers were arrested. In the Shakhty Trial and Industrial

[29]Nove, *An Economic History of the USSR,* pp. 172–180; and Conquest, *Harvest of Shame,* pp. 22–24.
[30]Nove, *An Economic History of the USSR,* pp. 257–258.

Party Trial the state terrorized the "class enemy." Culture was politicized, with radical attacks on the People's Commissariat of Enlightenment.[31]

But the regime jettisoned class war in 1931 as counterproductive to the state. In the Great Retreat that followed, the state emphasized traditional culture and discipline, ended the harassment of bourgeois specialists, and revived the tsars and military leaders as great heroes.[32] The Stalinists repressed the radical Marxists, denounced wage egalitarianism, increased the status and authority of the rising professional and managerial class, and ended strong preference for lower-class elements in promotion. This was not a retreat to NEP, for it was marked by militancy, Marxist orthodoxy, a fervent revolutionary utopianism, and great privileges for the new elite. The old Marxist emphasis on proletarian internationalism and solidarity with the Western working class was replaced by a new Russian nationalism.[33]

In line with the new conservatism, Stalin claimed great powers in many areas in the 1930s. Writers were told to promote socialist realism and the state attacked modernism in the arts. Traditional education was revived with grades, uniforms, and formal teaching. Experimentalism in personal life ended as abortion and divorce became much harder to obtain. Stalin was glorified, together with tsars, such as Peter the Great and Ivan the Terrible, and Russian nationalism was revived.

LIFE IN THE 1930s

Life in the Soviet Union during the 1930s was extremely turbulent. For those under attack—priests, kulaks, minority intellectuals, Communist bureaucrats, many peasants—life could be extremely dangerous and even deadly. One's fate was decided by a remote government that one day would simply and arbitrarily sentence one to lose nearly all of one's possessions and deport one to Siberia or even to be shot. For these millions, life was repressive and gloomy. Life in the labor camps of Siberia seemed a slow death—and often was.

But for the tens of millions of peasants who moved to the cities, for the hundreds of thousands of workers rapidly promoted to high positions, to the millions of new students in vastly expanded high schools and colleges, life could be a heady experience. There were fewer than 150,000 university students in 1929; there were more than 800,000 in 1939. For them, the 1930s meant enormous opportunity and unimagined expansion of their chances for success and advancement. This was especially true after the 1937 Great Purges opened

---

[31]See, for the best account, Sheila Fitzpatrick, editor, *Cultural Revolution in Russia, 1928–1931,* Indiana University Press, Bloomington, 1978.

[32]The parallels here with other postrevolutionary societies, such as Bonapartist France and Deng's China, are fascinating. The new regime, like the Stalinist regime, brought back significant elements of the old culture, abandoned radical experimentation, strengthened ties with the old patriarchal male authority in the countryside, and established a more stable order.

[33]Jerry Hough, "Cultural Revolution and Western Understanding of the Soviet System," Fitzpatrick, *Cultural Revolution in Russia, 1928–1931,* pp. 240–250.

the doors for hundreds of thousands to gain rapid promotions. The sense of building a new Russia, the advance of peasants into urban society, the provision of social services, elimination of unemployment, and access to advancement and culture made this an exciting time for millions of Russians, who would form the base for Stalin's new Russia.

All this came at a high cost. Life was tough in Soviet cities with labor discipline, fines for absenteeism, and harsh punishments. Rationing, huge price differentials between private and governmental markets, shortages, lines, low-quality goods, and neglect of consumer goods were facts of life. By 1940 real wages in cities were 30 to 40 percent lower than in 1930. In Moscow in 1935, 25 percent of the citizens lived in dormitories (often several to a room), 5 percent lived in kitchens or corridors, 24 percent had less than one room, 40 percent had one room, and only 6 percent had more than one room. Living space was atrocious, goods were short, strains on families were tremendous, privacy and personal life were constrained, and long lines were the norm. The doubling of the size of the urban population in ten years without significant new building was reflected in these figures.[34]

UKRAINIAN FAMINE

One of the most horrible aspects of the 1930s was the Ukrainian famine.[35] Ukraine traditionally was one of the hotbeds of anti-Soviet sentiment. During the Civil War it had provided fertile ground for Whites like General Anton Denikin, and it took three Red Army campaigns before it was subdued by 1920. However, Ukraine and the North Caucasus were vital agricultural areas, producing 50 percent of the marketable grain surplus. Ukrainian nationalism and religious sentiment were a thorn in the side of the government in Moscow. Already in the early 1930s there had been a major Soviet attack on the kulaks and on intellectuals and priests in the Ukraine.

Stalin and his top associates were determined to extend their control over Ukraine, especially the countryside. By the end of 1932, poor weather and high grain requisition targets produced a famine in the Ukraine and North Caucasus. Some Ukrainian Communists, led by Iona Yakir (commander of the Ukrainian Military District) and Vasilii Chubar (head of the Ukrainian government and the head of the Kharkov party organization) tried to get the quotas lowered and grain imported from elsewhere. But the Stalinists in Moscow refused, seeing both an opportunity to crush Ukrainian resistance and a threat to their ambitious plans of industrialization if they lowered the quotas. Instead, they enforced high quotas and ordered a blockade to prevent Russian grain from flowing to Ukraine and Ukrainians from moving to Russia. This was accompanied by a campaign against Ukrainian cultural, religious, and intelligentsia figures, who were denounced as class enemies. The government pro-

---

[34]Nove, *An Economic History of the USSR*, pp. 247–252.
[35]See Conquest, *The Harvest of Sorrow*, for a full treatment of the Ukrainian famine.

vided bread only to the Ukrainian cities, prevented Ukrainian peasants from going to the cities for help, and continued to export grain from famine areas. Unlike 1922, this time it was even prohibited to mention that there was a famine in Ukraine. Even in the famine year of 1933 there continued to be some grain exports abroad.

The results were incredible. No less than 20 percent of all Ukrainian peasants died in the famine, with the figure varying from 10 to 100 percent in different villages. The local elite and the urban dwellers survived, but 5 million Ukrainian peasants and 2 million peasants in the North Caucasus and elsewhere died. Rampant cannibalism resulted. Millions of children and old people died agonizing deaths. Suddenly, in March 1933, the government stopped collecting grain and by May 1933 the famine was over. Large numbers of Russian peasants and students were sent to the Ukraine, and the famine stopped as quickly as it had begun. The result? As Robert Conquest declared,

> So the Ukraine now lay crushed: its Church destroyed, its intellectuals shot or dying in labor camps, its peasants—the mass of the nation—slaughtered or subdued. Even Trotsky was to remark that "nowhere do repression, purges, subjection and all types of bureaucratic hooliganism in general assume such deadly proportions as in the Ukraine in the struggle against powerful subterranean strivings among the Ukrainian masses towards greater freedom and independence."[36]

GREAT PURGES *(YEZHOVSHCHINA)*

Although there is controversy over the reasons behind the Great Purges, there is little dissension over the main course of events.[37] The purges were unique in Soviet history for their huge scale, method of show trials, secrecy, and occurrence in a time of calm and relative prosperity. The Stalinists claimed that the government detected a huge conspiracy led by top leaders in all bureaucracies who were conspiring with German, Polish, British, and Japanese intelligence. Their goal was to kill leaders, cripple Soviet military capability, dismember the country, restore capitalism, and sabotage the economy. Once uncovered, many of the leaders confessed and were tried and punished.

This official version is now discredited, and two alterative views have emerged. One, developed by Robert Conquest and most Sovietologists, saw a vast conspiracy led by Stalin and his top associates to liquidate the bulk of the bureaucratic elite.[38] Their goal was to eliminate wavering elements, to liquidate a possible alternative leadership in case of war, to provide an explanation for the low standard of living and suffering in the 1930s, to provide upward

---

[36]Conquest, *Harvest of Sorrow*, p. 272. The official Soviet view denying the massive fatalities was long accepted inside the country but now is discredited within the FSU.
[37]For works focusing on the Great Purges, see Conquest, *The Great Terror;* and a recent revisionist work by Getty, *Origins of the Great Purges.*
[38]Conquest, *The Great Terror.*

mobility for millions of the younger generation, and to cow the population into submission for the new totalitarianism.

A group led by J. Arch Getty analyzed it quite differently.[39] They did not deny Stalinist complicity, but saw no conspiracy. Rather they stressed a complex pattern of unstructured, erratic, and indecisive decision making. The Great Purges were not of whole cloth but rather an incremental, confused, and contradictory process with numerous issues such as nationalities, industrialism, Stakhonovism, foreign policy, and new cadres at the core.

The main events were clear enough. In August 1936 the government opened the second trial of Zinoviev and Kamenev, who were accused of trying to kill Stalin and five party leaders. The defendants, subjected to lengthy interrogations and promised leniency if they cooperated, pled guilty and abased themselves in public. Nevertheless, all sixteen defendants were shot. The spectacle of former leaders of the opposition publicly confessing to terrorist deeds and being executed marked the start of the Great Purges.

Evidently, large elements in the party were not prepared to go any further and a September 1936 plenum saw further charges dropped against the leaders of the rightist opposition, Bukharin and Rykov. Stalin replaced the doubting Yagoda, head of the secret police, with Nikolai Yezhov and staged the next show trial in January 1937. Not able to put the rightists on trial, he settled for the Trotskyists led by Pyatakov, Radek, Serebryakov, and Sokolnikov in the Trial of the Seventeen. They were convicted of trying to restore capitalism, overthrow the government with German and Japanese help, and carry out espionage, wrecking, and terror. A mass rally of 200,000 Muscovites, led by Khrushchev and Shvernik, called for their executions and the prosecutor, Andrei Vyshinsky, screamed at them,

This is the abyss of degradation!
This is the limit, the last banditry of moral and political decay!
This is the diabolical infinitude of crime![40]

The executions of these men led to strong resistance to the purges at the Central Committee plenum in February and March 1937. Stalin, deploring wrecking and espionage, stood with the Party masses against the bureaucratism, favoritism, and nepotism of the elite. The hard-line Stalinists triumphed and decided to use terror and antibureaucratic populism to remove the middle levels of the party and government and attack the elites that stood in their way.

The next major victim was the Red Army, whose guns stood in the way of an all-out assault. Many of the best officers, led by Marshal Mikhail Tukhachevsky, were only nominal Stalinists. In June 1937 Tukhachevsky and a group of army commanders, mostly in their forties, were tried in secret and shot for an alleged plot to seize the Kremlin. This led to a wave of violence in 1937 and 1938 that eliminated tens of thousands of officers. Three of five marshals, eight of eight admirals, eleven of eleven vice commissars of defense,

[39]Getty, *Origins of the Great Purges.*
[40]Conquest, *The Great Terror*, p. 179.

fourteen of sixteen army commanders, sixty of sixty-seven corps commanders, 136 of 199 divisions commanders, and almost 70 percent of the political workers were purged.[41]

During 1937 the purge relentlessly reached out everywhere. The majority of government commissars were arrested. In August 1937, in Ukraine a Politburo commission of Molotov, Yezhov, and Khrushchev removed all but one member of the Politburo, Secretariat, and Orgburo, 99 of 102 members of the central committee and all seventeen commissars of the government. In June 1938, eighty-five of the eighty-eight members of the new Ukrainian Central Committee were new members.[42] After carrying out the purge, Khrushchev became first secretary of the Ukrainian party in 1938.

In 1937 the terror spread throughout the population. The regime arrested millions of people for anti-Soviet behavior, membership in churches or religious sects, past anti-Soviet behavior, and having contacts abroad. Millions were sentenced under Article 58, Section 10 of the Constitution for counterrevolutionary behavior or intent. Perhaps 1 million people were shot and another 8 million, 80 percent of whom were males, were sent to labor camps.[43] Working under the scrutiny of 250,000 trained NKVD camp guards, they suffered from isolation, cold, and disease. Perhaps 50 percent died within two or three years in a typical camp.[44]

The last great purge trial of the rightists, led by Nikolai Bukharin and Genrich Yagoda (former secret police head), was held in March 1938. Bukharin's veiled refutation of the charges made no difference as nearly all were shot.[45]

The purges reached their climax as three members of the Politburo—Eikhe, Kossior, and Chubar—were arrested and a second wave of arrests swept the army and the hitherto sacrosanct Far Eastern Red Banner Army. In December 1938 Lavrentii Beria replaced Yezhov and soon executed Yezhov and his men.

The new regime was crowned with the holding of the Eighteenth Party Congress in March 1939. The old elite was replaced by new men who had proven themselves in the purges. Andrei Zhdanov and Nikita Khrushchev were made full members of the Politburo. Exactly 3 percent of the delegates to the 1934 Party congress were reelected in 1939. The majority of the delegates had been liquidated, as had been 70 percent of the members of the old Central

---

[41]Conquest, *The Great Terror*, chapter 13.

[42]Conquest, *The Great Terror*, chapter 8.

[43]According to secret documents released in 1990, the 1939 census revealed that the NKVD were holding 3.5 million people, of whom 2.8 million were males. See *Journal of Soviet Nationalities*, vol. 1, no. 4, Winter 1990–1991, pp. 164–167.

[44]For the best description of the camps, see Alexander Solzhenitsyn, *The Gulag Archipelago*, Harper and Row, New York, 1974–1985, 3 volumes. For an account by a survivor of the camps, see Evgeniia Ginzburg, *Journey Into the Whirlwind*, translated by Paul Stevenson, Harcourt, Brace, New York, 1967.

[45]See George Katkov, *The Trial of Bukharin*, Stein and Day, New York, 1969; Stephen Cohen, *Bukharin and the Bolshevik Revolution*, Alfred Knopf, New York, 1973.

Committee (98 of 130) and 80 percent of the members of the old Council of People's Commissars. Seven members of the 1934 Politburo were gone, and even some newer members (like Eikhe and Yezhov) had been shot. The Great Purges created a new political system built around forced adulation of Stalin.

Stalin reduced the national and regional Party secretaries from 41 percent of the members of the Central Committee in 1934 to 14 percent in 1939.[46] Hundreds of thousands of younger men were swept ever upward with spectacular promotions. In 1935 Leonid Brezhnev and Alexei Kosygin were graduating from technical institutes; in 1939 Kosygin was People's Commissar of Textile Industry and Brezhnev was the regional secretary for an important province. The new leaders for the next forty years now appeared on the scene.

The 1930s were an extraordinarily turbulent decade. Its positive accomplishments—a stronger heavy industrial base, a much expanded Red Army, a more urbanized and educated society—greatly enhanced the Soviet capacity to withstand the Nazi invasion of 1941. At the same time collectivization and dekulakization, the Ukrainian famine, and the Great Purges substantially weakened the Soviet Union, terrorized a significant part of the population, and alienated the Soviet Union from the rest of the world. More than any other decade, the 1930s was truly a decade when what you thought of it depended on which part of it you chose to look at.

[46]Getty, *Origins of the Great Purges,* conclusions.

11

World War II (1941–1945) and the Final Years of Stalin (1945–1953)

Until the middle of the 1980s, with the ascension of Mikhail Gorbachev, World War II (or the Great Patriotic War) was the dominant formative experience for Soviet leaders.[1] Visitors to the Soviet Union were struck by the plethora of monuments to the war, of war veterans with their medals, of brides going to the war monuments, and of the volubility of Russians on this topic above all else. The Russians produced over 15,000 volumes on the war. As Susan Linz has observed,

> World War II provided an important watershed for the Soviet Union. Economically, it was the first real test of the Soviet system of central planning. Politically, it thrust the USSR into the world arena as a major world power. Socially, it provided a cohesive force previously lacking in Soviet society.[2]

To Americans, for whom World War II was a distant and "good war," this seemed puzzling.[3] No bombs dropped on American soil, no foreign troops raped, pillaged, and plundered the population. The casualties were relatively modest—300,000 fatalities—and the gains enormous—superpower status, atomic monopoly, economic boom, an end to the Great Depression.

For the Soviet Union the war was a catastrophe of the first order. The statistics numb the mind—26 million dead, 18 million casualties, 25 million homeless, 25 percent of the economy destroyed. In the occupied territories

---

[1]Gorbachev, born in 1931, was the first leader of the postwar generation. Although he did live under German occupation for eight months, he neither fought in the war nor felt it to be the critical event in his life.

[2]Susan Linz, "Introduction: War and Progress in the USSR," in Susan Linz, editor, *The Impact of World War II on the Soviet Union*, Rowman and Allanheld, Totowa, New Jersey, 1985.

[3]See Studs Terkel, *The Good War: An Oral History of World War II*, Pantheon, New York, 1984.

thousands of factories and hundreds of cities lay in ruin, 50 percent of urban housing was destroyed, and over 65 percent of the horses and pigs had been killed.[4] For over one thousand days, from June 1941 until June 1944, the Soviet Union endured the attack of the German Wehrmacht and Luftwaffe. The Russians lost three to five times more soldiers than the Germans, watched millions of people be slaughtered by the fascists, yet endured and triumphed. The United States and England played a substantial role in this victory. Yet in the end it was the Soviet people that suffered the bulk of the casualties and endured most of the suffering on a scale exceeded only by that of European Jews.

The story of the war was one of tremendous agony, pain, and suffering, culminating in the raising of the red flag over the Reichstag building in Berlin. No army in history has suffered such enormous defeats and losses and come back to achieve a total victory. Why did the Russians suffer such enormous losses early in the war, how did they manage to continue in the war, and what factors enabled them to recover and attain ultimate victory?

EARLY DISASTERS AND BRIEF REDEMPTION: 1941

The Germans planned an enormously ambitious "Operation Barbarossa" for the defeat of the Soviet Union in a ten-week summer campaign. They hoped to destroy the Soviet armed forces, capture Moscow and Leningrad, occupy the Ukraine and Caucasus, and reach a line 1000 miles deep inside the Soviet Union. In the first phase their air and ground thrusts would reach deep inside the country, create chaos, disrupt supplies, and destroy the armies west of the Dvina and Dnieper. In phase two they would take Leningrad, Moscow, and Ukraine; and in phase three, advance to the line from Arkhangel in the north to the Volga in the south. With 170 divisions split among three army groups, they would destroy the 150 divisions of the Red Army and achieve great successes.[5]

The Germans reckoned on a number of key factors. They had enormous battle experience from the earlier campaigns in France, the Low Countries, and Poland, and they had never been beaten. The advantage of surprise would be decisive in the early going. German equipment was superior, and the German soldiers knew how to use it. German commanders were better educated and better experienced than their Soviet counterparts. The Germans would have localized quantitative, as well as qualitative, superiority over a partially mobilized Soviet army. German morale was higher. Soviet armies, their supply dumps, and their military industry were too far forward and so were susceptible to German blitzkrieg tactics. Supported by a strong industrial base, exten-

---

[4]Alec Nove, *An Economic History of the USSR*, Penguin Books, Harmondsworth, England, 1982, p. 283.
[5]For the best description of the battle of Moscow and other campaigns, see John Erickson, *The Road to Stalingrad*, Weidenfeld and Nicholson, London, 1975.

GERMAN INVASION OF RUSSIA, 1941

NORWAY

SWEDEN

FINLAND

USSR

ESTONIA

Baltic
Sea

LATVIA

LITH.

Leningrad

Novgorod

Moscow

Tula

Minsk

Voronezh

Stalingrad

BELORUSSIA

GERMANY

UKRAINE

Rostov

SWITZ.

HUNGARY

ITALY

CROATIA

RUMANIA

Black Sea

GEORGIA

BULGARIA

ALBANIA

TURKEY

GREECE

SYRIA

IRAQ

LEBANON

Mediterranean   Sea

PALESTINE

JORDAN

SAUDI
ARABIA

LIBYA

EGYPT

German Conquest

sive campaign experience, and strong education and training, the Germans felt invincible. Red Army performance in the Winter War with Finland had been wretched. German racist propaganda about their innate superiority over the Slavs did the rest.[6]

The scale of the early Soviet defeats was enormous. On the first day of the war (June 22, 1941) German air raids destroyed over 1000 Soviet planes. Within ten days the German army seized much of the Baltics, western Belarus, and western Ukraine. By September the Germans had taken 600,000 prisoners in the Kiev salient. By late September the Germans were on the move towards Moscow, Leningrad, and through Ukraine. The Germans had lost 500,000 men; the Russians, 3 million, nearly 50 percent of their strength.[7]

In October and November the Germans were stopped, for the first time ever in World War II, in front of Moscow. Despite panic in the streets of Moscow in the middle of October as the Germans drew ever nearer and the government was evacuated to Kuibyshev, Stalin reasserted control. On November 7 Stalin took the salute of the soldiers marching towards the front only forty miles away. In December the Red Army counterattacked and threw the Germans 100 to 150 miles back from Moscow. Over 500,000 Russian civilians died that horrible winter in besieged Leningrad as the Red Army could not break the German siege.[8] Russian nationalism as the war drew close to the Russian heartland, the onset of winter, overstretching of German supply lines, German tactical errors, and the tentative emergence of a new Red Army had made the difference. At a cost of over 4 million losses, the Red Army finally slowed the Germans, who suffered 750,000 casualties by the end of November.[9]

CONTINUED DEFEATS AND THE BEGINNING OF HOPE: 1942

The initial victories in front of Moscow did not signal a general shift in favor of the Red Army. The Soviet war effort was greatly harmed by the loss of territory with almost 40 percent of the population and could not replace its huge losses of men and equipment. Allied aid came in only limited quantities in 1942 and no serious second front was opened, only the limited North African campaign in November 1942. However, the Germans too had suffered in 1941 and would be able to advance only on one front in 1942, not on three as in 1941.

The year 1942 was a severe test for the Soviet Union as German armies swept forward in Ukraine and towards Stalingrad and the Caucasus oil fields.

[6]Alec Nove, *Stalin and Afterwards*, Allen and Unwin, London, 1982, chapter 3.
[7]Roy Medvedev, *Let History Judge*, translated by Colleen Taylor, Alfred Knopf, New York, 1972, chapter 12.
[8]See Harrison Salisbury, *The 900 Days: The Siege of Leningrad*, Harper and Row, New York, 1969. This number was almost twice all American military fatalities in World War II on both fronts.
[9]Alexander Werth, *Russia At War, 1941–1945*, Dutton, New York, 1964, chapter 10 for details on this critical period in Moscow with air raids, demoralized Russians, stampedes, sullen soldiers, and the evacuation of the government.

In May the Germans occupied the Crimea, save for Sevastopol, and crushed a Russian offensive aimed at retaking Kharkov. By June the Germans were in Kursk, in July in Rostov, and by September reached Stalingrad and the North Caucasus. In three weeks the Germans advanced 250 miles, an echo of 1941. In September the German army tried to storm Stalingrad.

Stalingrad! The name connoted the entire ferocious war on the Eastern front. Stalingrad was an industrial city of 450,000 people on the Volga, with no natural or artificial defenses. The battle was fought street to street, house to house, and floor to floor. Under Generals Chuikov, Lopatin, and Zhukov, the Red Army slowly gave ground until it held only a thin strip a mile and a half wide on the river. Then in November 1942 a Red Army counterattack crushed the Rumanian, Hungarian, and Italian troops on the German flanks, and caught 285,000 German troops inside Stalingrad. In December 1942 the Red Army stopped an attempt by General Von Manstein to relieve Stalingrad. Hitler forbade a breakout by Field Marshal von Paulus, who surrendered at the end of January. This was a crushing defeat from which the German army never recovered.

THE TURNING POINT: 1943

By 1943 the tide of battle had turned for the allies. The British victory at El Alamein (November 1942) and the Anglo-American victories in North Africa merged with American victories in the Pacific. The victory at Stalingrad, stabilization of the war economy, promotion of many battle-tested commanders, and arrival of large quantities of Allied aid helped turn the tide in the east.

By the end of 1943 the Russians had driven the Germans from two-thirds of occupied Soviet territory. In May 1943 a German counterattack retook Kharkov, only to lose it back to the Red Army. The key event was the battle of Kursk-Orel in the summer of 1943, the last great German offensive (Operation Citadel) of the war in the east. There, more than 6000 tanks and self-propelled guns duelled, making it the greatest tank battle in history. In one small village 1700 tanks and self-propelled guns were engaged on both sides. Elaborate German offensive preparations were stymied by a deeply echeloned Soviet defense zone. After defeating the German attack, the Russians cleared large sections of Ukraine and part of western Russia by the end of the year. The Red Army took Orel, Belgorod, Kharkov in the summer, Smolensk in September, and Kiev by November. By the Teheran Conference in November and December 1943, the Red Army was clearly winning its war.

TEN DECISIVE BLOWS: 1944

In 1944 the Red Army drove the German army from Soviet soil and moved into Eastern Europe. In June 1944 the Anglo-American forces opened the crucial second front in Normandy and reached Paris in August. The Third Reich, facing 4.5 million men in the west, 1.0 million men in the south, and 6.5 million

RED ARMY INVASION OF GERMANY, 1943-1944

NORWAY

SWEDEN

FINLAND

USSR

ESTONIA

Leningrad

Novgorod

Moscow

Baltic Sea

LATVIA

Tula

LITH.

Minsk

Voronezh

BELORUSSIA

Stalingrad

GERMANY

UKRAINE

Rostov

Odessa

SWITZ.

HUNGARY

Black Sea

GEORGIA

ITALY

CROATIA

RUMANIA

BULGARIA

ALBANIA

TURKEY

GREECE

SYRIA

IRAQ

LEBANON

Mediterranean   Sea

PALESTINE

JORDAN

SAUDI ARABIA

LIBYA

EGYPT

Russian Reconquest

men in the east, and hammered by Anglo-American air attacks, began to crumble. The opening of the second front in 1944 forced the Germans to move dozens of divisions to the western front, which rose from 65 divisions in 1943 to 120 divisions in 1944 and 1945. This substantially contributed to final Soviet victory.[10]

The Red Army reached its optimal efficiency at this time. Together with its vast military production, large supplies of Allied aid (overall 11 billion dollars) gave it needed mobility and foodstuffs. The Red Army, after the devastating early defeats, had regained its confidence. Stalin relied on a group of professional officers, led by Marshal Georgii Zhukov, and the overall quality of the officer corps was much improved over 1941. The regaining of occupied territory bolstered morale and increased the resource base for manpower recruitment and war production. With the German army increasingly forced to transfer dozens of divisions to the western front, the Soviet army now faced an increasingly demoralized and depleted, though still dangerous, enemy.

The ten blows that drove back the Germans began in January 1944 with an end to the encirclement of Leningrad. For 800 days the people of Leningrad suffered indescribable hardships as 600,000 to 900,000 civilians had died.[11] In the next blow, in February and March the Red Army drove the Germans out of Ukraine, ending the nightmare of mass extermination, shooting, and the forcible deportation of millions of Ukrainians to the Third Reich as slave laborers. In March the Red Army followed up with a third blow that seized the Crimea.

In June the Red Army took the offensive, ousting the Finns from Karelia. This evened the score for the disasters suffered in the Winter War with Finland. The most important blow was the fifth one, inflicted by the Red Army in June 1944 in coordination with the Anglo-American landing at Normandy. A huge force of 146 divisions (1.5 million men, 5000 tanks, and 6000 planes) caved in Army Group Center, seized Minsk and Vilna, and by July was on the banks of the Vistula opposite Warsaw. Here they rested until January. This proved highly controversial, as the Red Army sat idle while the Germans crushed the Warsaw uprising late that summer and early fall. The sixth blow came in Galicia, that favorite fighting ground of World War I, where the Red Army reached Lvov. In August and September the Red Army forced the surrender of Rumania (which switched sides) and Bulgaria. The eighth blow in October took the Red Army into Belgrade and in November advanced it close to Budapest. The ninth blow freed the Baltics from German occupation. The last and final blow wrested Petsamo in northern Norway from German hand.

TOTAL VICTORY: 1945

In 1945 the Red Army, having marched from the Polish border back to Moscow and Leningrad and Stalingrad, advanced on Berlin. In January 1945 the Rus-

[10]Jonathan R. Adelman, *Prelude to the Cold War: Tsarist, Soviet and United States Armies in the Two World Wars*, Lynne Rienner Publications, Boulder, Colorado, 1988, p. 175.
[11]See Salisbury, *The 900 Days: The Siege of Leningrad*, for a description of these horrors.

sians enjoyed a three to one advantage in manpower and cannons and a six to one advantage in tanks over the Germans.[12] The enormous assault of 275 divisions was led by Ivan Konev in the North Carpathians, Georgii Zhukov in central Poland, Konstantin Rokossovsky in northern Poland, and Ivan Chernyahovsky in eastern Prussia. In January they tore an enormous hole in German defenses and took Warsaw and Krakow. In February Budapest fell after a harsh struggle, only to see a determined German offensive blunted in Western Hungary around Lake Balaton in March. In April 1945 the Red Army entered Vienna and prepared to drive on Berlin.

In a ten-day relentless assault, the Red Army, with over 2 million soldiers, smashed through the last German defenses, entered Berlin, and placed the red flag above the Reichstag. Hitler committed suicide, and the Third Reich was liquidated, after having caused the deaths of 50 to 60 million people. But 80,000 Russians died and over 225,000 were wounded in the final drive on Berlin, more than the Allies lost in all of 1945 in the West.[13]

ECONOMIC PROBLEMS OF THE WAR EFFORT

The Soviet war effort was handicapped by a number of factors. In the first five months of the war the Soviet Union lost territory with over 35 percent of its population, 300 major arms factories, 38 percent of the grain, 41 percent of the railroads, 58 percent of the steel, and 63 percent of its coal. In November 1941 the German invasion reduced Soviet industrial capability to 52 percent of the prewar level. German advances in the spring and summer of 1942 took further productive territory. In 1940 the Soviet Union produced 18.3 million tons of steel; in 1942, 8.1 million tons. In 1942 Soviet industrial production declined 24 percent from the already depressed 1941 level. In 1942 Soviet grain production was a minuscule 32 percent of the 1940 figure.[14]

Allied aid, hampered by a late start, lengthy and difficult lines of transportation, and competing war priorities, reached the Soviet Union largely after the severe crisis of the first eighteen months of the war had passed. American Lend Lease aid (11 billion dollars) accounted for 9 percent of Soviet national income in 1942, 18 percent in 1943, and 17 percent in 1944. While the Soviets produced the bulk of their own weapons, American aid was instrumental in providing the Red Army with mobility (almost 500,000 trucks), specialized fuels and supplies, and desperately needed food.[15]

Soviet economic capabilities, hampered by weakened industrial capacity, low levels of education (the average soldier had four years of education), and

[12]See Erickson, *The Road to Berlin,* for the definitive story.
[13]Adelman, *Prelude to the Cold War: Tsarist, Soviet and United States Armies in the Two World Wars,* p. 192.
[14]Nove, *An Economic History of the USSR,* chapter 10.
[15]Mark Harrison, "Resource Mobilization for World War II: the U.S.A., U.K., U.S.S.R., and Germany, 1938–1945," *Economic History Review,* vol. XLI, no. 2, 1988, pp. 171–192.

inferior technological infrastructure, lagged behind those of Nazi Germany, which occupied most of Europe for four years. Germany produced almost $90 billion worth of war supplies to $50 billion worth for the Soviet Union.[16]

Soviet industry, shaking off the impact of the Great Purges, was modernizing when the war started. A startling 77 percent of Soviet industrial assets were in the path of the oncoming German army in the west. While work had begun in the east, it was far from adequate for the load of a total war. Russian designers lacked the war experience of their German counterparts.[17]

From June 1941 until June 1944 the Germans maintained the bulk of their active troops on the eastern front. From June 1941 until July 1943 the Germans kept 150 to 190 divisions on the eastern front compared to 50 to 65 divisions on other fronts.[18] Even after D-Day, with the exception of the Battle of the Bulge in December 1944, the Germans kept two-thirds of their forces in the east. Also, as seen by the massive German surrenders in the west beginning in March 1945 and hardened resistance right up to the Battle of Berlin in the east in April 1945, they fought harder in the east. Statistics tell the story: In Europe, the Russians lost 8.6 million soldiers killed in battle, the United States 140,000 soldiers.[19]

HOW DID THEY DO IT?

Economics

How was traditionally backward Russia, facing superior German military power and military industry and having lost its best industrial and human resources, able ultimately to win the war? Certainly the Allies played their role, but in the grim days of 1941 and 1942 their contribution was more exhortatory than substantial. How then, in 1942, did the Soviet Union produce 24,700 tanks and 25,400 planes? And during the war how did it produce 490,000 artillery pieces, 137,000 planes, and 102,000 tanks and self-propelled guns, a tremendous accomplishment?[20]

The Soviet economy in the 1930s, essentially a war economy in peace time, had laid a strong base for this war effort. During the war the Russian production of $50 billion worth of war supplies matched the $50 billion German effort on the eastern front.[21] The Soviet economy was able to shift rapidly to war production with a minimum of disruption. The 1930s transformation greatly increased both the industrial base and trained tens of millions of workers. The massive evacuation of 25 million people and over 1500 factories eastward in 1941 was critical to future success.[22]

---

[16]Ibid.

[17]Nove, *An Economic History of the USSR,* chapter 10.

[18]Adelman, *Prelude to the Cold War: Tsarist, Soviet and United States Armies in the Two World Wars,* p. 131.

[19]See Adelman, *Prelude to the Cold War: The Tsarist, Soviet and United States Armies in Two World Wars.*

[20]Nove, *An Economic History of the USSR,* pp. 273–274.

[21]Harrison, "Resource Mobilization for World War II: the U.S.A., U.K., U.S.S.R., and Germany, 1938–1945," *Economic History Review,* p. 191.

Mark Harrison summarized the importance of Soviet military preparation in the 1930s to ultimate success:

> The only country to attempt the building of a true military counterweight to German dispositions . . . only in the Soviet Union did defense production in the 1930s approach the same order of magnitude as that of Germany, and of all Germany's adversaries the Soviet economy devoted the highest peacetime proportion of national income to defense—perhaps 20 per cent in 1940, more than the proportional burden on Germany's national economy in 1938.[23]

During the war the regime lowered the standard of living a stunning 40 percent. Clothes and footwear became scarce, heat was at times inadequate, and food rationing left many people near the edge of starvation—and sometimes over it. Housing was so poor that in the coal mines a typical coal miner had 13 square feet, less than the size of a modern bathroom, for his total living space.[24]

There was a ruthless mobilization of labor into the work place. While in Germany millions of women stayed at home, the Soviet leaders mobilized every youth, woman, and older person able to work. They enforced military discipline in war industry. There were no holidays, no compensation for days missed, and no leaving the job. Food rationing was tied to job category. By the end the Soviet economy was producing its maximum potential.[25]

Soviet military efforts in 1941 and 1942 transformed the German blitzkrieg into a war of attrition, which ultimately favored the Allies. Even in the early days of the war the system functioned well in converting the economy to full war mobilization. By 1942 the Soviet Union spent a higher proportion of its GNP on the war than any other power. Popular support for the war effort and willingness to carry out arduous tasks was critical to survival.[26]

The movement eastward of over 25 million people and 1500 major factories in 1941 and 1942 was an unprecedented task. The ability to reassemble part of the Soviet economy in the eastern zone was an enormous accomplishment.

The material aid offered by the Allies allowed the Soviet economy to focus on producing a small number of standardized items with accompanying economies of scale. Soviet spokesmen admit that American aid shortened the war by twelve to eighteen months.[27] Allied aid was critical to the great victories in the final two years of the war.

---

[22]This feat, judging by the disorganization of the Tsarist war effort in 1914, would likely have been well beyond Russia's capacities in World War I.

[23]Harrison, "Resource Mobilization for World War II: the U.S.A., U.K., U.S.S.R., and Germany, 1938–1945," *Economic History Review,* p. 174.

[24]Nove, *An Economic History of the USSR,* pp. 276–277.

[25]Nove, *An Economic History of the USSR,* pp. 277–279.

[26]In 1941, especially in the nationality areas, the will to fight was weak, and there was much collaboration with the enemy. By 1942, German defeats, German barbarism, Western invasion of North Africa, and Soviet mobilization helped the Red Army turn the tide and regain its fighting ability.

[27]Conversation in Moscow at Soviet Academy of Sciences, April 1990.

Politics

There were a number of political factors in the final victory. Despite its deficiencies, the political system proved superb at mobilizing the population for war. Within a few days after the beginning of the war, it kicked into high gear. The millions of Communists who had joined the Party before the war, and the 6 million enrolled during the war, provided the glue both in Soviet territory and in German-occupied partisan territory. The system, harsh and tightly run, was essential to victory.

Stalin, for all his faults, adroitly maneuvered during the war.[28] While Hitler alienated the Soviet people, Stalin courted them with the conviction that this was their war. The war was fought not for socialism but for the fatherland and nationalism. In July 1941 Stalin invoked the great patriotic war of 1812 against Napoleon as his model and called the Soviet people his "brothers and sisters." Stalin, by appearing in Moscow for the October Revolution celebration in 1941 and by invoking the great Tsarist ancestors, effectively manipulated Russian nationalism. He abolished the Comintern in 1943 and restored Tsarist military ranks. Stalin became a rallying point, a unifying symbol for the Soviet people, the Little Father of the people.[29]

This appeal went beyond Russian nationalism. He appealed to the religious by dissolving the League of the Militant Atheists in 1941, appointing the Metropolitan of the Russian Orthodox Church to a Soviet commission on German war crimes in 1942, and meeting with the Patriarch of the Russian Orthodox Church in 1943. In September 1943 Stalin restored the status of the Church and agreed to a Concordat with it. For the Moslems, he created a Central Direction for Moslems and a Mufti of Tashkent in October 1942. For the Jews he created the Jewish Anti-Fascist Committee with contacts in the West. For the peasants he allowed a major expansion of private plots during the war, turned a blind eye to runaway prices on the peasant markets and tolerated (or perhaps even spawned) recurrent rumors that things would be better after the war.

By contrast, Hitler did everything possible to alienate the 70 million Soviet citizens now under his control.[30] Millions of Soviet citizens in the western territories greeted the German army with enthusiasm and were prepared to rally to Hitler's cause. Instead, contemptuously dismissing them as *untermenschen* (inferior people), he raped, pillaged, and plundered them. He refused to make concessions to the nationalist desires of the non-Russians for independence until it was too late. For the peasants yearning to be free of the collective farms, he refused to disband the farms. For Jews and disaffected Communists, he offered mass extermination. For millions of Soviet citizens, especially Ukrainians, he ordered forced emigration to the Third Reich to work

---

[28]See Alexander Werth, *Russia At War*, E.P. Dutton, New York, 1964, for a portrayal of life in the Soviet Union during the war.
[29]The battle cry was "For Stalin, for the Motherland."
[30]There were 80 to 85 million people in the conquered territory but 10 to 20 million of them fled eastward to Soviet lines.

as slave laborers. He refused to restore the Church, limited the population to only elementary education, and had 3 million Soviet prisoners of war starved to death. Hitler's policies massively alienated the population and drove them into the arms of the partisans.[31]

Military

Militarily, there was a dramatic turnaround during the war. At the beginning of the war, the Red Army was still suffering serious consequences from the Great Purges that had decimated the officer corps, the poor leadership of the "Horse Marshals" that ran the Soviet army, and the weak and unimaginative leadership of Stalin. The Germans seemed invincible, the Red Army lacked modern equipment and training, and the quality of the officers left much to be desired. The Stalinist strategy of static defense, the lack of a well-organized command structure, and excessive reliance on the center also hindered the Red Army. The staggering early losses of men, material, and territory plagued the army for many months. But by 1942 a new generation of officers came to the fore, experienced professionals (Zhukov and Konev) replaced the Horse Marshals (Budenny, Voroshilov, Kulik, Mekhlis), and Stalin increasingly gave them more power. War gave the officers the training and experience so many had lacked in June 1941, but at a great price.[32]

The massive economic transformation in the 1930s played a key role in the survival of the Soviet Union. During the 1930s the Soviet Union had been the leading power outside of Germany in developing its military prowess. During the war the State Defense Committee and Supreme Headquarters proved adept in running the war effort. The recruitment of over 5.3 million people to the Party during the war was a major asset.

Another major factor was German military errors. The initial German war plan was extremely unrealistic in postulating enormous gains and the destruction of a huge country like the Soviet Union in such a short time. The Germans, once the war started, were never able to decide on whether to disperse (and continue a three pronged attack) or concentrate on key objectives (as Moscow). Their political program of genocide, barbarism, and slavery greatly promoted the cohesion and fighting capability of the Red Army in 1943 and 1944. The dominance of Hitler, a military novice, over the German professional officers was another asset for the Red Army. Stalin learned from some of his mistakes; Hitler did not.[33]

After early disasters, the Red Army and the Soviet people rallied to play a key role in the destruction of the Third Reich. In the process much of their

---

[31]Helene Encarrere D'Encausse, *Stalin: Order Through Terror,* Viking Press, New York, 1978, chapter 5; and Alexander Dallin, *German Rule in Russia, 1941–1944,* Macmillan, London, 1957. What is particularly interesting is that there was considerable dissension within the German hierarchy on how to deal with the eastern territories and whether there should be different treatment of different minorities.

[32]See Seweryn Bialer, editor, *Stalin and His Generals,* Pegasus, London, 1970.

[33]See Adam Ulam, *Stalin: the Man and his Era,* Beacon Press, Boston, 1973, chapter 12.

economy was shattered, tens of millions of their people killed and tens of millions more injured, and their land subjected to German barbarism. Outside of European Jews devastated in the Holocaust, the Soviets lost the highest percentage of their people in the war. In the end, in alliance with the United States and England, the Soviet Union emerged bloodied but triumphant. The war laid the basis for a new relationship between the regime and the population after the death of Stalin.

In Churchill's memorable phrase, the Red Army "tore the guts" out of the German army. German statistics have shown that from June 1941 until June 1944 the Germans lost 4.2 million soldiers on the eastern front and only .3 million soldiers on other fronts.[34] The war thrust the Soviet Union into superpower status over a prostrate Germany and Japan.

THE FINAL YEARS OF STALIN (1945–1953)

The final years of Stalin followed the great and unexpected triumph in World War II. Stalin had brought the nation from the depths of despair under the oppressive heel of German occupation in 1941 and 1942 to the glorious triumphs of 1944 and 1945. A new Soviet Union emerged by 1945. No longer a weak and backward country, it had become a nascent superpower bestriding Eastern Europe and dividing Germany with the United States, France, and England. With Japan and Germany in ruins, its economy was the second greatest in the world.

The war forged a national unity long lacking in the Soviet Union. In 1941 the list of dissatisfied elements was a long one—the Ukrainians (famine and Great Russian chauvinism), the peasants (dekulakization and collectivization), the workers (low standard of living), the religious (persecution), the old bourgeoisie and aristocracy (persecution), and many Communists (Great Purges). The war unified the country around Stalin and the Soviet system, which had won such a great victory. By 1945 most hoped that peace would bring blessed calm and relief after the severe trials of war.

These hopes were to prove ephemeral in the final years of Stalin. At the same time Stalin neither resumed the radical programs of the 1930s nor imposed mass terror on the population. There was a curious formlessness to the final years of Stalin. In the postwar years events adopted a muted and hushed tone, reflective of the decrepitude and decline of its supreme leader. And yet one cannot simply define Soviet politics in the 1945–1953 period as the life of Stalin writ large. Bureaucratic interests and political clashes were strong and the outcomes of this period often decisively reversed in the following decade. There is a striking contrast between the great victory in the war, after so much sacrifice, and the relatively depressed attitudes in the final years of Stalin.

The end of the war left the Soviet Union in a paradoxical position. The war had transformed the Soviet Union from a weak power to a nascent superpower. Yet this position masked enormous problems within the Soviet Union itself. Its

[34]Adelman, *Prelude to the Cold War: Tsarist, Soviet and American Armies in the Two World Wars*, p. 171.

situation was very different from that of the United States, which emerged in 1945 with an unscathed war economy, its economic output almost 50 percent of the world's GNP, a massive army, air force, and navy, and an atomic monopoly.

The Soviet Union had lost not 300,000 dead, as the United States had, but 26 million dead and 25 million wounded or maimed. Fully 25 percent of the Soviet population was killed or injured in the war. In 1945, 25 million people were homeless, their "homes" consisting of makeshift hovels or holes in the ground. The war and German scorched earth strategy destroyed 25 percent of the GNP, 50 percent of the railroad lines, 17 million cattle, 98,000 collective farms, and 1700 towns. Major cities like Stalingrad, Kiev, and Kharkov were largely a heap of rubble, awaiting excavation and reconstruction. The famine of 1946 left agricultural production at a level 14 percent *below* the level of 1913, over thirty years earlier.

All Soviet leaders agreed on the necessity of rapid industrial reconstruction and massive demobilization of the 12 million-man army (reduced to 2.8 million men by 1948). The key questions were how ambitious the economic plans should be and what kind of politics should be pursued. One variant, pursued by Malenkov after Stalin's death, was for moderate growth with a balance between consumer goods and heavy industry and a policy of conciliation with the population. This "New Course" policy wanted to build on the relative liberalism of Soviet wartime politics, the economic accommodation with peasants over expansion of private plots, and the political accommodation with the population in the antifascist war effort. Such a line sought to address the glaring weaknesses of the Soviet state—the primitive villages, poor consumer goods, terrible housing, backward aspects of industrial structure, weak agricultural sector, and pervasive system of terror. It argued that all traitors were either destroyed in the Great Purges or liquidated in the war. In foreign affairs it similarly called for accommodation with the West, a relatively open posture towards Western influences, and international detente.

The alternative Stalinist policy called for stringent isolation from the West, rapid expansion of heavy industry, repression of all liberal influences, and a tough line towards the West. This policy wanted to build on the Stalinist strengths of being an ascent superpower with the world's second greatest military and industrial power, solid scientific achievements, and some modern aspects of agricultural sector (as modern harvesters). It sought to build on Soviet strengths and project power in the international arena.[35] It saw the West as a threat to the Soviet Union. Recalling the origins of the Decembrist Revolt in 1825 in the exposure of Russian officers to the corrupting influence of France in the Napoleonic campaigns, the Stalinists argued for the isolation of Russia from the West. They pointed to domestic cosmopolitans, especially intellectuals and Jews, and those tens of millions of Russians who had been forced laborers in the Third Reich, soldiers in the Red Army invasion of Central Europe, or those living under German occupation as especially dangerous.

In the immediate postwar era the debates were led by Andrei Zhdanov and

---

[35]See Nove, *An Economic History of the USSR*, p. 321.

Evgen Varga, a Hungarian-born economist. Zhdanov held that exposure to the West meant that Soviet weaknesses would be relentlessly exploited by an aggressive Western imperialism. Only a firm policy of isolation, Russian chauvinism, and intensified orthodoxy could fend off the West and build a firm foundation for future growth. By contrast, the academician Varga held that the West too would have to rebuild and that both socialism and capitalism would develop without further crises. In some ways Varga was a forerunner of Gorbachev.

These debates were complicated by the slow evolution of the Cold War in the 1945–1948 period, the beginning of the disintegration of colonial rule in the Third World, the famine of 1946, and the slow decline in Stalin's powers. As Stalin aged (he reached 70 in 1949), he became increasingly suspicious of everyone, denouncing close associates (Molotov and Voroshilov) as British spies and leading intellectuals, (Ilya Ehrenburg and Alexei Tolstoy) as agents of foreign imperialism. By 1949 he had sent Molotov's wife into exile, isolated himself from the world, and insisted that his food be first tasted by his associates.

Stalin dominated the policy process in the postwar era. He worked closely with a small group of compatriots, such as Georgii Malenkov, Lavrentii Beria, Nikita Khrushchev (after 1949), Nikolai Bulganin, and Vyacheslav Molotov. At his dacha and retreats they frequently met at dinners that lasted into the early morning hours and argued over all the important policy issues. Specific commissions within the Politburo ("quintets," "sextets," and "novenaries") dealt with specific problems. The highly centralist regime was shrouded in secrecy. There were few Central Committee plenums and only one Party Congress in 1952. Stalin rarely spoke in public. The regime endlessly praised Stalin and Russian achievements, censored anything considered deviant, frequently reorganized the state structure, and functioned at a minimal intellectual level.

At lower levels there were intensive bureaucratic struggles and individual scholars putting forth proposals in the newspaper and conducting sanctioned social experiments. There were also local Stalinists performing similar functions. The seemingly centralized, rigid, and repressive command structure hid a much more complex reality.[36]

Despite bloodcurdling calls against intellectuals, the great majority of those attacked survived the period intact. The focus of attack was the Jews, who were largely spared only by Stalin's death. There was no mass terror, and many under attack, such as Evgen Varga, even remained in their positions. By 1945 fully 65 percent of Party members had joined during the war and 40 percent of the members were soldiers enlisted in combat. Although few had much education or knowledge of Marxism, there was no mass purge.[37]

The army was singled out for greater attention. Many leading officers were

[36]See Jerry Hough and Merle Fainsod, *How the Soviet Union is Governed*, Harvard University Press, Cambridge, 1979, chapter 5; and Nove, *An Economic History of the USSR*, p. 287.
[37]D'Encausse, *Stalinism: Order Through Terror*, chapter 7.

retired or exiled to the provinces (Zhukov). But, there was no mass purge of the officer corps. Despite his anger at the non-Russian nationalities, Stalin confined his actions to small nationalities, sparing the larger ones, such as the Ukrainians, from massive reprisals. Despite all the maneuvering and the Leningrad Affair, the great majority of the top leaders in 1949 and 1952 were the same people as in 1939. Their rank order may have changed, but their ranks were largely the same. In 1939 the top ten members of the Politburo were Stalin, Molotov, Voroshilov, Kaganovich, Mikoyan, Andreyev, Khrushchev, Zhdanov, Beria, and Kalinin. In 1949 all were still in the leadership, with the exception of Kalinin, who had died.

All these trends were indicated already by 1946 and 1947. In September 1945 the State Defense Committee was abolished and in February 1946 the first elections were held for the Supreme Soviet. By March 1946 the new order of normalization was reflected in the change of the title of the Council of People's Commissars to the Council of Ministers, the traditional prewar title.

Stalin tried to regain control over various elements who had gained autonomy during the war. He tamed the army, reshuffled his lieutenants, and sent millions to forced labor camps. While new lieutenants, such as Andrei Zhdanov and Nikita Khrushchev (beginning in 1949 after Zhdanov's death) rose, the older lieutenants, like Molotov, Malenkov, and Kaganovich, retained significant power.

Stalin also tried to increase his power through his publications, which set him up as the final authority on many intellectual matters. In 1950 his essay on linguistics quelled disputes in this area. In 1952 his "Economic Problems of Socialism" sought to definitely resolve the future economic course of the Soviet Union. In this, he sought to emulate Lenin, who had often been seen as much as a theoretician as a politician.

ECONOMIC POLICY

In economic affairs, Stalin took a leading role in pushing a highly centralized and conservative style of decision making. In industry Stalin emphasized producing the same designs with a freeze on innovation (no use of plastics or nonsolid fuels). Weak industries were to remain weak and the traditional favorites, such as heavy industry, were given high priority, receiving 88 percent of investment in industry. Agriculture, consumer goods, and housing were given low priority, and the standard of living remained low. The housing shortage saw four families sharing a four-room apartment, and whole families living in but one relatively small room. Even by 1952 the real wages of workers were only 70 percent of the 1928 level. The state wiped out the bulk of peasant savings by a 1947 conversion of currency. Only in 1947 did rationing begin to come to an end. Politics dominated economics, and central intervention was ever more stultifying of initiatives.[38]

[38]Nove, *An Economic History of the USSR,* chapter 11; and D'Encausse, *Stalin: Order Through Terror,* pp. 136–138.

The plans, however, were ambitious. Under the Fourth Five Year Plan (1946–1950) the goal was to exceed the 1940 level. This was not easy given the enormous wartime destruction of the Soviet economy and the end of Lend Lease in 1945. The 1948 Plan for the Transformation of Nature (later largely abandoned) envisioned vast canals, forest belts, and hydroelectric plants.

Nowhere were the problems more evident than in 1946, with the worst natural drought since 1891 in the Volga and Ukraine. The population wanted to relax, not work harder. Millions of soldiers and civilians returned home and many volunteers, teenagers, and elderly abandoned the economy. Food rationing was continued into 1947, and industrial production fell 17 percent under the demands of conversion from a military to civilian economy. Inflation leaped ahead in the wake of serious consumer shortages. By 1947, though, reconstruction was under way, and in 1950 industrial output did exceed that of 1940. In 1952 industrial production was almost double that of 1940, though consumer goods had only regained the meager 1940 level. Putting back into operation the vast damaged enterprises of the occupied areas yielded great benefits.[39]

But while the Stalinist plan did yield real benefits in industry, it continued to walk on that Achilles heel, agriculture. The war devastated an agricultural sector still reeling from collectivization in the 1930s. In 1946 there were fewer horses and sheep in the countryside than in 1913. On top of this was the devastating 1946 famine, the worst in over fifty years in the Ukraine and Volga. Many millions of peasant soldiers, killed or maimed in the war or preferring to move to the cities, never returned home. The peasants were short of tractors, oxen and horses, fuel, and seeds, and even cannibalism was not unknown as the old, invalids, unfit, and women struggled to cope with the famine. Only by 1950 had agricultural production equaled the 1913 level.[40]

The Stalinist response was not to attempt reconciliation with the peasants but to intensify the harsh regimen. In September 1946 the peasants were ordered to return all collective property taken over during the war. Discipline was increased, tax rates remained severe, and new laws expropriated 90 percent of their wartime savings. A new Council of Kolkhoz Affairs under Andreyev sought to revive agriculture. Agricultural prices remained lower than the cost of transportation for some commodities such as potatoes. There was a vast plan of massively reducing the number of kolkhozy (agricultural communes, which fell from 250,000 to 97,000) and hence expanding their size. In 1950 the basic unit of the collective farm was changed from the link, a group of six to nine who were often family members, to the brigade of over one hundred people. Attacks on private plots continued apace. Other schemes, such as Khrushchev's 1950 Agrocity proposal of turning villages into semimodern rural centers, and the Stalinist plan for the transformation of nature in 1949, were considered.[41]

---

[39]Nove, *An Economic History of the USSR*, chapter 11.
[40]Nove, *An Economic History of the USSR*, chapter 11.
[41]Nove, *An Economic History of the USSR*, chapter 11.

The lot of the peasants remained primitive and backward. Grain production per capita in 1952 was lower than in 1913. In 1949 collectivization was extended to the Baltics. For one year's work the average peasant received a cash income that would not even buy a poor quality suit—and it took twenty days' pay to buy a bottle of vodka. With excessive bureaucratic centralism, very low agricultural prices, weak investment, minimal incentives, and excessive taxes on private plots, the peasants staggered along, isolated from the regime, passive, and dependent for survival on their private plots and own animals.[42]

ZHDANOVSHCHINA

The main political trend in the postwar era was the growing policy of cultural and intellectual repression, driven by Russian nationalism and anti-Semitism. This policy was called *zhdanovshchina,* named after Andrei Zhdanov, who died in 1948. It continued after his death and represented the policy of Stalin. Stalin intended to cut the Soviet Union off from pernicious Western influences.

One aspect of this policy was an emphasis on traditional Russian nationalism, chauvinism, and patriotism, which had been prominent features of Tsarist Russia and had been revived in the war years. In his May 1945 victory toast, Stalin drank a toast solely to the Russian people, whom he called primarily responsible for victory in the war. Stalin, although himself a Georgian, hailed the Russians as the elder brothers of the minorities, as a nation that inspired, taught, and promoted socialism and culture. Stalin exalted Russians, as had the tsars, as civilizers, masters, and protectors of lesser nationalities. His minions soon proclaimed that nearly all Western scientific inventions, from the electric lamp to the radio, had actually been made by Russians. He hailed the great Russian tsars, including Ivan the Terrible and Peter the Great.

This Russian nationalism meant oppression for the nationalities within the Soviet Union. During the war Stalin transferred over 1 million people belonging to seven minority nationalities, including the Volga Germans and Crimean Tatars, to Central Asia and Siberia for their anti-Soviet behavior.[43] In 1948 and 1949 almost 600,000 Balts would be forcibly exiled from the Baltics for their "heinous" attitudes. This followed similar mass deportations from Western Ukraine, Western Belarus, and Bessarabia, all retaken at the end of the war. Histories of the non-Russians condemned their resistance to Tsarist Russian annexations, attempts to maintain a separate culture, and desire to promote "deviant" views such as Islam and bourgeois nationalism. Books glorified the Russians and Slavs and virtues of Tsarist Russia, to the exclusion of the non-Russians.[44]

A second aspect of this policy was an open attack on intellectuals, who are

[42]Nove, *An Economic History of the USSR,* chapter 11.
[43]See Robert Conquest, *The Nation Killers: The Soviet Deportation of Nationalities,* Macmillan, New York, 1970.
[44]D'Encausse, *Stalinism: Order Through Terror,* chapter 7.

rarely popular in any society. Stalin pandered to the peasants and bulk of urban dwellers, who had less than an elementary education and had come only recently from the countryside. They often viewed bureaucrats and intellectuals as responsible for their problems.

In 1946 Zhdanov denounced the poet Anna Akhmatova as a "whore" and the humorist Mikhail Zoshchenko as a "literary swindler" and formalist, pandering to the West. Zhdanov attacked such foreigners as Albert Einstein and Jean Paul Sartre, declaiming "Could they have endured what we endured?" Evgen Varga was attacked and his Institute of World Economy abolished for daring to suggest that capitalism might stabilize after the war. Zhdanov even gave the famous Soviet composer Sergei Prokofiev a piano lesson in "Communist music" and belittled the "formalism" of Dmitrii Shostakovich and Aram Khachaturian. The regime blasted wave mechanics, cybernetics, psychoanalysis, and genetics. Charlatans like Trofim Lysenko soon came to dominate branches of science.[45]

The regime went further, even deifying Stalin. The great victories of World War II, the long tradition of Tsarist authority figures, the remoteness of Stalin, and the low educational level of the population enhanced the effectiveness of this effort. The state built enormous monuments to Stalin, staged extensive celebration of his seventieth birthday, distributed 20 million copies of his writings, and attributed infallibility to him on all key issues of the day.[46]

A further step was stress on the superiority of the Soviet system. Stalin in his February 1946 speech argued that the war showed the superiority of the Soviet system over the decadent West. By February 1947 he was banning marriages with decadent foreigners. Stalin promoted a modern version of the Tsarist concept of Russia as the Third Rome, uncontaminated by the degeneration of the West.

The campaign against Jews and "rootless cosmopolitans" came to full flower after 1948. Anti-Semitism had been nurtured by many tsars and bureaucrats who advanced the slogan "Beat the Jews and Save Russia." Tsar Nicholas II was a member of the anti-Semitic Black Hundreds and approved of pogroms against Jews. Although Lenin condemned anti-Semitism, by the late 1930s anti-Semitism was rising in the Party. The violent anti-Semitism of Nazi Germany penetrated Russia during the 1941–1943 period of German occupation. The Germans slaughtered over 1 million Soviet Jews during the Holocaust. After 1937 Stalin excluded Jews from top positions in the Party, army, government, and secret police, confining them to a role as a technical intelligentsia.

Stalin was not a crude anti-Semite of the Nazi variety. There were Jews in leading positions (Lazar Kaganovich and Maxim Litvinov), his mistress was Jewish (Rosa Kaganovich), and there were more Jews in the Central Committee in 1930, after his rise to power, than before it. His educational policies in the

---

[45]Adam Ulam, *Stalin: The Man and His Era*, Viking Press, Boston, 1973, chapter 13; and D'Encausse, *Stalinism: Order Through Terror*, chapter 7.

[46]Roy Medvedev, *Let History Judge*, Alfred Knopf, New York, 1972, chapter 14.

1930s benefited Jews, who outnumbered Ukrainians in the universities even though there were over ten times more Ukrainians than Jews in the population. It was Soviet arms, not American arms (for the United States maintained an arms embargo in 1948), that helped establish the state of Israel in 1948—and the Soviet Union was the first state to recognize Israel.

However, by the late 1940s Stalin decided to move against Soviet Jews, a small group of several million people without strong popular support but with considerable public visibility. With relatives in the West and a strong orientation towards Western culture and a critical view, they seemed to personify the "rootless cosmopolitanism" Stalin sought to obliterate. The enthusiastic reaction of Soviet Jews to the creation of the state of Israel and the desire of many Jews to emigrate to Israel seemed treasonous to Stalin. In 1948 the wartime Jewish Anti-Fascist Committee was abolished and its members, led by the famous actor Solomon Mikhoels and the former Assistant Foreign Commissar Solomon Lozovsky, were shot in 1949 and 1952. By 1952 thirty leading Soviet Jewish intellectuals and poets, led by Peretz Markish, were dead.

The high point came after a series of anti-Semitic purge trials in Eastern Europe. In January 1953 the press disclosed that nine leading Kremlin doctors, of whom seven were Jews, had been arrested as agents of American, British, and Zionist intelligence (the Jewish relief organization, the Joint) on charges of poisoning two former Kremlin leaders and intending to poison a number of other top leaders. In this "Doctors' Plot" likely victims included Beria, Malenkov, Molotov, and perhaps Andreyev and Voroshilov (both had Jewish wives). Thousands of Jews were expelled from medical schools, hospitals, and various institutions. Hooligans beat up Jews in the streets, and books by Jewish authors were removed from the shelves. Jews were denied many jobs and quotas were lightened in higher education. By March 1953 Jews were purged from top Party, secret police, judicial, and ministerial positions. Jewish cultural institutions were closed and Jewish organizations disbanded. Stalin made plans to expel the Jews from the major cities and resettle them in ghettos in Central Asia and the Far East. All these plans came to naught when Stalin died in March 1953, the doctors were exonerated, and formal, violent anti-Semitism vanished from the press.[47]

LENINGRAD AFFAIR

The major purge of the postwar era came in Leningrad after the death of Andrei Zhdanov in 1948. Zhdanov had been a rising young star in the Soviet firmament, only to have his life cut short with a notable assist from alcoholism. Lavrentii Beria and Georgii Malenkov saw this as an opportunity to eliminate Zhdanov's associates in Leningrad and Moscow. Early in 1949 a massive purge swept away the bulk of Zhdanov's associates. The most notable victims were the Politburo member and head of Gosplan (Nikolai Voznesensky), the Russian

---

[47]Medvedev, *Let History Judge,* chapter 13.

Education Minister (Voznesensky's brother), the secretary of the Leningrad party organization (Popkov), the Prime Minister of the Russian Republic (Mikhail Rodionov), and the head of the Leningrad Soviet (Aleksei Kuznetsov). Thousands of other Leningrad officials in the party, scientific, educational, and factory elite were shot or sent to Siberia.

There were no public trials and Voznesensky was evidently found innocent at his first secret trial. The case, unlike the Great Purges, was hushed up and may have had more connection with the succession struggle than with Stalin's own wishes. Aleksei Kosygin managed to survive the purges and later rise to the top of Soviet politics.[48]

NINETEENTH PARTY CONGRESS

Less than five months before Stalin died in March 1953, the Party suddenly held its Nineteenth Party Congress, the first in thirteen years. Stalin, already very sick, gave only a brief report lasting seven minutes, rather than the usual five or six hours. Georgii Malenkov gave the main report, and others, such as Khrushchev and Saburov also gave important reports. Most striking was the creation of a new twenty-five-member Presidium to replace the old eleven-member Politburo and the Orgburo. One-third of the Presidium's members had not even been delegates at the last Party Congress in 1939. At the congress the ill Stalin asked to be relieved of his position as General Secretary—and debate continues on whether or not this was accepted. Stalin attacked his old colleagues Molotov and Mikoyan, yet they were not removed from power. There were no mass purges, save the Leningrad Affair, which had already been completed at this time.

The final congress of the Stalin era epitomized the final years of Stalin. An ailing and suspicious Stalin was evidently laying plans for a new, great purge, to be signalled by a pogrom against the Jews and their "voluntary" removal to a distant exile. After that, Stalin apparently planned to remove many of his trusted lieutenants and shrink the Presidium back to its normal size. Yet by early 1953 he had not accomplished this. With the lessons of 1937 fresh in their mind, perhaps Stalin's likely victims were not entirely idle. The stasis and stagnation continued for several more months until Stalin became severely ill in March 1953 and suddenly died, opening the door to a new era.[49]

The aging Stalin gradually lost control in the postwar era. Much like Mao Zedong in his final years, Stalin was too powerful and important to be ousted, but too far removed from the urgent demands of political reality to be followed. His program of virulent Russian nationalism, anti-Semitism, confrontation with the West, anti-intellectualism, and deification of the leader—in itself a striking Russian anticipation of the Chinese Cultural Revolution in Mao's final years—

---

[48]See *Khrushchev Speaks*, University of Michigan Press, Ann Arbor, 1963, p. 10; and *Khrushchev Remembers*, translated by Strobe Talbott, Little Brown, Boston, 1974, chapter 8.
[49]Ulam, *Stalin: The Man and His Era*, chapter 14.

was, like its Chinese variant, to be undone soon after his death. In his final years the aging leader, again much like Mao, reached back to the formula that had worked so well for him in an earlier period, in this case the 1930s, and tried to apply it under radically different circumstances. The result was a standoff between Stalin and much of the leadership. Only the removal of the old leader could open the door to a new Soviet orientation.

12

Khrushchev Era

The turbulent years following the death of Stalin in March 1953 stand out against the inertia of the late Stalin era and the bureaucratic conservatism of the Brezhnev years. The arrest and execution of Beria, the rise and fall of Malenkov, the rise of Khrushchev, his near ouster in 1957 and overthrow in 1964, and his numerous and flamboyant policy proposals marked this exciting era, which foreshadowed the Gorbachev era.

WHO WAS KHRUSHCHEV?

Nikita Khrushchev, like Joseph Stalin, seemed an unlikely leader of the Soviet Union.[1] In March 1953 Khrushchev ranked only number five in the Party. How could Khrushchev compare with Georgii Malenkov, Stalin's presumed heir apparent, or with Lavrentii Beria, the ruler of a vast secret police empire? What about Vyacheslav Molotov, for years the man closest to Stalin, or Lazar Kaganovich, Khrushchev's patron and powerful member of the Politburo? Khrushchev arrived in Moscow only in 1950, when his rivals had already been there for decades. He was a colorful and self-reliant man, an uncultured man, in a sea of cautious bureaucratic maneuverers.

Khrushchev was born in 1894 in a mud hut with a ragged thatch roof in the Russian village of Kursk. His grandfather was a serf, and his father, like Stalin's, a seasonal worker. Khrushchev left school at nine to herd cows. By

---

[1]See Edward Crankshaw, *Khrushchev: A Career*, Viking, New York, 1966; Frank Roberts, "Encounters With Khrushchev," in Martin McCauley, editor, *Khrushchev and Khrushchevism*, Indiana University Press, Bloomington, 1987, chapter 12; and Carl Linden, *Khrushchev and the Soviet Leadership*, Johns Hopkins University Press, Baltimore, 1990, chapter 7.

fifteen he was a fitter in a Donbass coal mine. After the October Revolution he joined the Red Army, and he became a Bolshevik in 1918. By the middle 1920s he had become literate, graduated from mining school, and he began to work full time for the Party. In 1929 he ran the Party cell in the Industrial Academy in Moscow. Within five short years, under the tutelage of Kaganovich, he became Moscow Party boss and helped build the Moscow subway. He enthusiastically supported Stalin and the Great Purges. In January 1937, at a rally of 200,000 Muscovites, he attacked the "murderers" in the Party and declaimed that "Stalin is our banner. Stalin is our will. Stalin is our victory." He called on the Party to "finish off and wipe out all the remnants of these vile murderers, fascist agents, Trotskyites, Zinovieties, and right wing accomplices."[2] He ran the Ukrainian Party machine from 1938 to 1949, not hesitating to carry out massive purges.

During the war years he was a leading political commissar in the army. After a brief demotion in 1947, he bounced back and in 1950 moved to Moscow, evidently as part of Stalin's desire to balance the rise of Malenkov. His proposal to build vast agrotowns in the countryside (agro-cities) showed his basic temperament.

His personality was both an asset and a liability. His coarse, often drunken, savage, bullying style hardly marked him as Stalin's successor. His rashness, impulsiveness, and propensity for risk taking often led him into trouble. On the positive side his quick wit, earthy humanity, intense curiosity, powerful personality, and strong ego did stand him in good stead. It was the weakness of his enemies added to his own cunning, his political base in Moscow and Ukraine, and his populism that drove him forward.[3]

THE RISE AND FALL OF GEORGII MALENKOV: 1953–1955

Stalin's death in March 1953 was fortunate for the old Stalinists.[4] Stalin seemed to be preparing a great purge of the Jews and many key associates, such as Beria, Voroshilov, Kaganovich, and Molotov. The new leaders moved quickly to consolidate power.

Within two weeks of Stalin's passing, Georgii Malenkov, the heir apparent, was forced to yield the leadership of the Party to Khrushchev. The First Secretary ran the Party organization, and the Chairman of the Council of Ministers ran the government. The Party post had been important under Stalin, but it was uncertain which would be more important in the future. Lenin, for example, had been head of government, not the Party. A troika of Malenkov (Prime Minister) and Beria and Molotov (First Deputy Prime Ministers) ran the country. Below them in order came Voroshilov, Khrushchev, Bulganin, Ka-

[2]Crankshaw, *Khrushchev: A Career*, pp. 106, 114.
[3]See Roberts, "Encounters with Khrushchev," in McCauley, *Khrushchev and Khrushchevism*, chapter 12.
[4]This has fueled speculation that his death may not have been accidental, that men like Beria may have accelerated it. However, there is no firm evidence, and the aging Stalin may simply have brought about his own downfall.

ganovich, and Mikoyan.[5] Malenkov ran the government, Khrushchev the Party, Beria the secret police, Bulganin the military, and Mikoyan trade. At Stalin's funeral only members of the troika gave orations.[6]

Most Soviet specialists expected a continuation of "Stalinism without Stalin," of a continued totalitarianism. In foreign affairs, the Korean War and Cold War presented serious dangers. The terror of the Great Purges and the Leningrad Affair hovered over the new leaders. The standard of living was abysmally low, especially in housing, consumer goods, and food. Grain production was lower than before 1940, and meat production below the 1916 level. Overcentralization, poor quality, and a general conservatism plagued industry. The state-dominated agriculture, which received few resources from the state, produced little in return.[7]

The leaders reinstated normal business hours for ministries (Stalin had preferred to work late at night), reduced the Presidium to its normal size, and purged Stalin's personal clique (Alexander Poskrebyshev, the commandants of the Kremlin Guards, the Kremlin and the Moscow Military district, and Stalin's son). They exonerated the accused in the Doctor's Plot and Mingrelian Plot (an obscure plot of the early 1950s aimed at Beria's native Mingrelian tribe in Georgia) and freed Mrs. Molotov from a labor camp. They instituted regular meetings of the Presidium and Central Committee and allowed greater freedom of discussion of policy issues.

However, there could be no personal security as long as the master of hundreds of thousands of secret police troops and millions of labor camp inmates sat in the troika. Beria's brutality, cruelty, and double-dealing were notorious in the Kremlin. In June 1953 Beria was arrested, evidently by top military officers, at a Party meeting. He was soon tried and executed along with a number of other top secret police officials. The government sharply reduced the powers of the secret police, thereby removing the threat to the other leaders and also weakening Beria's ally, Malenkov.[8]

Opposition to Khrushchev began to crumble. Molotov, in his early sixties, was deeply identified as Stalin's alter ego and a faceless bureaucrat. Malenkov, physically unimpressive, relatively cold and remote, was stained by his role as an accomplice of Yezhov in the Great Purges and Beria in the Leningrad Affair. Kaganovich (Jewish) and Mikoyan (Armenian) never offered a real challenge for the leadership, and Voroshilov was too old.[9] The massive problems facing the country added to the woes of the succession.[10]

[5]Alec Nove, *Stalinism and After,* Allen and Unwin, London, 1982, p. 121.

[6]Malenkov's famous forged photograph of himself with Mao Zedong did not prevent his loss of power.

[7]Nove, *Stalinism and After,* chapter 5; and Jerry Hough and Merle Fainsod, *How the Soviet Union Is Governed,* Harvard University Press, Cambridge, 1979, chapter 6.

[8]See Tadeusz Wittlin, *Commissar,* Macmillan, New York, 1970.

[9]See Nove, *Stalinism and After,* chapter 5; and Roy and Zhores Medvedev, *Khrushchev: The Years in Power,* translated by Andrew Durkin, Columbia University Press, New York, 1976, chapter 1.

[10]Carl Linden adumbrated the orthodox and reform courses well in his book on Khrushchev written originally in the 1960s. See Carl Linden, *Khrushchev and the Soviet Leadership,* Johns Hopkins University Press, Baltimore, 1990, chapter 1.

MALENKOV'S NEW COURSE

Malenkov's response to the political problems was to initiate a "New Course" policy in 1953 and 1954. Abroad, he ended the Korean War in July 1953 and pushed for the Austrian State Treaty of February 1955. In an August 1953 speech instituting his "New Course," Malenkov promised to improve the food supply, institute tax reform, lessen delivery quotas for farmers, and increase raw materials for light industry. He wanted to consolidate the collective farms and provide more incentives for them. He canceled tax arrears and reduced by 50 percent the tax on private holdings of collective farmers.

The New Course emphasized more and better-quality consumer goods for a depressed population. For the first time in a quarter century the rate of production of consumer goods was set to increase more rapidly than that of heavy industrial goods. The plan increased the quality of housing, hospitals, and schools on the institutional front and the provision of potatoes and vegetables.[11] The New Course allowed for more cultural diversity, as reflected in the publication of Ilya Ehrenburg's novel, *The Thaw*. Stalin was for the moment neither a villain nor a great hero.

The New Course gained public approval but was deeply flawed. Party apparatchiki and the military-industrial complex resisted the cuts in defense spending. Malenkov, with hands stained by the Great Purges and Leningrad Affair, never faced up to the issue of Stalin's crimes. Only 16,000 of many millions of victims and labor camp inmates were released.[12] Malenkov lacked the resources to dramatically increase consumer goods. Reductions in the price of retail and agricultural goods without an increase in production only increased lines and the gap between free and official prices. The elimination of "voluntary" bond sales increased the gap between wages and goods. The rise in agricultural procurement prices was costly for the budget. His program to increase popular income and production of consumer goods, food, and housing while continuing stress on industrial and military products was economically unwise. By refusing to adjudicate the competing claims, he set the stage for his fall.[13]

KHRUSHCHEV'S AGRICULTURAL INITIATIVES

Khrushchev dominated the rural scene. A product of the countryside who had run Ukraine for thirteen years and been Stalin's agricultural specialist, Khrushchev knew more about agriculture than any top leader outside of Andreyev. His frequent tours of the countryside gave him a first-hand perspective lacking in others.

In September 1953 Khrushchev revealed just how terrible things were in the countryside. He cited statistics on the abysmal level of grain (25 percent

---

[11]See Basil Dmytryshyn, *USSR: A Concise History,* Charles Scribners, New York, 1973, pp. 279–280.
[12]Medvedev, *Khrushchev: the Years in Power,* chapters 1, 2.
[13]Alec Nove, *An Economic History of the USSR,* Penguin, Harmondworth, England, 1976, chapter 12.

lower per capita than in 1913) and meat production (lower than 1916). In 1953 Soviet yields in agriculture were only one-third those of Europe. Collective farms provided peasants with a minimal income which was supplemented by their private plots. Huge war losses further depressed an already backward sector, which received only 14 percent of all state investment.[14]

The peasants were still bitter over the repression of the early 1930s, the expropriation of their land, the hypercentralized and remote command system, the perversities of the planning process, and the huge bureaucratic structure. They were alienated by the lack of labor incentives, the misallocation of capital, the lack of animal and mechanical power, the poor storage facilities and transportation network, and the basic hostility of the regime to their interests. Waste, corruption, stealing, and indifference were at the core of this system. In 1952 procurement prices were below the cost of production, and sometimes even transportation.[15]

Khrushchev, the eternal optimist, believed that it was possible to make the rural sector a productive socialist sector. In September 1953 he increased procurement prices for vegetables by 40 percent, for milk and butter by 200 percent, and for meat and poultry by 550 percent. Khrushchev increased agricultural investment and the production of fertilizers and agricultural equipment. He wrote off farm debts, provided funds to pay most transport costs, decreased taxes, and strongly promoted the production of tractors. He sent 30,000 Communists to rural areas to strengthen the Party.[16]

Khrushchev proposed an end run around the mammoth rural problems. In February 1954 he called for a Virgin Lands program to develop 74 million acres of marginal farm land in the Urals, Siberia, and Central Asia. No fewer than 300,000 volunteers, 50,000 tractors, and 6000 trucks were deployed in this campaign to open the eastern region, a territory with arable land equal to that of Canada. This was a daring ploy, given the high risk of drought in these marginal agricultural lands, usually left fallow for grazing by nomadic cattle, and the enormous problems of starting up agriculture in a primitive and remote region with minimal resources. Good 1954 and 1956 harvests seemed to vindicate this strategy, which produced over 65 percent of the increase in grain production between 1953 and 1963.[17] Khrushchev then proposed in January 1955 a massive program to plant 70 million acres with corn for fodder.[18]

Khrushchev's program faced daunting problems. It was highly improvisational and daring without adequate resources to back it up. Khrushchev stressed socialism and the elimination of private plots at a time when most

[14]G.E. Smith, "Agriculture," in Martin McCauley, editor, *Khrushchev and Khrushchevism*, Indiana University Press, Bloomington, 1987, chapter 6.

[15]Dmytryshyn, *USSR: A Concise History*, pp. 276–278; and Smith, "Agriculture," in McCauley, *Khrushchev and Khrushchevism*, p. 102.

[16]Medvedev, *Khrushchev: the Years of Power*, chapter 3; and Nove, *An Economic History of the USSR*, pp. 327–329.

[17]Smith, "Agriculture," in McCauley, *Khrushchev and Khrushchevism*, p. 104; and Medvedev, *Khrushchev: Years of Power*, pp. 58–59.

[18]Dmytryshyn, *USSR: A Concise History*, pp. 278–279.

peasants wanted their own lands and less socialism, not more. Private plots remained, but only at the margin of agriculture. His stress on increased size of farms and more machinery represented a form of "gigantomania" not well suited to Russian conditions. In the short run, however, his program and his frequent trips around the country helped to position Khrushchev to succeed Malenkov in 1955.

THE YEARS OF ASCENT AND TRIUMPH: 1955–1957

In February 1955 Khrushchev ousted Malenkov as the Prime Minister. Malenkov admitted his "guilt" in agriculture (actually Khrushchev's area), his "inexperience" in administration (actually his strong suit), and his error in opposing heavy industry. Riding support from a military-industrial complex upset at Malenkov's program, Khrushchev replaced Malenkov with Bulganin, promoted eleven men as marshals of the Soviet Army, and added proteges (Mikhail Suslov and Aleksei Kirichenko) to the Politburo. Anastas Mikoyan, Mikhail Saburov, and Mikhail Pervukhin were all made First Deputy Prime Ministers. Khrushchev rapidly showed off his new power with state visits to India, Burma, Afghanistan, and Geneva, where he met U.S. President Dwight Eisenhower. He approved new initiatives with the Americans (spirit of Geneva), signed the Austrian State Treaty, created the Warsaw Treaty Organization, and initiated arms sales to the Arab Middle East (Egypt). Yet Khrushchev's enemies (Malenkov, Molotov, and Kaganovich) remained on the Politburo.

At the Twentieth Party Congress in February 1956 Khrushchev boldly struck out at his foes in the famed "secret speech."[19] The Congress was a triumph for Khrushchev, who gave the opening address, read the report for the Central Committee, and watched the Congress approve his followers for membership in leading bodies and the new Sixth Five Year Plan. At the Congress 25 percent of the delegates came from Khrushchev's strongholds in Moscow and Ukraine. The Congress backed Khrushchev by replacing over 40 percent of the members and 60 percent of the alternate members of the Central Committee.

In February 1956 there were several million inmates in the labor camps and only minor limitations of police power.[20] The regime neither praised nor repudiated Stalin. In his secret speech, Khrushchev defended Stalin's actions before 1934 but condemned him for the Great Purges, Leningrad Affair, deportation of national minorities during the war, Doctors' Plot, and other atrocities. Khrushchev lambasted Stalin for his "cult of personality," errors in

---

[19]Although the speech became widely known inside and outside the country, its contents were considered so inflammatory that it was not actually published as part of the Congress proceedings.
[20]For the most detailed treatment of rehabilitation, which ended in 1959, see Albert Van Goudoever, *The Limits of DeStalinization in the Soviet Union,* translated by Frans Hijkoop, St. Martin's Press, New York, 1986.

war leadership, personal megalomania, and persecution phobia. He left open the question of responsibility for Kirov's murder. Soon, millions of people were released from the camps in 1956 and 1957 and millions others who had died were rehabilitated.[21]

Khrushchev tried to discredit not only Stalin but also the remaining Stalinists in the leadership. Although Khrushchev's hands were not clean, they were whiter than those of Kaganovich, Malenkov, and Molotov, who, as Stalin's close aides, were directly implicated in the Great Purges. The Leningrad Affair could be laid directly at the hands of Malenkov and his ally Beria.[22]

Khrushchev's triumph was only temporary. In June 1956 he removed Molotov from the Foreign Ministry, replacing him with Alexander Shelepin, and Kaganovich from the State Committee on Labor and Wages. By fall, the attack on Stalin had unleashed massive unrest in Eastern Europe. In October the Politburo backed off and allowed Wladyslaw Gomulka to become head of the Party in Poland; in November in Hungary only Soviet tanks restored Soviet power in a large-scale bloodbath that killed thousands of Hungarians and sent over 100,000 Hungarians into exile. Conservative bureaucrats, aligning with the old Stalinists, soon launched a powerful counterattack at the weakened Khrushchev. A December 1956 Central Committee plenum abandoned the next Five Year Plan and approved Pervukhin as the new overlord of planning. The Central Committee revised downwards the industrial targets approved earlier at the Congress. By January 1957 Khrushchev was forced to partially rehabilitate Stalin.

Khrushchev soon counterattacked as the situation stabilized in Eastern Europe. By February 1957 he was strong enough at a new Central Committee plenum to reverse the verdict of the December plenum and attack the power of his enemies in Moscow. He called for the abolition of thirty-three central ministries and dispersal of their functions to 105 regional economic councils (*sovnarkhozy*). This would greatly weaken the central bureaucracies, eliminate ministerial empires, and end the problems of regional-central coordination. Regional committee would control most local factories, save for those in weapons, chemicals, and electricity.[23]

But this plan too was deeply flawed. There were too many regional councils and too little central supervision and coordination. Most big factories received many supplies from outside their regions and supplied consumers outside their regions. The inevitable result was chaos, localism, ignoring of technological innovation, reorganizations, and the final restoration of central ministries. Key economic problems, such as isolation from foreign science, stress on quantity over quality, small rewards for progress, fragmentation, and coordination, remained serious.[24]

---

[21]Medvedev, *Khrushchev: The Years of Power,* chapters 1 and 2.
[22]Hough and Fainsod, *How the Soviet Union Is Governed,* chapter 6.
[23]See Nove, *An Economic History of the USSR,* chapter 12, and *Stalinism and Afterwards,* chapter 6.
[24]See Alec Nove, "Industry," in McCauley, *Khrushchev and Khrushchevism,* chapter 4; and M. J. Berry, "Science, Technology Innovation," in McCauley, *Khrushchev and Khrushchevism,* chapter 5.

In May 1957 Khrushchev rashly called for a Soviet version of the Chinese Great Leap Forward, with the Soviet Union to overtake the United States in meat, milk, and butter production per capita by 1961. This would require a tripling of Soviet output without any change in resources. His attention to agriculture did result in a 60 percent increase in rural income between 1952 and 1957. State procurement of grain increased 85 percent between 1953 and 1958.[25]

The showdown came in June 1957. Taking advantage of Khrushchev's trip to Finland, the old Stalinists on the Presidium called for a vote on ousting the impetuous Khrushchev. Led by Malenkov, Molotov, and Kaganovich, they secured a seven to four majority, with only Suslov, Mikoyan, and Kirichenko supporting Khrushchev. At this point, the game should have been over, with Malenkov restored as Prime Minister, Molotov appointed First Secretary of the Party, and Khrushchev demoted to Minister of Agriculture. But Khrushchev refused to accept the vote and demanded a Central Committee vote that would be, for the first time since 1926, a free vote. Here, with the aid of Defense Minister Zhukov, the head of the Committee of State Security Ivan Serov, and all but one of the Presidium alternate members, he was able to overturn the Presidium verdict and bring in hundreds of Central Committee members from all over the Soviet Union for an emergency meeting. Zhukov used military aircraft to fly in Central Committee members from all over the country. At a protracted eight-day meeting of the Central Committee, Khrushchev carried the day, especially with the younger Communists, who wanted a decisive break with the old Stalinists. Khrushchev also won over Voroshilov, Bulganin, Pervukhin, and Saburov, who originally had backed the old Stalinists. Initially, it had been touch and go, and even after victory Khrushchev was unable to expel the opposition from the Party or continue his anti-Stalin campaign. Perhaps 70 percent of the Central Committee favored him. After it was over, he sent Molotov as Ambassador to Outer Mongolia, Malenkov to direct a power station in Central Asia, and Kaganovich to run a cement factory in Sverdlovsk. All four of the leaders were ousted from the Central Committee and Presidium, and in 1958 Bulganin was ousted and in 1961 Voroshilov. Khrushchev added eight new members to the Presidium, including Brezhnev, Zhukov, and Frol Kozlov.[26] In October 1957, to complete the sweep, he purged the outspoken Defense Minister Zhukov from the Presidium. Given Zhukov's key role in Khrushchev's victory in June, it was imperative to put the military back in its proper place.

NEW INITIATIVES: MTS AND EDUCATION (1958)

Now at the height of his powers, Khrushchev in 1958 returned to agriculture to continue his reforms. In April 1958 he was chairman of the Council of Ministers and First Secretary of the Party. The launching of Sputnik in October 1957

---

[25]Nove, *Stalinism and After,* chapter 12.
[26]Medvedev, *Khrushchev: The Years of Power,* chapter 7; Linden, *Khrushchev and the Soviet Leadership,* chapter 3; and Crankshaw, *Khrushchev: A Career.*

elevated Soviet prestige. By 1958 grain output was 70 percent higher than 1953 and grain requisitions had almost doubled.[27]

In 1958 Khrushchev abolished the machine-tractor stations, a mainstay of Stalinist agriculture since 1930. This eliminated the dual subordination of the peasants to the kolkhoz and the machine-tractor station, by folding remnants of the latter under the kolkhoz. He stressed state farms, which after the Virgin Lands campaign incorporated 25 percent of all land, compared to 10 percent in 1952.

Unfortunately, as with everything Khrushchev did, abolishing the machine-tractor stations was done too quickly. Forced to buy the stations' machines (old and new at the same price), shops, and buildings and lacking repair stations, the kolkhozs went deep into debt and were unable to use much of the equipment. Furthermore, 50 percent of the technical personnel of the MTSs moved to the cities, further compounding the problem.[28]

In April 1958 he attacked Soviet education for overemphasis on traditional education and for promoting 55 percent of the students to the eighth grade. By December Khrushchev demanded stress on physical labor for all students and part-time work in factories and plants for high school students. He wanted to expose all students to work and ease access for workers and peasants to higher education. This was widely unpopular and was later reversed, but it fit Khrushchev's background and desire to integrate education and the workplace.[29]

The Twenty-First Congress in 1959 exalted Khrushchev and purged Bulganin for his role with the Anti-Party Group in 1957. Other participants in that action, namely Voroshilov and Pervukhin, managed to hold their positions. The Congress added Nikolai Podgorny and Dmitrii Polyansky, two future members of the Brezhnev team, to candidate membership in the Presidium.

KHRUSHCHEVIAN INNOVATIONS: 1960–1962

By the early 1960s many of Khrushchev's innovations were no longer working. His 1957 industrial decentralization scheme was being revised year by year. By 1962 there were only forty-two regional economic councils, and significant power over construction, new designs, and technology had been given back to the center. Duplication, parallelism, and dissipation of efforts were the rule of the day. Yet in 1962 Khrushchev struck back in the Party arena, with a new scheme to divide the Party into two parts at the lower levels. All key regions were divided into industrial and regional Party committees, each with a separate staff. This widely unpopular maneuver created two Party first secretaries and two executive committees for each region.[30]

[27]Linden, *Khrushchev and the Soviet Leadership,* p. 37.
[28]Ibid., chapter 8.
[29]Donald Treadgold, *Twentieth Century Russia,* Westview Press, Boulder, Colorado, 1990, chapter 29.
[30]Hough and Fainsod, *How the Soviet Union Is Governed,* chapter 6; and Barbara Chotiner, *Khrush-*

His agricultural policies yielded little benefit, as grain production in the early 1960s ran a paltry 10 percent ahead of its level in the late 1950s.[31] At times he was acutely embarrassed, as in the famous Riazan fiasco. In 1959 the head of the Riazan oblast promised to double meat output in a year—and he did, by slaughtering all local livestock and buying cattle elsewhere to fulfill the campaign. When this became known in 1960, the secretary committed suicide and Khrushchev lost face.[32] The Virgin Lands experiment began to go awry. Soil erosion, lack of standardized agricultural methods, and remoteness from the center of the country led to costly failures. So, too, did Khrushchev's program to grow corn, regardless of the suitability of the climate, at the expense of all other crops after 1957. Attempts to reorganize the Ministry of Agriculture and relocate it in rural areas met with disaster.[33]

His anti-Stalin campaign also ran aground in 1961 at the Twenty-Second Party Congress. There he tried to expel Molotov, Malenkov, and Kaganovich from the party for their role in the Great Purges and other Stalinist excesses. Khrushchev attacked Kaganovich as a sadist and provided documents showing the culpability of the leaders of the Anti-Party Group for the "mass slaughter" of the Great Purges. Yet the Party elite refused to expel or indict them or even open their cases, although it did approve removing Stalin's body from Lenin's mausoleum. Conservatives, such as Suslov and Kozlov, came to the fore as a number of Khrushchev's allies lost their positions.[34]

Yet at this same congress Khrushchev laid out an ambitious Party program to exceed the American standard of living by 1970 and achieve the basics of communism by 1980. Khrushchev brashly proclaimed that by 1980 the Soviet Union would achieve a 500 percent increase in industrial production, a 350 percent increase in labor productivity, the production of 250 millions tons of steel, and a rapid increase in consumer goods. Khrushchev proclaimed that by 1980 the Soviet consumer would surpass the American consumer, transportation, utilities, and housing would be free, there would be a cornucopia of free nurseries, kindergartens, books, clothes, education, and hot lunches for all. All this would be achieved with a 400 percent increase in the national income and a 250 percent increase in per capita income.[35]

Bolstered by space exploits, such as Yuri Gagarin's becoming the first man to orbit the earth in April 1961, and the development of heavy rockets, Khrushchev unsuccessfully challenged the West in the 1961 Berlin crisis and the 1962 Cuban Missile Crisis. He reduced the size of the Soviet military from 5.6 million men in 1956 to 3.0 million in 1961 and made plans for further major reductions before they were frozen by the Berlin crisis of 1961.

---

chev's Party Reform, Greenwood Press, Westport, Connecticut, 1984.

[31]Smith, "Agriculture," in McCauley, *Khrushchev and Khrushchevism*, p. 108.

[32]Medvedev, *Khrushchev: The Years of Power*, chapter 9.

[33]Ibid., chapters 10–11.

[34]See Van Goudoever, *The Limits of DeStalinization in the Soviet Union*, p. 91.

[35]Dmytryshyn, *USSR: A Concise History*, chapter 9.

BEFORE THE FALL: 1962–1964

Many of Khrushchev's programs were in deep trouble even before he was ousted in October 1964. In agriculture he had promised a 70 percent increase by 1965, but achieved only 10 percent. The kolkhozs were overburdened with payments from the elimination of the MTS and there were too few technicians to run the machinery. The rural areas were groaning under the endless campaigns initiated from above without concern for local problems. The relations between center and periphery remained far too weighted towards the center. Repeated reorganization of the state machinery achieved little. The attack on private plots only further reduced incentive to produce for market. The inherent weakness of the Virgin Lands program was a perennial problem. The campaign to quintuple output of fertilizer by 1970 was totally unrealistic. Khrushchev set impossible goals, interfered and reorganized far too much, and neglected the basic interests of the peasants. His failure was noticeable when in 1964 agricultural production was only 13 percent above the 1958 level.[36]

How, then, did Khrushchev remain in power? It is important to remember that the Soviet economy was still functioning relatively well. In 1965 national income was 58 percent higher than it had been in 1958, industrial production 84 percent higher, steel production 91 percent higher, and oil production 243 percent higher.[37] The problem then, unlike now, was not the performance of the economy but the specific policies of Khrushchev. His boasts of overtaking the United States by 1970 and achieving full communism with free housing, meals, and a 35-hour week by 1980, were simply fantasies, without any base in reality.

In many ways this epitomizes the Khrushchev era. He tried to implement radical populist and utopian programs without fundamentally changing the nature of the system. His stress on mass participation, regional economic councils, bifurcation of the Party, appeals to the Central Committee over the Presidium, adding experts to many policy bodies, and repeated major changes sought to shake up the highly centralized bureaucratic structure. All this was to be done without terror and with the support of strong elements within the system. Yet he himself exercised enormous power, without restraint, and he often acted recklessly and without foresight.[38] But in the end he failed to dismantle the strong power base of the privileged bureaucracy which, by October 1964, was unified in its determination to overthrow him.[39]

By the fall of 1964 he had succeeded in deeply alienating all the key power bases of Soviet politics. Much of the military was offended by the deep cuts in ground forces, the forcible demobilization of over 100,000 officers, and the lack of any clear role for the traditional mainstays of the military—the ground forces

---

[36]Nove, *Stalinism and After,* chapter 6, and *An Economic History of the USSR,* chapter 12.
[37]Nove, *An Economic History of the USSR,* p. 353.
[38]See Ronald Hill, "State and Ideology," and Graeme Gill, "Khrushchev and Systemic Development," in McCauley, *Khrushchev and Khrushchevism,* pp. 36–51.
[39]See Martin McCauley, "Khrushchev As Leader," in McCauley, *Khrushchev and Khrushchevism,* chapter 1.

and tactical air force. The secret police was maimed by his continuing attacks on Stalin, frequent attacks on their past deeds, and the lack of a legitimate role in Soviet society. The Party apparatchiki were appalled by his 1962 bifurcation of the Party, his extravagant boasts and promises, the lack of any systemic thrust to his policies, and his policies of rotation of one-third of the elite at every congress. The industrial bureaucracies were still reeling and trying to undo his 1957 implementation of regional economic councils that had decimated their power and status. The agricultural ministry was trying to recover from being sent to the countryside and being expected to conduct numerous and unrealistic agricultural campaigns. The intellectuals were disappointed by his anti-intellectualism, educational policies, and lack of support for a real thaw in Soviet culture. His spectacular foreign policy failures in the Berlin crisis of 1961 and Cuban Missile Crisis of 1962 undercut his authority.

And so, in October 1964, a conspiracy was hatched while Khrushchev was on vacation at the Black Sea. Despite all the forces on their side, his opponents still must have wondered whether they could succeed. For in 1957 Khrushchev had managed to beat back the Anti-Party Group, and he still retained considerable powers. Now the coup was led by three senior leaders of the party (Brezhnev, Suslov, and Kosygin). At the Presidium meeting held on Khrushchev's return to Moscow, they castigated him for "harebrained" scheming, for being too old and too uncontrolled, for alienating so many segments of Soviet society and politics, and for wielding absolute authority. Suslov led the conspirators, decrying Khrushchev's arbitrary, uncouth style and cult of personality. He was denounced for extravagant promises, for denigrating ideology, for demagoguery, and extreme personal conceit. His errors in domestic and foreign affairs were thoroughly covered. Mikoyan on the Presidium tried to defend Khrushchev, but he was a lone voice in the wilderness.

Khrushchev was alone, and after his fall not one other member of the Presidium was ousted with him. Only the heads of Pravda and radio and television were ousted. The public response was apathetic, and the flamboyant Khrushchev era ended, like the Gorbachev era, not with a bang but with a whimper. He went into the night with a pension, car, villa, and a small staff to attend him and guard him.[40]

Twenty-five years later, Gorbachev surely mulled over the lessons of Khrushchev's failure. Gorbachev worked hard to keep good relations with the secret police and military, who were important in Khrushchev's ouster. He never made flamboyant promises or resorted to the kind of demagoguery that got Khrushchev into such trouble. He avoided the cult of personality that so outraged many after the excesses of Stalin. Gorbachev tried to outflank the conservative bureaucrats by exposing them to popular indignation through elections to the Congress of People's Deputies and through creation of a meaningful alternative to his Party role in his government role. He also cultivated the West, rather than alienating it, and thereby avoided spectacular

---

[40]William Hyland and Richard Shyrock, *The Fall of Khrushchev*, Funk and Wagnalls, New York, 1968, chapter 8; and Crankshaw, *Khrushchev: A Career*, chapter 20.

failures like the Cuban Missile Crisis and Berlin crisis. Surely one of the most rapt readers of the chapters of Khrushchev's life had to be Gorbachev, who, as he sought to similarly reform Soviet society, wanted to avoid Khrushchev's fate. Yet, in the end, he too fell, but this time to the popular wrath that he unleashed rather than to the conservative bureaucrats whom he bested in the August 1991 coup.

13

Brezhnev Years

The eighteen years of Brezhnev's rule, which began during the Johnson presidency and ended during the Reagan presidency, represented the last hurrah for the Stalinist polity and economy. The Soviet Union achieved strategic nuclear parity with the United States, watched the United States humiliated in Vietnam, extended its influence and power in the Third World, and became a superpower. At home the standard of living of the population, especially in the first thirteen years of the Brezhnev era, increased steadily. Compared to the *sturm und drang* of the preceding Stalinist and Khrushchev era and the turmoil and chaos of the ensuing Gorbachev and Yeltsin eras, the Brezhnev era stands out as an oasis of stability, almost like the golden era of the 1920s. It was precisely the stability and tranquillity of the era and the overextension of Soviet resources abroad and in the military sector that laid the basis for the sharp decay and petrification of the final years of Brezhnev and disintegration of the Soviet Union under Gorbachev.

WHO WAS BREZHNEV?

The choice of Leonid Brezhnev to head the party continued the tradition of selection of leaders who seemed relatively implausible to Western observers. He had the correct characteristics and was representative of the generation that Stalin raised to power after 1937. He was a generalist from a small town or rural area with technical education. A Russian, Brezhnev had a distinguished war record as a commissar at Stalingrad. He came from the lower classes and was even, in a rare departure from the norm, Khrushchev's choice to succeed him.

Brezhnev held significant posts in the government (President), military (head of the Political Administration of the Navy), and the Party. He worked in both the nationality areas (Ukraine, Moldavia, Kazakhstan) and Russia. He had an engineering background, training in agriculture and industry, and a history of lengthy service as a Party apparatchik. He had few known enemies in the Party and was considered a tough leader.

And yet he seemed implausible. Brezhnev was a backslapping moralizer, a cautious manipulator without any broad vision of the future. A man of low ambitions, he seemed a relatively uninspiring Party hack. His predecessors, with strong visions of the future, favored a relatively simple and austere life. Brezhnev loved the good life—expensive clothes, luxurious and fast cars, yachts, government dachas, seats in the stadium for soccer, boar and duck hunting. His stable of Rolls Royces and Mercedes was not inferior to that of many rich Westerners.[1]

A Soviet joke captures his love for luxury: Brezhnev invites his mother to the Kremlin and shows off the vast opulence at his command. His mother, shrouded in black, fails to show any approval. Then he takes her to his dacha on the Black Sea, and again she shows no approval. Finally, in desperation, Brezhnev turns to his mother and says, "Mama, look at all these things that I have. Aren't you proud of what I accomplished?" And his mother responds, "I just have one question for you." He says, "What?" She says, "What are you going to do when the Reds come back?"

Brezhnev was a Russian born in 1906 in a provincial small town to working-class parents who had toiled for two generations in the steel mills of Dneprodzerzhinsk for foreign companies in Ukraine. He grew up in one room with crude brick walls and earthen floors, in the overcrowded and unsanitary living conditions of an industrial settlement. After graduation from high school, he left town in 1923 to study at the Kursk Technicum. He joined Komsomol that year, but he did not join the Party (as a candidate member) until 1929. In the early 1930s Brezhnev participated in the campaigns to expel the kulaks in the Urals and to seize grain during the Ukrainian famine. He spent five years working as a stoker and fitter in a plant.

In 1935 Brezhnev graduated as a metallurgical engineer. Associated with Khrushchev, he leaped ahead during the Great Purges. By 1939 he was the number five man in the Party of a major industrial province. In the war he helped evacuate the region in the face of the advancing Germans and served as Deputy Chairman of the Political Administration of the Southern Army Group. In 1945 Brezhnev was a major general who helped administer Czechoslovakia and marched in the victory parade in Red Square that June.

After the war he supervised the reconstruction of Zaporozhe province as the Party oblast secretary, and then moved to Dnepropetrovsk. After winning the Order of Lenin in 1947, Brezhnev was sent in 1949 to run the Moldavian

---

[1]For good biographies of Brezhnev, see John Dornberg, *Brezhnev: The Masks of Power*, Andre Deutsch, London, 1974; and Paul Murphy, *Brezhnev: Soviet Politician*, McFarland and Company, Jefferson, North Carolina, 1981.

Republic for over two years. By 1952 he became the number one candidate member of the Presidium (the Politburo of the time) and the number three member of the Secretariat at the Nineteenth Party Congress. In October 1952, as number seventeen in the Party, he stood near Stalin on Lenin's mausoleum.

Losing out in the maneuvering after Stalin's death, Brezhnev in March 1953 lost both his key positions. He was demoted to a position in the military (head of the Political Administration of the Navy) and began his comeback in June 1953 by helping to throw the Red Army against Beria. In 1954 Khrushchev sent him to run the Virgin Lands program in Kazakhstan. By 1956 his patron rewarded his successful efforts to nearly double grain production in Kazakhstan by making him a candidate member of the Presidium. The ouster of the Anti-Party Group and Brezhnev's support for Khrushchev led to his promotion to full membership in the Presidium in June 1957. For the next several years he helped run the missile program.

In 1960 Khrushchev named him to replace the aging Voroshilov as President of the Supreme Soviet, the nominal President of the country. Taking full advantage of this usually nominal post, Brezhnev became a world traveler, especially in the Third World. As had happened in 1953, in July 1960 he lost an inter-Party struggle and was purged from the Secretariat by the rising Frol Kozlov. But Kozlov's star waned, and in 1963 Kozlov suffered a heart attack. In 1962 Brezhnev stood next to Khrushchev on the reviewing stand for May Day and in July 1964 he left the Presidium for the Secretariat. In 1964 the fifty-eight-year-old Brezhnev, already Khrushchev's heir apparent, took the plunge in overthrowing Khrushchev.

Brezhnev brought to power a distinctive political viewpoint. A pragmatist, he undertook no great initiatives to revive Soviet society and broke no new ideological ground. His notion of "developed socialism" to explain why communism had not been achieved was simply a way to make ideology fit reality. He would neither re-Stalinize nor de-Stalinize Soviet society. For him, as seen in the 1977 Constitution, the Soviet Union was a developed socialist society whose problems could be resolved by the scientific-technological revolution, planning, national integration, and the timetable of communism. The party was to be the vehicle of resolving all conflicts. The 10 million cadres with higher education in the economy provided a sound base for achieving the professional administrative level that would drive the Soviet economy and society to greater successes.[2] He relied heavily on his Dnieper Mafia (his friends from Dnieper-petrovsk) and former associates from the Urals, Moldavia, Kazakhstan, armed forces, Supreme Soviet, and Central Committee.

Riding the tide of conservative reaction to Khrushchevian radical and erratic populism, Brezhnev opposed campaigns to transform society and stressed the need for stability and predictability. Brezhnev emphasized the virtues of selective reforms and budgetary redistribution. He opposed popu-

---

[2]Donald Schwartz, editor, *Resolutions and Decisions of the Communist Party of the Soviet Union*, vol. 5 (*The Brezhnev Years*), University of Toronto Press, Toronto, 1982, pp. 29–33; and Seweryn Bialer, *Stalin's Successors*, Cambridge University Press, Cambridge, 1980, chapter 8.

lism, preferring a bureaucratic regime responsive to popular needs. He increased the use of public opinion polls, made the Party more responsive to the citizenry, and improved legal norms and channels for specialist input. He also prosecuted dissidents, restricted public admission to the Party, ended de-Stalinization, and increased the power of the Party.[3]

BREZHNEV IN POWER: 1964–1965

Brezhnev, in cooperation with Kosygin, Podgorny, and other leading party and military officials, was able to easily sweep Khrushchev away. This was the only successful ouster in Soviet history of a leader who had been in power for more than four years. It was a measure of Khrushchev's isolation that no other members of the ruling elite were ousted apart from his relatives.

The major question for Brezhnev and his allies now was how to govern the Soviet Union. By overthrowing Khrushchev, they gained the support of the disgruntled bureaucracies against Khrushchev's radical populism, utopian promises, and failed organization schema. Now, several possible routes were open to the new leaders. One was a conservative reorganization of the system, to wring the remaining benefits out of the neo-Stalinist command economy. A second was to make substantial reforms, but in a more orderly fashion and at a more measured pace. The third was to attempt a radical reorganization of the society. The third, given the players who supported the new regime, was never in the cards. Brezhnev represented the more conservative of the two remaining routes and Kosygin the more liberal one, but initially, all united in undoing Khrushchev's more outlandish organizational schemas. As *Pravda* proclaimed in October 1964:

> The Leninist party is the enemy of subjectivism and drift in Communist construction. Wild schemes; half baked conclusions and hasty decisions and actions divorced from reality; bragging and bluster; attraction to rule by fiat; unwillingness to take into account what science and practical experience have already worked out—these are alien to the party. The construction of communism is a living, creative undertaking. It does not tolerate armchair methods, one-man decisions or disregard for the practical experience of the masses.[4]

The new leaders ended the bifurcation of the Party in November 1964 and eliminated the *sovnarkhozy* (regional economic councils) by September 1965. They promised to eliminate wild campaigns and "harebrained" scheming and commit to more scientific and pragmatic decision making. Only Khrushchev's relatives, like Alexei Adzhubei, were ousted and men like Kozlov were retired on health grounds. Older veterans, such as Mikoyan and Shvernik, were allowed to retire with honor. Many of Khrushchev's purge victims, such as

[3]George Breslauer, *Khrushchev and Brezhnev As Leaders Building Authority in Soviet Politics,* Allen and Unwin, London, 1982, chapters 8, 15.
[4]*Pravda,* October 17, 1964.

Vladimir Matskevich (Minister of Agriculture), Fyodor Kulakov (chairman of Central Committee department for agriculture), Vladimir Shcherbitsky (Prime Minister of Ukraine) and Dinmukhamed Kunayev (head of the Kazakhstan Communist Party) were returned to power. Some younger leaders, such as Pyotr Shelest (Ukraine) and Alexander Shelepin (KGB), were promoted to full membership on the Politburo, and Pyotr Demichev was promoted to candidate member in November 1964. The new leaders promised routine and stability and an end to threats to the positions of the elite. Brezhnev personally backed gentle change and the traditional role of the Party in the economy.[5]

A stable elite emerged to run the society. A ruling oligarchy headed but not dominated by Leonid Brezhnev, the new Secretary-General of the Party, now took power. In the early years Brezhnev did not seem unduly ambitious and acted largely as a power broker and chairman of the board, who did not enjoy the overwhelming power of a Lenin or a Stalin. He put forth no radical programs of change and accepted distinct limits on his role.

Kosygin emerged as the relatively liberal head of the government, with responsibility for the economy and defense. Podgorny was number two in the Secretariat and helped run defense, the state, and the legislature. Andrei Kirilenko took responsibility for the Party and industrial management while Suslov ran ideology, international communism, and relations with China. Shelepin was given a major role within the Party-state control committee, which he chaired.

The new regime provided security and tenure for the elite. There were no major purges from 1964 until 1973. Only in the middle 1970s were there substantial purges (Gennady Voronov, Pyotr Shelest, Alexander Shelepin, Dmitrii Polyansky, Nikolai Podgorny and Kirill Mazurov).[6] But the core leaders, except for Podgorny, remained intact through the 1970s. The regime recruited numerous new, but relatively old, leaders to the Politburo throughout the 1970s. The eight recruits after 1971 included the future contenders for power in 1982 (Grigorii Romanov, Konstantin Chernenko, Mikhail Gorbachev, Yuri Andropov) and four other aged leaders (Andrei Gromyko, Andrei Grechko, Dmitrii Ustinov, Nikolai Tikhonov). At the last four Party congresses of the Brezhnev era 79, 77, 83 and 89 percent of the full members were reelected.[7]

All major institutions were given significant autonomy in their respective areas. The leaders opposed radical change and de-Stalinization and supported the bureaucratic prerogatives of Party and state officials. They lessened dog-

---

[5]See Donald Kelley, editor, *Soviet Politics In the Brezhnev Era*, Praeger, New York, 1980, chapter 1; Dornberg, *Brezhnev: Masks of Power*; Bialer, *Stalin's Successors*, chapter 4; Schwartz, *Resolutions and Decisions of the Communist Party of the Soviet Union*, vol. 5 *(The Brezhnev Years)*, chapter 1; and Breslauer, *Khrushchev and Brezhnev*, chapter 8.

[6]It should be noted that these purges were simply ousters from their posts, without any of the violent consequences or mass characteristics of Stalin's Great Purges.

[7]Seweryn Bialer, "Political System," in Robert Byrnes, editor, *After Brezhnev: Sources of Soviet Conduct in the 1980s*, Indiana University Press, Bloomington, 1983, chapter 1; and Schwartz, *Resolutions and Decisions of the Communist Party of the Soviet Union 1964–1981*, vol. 5 *(The Brezhnev Years)*, pp. 3–4.

matic controls over the sciences and society, expanded the role of experts, eliminated mass terror, institutionalized the role of key bureaucracies, and sought to respond to popular aspirations. The keynotes of the new regime were dullness, methodical and cautious behavior, gradualism, and order. They sought to improve the popular standard of living, revamp the weak agricultural sector, and improve the food situation. The new oligarchy ended the struggle against bureaucratism, opposed doctrinal innovations, and downplayed any chiliastic hopes of attaining communism. They reasserted traditional values, attacked renegades and dissidents, denigrated bourgeois accomplishments, and proclaimed the greatness of Soviet-style socialism. They accepted the basic premises of the neo-Stalinist command economy, with its supercentralization, lack of autonomy for its subunits, detailed and strict planning, addiction to quantity, and lack of a self-regulating and generating mechanism.[8]

Brezhnev was especially interested in promoting a stable economy which would rely on expert advice and avoid Khrushchev's resort to panaceas. There would be no appeal to the masses but rather a reliance on scientific methods of operation to drive society forward. The regime promoted administrative stability, accommodation to the wishes of Soviet officials, and rationalization of the society. The regime granted in effect virtual life tenure to many elite and mid-level bureaucrats.

During the 1960s men such as Kosygin, Podgorny, and Shelepin enjoyed real power. Only during the 1970s did Brezhnev emerge as nominally the predominant leader. Chairman of the Constitution Committee and chairman of the Russian Party Bureau, in 1966 he was confirmed as General Secretary of the party. Not for a decade would his power formally increase, and even then it would be more on paper than in reality.

BREZHNEV'S AGRICULTURE POLICIES

Brezhnev was well aware of the failures and importance of the rural sector.[9] With first-hand knowledge of rural poverty, he rejected the coercion and neglect of Stalin and the radical quick fixes of Khrushchev. He stressed massive investment of tens of billions of rubles, even 25 to 30 percent of all state investment. He was convinced that with enough tractors, combines, chemicals, private incentives, and raised procurement prices, the rural sector could thrive. Scientific management and pragmatism could sharply upgrade the depleted rural sector. Like Khrushchev he pushed for state farms, whose number rose 70 percent during his tenure.[10]

[8]Bialer, "Political System," in Byrnes, *After Brezhnev: Sources of Soviet Conduct in the 1980s,* chapter 1.
[9]Here and throughout the text where we refer to Brezhnev's actions, we really mean the actions of his administration, rather than of him personally. This is especially important given the power of his aides and allies throughout his administration.
[10]Kolkhozs declined a corresponding 25 percent in number. Roy Laird, "Political Economy of Soviet Agriculture Under Brezhnev," in Donald Kelley, editor, *Soviet Politics From Brezhnev to Gorbachev,* Praeger, New York, 1987, chapter 3.

Nevertheless, Brezhnev's agricultural policies failed. Government policy could not rectify the problems of the inherently poor climate, a short growing season, great distances to market, and a huge, bureaucratic, and politicized system. Recurrent harvest disasters, pushed by low productivity, low yields, enormous waste, theft, spoilage, and inadequate transportation and storage, plagued agriculture during the Brezhnev years. Private incentive remained minimal with 15 million private plots averaging less than one acre apiece. Despite its huge investments, the regime still needed massive imports of grain. Food output per capita by 1980 was barely half the American level and food output had increased 26 percent in the first ten years of Brezhnev's rule.[11]

Brezhnev made significant incremental changes but never any fundamental changes in agriculture.[12] The government, reversing the Khrushchevian policy of trying to eliminate private plots as the last vestige of capitalism, restored farms plots to their old size, reinstated old norms for private livestock, and increased the marketing system for privately grown food. In March 1965 Brezhnev attacked Khrushchev for his mistakes in planning, pricing, finance, and credit, for weak investment and poor standards. Brezhnev called for long-run stable prices, reasonable plans, a stronger technical base, better organizational work, and an end to campaigns that ignored local conditions. He stressed the need to increase rural income, hike procurement prices, and strengthen local autonomy. The government guaranteed peasants a minimal wage and canceled debts and discriminatory rural taxes.[13]

In 1966 the regime launched a long-range program with large scale capital investment in agriculture. Brezhnev pushed improvements in land fertility, land reclamation, irrigation of arid regions, water development and management, and capital effectiveness. All this was to increase production and offer material incentives with the mechanization of agriculture, use of fertilizers, and subsidization of the rural sector. In 1968 Brezhnev encountered strong resistance to plans to further increase mechanization of agriculture, chemical production, and land reclamation. By 1970 a Central Committee plenum emphasized more land reclamation, increasing chemical fertilizer production and subsidization of the rural sector, incentives for overfulfillment of the plan, rural research, and micromanagement of agriculture. These policies in the 1960s led to a 70 percent increase in agricultural output, but the trend was soon reversed.[14]

The failure of these policies and major harvest disasters and failures forced a large-scale long-term agreement to import American grain. In 1974 the regime launched a massive 35 billion ruble program of land reclamation and social development of the Non-Black Earth Region. In 1976 the regime revived the

[11]Gail Lapidus and Robert Byrnes, "Social Trends," and Roy Laird, "Political Economy of Soviet Agriculture Under Brezhnev," in Kelley, *Soviet Politics From Brezhnev to Gorbachev*, chapters 3–4.

[12]The great difficulties of Gorbachev and Yeltsin in trying to modernize and privatize the rural sector may demonstrate that Brezhnev was not totally irrational.

[13]Breslauer, *Khrushchev and Brezhnev*, chapter 15; and Schwartz, *Resolutions and Decisions of the Communist Party of the Soviet Union*, vol. 5 *(The Brezhnev Years)*.

[14]Schwartz, *Resolutions and Decisions of the Communist Party of the Soviet Union*, vol. 5 *(The Brezhnev Years)*, pp. 20–24, 74–78, 135–141, 158.

idea of interkolkhoz associations, first begun in the late 1950s. The ideological goal was to move towards socialism by industrializing agriculture and promoting state farms. In 1978 Brezhnev, at a Central Committee plenum, acknowledged the failures of agriculture but continued his support for large capital investments and subsidization of the rural sector. He blamed inadequate mechanization, poor interfarm cooperation, and construction bottlenecks for slowing the plan. In 1981, at the Twenty-Sixth Party Congress, Brezhnev one last time turned to large land reclamation and large-scale investment as the panaceas for his stillborn Food Program. He also restated the need for increased private agriculture.[15] By the end of the Brezhnev era, the country needed massive imports of food to maintain agriculture even at a level far below that of the West. Agriculture remained the Achilles' heel of the Soviet Union, a legacy of the distortions of the Stalin era that had starved agriculture and turned it into an internal colony.

SOVIET INDUSTRY

Brezhnev inherited a difficult economic situation as the economic boom of the Khrushchev era subsided. There were no massive new inputs of capital, natural resources, and labor to fuel substantial increases in the economy. The 7 to 10 percent yearly increases in industrial output of the late 1950s faded to 5 percent in the 1960s and 3 to 5 percent in the 1970s. The civilian work force that grew 2.3 percent a year in the 1960s increased by only 1.4 percent in the 1970s and .5 percent in the 1980s. The supply of cheap natural resources became increasingly expensive to find and transport while the demand for them grew sharply. With growing popular demand for a higher standard of living, the regime could not maintain a high savings and investment rate. The expanded superpower role ate up significant resources, with 10 to 20 percent of GNP going to the military.

Brezhnev hoped to improve, not radically alter, the neo-Stalinist command economy. Supported by the major bureaucratic actors, he improved the technological functioning of the economy and strove to eradicate waste. He believed in the superiority of the system that had brought victory in World War II and made the Soviet Union a superpower. Brezhnev did improve the low standard of living. He boosted the output of cars from under 200,000 in 1966 to over a million a year by the late 1970s. He raised housing starts to over 2 million a year to provide all urban dwellers with their own apartments, replete with electricity, indoor toilets, hot water, gas, and heat.[16] By the late 1970s more than 85 percent of the population owned radios, televisions, and refrigerators. Wage reforms raised pensions and minimum wages and provided peasants with social security and insurance against bad harvests. Brezhnev saw consumer goods production increase 5 percent a year in the late 1960s, only to watch it

---

[15]Schwartz, *Resolutions and Decisions of the Communist Party of the Soviet Union,* vol. 5 *(The Brezhnev Years),* pp. 24, 239–240.

[16]Housing was dreary. An average family of four in the late 1960s had 320 square feet of living space, barely 25 percent of the American level, and of much lower quality.

dwindle to an annual increase of less than 2 percent a year by 1981. By 1976 national income had doubled, personal services more than doubled, and consumer durables were more plentiful than before 1964.[17]

Brezhnev emphasized a gigantomania that echoed the Stalinist era, with its enormous projects assuming huge economies of scale. These vast projects—the Kama power station, the Togliatti automobile factory, the Samotlor oil field, the Baikal-Amur railroad, the Kama truck plant, the Ural pipelines, the Orenburg natural gas pipeline, the Kursk metallurgical complex—were outdated relics whose cost and waste often exceeded their value.

Brezhnev emphasized the role of natural resources in an era of rising commodity prices. Occupying one-sixth of the world's earth surface, the Soviet Union possessed enormous natural resources. He directed 16 percent of investment to develop oil, natural gas, and atomic power plants. The results were encouraging as the country produced 3 million barrels a day of oil in 1960 and 12 million barrels a day in 1980. But the costs of production soared as the cheap oil and gas were exhausted and there was no conservation and huge waste with such cheap resources.[18] Energy development, together with industrial pollution, massively damaged the environment.[19]

Brezhnev put his faith in scientific-technical progress, a return to traditional Stalinist institutions, and marginal incremental changes. He ended the *sovnarkhozy* in 1965 and endlessly tinkered with middle-level management, plan indicators, plan flexibility, and Party coordination of the economy to improve the economy. He opposed the stronger reforms of the economy proposed in 1965 by Kosygin as incompatible with the basic direction of the economy. It was this commitment to the traditional forms of a neo-Stalinist command economy in inexorable decline that led to the petrification and decay of the final year of Brezhnev.

In Brezhnev's early years there was a lively debate over economic reform, with Kosygin, the Prime Minister, strongly in the forefront. In 1965 Kosygin advanced plans for economic reforms, including enhanced autonomy for enterprises, a decreasing number of performance indicators, increasing stress on profitability, emphasis on production associations at the intermediate phase, and overall decentralization. But in December 1965 Brezhnev signaled a more conservative tone by putting his faith in managerial cadres and enhanced party control over the economy.

Although the Twenty-Third Party Congress in 1966 saw no new economic direction, Brezhnev in 1967 proclaimed the need for "scientific management." By 1971 the growth rate of light industry and consumer goods exceeded that of heavy industry, thereby raising the average standard of living. Brezhnev improved pensions, minimum wages, consumer goods, and rural benefits.

---

[17]Bialer, *Stalin's Successors,* chapter 8; and Gail Lapidus, "Social Trends," in Robert Byrnes, editor, *After Brezhnev: Sources of Soviet Conduct in the 1980s,* Indiana University Press, Bloomington, 1983, chapter 4.

[18]Unfortunately for the Soviet Union, costs soared with 80 percent of the population living west of the Urals and 80 percent of the resources lying east of the Urals in remote and frigid places.

[19]Robert Campbell, "The Economy," in Byrnes, *After Brezhnev: Sources of Soviet Conduct in the 1980s,* chapter 3.

However, problems began to pile up in industry. Light industry lacked the technology, status, and investment to meet the new demands. A weak service sector, the poor retail distribution, a terrible product mix, and the poor quality of goods harmed the drive to aid the consumer.[20] At the end of the 1960s, the industrial growth rate continued to decline. In 1967 an experiment at the Shchekino chemical complex in Tula gave management the right to fire workers, reorganize management, mechanize labor, combine jobs, and introduce progressive work norms without central interference. In October 1968 the Central Committee gave this plan its approval, but in December 1969, Brezhnev, alarmed at such enterprise autonomy, differential pay rates, and unemployment, got the Central Committee to condemn such reforms. He denounced the plan as irresponsible, undisciplined, and unconscientious for challenging the neo-Stalinist command economy and bureaucratic institutions. Instead, he propounded the need for labor and Party discipline and centralized control of the economy. Brezhnev called for better scientific management, tighter discipline, and enhanced reliance on cadres and economic principles. Two months later Brezhnev declared that he would hold higher state and Party bodies responsible for failures in the economy.[21]

At the Twenty-Fourth Party Congress in 1971, Brezhnev intensified his commitment to scientific-technical progress as the answer to the problems of the Soviet economy. He called for the use of computers and scientific methods to automate management. His emphasis on discipline, ideology, legal norms, and Party monitoring of the economy represented a retrograde effort to make the crumbling system work better by traditional means.

By the Twenty-Fifth Congress in 1976, increasing economic problems did not bring a concomitant response from the government. Rather Brezhnev continued to echo his faith in scientific-technical progress, the need to divert resources to rural areas, increase consumer goods, and enhance foreign economic relations. In 1978 and 1979 a frustrated Brezhnev attacked waste, inefficiency, ineffective transportation, inadequate mechanization of the economy, weak consumer sector, poor quality, and unfinished goods in the economy. His answers were hardly creative: Management was to blame and enhanced discipline, tougher laws, daily supervision of management, and more sector monitoring would be the solution. In 1980 he acknowledged the massive problems in the light industrial sector. His solutions: Attack management, create consumer cooperatives, stress research and development. Brezhnev was aware of many of the economy's problems but was unwilling to consider more radical suggestions to resolve them.[22]

In addition, the relentless push towards heavy industrialization had cre-

---

[20]Schwartz, *Resolutions and Decisions of the Communist Party of the Soviet Union*, vol. 5 (*The Brezhnev Years*), pp. 50–111.

[21]Schwartz, *Resolutions and Decisions of the Communist Party of the Soviet Union*, vol. 5 (*The Brezhnev Years*), pp. 114–115, 143–144.

[22]Schwartz, *Resolutions and Decisions of the Communist Party of the Soviet Union*, vol. 5 (*The Brezhnev Years*), pp. 16, 152–274. The failure of Gorbachev's and Yeltsin's reform efforts may suggest that he was aware of the high cost and problems associated with serious reform.

ated massive environmental problems. Under Brezhnev for the first time serious efforts were made to improve the ravaged environment. In 1970 the government created a national water code, in 1974 a national environmental plan, and in 1978 a new State Committee for Hydrometereology and Oversight of the Environment. This was too little too late. Weak enforcement rarely shut down offending polluters, and a weak inspectorate lacked the manpower and funds to take tough measures. The effort had only marginal impact and left a massive problem for Gorbachev.[23]

SOVIET INSTITUTIONS

The core of Brezhnev's politics was his attitude to the key Soviet institutions—military, secret police, government, and Party—in Moscow. Historically, Communist leaders had seen these key governing institutions in widely varying ways. To radicals like Mao Zedong in China, they represented conservative, anti-revolutionary forces, against whom Mao struggled in the Cultural Revolution in China. In the Soviet Union, Stalin first greatly increased the powers of these bureaucracies, then submitted them to a massive and devastating purge in the Great Purges. After gaining power by 1955 Khrushchev often attacked the bureaucracies, seeing them as hostile to his reform program.

By contrast, Brezhnev saw in these bureaucracies a necessary, powerful, and conservative force to hold together society. Brezhnev created a decision-making process that granted enormous powers of autonomy and substantial yearly budget increases to the relevant bureaucracies. All the leading cadres were granted virtual lifetime tenure in office in return for their loyalty. This pluralistic, bureaucratic, oligarchical decision making firmly rooted the Brezhnev years in a conservative yet strong mold.

Brezhnev identified himself strongly with the core values guiding these bureaucracies. He too opposed liberal democracy and supported the one-party state, with its neo-Stalinist command economy and polity. He distrusted independent views and spontaneous political behavior. Brezhnev was a strong Russian and Soviet nationalist, firm in his desire to keep the Soviet Union under Russian control. Like the bureaucrats, he did not want to reshape society or foster utopianism. Rather he saw the future in terms of material-technical progress driven by the scientific-technological revolution. Although a minority within the bureaucracies thought otherwise, the majority were strong supporters of those core values which Brezhnev epitomized.[24]

The Party received great prominence under Brezhnev, who took the old Stalinist title of Secretary-General of the Party. Brezhnev stressed the need for a stable Party to provide the leading role in society. He acted as a power broker accommodating diverse interests within the Party. He emphasized the need to

---

[23]Thane Gustafson, "Environmental Policy Under Brezhnev: Do the Soviets Mean Business?," in Kelley, *Soviet Politics From Brezhnev to Gorbachev,* chapter 6.
[24]Bialer, *Stalin's Successors,* chapter 9.

trust cadres and give them security in their positions. No less than 18 percent of adult urban males and 33 percent of those with higher education were Communists. Cooperation, consensus, and stability were the bywords.[25]

An October 1964 Central Committee plenum ended the bifurcation of the Party and denounced Khrushchev's endless reorganizations. The Party was restored to its old role of running the economy as local Party organs coordinated and controlled industrial, agricultural, and public organizations. Party cadres, ensured stability in office, received management-oriented training. Purges were so minimal that the Twenty-Fourth Party Congress call for an exchange of Party documents led to the ouster of 1.5 percent of Party members for inactivity, passivity, and undiscipline. Brezhnev routinized the collective leadership, increased the number of Central Committee plenums, decreased irregular procedure, and increased the rules of local Party organizations.[26] Brezhnev and his colleagues ended the Khrushchevian attack on Stalin. There was no full-scale rehabilitation of Stalin, only a mild rehabilitation.

Equally pleased were the secret police and the military. Khrushchev had repeatedly pilloried and savaged the secret police, who lost their prestige and many functions. Brezhnev lionized the secret police as an exemplary organization. Yuri Andropov (1967–1982) successfully professionalized the KGB and emphasized psychological pressure over brute force. The secret police repressed the dissident movement, which emerged as a major force for the first time in Soviet history at this time, countered Western espionage, and played a role on the public stage.

Similarly, the Soviet military was grateful to Brezhnev. The Khrushchev era had been a harrowing one for much of the military. Khrushchev repeatedly slashed the size of Soviet ground forces and questioned their value. They had been humiliated in the 1962 Cuban Missile Crisis. Brezhnev now provided real increases in budgetary allocation and professional autonomy to each of the services and branches of the Soviet military. By 1970 they had reached strategic parity with the Americans and in the 1970s exported their capabilities abroad, from Angola and Ethiopia to Egypt and Afghanistan. So strong was their professional autonomy that at the first SALT negotiation in 1971 a civilian member of the Soviet negotiating team admitted that only the military knew the classified details of the Soviet military posture.

Brezhnev undertook a strong and sustained arms buildup that greatly pleased the military. Brezhnev upgraded the Warsaw Pact, restored the role of the ground forces, greatly increased military manpower to 4 million men, and provided doctrinal justification for the roles of all services.[27] In the first three five-year plans of the Brezhnev era, military spending increased almost 100 percent, 63 percent, and 60 percent. A modern blue-ocean navy appeared for the first time. Massive strategic rocket forces with 1400 ICBMs and 1.8 million

---

[25]Kelley, *Soviet Politics From Brezhnev to Gorbachev,* chapter 2; and Bialer, *Stalin's Successors,* chapter 9.
[26]Schwartz, *Resolutions and Decisions of the Communist Party of the Soviet Union,* volume 5 (*The Brezhnev Years*), pp. 7–93.
[27]During the Khrushchev era the role of ground forces, tactical air power, and air defenses had been in limbo.

ground forces with 50,000 tanks (albeit many old), 20,000 cannons, 4800 fixed-wing airplanes, strong transport capacity, and a large ground-air defense program highlighted this program. While American military spending declined sharply after Vietnam, the Soviet Union underwent a protracted military buildup, fueled by yearly raises of 4 to 5 percent.[28]

Finally, state and public organizations found a definite role in the new corporatist order. Although this was contrary to Marx's notions of the withering away of the state or Khrushchev's attempt to increase the popular role in state administration, it fit in nicely with the expanded role of states in developed countries in the middle of the twentieth century. In the Brezhnev era the Komsomol and trade unions continued their traditional mobilization and politicization work. Brezhnev upheld the role of the state and widened the notion of socialist legality and law to support the new stabilization. The roles of militia, procurators, and the courts was widened; the secret police was kept firmly under the Party. Overall, there was a limited increase in organizational and jurisdictional power for such organizations. Rather than decaying, the power of the state naturally grew under the Brezhnev years.[29]

BREZHNEV AND THE MINORITIES: NATIONALITIES AND DISSIDENTS

Brezhnev pursued a conservative, but not extreme, policy towards minorities. He eschewed both the violent suppression of the Stalinist era and the relative tolerance and openness of the 1920s. He pursued a policy of modulated repression aimed at maintaining central power at the lowest cost. Although Brezhnev felt that Russian domination was right and natural, the declining number of Russians in the population of the USSR (now 53 percent) called for a more sophisticated policy than Great Russian chauvinism.[30]

Brezhnev decided to co-opt assimilated Ukrainians and thereby neutralize and absorb the largest non-Russian element in the country. While continuing to repress Ukrainian nationalism, he massively promoted the Ukrainian managerial and technical elite to positions in Moscow. Over one hundred Ukrainians, including Nikolai Podgorny, Dmitrii Polyansky, Nikolai Tikhonov, Marshal Kirill Mosklenko, and Marshal Andrei Grechko, rose to the highest positions in Soviet society.

Brezhnev tried hard to co-opt local non-Russian elites. In Central Asia and Moslem areas he tolerated extensive corruption by local elites in order to retain their loyalty. At the national level he had several national minorities in the Politburo.

Nonetheless, Brezhnev maintained Slavic domination of the elite. Seweryn

---

[28]Coit Blacker, "Military Forces," in Kelley, *Soviet Politics From Brezhnev to Gorbachev*, chapter 3; and Paul Murphy, *Brezhnev: Soviet Politician*, McFarland, Jefferson, North Carolina, 1981, chapter 22.
[29]Schwartz, *Resolutions and Decisions of the Communist Party of the Soviet Union*, vol. 5 (*The Brezhnev Years*), pp. 25–29.
[30]See Bialer, *Stalin's Successors*, chapter 10.

Bialer has compiled figures showing that 98 percent of the 150 top central party officials, 98 percent of 150 top armed forces commanders, and 97 percent of government ministers were Slavs. In all republics the head of the KGB, the top military commander, and second secretary of the republican party organization were Russians.[31]

Brezhnev was hostile towards religion and isolated national minorities. For Brezhnev, religion represented antiquated views that needed to be destroyed by progressive socialism. At the same time his approach, more legalistic than that of Khrushchev, eased pressure on many religions. Especially after the Israeli victory in the Six Day War in 1967, Brezhnev restricted Jewish entrance to universities and elite positions, but under pressure from the United States, he allowed nearly 300,000 Soviet Jews to emigrate in the 1970s.[32]

This duality reflected the Brezhnevian approach to human rights. Brezhnev wanted to destroy all dissent, albeit without the violence and coercion of the Stalin era. He dashed the hopes for liberalization raised by the thaw of the Khrushchev era. Censorship was especially tight on all expressions of literary thought. In 1965 and 1966 the government tried and convicted Andrei Sinyavsky and Yuri Daniel for anti-Soviet behavior and thought.

Dissent took many forms in the Brezhnev era. There were the universalist groups, such as the branch of Amnesty International, the Human Rights Group, and the Initiative Group. There were particularist groups reflecting nationalities, religions, labor organizations, and professional associations. Forms of protest took numerous forms, from poems, letters, and stories to the *samizdat* (self-publication) of underground literature. Demonstrations were frequent until KGB repression curbed them in the early 1970s. Dissidents came largely from the urban middle class and were usually older people. During the 1970s the government suppressed the *Chronicle of Current Events*, arrested Natan Shcharansky, sent many leaders into forced emigration (such as Alexander Solzhenitsyn) and internal exile (Andrei Sakharov), and broke the back of the movement. Government repression counteracted the stimulus given to the movement by the 1968 Soviet invasion of Czechoslovakia and the 1975 Helsinki Accord guaranteeing human rights.[33]

THE YEARS OF HOPE AND PROGRESS (1965–1975)

During its first decade the Brezhnev team made discernible progress. At the Twenty-Third Party Congress in 1966 the regime consolidated its power and Brezhnev was formally made Secretary-General of the Party. In 1967 Andropov became head of the secret police and Grechko, Brezhnev's friend, replaced Rodion Malinovsky as head of the military. The Six Day War in 1967 led to the

---

[31]Bialer, *Stalin's Successors*, chapter 10.
[32]The regime continued to harass potential emigrés and to prevent thousands of refuseniks from emigrating at all.
[33]David Kowalewski, "Trends in Human Rights Movement," in Kelley, *Soviet Politics From Brezhnev to Gorbachev*, chapter 7; and Maurice Friedberg, "Cultural and Intellectual Life," in Byrnes, *After Brezhnev: Sources of Soviet Conduct in the 1980s*, chapter 5.

demise of Nikolai Yegorichev as head of the Moscow Party Committee and the fall of Alexander Shelepin, upset over Soviet failure to help the defeated Arabs. After 1969 Brezhnev gained increased prominence at the expense of Kosygin and Podgorny. At the Twenty-Fifth Party Congress in 1976 Brezhnev praised the KGB, the scientific-technical revolution, and the role of officials acting with tact, restraint, and under socialist legality. He emphasized the need for consumer goods, which now grew faster (48 percent) than heavy industrial goods (45 percent), and private plots. At the Congress three allies (Kulakov, Shcherbitsky, and Kunayev) joined the Politburo, and members of his Dnieper Mafia joined the Central Committee. The Congress reaffirmed its support for Brezhnev's peace policy, trip to the United States, and promotion of *ostpolitik* with the West Germans. But the late meeting of the congress, which failed to coincide with the one hundredth anniversary of Lenin's birth, indicated the difficulties still faced by Brezhnev in consolidating his power.[34]

The year 1972 was climactic, with Richard Nixon's famous visit to Moscow and the intensified bombing of Vietnam. The worst weather in fifty years led to a severe agricultural shortfall and agreement to spend 2 billion dollars to import 28 million tons of grain from the United States. Despite this setback, Brezhnev's power grew as detente with the United States blossomed. The former head of the KGB (and later Foreign Minister and head of Georgia) Eduard Shevardnadze replaced the corrupt Georgian party boss Mzharadze. In 1973, at the time of his trips to West Germany and the United States, the Politburo expelled Shelest and Voronov and added Grechko (head of the military), Andropov (head of the KGB), and Gromyko (Foreign Minister). This seemed to reflect a broadening of the bureaucratic base of the Politburo. In his speeches Brezhnev downplayed consumer goods and focused on agriculture, Siberian development plans, and defense spending.[35]

THE FINAL YEARS OF BREZHNEV: DECAY AND PETRIFICATION (1976–1982)

The final years of Brezhnev, the years of stagnation and immobility as the leader and his allies aged noticeably, should be seen in the broader perspective of the relation between age and politics. In the West, there have been notable older leaders in their seventies and even eighties—Konrad Adenauer in Germany, Charles de Gaulle in France, Winston Churchill in England, Ronald Reagan in the United States, and Golda Meir in Israel. Yet for the most part, the democratic electoral process and clashes within parties have tended to winnow out the older leaders in favor of younger leaders who projected the requisite dynamism and appearance. As leaders aged in the West, they increasingly found themselves challenged, often successfully, by younger leaders. Many of

[34]Breslauer, *Khrushchev and Brezhnev*, chapters 11–12; and John Dornberg, *Brezhnev: Masks of Power*, Andre Deutsch, London, 1974, chapter 13.
[35]Dornberg, *Brezhnev: Masks of Power*, chapters 15–16; Murphy, *Brezhnev: Soviet Politician*, chapter 24; and Breslauer, *Khrushchev and Brezhnev*, chapter 12.

these older leaders came to power because of special circumstances, such as the war in England and France, the lack of suitable leaders not identified with fascism in Germany, and a leadership crisis in Israel that needed a temporary solution.

The situation in the Soviet Union was very different. Lenin, Stalin, Brezhnev, Andropov, and Chernenko died in office, leaving Khrushchev the only aging leader to have been removed. Many other Communist leaders, such as Mao Zedong, Josip Tito, Enver Hoxha, Klement Gottwald, and Ho Chih Minh, also died in office. There was no electoral process, no intra-Party competition to remove aging leaders. Aging leaders could be reasonably assured of lifetime tenure in office, as long as their tenure was mildly successful.

Communist political history showed no correlation between age and conservatism. An aging Stalin in his early seventies fought the West in Korea and prepared massive purges at home. Mao Zedong at seventy-three launched the Great Proletarian Cultural Revolution in China. Ho Chih Minh in his seventies urged vigorous prosecution of the war with South Vietnam and the United States. Even now a spry sixty-three-year-old Boris Yeltsin pushes radical reforms in post-Communist Russia.

Aging leaders tended to resort to policies that had worked well for them in their youth. For Stalin, the Great Purges, for Ho the war against the French, and for Mao the civil war (Yenan era) provided the models for their actions in old age. So too did the aging Brezhnev, whose early career had been promoted by intrigue within the Party machine, turn once more to the Party elite to sustain him. There was no sense of motion in the regime, no end to the war in Afghanistan, no reforms or turnover within the Party, no serious attempts to fix the failing economy.[36]

By the late 1970s the Brezhnev regime began to lose any dynamism and fall into immobility.[37] Brezhnev, now past seventy and ill, was increasingly surrounded by his old cronies. Remembering what had happened to Khrushchev at seventy, Brezhnev and his allies refused to promote younger leaders who could challenge him. Brezhnev became increasingly vainglorious and insistent on his prerogatives. In 1975 he was hailed for his modest role in the great victory of World War II. In 1976 he became a Marshal of the Soviet Union, even though his role in World War II as a political commissar did not merit the rank. His role as chairman of the Defense Council and Commander-in-Chief of the armed forces was publicized. In 1977 he ousted his long-time ally Podgorny from the Presidency so that he could become President. Nepotism and corruption flourished as the top was increasingly seized by paralysis. His son Yuri Brezhnev became Deputy Foreign Trade Minister, his son-in-law Yuri Churbanov became Deputy Minister of the Interior and his brother-in-law Semen

---

[36]The war in Afghanistan, which started with Soviet military intervention in December 1979, quickly acquired some (but not all) of the characteristics of the Vietnam War for the United States.
[37]For views on the final years of Brezhnev, see Dusko Doder, *Shadows and Whispers: Power Politics Inside the Kremlin From Brezhnev to Gorbachev*, Random House, New York, 1986; Bialer, *Stalin's Successors*, chapter 6; and Kelley, *Soviet Politics From Brezhnev to Gorbachev*, pp. 13–15.

Tsvigun Deputy Chairman of the KGB. Even his personal physician, Yevgeny Chazov, was elevated to a special position. Brezhnev was general secretary of the Party, president of the government, head of the Defense Council and commander-in-chief of the armed forces. Brezhnev's chief-of-staff, Konstantin Chernenko, became a full member of the Politburo and even offered a challenge for the leadership after Brezhnev's demise.

The elite grew old together with Brezhnev.[38] Although after the 1937 Great Purges the Soviet government had been the youngest in the world, the survival of many of these same men into the late 1970s made it the oldest government in the world. In 1978 the average age of the members of the Council of Ministers and of the high command of the Armed Forces was sixty-five. In 1980 the average age of a full member of the Politburo was seventy, of the Secretariat sixty-seven, and of the Presidium of the Council of Ministers sixty-eight.

When old cadres became incapacitated or died, they were replaced by other old cadres. In 1976 the sixty-eight-year-old Ustinov replaced the seventy-three-year-old Grechko as Defense Minister and the sixty-nine-year-old Minister of Ship Building was replaced by another sixty-nine-year-old man. Two of the five members purged from the Politburo were the youngest members. By 1978 the members of the Politburo were thirteen years older than those in 1965.

The trend was first evident after the Twenty-Fifth Party Congress in 1976. The lavish praise of Brezhnev echoed the late Stalin era in its fulsomeness and insincerity. Brezhnev's report became the resolution of the Congress. His report hailed law and order, the courts, the KGB, and the forthcoming constitution. Brezhnev supported the industrialization of agriculture, slow development of light industry, strong development of the military and heavy industry, big land reclamation in the Non-Black Earth areas, import of foreign technological goods, and automation of planning. At the Congress Polyansky was ousted for agricultural failures (Shelepin had been ousted the previous year) and Defense Minister Ustinov and Leningrad Party chief Romanov became full members of the Politburo.[39]

By the late 1970s Brezhnev was increasingly critical of Gosplan and individual corrupt officials but had no real program to fix the mounting problems. Bottlenecks were growing in the energy field, transportation, and agriculture. Consumer goods were lagging under the priority for the military and the mismanagement of the economy. He brought in some new talent, such as Mikhail Gorbachev to the Secretariat in 1978, but it was too little too late.[40]

The stagnation was clearly evident at the Twenty-Sixth Party Congress in 1981, which met in the wake of the failure of the Soviet intervention in Afghanistan, launched in December 1979. The backdrop was one of Cold War

---

[38]For an excellent summary of this process, see Bialer, *Stalin's Successors*, chapters 5 and 6.

[39]Schwartz, *Resolutions and Decisions of the Communist Party of the Soviet Union*, vol. 5 (*The Brezhnev Years*), pp. 237–258; Breslauer, *Khrushchev and Brezhnev*, chapter 13; and Murphy, *Brezhnev: Soviet Politician*, chapter 25.

[40]Schwartz, *Resolutions and Decisions of the Communist Party of the Soviet Union*, vol. 5 (*The Brezhnev Years*), pp. 254–276.

and rising East-West tensions. Brezhnev, attacking economic inefficiency, put forth a food program stressing rural development, more private incentives, and Non-Black Earth development that broke little new ground. His economic plan, with stress on heavy industry, priority for military goods over consumer goods, discipline, and better labor conditions, in the Eleventh Five Year Plan, represented old wine in new bottles. The party was to create a Letters Department of the Central Committee to improve conditions. His attack on decentralization and continued emphasis on centralism showed his commitment to a neo-Stalinist command polity and economy. With the economy in decline, agriculture a disaster area, and the Cold War revived, he offered little to revive the country.[41]

By the early 1980s the growth rate of the economy dropped to nearly zero. Some Soviet officials later claimed that if oil and vodka were ousted from the statistics, there was no growth at all in the Soviet economy.[42] Poor harvests, and the large-scale loss of 20 to 35 percent of the harvests to negligence, poor infrastructure, and corruption led food imports to skyrocket from 700 million dollars in 1970 to 7 billion dollars in 1980. Corruption, inefficiency, alcoholism, and criminality plagued the economy. Corruption, cynicism, and pessimism were widespread.[43]

But the increasingly inert Brezhnev, shielded from reality, comfortable with his old cronies, and dependent on the bureaucracy, did nothing. On his seventy-fifth birthday in December 1981, the aging Brezhnev received a new Order of Lenin. Eight columns of headlines and 75 percent of the space in the major newspapers were dedicated to the event.

Major forces within the Soviet elite, sensing his impending demise, went on the attack. In December 1981 a scathing satire in a Leningrad literary magazine signaled an attack on the declining Brezhnev. A month earlier there had begun a crackdown on corruption in several nationality areas, which soon reached into Brezhnev's inner circle. His brother-in-law, Semen Tsvigun, the First Deputy Chairman of the KGB, committed suicide over a scandal, and Brezhnev did not dare sign his obituary. Later in January the KGB arrested Boris the Clown, the boyfriend of Brezhnev's daughter Galina in a scandal involving diamonds and official corruption. In March, the head of the trade unions, Alexei Shibayev, was fired for corruption, mismanagement, and outrageous behavior.

In March 1982 Brezhnev took a trip to Tashkent with Sharif Rashidov, a candidate member of the Politburo, who suddenly died. The shocked Brezhnev had to be hospitalized and returned to Moscow on a stretcher. In April, on the anniversary of Lenin's birth, he appeared weak and thin in public as he shuffled along. That summer, while Brezhnev vacationed, corruption in-

---

[41]Breslauer, *Khrushchev and Brezhnev,* chapter 14; and Schwartz, *Resolutions and Decisions of the Communist Party of the Soviet Union,* vol. 5 (*The Brezhnev Years*), pp. 285–287.
[42]Private conversation with Pavel Bunich, economist and member of the Central Committee, August 1988, Telluride, Colorado.
[43]Doder, *Shadows and Whispers,* chapter 1.

creased. The Israelis invaded Lebanon and the British the Falklands but Brezhnev remained aloof. In September he went to Baku, where he read the wrong speech until he was cued by his advisors. Noticeably shaky in public and private, Brezhnev now appeared to be teetering on disaster, and in November he died of a heart attack.[44]

During the last year of Brezhnev's life, the most noticeable figures in Soviet life were Yuri Andropov and Konstantin Chernenko. Chernenko, as Brezhnev's chief-of-staff, used his position to advance himself as the guardian of Brezhnevism, with or without Brezhnev. By contrast, Andropov, the head of the KGB from 1967 to 1982, put himself at the head of reformist forces. But although he probably was behind much of the KGB attacks on Brezhnevian corruption, he too had serious problems. Andropov was himself in poor health, had never been a secretary of the Central Committee before May 1982, and was associated with the secret police. Yet with his intelligence, connections to the secret police and military, and demonstrated honesty, Andropov would be a formidable figure for the ailing Brezhnev in his final year in power.[45]

The disabilities of Andropov and Chernenko signaled the start of a lengthy succession crisis. The only strong younger figure, Mikhail Gorbachev, had come to Moscow in 1978 and become a full member of the Politburo in 1980. His ascent to power represented a long and arduous process, although speeded by the demise of a number of Politburo members through old age, ill health, or death.

[44]Doder, *Shadows and Whispers,* chapters 2–4.
[45]Doder, *Shadows and Whispers,* chapter 5.

PART THREE

The Current Time of Troubles

In these six chapters we turn to the revolutionary events that still dominate the world headlines. The dramatic events of October 1993, when Yeltsin used massive force to suppress the conservatives in parliament and killed over 100 people, show just how tenuous the hold of the reformers is on Russia. And elsewhere, especially in the Transcaucasus, Central Asia, Ukraine, and Belarus, the reformers are even weaker, and there is little move toward democracy, capitalism, and nation building. These chapters begin by reviewing the post-Brezhnev crisis and the traumatic developments of the Gorbachev era. The following four chapters highlight current and past developments in the fifteen, largely unfamiliar, states that have emerged from the wreckage of the former Soviet Union. Only by understanding what has gone before in these new states can we hope to understand fully the enormous challenges and difficulties facing these new regimes. Now Moscow no longer decides everything; it does matter what happens in Kiev, Minsk, and even Tashkent. This requires the student to master considerably more material, but, it is to be hoped, to good purpose.

14

The Interregnum (1982–1985)

Brezhnev's refusal to elevate a younger generation to the center of power intensified the succession crisis. Between 1979 and 1982 the leaders of the Brezhnev era either died (Brezhnev, Kosygin, Suslov) or were gravely ill (Kirilenko). Prime Minister Tikhonov, Defense Minister Ustinov, and Foreign Minister Gromyko were too old and the latter two too specialized to lead the party. Dunmukhamed Kunaev and Arvid Pelshe were both old and not Russians. Mediocrities like Viktor Grishin from the Moscow Party machine were likely only as compromise choices.[1]

Yet after the stagnation of the Brezhnev era, many in the elite were eager for a strong leader to deal with mounting Soviet problems. After nearly forty-five years of rule by the Brezhnev generation that advanced after the Great Purges, a blocked middle-aged generation was eager for advancement and for a new policy to deal with the mounting problems. The detente of the 1970s had degenerated into a mini-Cold War with the United States, an endless war in Afghanistan, and a crisis with Solidarity in Poland. The economy continued its inexorable decline with four straight terrible harvests. The military continued to absorb a disproportionate part of the nation's resources. Social problems, such as alcoholism, corruption, and bureaucratism, continued to grow, as did problems with the nationalities.[2]

Meanwhile, there was still no orderly succession process. Each previous succession had represented the changing political characteristics of the Soviet

---

[1]Dimitri Simes, "National Security Under Andropov," *Problems of Communism*, vol. 32, no. 1, January–February, 1983, p. 32; and Jerry Hough, "Soviet Succession: Issues and Personalities," *Problems of Communism*, vol. 31, no. 5, September–October, 1982, p. 51.
[2]See Martin McCauley, editor, *The Soviet Union After Brezhnev*, Holmes and Meier, New York, 1983, for chapters on the various problems facing the Soviet Union in 1982.

system. Now, without a logical successor to Brezhnev, the system faced even greater problems than usual.

CANDIDATES

The number of candidates for the mantle of Brezhnev was small. There was no logical candidate—no middle-aged Russian with broad experience in the Party apparatus, prior posts in the nationality areas, and political views in the mainstream of the Party. Most of the candidates were too old or too ill. Younger candidates were too new to Moscow (Mikhail Gorbachev) or worked outside of Moscow (Georgii Romanov).[3]

Konstantin Chernenko and Yuri Andropov emerged as the leading candidates. Each would have been fatally flawed under normal conditions. The unsophisticated Chernenko was poorly educated, with only a correspondent degree from the Kishinev Pedagogical Institute. He had no experience in running a major Party or economic unit or in foreign affairs, and no war experience. A poor speaker, he came across as a dullard best suited to be back in the border guards of the 1930s. Over seventy, he suffered from poor health. He had become a full member of the Politburo only in 1978. Chernenko lacked an independent image and was known mainly as an aide to Brezhnev, a Brezhnev clone, a colorless staff person.

Yuri Andropov also had serious problems. Unlike Chernenko, he had never been an insider and lacked a powerful patron. With a cool and aloof personality, Andropov lacked both a political persona and a political machine behind him. He had never been a regional Party secretary, run an economic unit, or served in the army. Worst of all, he had been the head of the KGB for fifteen years. No less than five heads of the secret police (Yagoda, Yezhov, Beria, Abakumov, Merkulov) had been shot. Andropov was sixty-eight years old and in poor health. As late as 1981 he had been ranked eighth in the party. If Brezhnev had died in 1980 while Mikhail Suslov was alive and Yuri Andropov ran the secret police, Andropov could not have contended for the leadership. If Brezhnev had died in 1983 or 1984, Andropov would have been dying or too ill to contend.[4]

Chernenko offered "Brezhnevism without Brezhnev." Precisely because he was not vigorous, young, or capable, he posed no threat to the remaining kingmakers in Soviet politics. Chernenko would not rock the boat, and he could be trusted to maintain the traditional prerogatives and policies of the Party apparatus.

Andropov, on the other hand, was the logical choice for those interested in

---

[3]For articles on the succession crisis, see Hough, "Soviet Succession: Issues and Personalities," and Sidney Ploss, "Soviet Succession: Signs of Struggle," in *Problems of Communism,* vol. 31, no. 6, November–December, 1982.

[4]Joseph Nogee, editor, *Soviet Politics: Russia After Brezhnev,* Praeger, New York, 1985, pp. 10–11.

serious change. He appealed to disciplinarians, impressed by his record at the KGB, and reformers, who felt that as an honest and incorruptible outsider he could lead them out of the current morass. Andropov seemed intelligent and vigorous, with very capable advisers (Georgii Arbatov, Fedor Burlatsky, Oleg Bogomolov, and Alexander Bovin). His years in Hungary and at the KGB made him knowledgeable in foreign affairs.

THE STRUGGLE FOR SUCCESSION IN 1982

Andropov evidently did not wait for Brezhnev to die to launch his bid for power. In December 1981 the literary journal *Aurora* in Leningrad published a satire about a seventy-year-old writer who had disappointed his admirers by failing to die, a man who "isn't even thinking of dying." The author concluded, "But I think that he will not keep us waiting very long. He will not disappoint us. We all believe in him. We want him to finish those labors that he has not yet finished and hasten to gladden our hearts."[5] In January 1982 Mikhail Suslov, the party watchdog, learned of a scandal in illegal diamond trading linking Boris Buryatia and Brezhnev's daughter, Galina. After evidently being confronted by Suslov, Semen Tsvigun (Brezhnev's brother-in-law and First Deputy Chairman of KGB) killed himself. Brezhnev did not sign Tsvigun's obituary and Suslov, perhaps overcome by the strain of the affair, died as well. The next month the government arrested Boris Buryatia and Anatoly Koleva-tor, the director of the circus. With censorship miraculously lifted, an aging Brezhnev was shown on television weeping at the funeral of an old friend.

In March 1982 Brezhnev suffered a stroke on his return from Tashkent and was disabled. In April a newly visible Andropov gave the annual Lenin speech. In May the Politburo promoted the rising Andropov from the KGB to Suslov's old post in the Central Committee Secretariat. In August Andropov succeeded in ousting one of Brezhnev's closest and most corrupt allies (Sergei Medunov, boss of Krasnodar). In September Soviet television caught Brezhnev in Baku looking ludicrous as he read the wrong speech to an audience.[6]

Yet all was not smooth for Andropov. In October 1982 Chernenko still ranked ahead of Andropov at an important political meeting. In early November Viktor Grishin, a Chernenko ally, gave the speech commemorating the October Revolution.[7]

When Brezhnev suddenly died in November 1982, after spending three

[5]Anthony D'Agostino, *Soviet Succession Struggles,* Allen and Unwin, Boston, 1988, p. 215.

[6]For 1982 see Jonathan Steele and Eric Abraham, *Andropov in Power,* Doubleday, Garden City, New York, 1984, chapter 7; Zhores Medvedev, *Andropov,* W.W. Norton, New York, 1983, chapters 2, 9; Ilya Zemtsov, *Chernenko: The Last Bolshevik,* Transaction Books, New Brunswick, New Jersey, 1989, chapter 5; and Donald Kelley, *Soviet Politics From Brezhnev to Gorbachev,* Praeger, New York, 1987, chapter 2.

[7]Boris Meissner, "Transition in the Kremlin," *Problems of Communism,* vol. 32, no. 1, January–February, 1983.

hours in the bitter cold on the reviewing stand for the October Revolution parade, Andropov successfully went on the offensive. Evidently the elders of the Politburo, Foreign Minister Gromyko and Defense Minister Ustinov, teamed with younger members, such as Gorbachev and Romanov, to provide the critical votes. The Central Committee, which was more favorable to Chernenko, was presented with a *fait accompli*.[8]

WHO WAS ANDROPOV?

Yuri Andropov's life was only somewhat unconventional. Like most Soviet politicians, he came from a lower-class background in the provinces. He was born in 1914, the son of a railroad worker and perhaps station master in a remote part of Stavropol province. He drifted through a series of jobs as a movie projectionist, Volga boatman, telegraph operator, and factory worker. With only an elementary school education, his future seemed bleak. But in 1930 he joined the Komsomol and in 1936 graduated from the Rybinsk technical college for water transport, hardly a great educational institution. The Great Purges opened the door and the young Andropov at age twenty-four in 1938 was the first secretary of the Yaroslavl Komsomol organization. In 1939 he joined the Party and in 1940 ran a republic-level Komsomol organization in Karelo-Finland.

His wartime years were not fortunate. He helped run the partisan movement in his region but in 1944 was demoted to deputy secretary for the small Party organization in Petrozavodsk, a town with 50,000 people and no industry. Evidently with the help of veteran Finnish Communist Otto Kuusinen, he became the second secretary of the Karelo-Finnish Party organization in 1947 and survived a purge of the region. Suddenly he was called to Moscow in 1951 and appointed inspector, and later head, of a section of a department of the Central Committee, a heady promotion for the thirty-seven-year-old Andropov. After Stalin's death he was demoted and shipped off to Hungary to serve as a counsellor in the Soviet Embassy, usually a place of exile.

Andropov turned this lemon into lemonade, and Hungary became his greatest triumph. Made Soviet Ambassador to Hungary in 1954, he performed masterfully during the 1956 Hungarian Revolution. He returned to Moscow in 1957 to head an important Central Committee department dealing with ruling parties in Eastern Europe and Asia. By 1961 Andropov had become a full member of the Central Committee and in 1962 a Central Committee Secretary. During his ten years in the Central Committee, his professionalism, hard work, puritanism, and toughness impressed Brezhnev and other Party leaders.

In his fifteen-year reign at the KGB (1967–1982), Andropov kept the KGB under Party control, modernized foreign and domestic espionage, streamlined training methods, reined in overzealous subordinates, and rebuilt morale, shattered during the Khrushchev era. He improved the damaged reputation of

---

[8]Zemtsov, *Chernenko: The Last Bolshevik*, chapter 5.

the KGB, which became an efficient and sophisticated organization, utilizing modern technology and psychological techniques. He further enhanced the KGB image through its campaign against corruption. The largely successful conclusion of the campaign of repression and intimidation against dissidents, without deeply alienating the West, boosted Andropov's stock in Moscow. In May 1982 Andropov transferred from the KGB to the Central Committee Secretariat, from which he launched his successful bid for power in November 1982.

THE ANDROPOV INTERLUDE

Andropov's rule lasted for only seventeen months, during thirteen of which he was terminally ill and on kidney dialysis. His tenuous control of the Politburo did not extend to the Central Committee and many regional Party organizations. Yet, as Seweryn Bialer concluded in the 1980s,

> Andropov did leave his mark on the Soviet Union. He represented a style of leadership, a direction of personnel policies, a sober assessment of the situation and a desire to improve performance, which acted as a model for many, and perhaps most, members of the leadership, elite and political public. Without any doubt he remains an object of reverence in Gorbachev's Russia and for Gorbachev himself. This in itself makes analysis of his short rule significant for understanding the Soviet Union in the mid-1980s.[9]

Within seven months of taking power, Andropov took all the key positions—head of the Politburo, chairman of the Defense Council, chairman of the Presidium of the Supreme Soviet—that it had taken Brezhnev thirteen years to acquire. He downgraded Chernenko and promoted his allies, especially Gorbachev. By early 1984 Andropov's team had purged almost 15 percent of the members of the Central Committee and government ministers and over 20 percent of the first secretaries of the regional and provincial Party committees. By the end of 1983 Andropov allies (Vitalii Vorotnikov, Mikhail Solomentsev, and Geydar Aliyev) were full members of the Politburo while Viktor Chebrikov (head of the KGB), and Yegor Ligachev were candidate members. New Central Committee Secretaries included such future leaders as Nikolai Ryzhkov, Yegor Ligachev, and Georgii Romanov. Gromyko was the new First Deputy Prime Minister. Gorbachev became Andropov's clear heir, and after April 1983 he had broad responsibilities for light industry, personnel, the military, the police, and agro-industry.[10]

Andropov launched a sweeping campaign against corruption and lack of

[9]Seweryn Bialer, *The Soviet Paradox: External Expansion, Internal Decline*, Alfred Knopf, New York, 1986, p. 90.
[10]D'Agostino, *Soviet Succession Struggles*, pp. 217–218; Nogee, *Soviet Politics: Russia After Brezhnev*, p. 10; Bialer, *The Soviet Paradox: External Expansion, Internal Decline*, p. 91; and Federal Institute for East European and International Studies, *The Soviet Union 1984/85: Events, Problems, Perspectives*, Westview Press, Boulder, Colorado: 1986, pp. 12–38.

discipline in the economy. He sought to mobilize popular support against alcoholism, corruption, and theft of public property. He thought the system could be made to work if massive corruption and labor shirking (absenteeism, laziness, drunkenness, theft of property) could be reduced at all levels. Since almost one-third of all workers were absent at any time and 90 percent were missing in the final hour of the day, there was great room for improvement. Andropov began by firing the old Brezhnevites and thousands of corrupt officials and installing in their place tough policemen like Geydar Aliyev (First Deputy Prime Minister), Viktor Chebrikov (head of the KGB), and Vitalii Fedorchuk (head of the Ministry of Internal Affairs). In January 1983 the regime increased punishments for crimes against the state. Police carried out massive daytime sweeps of public shops and arrested those absent from work. In September 1983 a new law on labor collectives called on them to enforce discipline, increase liability for damage done on the job, and deduct a day's vacation for anyone absent more than three hours on a given day.[11]

Andropov decisively repressed all dissident and emigration movements and attendant cultural liberalism. Although 51,300 Jews had emigrated in 1979, only 2700 emigrated in 1982, 1300 in 1983, and 960 in 1984. There were shrill attacks on Zionism and the Jewish Anti-Zionist Committee was created in April 1983. Similarly, the emigration of Soviet Germans dropped to 2000 in 1982, 1000 in 1983, and 470 in the first six months of 1984. Laws were tightened against dissidents and hundreds of dissidents were arrested. The government formally warned dissidents such as Roy Medvedev and declared Andrei Sakharov a security risk. The amnesty in December 1982 on the sixtieth anniversary of the founding of the USSR pointedly excluded political prisoners.[12]

Despite his repression of dissident and emigré movements, Andropov promoted a new openness in style that indicated that Stalinism, despite the repression of dissidents, was not on the agenda. He increased consultation with experts, published reports of Politburo meetings, promoted frankness in reports on government work, and responded to public complaints. He ended sloganeering and the public ignoring of serious problems. Andropov tried to be frank and open in his speeches, to lay the base for significant changes in the structure and method of governing.[13]

In planning he decreased plan targets and increased the rate of investment. He favored greater enterprise autonomy and more stress on technological innovation. Andropov called for material incentives and personal responsibility and discipline. In agriculture he favored greater freedom for brigades of fifty to one hundred people to organize their own work. He initiated the July 1983 experiment in five industrial ministries to increase the role of managers and

[11]Robert Sharlett, "Soviet Legal Policy Under Andropov: Law and Discipline," in Nogee, *Soviet Politics: Russia After Brezhnev,* chapter 5; Medvedev, *Andropov,* chapter 15; and Stephen White, *Gorbachev in Power,* Cambridge University Press, Cambridge, 1990, pp. 10–12.
[12]Federal Institute for East European and International Studies, *The Soviet Union 1984/85,* chapters 12, 16; Steele and Abraham, *Andropov in Power,* chapter 8.
[13]White, *Gorbachev in Power,* pp. 10–12.

their autonomy, decrease the role of central indicators, promote technology, and allow workers to be fired. However, he never challenged the idea of a centrally planned economy.[14]

THE ANDROPOV SUCCESSION

Four months after taking office, Andropov was already on a kidney dialysis machine. He last appeared in public at a Politburo meeting in September, 1983. Taken seriously ill in January 1984, he died the next month.[15]

His death provoked a four-day power struggle, as his supporters disintegrated as a cohesive bloc. Even today, a decade later, the actual events are somewhat obscure. The heir apparent, Mikhail Gorbachev, was too young (53) and vigorous for the thinning ranks of the party elders, such as Nikolai Tikhonov (78), Dmitrii Ustinov (75), Andrei Gromyko (74), Konstantin Chernenko (72), Dinmukhamed Kunaev (72), and Viktor Grishin (69). This time they did not divide, fearing correctly that a new and vigorous leader would sweep them away. Yet the movement for change had significant public and institutional support from the middle-aged generation.

The result was a massive power struggle among the main contestants for power. The leading contenders were Konstantin Chernenko, Mikhail Gorbachev, and Georgii Romanov. Chernenko's problems, as we saw earlier, were legion. Romanov had only moved to Moscow from Leningrad in 1983. He had limited education (evening school for higher education), no knowledge of or experience in foreign affairs, and a reputation for being ruthless and imperious. Gorbachev seemed the most logical choice—vigorous, intelligent, experienced, well educated. But he had moved to Moscow only in 1978 and had been a full member of the Politburo only since 1980.

Chernenko made a comeback as Andropov had slipped from sight. He gave the October Revolution Day speech in 1983 and in January 1984 published a new edition of his speeches. Not all was smooth as the December 1983 Central Committee Plenum advanced a number of Andropov supporters. But without Andropov there was no coherence to the opposition. And Gorbachev could bide his time.

In the end a compromise was reached. The Gorbachev forces would not stop Chernenko from ascending to the top. His poor health and general political weakness made him a minimal threat. This, coupled with his mediocre abilities, made him a perfect lame duck. In turn, the Chernenko forces would accept Gorbachev as the number two man in the leadership, who would eventually take the top spot after Chernenko's demise. Gorbachev would become the *de facto* Second Secretary of the Party and number three in the leadership after

---

[14]Steele and Abraham, *Andropov in Power,* chapter 8.
[15]The best summaries of the rise of Chernenko are in Mark Zlotnik, "Chernenko Succeeds," *Problems of Communism,* vol. 23, no. 2, March–April 1984; Zemtsov, *Chernenko: The Last Bolshevik;* and Kelley, *Soviet Politics From Brezhnev to Gorbachev,* chapters 3–4.

Chernenko and the aged Tikhonov. He would chair the Foreign Affairs Commission of the Council of Union of the Supreme Soviet and travel abroad (as to London in December 1984). Chernenko would accept collective rule of the elders (Tikhonov, Ustinov, Gromyko), not rock the boat, and continue some of Andropov's experiments.[16]

WHO WAS CHERNENKO?

Konstantin Chernenko's rise to power was most unexpected.[17] Born in a Siberian village in 1911, he went to work as a hired farm hand by age twelve and completed only elementary school. In 1929 he entered the Komsomol and in 1930 became a border guard in the harsh conditions of Siberia. The Stalinist Great Purges lifted him from obscurity, and by 1941 he was the secretary of the Krasnoyarsk regional Party committee in charge of propaganda. During the war he went to the Higher School for Party Organizers in Moscow. In 1945, the party sent him to Penza and then to Moldavia in charge of propaganda. There he hitched his star to that of the new Party boss, Leonid Brezhnev.

The rest of his career was due solely to Brezhnev's favor. When Brezhnev moved to Moscow in 1956 as Central Committee Secretary, he brought along Chernenko as head of the Agitation and Propaganda Department. When Brezhnev became titular President of the country in 1960, Chernenko became head of its Secretariat. When Brezhnev became General Secretary of the Party in 1964, Chernenko became head of the powerful General Department of the Central Committee, where he was responsible for preparing the agenda for the Politburo and helping execute its decisions. By 1971 Brezhnev made Chernenko a full member of the Central Committee and in 1978 a full member of the Politburo. He was defeated by Andropov for the succession in November 1982.

CHERNENKO ERA

Unlike Andropov, Chernenko came to power without a mandate for change. His appointment reflected the deadlock in Soviet politics. Andropov had defeated him for the leadership in 1982 and at seventy-two, old and in failing health, Chernenko neither could nor would do much. His power was circumscribed by the Old Guard and by the deal he had made with Gorbachev. During his thirteen-month reign, Chernenko held two Central Committee plenums but made no significant personnel changes in the Politburo. Only 11 percent of the members of the Council of Ministers were replaced during his reign. His

[16]For a view of this, see Heinz Brahm, "Secretaries General Come and Go," in Federal Institute for East European and International Studies, *The Soviet Union 1984/85,* chapter 1.
[17]For biographies of Chernenko, see Zemtsov, *Chernenko: The Last Bolshevik;* K. C. Chernenko, *Speeches and Writings,* second edition, Pergamon, Oxford, England, 1984; and Mark Zlotnik, "Chernenko's Platform," *Problems of Communism,* vol. 31, no. 6, November–December, 1982.

attempts to foster a cult of personality were a failure. A terrible harvest and growth rate of less than 2.5 percent in 1984 marked his time in office.[18]

Chernenko did pursue several policies. One, as seen in the ouster of the aggressive Nikolai Ogarkov (chief of staff) and his replacement by Sergei Akhromeyev, was to limit the role of the military and reduce military spending. The mediocre Sergei Sokolov replaced the powerful Defense Minister Dmitrii Ustinov, who died in December 1984, and Sokolov was not put on the Politburo.[19] Chernenko tried to return to the Brezhnev policy of extensive development of agriculture. In October 1984 the government announced a new long-term program for land improvement which stressed massive increases in acreage and redirection of water from Siberia to Central Asia and the Caucasus. Chernenko emphasized consumer goods and a food program. He continued Andropov's campaigns against inefficiency and corruption, but without enthusiasm. He stressed the role of workers in management and new introduction of technology.[20]

Chernenko supported increasing the responsiveness of the Party to the people by sociological research, public opinion polls, and letters from the public. He advocated more debates and less secrecy within the Party, but reassured the Party elite that he would not threaten their job security. Condemning Great Russian chauvinism, he favored a pragmatic policy towards nationalities.[21]

His hard work schedule and addiction to lengthy speeches accelerated the worsening of his emphysema. By July 1984 he was very ill and had to be supported by bodyguards. Chernenko was not seen in public for almost two months. After December he could walk no more than a few steps, and he died in March 1985.[22]

The Andropov and Chernenko eras in retrospect wasted valuable time, making the possible success of any reformist leader more difficult. Taken together with the incapacity of Brezhnev after the late 1970s and the inevitable several years it would take any new leader to consolidate his power, it meant that a full decade would be lost before a reformist leader could deal with the mounting problems of the regime. This only added to the burden of Mikhail Gorbachev, who inherited these problems in 1985.

---

[18]White, *Gorbachev in Power*, chapter 1; and Federal Institute for East European and International Studies, *The Soviet Union 1984/85*, chapter 3.

[19]See Timothy Colton and Thane Gustafson, editors, *Soldiers and the Soviet State*, Princeton University Press, Princeton, pp. 72–74.

[20]Ian Derbyshire, *Politics in the Soviet Union From Brezhnev to Gorbachev*, W. and R. Chambers, Cambridge, England, 1987, pp. 95–104.

[21]Mark Zlotnik, "Chernenko's Platform," *Problems of Communism*, vol. 31, no. 6, November–December 1982, pp. 70–74.

[22]Zemtsov, *Chernenko: The Last Bolshevik*, chapter 6.

15

The Gorbachev Era

The Gorbachev era was a period of great triumph and failure, of Gorbachev's winning the Noble Peace Prize in 1990 and presiding over the disintegration of the Soviet Union in 1991. We must understand the great problems facing Gorbachev as he sought to bring change to a lagging superpower, a country beset by declining life expectancy, horrendous consumer goods, a weak agricultural sector, and isolation from the West—but still a military superpower with a strong heavy industrial base, large scientific establishment, and a well-educated, predominantly urban population. In six years he did carry out many reforms and laid the base for Yeltsin's leap towards capitalism, democracy, and nationhood. Like most reformers in a revolution, he moved too slowly, inhibited by his own ties to the old order (to socialism and the Soviet Union) and a lack of awareness of the depth of the problems. In the end he was overtaken by true revolutionaries. This does not lessen our debt to him for ending the Cold War and paving the way to a more humane, democratic, peaceful, and open post-Soviet society.

WHO WAS MIKHAIL GORBACHEV?

Like most Soviet leaders, Gorbachev came from humble origins.[1] He was born in 1931 in Privolnoe, a village of 3000 people, in Stavropol province in the Northern Caucasus. His religious grandmother had Gorbachev baptized at

---

[1]There have been a plethora of works on the Gorbachev years. On Gorbachev the man see Zhores Medvedev, *Gorbachev*, W.W. Norton, New York, 1986; and Dusko Doer and Louise Branson, *Gorbachev: Heretic in the Kremlin*, Viking, New York, 1990. For further biographies see Neil Felshman, *Gorbachev, Yeltsin and the Last Days of the Soviet Empire*, St. Martin's Press, New York, 1992, chapter 3; and Marshall Goldman, *What Went Wrong With Perestroika*, W.W. Norton, New York, 1991, chapter 4.

birth. His father came from a line of free peasants rather than serfs. One grandfather may have been sent to Siberia in the 1930s, and the other, chairman of his kolkhoz, was imprisoned for over a year as an enemy of the people. During the early 1930s half of Gorbachev's family starved to death in a local famine. During the war the Germans occupied his village, which was not in a war zone, for eight months. His father, a tractor and combine operator, fought in the Red Army, and his uncle was killed in the Battle of Kursk-Orel. The war disrupted his schooling and he worked eleven to twelve hours a day during summers as a combine operator. In 1949 his summer activities won him an Order of the Red Banner of Labor for overfulfilling grain quotas.

With high intelligence, good grades (silver medal in high school), a lower-class background, and the award, he was a natural candidate to go to school in Moscow. He arrived in Lenin Hills in 1950 with all his belongings in one small suitcase, and in 1955 he graduated with honors from Moscow State University Law School and joined the Party. At the university he met and married Raisa Titorenko, a gold medal high school graduate, who would have a major influence on his thinking. After graduation, he returned to Stavropol, a city of 130,000 people with one main street, 750 miles from the glitter of Moscow. He began at the bottom by heading a department in the Stavropol City Komsomol and worked his way up through the machine. Over time, Gorbachev gained patrons, such as Fyodor Kulakov and, perhaps, Mikhail Suslov, then current and former Stavropol Party bosses. By 1960 Gorbachev headed the Stavropol Komsomol organization and in 1961 attended his first Party congress as a delegate. He obtained a degree as an agronomist from the Stavropol Agricultural Institute in 1967. He also traveled to Europe, first France and then Italy.

In 1970, at the age of thirty-nine, he became First Party Secretary for Stavropol region (over 2 million people), which included the best agricultural province and the top resort area in the country. He belonged to an elite of roughly a hundred first secretaries of key regions. During the 1970s Gorbachev met and impressed the vacationing Yuri Andropov and conducted agricultural experiments. In 1978 Gorbachev was called to Moscow as a Central Committee secretary in agriculture to replace Fyodor Kulakov. Gorbachev was not able to improve the dismal national performance of agriculture, but within two years he was a full member of the Politburo.

MIKHAIL GORBACHEV: THE HEIR (1982–1985)

Gorbachev rose quickly in Moscow in the leadership vacuum of the late Brezhnev era. After Brezhnev's death, Gorbachev became second in command to Andropov and ran the Secretariat in his absence. In February 1984 he supported the ailing Chernenko in return for a role as number two in the Party. With Chernenko declining in health, Gorbachev began to chair Politburo meetings that summer. In December he supported market socialism and an industrial revolution. His visit to London led Margaret Thatcher to proclaim, "This is a man with whom we can do business."

Normally, Gorbachev's weaknesses—a poor agricultural record, no ties to

military-industrial complex, weakness in foreign policy, no record in nationality areas—would have disqualified him for the top post in March 1985 after
Chernenko died. But these were not normal times. The bulk of the Old Guard
was dead or dying. Pragmatic conservatives (Andrei Gromyko, Viktor Chebrikov, and Yegor Ligachev) evidently backed the tough but reform minded
Gorbachev. So did Mikhail Solomentsev, Geydar Aliyev, and Vitali Vorotnikov,
nonvoting Politburo members such as Eduard Shevarnadze and Nikolai
Ryzhkov, and most provincial Party secretaries. The absence of Vladimir
Shcherbitsky (in United States) and Dinmukhamed Kunayev (in Alma Ata)
deprived the Grishin camp of momentum. In his nominating speech Gromyko
slid over Gorbachev's thin record and emphasized his brilliance, toughness,
and leadership ability. He declared, "This man has a nice smile but iron teeth."[2]

GORBACHEV'S INITIAL CAUTIOUS MOVES (1985–1987)

Gorbachev began by consolidating his position, eliminating his enemies, and
promoting his friends and allies. Gorbachev masterfully used the media and
traveled throughout the country to establish his authority. In 1985 he purged
key rivals (Georgii Romanov and Viktor Grishin) and retired Prime Minister
Nikolai Tikhonov. A new generation entered power—Prime Minister Nikolai
Ryzhkov, head of the Moscow Party machine Boris Yeltsin, Foreign Minister
Eduard Shevardnadze, and Central Committee Secretary Yegor Ligachev.
Many of these men would later fight him from the right (Yegor Ligachev,
Geydar Aliyev) or the left (Boris Yeltsin, Eduard Shevardnadze).[3] By 1986
almost half of the members and candidates of the Central Committee were new
men. Gorbachev's firing of Yuri Brezhnev (son of Leonid Brezhnev) as First
Deputy Minister of Foreign Trade and Dinmukhamed Kunayev (party boss of
Kazakhstan) in 1986 sent a clear message to the old Brezhnevites. But the
massive rioting in Alma Ata over Kunayev's ouster showed the depth of
nationality resentment of Russian domination of the Soviet Union.

The Gorbachev program stayed close to the old Andropov program of
revitalizing the system from within. To combat massive drunkenness, Gorbachev raised the drinking age from eighteen to twenty-one, instituted stiff
penalties for public drunkenness and operation of private stills, banned alcohol
from state receptions and banquets, restricted hours of sale for alcohol, and
ordered a sharp increase in the price of alcohol. In agriculture, he forbade
peasants to move to the cities, increased agricultural procurement prices to
make the countryside more appealing and raise productivity, and created a
supercentralized State Agricultural-Industrial Committee. In economics, the

---

[2]For an interesting view of what happened, see *Inside Gorbachev's Kremlin: The Memoirs of Yegor
Ligachev*, translated by Catherine Fitzpatrick, Michele Berdy, Dobrochna Dyrcz-Freeman, Pantheon,
New York, 1993; and Christian Schmidt-Hauer, *Gorbachev: The Path to Power*, translated by Ewald
Osers and Chris Romber, Salem House, Topsfield, Massachusetts, 1986, chapter 1.

[3]See *Inside Gorbachev's Kremlin: The Memoirs of Yegor Ligachev;* and Baruch Hazen, *Gorbachev and His
Critics*, Westview Press, Boulder, Colorado, 1990, chapter 1.

party approved a year 2000 plan to double production, improve the standard of living by 60 to 80 percent, quintuple nuclear energy production, and produce 1.3 million cars a year. At the Twenty-Seventh Party Congress a new super-agency ran energy policy, and the Twelfth (and last) Five Year Plan emphasized machine building, electronics, energy-saving techniques, long-run planning, enhanced autonomy of farms, and more decentralized economic planning.[4] But all of these traditional nostrums failed and were abandoned within the next several years. Gorbachev also continued press censorship, repression of dissidents, and severe limits on Jewish emigration.

Yet from the beginning Gorbachev realized the need for some change. During 1985 he proclaimed that *perestroika* (rebuilding) of the economy and society could bring the Soviet Union back on the track of progress and development. In 1986 he formally endorsed the limited goals of the 1920s NEP and called for *glasnost* (openness), meaning the demise of censorship, a free flow of information to the population, and a plurality of views in the public and media. In response, the theater and cinema unions installed reform leaders, who unleashed a flood of almost 100 previously unreleased films. Newspapers became freer and more critical and television more interesting with faster and freer reporting of disasters and political issues.[5] In 1986 the dissident Anatol Shcharansky was allowed to go to Israel and another dissident, Andrei Sakharov, was recalled from exile in Gorky to Moscow.

But overshadowing this was the dark cloud of the March 1986 explosion of the Chernobyl nuclear reactor 80 miles from Kiev. For nine days there was no official statement and eighteen days passed before Gorbachev appeared on television. Evidently several hundred people died, over 100,000 people were evacuated, and billions of rubles were spent on cleanup. Chernobyl accelerated the reform process by opening up the media to show the dark side of Soviet life and revealing the irrationality of the old order.

GORBACHEV: THE TURNING POINT (1987)

Gorbachev soon realized that marginal incremental steps were not working in the face of strong conservative and bureaucratic opposition. In July 1987 the Politburo called for purging 500,000 government officials. By August 1987, 25 percent of all the regional party secretaries, 77 percent of the deputy chairmen of the Council of Ministers, 80 percent of the commanders of military districts and groups, and 50 percent of the lower-level commanders were ousted. Almost 50 percent of the leading provincial Party figures were replaced.[6]

---

[4]Stephen White, *Gorbachev in Power*, Cambridge University Press, Cambridge, 1990, chapter 4; and Medvedev, *Gorbachev*, chapter 9.

[5]Jutta Scherrer, "History Reclaimed," in Abraham Brumberg, editor, *Chronicle of a Revolution*, Pantheon, New York, 1990, pp. 90–107; Josephine Wall, "Glasnost and Soviet Culture," *Problems of Communism*, vol. 38, no. 6, November–December, 1989, pp. 40–50; Doder and Bramson, *Gorbachev: Heretic in the Kremlin*, chapter 5; and Alec Nove, *Glasnost in Action*, Unwin, Hyman, Boston, 1989, chapter 6.

[6]Hazen, *Gorbachev and His Critics*, chapter 9.

In 1987 Gorbachev, pointing to the need for "radical change," supported the idea of subjecting the Party to the rule of law, democratizing the Party with secret ballots and open multiple nominations, and allowing non-Communists to have leading posts in society.[7] The purge of Brezhnev allies in the Politburo and shrill attacks on Brezhnev at the January 1987 Central Committee plenum signaled a new offensive. By arresting Yuri Churbanov (Brezhnev's son-in-law) and sending him to labor camp for twelve years, Gorbachev intensified the reform movement.[8] The spectacular feat of the young German Matthias Rust, flying 400 miles across Soviet territory into Red Square on Border Guards Day in May, was a blow to the Soviet military. Gorbachev responded by firing dozens of top defense officials, including Defense Minister Sergei Sokolov and Air Marshal Alexander Koldunov, and promoting Dmitrii Yazov to the post of Defense Minister ahead of numerous better-qualified candidates.

After fending off Ligachev's attacks and preventing him from speaking at the June 1987 Central Committee plenum, Gorbachev promoted four protégés to the Politburo. Declaring that the country faced a "pre-crisis situation," he called for a radical economic reorganization with self-reliant industrial and agricultural economic units and price and bank reforms. Perhaps 15 percent of the 48,000 state enterprises could be liquidated, and by January 1990 all enterprises were to be under self-management.[9]

In the first open clash at a Party plenum in over sixty years in October 1987, Boris Yeltsin attacked Gorbachev's cult of personality, denounced Ligachev for sabotaging *perestroika,* and railed against Party privilege. Yeltsin called Ligachev "an intriguer" of the old school who engaged in "obstructionism" and deserved Party censure. Ligachev savaged Yeltsin for his morals and purges in Moscow. Gorbachev in turn backed the ouster of Yeltsin from his Moscow Party post. At the followup Moscow Party Committee meeting, Gorbachev blasted Yeltsin for his pomposity, political errors, personal ambitions, and poor job performance. Yeltsin attacked the privileges and abuses of the elite and institutional sabotage of his directives. After the pseudo-show trial, Yeltsin, admitting his guilt in the traditional Bolshevik fashion, was replaced as Moscow Party secretary.[10]

On the seventieth anniversary of the October Revolution, Gorbachev rehabilitated Stalin's victims, praised Khrushchev's courage, and condemned Stalin for "unforgivable" crimes and "outright crimes and abuses of power." Yet

---

[7]Roy Medvedev and Giulietto Chiesa, *Time of Change,* translated by Michael Moore, Pantheon, New York, 1989, chapter 4; and Peter Frank, "The Political Framework," in Christopher Donnelly, editor, *Gorbachev's Revolution,* Janes, Medford, England, 1989, chapter 1.

[8]While I was in Moscow in June 1988 as a guest of the Soviet Academy of Science, a member of Gorbachev's Presidential Council emphasized that the West had overlooked the deeper significance of the Churbanov trial in terrorizing the Brezhnev holdovers with the threat of trial and exile to Siberian labor camp.

[9]Peter Frank, "The Political Framework," in Donnelly, *Gorbachev's Revolution,* chapter 1; White, *Gorbachev in Power,* chapter 4; and Doder and Branson, *Gorbachev: Heretic in the Kremlin,* chapter 13.

[10]Medvedev and Chiesa, *Time of Change,* chapters 4–5; and Hazen, *Gorbachev and His Critics,* chapter 4.

Gorbachev disappointed reformers by not going further and by his dismissal of Yeltsin. He also celebrated the seventieth anniversary of the KGB, while remaining distant from the military, but the KGB supported the reform program only with reservations.[11]

GORBACHEV: THE TIME OF TROUBLES (1988–1989)

Gorbachev entered the second phase of his reform drive optimistic that he would succeed. He had consolidated his power and eliminated most of his enemies. With strong central control he thought he could push reform and seize the initiative. He had mastered the threat from the right, and the left appeared weak. Both lacked strong institutional support or leadership, and the Soviet economy continued to grow. Yet the more Gorbachev moved in a radical direction, the weaker his position became and the stronger became that of his leading rivals, mainly Boris Yeltsin. He had unleashed forces over which he would soon lose control.[12]

The February 1988 announcement of Soviet withdrawal from Afghanistan symbolized Gorbachev's determination to improve relations with the West, cut losses abroad, and focus on domestic reforms. Intellectual pluralism took hold for the first time since the 1920s with discussion of previously banned themes (the war in Afghanistan, life in labor camps, and the harshness of life in the Soviet army) and reports of the discovery of mass graves of Stalin's victims in Ukraine, Russia, and Siberia.[13]

Gorbachev took on the government bureaucracy. In January 1988 *Pravda* called for a 50 percent reduction in the size of the bureaucracy, later trimming the figure to 30 to 40 percent. By March 1988 the government had dismissed 60,000 officials in the Ministry of Internal Affairs. By July 1988, 400,000 bureaucrats had lost their Volga sedans and chauffeurs.[14] The government released many dissidents and rehabilitated numerous "enemies of the people" while the KGB revealed many cases of official abuse and corruption.

Gorbachev tried to mobilize new support. He turned to the Russian Orthodox Church, which had perhaps 50 million followers. In 1917 the Russian Orthodox Church had 79,000 churches and chapels and 51,100 bishops and priests; in 1988, 7000 churches and 7400 priests and deacons. On the millennium of Christianity in Russia, Gorbachev met with Church leaders and

[11]Hazen, *Gorbachev and His Critics,* chapter 6.

[12]Anders Aslund, "Gorbachev, Perestroyka and Economic Crisis," *Problems of Communism,* vol. 40, nos. 1–2, January–April 1991, p. 29.

[13]See Nove, *Glasnost in Action,* chapters 2–6; White, *Gorbachev in Power,* chapter 3; and Woll, "Glasnost and Soviet Culture," *Problems of Communism.*

[14]For Americans used to two-car families, the importance of this reform may seem hard to grasp. But in a society where the vast majority of people do not own cars and where the car and chauffeur were the ultimate symbol of power and authority, the impact was considerable. When I was in Moscow in June 1989, I heard Soviet bureaucrats deriding a fairly powerful government official by sneering, "Why, he doesn't even have a Volga and chauffeur—he has to pay for his own!"

promised no further persecution of believers, the transfer of holy relics from the Kremlin to the Church, the televising of church services on Easter, the reopening of hundreds of churches, and mention of God in the newspapers. In 1989 Gorbachev met the Pope in the Vatican and later signed a pact to normalize relations.[15]

Gorbachev tried to alter the old Party-dominated legal system. He made judges independent with ten-year terms, promoted the presumption of innocence for defendants, and enacted new criminal legislation. By 1989 these changes had created the outlines of new Fundamental Principles for a new legal order.[16]

At the February 1988 Central Committee plenum Gorbachev conceded that an "acute struggle" lay ahead. In March 1988 a letter by Nina Andreyeva, a chemistry teacher, lashed out at Gorbachev reforms, cosmopolitan society, the Western threat, nihilism, and Jews and praised Stalin as a true Leninist. With Gorbachev in Yugoslavia, only one journalist in *Moscow News* dared to criticize the letter. But with public support and a Politburo majority, Gorbachev went on the offensive and demoted Ligachev. By May 1988, 66 percent of all ministers and 61 percent of the first secretaries of regional party organizations were changed under Gorbachev.[17]

The massive battle came at the spectacular Nineteenth Party Conference, the first such conference since 1941.[18] The conservative-dominated Party apparatus largely controlled delegate selection and prevented any major purge of the Central Committee. The conference did give Gorbachev a mandate for continued reforms, conducted open and passionate debate, and approved Gorbachev as the new President of the country (chairman of the Supreme Soviet). Public demonstrations in many cities reinforced Gorbachev's power.

Gorbachev called for a powerful popularly elected parliament, reorganization of the Party apparatus, an increased role for the Central Committee, electoral reform for a democratic party, and legal reforms. He envisioned socialism with a human face, with an advanced economy, enterprise autonomy, high culture, democratic traditions, legal guarantees, and equality for all nationality minorities. He descried "command-style methods" that "hinder socialist development" and called for new legislation that implied that "everything not prohibited by the law is allowed."[19]

At the conference Yeltsin appealed for direct and secret elections in the

---

[15]John Dunlop, "Gorbachev and Russian Orthodoxy," *Problems of Communism,* vol. 38, no. 4, July–August 1989; and Bohdan Bociurkiw, "The Ukrainian Catholic Church Under Gorbachev," *Problems of Communism,* vol. 39, no. 6, November–December, 1989. The preference for the Russian Orthodox Church led to serious conflict with its rivals, such as the suppressed Ukrainian Catholic Church.

[16]William Butler, "Toward the Rule of Law," in Brumberg, *Chronicle of a Revolution,* pp. 72–89.

[17]Nove, *Glasnost in Action,* chapter 3; Hazen, *Gorbachev and His Critics,* chapters 2–3; and Medvedev and Chiesa, *Time of Change,* chapter 7.

[18]The most detailed recounting of the Nineteenth Party Conference is to be found in Dawn Mann, *Paradoxes of Soviet Reform: The Nineteenth Party Conference,* Center for Strategic and International Studies, Washington, D.C., 1988; and Baruch Hazen, *Gorbachev's Gamble–The Nineteenth All Union Party Conference,* Westview Press, Boulder, Colorado, 1990.

[19]White, *Gorbachev in Power,* chapter 7; and Hazan, *Gorbachev and His Critics,* chapter 7.

Party and the government and for his own rehabilitation and declared, "After all, in seventy years, we have not resolved the main questions—feeding and clothing the people, establishing the service sphere, resolving social questions." Ligachev harshly attacked Yeltsin as a "destructive force," defended Party privilege, attacked the moral decay of the country, and took partial credit for the election of Gorbachev in 1985 by a bloc of conservative reformers (Chebrikov, Solomentsev, Gromyko, himself). The conference refused to rehabilitate Yeltsin.[20]

The conference concluded by creating a strong presidency. There was to be a partial transfer of power from the Party to the local soviets. There would be competitive elections within the Party and a ten-year limit on serving in Party and government posts. Party secretaries, while facing no retirement age, would need to stand for election and be limited to two terms in the future. The new legislature, the Congress of People's Deputies, would be partially popularly elected and have significant powers.[21]

After a conservative attack in August 1988 by Ligachev, Marshal Serge Akhromeyev, and KGB head Viktor Chebrikov, Gorbachev counterattacked. Meeting in secret without Ligachev and with only four days' notice, the Central Committee plenum approved the ouster of four members from the Politburo, downgraded Ligachev from his number two post and promoted four Gorbachev allies. Only Gorbachev and Shevardnadze remained from the 1985 Politburo. The plenum restructured the Politburo by creating six topical committees. Gorbachev was the master of the Politburo and the Central Committee bureaucracy, with the Central Committee the only holdout. By the end of 1988 Gorbachev had changed 66 percent of the regional, territorial, and union republic Party secretaries and 70 percent of the district and city Party secretaries.[22] In November 1988 Gorbachev legalized private ownership of agriculture. In December 1988 the Supreme Soviet formally approved the new political structure with a powerful presidency, a new national legislature with broad authority, limited terms in government positions (ten years), competitive elections, and an independent judiciary.[23]

Demonstrations in the Baltics in 1987 presaged the wave of ethnic violence and passions that emerged in 1988 in the Transcaucasus and the Baltics. In February 1988 ethnic violence exploded in an obscure, predominantly Armenian part of western Azerbaijan known as the Nagorno-Karabakh Autonomous Region.[24]

Politically, 1989 was the year Gorbachev finally mastered the Party appa-

---

[20]Hazan, *Gorbachev's Gamble—The Nineteenth All Union Party Conference*, chapter 46.

[21]Hazan, *Gorbachev's Gamble—The Nineteenth All Union Party Conference*, chapter 8.

[22]Peter Frank, "The Political Framework," in Donnelly, *Gorbachev's Revolution*, chapter 1; and Hazan, *Gorbachev and His Critics*, chapters 3, 6.

[23]Yet at the time the Armenian earthquake of December 1987, with the deaths of tens of thousands of victims, overshadowed this progress. See Doder and Branson, *Gorbachev: Heretic in the Kremlin*, chapters 18–19.

[24]For a broader analysis see chapters 17 and 19. See Mark Saroyan, "The 'Karabakh Syndrome' and Azerbaijani Politics," *Problems of Communism*, vol. 39, no. 5, September–October 1990, and Ronald Suny, "Nationalities and Nationalism," in Brumberg, *Chronicle of a Revolution*.

ratus. The Central Committee had eluded him. The success of the March 1989 elections to the Congress of People's Deputies (see below) gave him momentum to purge ninety-eight members of the Central Committee and twelve members of the Central Audit Commission, including ten former Politburo members of the Politburo and Central Committee secretaries, and eleven marshals and generals. By June 1989, 105 of 115 members of the 1984 Council of Ministers had been replaced under Gorbachev. In September he removed three full members and two candidate members and promoted four allies to the Politburo. By December nearly all provincial secretaries, 100 percent of republic first secretaries and 90 percent of the 1985 Politburo had been changed. In the Politburo, sixteen of nineteen had been appointed during the Gorbachev era.[25]

Gorbachev's other accomplishment was the holding of elections to the Congress of People's Deputies in March 1989. Here there were mass rallies and a spirited election campaign with nomination by selection of a conference in a constituent or social group. The Party nominated 100 candidates for its 100 reserved seats and 750 seats were reserved for public organizations. No fewer than 2884 people ran for 1500 seats. The vote in March by 173 million people (90 percent of eligible voters) stunned the conservatives. One-third of leading Communists and thirty regional Party leaders were defeated. Leningrad First Party Secretary Yuri Solovyev ran unopposed but still lost. He received 110,000 votes—but 130,000 voters crossed his name off. The mayors of Moscow, Leningrad, and Kiev, the commander of Soviet troops in East Germany, and the admiral of the Northern Fleet, the president of the Lithuanian Supreme Soviet, and the chairman of the Estonian KGB were all defeated. In Moscow Boris Yeltsin won 89 percent of the vote.[26] This election was a major gain for Gorbachev in his battle with conservatives.

The holding in June 1989 of the first parliamentary session of the Supreme Soviet elected by the Congress of People's Deputies was an historic moment. The new parliament eliminated twenty-five ministries and retained fifty-seven ministries, rejected six nominees for ministers, and showed surprising energy in its first three-week session. Its televised session, with deputies openly speaking their minds, was a stunning moment in Soviet history.[27]

This success may have helped prompt Gorbachev's decision not to intervene in the affairs of Eastern Europe. The end of Soviet control of Eastern Europe ended the drain on Soviet resources and focused the debate on the need for radical domestic reforms.

The momentum for change now moved out of Gorbachev's control. Boris Yeltsin outbid him on the political left and popular fronts were able to outbid him on the nationality front. A 1989 Academy of Social Sciences poll found that while the ideal of *perestroika* was popular, no fewer than 75 percent of the citizens felt uninvolved in events, 66 percent were uninterested in *glasnost* and most cared more about consumer goods and housing than politics.[28]

---

[25]Hazan, *Gorbachev and His Critics,* chapter 9; and White, *Gorbachev in Power,* chapters 1, 7.

[26]Hazan, *Gorbachev and His Critics,* chapter 8; and White, *Gorbachev in Power,* chapter 2.

[27]White, *Gorbachev in Power,* chapter 2.

[28]White, *Gorbachev in Power,* pp. 189–207.

percent), investment (20 to 30 percent), development (70 to 80 percent) and government spending (10 percent). All state property except apartments, including 460,000 industrial firms and 760,000 small firms, should be sold off; private property was to be the key to the new order. Shatalin wanted to give land to the peasants and reduce military spending 10 percent and KGB spending 20 percent. Government experts under Prime Minister Ryzhkov prepared a more conservative and gradualist plan with smaller cuts and a longer timetable.[42]

Gorbachev vacillated and then, in October 1990, opposed the radical plan, afraid of the political consequences of too-rapid economic change. Already the previous month parliament had voted to give him emergency powers for eighteen months to impose wage, price, finance, budget, and law and order decrees to restore the economy and stop the slide. Gorbachev, together with Abel Aganbegyan, proposed their Basic Guidelines on Economic Stabilization and Transition to a Market Economy. They suggested a new, looser union of republics, but without any right of secession. They would free 30 percent of wholesale prices while allowing another 30 percent to rise to a ceiling, leaving 40 percent frozen. Administrative means would continue to hold down inflation. The plan would limit the budget deficit to only 25 to 30 billion rubles. The government would begin the process of selling off state property. The Supreme Soviet approved the program, which was promptly denounced by Yeltsin as a move by the center to keep control of the economy.[43] In December 1990, Gorbachev fired Ryzhkov as Prime Minister, Bakatin as Minister of Internal Affairs, and Shatalin as adviser.

Gorbachev was unable to carry through his reforms. In March 1990 the government allowed individuals to own land, but a survey found that 40 percent of farmers opposed private ownership of the land under any condition, 34 percent under some conditions, and only 17 percent supported it. Land tenure was not guaranteed to farmers, who remained dependent on hostile managers for needed inputs. Few farmers were willing to take risks for uncertain returns in a hostile environment. In April 1990 there were only 20,000 private farms in the Soviet Union, and only 240 of them in Russia.[44]

GORBACHEV'S DEMISE (1991)

His move to the right in late 1990 solidified his ties to the powerful central institutions and also set the stage for the August coup attempt. In January 1991 the Soviet army suppressed demonstrations and reasserted control violently in

---

[42]Aslund, "Gorbachev, Perestroyka and Economic Crisis."

[43]Aslund, "Gorbachev, Perestroyka and Economic Crisis"; and Braun and Day, "Gorbachevian Contradictions."

[44]Barbara Chotiner, "On Communist Agriculture," *Problems of Communism,* vol. 39, no. 2, March–April 1990; Karen Brooks, "Soviet Agriculture's Halting Reform"; and Goldman, *What Went Wrong With Perestroika,* chapter 5.

Riga and Vilnius. Attempts to form a National Salvation Committee to restore Soviet control failed. Gorbachev's conservative nominee for Prime Minister— Dr. Valentin Pavlov, later a coup plotter—narrowly squeaked through the Congress of People Deputies, as did Boris Pugo (another plotter) as Minister of Internal Affairs. New legislation allowed joint military-police patrol of violence-torn areas.

At the same time that he moved to the right, Gorbachev also moved towards the center. He took a new, softer line on the Baltics. In March 1991 a referendum was held on preserving the USSR as a renewed federation with equal sovereign republics.[45] Six republics refused to hold elections. Turnout was 75 to 95 percent of the population, and roughly 70 percent of the Slavs and over 90 percent of the Central Asians approved this referendum.[46] In May and June Gorbachev cut a deal with nine of the fifteen republics. This agreement restructured the Soviet Union. It maintained a federal system of finance, credit, and taxation. Central government ministries would lose 30 percent of their budget, and privatization would come mainly in the republics. Many defense industries would become civilian industries. This set the stage for the new union treaty, set to be ratified in August, which conservatives opposed for reducing central power.

Gorbachev began to move towards market reform. In April 1991 the government undertook a major price reform with partial compensation for workers. Meat, bread, and grain prices soared over 200 percent; eggs, tea and oil 100 percent; and passenger fares 70 to 140 percent. Now one-third of all retail prices were free and 40 percent under contract. The reaction was more passive than expected.

Popular sentiment backed reform. In June 1991 Boris Yeltsin won 60 percent of the vote in the Russian republic to become its first popularly elected President. In Leningrad 55 percent of the voters approved a nonbinding referendum to change the name of the city back to the Tsarist Saint Petersburg. Later that month Gorbachev defeated a conservative attempt in the parliament to enhance the powers of the more conservative Prime Minister Valentin Pavlov and carry out what many saw as a "constitutional coup."

The conservatives, whose power had been enhanced by Gorbachev's appointments to key positions, decided to seize power before the new union treaty, which would grant enhanced power to the republics, was ratified. The leaders of the August coup—Vladimir Kryuchkov (KGB), Boris Pugo (Ministry of Internal Affairs), Dmitrii Yazov (Defense Ministry), Valentin Pavlov (Prime Minister), and Gennady Yanayev (Deputy President)—were the leading bureaucrats aligned with Gorbachev.[47] They believed that by putting Gorbachev under house arrest and transferring power from a "sick" Gorbachev to a "well"

---

[45]Soviet federalism, with its notion of central domination of nationality areas, differs from American federalism with its notion of reserving important roles for the states.

[46]*Izvestiya*, March 27, 1991.

[47]For Gorbachev's version of the coup, see Mikhail Gorbachev, *The August Coup*, Harper Collins, New York, 1991.

Yanayev, they could seize power bloodlessly with little opposition. As had happened with the arrest of Khrushchev, another misguided reformer in 1964, the public would remain inert and the military-security forces would quell any unrest. They might even be able to get Gorbachev to endorse the coup. The Soviet public would grumble but do nothing.

The State Committee for the State of Emergency of the USSR was a resounding failure. Their proclamation, "There is mortal danger for our motherland. The country has become ungovernable," fell on deaf ears. Their decision to suspend all parties, ban nearly all publications and meetings, lower prices, and raise wages was ignored. Gorbachev refused to sanction the coup or the state of emergency. The coup leaders lacked a real program and fought among themselves. The country, which several years earlier might not have resisted, now showed some signs of the impact of the reforms. Important military and KGB commanders opposed the coup. The coup leaders failed to seize Yeltsin or cut off communications with the West. Boris Yeltsin mobilized domestic and foreign support against the coup. Jumping onto a tank in front of the White House (Russian parliament building), he rallied 50,000 to 100,000 people against this "right wing, reactionary, unconstitutional coup." The next day the Russian parliament unanimously denounced the coup. Public sentiment swung decisively against the coup plotters, backed by only 10 percent of the population in one poll. Within three days it fell apart, Gorbachev returned to Moscow, and Yeltsin saw his popularity soar. Three people were killed in the coup, which decisively ended the power of the old order.[48]

In the aftermath the deep role of the Party in the coup was revealed and the coup plotters were arrested (save for Pugo, who killed himself). In front of the Russian parliament Yeltsin humiliated Gorbachev by demanding he read the minutes of his own Cabinet shortly before the coup. Gorbachev quit as General Secretary of the Party, which was soon dissolved. Few mourned the end of the Party. A September 1991 poll found that only 2 percent of the people had real confidence in it. Flags of the new Russian Republic replaced the old Soviet flags. Statues of Lenin and Dzerzhinski were toppled. By September 1991 ten republics had declared their independence, with two more to follow in the coming months.[49]

In the final months of 1991, Gorbachev, saddled by the fact that all the coup leaders were his close associates, saw his popularity plummet. His attempts to maintain the Soviet Union were rebuffed by republic after republic that preferred independence and sovereignty. In November 1991 nine of the fifteen republics backed a transformed union with direct elections of a president and a bicameral legislature. In December the vote by over 90 percent of Ukrainians for independence sank that idea. By December 1991 Yeltsin outmaneuvered Gorbachev by meeting in Minsk with the leaders of Belarus and Ukraine and creating a new Commonwealth of Independent States. Eight other republics joined this commonwealth, but not the Baltics and Georgia. This was not a state

---

[48]Felshman, *Gorbachev, Yeltsin and the Last Days of the Soviet Empire,* chapter 1.
[49]White, *Gorbachev and After,* chapter 7.

but an association that lacked a parliament or president. Late in December Gorbachev quit as President of the Soviet Union, which was officially dissolved on January 1, 1992.[50]

WHY GORBACHEV FAILED

Why did Gorbachev, a man with seemingly so many assets, fail and have to preside over the dissolution of the Soviet Union? Perhaps Alexis de Tocqueville said it best 150 years ago, "The perilous moment for a bad government is when that government tries to mend its ways."[51] Gorbachev's popularity plummeted from 80 percent approval in 1987 to 20 percent in 1990 and near 3 percent in December 1991.[52] He wasted (perhaps unavoidably because of conservative pressure) his first two years in office before seriously approaching the reform issue in the summer of 1987—an issue that should have been approached perhaps ten years earlier during the Brezhnev era. The hour was already late, and even then it was 1988 before he truly accelerated the reforms.

His economic record was horrid, with GNP declining 10 percent in 1990 and 14 percent in 1991.[53] Budget deficits soared from 25 billion rubles in 1985 to 100 billion rubles in 1988 and 200 billion rubles in 1990. There was a huge monetary and fiscal crisis, reflected in a massive ruble overhanging the economy. Long lines, rampant black market activity, rationing, shortages, increasing poverty, and inflation marked the Gorbachev era. In 1991 there were 1000 joint ventures (300 of them somewhat successful) with foreigners in the Soviet Union; 20,000 in China. In agriculture his record was poor. The average harvests of 200 million tons of grain meant that 30 to 40 million tons of grain had to be imported each year. Gorbachev undermined the old system by eliminating the power of the five year plans, Gosplan, and Gossnab but created little new. He left the Soviet Union in the Sinai between the old (Egypt) and the new (Promised Land).[54]

Politically, he completely lost the confidence of the people, only 3 percent of whom supported him at the end. By early 1991, 17 percent of the population wanted to leave the country, and almost 500,000 people had emigrated in 1990. Yet this was not because of a popular desire for democracy. A 1991 poll found only 4 percent had real confidence in the new parties and 70 percent wanted a person who could lead the people and maintain order. Gorbachev had lost the mantle of leadership by failing to respond to demands for economic growth

---

[50]White, *Gorbachev and After,* chapter 5.

[51]Alexis de Tocqueville, *The Old Regime and the French Revolution,* Doubleday Anchor, New York, 1955, p. 177.

[52]White, *Gorbachev and After,* chapter 7.

[53]There is much dispute over these figures. White, for example, gives a decline of 2 percent for 1990 and a noncomparable 17 percent drop in national income in 1991. See White, *Gorbachev and After,* chapter 4.

[54]Goldman, *What Went Wrong With Perestroika,* chapters 4, 6; Gertrude Schroeder, "The Soviet Economy on a Treadmill of Perestroika: Gorbachev's First Five Years," in Harley Balzer, editor, *Five Years That Shook the World,* Westview Press, Boulder, Colorado, 1991, chapter 1.

institutions, property rights, enforceable decrees, law and order, and functioning political institutions added to massive budget deficits hindered the creation
of a functioning market economy. However, the lack of revolution or chaos, the
liberalization of prices, an exploding private sector (now 20 percent of GDP),
the unification of exchange rates, an end to the lines, and an abundance of
goods in the stores showed that some progress had been made.

There were some areas of strength. By 1993 the private sector created 25
percent of the gross domestic product. No fewer than 40 percent of Russians
worked full time or part time in the private sector, compared to 10 percent in
1990. By the end of 1993 it seemed likely that 5000 medium and large companies would be privatized. Over 250,000 private farms had been created during
the last three years. Substantial foreign assistance, although perhaps less
than the 43 billion dollars promised at the April 1993 Tokyo G-7 summit,
would help the economy. Part of the massive reduction in industrial output
was good in that it eliminated useless heavy industrial products. Some real
roots for capitalism had been planted in Russia.[8]

The transition of Russia to nationhood has similarly been traumatic. Russia
has failed to develop an effective policy to deal with the "near abroad"—the
other fourteen states that were created in the aftermath of the dissolution of the
CIS. Yeltsin has sanctioned the use of force by renegade army units (Moldova,
Georgia), made light in private of the capabilities of the other leaders (spring
1993), and publicly threatened to revise borders of other countries, including
Ukraine (1992). The search for a viable Russia without imperial overtones is
likely to be a long one.

WHO IS BORIS YELTSIN?

Boris Yeltsin, the first and current elected Russian leader, is a revolutionary
turned statesman. As a heretic and radical he claimed many firsts: the first
person since Trotsky to publicly criticize the Party leader and call for his
resignation, the first member of the elite to quit the Party, the first to make a
comeback from oblivion after being ousted from the elite, the first to remove
Lenin's picture from his wall. He transformed Soviet vocabulary with subver-
sive words like pluralism, opposition, splitting, multiparty system, totalitarian
socialism, and factionalism.[9]

Yeltsin was born and baptized in 1931 in a village in the middle Urals 875
miles east of Moscow. That same year his grandparents, denounced as kulaks,
lost their property and were deported to the far north, where his grandfather
soon died. In 1935 his uncle was arrested for sabotage and sentenced to a long
term of forced labor in exile. In 1937 during the Great Purges his father was
arrested and spent several months in jail. After release his father worked as a
mechanic and his mother as a seamstress. Yeltsin grew up in the dire poverty
of the 1930s and the even harsher conditions of the war years. A highly

[8]John Guardiano, "A Free Market Revolution," *The World and I*, August 1993.
[9]See Vladimir Solovyov and Elena Klepikova, *Boris Yeltsin*, G.P. Putnam's Sons, New York, 1992.

intelligent boy, he graduated from the Construction Department of the Urals Polytechnic Institute in 1955. While at school he spent one summer traveling as a hobo across the entire vast country. After graduation he spent fourteen years as an industrial manager in the construction business and joined the Party in 1961. In 1968 Yeltsin became the head of the Department of Construction for the Sverdlovsk oblast committee. In 1976 he became the Party boss for the vast Sverdlovsk region, a post he would keep for nine years. In 1985 he went to Moscow to become an important member of the Gorbachev team. After eight months as head of the Central Committee Department of Construction, Yeltsin became Moscow Party boss in December 1985. From 1986 until 1988 he was a candidate member of the Politburo. In October 1987 he was publicly humiliated and fired by Gorbachev, who soon restored him to a leading post in the USSR State Committee of Construction. Plotting his comeback, he ran and won a post as deputy to the Congress of People's Deputies in March 1989. In June 1990 he won election as head of the Russian Republic Supreme Soviet. In June 1991 he became President of the Russian Federation. In August 1991 Yeltsin led the successful opposition to the security coup that had imprisoned Gorbachev. In December 1991 Yeltsin engineered the demise of the Soviet Union and formation of the CIS. Since then he has been the major leader of both Russia and the CIS.

UKRAINE

Ukraine is the most important non-Russian state emerging from the former Soviet Union. With 52 million people, Ukraine is the fifth most populous state on the European continent, only slightly behind France and Italy. It is the most populous state in Eastern Europe (outside Russia), considerably larger than Poland and dwarfing Hungary, Rumania, the Czech Republic, and Bulgaria. Its 240,000 square miles, running a maximum of 600 miles by 800 miles, make it the second largest land mass in Europe after Russia. Ukraine is blessed with a moderate climate and black soil for two-thirds of its territory. A borderland on the southeastern fringe of Europe (hence the name Ukraine), on the threshold of Asia, and on the fringes of the Mediterranean, Ukraine was on the main routes from Europe to Asia and exposed to many cultures. Its private farms before the Communist era provided a legacy of rich farm land. However, it lacks natural borders, with 95 percent of the country being vast plains, so foreign domination was the dominant historical theme for Ukraine for a millennium.

Now, after the dissolution of the USSR, Ukraine has inherited a substantial nuclear and conventional military capability. With 176 ICBMs and thirty nuclear-capable bombers carrying 1656 strategic nuclear weapons and with large ICBM plants on its soil, Ukraine in 1993 was the third greatest nuclear power in the world.[10] This nuclear stockpile was far greater than the several

---

[10]*The New York Times*, June 21, 1993. Ukraine has promised to eliminate its large nuclear capabilities but, unlike Belarus and Kazakhstan, has refused to implement a 1992 agreement with the United

hundred nuclear weapons possessed by France, Israel, China, and India. Its stated goal of a 400,000 man army would give it an army exceeding that of England, France, Germany, or Japan, and one with strong technical capabilities inherited from the former Soviet army. With 600,000 Ukrainians serving in the Soviet army in 1991, there is a strong nucleus around which to build a new army. The Ukrainian army has inherited thousands of tanks in the three military districts on its soil. Similarly, the dispute over the Black Sea Fleet demonstrated the potential for Ukraine to build an excellent navy of 50,000 men. Many leading officers in the former Soviet army, from the late Defense Minister Marshal Andrei Grechko on down, were Ukrainians.

Ukraine has been of vital strategic importance in this century, especially for Germany and Russia. In World War I the occupation of Ukraine was the centerpiece of Imperial Germany's Mitteleuropa plan. In March 1918, in the Treaty of Brest-Litovsk, the Germans gained permanent control of the Ukraine as the key to their imperialist thrust in the east. Only the German defeat in November 1918 rescued Ukraine from its fate as a permanent colony of Germany. Instead, Russia made three invasions, in 1918, 1919, and 1920, to reintegrate a largely unwilling Ukraine into the new Soviet Union. In World War II in the summer of 1941 Hitler turned his forces south to secure Ukraine as the key to his plan for a new order in the east. German occupation of Ukraine was essential to German strategic thinking. In their retreat, the Germans demolished 99 percent of the industrial capability of the occupied areas. The fact that former Secretary of State Henry Kissinger in October 1991 became a consultant to the Ukrainian Foreign Ministry showed the ongoing importance of Ukraine in the 1990s.

The economic potential of Ukraine is significant. Ukraine, the proverbial bread basket of the Soviet Union, produced one-third of the agricultural output of the Soviet Union, a grain output similar to that of Canada. Its industrial output by 1990 was estimated at 175 times that of 1922, and was 20 percent of all Soviet output. Massive power plants, including 25 percent of all nuclear power plants (like the notorious Chernobyl plant), extensive light industry, and strong metallurgical and mining industries characterized Ukraine. Ukraine produced 40 percent of all steel in the Soviet Union, which led the world in steel production. It also produced 34 percent of all Soviet coal and 51 percent of all pig iron. The economy is well served by major ports, most importantly Odessa. Although GNP is very hard to estimate, it would probably be in the 100 to 200 billion dollar range, once again dwarfing that of most of Eastern Europe.[11]

Yet serious economic problems remained. For over seventy years the Ukrainian economy was tightly integrated into the Soviet economy. Over 90

States for ratifying the Strategic Arms Reduction Treaty or to join the Nuclear Non-Proliferation Treaty as a nonnuclear state. In the summer of 1993 these matters were still under negotiation with the United States. Nationalists and industrialists have opposed the surrender of Ukrainian nuclear weapons.

[11]Orest Subtelny, *Ukraine: A History,* University of Toronto Press, Toronto, 1988, chapter 25. Neither the World Bank nor IMF are willing to make an official estimate, thereby making any GNP estimate purely speculative.

percent of all oil had to be imported, usually from Russia or now Iran. Without these ties, the economy lacks many of the natural resources, inputs, and goods it received from Russia and other parts of the Soviet world. Its goods, while desirable, are largely noncompetitive on the world market. The 1970s and 1980s were periods of low or minimal growth for its aging and inefficient industries. Many steel and chemical works and coal mines will need to be closed, thereby deindustrializing Ukraine in part. The cost of cleanup for widespread environmental degradation, as symbolized by the Chernobyl disaster, will be massive. Slowness of reform and antiquated smokestack industries have remained serious problems, thereby creating "the economic devastation that is in place at the start of the 1990s." As David Marples observed,

> One characteristic of the Ukraine's economy in the period since 1985 has been its almost total failure to adjust to the new conditions of life, such as self-accounting and self-financing at the factory level. It possesses the oldest industrial region in the Soviet Union. Factories and steel works, especially in Eastern Ukraine, are technically outdated, environmentally dangerous, releasing large quantities of toxic byproducts.[12]

The social situation became critical during the Brezhnev and Gorbachev years, posing a serious problem in the Kravchuk era. In the 1980s very low birth rates resulted from the difficult social environment. Living quarters were cramped, life spans were declining, and the number of retirees increasing significantly. Almost 65 percent of the work force consisted of industrial workers. Ukrainian wages were significantly lower than Russian wages. The standard of living lagged significantly behind that of Eastern Europe, which in turn was far behind Western Europe. Even under the Communists no less than 45 percent of the population lived in poverty, 10 percent in dire poverty, and only 5 percent at an elite level. Alcoholism was pervasive, basic products were lacking, and food was often rationed. Chernobyl caused massive degradation, forced 135,000 Ukrainians to abandon their homes, and impacted over 1000 towns and villages and 12 percent of all Ukrainian territory.[13]

The new Ukrainian state functions in the unstable geopolitical environment of Eastern Europe, Central Asia, and the Middle East. Eastern Europe itself is rather volatile. Czechoslovakia in 1993 broke apart into two constituent states, albeit peacefully. Yugoslavia has been plunged into a bitter and bloody civil war which may have claimed over 100,000 lives and continues to this day. Rumania has been marked by recurrent local violence and instability. In Bulgaria the defeated Communists in the last election still polled one-third of the vote. The movement towards democracy in the region is weak and tentative, largely focused in the northern tier of Poland, Hungary, and the Czech Republic. As for Russia, its economy has been a disaster while its political instability has grown in the last year.

Yet there are even deeper problems in the nearby region. Central Asia has

---

[12]David Marples, *Ukraine Under Perestroika*, St. Martin's Press, New York, 1991, p. 5.
[13]Marples, *Ukraine Under Perestroika*, chapter 1.

held together quite well in the early going (apart from Tajikistan), but the rise of Islamic fundamentalism in the region, continuing poverty and backwardness, and the competition of Turkey, Iran, and Russia for influence do not bode well for future stability. In the Middle East tensions, as ever, remain high in the wake of the incomplete Allied victory in the Persian Gulf War. One nation (Israel) has nuclear weapons, another has chemical weapons (Syria), and two others are hard at work on nuclear projects (Iran and Iraq). The massive sale of Western, Russian, and Chinese weapons in the region has even increased in the last several years.

The potential ethnic problems for Ukraine are serious. Ukraine has repeatedly been a cauldron of hatreds and the scene of repeated ethnic slaughter. The Russians are blamed for massively repressing Ukrainian culture, allowing 5 to 7 million Ukrainians to die in the 1932–1933 famine (while food was being exported abroad), forcibly imposing collectivization and dekulakization in the early 1930s, and running the Great Purges of the late 1930s. Polish rule was no more beloved and was blamed for massive Polonization and repression of Western Ukraine in the interwar period. In the middle of the seventeenth century, the hetman Bohdan Khmelnitsky led a revolt against the Poles that led only to Russian rule. The Germans are associated with the barbarism of World War II, which included massive killing and slaughter, forced deportation of several million Ukrainians to Germany, repression of all Ukrainian consciousness, and the wholesale destruction of Ukraine during the German retreat. The Rumanians are associated with their occupation of part of the Ukraine during World War II.

Ukraine was the locale for violent anti-Semitism on a scale rarely seen elsewhere in Europe before the Holocaust. In the seventeenth century the Khmelnitsky forces slaughtered tens of thousands of Ukrainian Jews. During the Civil War the Whites under General Denikin and the partisans under Simon Petlyura and Nestor Makhno massacred 50,000 to 100,000 Ukrainian Jews and left 300,000 orphans. During World War II Nazi Germany killed over 1 million Soviet Jews on Ukrainian soil, symbolized by the mass murder of tens of thousands of Jews at Babi Yar outside of Kiev in 1941.

And yet, and here is the rub, Russians, Germans, Poles, and Jews are vital to the success of any Ukrainian enterprise. Despite its resentment of Russia, Ukraine is strongly linked economically to Russia, also the strongest military power in the region. Without large-scale German investment and guarantee of its independence, Ukraine will flounder. It needs good relations with its Polish and Rumanian neighbors. Ukraine needs the Jewish intelligentsia to be competitive in the international arena.

None of this is guaranteed. Russians remain rather hostile to Ukraine, as a result of both past Russian chauvinism and numerous disputes over nuclear and convention weapons, uncertain boundaries (Crimea), and economic issues (pace of transition to capitalism and democracy).[14] Germany, burdened by its

---

[14]At a conference of the Association of Professional Schools of International Affairs with the Russian Foreign Ministry in Washington, D.C. in April 1993, the author was struck by the uniform

new role in an expanding and conflict-ridden Europe, by large-scale immigration (technically asylum seekers), by massive spending on East Germany, is hardly likely to give Ukraine a high priority in its thinking, especially vis-à-vis a much more important and troubling Russia. Poland and Rumania have their own difficult agendas and do not appreciate being in the shadow of formerly subordinate Ukraine. Finally, the Jews have another option and, with memories of mass persecution and an uncertain Ukrainian future, will be emigrating in large numbers abroad to Israel and the United States. Many observers expect that within ten years the majority of Ukrainian Jews will be in Israel and the United States.

Internal divisions within Ukraine remain strong. There are 11 million Russians and perhaps 1 million Jews compared to 42 million Ukrainians. With 35 percent of all Ukrainians intermarrying, with 20 percent of all Ukrainians declaring that Russian is their mother language, and another 56 percent declaring a strong knowledge of Russian as a second language, the Russian base in Ukraine is strong, especially in eastern Ukrainian cities.[15] There is a geographic division between a more independent western Ukraine, formerly largely under Polish and Austrian rule, and a more conservative eastern Ukraine largely under Russian influence. There is religious division between Ukrainian Catholics and local divisions of Russian Orthodoxy.[16] There is a strong urban versus rural conflict, as well as a division bewteen the local Ukrainian anti-Communist intelligentsia (Rukh) and the Russian and Russified Ukrainian former Communist apparatus (current President Leonid Kravchuk).[17]

The drive for Ukrainian independence was markedly slower than that of the Baltics. Ukraine was a high priority for Moscow, both on economic and political grounds. Ukraine had always lacked a national identity of independence. Ukraine lacked the quasi-autonomous institutions that Poland possessed in the Roman Catholic Church and Solidarity in the 1980s. Foreign support for Ukrainian nationalism was minimal and confined to small Ukrainian diaspora communities with little political clout. Russian control was very

---

and strongly anti-Ukrainian attitudes of the Russian participants. They were highly educated professionals at the Diplomatic Academy and Institute of World Economy in Moscow. Yet they openly talked with approval of the statement of the Russian Ambassador in Warsaw telling the Poles not to deal too closely with Ukrainians for their current status as an independent nation was likely to be only temporary.

[15]See Nadia Diuk and Adrian Karatnycky, *The Hidden Nations*, William Morrow, New York, 1990, p. 266.

[16]See David Little, *Ukraine: The Legacy of Intolerance*, U.S. Institute of Peace, Washington, D.C., 1991, chapter 3. In January 1990 the Russian Orthodox Church in Ukraine reorganized as the Ukrainian Orthodox Church. In 1990 there were mass takeovers of churches formerly belonging to the Russian Orthodox Church by Ukrainian Catholics (Uniates) in Western Ukraine.

[17]Among the relevant and useful works on Ukraine are Marples, *Ukraine Under Perestroika*, on the Gorbachev era; Little, *Ukraine: The Legacy of Intolerance*, on religious historical problems; Subtelny, *Ukraine: A History*, an excellent review of Ukrainian history; Ivan Rudnytsky, *Essays in Modern Ukrainian History*, Harvard University Press, Cambridge, 1987, a broad review; and John Armstrong, *Ukrainian Nationalism*, Columbia University Press, New York, 1963, on World War II.

strong in the major cities and Eastern Ukraine. The main theme of Ukraine's history for over a millennium had been foreign dominance.

Russian control rested on many factors. By the 1980s there were 3 million Ukrainian Communists, and Ukraine was tightly integrated politically and economically with Russia. The power of a strong, conservative Party apparatus for many years under Vladimir Shcherbitsky (until late 1988) seemed a solid rock of Russian control. An extensive KGB presence, the state occupation of the political sphere for generations, and the memory of former harsh repression of Ukrainian identity in the 1930s and 1960s reinforced Russian rule.

Ukrainian elites received significant privileges from the state. The peasants, largely aged, female, and poorly educated, were tied to the state for their meager existence. There was little foreign pressure or support for Ukrainian independence. Millions of Ukrainians living outside Ukraine had seemingly become denationalized and largely Russified. Over 50 percent of all Ukrainian children attended Russian language schools, with the figure reaching 77 percent in Kiev. Ukrainian language schools were largely absent from a number of Ukrainian cities, especially in eastern Ukraine. In 1990 Ukrainian historian Orest Subtelny argued that most Ukrainians accepted the Soviet Union as legitimate on multiple grounds—pride in the power of the Soviet Union, gratitude for increased income, upward mobility, and social services and access to mass education. The spread of religious and capitalist consumer values and resentment of Moscow's domination were undermining this support.[18] As late as 1990 Alexander Motyl wrote that Russian domination of Ukraine had been considered normal and legitimate since the 1920s and even then

> most Ukrainian citizens of the Soviet Union accept the authority of a powerful state that goes out of its way to bestow material blessings in return for one thing only—acquiescence in its existence.[19]

Only in the spring of 1990 did reformers come to dominate western Ukraine and, in 1991, eastern Ukraine.

Ukrainian history began over a millennium ago as a part of Kievan Rus, that cradle of the Russian, Belorussian, and Ukrainian nations. In 988 Prince Vladimir of Kiev accepted Christianity as the official religion, with a Byzantine orientation. Kievan Rus was not a modern state, for it lacked centralized government or specialized bureaucracies. Rather it was a loose confederation of princes and influentials that lasted for almost four centuries until the Mongols seized Kiev in 1240. This was a decisive moment, for it ended the unity of the region and led to different national futures for the constituent members of Kievan Rus. Its center in Kiev, the future capital of Ukraine, symbolized the centrality of Ukraine to the future Russian endeavor. The confusion over whether this was a Ukrainian state or more a Slavic unit has

---

[18]Subtelny, *Ukraine: A History,* chapter 25.
[19]Alexander Motyl, *Why Non-Russians Don't Rebel,* Cornell University Press, Ithaca, 1991, p. 70. As he declared, "Rebellion, revolt and insurrection will be well-nigh impossible. . . . Because they cannot rebel, non-Russians will not rebel." (p. 170)

created ambiguities ever since in Ukrainian history. The beginning of the Mongol period also represented the foreign domination of Ukraine that has characterized most of its history.[20]

The end of Kievan Rus and the Mongol invasion led to different fates for Ukraine and Russia. While Russia suffered under the Mongol yoke for 150 to 250 years, most of Ukraine and Belarus came under the Grand Duchy of Lithuania, another alien ruler, later amalgamated into the Polish-Lithuanian Commonwealth (after 1385). Ukraine became an important peripheral province whose elites supported the kingdom for cultural and political reasons. This alien rule lasted for four centuries until the middle of the seventeenth century. Cossacks, who were free men on the periphery of Ukraine, became increasingly successful in battles against the Tatars and Ottoman Turks.

The great revolt of 1648 had major significance for Ukrainian history and is still remembered today. In May 1648 the Cossacks, under Hetman Bohdan Khmelnitsky, allied with the Crimean Tatars and won a crushing victory over the Poles.[21] In the aftermath the Cossacks massacred tens of thousands of Jews, killed local nobles and priests, and burned Catholic churches. In September 1648 the Cossacks again crushed a Polish force. In November 1648 Jan Casimir ascended the Polish throne. The revolt waned as famine and plague decimated the Ukrainians while the Tatars desired to return home. There ensued years of inconclusive war. After a 1649 Polish offensive, the Treaty of Zboriv banned the Polish army and Jews from three provinces, provided an amnesty, and allowed Polish nobles to regain their estates. In 1651 the withdrawal of the Tatars allowed a Polish victory, which was negated the following year by a major Cossack victory. Yet the Cossacks were not strong enough to prevent recurrent Polish attacks. In 1654, in the famous and much-disputed Treaty of Pereislav, Khmelnitsky accepted an Orthodox Moscow as overlord of Ukraine as the price of survival. By 1656 Russia reached a peace agreement with Poland and the following year Khmelnitsky died.

Khmelnitsky ultimately failed to achieve and maintain statehood at this critical juncture. Against expansionary Poland, Russia, and Ottoman Turkey, Ukraine lacked internal cohesion and discipline, well-defined and obtainable goals, and viable institutions. The revolt could not go beyond replacing a foreign Polish elite with a Ukrainian elite. Massive internal strife arose over which nation should be the overlord and whether Ukraine should be a unique society of free Cossack farmers or a more typical neofeudal society. Khmelnitsky also launched failed campaigns against Moldavia and Poland and never came to terms with Turkey. The Khmelnitsky revolt opened the door for the Russians, who retook most of Ukraine and ousted the Turks. Already by 1649 the Russians had reached the Pacific and would now expand southward.

---

[20]For the historical development of Ukraine, the principal source has been Subtelny's excellent work, *Ukraine: A History.* See also for modern Ukrainian history Ivan Rudnytsky, *Essays in Modern Ukrainian History,* Harvard University Press, Cambridge, 1987.

[21]The Cossacks were an important independent social group on the frontiers of the Russian Empire. They were granted certain privileges in exchange for military service.

Nevertheless, despite his failures and massacres, Khmelnitsky engendered "instinctive, unbounded admiration for Batko (father) Bohdan."[22] However, as Subtelny has depicted this period,

> In the decades following Khmelnitsky's death, bitter conflicts over these issues pitted Ukrainians against each other. Civil strife, foreign invasion, and further devastation of an already despoiled land ensued. In Ukrainian historiography, the tragic spectacle of Ukrainians dissipating the tremendous energy and resolve that had been generated by the 1648 uprising in seemingly endless, self-destructive conflicts is often called the Ruin (Ruina). Twenty years after Khmelnitsky's death, the successes that had been scored against a common foe were canceled out by woeful inability of Ukrainians to unite towards a common goal.[23]

The period of ruin after Khmelnitsky's death was extremely confusing and painful for Ukraine. A council of military officers together with the elected hetmans ran Ukraine. Internal divisions were sharp and in 1658 two Cossack armies battled each other. Yet a massive Russian invasion that year failed to subdue Ukraine. In 1659, after a new Russian invasion, the Ukrainian hetman Yuri Khmelnitsky (son of Bohdan) signed a treaty with Moscow which forbade Cossacks to go to war, allowed Russian garrisons in major towns, Russian direction of Ukrainian foreign policy, and Russian approval of hetmen. In 1660 Russian defeats at the hands of the Polish army saw a temporary division of Ukraine. By 1663 Yuri Khmelnitsky had retreated to a monastery and Ukraine was rent by insurrections and divided between Russia and Poland.

By 1667 in the Treaty of Andrusovo Poland and Russia formally divided Ukraine on the Dnieper River with Kiev and the Left Bank under Russian control. This was reaffirmed in the 1686 Treaty of Eternal Peace between Russia and Poland. Russia, the would-be overlord of Ukraine, gave half of Ukraine to the Poles, who could not prevent repeated invasions by Russians, Turks, and Tatars in the 1660s and 1670s. By 1686 all of Ukraine was under foreign rule. In a matter of several decades Ukraine had changed from a potentially important nation to object of civil war, foreign invasions, and partitions.

Over the next century and beyond Russia, needing Ukrainian help against the Ottoman Turks, slowly tried to absorb its part of Ukraine. It eliminated the independence of the Ukrainian Catholic Church, prohibited the use of the Ukrainian language in books, and integrated Ukrainians into the army. Cossacks were used against Poland, the Tatars, and Ottoman Turkey. In 1722 Peter the Great abortively tried to eliminate the election of the Cossack hetman, which was finally accomplished only in the 1780s. In 1783 serfdom was introduced in Ukraine and in 1775 the independence of the Zaporozhie Host

---

[22]Subtelny, *Ukraine: A History,* chapter 9, especially p. 138. As Subtelny further asserted, "For the vast majority of Ukrainians, both in his day and up to the present, Khmelnitsky towered as a great liberator, as a heroic figure who by force of his personality and intellect raised Ukrainians from a centuries-long miasma of passivity and hopelessness and propelled them toward national and socio-economic emancipation." (p. 138)
[23]Subtelny, *Ukraine: A History,* p. 138.

was ended. Large numbers of Russians moved to Ukraine. Within a little over a century the political and administrative autonomy of Ukraine ended. Attempts at resistance, such as that of Ukrainian Hetman Ivan Mazepa to support Sweden against Russia, ended with defeat at the Battle of Poltava (1709) and hastened Russian repression of all opposition. By the late eighteenth century Russia had forced Ukrainian obedience to Moscow, coordinated Ukrainian government, economy, and culture with those of Russia, and extracted maximum benefit from the relationship.[24]

The three partitions of Poland (1772–1795) that saw Russia, Prussia, and Austria eliminate an independent Poland deeply impacted Ukraine. From 1770 to 1917, 80 percent of Ukrainians came under Russian rule; the remainder were under the Austro-Hungarian Empire. The Russian Empire, with absolutist autocracy, a strong and reactionary bureaucracy, and stringent police policies, treated Ukraine as part of Russia. The Tsars denied the existence of Ukrainian language or culture, sought to suppress Ukrainian national identity, and denied the existence of any borders for a Ukrainian state. Imperial policies were applied on the Left Bank in the 1780s but not for fifty years on the Right Bank. The government promoted Russification by closing Polish schools, creating Russian schools, stripping 60,000 Polish nobles of nobility and exiling many, replacing Poles with Russians in the Ukrainian bureaucracy, ending Western legal codes, and eliminating the Greek Catholic Church.[25]

The Austrian Empire (later the Austro-Hungarian Empire) similarly tried to fit Ukrainians into their mold. While Russians were imposing serfdom on the Left Bank, Austrians were dismantling it in western Ukraine. Austria similarly had a major impact on western Ukrainians. However, there was no parallel to the Russification policy in the rest of Ukraine given the polyglot nature of the Hapsburg Empire. After the 1848 revolution in Galicia, the Austrians abolished corvee labor (two to three days' work a week for the lords) and supported Ukrainians against the Poles. The grateful western Ukrainians supported Austrian absolutism and reactionary rule against Poles and Hungarians fighting for independence and for liberal democracy.

The 1861 Russian emancipation of serfs had a major impact on Ukraine where 42 percent of the population were serfs (compared to 35 percent in Russia). So too did the creation of local government *(zemstvo)* by the nobles and increasing emphasis on legality versus autocracy. Yet the peasants and serfs remained unhappy with the high cost of paying for the land and with the fact that the landlords kept half of the land, and the better part at that. Furthermore, peasants and liberated serfs were still not equal, but rather remained isolated from the general population. They needed passports to travel to cities, came under special courts with great powers over them, had to pay a head tax, and lived under the rule of their village elders.

---

[24]Stephan Horak, "Russian Expansion and Policy in Ukraine, 1648–1791," in Michael Rywkin, editor, *Russian Colonial Expansion to 1917*, Mansell Publishing Ltd., London, 1988, chapter 6.
[25]The Greek Catholic Church, or the Uniate Church, in its sixteenth-century agreement with Rome, reunited with Rome while retaining Slavonic liturgy.

In these benighted conditions, national consciousness remained primitive, as did living conditions in general for the bulk of the population. Ukraine was not a historic nation like Poland or Georgia. Nationalism came late to Ukraine, beginning to take shape only at the end of the nineteenth century and becoming a serious force after 1917. The upper classes and the bulk of the educated population were Russified or non-Ukrainians and the cities remained predominantly in the hands of non-Ukrainians. In 1897 Ukrainians made up only 22 percent of the population of Kiev.[26] The lures of career, recognition, and money to ambitious Ukrainians, especially with little likelihood of any Ukrainian autonomy or independence, were powerful in the nineteenth century. Even Ukrainian university students at the end of the nineteenth century tended to be antinational. Most emerging parties, ranging from radical Marxists and Bundists to moderate Kadets to reactionary Black Hundreds, consisted of intelligentsia elements either hostile or indifferent to Ukrainian nationalism. Even the 1905 Revolution had little impact in this area, and Ukrainian consciousness remained low. The First Duma elected in 1906 did have a Ukrainian club of forty members in favor of autonomy; subsequent Dumas simply ignored Ukrainian interests. Until 1914 Ukrainian nationalism remained weak, limited to the better-off peasantry and local intelligentsia.

Even the industrial revolution that swept through the Russian Empire in the late nineteenth century had limited effects in Ukraine. The locus of power in Ukraine remained in the rural areas, which suffered from overpopulation, land shortages, and dire poverty. In the 1890s fully 68 percent of the population was unemployed, underemployed, or living from hand to mouth. Poor peasants, with less than three acres of land, constituted half of the population and lived in serious poverty. In 1897 there were 400,000 industrial workers toiling under harsh conditions for low pay ten to fifteen hours a day, six days a week. Foreigners and non-Ukrainians predominated in the industrial boom in Ukraine. The local bourgeoisie was insignificant. Even in 1900, 87 percent of all Ukrainians lived in rural areas. In Odessa, the most dynamic city, only six percent of the population were Ukrainians. Ukrainians were absent from modernization. Only 25 percent of the leading workers and 10 to 25 percent of the intelligentsia were Ukrainians.

Russians and Jews made up over 65 percent of the urban population in Ukraine. The cities and towns were centers of Russian imperial administration, strongholds of Russian language, culture and non-Ukrainians and Russified Ukrainians. In 1900 fully 26 percent of the population of Ukraine were Russians, Jews, and Poles. The Russians, Orthodox in religion and loyal agents of the empire, were hostile to any form of Ukrainian nationalism. So too were the Poles, a more elite element, who saw Ukraine as part of Poland rather than Russia. The 2 million Ukrainian Jews, largely poor traders and artisans and often religious, stood outside of the Christian world. Frequently victimized in the pogroms of 1881 and 1903–1905, they were deeply alienated from the

---

[26]Chauncy Harris, "The New Russian Minorities: A Statistical Overview," *Post-Soviet Geography*, vol. 34, no. 1, January 1993, p. 18.

Ukrainians. Overall, then, the peasants were Ukrainians, the landlords and government officials were Russians and Poles, and the commercial elements were Jews.[27]

The decisive moment was to be World War I. In 1914 there was the first massive demonstration against ignoring the centenary of the famous Ukrainian poet, Taras Shevchenko. Yet even there the change from the idea of Ukrainians as an ethnic mass to cultural, political, and self-conscious nation was developing very slowly. The hostility of both the Russian Empire and Russian populace to Ukrainian nationalism included even the usually open-minded Russian intelligentsia. The Ukrainian peasant masses were illiterate, with little or no political consciousness. The Russian willingness to accept Russified Ukrainians as Ukrainians (here Little Russians), while simultaneously repressing the Ukrainian language and Ukrainian nationalists, continued to have an effect. So too did Russian dominance of the cities. These aspects helped determine the ultimate failure of Ukrainian nationalism by 1920.

The massive defeats suffered by the Russian Imperial Army in the war undermined its authority and capacity to control the Ukrainians. The defeats suffered by the Russian army in Galicia led over 1 million soldiers to retreat in disorder into Ukraine. The rapid success of the 1917 February Revolution, like the 1991 August coup, led to the loss of central Russian control over Ukraine and emergence of a Ukrainian government. By March 1917 a moderately pro-Ukrainian nationalist Central Rada dominated by Social Democrats vied with the radical Kiev Soviet for control of Ukraine. The Bolsheviks were very weak in Ukraine, as they relied on Russian Marxists and a small industrial working class. In 1918 they had 5000 members compared to 300,000 members of the Ukrainian Socialist Revolutionaries. Under these conditions the success of the Bolshevik October Revolution in the twin capitals led to the decision of the Central Rada to demand an autonomous Ukrainian Republic. In December 1917 elections the Bolsheviks won a mere 10 percent of the vote. By January 1918 the Central Rada was calling for Ukrainian independence. Although the Central Rada commanded popular support and pushed for self-government and a democratic parliamentary regime, it soon failed. Without a bureaucracy, it could not penetrate the countryside. Without an army it could not ward off the more powerful forces of Germany and Russia. Since most educated people were Russians or Russified Ukrainians, it was weak in the city. Yet it began the process of nation building.[28]

Undeterred by the popularity of the Central Rada, the Bolsheviks launched their first invasion of Ukraine. By January 1918 Kiev was in the hands of the Bolsheviks. But this first experiment was very brief as the Treaty of Brest-Litovsk ceded Ukraine to Germany. In February 1918, 450,000 German and Austro-Hungarian troops invaded and occupied Ukraine in three weeks. The Germans created a puppet regime under Hetman General Pavel Skoropadsky, a former aide de corps to Tsar Nicholas II, a quasi-monarchist and Russified

---

[27]Subtelny, *Ukraine: A History,* chapter 15.
[28]For a good review of the 1917–1920 period, in addition to the Subtelny volume, see John Armstrong, *Ukrainian Nationalism,* Columbia University Press, New York, 1963, chapter 1.

Ukrainian aristocrat. Like Vichy France and other puppet regimes, the Skoropadsky regime promised to "save the country from chaos and lawlessness." It revoked the Bolshevik nationalization of large estates and supported the Cossacks and large landowners. Like Marshal Petain in Vichy France, the regime drew on a strong, professional civil service, the old police force, and conservative support. It was fatally handicapped by its support of Germany and its Russified facade. The regime helped Germany exploit Ukraine for the benefit of the German war effort. The Skoropadsky regime, resting on German support, could not deal with Ukrainian nationalism or social reform. The defeat of Germany in November 1918 and the December German evacuation of Kiev led to the downfall of the puppet regime. However, its mere existence showed the possibility for a Ukrainian regime.

The withdrawal of German forces from Ukraine led to sheer chaos. The immediate winner was the Ukrainian Directory of Simon Petlyura and Vlodymyr Vynnychenko, who proclaimed a Ukrainian National Republic in Kiev in December 1918. Petlyura would be rapidly discredited for his alliance with Poland, his inability to maintain law and order, and his ignoring the demands of the peasants. That same month 60,000 French troops landed in Odessa and in February the Red Army invaded for a second time. Chaos rapidly ensued. Orest Subtelny summarized the fateful year 1919:

> In 1919 total chaos engulfed Ukraine. Indeed, in the modern history of Europe no country experienced such complete anarchy, bitter civil strife and total collapse of authority, as did Ukraine at this time. Six different armies—those of Ukrainians, Bolsheviks, Whites, Entente, Poles and anarchists—operated on its territory. Kiev changed hands five times in less than a year. Cities and regions were cut off from each other by numerous fronts. Communications with the outside world broke down almost completely. The starving cities emptied as people moved into the countryside in their search for food. Villages literally barricaded themselves against intruders and strangers.[29]

Literally hundreds of partisan bands battled each other in a kaleidoscopic spectacle in Ukraine. Esther Markish, an observer of the pogrom in Ekaterinoslav during the Civil War, has well remarked the anarchy and the pogroms:

> My awareness of time began with that autumn night when the streets were slimy with mud and blood. . . . Who was doing the killing? The Whites? The Greens? Makhno's partisans? Petlyura's partisans? In Ekaterinoslav power changed hands every day. It would happen that one quarter of the town was occupied by the monarchists, the other by the anarchists. It must seem funny to people today. The anarchists would leave, the Reds would arrive; then the Whites decimated the Reds, after which a band of peasants would approach the town, drawn by the prospect of looting. All these comings and goings took place at night. Two groups of men would clash and fight, one of which would retreat, abandoning their dead and wounded.[30]

[29]Subtelny, *Ukraine: A History,* p. 359.
[30]Quotes in Michael Glenny and Norman Stone, *The Other Russia: The Experience of Exile,* Viking, New York, 1991, pp. 169–170.

Our experience of the horrors of the Armenian genocide in World War I, the Jewish Holocaust in World War II, and the massive depredations of ethnic cleansing in Bosnia have inured us to the horrors of the Ukrainian civil war. Markish, then a seven-year-old child, tells the terrifying story of how a squad of Nestor Makhno's partisans rounded up a group of twenty Jews (including her father) in the town, ordered them to take off their clothes and lined them up against the wall to shoot them. Only Makhno's intervention saved them. More common was the fate of those not rescued, who had no intercessor to fend off the many partisans who preferred to slaughter Ukrainian Jews at will.

The second Bolshevik invasion did a little better than the first one. In January 1919 the Red Army took Kharkov, in February Kiev. Bolshevik rule lasted seven months. Russians predominated in this alien regime that refused to use Ukrainian language, allied itself closely to Russia, forcibly seized grain from the peasants, and supported rural collectivization of agriculture. The regime became ever more unpopular. In June 1919 White General Denikin invaded Ukraine and by August the second Bolshevik government had been forced back to Russia. Yet Denikin too, as an anti-Ukrainian Russian chauvinist who backed the old order, was soon not welcome in Ukraine. In 1920 the third Bolshevik invasion of Ukraine was finally successful, as the Red Army won the Civil War. This time the Bolsheviks demonstrated a learning curve not noticeable in their enemies. The new Bolshevik government included many Ukrainians, used Ukrainian language, avoided radical social experimentation, and built a strong army and bureaucracy. In the end 30 million Ukrainians found themselves in the Soviet Union, largely against their will. The Ukrainian national movement was underdeveloped, the peasants remained politically unconscious and unorganized, the cities were bastions of Russophile sentiment, the eastern Ukraine opposed the Whites, and foreign powers showed little interest in supporting Ukrainian independence. The Bolsheviks were well led and organized and had learned from their experience. Overall, the Poles in Galicia and Russians in eastern Ukraine were simply too strong and the Ukrainians too poorly organized. Once more, Ukraine was partitioned among Russia and Poland.

The 1920s were the happiest period in Ukrainian history before the current era. After the horrors of the Civil War that had killed 1 to 2 million Ukrainians, peace, even at the hands of the Bolsheviks, was welcomed by many. In 1922 the Ukraine, with 26 million people (20 percent of them non-Ukrainians), became one of the four republics in the new Union of Soviet Socialist Republics. There was recognition of a Ukrainian republic, language, and culture. Fully 97 percent of Ukrainian children were taught Ukrainian, and Ukrainians were a majority in the universities. The cities became increasingly Ukrainian as industry revived and peasants moved from the countryside to the city. There was innovation and experimentation in education and culture. Literacy rose from 24 percent of the population to 57 percent. Unlike the tsars, the Bolsheviks acknowledged the Ukrainian nation within a territorial-administrative framework and promoted the education and development of Ukraine.

The 1930s, though, were a nightmare for Ukraine. The decade was a time of terror. In order to destroy fierce resistance to collectivization that took the forms of violence and mass destruction of 50 percent of the livestock, Stalin resorted to harsh repression. No fewer than 850,000 Ukrainians were deported. In 1932–1933 Stalin allowed 5 million Ukrainian peasants, 22 percent of the total, to starve to death in a famine. Throughout this time food was being exported from the Ukraine and total grain production in Ukraine was only 12 percent below the average for the past four years. Yet quotas had been raised a stunning 44 percent, provoking starvation at home. Peasants ate rats, pets, bark, leaves, and garbage, even resorting at times to cannibalism. Robert Conquest in his eloquent work, *The Harvest of Sorrow,* has recollected this dreadful period:

> Outside the villages and even the small towns in Kiev and Vinnytsa Provinces, piles of human bodies to the number of several thousand lay on the frozen ground with no one strong enough to dig the graves. The village of Matkivtsi, Vinnytsia Province, had 312 households and a population of 1293. Three men and two women were shot for cutting ears of corn in their own garden plots and twenty-four families were deported to Siberia. In the spring of 1933 many died. And the rest fled. The empty village was cordoned off. . . . A Russian friend of the author's similarly tells of his father in the Komsomol, who belonged to a squad which went to villages with the whole population dead . . . to put up "no entry" signs around them for health reasons—there being no possibility of burial of the many corpses.[31]

In 1933 Russians arrived to run the Ukrainian Communist Party, ending the rule of Pavel Postyshev. The new leaders purged 100,000 Ukrainian Communists and 80 percent of the leading authors in the region. In the Great Terror of 1937–1938 over one-third of all Communists (170,000 Communists), 100 percent of the top seventeen government ministers, and perhaps 90 percent of the Ukrainian Central Committee were purged. Ukrainians were a significant element of the 3 to 12 million inmates of the labor camps in Siberia and elsewhere. By the end of the decade all pretense of limited Ukrainian self-rule was at an end. Hundreds of thousands of Russians moved to Ukraine in the 1930s, which had over 3 million Russians and 1.5 million Jews by 1939.[32] Russian had become a compulsory language by the end of the decade. Stalin's Moscow emissaries enforced central rule, idealized everything Russian, and liquidated local autonomy. Stalin had smashed the Ukrainian intelligentsia and peasantry, the twin bases for Ukrainian nationalism, and set back Ukrainian nation building by decades.[33]

Only now that the Russians have published the secret 1937 census do we know the full scale of the horrors. From 1926 to 1937 non-Ukrainians in the

---

[31]Robert Conquest, *The Harvest of Sorrow,* Oxford University Press, New York, 1986, p. 250. This book is a fascinating and devastating testimony to the horrors visited on Ukraine by Stalinism in this era.

[32]The Jews were largely indigenous while the Russians were largely migrants. The Jews overwhelmingly sided with Russians, whom they saw as progressive and protectors, against Ukrainians. For the data from the heretofore secret 1937 census see "Research Materials," *Journal of Soviet Nationalities,* vol. 1, no. 4, Winter 1990–1991, p. 159.

[33]Conquest, *The Great Terror.*

Soviet Union increased from 116 million to 136 million people, a gain of 20 million or an 18 percent increase. Ukrainians *decreased* from 31.2 million people in 1926 to 26.4 million in 1937, a 4.8 million decrease. Assuming that Ukrainians had grown at the same rate as the rest of the population (and this still does not take into account the general terror), they should have increased by at least 5.4 million people. This suggests a total loss of roughly 10 million Ukrainians. More than 5 million Ukrainians died in the famine, millions more were not born under those harsh conditions or perished in collectivization and Great Purges. Overall losses for the decade were thereby roughly 25 percent of the expected population.[34]

Stalin decided to carry out a radical transformation through collectivization, industrialization, and modernization, to end the dichotomy between Sovietized cities and the traditional countryside. He wanted to smash remaining anti-Russian national strongholds outside Russia and to destroy peasant resistance to communism. In the 1930s revolution from above and mass industrialization transformed the area until by 1940 Ukrainian industrial output was seven times that of 1913. Ukraine, especially in Donbas-Krivoi Rig, Kharkov, and the Dnieper power plant, emerged as the second most important industrialized part of the country. Mass movement to the cities eroded the gap between city and countryside in Ukraine.

The time of troubles was not over for Ukraine; it was just beginning. The August 1939 Molotov-Ribbentrop Pact allowed the Red Army to march into western Ukraine (and western Belarus) in September. From September 1939 to June 1941 Moscow tried fervently to integrate the region into the rest of Ukraine and the Soviet Union. Ukrainian nationalists were happy with this unity, which had been severed for almost 300 years, but they found that the price was awesome. Moscow deported 500,000 to 1 million Ukrainian politicians, landlords, merchants, bureaucrats, lawyers, officers, priests, and nationalists to Siberia and elsewhere. They expropriated land from the landlords and made Russian the dominant language. By the summer of 1941, many Ukrainians, especially in western Ukraine, hailed the invading Germans as conquering heroes. The Metropolitan of Kiev declaimed, "We greet the victories of the German Army as that of a deliverer from the enemy." Most Ukrainian nationalists similarly hailed the German cause. This did not last long.[35]

By October 1941 the German army dominated Ukraine. In their retreat the Red Army evacuated hundreds of industrial plants while the secret police carried out massacres and left agents behind. The Germans soon proceeded to massively alienate the population. By October 1941 they had arrested and executed much of the leadership of the OUN (the Ukrainian nationalist organization) that had welcomed them. The Nazis saw Ukrainians as subhuman

---

[34]"Research Materials," *Journal of Soviet Nationalities*, pp. 158–159. The actual losses may have been even higher. The fertility rate in the Ukrainian countryside, which housed the majority of Ukrainians in this period, was quite high. Also, the expected growth rate would probably be higher than 18 percent over eleven years for the country, except that massive losses were sustained by non-Ukrainians as well.

[35]For the section on World War II, see Subtelny, *Ukraine: A History*, chapter 23; and Armstrong, *Ukrainian Nationalism*, chapters 2–7. The quotation is on p. 81 in the Armstrong volume.

Slavs, fit to be slaves for the superior Aryan race. The majority of 1 million Ukrainian POWs were starved to death in special camps. Over 2 million Ukrainians, under harsh labor discipline and for very low wages, were sent to Germany as slave laborers for the Third Reich. Often seized at random, the Ukrainians were sent over one thousand miles in unheated cattle cars sealed with barbed wire. A systematic program to ruralize Ukraine and redirect food surpluses to the Third Reich saw Kiev lose 60 percent of its population. From Kharkov 120,000 Ukrainians were sent to Germany, 30,000 were executed, and 80,000 starved to death. All higher educational institutions were closed, and Ukrainians were allowed only three or four years of education. The Germans banned Ukrainians from theaters, restaurants, and public places. Massive punitive raids against partisans burned hundreds of villages and killed hundreds of thousands of Ukrainians.

A worse fate was reserved for Ukrainian Jews, who in 1941 were herded into fifty ghettos and 180 concentration camps. Starting with the massacre of tens of thousands of Jews at Babi Yar ravine outside of Kiev in September 1941, the Germans exterminated 850,000 Ukrainian Jews by 1944.

The Germans divided Ukraine into four parts, three under German, Polish, and Rumanian auspices, the final one solely for Ukraine. Ukrainians were banned from holding office in these all-German governments. The hated collectives were preserved and peasants made to work from dawn to dusk. Ukraine provided the bulk of Soviet agricultural produce for the Third Reich.

The great bulk of the population soon grew to detest the Germans as much as the Russians. They remained uncommitted as relatively small groups fought on one of three possible sides. Partisan warfare was difficult in the largely open country, apart from northern woods and swamps and Carpathian mountainous regions. Ukrainian partisans on the Soviet side numbered perhaps 50,000 men under the command of Timofei Strokach, a senior secret police official. Another 30,000 to 40,000 men fought in UPA (the Ukrainian Insurgent Army, which fought both the Soviet army and German army). Perhaps 200,000 men served in the German army and 2 million men, largely recruited before June 1941 or after the Soviet reoccupation of Ukraine in 1944, in the Soviet army. Most Ukrainian organizations collaborated with the Germans at some point in the war, if only for tactical reasons.

By August 1943 the Red Army had retaken Kharkov and by March 1944 all but western Ukraine. The Red Army promptly drafted most men between eighteen and fifty, repressed Ukrainian nationalists, and re-Sovietized the economy and polity. By October 1944 the Red Army was master of all of Ukraine. The losses were staggering, even more so after the German scorched-earth policy in a 200-mile-wide zone. The war killed over 5 million Ukrainians, left almost 10 million homeless, and levelled 700 cities, 28,000 villages, and 16,000 industrial enterprises. By 1945 industrial production was 26 percent that of 1940 and famine threatened in 1946. But Ukraine was unified for the first time since 1654 with all Ukrainians in one state. In 1944 Ukraine took a seat at the United Nations.

In the postwar era the reinstated Soviet government waged a bitter and violent struggle with the UPA for control of Ukraine. Tens of thousands died in this struggle, which saw Moscow regain control of western Ukraine by 1948. The bulk of western Ukraine had never been a part of Tsarist Russia, let alone Soviet Russia, until now. Largely Eastern Rite Catholics with a Central European culture and strong Ukrainian nationalism, western Ukrainians resisted the Russians for years. In the process Moscow used secret police units to root out the nationalists by deporting 500,000 western Ukrainians, planting informers in all villages, carrying out propaganda, and using all forms of torture. The hard-line Russification policy of Stalin in his final years further alienated Ukraine. But the government also successfully reconstructed the devastated Ukrainian economy by the end of the 1940s. Many Ukrainians, while alienated by the regime, nevertheless hailed the social and economic modernization, the expulsion of Poles, and the uniting of all Ukrainians in one state.

The death of Stalin brought significant changes to Ukraine. In his brief bid for power after March 1953, secret police chief Lavrentii Beria had supported major concessions to Ukrainian nationalism. The accession of Nikita Khrushchev to power meant that a native son was in power. A Russian born and raised in Ukraine, Khrushchev had conducted the purge of Ukrainian Communists in the Great Purges, run Ukrainian partisans in the war, and supervised the economic reconstruction of Ukraine and integration of western Ukraine before his move to Moscow in 1949. Many of his policies were popular in Ukraine. In 1954 the regime gave Crimea to Ukraine.[36] Under Khrushchev (1955–1964) the denunciation of Stalin, purge of the secret police, end of mass arrests, terror, and purges, promotion of legality, cultural thaw, encouragement of Ukrainian culture, and greater tolerance for Ukrainian nationalism were all popular. So too was the rising standard of living and the move towards regional economic councils that promoted Ukrainian economic autonomy. After the horror of the Stalin era, Khrushchev's populist touch and promotion of agricultural experiments in Ukraine made him locally popular. Many Ukrainians belonged to Khrushchev's personal clique. Three men promoted to Soviet Marshals (Rodion Malinovsky, Andrei Grechko, and Kirill Moskalenko) were Ukrainians as were three rising stars in Soviet politics (Peter Shelest, Dmitrii Polyansky, and Nikolai Podgorny). The list of Ukrainians promoted to high places in Moscow during the Khrushchev era fills much of a single-spaced page in Seweryn Bialer's *Stalin's Successors*.[37] Even the Ukrainian Communist Party now came increasingly under the control of Ukrainians rather than Russians.

The Brezhnev era was more mixed for Ukraine. The rising prosperity of the early years and stagnation, corruption, and decay of the latter years both impacted Ukraine. Similarly divergent were the two men who dominated Ukraine during the long Brezhnev era. Petr Shelest, who advanced under Khrushchev and ruled Ukraine from 1963 until 1972, was quite popular for his

---

[36]In the post-Soviet world largely Russian and Russified Crimea has become one of several bones of contention between Russia and Ukraine. The transfer of Crimea to Ukraine in 1954 was a move to bolster Ukrainian attitudes towards the Soviet Union.

[37]Seweryn Bialer, *Stalin's Successors*, Cambridge University Press, Cambridge, 1979.

support of Ukrainian autonomy and Ukrainian culture. He fell afoul of the increasing conservatism of the Brezhnev group in the early 1970s, when he was displaced by Vladimir Shcherbitsky, who ruled until deposed in late 1988. Shcherbitsky ran a conservative, traditional machine that was unresponsive to liberalizing trends from Moscow in the Gorbachev years. Yet at the same time his hard-nose rule made it very difficult to displace him. For there was a strong base for Russian rule in the eastern Ukraine among the 11 million Russians and millions of Russified Ukrainians and Jews. His machine was based in the large cities dominated by Russians rather than in the rural areas dominated by Ukrainians. Not until the 1970s did the majority of Ukrainians live in urban areas.

Thus, by the beginning of the Gorbachev era a traditional, pro-Moscow Russian machine was well in place in Ukraine and would oppose and slow all his reforms.[38] The strength of pro-Moscow forces slowed the growth of Ukrainian independence forces. The first major demonstration came only in July 1988, when 50,000 Ukrainians protested local conditions in Kiev. In 1988 and 1989 nationalist forces such as Rukh, which held its first congress in September 1989, and the Popular Movement for Ukraine held demonstrations. In March 1990 Ukraine carried out its first multicandidate elections, with the democratic opposition gaining one-third of the seats.

In July 1990 the Ukrainian legislature formally declared its sovereignty. Gorbachev's ill-fated referendum on keeping the Soviet federation together in March 1991 accelerated the trend towards independence. While 70 percent of Ukrainians voted in favor of union with Russia, a stunning 80 percent voted in favor of Ukrainian sovereignty. The increasing disintegration of Moscow, the acceleration of nationalist sentiment beyond Western Ukraine and the failure of the August coup led to an August 1991 declaration of independence by the Ukrainian parliament. Soon afterwards Ukraine enacted laws to create its own army, eliminate the KGB, create its own secret police, and institutionalize itself as a state. In December 1991 a Ukrainian referendum on independence saw 84 percent of all voters go to the polls and give an overwhelming 90 percent endorsement to independence. Support ranged from 95 percent in western Ukraine to 54 percent in largely Russian Crimea. In the presidential race the Communist leader, Leonid Kravchuk, won 62 percent of the vote compared to 23 percent for Vyacheslav Chornovil, the Rukh candidate. Kravchuk himself, the former Second Secretary of the Ukrainian Communist Party Central Committee in charge of ideology and a clever pragmatic politician, won heavily against a broad field. He benefited from incumbency, his skillful use of the infrastructure, and strong resources. Kravchuk and Ukrainian opposition to continuation of the Soviet Union helped sink it and Gorbachev and create the new CIS.

Even today much of this machine—heavily bureaucratic and statist in

---

[38]For a good overview of the most recent period, see Commission on Security and Cooperation in Europe, *Human Rights and Democratization in the Newly Independent States of the Former Soviet Union*, Government Printing Office, Washington, D.C., 1993, pp. 50–75.

nature—remains the basis for the more conservative former Communists, led by Leonid Kravchuk, to oppose the more radical Ukrainian nationalists in Rukh. Any real multiparty state is still far away. Only the heavily factionalized Rukh represents a large constituency. In 1992 Kravchuk gained parliamentary approval for a heavily presidential system whereby he could appoint large number of appointees, mostly former Communists, to run localities. In June 1993 Kravchuk demanded a virtual dictatorship, with personal control of the government, army, and secret police, and his Prime Minister Kuchma running the economy on a daily basis. Parliament has resisted this demand and the outcome is uncertain. The majority of the parliamentary deputies, elected under the Communists in 1990, are still former Communists. Much of the media has remained state-owned and significantly proregime, with little criticism allowed. With much of the old machine still in power, progress towards democracy and a market economy has been slow. The legal system has remained largely in the predemocratic era. Much of the population still views democracy as an alien concept. As the 1993 Commission on Security and Cooperation in Europe report on Ukraine put it:

> Perhaps the most fundamental challenge in building a lasting democratic, rule-of-law state is to change the deeply ingrained attitudes among the population as a whole that can act as a significant barrier to wide-reaching reform. Simply put, democracy remains an alien concept to a significant portion of the population. It did not emerge from experience, it was simply declared. Hence, even under optimal circumstances, it will take time to develop a "culture" of democracy. While the form of the totalitarian state has disappeared, the substance has not.[39]

However, parliament has not been a pure rubber stamp. Its October 1992 no-confidence vote against Prime Minister Vitold Fokin brought down his government and led to the formation of a new government under Leonid Kuchma, the former head of a ballistic missile plant. In June 1993 it overwhelmingly refused to rubber stamp Kravchuk's desire to replace Kuchma's government with a virtual one-man dictatorship. A new constitution with guarantees of many basic human rights is being actively debated and discussed. Citizenship is available to all those residing in Ukraine, regardless of ethnic or religious background. Numerous laws protecting human rights have been passed by parliament in the last two years. Numerous laws on democracy and market economy have been passed. Treatment of minorities, such as Russians and Jews, has been relatively good, and Kravchuk has travelled frequently to Moscow and even to Tel Aviv.[40]

---

[39]Commission on Security and Cooperation in Europe, *Human Rights and Democratization*, p. 50.

[40]The large Russian population has not suffered under Ukrainian rule. As for Jews, often victims in the past, President Kravchuk has been solicitous of Jewish interests and even made a state visit to Israel in 1992. Over 100,000 Ukrainian Jews have emigrated abroad, mainly to Israel, a Jewish day school has opened in Kiev, and a Yiddish radio station has begun broadcasting in Chernyvitsy. In 1991 Ukraine did commemorate officially the fiftieth anniversary of the Babi Yar massacre outside Kiev.

Ukraine has created its own armed forces, currently in excess of 700,000 men. Even when reduced to 500,000 men or less, it will be larger than the German armed forces and five times the size of the American forces in Europe. Soviet military academies are now Ukrainian military academies, stressing Ukrainian history, language, and identification. Although 4000 tactical nuclear weapons were transferred to Russia in 1992, 176 ICBMs with 1240 nuclear warheads and 20 bombers with 160 nuclear warheads remain in the Ukrainian arsenal.[41]

Kravchuk's great success came as the avatar of Ukrainian nationalism. In December 1991 his anti-Soviet posture helped overthrow Gorbachev and the Soviet Union. In 1992 and 1993 Kravchuk repeatedly stood up to Russia and fought for Ukrainian interests in the CIS, over the Black Sea Fleet, Crimea, and nuclear weapons. Summit meetings with Boris Yeltsin enhanced his image, especially given the tendency towards Great Russian chauvinism emanating out of Moscow. He did open up the mass media and stop the massive surveillance by the security police. Kravchuk worked with Kuchma, the new reformist Prime Minister, who initiated a massive anticorruption campaign after election in October 1992.

Other problems do remain. The Kravchuk government has been unable and unwilling to implement serious economic reforms. Ukraine has lagged well behind Russia in privatizing firms, in liberalizing internal trade, and in receiving international aid. Proposals for economic reform in 1992 and 1993 have not been seriously implemented, even during the six-month rule by government decree at the end of 1992 and first half of 1993. Battles between President Kravchuk, the more popular Prime Minister Kuchma, and the conservative parliament, have hampered change.[42] Even reformers, such as Deputy Prime Minister Vlodymyr Lanovy, asserted in 1992:

> Ukraine . . . is unprepared for independent implementation of the reforms because its economy is not under full control of the state. . . . It is part of the economy of another state and is still regulated largely from Moscow.[43]

Kravchuk fired Lanovy in July 1992 for being too devoted to reform. Prime Minister Vitaly Fokin, fired in October 1992, was the former head of Ukrainian Gosplan. Over 99 percent of all industry remained by 1993 in the hands of the government. Rampant inflation, 1600 percent in 1992 and running at over 2500 percent in 1993, preserved jobs but at a devastating cost to the economy. In 1992 agricultural production fell 18 percent, industrial production over 15 percent, and the budget deficit was a massive 44 percent of the budget. In 1993 the ten trillion karbavonets budget deficit was actually greater than revenues. The economic slide exceeded that in Russia, with the new Ukrainian currency

---

[41]See Nadia Diuk and Adrian Karatnycky, *New Nations Rising,* John Wiley and Sons, New York, 1993, chapter 3.

[42]Simon Johnson and Oleg Vostenko, "Ukraine Slips Into Hyperinflation," *RFE/RL Research Report,* vol. 2, no. 6, June 25, 1993, pp. 24–25.

[43]Diuk and Karatnycky, *Rising New Nations,* p. 98.

decreasing 30 percent relative to the virtually worthless ruble in the first half of 1993. In February 1993 the Ukrainian cabinet approved major economic reform but it was not implemented. By 1993 Ukrainian inflation, at 50 percent a month, was approaching hyperinflation, which would completely destroy the economy.

Kravchuk's unwillingness to move seriously towards capitalism reflected popular attitudes. A May 1993 poll found only 22 percent of Ukrainians supported a market economy, compared to 26 percent who preferred a planned economy. Yet at the same time only 8 percent of Ukrainians were happy with the economy while 55 percent were unhappy.[44]

The Crimea, with 1.5 million Russians, 800,000 Ukrainians, and 200,000 Tatars, remained a stumbling block between Ukraine and Russia. In May 1992 the Crimean parliament, by a vote of 118-28, declared its independence from Ukraine, then reversed itself to request status as a semiautonomous region. The Russian parliament in 1992 annulled its 1954 transfer of Crimea to Ukraine.

Ukraine has been ambivalent over the extent of its linkage to CIS. The issues of nuclear and conventional weapons, borders with various Eastern European countries, foreign investment, and nation building crowd an agenda dominated by slow movement towards democracy and capitalism. So too are religious antagonism among the three main Christian churches with different relationships to Moscow and Rome. Battles with Russia over money (dividing up Soviet debts and assets), nuclear weapons and the Black Sea Fleet, the Crimea, and the fate of over 11 million ethnic Russians in Ukraine highlight the difficulties between the two major powers. It is no accident that Kravchuk is more popular in western Ukraine than in the more Russified eastern Ukraine.[45] Rising prices for Russian oil have also been a sore point. Several agreements over the division of the 350-ship Black Sea Fleet anchored at Sevastopol, the latest in June 1993, reflect the serious problems between Russia and Ukraine. In May 1992 Kiev signed the Lisbon protocol as a prerequisite to signing the START treaty and promising to allow Russia to control its nuclear weapons. By June 1993 this was a dead letter, as Kravchuk seemed to move toward the idea of keeping some nuclear weapons (specifically forty-six SS-24 missiles and 600 short-range nuclear weapons). Then by the fall of 1993 Kravchuk seemed to be moving towards giving up the nuclear weapons in return for substantial American aid. With previous Black Sea and nuclear deals never implemented, these disputes seemed likely to continue for years.

By the fall of 1993 Ukraine remained gripped in a political deadlock between the old conservative forces and the new reform forces. Discernible progress existed in the form of Ukrainian nationhood, the holding of elections,

---

[44]Kathleen Mihalisko, "Ukrainians and Their Leaders at a Time of Crisis," *RFE/RL Research Report*, vol. 2, no. 31, July 30, 1993.

[45]Ukrainians form 26 percent of the population in Crimea, 51 to 55 percent in the Donetsk, Odessa, and Luhansk regions, and over 90 percent in western Ukraine. Furthermore, 4.5 million Ukrainians speak Russian as their native language. See Susan Stewart, "Ukraine's Policy Toward Its Ethnic Minorities," *RFE/RL Research Report*, vol. 2, no. 36, September 10, 1993.

an increasing role for the parliament, and a more active media. Yet the power of the old apparatus (epitomized by Kravchuk), the failure to make serious moves towards capitalism, and the fragility of the democratic experiment are warnings that the path to democracy, capitalism, and nationhood is still very tenuous.

BELARUS

The creation of an independent Belarus of 10 million people on 80,000 square miles of territory is one of the more interesting modern phenomena.[46] The name change reflects a move away from the Russian Belorussia to the native Belarus. For the last 1100 years there has been a Belorussian people and culture, but only for the briefest of times an independent state. Rather Belorussia has always existed as part of a largest state in the region, whether Kievan Rus, Mongol, Polish-Lithuanian, or Russian. This poses serious difficulties for its future development as an independent state. So too has its close integration into Russia in recent times. It was the only major Slavic state with net outmigration. With 30 percent of all Belorussians calling Russian their native language and another 55 percent with Russian as their strong second language, Belarus had the weakest native language identification rate of any of the fifteen republics— and by a wide margin. This is in addition to the significant Russian-Ukrainian element, which is 17 percent of the population.[47] Belorussian nationalism has been much weaker and more recent than Ukrainian or Baltic nationalism. Belarus has been by far the most conservative and Russified of the fourteen non-Russian republics. It also emerged as one of four nuclear states after the dissolution of the Soviet Union, and the one most willing to give up its eighty-two SS-25 nuclear-tipped missiles.

In recent times there has been a marked nativization of Minsk, the capital. In 1959 only 64 percent of its citizens were Belorussians; by 1989 the figure had climbed to 72 percent. Russians formed 20 percent, Ukrainians and Jews each 3 percent of the population. This has been critical for the assertion of Belorussian nationalism.[48]

In its earliest history, Belarus, together with Russia and Ukraine, was a part of Kievan Rus from the time of Rurik (862) until the Mongol conquest (1240). Like the other peoples, the Belorussians accepted Christianity at the time of Prince Vladimir I in 988. The Mongols, while smashing Kievan Rus in the thirteenth century, did not reach Belarus, which led to a prolonged isolation from the Russians. Seeking protection against the Mongols and Teutonic

---

[46]For the discussion on Belarus, or Belorussia, see Nicholas Vakar, *Belorussia: The Making of a Nation*, Harvard University Press, Cambridge, 1956; and Ivan Lubachko, *Belorussia Under Soviet Rule, 1917–1957*, University of Kentucky Press, Lexington, 1972.

[47]Duik and Karatnycky, *The Hidden Nations*, p. 266.

[48]Mikhail Guboglo, "Demography and Language in the Capitals of the Union Republics," *Journal of Soviet Nationalities*, vol. 1, no. 4, Winter 1990–1991, pp. 7, 13.

Knights, Belarus became a vassal to the Grand Duchy of Lithuania, later the Polish-Lithuanian Kingdom. This lasted in various forms for over 450 years, until the latter part of the eighteenth century. During the three Polish partitions, from 1772 to 1795, Tsarist Russia took over Belarus and attached it to the Russian Empire. A thoroughgoing Russification policy after the 1863 Polish revolt eliminated Poles from the government, closed Roman Catholic monasteries, and promoted Russian as the only language of administration, education, and law. Belorussian nationalism remained a minor force until the end of the nineteenth century.

In 1900 Belorussians were overwhelmingly rural while non-Belorussians (Poles, Jews, and Russians) dominated the leading professions and businesses and the major cities. In 1897 Belorussians were 4 percent of the population of Vilnius. There was no institution of higher education, and the bulk of the Belorussians were illiterate. In the 1905 Revolution the local masses were largely indifferent to the revolution, and there were no major uprisings. In the elections for the First Duma the local nationalities (Russians, Poles, Jews, and Lithuanians) all ran their own tickets, but there were no Belorussian tickets. During the 1906–1916 period not a single deputy from Belarus mentioned his own Belorussian consciousness, though numerous other nationalities trumpeted their own concerns. Only now did a lesser Belorussian nationalism emerge, and it was largely confined to clubs and perhaps 3000 to 4000 Belorussian nationalists. The native language had no literary tradition or written form. "Indeed, Polonized on one hand, Russianized on the other, the Belorussians were as if they did not exist as a people."[49]

Even World War I failed to nationalize the masses. Divisions continued to plague Belarus. Various local groups formed after the February Revolution failed to mention national rights. In April 1917 Belorussian elections failed to return a single Belorussian nationalist. In the November 1917 Constituent Assembly elections the nationalists won all of 27,000 votes. The First Belorussian Convention in December 1917 after the October Revolution saw the predominance of Russian parties over Belorussian parties. The appearance of the Red Army smashed even this modest attempt at autonomy.

But the Treaty of Brest-Litovsk forced a Bolshevik retreat from Belarus at the hands of the Germans. Under the umbrella of German rule a Belorussian National Republic functioned for ten months. Without the benefit of real power, elections, or international recognition, subservient to the Germans, it yet made an important contribution to the cause of Belorussian independence. The invading Red Army in December 1918 sent it packing to German exile and proclaimed a Belorussian Socialist Republic in Minsk that lasted less than four months. The April 1919 Polish invasion found popular support among Belorussians, who praised Marshal Pilsudski, of Lithuanian Belorussian origin. However, the Poles wanted to subordinate Belarus, not give it independence. By August 1920 a Red Army counterattack brought Bolshevik rule back to Belarus

[49]Nicholas Vakar, *Belorussia: The Making of a Nation*, Harvard University Press, Cambridge, 1956, p. 74.

for the third time in three years. A Polish counterattack retook western Belarus, leaving eastern Belarus in Russian hands. This was confirmed in the 1921 Treaty of Riga.

During the interwar period western Belarus, with 5 million people, was under Polish occupation. After early enthusiasm for Polish rule and free election in 1923, Belorussian representatives began to turn against Poland. In 1924 the Poles cracked down on Belorussian nationalism, closing schools, confiscating newspapers, and imposing heavy taxes and corporal punishment. Large-scale repression continued throughout the 1930s as the Poles tried to eradicate Belorussian nationalism and culture. By 1935 there were no native Belorussian representatives left in the Polish parliament. Over 100 churches were closed, the clergy could use only the Polish language, the Roman Catholic Church was imposed on the population, cultural institutions and schools were liquidated, and Belorussian nationalists were sent to camps.

In eastern Belorussia, also with 5 million people, the 1920s saw a Soviet policy favoring Belorussian national culture. The Belorussian language became first among equals, and thousands of elementary schools used it. During this golden era of Belorussian culture, most emigrés returned to found a new university, a large dictionary of the Belorussian language, and new libraries. The good times could not last with the rise of Stalin in Moscow. By the fall of 1929 all Belorussian nationalists were in jail. In the early 1930s some were shot and most exiled for the crime of bourgeois nationalism. Massive purges in 1936 and 1937 completed the elimination of the old elite. In their place came a new, Sovietized elite, which spoke Russian and was better educated and loyal to Moscow.

The Molotov-Ribbentrop Pact in August 1939 opened the door for World War II and the Russian occupation of western Belorussia and western Ukraine. The population welcomed the reunification of Belarus and gave its approval in a formal National Assembly in November 1939. In 1940 a large-scale purge liquidated the leaders of western Belorussia and deported tens of thousands of kulaks and intelligentsia. A passive population watched in bitterness.

Under these circumstances most Belorussians welcomed or tolerated the German invaders who occupied Belarus in three weeks in June and July 1941. However, the Nazis would rapidly transform this friendship or passivity into hatred. The Germans killed over 80 percent of Belorussian Jews in the Holocaust, maltreated Soviet POWs, kept the collective farms, showed contempt for Slavic "inferiors" (*untermenschen*), forced laborers to work in the Third Reich, and repressed the bulk of the majority. Belorussian Nazis never numbered more than a few hundred, but Moscow poured in thousands of its own partisans and stepped up daily broadcasts. By 1943 the Red Army counted on several hundred thousand loyal guerrillas. Very belated German attempts to woo Belorussian nationalists were thwarted by continued Red Army advances.

Liberated by the Red Army in 1944, a new unified Belorussian Soviet Socialist Republic was created. War losses were horrifying: over one million houses and farm buildings destroyed, 80 percent of Minsk and 95 percent of Vitebsk devastated, 85 percent of industry and 100 percent of machine-tractor stations levelled. In 1945 Belarus, like Ukraine, was admitted to the United Nations as compensation for massive war losses, and in 1951 it gained its own flag. The bulk of its Jews were dead or scattered, and the Poles removed to Poland, while Belorussians from Poland and Lithuania migrated to their homeland. Almost 3 million people were killed during the war. By 1959 Belorussians formed almost 70 percent of the urban population compared to 35 percent in 1939. Russians made up most of the rest. In the 1960s and 1970s Belorussia industrialized rapidly. By 1979 only 20 percent of all Belorussians were collective farmers. Large-scale modernization promoted massive urbanization and educational accomplishments.[50]

Ethnic assimilation continued apace in the 1960s and 1970s. In 1979 Belorussians had the lowest rate of nationalities regarding their own language as their native tongue (74 percent), a figure which declined to 71 percent in 1989. There has been strong intermarriage with Russians and many interethnic contacts, as well as some migration to Russia.

The 1980s saw both rapid socioeconomic modernization of Belarus and emergence of an incipient nationalist movement. With strong capital investment, relatively advanced industries (machinery, chemicals, textiles, electronics), a good location near Europe, and an extensive transportation network, Belarus continued rapid economic advance in the 1980s. However, the closeness to Chernobyl, the spreading ethnic consciousness in the Soviet Union, the revelation of mass Stalinist graves, and outside pressures promoted a small but significant ethnic consciousness. In February 1989 over 50,000 people attended a demonstration in Minsk for the Renewal Belorussian Popular Front for Perestroika. The national flag and nationalist symbols were displayed at the meeting.

Yet Belarus was slow to assert its independence from Moscow. Multiparty elections held in March 1990 put the pro-Russian Belorussian Communists firmly in control of the parliament. In April 1990 riots erupted in Minsk in protest over price rises. In Gorbachev's March 1991 Referendum on the Soviet Union, 83 percent of the voters backed union with Russia. Only the failed August 1991 coup attempt in Moscow prompted the Belarus Supreme Soviet to declare independence. In 1992 Belarus signed an agreement with Moscow to coordinate economic and reform strategies with Russia and to transfer its nuclear weapons to Russia.

Even more than in Ukraine, the old-line Communist political machine has held on to power in Belarus. The Communists continued to hold the majority of key posts. The parliament remained under the control of former Communists, and new elections were advanced to March 1994. A reactionary government led by Prime Minister Vyacheslav Kebich continued to thwart democratic processes and the leadership of the popular reformist parliamentary chairman Stanislav Shushkevich, who pushed hard for independence from Russia. Belarus itself has the most extensive alliance with Russia of any state in CIS. An

[50]Ralph Clem, "Belorussians," in Graham Smith, editor, *The Nationalities Question in the Soviet Union,* Longmans, London and New York, 1990, chapter 7.

agreement in July 1992 provided for a unified credit and financial system, a unified ruble zone, coordinated budget, tax, and credit policies, and military cooperation. Russia gained control over Belarus nuclear weapons and its 30,000-man special nuclear forces for a period of seven years. In March 1993 a further agreement provided for economic, political, and even military union with Russia. As elsewhere, there are no real political parties, only various associations. Strikingly, in 1992 less than 30 percent of the soldiers and 20 percent of the staff of the Belarus armed forces were Belorussians. The Russian Orthodox Church, traditionally a symbol of Russification, has remained the strongest church in Belarus. The government has continued to control the media, and especially newspapers, all of which it has subsidized. Even emigration has remained under old Soviet legislation and standards.[51]

Progress towards a market economy has been slow, with the Belarus economy closely tied to the Russian economy.[52] No less than 50 percent of Belarus industry (with 300,000 workers) had been in military industry. Without serious economic reform, industrial production dropped 12 percent in 1992 and is projected to drop 20 percent in 1993 and again in 1994. By 1993 military orders had plumetted to 10 percent of the 1990 level and the army was increasingly outdated. Although there has been some progress—elections were held for parliament in 1990 and will be held again in 1994, minorities are protected by the government, some small steps toward a market economy have been taken—the overall record is weak. Even nation building will take significant period of time. This has reflected the popular conservatism. As a 1993 report concluded about Belarus:

> The population of Belarus is clearly conservative—to say nothing of the parliamentary old-guard majority—and certainly is in no hurry to risk the sort of social turmoil that has befallen other former Republics. It is notable that the public reaction to parliament's cavalier dismissal of its referendum petitions appears to have been muted, to say the least. In most other former republics, the reaction would have been vehement.[53]

---

[51]See Diuk and Karatnycky, *New Nations Rising*, pp. 260–283.
[52]Kathleen Mihalisko, "Belarus: Neutrality Gives Way to 'Collective Security,' " *RFE/RL Research Report*, vol. 2, no. 17, April 23, 1993.
[53]Commission on Security and Cooperation in Europe, *Human Rights and Democratization in the Newly Independent Former Soviet States*, Government Printing Office, Washington, D.C., 1993, p. 84.

17

Emerging Nation States: Transcaucasus

The Transcaucasus, including Armenia, Georgia, and Azerbaijan, is a group of small nations with enormous political difficulties. Their populations range from 3 million (Armenia) to 5.5 million (Georgia) to 7 million (Azerbaijan), all with significant outmigration. In the 1989 census 98 percent of Azerbaijanis and Georgians claimed their native language as their first language, while 92 percent of Armenians did so. One-third of Azerbaijanis and Georgians claimed a good knowledge of Russian as a second language, and almost half of Armenians did so. Armenians (97 percent) dominated Yerevan, while Azeris (62 percent) and Georgians (66 percent) controlled Baku and Tbilisi.[1]

Since independence in 1991 the region has been plagued by a war between Armenia and Azerbaijan over Nagorno-Karabakh that started in 1988 and civil wars within Georgia and Azerbaijan. International pressures from Russia, Iran, and Turkey have complicated the problems. All three states have experienced economic hardship, a sharp decline in the standard of living, and rising crime rates. Major refugee flows and ethnic hatreds have fueled dire problems in the region. As a series of Kennan Institute seminars in March 1993 observed:

> Ongoing ethnic disputes, together with the collapse of interrepublic economic ties of the Soviet system, have hindered economic reform in the three countries of the Caucasus, brought sharp declines in the standard of living and created opportunities for outside powers to expand their influence in the region. The future of these states remains bound to Russia, as their ability to sustain democratic polities and move toward market economies largely depends on

[1]Nadia Diuk and Adrian Karatnycky, *The Hidden Nations,* William Morrow, New York, 1990, p. 266; and Mikhail Guboglo, "Demography and Language in the Capitals of the Union Republics," *Journal of Soviet Nationalities,* vol. 1, no. 4, Winter 1990–1991, pp. 23, 25, 26.

the future political orientation of the Russian state and the manner in which it defines its national interest.[2]

Weak and inexperienced politicians, drawn into ethnic conflicts, have neglected key economic changes and failed to make necessary reforms. There was almost no preparation for independence, and there was a lack of skilled administrators and politicians. Rather, as Paul Henze, a RAND consultant has observed, there was the Russian legacy of

> distorted economies oriented towards the imperial center, economic and environmental devastation, territorial and administrative boundaries devised for purpose of central control and deliberatively cultivated ethnic and national antipathies. . . . The classic Russian approach has always been to play one nationality against the other and, unfortunately, this is still going on.[3]

The nearby Middle East has shown the negative impact of ethnic strife on creating democracies, capitalism, and new nations.[4]

ARMENIA

Soviet Armenia, with 11,000 square miles, is but 10 percent of historic Armenia, whose most famous symbol, biblical Mount Ararat (where Noah's Ark came to rest), rests in Turkey.[5] Its population of 3 million people make it the smallest of the republics in CIS. Its Armenian Orthodox Church, established in the fourth century, is one of the oldest Christian churches, with an offshoot even in the Armenian Quarter of the Old City of Jerusalem. Armenia has battled Azerbaijan over Nagorno-Karabakh, a mountainous, largely Armenian territory within Azerbaijan, since the early 1920s. In 1992 and 1993 Armenian forces opened two corridors to Nagorno-Karabakh and occupied 20 percent of Azerbaijani territory. Repeated mediation and meetings between Armenia and Azerbaijan have failed to resolve the conflict.

The Azerbaijani blockade of Armenia, begun in 1989, had a severe impact on Armenia as rail lines to Armenia must cross Azerbaijan. The Turkish refusal to open its border with Armenia and talk of a formal alliance with Azerbaijan in the spring of 1993 has reinforced the power of the blockade. The local

---

[2]"Caucasus: Ethnic Conflict and Economic Decline," *Kennan Institute Meeting Report,* vol. 10, no. 14, April 1993.

[3]"Caucasus: Ethnic Conflict and Economic Decline," *Kennan Institute Meeting Report.*

[4]In the case of Lebanon, a civil war raged for sixteen years from 1976 until 1991 with as many as 150,000 deaths. Only Syrian military intervention into Beirut and occupation of 60 percent of the country (Israel occupies another 5 percent) ended this strife.

[5]For discussions of Armenian history, see Christopher Walker, *Armenia: The Survival of a Nation,* St. Martin's Press, New York, 1980; and Nadia Diuk and Adrian Karatnycky, *New Nations Rising,* John Wiley and Sons, New York, 1993, chapter 5. The history of Armenia, especially of its relationship with Turkey, is highly controversial, and there is significant variation in the ways different authors have dealt with the subject matter.

economy is devastated and misery is widespread. The old command economy remains in place in wartime. With Russian oil supplies blocked, energy is very scarce and only ten of Armenia's 400 largest industrial enterprises are working in 1993. All education institutions are closed, trash is not collected, and infant mortality rates are rising. Despite military successes, Armenia is suffering, and its transition to democracy and capitalism slowed to a crawl. Only nation building, with a common enemy (Azerbaijan, Turkey), is making progress. Yet for Armenians the importance of Nagorno-Karabakh is such that it seems unlikely that any short-term solution is possible.[6]

As one distinguished author describes Armenian history:

> From the time of Armenia's loss of sovereignty over her lands, many centuries ago, until the present borders were fixed in 1921, the country has been characterized by misrule, by invasion, by imperial rivalry and in more recent times by outright and deliberate massacre.[7]

A country of volcanic tablelands set amidst soaring mountains, exposed to East and West, and with a harsh climate, Armenia has had a turbulent and traumatic history. It traces its history to the ancient kingdom of Urartu 3000 years ago. Armenia was a satrap of Alexander the Great 2300 years ago and then a semiautonomous state between eastern (Persian) and western (Roman) empires. In 301 it was one of the first states to embrace Christianity, and in the following century to create a distinctive alphabet and literary tradition. In 642 the Arabs took Yerevan, which became an autonomous tributary state. In 1041 it was integrated into the Byzantine Empire, only to be retaken by the Turks in 1064. In 1236 the Mongols took Armenia, and in 1386 and 1388 Tamerlane arrived with mass destruction. Armenian sovereignty over Cilicia ended in 1375. In 1502 the Persians conquered Armenia which, for the next two centuries, was divided between Persia and Turkey.

After 1762 the rising power in the Caucasus was Russia, whose forces took Yerevan in 1804 and Baku in 1806. A Persian attack was met by a successful Russian counterattack, which retook Yerevan in 1827. After this the Christian Armenians looked for Russian help against the Persian and Turkish Moslems. The Crimean War took place partly on Armenian soil. After 1881 Russian policy grew increasingly harsh, and after 1896 openly anti-Armenian. This was part of the broader crackdown in Russia after the assassination of Tsar Alexander II in 1881. In 1905 the Russians did nothing to stop the Azeri slaughter of over 1000 Armenians in Baku in February, the June pogrom in Yerevan, or the September killing of 1500 Armenians in Baku. After 1907 Armenian nationalists (Dashnaks) supported the liberation of Turkish Armenia and autonomy for Russian Armenia.

Life was even worse for the Armenians in the Ottoman Turkish Empire. After 1514 half of Armenia was in the Turkish Empire and after 1534 so too was most of the rest of classical Armenia. Armenia formed the border between

---

[6]"Caucasus: Ethnic Conflict and Economic Decline," *Kennan Institute Meeting Report.*
[7]Walker, *Armenia: The Survival of a Nation,* p. 11.

Persia and Russia. Although Armenians had a significant role in running the empire, Armenians as a group suffered from being designated as an inferior Christian minority. In an 1894 massacre several thousand Armenians died, and in 1895 perhaps as many as 50,000 were killed. After an Armenian revolutionary attempt failed in 1896, over 5000 Armenians were brutally murdered. The 1908 Young Turk Revolution promoted a Pan Turkism that was violently anti-Armenian. After early Turkish defeats in World War I, the regime decided to eliminate Turkish Armenia. Mass murders and forced marches into deserts and marshlands killed as many as 1.5 million Armenians, forcibly Islamicized 200,000 Armenians, and sent 250,000 starving Armenians fleeing to Russia. This Armenian Holocaust threatened the existence of the Armenian community and promoted a passionate desire for Russia to protect Armenia against the Turks. Armenians hailed Russian victories in the region in 1916.

In 1917 Dashnaks participated in a Provisional Government for the Transcaucasus after the February Revolution. The Treaty of Brest-Litovsk, with its loss of Kars, Ardahan, and Batu to the Turks, threatened Armenia, as did the Turkish invasion of Western Armenia and the ensuing massacres of Armenians. At May 1918 peace talks, the advancing Turks demanded all of Armenia. The June 1918 Treaty of Batum left Armenia with a tiny state of 4200 square miles, including 600,000 Armenians (50 percent of them refugees) and 100,000 Azeris. Armenia faced chaos, war, disaster, and starvation. In September 1918 the advancing Turks took Baku and killed 20,000 Armenians. Even the Allied victory in World War I and Turkish withdrawal in the final months of 1918 led to further atrocities.

At the 1919 Paris Peace Conference the Allies did not back an independent Armenia and its territorial demands for more than a rump state. In August 1918 the British evacuated the Caucasus and the Nationalists under Mustafa Kemal came to power in Turkey. An ensuing Russo-Turkish alliance seemed to threaten Armenia as the Turkish nationalists in February 1920 demanded control of all of Turkish Armenia. In January 1920 the Allies finally recognized Armenia but provided no aid apart from relief supplies. In April 1920 the Red Army invaded the region and took Baku. The Soviet Union opposed Armenian territorial demands but was willing to negotiate some help. In September 1920 the Congress of Peoples of the East in Baku was notably pro-Moslem and anti-Armenian. Isolated, deserted by its friends, faced by Turkish desire to destroy it, ravaged by internal economic and social problems and lawlessness and a September 1920 renewed Turkish advance in the region, Armenia pondered its fate. In October 1920 Turkey retook Kars and slaughtered 6000 Armenians, and in November the Turkish army seized Alexandropol. By November 1920 the Turkish army was 25 miles from Yerevan.

In desperation in December 1920 the Armenian government handed power to the Communists, who called in the Red Army. The dream of Armenian independence was shattered, but at least Armenia continued to exist. In February 1921 a Dashnak uprising held Yerevan for six days before the Red Army liquidated the insurgency. Eastern Armenia became part of the Soviet Union; western Armenia went to Turkey. In 1922 Armenia was absorbed in the new Transcaucasus state, only to reemerge as formally independent in 1936. In 1930 Armenian mountaineers rebelled unsuccessfully against collectivization, with Zangezur holding out until 1934.

Soviet achievements were quite real. By 1927 land under cultivation rose from 30 percent of the pre-war level to 90 percent. Starvation, which claimed thousands of lives in 1920, was a thing of the past. The regime repaired the roads and carried out major irrigation projects. But slow industrialization, the movement of peasants to the cities, and the huge number of refugees kept unemployment high in the 1920s. Even by 1929 only 13 percent of the population were workers.[8]

In the 1930s Stalin's massive transformation from above affected Armenia. Forced collectivization reached 80 percent of households by 1936, while industrialization radically modernized the economy. In 1936 tens of thousands of Armenians were jailed and some shot, but there was no genocide aimed at Armenians. No fewer than 40,000 Armenians fled from Turkey to Russia. During World War II, despite some collaboration with Nazi Germany, the bulk of Armenians were loyal to the Soviet Union. Some 300,000 to 500,000 Armenians served in the Red Army, with 32,000 being decorated for bravery and fifty attaining the rank of general.

In the postwar decades repression tailed off as the modernization process continued. Armenians, though upset with various Soviet policies, remained well aware of the dangers posed by a resurgent Turkey. Soviet authorities in the Khrushchev and Brezhnev eras were more tolerant. After a 1965 demonstration to commemorate the fiftieth anniversary of the Armenian Genocide, the regime adopted the anniversary and created a monument.

Under Gorbachev Armenians, ever leery of Turkey, focused their demands on the small, largely Armenian territory of Nagorno-Karabakh, which had been part of Azerbaijan after 1921. Gorbachev, deferring to Moslem sentiment, was cautious. In October 1987 demonstrations began in Yerevan, and in February 1988 the Nagorno-Karabakh Supreme Soviet voted to unify with Armenia. One million Armenians demonstrated in February 1988 over this issue. That month several hundred Armenians were killed in a pogrom in Sumgait in Azerbaijan. In March 1988 Red Army troops entered Nagorno-Karabakh as the Armenian Supreme Soviet laid claim to the disputed territory. In May 1988 Gorbachev fired the first secretaries of the Armenian and Azerbaijan Communist Parties. By November 1988, 150,000 Azeris fled to Azerbaijan, and 180,000 Armenians fled to Armenia from Azerbaijan. In December 1988 a massive earthquake in Yerevan killed 100,000 Armenians and left 500,000 homeless.

Even by 1993 the dispute had not been resolved. Armenian troops won major victories in opening two corridors between Armenia and Nagorno-Karabakh, with over 3000 dead and over 350,000 Armenians and 500,000 Azeris refugees. By the fall of 1993 Armenia had seized 20 percent of Azerbaijani territory, but an Azerbaijan blockade of Armenia had crippled its economy and left it destitute.

---

[8]See Edmund Herzig, "The Armenians," in Graham Smith, editor, *The Nationalities Question in the Soviet Union,* Longmans, London and New York, 1990, chapter 9.

As for democracy and capitalism, the record has been mixed.[9] Armenia has made the best progress in the Transcaucasus in moving to democracy. However, despite land reform, the war has halted moves towards economic reforms. Ethnic hatreds have led to the flight or expulsion of most of the 200,000 Azeris who lived in Armenia prior to 1988. Fully 60 percent of the members of parliament do not belong to a party. In October 1992 elections fewer than 20 percent of voters turned out to fill vacant parliamentary seats.

In May 1990 Armenia held parliamentary elections that brought to power Levon Ter-Petrossyan, a non-Communist head of the Armenian Pan-National Movement. An antiquities scholar, he has a reputation as a reasonable, skillful moderate. Armenia was also the only Soviet republic that sought its independence in conformity with Soviet law. In August 1990 the new parliament voted for a legal transition to independence. In August 1991 the failed Moscow coup accelerated the move to independence, and the Armenian Communist Party dissolved itself. In September 1991 Armenia held a referendum on independence with a turnout of 95 percent of eligible voters and a 99 percent yes vote. Two days later the Armenian parliament declared its independence and sought negotiations with Moscow for Russian recognition, which was important, given the war with Azerbaijan and poor relations with Turkey. In October 1991, elections for President of Armenia gave Ter-Petrossyan 83 percent of the vote, an endorsement of his pragmatism and desire for good relations with Moscow.

The long and tragic history of Armenia, its bitter rivalry with Turkey and Turkish Moslems (Azeris), and the massive killings in the region are a sobering reminder that the bloody history of Europe has been replicated in other areas of the world. The creation of an independent Armenia, while laudatory, has created and reinforced tensions in the Transcaucasus. Armenia has achieved a political stability lacking in Georgia or Azerbaijan. Although there has been opposition to Ter-Petrossyan, there have been no coups to overthrow the leader (as in Georgia) or marches on the capital (Azerbaijan). This stability had allowed Armenia to make significant process towards a legal democratic state. A new constitution has been proposed but not yet accepted.

GEORGIA

Like Armenia, Georgia has a relatively short history as part of the Russian sphere, one dating only to 1801.[10] Also like Armenia, this has been a small, embattled, Christian country with an ancient history over 3000 years long. Five million people live in Georgia, only 60 percent of whom are ethnic Georgians.

[9]See Commission on Security and Cooperation in Europe, *Presidential Elections and Independence Referendums in the Baltic States, the Soviet Union and Successor States*, Washington, D.C., August 1992, pp. 65–82.
[10]For Georgian history see Ronald Suny, *The Making of the Georgian Nation*, Indiana University Press, Bloomington, 1988; and David Lang, *A Modern History of Soviet Georgia*, Grove Press, New York, 1962.

But 90 percent of all Georgians in the world live in Georgia, a much higher percentage than for Armenians.

Under the leadership of former Soviet Foreign Minister Eduard Shevard-nadze, Georgia retains a high profile, as during the Stalin era. It was the first post-Soviet state to overthrow a democratically elected leader in a coup in 1992. Georgia has remained embroiled in several civil wars, in both South Ossetia and Abkhazia. Abkhazia is an autonomous republic of Georgia, with a popula-tion 17 percent Abkhazian and 45 percent Georgian, bordering the Black Sea. Intermittent armed conflict has continued since August 1992. Russian troops have supported Abkhazian nationalists out of their interest in maintaining access to the Black Sea. In September 1993 Abkhazian nationalists, with support from local Russian forces, overran all of Abkhazia and forced Shevardnadze to flee the capital of Sukhumi. By contrast, a cease-fire was negotiated in South Ossetia in November 1992, where 70,000 Ossetians, desiring to integrate with North Ossetians in Russia, lived with 30,000 Georgians. Russian interest in Georgia has been strong. As Tedo Japaridze, the National Security Advisor of the Georgian Republic, declared in Washington in March, 1993, "We under-stand that Russia, as a major geopolitical component, [will] have interests in the Caucasus."[11]

In ancient mythology Jason sailed to Colchis (now western Georgia) to steal the Golden Fleece, and Prometheus was chained to a rock in Georgia. With mountains for refuge and set between two continents, Georgia inevitably had a stormy history. Xenophon marched through here in 400 BCE and the Romans under Pompey garrisoned Georgia and made it part of the Roman Empire several centuries later. Despite the invasions, Georgia often maintained a precarious independence as a kingdom in the Greco-Roman world. In 330, less than thirty years after the Armenians, the Georgians accepted Christianity under Saint Nino. The area was fought over by Romans, Persians, and Byzan-tines. In 550 the dominant Persians abolished the local monarchy. In 645 the ascendant Arabs seized Tbilisi for Islam and Georgia became fragmented. It was reunited in 1121 under King David, who ended almost four centuries of Islamic rule. Georgia reached new heights under Queen Tamar, only to fade after the Mongol invasion of 1236. Tamerlane later wreaked havoc on Georgia. By the sixteenth century Persia and Ottoman Turkey both launched devastating invasions of the region. By the end of the century the Persians dominated eastern Georgia, and Turkey western Georgia. This rivalry continued in the seventeenth century, when the Turks seized Tbilisi in 1723. Endless invasions halved the local population by the seventeenth century.

Russian interest in the region vacilated, but in 1783 the Treaty of Geor-gievsk temporarily made the Georgian kingdom a Russian protectorate. Four years later, though, Russia withdrew and a 1795 Persian invading force burned Tbilisi and took 15,000 captives. In 1801 Russia annexed part of eastern Georgia and over the next thirty years the local monarchies became incorporated into the Russian Empire. After 1811 the independence of the local church was suppressed, as were the two leading local monarchies. In 1826 Persian forces

[11]"Caucasus: Ethnic Conflict and Economic Decline," *Kennan Institute Meeting Report.*

overran part of Georgia before being routed by the Russian army. In 1832 a local noble conspiracy against Russian authority was smashed. Reforms under Viceroy Vorontsov (1832–1855) pacified the Georgians, absorbed the Georgian nobles as Russified nobles, and provided stability. Serfdom was abolished in 1864 but nobles retained 50 percent of the land. In the Russo-Turkish War of 1877–1878 the Russians recovered significant Georgian territory lost to the Ottoman Turks in the sixteenth century. By the late 19th century Georgians were

> still a divided, defeated, inchoate people, sharing an ethnicity with recogniz-
> able cultural features. Despite periods of unity and glory in the past, they had
> faced virtual extinction by the end of the eighteenth century and, except for a
> few nobles and clerics, possessed little sense of their own nationhood.[12]

Russian rule until 1881 stabilized the country, reunited Georgia, stripped the Georgian nobles of their leadership role, improved the economy, and enhanced national identity. But the harsh Russification and repression of the last two decades of the nineteenth century alienated Georgian society and promoted an anti-Russian national struggle. Although most Georgians were peasants, industrialization had created a significant working class by 1900. The class struggle came on top of a national struggle, with the largely rural Georgians fighting the imperial Russians while the urban Georgians fought the Armenians and Russians.

In the wake of Russian defeats in the war with Japan, the 1905 Revolution brought protest, insurrection, and repression to Georgia. In January 1905 echoes of Bloody Sunday in Saint Petersburg brought a general strike in Tbilisi. By March the whole area was in revolt. In June 1905 a new general strike brought martial law. In August 1905 sixty Georgians were massacred in a peaceful protest in Tbilisi's Town Hall. In October forty were killed in Black Hundreds riots. The power of the Social Democrats was strong throughout the year. In December 1905 a general strike led to an armed uprising that failed. In the following two years limited reforms saw the end of ethnic restrictions on working in the government bureaucracy, an end to Russian language predomi-nance, and the return of Church lands. In the Dumas in Saint Petersburg 90 percent of the Tbilisi delegates were Mensheviks, with a prominent Georgian (Irakli Tsereteli) heading the Second Duma's Menshevik faction.

By 1914 the Russians had gathered together the traditional Georgian lands, Mensheviks (a more democratic branch of the Social Democrats than the Bolsheviks) dominated political trends, and the workers and peasants were well organized. Russians still dominated the government and Armenians the economy, leaving Georgians the least powerful group in Georgia. The early phases of World War I saw the Russians in 1915 march into Turkish Armenia and in 1916 seize Erzurum and Trebizond. After the 1917 February Revolution, the Mensheviks under Noah Zhordania dominated Georgian politics and the Tiflis Soviet played a prominent political role.

After the October Revolution a Transcaucasus Provisional Government

---

[12]Suny, *The Making of the Georgian Nation,* p. 114.

dominated the region. In February 1918 the Russians prepared to abandon the Transcaucasus in the light of Turkish advances and the Treaty of Brest-Litovsk with Germany. In May 1918 Georgia declared its independence but came under German protection against the advancing Turks. It was now an independent state for the first time in 117 years, even if a protectorate. Only physical and political separation from Russia and the Turkish advance had brought independence. And it came at a price, for Germany was free to use Georgian railroads and ships to occupy key points in the country, to circulate the mark, conduct foreign diplomacy, and gain economic concessions.

In the June 1918 elections the Mensheviks won a stunning 82 percent of the vote. They proceeded to nationalize industry and make radical land reform, but without persecution of the landlords, middle-class elements, and nobles. They outlawed the Russian language in the Assembly, law, and army and carried out progressive social and economic legislation. In December 1918 an Armenian invasion of Georgia was repulsed. However, after the German defeat in World War I in November 1918, Georgia faced hostile Soviet Union, White Russians, Turkey, and Armenia without allies. The victorious British were hostile to the former German allies but left the region in 1920. The Whites under Denikin declared war on Georgia in 1919, but were beaten by the Red Army before they could attack.

As victory neared in the Civil War, the Red Army made ready to intervene in the region. In April 1920 the Red Army took Baku with little opposition. In April 1920 the Soviet leaders created a North Caucasus Bureau under Sergo Orzhonikidze, a Georgian, to coordinate policy in the area. At the same time a Communist uprising in Tbilisi was smashed. In May 1920 the Soviet Union and Georgia signed a treaty calling for freedom for Communist activity in Georgia. In December 1920 the Armenian Dashnaks agreed to Red Army occupation in return for protection from the Turks. With growing Soviet power and lack of Western intervention, the fate of Georgia was sealed, unless Moscow determined otherwise. In 1921 the little Georgian army had 32,000 soldiers, 500 machine guns, seventy-four cannons, and two tanks—a small, poorly equipped army with low morale. With Lenin ailing, the hard line of Stalin and Ordzhonikidze, Georgian Bolsheviks prevailed. The Red Army marched into Tbilisi in February 1921 as the Mensheviks held out for only a week. Menshevik rule was now over. In 1922 Lenin wanted Stalin punished for maltreatment of the Georgians but was too ill to enforce his way. In 1924 an armed uprising in Georgia was crushed in three weeks with 7000 to 10,000 deaths.

Georgians came to dominate the local government and party bodies. Many Georgians, from Stalin and Orzhonikidze to Eliava and Makharadze and Beria, became influential in Moscow. In Georgia the number of local Communists quadrupled to 33,000 by 1929. The New Economic Policy helped stabilize the economy in the middle 1920s. But except for the rise to power of a small group of Transcaucasians around Stalin, Stalin's rise to power in Moscow in 1929 did little to benefit the region. Radical collectivization engendered violent uprisings in the countryside in the early 1930s. In 1932 Beso Lominadze, secretary of the Transcaucasian Communist Party, helped lead the fruitless opposition to Stalin.

The key event here was the rise of Lavrentii Beria as First Secretary of the Transcaucasus Communist Party (later the Georgian Communist Party) from 1931 until 1938, when he moved to Moscow to head the notorious NKVD. Beria was a Mingrelian from Abkhazia in Georgia. Born into a peasant background, he joined the Party in 1917 while studying at the Baku Technical College. During the 1920s Beria was head of the Georgian secret police and chief secret police representative for Moscow in the Transcaucasus. During the 1930s he pushed the Stalinist policies of industrialization, collectivization, and modernization with considerable brutality. At the same time he pushed for native cadres and political mobilization while attacking local nationalism. Beria's 1933 purge ousted almost 10,000 Georgian Communists. A bureaucrat without popular base but personally close to Stalin, he became a member of the Central Committee in 1934. His 1935 lecture in Tbilisi falsifying Stalin as a hero of the Transcaucasus underground before 1917 paved the way for the Great Purges after 1937. Beria conducted two trials of Georgian Communists, mostly intellectuals associated with Tbilisi University. The suicide of Orzhonikidze in Moscow signaled the onset of the Great Purges. Beria after 1938 headed the secret police in Moscow, together with Georgians like Vsevolod Merkulov and Boden Kobulov (Moscow), Sergei Goglidze (Leningrad), Tsanava (Belarus), and Gvishiana (Maritime Provinces).

Georgia was spared German occupation during the war, a pleasant fate compared to the horrors visited on much of the country. Beria continued to rule Georgia from afar, and the main square in Tbilisi was named for him. The fading of Beria's power in Moscow after 1950 had local repercussions. The fabricated 1951 anti-Soviet Mingrelian Plot was aimed at the Mingrelian Beria. The growing anti-Semitism embodied in the 1952 Doctors' Plot also did not miss Beria, who had run the atomic project and sheltered many Jews. In April 1952 a local purge swept away 50 percent of the Central Committee members and many of the leading government bureaucrats.

The death of Stalin in March 1953 and the attempt of Beria to seize power, resulting in his arrest in June 1953 and execution in December 1953, were major events in Georgia. During Beria's brief bid for power, his protégés took over the Georgian Party. A number of Georgians were shot together with Beria, including Sergei Goglidze (former head of the Georgian secret police), Vladimir Dekanozov (former Soviet Vice Minister of Foreign Affairs), and Bobo Kobulov, (former Soviet Deputy Minister of State Security).

A new Georgia, more urbanized, industrialized, and modernized, emerged from the Stalinist era. Far from traditional colonial exploitation, the Russians had financed Georgian industrialization, promoted Georgians in government and Party positions, and emphasized local education and modernization. Georgians, not Russians and Armenians, increasingly dominated Georgia, with many Armenians returning to Armenia. By 1956 literacy was now 100 percent and a Georgia with no universities in 1913 had 39,000 university students and 2000 scholars in the local Academy of Sciences. At peace at home and protected by the Soviet army, unravaged by World War II, Georgia made significant gains. The attack on Stalin in Khrushchev's secret speech in February 1956 incited massive riots that led to a hundred deaths. A new leader, Vasili Mzhavanadze, ran the Georgian party from 1953 until 1972. This was a period of tolerant corruption and mild changes compared to the past. Russification was quietly shelved. By 1970 only 9 percent of the peasants and 37 percent of the urban Georgians spoke Russian. Even in Tbilisi the majority of Georgians were not fluent in Russian. Renationalization created a new traditional culture with Georgians forming over 80 percent of the students in higher education.

In 1972 the former head of the internal security forces, Eduard Shevard-nadze, came to power for thirteen years until called to Moscow as Foreign Minister. A firm administrator and mild reformer, he cracked down on rampant corruption (far greater than the usually tolerated corruption), drug abuse, and alcoholism. In 1978 a government attempt to promote the Russian language led to a protest by over 5000 students. By the 1980s Georgians would be very responsive to the implications of Gorbachev's reforms. Their national identity, now forged on a solid basis with a strong Georgian majority in key areas, was ready for separation from Moscow. Their Christian identity separated them from the nearby Moslem world as their Georgian language, customs, and history separated them from Russia. Their tragic past dealings with powerful neighbors induced caution in seeking independence. The elevation of Eduard Shevardnadze to the post of Soviet Foreign Minister from 1985 to 1990 highlighted the importance of Georgia in the broader world.

The slow Georgian drive for independence left the Communists in control until 1990.[13] In April 1989 on Bloody Sunday, Soviet troops killed nineteen people demonstrating in Tbilisi. In October 1990 Zviad Gamsakhurdia, a leading dissident and son of a famous writer, became the first freely elected president of Georgia as leader of the Round Table-Free Georgia bloc. In May 1991 he won an overwhelming mandate of 87 percent of the vote. Yet he also alienated many Georgians who saw him as a tyrant for his repression of opposition and the highly authoritarian style of rule that earned him the sobriquet the "Saddam Hussein of the Caucasus." The failure of the August 1991 coup in Moscow undermined his position, as his enemies accused him of conniving with the coup plotters. The head of the National Guard, Tengiz Kitovani, called him a traitor and set up his camp outside of Tbilisi. Increasing conflict led to open violence in December 1991. The next month the National Guard, together with other elements, forced Gamsakhurdia to flee. A Military Council took power and declared a state of emergency until August 1992. For much of 1992 various armed militia battled each other in the vacuum created by the lack of a legitimate government. In March 1992 Eduard Shevardnadze returned to Tbilisi and became chairman of a new State Council that replaced the Military Council. Gamsakhurdia from exile directed armed uprisings in his

---

[13]The following discussion draws heavily on the Commission on Security and Cooperation in Europe, *Report on Georgia's Parliamentary Elections,* Washington, D.C., November 1992; and on Diuk and Karatnycky, *New Nations Rising,* chapter 5.

native western Georgia. In August 1992 Shevardnadze lifted the curfew and pardoned those who had been in the Gamsakhurdia camp. The Gamsakhurdia followers were not mollified and began kidnapping local officials to Abkhazia, a practice that continued into 1993. They charged ongoing massive human rights violations against the Shevardnadze forces, including shootings, beatings, arrests, crimes, and closing of pro-Gamsakhurdia media outlets.

In October 1992, despite some irregularities and boycotts in western Georgia, 81 percent of the eligible voters turned out for Georgia's second free election. Shevardnadze, unopposed as in the Communist era, won 96 percent of the vote as Chairman of the Georgian Parliament. No fewer than twenty parties and blocs won seats in parliament, with perhaps two-thirds backing Shevardnadze. In November 1992 the new parliament formally elected Shevardnadze head of state. In April 1993 there were reports that Defense Minister Tengiz Kitovani, who had been instrumental in ousting Gamsakhurdia, was now plotting to overthrow Shevardnadze. In May 1993 Shevardnadze fired Kitovani, replaced him with twenty-seven-year-old General Giorgi Karkarashvili, and abolished the fractious Council for National Security and Defense. This may have prevented another coup.

Despite Shevardnadze's landslide and his popularity at home and abroad, severe problems remain on Georgia's path to capitalism, democracy, and nation building. Shevardnadze's control over the military and a multitude of armed groups and militia remained unclear, although strengthened by his actions in May 1993. Georgia has been unable to deal effectively with the desire of its ethnic minorities to assert their rights to self-determination. Open warfare raged in Abkhazia, with Russian troops, the Russian Supreme Soviet, and North Caucasians supporting the rebel side and overrunning the entire region in September 1993. In April 1993 Georgia formally protested Russian interference in its affairs and the continuing presence of Russian troops on its soil. Hundreds had been killed. The truce in South Ossetia, after two and a half years of civil war, remained tenuous and enforced only by the presence of Russian, Georgian, and Ossetian troops. Gamsakhurdia's supporters were still armed and unwilling to reconcile with Shevardnadze, whom they see as a representative of the old order. In April 1993, 5000 Georgians rallied for Gamsakhurdia in Tbilisi. With little economic reform, living standards declined sharply while prices soared. Western investment was hopeless without major economic reforms, privatization of land, and peace. Fully 60 percent of the largest factories closed down while natural gas and food deliveries from Russia and Ukraine were hampered by the civil war in Abkhazia. The government budget in 1993 was roughly 50 percent of all revenues.

The reliance on a single authoritarian figure—first Gamsakhurdia, now Shevardnadze—smacked more of the old authoritarianism than the new democracy. So too did the fact that the largest party in parliament (Peace Party) was largely a Communist organization. The government heavily controlled the media, firing editors who did not toe the state line. Demonstrators opposing the government have routinely been attacked, beaten, and arrested. Violence has continued unabated in western Georgia, a Gamsakhurdia stronghold. Both sides have trampled human rights. Relations with Russia, which seems to be backing Abkhazian and South Ossetian separatism, have been difficult.

The future, then, seems grim. But Shevardnadze does enjoy strong Western and American support and has good relations with Moscow. Together with his political capabilities and domestic support in Georgia, only time can tell whether he wants to—or can—push Georgia successfully down the road to the triple revolution of capitalism, democracy, and nation building. A start has been made; the rest will be decided in the future. Perhaps then Georgia will be able to overcome its image as "the most unstable, violence-ridden and violence-prone former republic" with its "lack of a legitimate government, the widespread violence, the virtual civil war and breakdown of normal structures of governance" in the past.[14]

AZERBAIJAN

As the only Transcaucasian republic with a predominantly Moslem population, Azerbaijan has been a special case.[15] It is a country trisected in loyalty: Its Shiite Islam and early and middle history have tied it to Iran; Islam, ethnicity, and language have tied it to Turkey; and politics for nearly two centuries has tied it to Russia. Relatively small, with 33,000 square miles, Azerbaijan is a state with 7 million people and a capital in the oil-famous city of Baku. It is bordered by the Caucasus in the north, the Caspian Sea in the east, Armenia in the west, and Iran in the south.

Azerbaijan in 1993 remained involved in the bloody military conflict with Armenia over Nagorno-Karabakh that has claimed several thousand lives since 1988. Azerbaijani defeats in 1992 and 1993 allowed Armenian units to create two strategic corridors between Armenia and Nagorno-Karabakh and seize 20 percent of Azerbaijani territory.[16] The Azerbaijani blockade of Armenia had caused it serious damage since 1989. The collapse of the Soviet Union thrust an unprepared Azerbaijan into independence in 1991. Unlike Armenia, it lacked a national democratic government, army, weapons, and armed militia. Only in June 1992 did democratic forces predominate with the election of Abulfaz Elchibey, the leader of the Azerbaijani Popular Front and a former jailed academic dissident, as president. Elchibey won 60 percent of the vote in the first election in over seventy years. However, the revolt of Colonel Surat Husseinov, fired for his defeats in February 1993, overthrew Elchibey in June 1993 when Husseinov's forces marched into Baku. This allowed Geydar Aliyev, a Politburo

---

[14]Commission on Security and Cooperation in Europe, *Human Rights and Democratization in the Newly Independent States of the Former Soviet Union,* p. 138.

[15]We rely here on three fine works, that of Audrey Alstadt, *The Azerbaijani Turks,* Hoover Institution Press, Stanford, 1992; Diuk and Karatnycky, *New Nations Rising,* chapter 5, for a general overview; and Tadeusz Swietochowski, *Russian Azerbaijan, 1905–1920,* Cambridge University Press, Cambridge, 1985, for the early period in particular.

[16]Not to overstretch the analogy, but the Arab-Israeli wars do leap to mind. The Israelis, a Westernized minority religious element outgunned and outmanned by their larger and stronger enemies, repeatedly won surprising and decisive victories over the Arabs in seven major wars.

member under Brezhnev and Gorbachev and former party boss of Azerbaijan, to establish his control in Azerbaijan by the fall of 1993. Military defeat, 1300 percent inflation, and economic hard times undermined support for Elchibey.

Azerbaijan, seeing a small Christian Armenia in a world of Turkish Moslems and an Islamicized Middle East, continues to believe in ultimate victory.[17] In August 1992 Azerbaijan formally took control of its border from Russian troops, who had been there after independence at the invitation of Azerbaijan.

An ancient land originally known as Medea, Azerbaijan suffered from numerous foreign invasions. Cyrus the Great of Persia invaded in the sixth century BCE, Alexander the Great of Macedonia in the fourth century BCE, and Pompey of Rome in the first century BCE. In the late Roman period Sasanian, Byzantine, and Turkish tribes all invaded the area. By the seventh century the predominant character of the land was Persian (now Iranian), hardly surprising given the power of its closest neighbor. In the seventh century the Arab invasion brought with it Islam, which has predominated ever since. By the eleventh century an influx of Turks had changed the ethnic composition to its current Turkish flavor. In the thirteenth century the Mongol invasion and subsequent invasion by Tamerlane lasted 200 years. By the fifteenth century a native Azerbaijan state emerged under the Shirvan shahs. From the sixteenth century to the middle of the eighteenth century, Persia ruled the area. What was most interesting, though, was that Azerbaijan had been the original base for the Safavid dynasty that ruled Persia and Azerbaijan. There were short interludes of rule by the Ottoman Turks (1578–1603) and Russians (1710–1730) during the Iranian period. The death of Nadiv Shah in 1747 ended Persian rule.

The next eighty years witnessed a tenuously independent Azerbaijan buffeted by the everlasting battle of Persia, Turkey, and Russia for control of the region. Azerbaijan was not a modern, unified independent state but rather a congeries of khanates, divided into mahal tribal units, further subdivided into sultanates. It was the Hobbesian world of all against all, set amidst massive international conflict and intrigue. Russia first expanded into the region during the 1722 campaign of Peter the Great and later, more persistently, under Catherine II (1763–1796). Two protracted Russo-Persian wars (1804–1812, 1828–1829) ended in Russian victories (even reaching Tabriz), despite popular support for the Persians. The 1829 Treaty of Adrianopole brought Russian rule to 500,000 Moslems living in one-third of Azerbaijan, with the remainder falling under Persian rule. The tsars favored the Shiite half of the population, promoting Sunni emigration.

Russia slowly pacified the region and eliminated the khanates and sultanates by 1860. Russian military rule was followed by the twenty-year reign of the relatively liberal Count Mikhail Vorontsov (1845–1865), the first Viceroy of the Caucasus. His strategy of co-opting native elites rather than Russifying them forcibly was quite successful. However, in the last two decades of the nineteenth century, Russia adopted more forceful measures and eliminated the post of viceroy.

Baku, the capital after 1859, became a boom town during the 1870s oil

---

[17]"Caucasus: Ethnic Conflict and Economic Decline," *Kennan Institute Meeting Report.*

frenzy. Baku, with Turkish Moslems forming only 20 percent of the population in 1913, was an alien island in a predominantly Turkish Moslem countryside. In 1913 Turkish Moslems accounted for 5 percent of the professionals, 11 percent of the workers, and 15 percent of the managers in the oil companies of Baku. In the cities there was only a small Turkish bourgeoisie, working class, and intelligentsia. Industrialization and modernization remained peripheral in Azerbaijan by World War I. The great majority of the population resided in the predominantly Turkish countryside.[18]

The 1905 Revolution, with its weakening of the center and greater tolerance for diversity, soon impacted Azerbaijan. Local protests following Bloody Sunday in Saint Petersburg led to the imposition of martial law in February 1905. Massive intercommunal violence broke out between Armenians and Moslems in Baku, Yerevan, and other cities, leaving 3000 to 10,000 people dead in the next year. The Russians supported the Moslems and then switched to backing the Armenians. Moslems were slow to take part in the broader political context of the 1905 Revolution. In August 1905 the First Russian Moslem Congress opened in Nizhnii Novgorod and took a moderate position. The few new weak parties did not survive the Tsarist repression of 1906–1907. However, the process of creating a national community continued, highlighted by the founding of the Musavat (Equality) Party in 1912.

The outbreak of World War I had a profound impact on the region. The exemption of Turkish Moslems from military service in the Russian army and the entry of Ottoman Turkey into the war on the side of Imperial Germany isolated the region. After initial Turkish victories, the Russian army, despite suffering 150,000 casualties, won impressive victories in 1915 (Armenia, Tabriz) and 1916 (Erzerum, Trebizond). Russian forces massacred Azeri villagers, while the Turks massacred Armenians on a greater scale.

The February Revolution ended the rule of a local viceroy and promoted numerous local power centers. There was the Provisional Government-sponsored Special Transcaucasus Committee, the more radical Tiflis and Baku Soviets, Moslem councils, nationalist parties (Armenian Dashnak, Turkish Musavat), and local branches of the Bolsheviks, Mensheviks, Socialist Revolutionaries, and Kadets. The Musavitists supported Turkish rights, Turkish nationalism, populism, and modernization. In voting in October 1917 the Musavitists led even in Baku, only to be outmaneuvered by the Bolsheviks. In November 1917, voting for the Constituent Assembly, the Musavitists won 63 percent of the vote in Azerbaijan and came in second in the Transcaucasus after the Georgian Mensheviks. In the February 1918 Transcaucasus Seim formed after the dissolution of the Constituent Assembly in Moscow, the Musavitists held the second most seats after the Georgian Mensheviks.

Elections, however, did not settle the fate of Azerbaijan and the Transcaucasus. The crumbling of the Russian Caucasus Front after the October Revolution brought huge military forces into the region. Despite winning only 4 percent of the vote in the Transcaucasus election, the Bolsheviks, with support

---

[18]Alstadt, *The Azerbaijani Turks,* chapter 3.

from Russia and the Armenians, dominated Baku. The Turkish Moslems, though numerically superior, lacked military experience, adequate weapons, and training. In a March 1918 battle for Baku 10,000 soldiers from the Baku Soviet and Armenian Dashnaks routed 10,000 Turkish Moslems. The victorious troops burned the Moslem quarter, killing perhaps 3000 Moslems and sending thousands fleeing the city.

A weak Soviet Union in the Treaty of Brest-Litovsk yielded Kars, Batum, and Ardahan to Ottoman Turkey. Turkish advances led to the April 1918 creation of an independent, democratic Transcaucasus republic. The next month its constituent parts—Azerbaijan, Georgia, Armenia—each declared their independence.

The Azerbaijan Democratic Republic lasted almost two years. Repeated occupations, border disputes, and internal battles limited its independence. From April to August 1918, its capital Baku was run by the Bolsheviks, who concluded an alliance with the Armenians. Ottoman Turkey signed a treaty with Azerbaijan but refused to recognize its independence, as it hoped to integrate Azerbaijan into the new Turkish empire. Its forces, organized as the Army of Islam, helped repel a Red Army offensive and seized Baku in August 1918. In the aftermath the Turks slaughtered 10,000 Armenians. The British, who had landed troops in Baku in August, were responsible for the killing of twenty-six Baku Commissars fleeing from a fallen Baku. The Azerbaijan government now moved to Baku.

A failing Ottoman Turkish Empire, beaten on all other fronts, could not hold onto its gains. In October 1918 Ottoman Turkey fell apart. British forces under Major General Thomson arrived in Baku the following month and stayed until August 1919. The British maintained a garrison in Baku, ran the railroad, directed the militia, internal security units, and armed forces, secured the ports, gathered intelligence, and interfered in local politics. They opposed the local republic and preferred a reintegration of the region under Russian rule. The British privatized industry and supported the Musavitists after the December 1918 election gave them legitimacy.

As the strongest group but without a parliamentary majority, the Musavitists relied on unstable coalition partners throughout the remainder of the period. There were five cabinets in less than two years. They faced huge tasks with little preparation. The Musavitists had to carry out moderate land reforms, reorganize the governmental administration, find qualified men to run the government, improve the weak educational infrastructure, and create a reasonable (40,000 man) army from diverse factions. Economic problems were endless, given the chaos of the Civil War and disruption of normal economic relationships. The government ran massive budget deficits, equal to 40 percent of expenditures.

Threats abounded to the independent regime. The Turks continued to want to reintegrate Azerbaijan into their empire. The British, intrigued by oil, meddled repeatedly. The weakened Soviet Union was not reconciled to the loss of the region. Local White forces also wanted Azerbaijani oil. In March 1919 the British helped to oust the White Russians from Baku. Only the Bolshevik defeats of General Denikin in October and November 1919 kept the Whites from trying to seize Baku. Armenia, too, angered by Ottoman Turkish massacres in 1915 and pogroms since then, remained hostile.

After the departure of the British forces in August 1919, Azerbaijan was finally free of occupation forces. Now it faced two fronts, a Russian front to the north and an Armenian front to the west. By January 1920 a Red Army counteroffensive against Denikin brought the Russian army to the gates of Azerbaijan. Local party forces were weak (4000 Azeri Bolsheviks), but Moscow was determined to regain the Tsarist patrimony and Baku oil. The Musavat party was further tainted by close association with British imperialism and the slaughter of Armenians. With a weak military and a beaten Turkey unable to come to its aid, internal political divisions, and defeatism, the Azerbaijan Parliament accepted a Russian ultimatum and surrendered power without a fight in April 1920. Territorial disputes, which still plague Azerbaijan, were temporarily settled. The border with Georgia was fixed, Zangezur went to Armenia, and Nakhichevan and Nagorno-Karabakh, despite Armenian majorities, went to Azerbaijan.

The consolidation of Soviet power in Azerbaijan was difficult and protracted. In 1920 there were uprisings in three parts of the republic. The Red Army was unable to quell armed resistance until 1924. The new regime implemented war communism, including nationalization of industry, mines, banks, and oil, monopoly of retail trade, and control of the media. In 1922 Azerbaijan lost its formal independence as it became part of the Transcaucasus Federation of the new Union of Soviet Socialist Republics. Georgians dominated the federation, which had few Azeri Turks in leadership posts. In 1925 Azeri Turks were a minority (43 percent) in the Azerbaijan Communist Party where non-Turks, mainly Russians and Armenians (like Sergei Kirov and Anastas Mikoyan), ran the show.

Moscow was aware of the deep anti-Communist sentiment. During the interwar period it resorted to recurrent terror and brutality to consolidate its rule. In the early 1920s the party killed or exiled thousands of former Musavitists, peasants, kulaks, and industrialists. From 1926 to 1933 the Party purged Turks who were seen as national communists and peasants who resisted collectivization. In the Great Terror the secret police destroyed nearly the entire native Party-state elite, much of the intelligentsia, and the old Bolsheviks—altogether, 120,000 people.

During the entire period from 1921 to 1953, Mir Jafar Bagirov was responsible for the terror and implementation of Moscow's policy. A 1917 Bolshevik, from the early 1920s until 1933 he was head of the security forces. From 1933 he served as both First Secretary of the Azerbaijan Central Committee and president of the government. His close association of Beria did not harm him.

World War II impacted Azerbaijan, even though the Germans were stopped at Stalingrad. Baku produced 70 percent of the oil and 90 percent of the aviation fuel used in the war. No fewer than 500,000 Azerbaijani soldiers fought in the war. At Stalingrad Caucasian and Central Asian natives accounted for nearly half the Red Army soldiers. The regime opened mosques, promoted local culture, and carried out mass propaganda while the Nazis treated Asians as inferior subhumans. And yet there was a noticeable lack of enthusiasm for the war against Germany. Almost 300,000 Moslems and Caucasians served in the German army. The desertion rate of Turks was high, and only 1.1 percent of 11,000 heroes of the Soviet Union were Azerbaijani natives.

The postwar era saw a reassertion of Russian domination and traditional Soviet policies. Bagirov continued to be Stalin's chief lieutenant in Azerbaijan. After Stalin's death, in June 1953 Bagirov was arrested and purged from the Party and government. In April 1956 he and other Beria cronies were executed. Bagirov's replacements in the Party were Imam Mustafayev (1953–1959), a mild geneticist, and Veli Akhundov (1959–1969), a medical doctor. The Soviet outreach to the Arabs and Third World under Khrushchev and Brezhnev increased the importance of the Turkish Moslems. After 1956 the regime granted increased autonomy to the republic, and by 1965 Turkish Moslems were a majority of the Party.

Azerbaijan again came back into the center of Soviet life during the lengthy reign of Geydar Aliyev (1969–1987). A native of Nakhichevan, Aliyev joined the party and secret police in 1945 after serving in a SMERSH (counterintelligence) unit during World War II. Having graduated from the Azerbaijan State University in 1957, he became a KGB major general in the 1960s. With the help of his boss, Semyon Tsvigun (Brezhnev's brother-in-law), he became head of the Azerbaijan KGB and then head of the Party (1969). In 1976 he became a candidate member of the Politburo and in 1982 was called to Moscow as a full member of the Politburo and First Deputy Chairman of the Council of Ministers of the Soviet Union. He would last until 1987, when he was purged in the Gorbachev era. In 1993 he made a comeback as leader of Azerbaijan after the overthrow of Elchibey government.

But for almost two decades Azerbaijan had one of the few leading Turkish Moslem politicians in the country deciding its destiny. From 1969 to 1974 Aliyev conducted a surprisingly massive purge (rivaling the Great Terror in extent but without violence) of the Azerbaijan elite. Aliyev ousted 67 percent of the members of the Council of Ministers, 75 percent of the Central Committee secretaries, 80 percent of the Communist Party bureau, 82 percent of the district Party committees, and 93 percent of the heads of Central Committee departments. A personal friend of Brezhnev, dynamic, and a smart leader with his own cult of personality and strong Mafia-like clique, Aliyev ruled Azerbaijan with a firm hand. He supported local culture and autonomy and battled corruption. During his rule there was little Russification of the population. In the 1989 census 98 percent of Azeri Turks claimed Turkish as their first language. Fully 63 percent said that they did not know Russian at all or very well. This was one of the lowest levels in the Soviet Union. Furthermore, 90 percent of Russians in Azerbaijan did not know the native language. There was a cultural resurgence of Azeri history and national literature with significant Azeri autonomy. Azeri Turks dominated Azerbaijan State University. Fully 85 percent of all students were Azeri Turks, far higher than their percentage in the population.

The rise of Gorbachev had little impact on Azerbaijan until the forced retirement of Aliyev in the fall of 1987. The dominant issue again was the escalating hatred between Azeri Turks and Armenians over Nagorno-Karabakh, which we have already covered from the Armenian side. In July 1988 the Armenian-dominated Nagorno-Karabakh Soviet voted to secede from Azerbaijan, a move blocked by the Azerbaijan Supreme Soviet. That month Moscow sent a high-level commission to the region for an investigation. The November 1988 mass demonstrations in Lenin Square in Baku prompted declaration of a state of emergency in the region in December and direct rule of Nagorno-Karabakh by Moscow in January 1989.

Rising ethnic tensions promoted the formation of the Azerbaijan Popular Front in the spring of 1989. It called for a blockade of Armenia, Azerbaijani sovereignty, local control, democracy, and equality. In December 1989 Armenia annexed Nagorno-Karabakh, a move rejected by Azerbaijan. Bloody clashes erupted as demonstrators broke down the frontier barriers to Iran. The Azerbaijan Popular Front seemed on the verge of taking power.

Moscow had other ideas. In January 1990 a bloody pogrom killed thirty-two Armenians in Baku. Gorbachev declared martial law and sent 11,000 KGB troops into Azerbaijan and Armenia. The violent occupation of Baku, suspension of the media, and repression of the Azerbaijan Popular Front left over a hundred dead and alienated the Azeris. Moscow thus kept the Communists in power and pushed Communist Party functionary Ayaz Mutalibov as party leader. Under martial law the October 1990 elections were blatantly biased and favored the Azerbaijan Communist Party. Opposition candidates won only 11 percent of the legislature's 360 seats. The Popular Front was suppressed for a year but Mutalibov's support for the August 1991 coup in Moscow and enthusiasm for CIS weakened his base. In December 1991 he agreed to the creation of a National Council of fifty members, evenly divided between his backers and those of the Popular Front. In early 1992 Armenian advances in Nagorno-Karabakh and the killing of hundreds of Azeris in Khojaly undermined his position. In March 1992 massive demonstrations forced his resignation in favor of Yakub Mamedov as Acting President.[19]

In May, though, Mutalibov staged a briefly successful coup that led the Supreme Soviet to reinstate him in office and cancel the elections scheduled for June. The Popular Front led demonstrations that smashed the coup in one day of fighting. Its leader, Isa Gambarov, became the Acting President of the National Council. The June 1992 election created a legitimate government under Abulfez Elchibey, who defeated four opponents. This government was non-Communist, pro-Western, and market oriented, the first such government in a former Moslem republic of the FSU. Elchibey saw Turkey and not Iran as

---

[19]The situation on recent events in Azerbaijan was drawn from the Commission on Security and Cooperation in Europe, *The Presidential Election in Azerbaijan*, Government Printing Office, Washington, D.C., June 1992; and Commission on Security and Cooperation in Europe, *Human Rights and Democratization in the Newly Independent States of the Former Soviet Union*, Government Printing Office, Washington, D.C., 1993, pp. 109–122.

a model for Azerbaijan and rejected Azerbaijani participation in CIS. But in June 1993 Elchibey was overthrown by Husseinov's forces and Aliyev came back to power, ending the semidemocratic interlude.

Violence and instability in the Transcaucasus is hardly surprising in view of the long and embattled history of the region, its weak economic underpinning, strong involvement by other powers, ethnic problems, and a long imperial history. The transition to capitalism and democracy has largely been thwarted and the transition to nationhood has become bloody and increasingly authoritarian. Can these dangers be overcome, or do they represent the future for other parts of the FSU that have thus far largely avoided the more extreme manifestations of the Transcaucasus that increasingly make them look like the FSU Balkans? Optimism is hard to generate at a time when there are civil wars in Georgia and Azerbaijan and a major battle going between Armenia and Azerbaijan.

18

Emerging Nation States:
Kazakhstan and Central Asia

The most obscure area for Americans is Central Asia, where five Turkish Moslem states—Kazakhstan, Kyrgyzstan, Turkmenistan, Uzbekistan, and Tajikistan—have emerged, divorced from Moscow by language, religion, customs, culture, and history.[1] A burgeoning Moslem identity and a strong sense of alienation from Moscow have combined there with ties to subnational (tribal), national (republic), supranational (Pan Islamic), and even federal (Soviet) structures. In 1989, 97 to 98 percent of Central Asians claimed their own languages as their first languages.[2] Yet until the granting of independence in 1991, there was little open resistance to Moscow.

There has been little transition to capitalism and democracy in the region. Soviet-style regimes run by former authoritarian Communists remain largely in place. Uzbekistan and Turkmenistan tolerate no opposition parties or free press. Tajikistan, suffering through a civil war, is even worse off as the regime has violently hunted down its opponents. Kazakhstan does allow opposition parties to function, though illegally, and only Kyrygyzstan has tolerated opposition parties and allowed a relatively free press. There is little transition to capitalism, save to some extent in Kazakhstan, and the new states must work hard to maintain themselves in light of over a century of Russian and Soviet

---

[1]For work on Central Asia, see Geoffrey Wheeler, *The Modern History of Soviet Central Asia*, Praeger, New York, 1964; Alexandre Bennigsen and Marie Broxup, *The Islamic Threat to the Soviet State*, St. Martin's Press, New York, 1983; Michael Rywkin, *Moscow's Muslim Challenge*, M.E. Sharpe, Armonk, New York, 1982; Teresa Rakowska-Harmstone, *Russia and Nationalism in Central Asia*, Johns Hopkins University Press, Baltimore and London, 1970; and more general works with sections on Central Asia, including Robert Conquest, editor, *The Last Empire*, Stanford University Press, Stanford, 1986; Nadia Diuk and Adrian Karatnycky, *The Hidden Nations*, William Morrow and Company, New York, 1990; and Graham Smith, editor, *The Nationalities Question in the Soviet Union*, Longmans, London and New York, 1990.
[2]Diuk and Karatnycky, *The Hidden Nations*, p. 266.

286

rule. There is the problem of over 1000 nuclear weapons in Kazakhstan, formerly a major test site for the Soviet military. Ethnic conflicts remain endemic, and extensive drug trafficking puts Central Asia second only to Burma in opium production. Extensive natural resources, including the largest gold mine in the world in Uzbekistan and large gas and oil reserves, offer some hope.[3]

The Moslem theme is the key that has set the region apart from Orthodox Christian, then atheist, Russia. Only Indonesia, Pakistan, India, and Bangladesh will each have more Moslems than the 50 million Moslems in these republics by the year 2000. The borders with Iran, Turkey, and Afghanistan reflect their geographic proximity to the Islamic Middle East. Islam remained strong in rural Central Asia, where 75 percent of the Moslems reside and 90 percent still obtain parental consent for marriage. In the 1970s, 92 percent of Moslems lived in homogenous Moslem families, and only 20 percent were atheists. Over 90 percent of all Central Asian Moslems performed the basic duties of Islam. Communal particularism was very strong here, walling them off from European and Russian influence.[4]

The Soviet interlude lasted less than seventy-five years in Central Asia, the Russian interlude less than 150 years, a brief space compared to 1400 years of a luminescent Persian-Turkish-Islamic civilization. For centuries Islamic civilization outshone European Christendom, suffering through the Dark Ages and early Middle Ages. Central Asia was then the intellectual center of the Islamic world, a seat of great empires and centers of learning. By the eighth century Islam had conquered most of the region dominated by Turkish nomads. Already by the tenth century Islamic traditions, practices, and laws were strongly entrenched in Central Asia. Islam predominated in the arts, architecture, literature (oral), music, and writing of the area. But by the thirteenth century, the end of the caravan routes (caused by a switch to sea routes to the Far East) isolated the region from international economic developments.[5]

Central Asian Moslems feel that Islam, despite massacres, transfers, proselytization, assimilation, and repression, has triumphed over six deadly enemies that set out to destroy it in the last 1200 years. The first were the Turkish Khazars who for 300 years blocked Arab expansionism and posed a serious threat to the Transcaucasus. By the middle of the ninth century Moslems formed a majority in the Khazar empire, and in 965 Kievan Rus destroyed Khazar power. The second threat came from the Buddhist Qara-Khitay that in the twelfth century conquered most of Central Asia. The Mongols in 1219 destroyed the Buddhist power but themselves posed a greater threat to Central Asia. The vicious Mongols after 1221 seized all the great cities, slaughtered their populations, and razed Bukhara and Samarkand. They ruled Central Asia as aliens for over a hundred years. But by 1340 the Islamicization of the Mongol

[3]For a good recent review, see "Nancy Lubin Examines the Complexities of Central Asia," *United States Institute of Peace Journal,* vol. 6, no. 4, August 1993, pp. 4–5.

[4]Rasma Karklins, *Ethnic Relations in the USSR,* Allen and Unwin, Boston, 1986, chapters 6–7.

[5]Wheeler, *The Modern History of Soviet Central Asia,* p. 28.

rulers ended this threat. In the seventeenth century the Kalmuks, nomadic followers of Western Mongol Buddhism, were a constant threat for 150 years. From the time they razed Khiva in 1603, Semireche in 1643, Balkagh and Tashkent in 1718, to their raids in 1723–1725 that again destroyed Tashkent and other major cities, they disrupted civilized life in Central Asia. Again an outside force, the Chinese Manchus, in 1757 saved Central Asia.[6] The two Russian threats—Tsarist conquest in the middle of the nineteenth century and Soviet rule after 1920—were repelled thanks to the 1917 and 1991 Revolutions respectively.

From 1000 to 1850 Turkish Moslems, with interruptions, ruled Central Asia and were closely integrated with Moslems in the Transcaucasus, Volga, and Crimea. The Soviet Union modernized the region, so that two-thirds of young Uzbeks now have secondary or higher education. Thanks to an explosive growth rate, the number of Moslems in the FSU will soar from 17 million in 1950 to 75 million in 2000 (50 million in Central Asia) and 141 million in 2050. The 25 million Uzbeks and 11 million Kazakhs are the largest groups.[7]

Central Asia, with 1.5 million square miles, has a diverse geography from the steppe of northern Kazakhstan to the semidesert of the rest of Kazakhstan to the desert in much of the rest of Central Asia and the mountains of the Pamirs and Tienshan.

Uzbekistan and Kazakhstan have been the two dominant republics. Kazakhstan, with 1.1 million square miles and 17 million people (and now with nuclear weapons), has been a major player in the region. Uzbekistan, with 20 million people, has been a huge cotton-producing area facing ecological disaster (Aral Sea). Its capital, Tashkent, has sometimes been an unofficial capital of Central Asia. Poverty is omnipresent. The World Bank calculated that in 1991 Uzbekistan produced an income of 1350 dollars per capita, Kyrgyzstan 1550 dollars and Tajikistan 1040 dollars (compared to 3220 dollars for Russia).[8]

The Russian conquest of Central Asia was a long, protracted, and complex matter, sharply different from the creation of the British and French empires. Russia itself had been under Asian dominance during the 250 years of Mongol rule. With its expansion to the Pacific in the seventeenth century, Tsarist Russia was a legitimate Asian power. When Russian soldiers and settlers moved into Central Asia, they did not have to cross oceans or feel as if they had left home. Like the American settlers going westward toward California in the nineteenth century, they simply moved overland to a new area while remaining tightly connected to the original base. There was no slave trade in Central Asia, no higher standard of living to attract the settlers. Islam was familiar to the

[6]Bennigsen and Broxup, *The Islamic Threat to the Soviet State,* chapter 2.
[7]Mikhail Bernstam, "The Demography of Soviet Ethnic Groups in World Perspective," and S. Enders Wimbush, "The Soviet Muslim Borderlands," in Conquest, *The Last Empire,* pp. 318–322; and Diuk and Karatnycky, *The Hidden Nations,* p. 267. In the same region, Xinjiang province in China is 60 percent Moslem Turks as well.
[8]*RFE/RL Research Report,* vol. 2, no. 20, May 3–7, 1993.

Russians who had lived under the Islamicized Mongols and by 1560 integrated the Tatar Moslem khanates of Kazan and Astrakhan into Russia.[9]

Much of Russian expansion was uncoordinated. The movement to Siberia and the Pacific took 135 years from 1555 to 1689. Many factors drove the eighteenth-century expansion from Siberia south into the steppes and Turkestan that ultimately seized Central Asia in the nineteenth century. There was competition with England, Turkey, and Iran, the desire for markets, the urge to reach Byzantium, and the predatory nature of the Cossacks. The collapse of the Great Tatar Horde left a vacuum in the region which encouraged Russian imperialism. Persia and Afghanistan supported the Russian drive from fear of British imperialism while a disintegrating China was too weak to stop the Russians. Central Asians, weakened by centuries of foreign invasions, massacres, and enslavement and lacking modern weapons, organization, or coordination, offered little resistance. Russian military operations in Central Asia from 1847 to 1873 cost only 400 dead and 1600 wounded.[10]

The Russian advance, which in 140 years seized a region with greater territory than India but only 9 million people, started in the 1730s. After Tsar Ivan the Terrible seized Astrakhan in 1556, the Russians by 1730 reached the steppes of Kazakhstan and in succeeding decades achieved nominal sovereignty over a number of local regimes. The 1 million square miles of Kazakhstan equalled 25 percent of the 4 million square miles of Europe. The Kazakhs, many of whom looked to Russia for protection against the Mongols and the Kokand khanate, were largely nomadic tribesmen who bred cattle on summer grazing grounds and then pastured them in winter. Ruled by local khans and sultans, they were divided into a series of clans built around a patriarchal family. The Kazakhs were engaged in perpetual tribal wars that diminished their ability to resist the relatively modern Russians. The gradual Russian advance slowly absorbed the area from 1730 until 1850.

In Turkestan the Russian moves came in a more settled region with a nomadic minority and 5 million people residing in the local Moslem khanates. However, there were no firm frontiers and the ruling dynasties of the Bukhara, Khiva, and Kokand khanates were less than fifty years old. There was only the most tenuous notion of a national existence. People did not see themselves as Bukharan or Khivan; their loyalties were to tribe, clan, and family. The local economies were largely neofeudal and primitive. Internecine warfare was common. The standard of living, and levels of government, literacy, medical care, poverty, and hunger resembled those of early medieval Europe over 500 years ago.

In the 1850s Russia began to built the same kind of forts in Turkestan that had marked her advance into Kazakhstan in the 1720s and onward. In 1864 a

[9]See Wheeler, *The Modern History of Soviet Central Asia,* chapter 1, for a good treatment of this subject.

[10]This is less than was lost on a single day of operations on the main fronts of World War I, where 9 million soldiers died in four years of fighting.

small Russian force of 4000 men took the holy city of Chimkent after defeating 12,000 Kokand warriors. In 1865 General Cherniayev took Tashkent when his force of 2000 men defeated 30,000 Moslem warriors. In 1868 Russian troops took Samarkand with a small force of 8300 men. By 1867 the Russian government created a Governor-Generalship of Turkestan under General Kaufman. By 1873 Khiva was a Russian protectorate. In 1876 the Russians dissolved the khanate of Kokand. By 1881 Turkmenistan was under Russian rule. The Russian conquest of Central Asia was completed by 1885. Russian superiority of organization, training, discipline, weapons, morale, leadership, technology, and skill told in this rapid conquest. Harsh temperatures (reaching 150 degrees Fahrenheit in the Khiva desert), long distances, and terrible roads often proved a greater problem than the local resistance.

The Russians consolidated their Central Asian empire from 1885 to 1917. By 1885 they controlled the borders with Persia and Afghanistan. The relatively despotic local Russian government was largely dominated by marginal military men prone to corruption and bribery. They maintained the khanates of Bukhara and Khiva at low cost. By 1898 the railroad extended to Samarkand. In 1914 Tashkent had 271,000 people, 31 percent of them Russian. Massive Russian and Ukrainian immigration brought 2 million immigrants into the region, where they made up 40 percent of the steppe population by 1911. Until 1916, 45,000 Russian troops kept order in Central Asia.[11]

The Russian treatment of the Moslems—Central Asian and otherwise—was exceptionally varied. The Russian slaughtered the Turkmen in 1881 and expelled over 2 million Cherkess, Abkhazians, Crimean Tatars (who migrated to Ottoman Turkey), and Kazakh nomads in the nineteenth century. The Russians assimilated the remaining Moslems in Bashkiria, Crimea, and the steppes who found themselves surrounded by alien Russian Orthodox. The government forcibly converted the Volga Tatars. They pursued a laissez-faire policy toward the Azeri Turks in the nineteenth century. The government actively tried to co-opt the elites in Kazakhstan and left alone the Ossetians and Kabardians. It offered an alliance to the Volga Tatars and exempted Central Asian Moslems from military service.

Moslem responses were also varied. Most natives (97 to 98 percent illiterate) were pacific. The conservatives sought to withdraw into Islam and preserve Islam under heathen rule. The more liberal strove to regain power through promoting a more modernized Islam. The radical conservatives, trying to build a theocratic state, sought cooperation with the rulers. The most militant, led by the Sufis, sought armed resistance. From 1824 to 1859 the Imam of Daghestan Shamil led a massive revolt in the region. In 1916 the Russian attempt to call up 430,000 Central Asian Moslems for war labor duty in the rear provoked a revolt that took six months to crush with almost 4000 Russians killed or missing.

By 1917 forty years of Russian rule had not radically changed Central Asia.

---

[11]This force of 45,000 Russians to rule 5 million Moslems was almost 40 times greater on a per capita basis than the 70,000 British soldiers deployed in India to rule 300 million natives.

In 1917, there were over 26,000 mosques and 45,000 mullahs outside of Bukhara and Khiva. There were 12 million Moslems and 2 million Slavs, who made up 29 percent of the Kazakhstan population and 4 percent of the rest of Central Asia. Only 1 to 3 percent of the Moslems were literate. There was no real Moslem intelligentsia, no national leadership, no idea of nationhood. Islam depended heavily on the traditional structures of family and clergy. Polygamy, early marriage, taboos, the veil, and rule by elders were common in Central Asia. The disintegration of Ottoman Turkey, anarchy in Persia, warlords in China, and the backwardness of Afghanistan meant that there were no attractive local Islamic or, in the case of China, non-Islamic powers to offset Russia.

In this context of very low political consciousness, traditional political views, and dire poverty, the radical socialism of the October Revolution found no echo. For Central Asian Moslems socialism was an alien, heretical, atheistic, European creed. The Russians made the revolution and continued to be the local rulers. The Moslem masses remained inert and passive, and the fragmented Moslem elite did not act. Rather, the Russians fought each for supremacy. As Rywkin has observed:

> The October Revolution in Central Asia was initially a settler's affair: this situation continued for two years while Turkestan was cut off from the rest of the country by events of the civil war. Menaced by Whites, threatened by Muslim nationalism and too weak to control the former Russian protectorates of Khiva and Bukhara, the authorities in Tashkent had only stranded Red Army units, railroad workers and a few leftist settlers to rely on. And settlers' support had to be bought by protecting their privileges. The breaking of the geographic isolation and arrival of metropolitan troops brought basic changes.[12]

There was some support for the Bolsheviks during the Civil War outside of the local Russian settlers. White Russian hatred of Moslems, Leninist promises of national self-determination, the role of the Georgian Joseph Stalin in running nationality policy, and the Moslem hope for using Bolshevism to destroy European Christianity and liberate Islam prompted some support for the Bolsheviks.

Moslems often saw the October Revolution as the beginning of the end of colonialism. Sultan Galiev (the leading Tatar National Communist) emphasized the great possibilities inherent in Bolshevism for liberating Islam. Moscow became for a short time the center of Third World revolution. Three Comintern congresses, and especially the famous Congress of the Toilers of the East in Baku in 1920, stressed the liberating role of Bolshevism.

In Turkestan the February Revolution led to the creation of a Provisional Government and Soviet, each composed solely of Russians, despite the presence of only 400,000 Russians and Ukrainians. In October 1917 the Tashkent Soviet, composed solely of Russians and openly excluding Moslems, seized power. In reaction, an All Moslem Congress in Kokand, while against inde-

[12]Rywkin, *Moscow's Muslim Challenge*, pp. 32–33.

pendence, formed a Kokand Provisional Government openly hostile to the Bolsheviks. But with the Moslem masses remaining inert, the Red Army was able to seize the city of Kokand, massacring 5000 to 10,000 Moslems. From 1917 to 1919 the Turkestani Russians were cut off from Moscow. Their excesses and brutality ultimately caused a strong Moslem backlash in the Basmachi revolt. The troops of the Tashkent Soviet seized Bukhara in March 1918 only to be routed. In Turkmenistan the excesses of the Military Commissar Frolov and his undisciplined and poorly armed troops led to an end of the Soviet role there.

In Kazakhstan the local government supported autonomy after the October Revolution. From January to March 1918 the Red Army seized the major cities with the support of the 1.5 million Russian and Ukrainian settlers. That summer hostile Cossacks liquidated their government. In 1919 anarchy reigned as different Russian factions battled it out. In the 1917–1920 period the Alash Orda ran an independent Kazakhstan government. By the fall of 1919 the Red Army returned to regain Soviet power. By 1920 the Bolsheviks, having won the Civil War elsewhere, made a dramatic comeback. In February 1920 the Red Army seized Khiva, in September 1920 Bukhara, both of which became people's republics. By December 1920 most of the steppe country and Turkmenistan was back in Soviet hands.

The Basmachi revolt showed that the local Moslem population could be stirred to resistance under certain circumstances. The brutality of the settlers and their Red Army, the massacres and looting, the mobilization of Moslems for the Red Army, and the food requisitions roused the Moslem peasant masses. Even some local forces went over to the rebels. Only the appearance of Frunze's Red Army from Russia liquidated the massive revolt.

The Basmachi revolt lasted almost two years after it flared up in the Fergana valley in January 1918. Only Moscow-directed army units finally suppressed it late in 1919. It was reignited in late 1920 when the Emir of Bukhara fled there after the Red Army seized Bukhara. With 40,000 men under the command of the emir, it took the Red Army almost a year to defeat the Basmachis in Fergana valley. At this point Enver Pasha (Turkish War Minister) arrived in Bukhara and rekindled the battle. Then in December 1921 his ally, Ibrahim Bek, with 20,000 troops retook Dushanbe. However, defections within the ranks of the Basmachis, a population tiring of war, and the death of Emir Pasha in battle in August 1922 again turned the tide. By December 1922 the Red Army had won back Eastern Bukhara and it pacified the region by late 1923.

The interwar period was a stormy one in Central Asia. At the tenth Party Congress in Moscow in 1921 the new regime condemned pan-Islamism and pan-Turkism. In 1923 the Party arrested Sultan Galiev, the most popular local leader supporting the regime. His advocacy of a single Turkic Communist Republic in Central Asia, strong and united, ran directly counter to Stalin's desire to divide and conquer the region in the service of a strong center in Moscow. The increase in private trade, end of economic exploitation, and lessening of political repression had a positive effect. But the expropriation of clerical property, the abolition of religious schools and Moslem courts, and the closing of thousands of mosques deeply alienated the population. The crushing of the Basmachi revolt led to a certain moderation. But in some places, such as Eastern Bukhara, 25 percent of the population fled to Afghanistan.

The decade from 1928 to 1938 saw massive and repeated purges that eliminated all of the former supporters of the new Soviet regime. In Kazakhstan every member of the first Politburo was shot. In 1937 in Uzbekistan there were three prime ministers in one year. A weak Party was decimated and a new one, from the upper crust of society, was recruited. After 1937 the Moslem Communists were not believers but an elite socioeconomic element. The bulk of the population (80 percent rural) stayed aloof from these changes. Soviet power brought collectivization, five-year plans, purges, large Russian industrial investment, attacks on religion, local nationalism, modernizing liberation of women, and literacy.

Tajikistan was an especially sad case. The bitterness and destruction of the protracted Civil War left a stinging legacy. Most local party cadres were illiterate as there was no real local intelligentsia. Wooden plows and hoes were the order of the day in the countryside. Teresa Rakowska-Harmstone has depicted the scene:

> Soviet rule in Tadzhikistan was established by Russian military action largely against the wishes of the local population which resisted it for a number of years. The civil authorities formed in the aftermath of military victory were dominated by Russian elements and faced a population still largely hostile to the new regime.[13]

Unable to sink firm roots, the regime resorted to divide and conquer tactics by splitting Central Asia in the early 1920s into five nations and a number of autonomous republics. Persian-speaking Tajiks, with an equal number of their brethren in Afghanistan, were especially receptive to such individual treatment. The government promoted rapid modernization from above, the creation of centrally dominated institutions, and strong Moscow-controlled political systems. The system preserved national languages and cultures, even creating the structure (but not the substance) of states to gain popular support. Russian settlers supported the regime but opposed land reform and collectivization. After the 1937 purges the First Secretary of the Tajikistan Communist Party (which had less than 5000 members) was a Russian secret police official. From 1926 to 1939 nearly 2 million Russians emigrated to Central Asia, where they now made up 9 percent of the population. By 1939 Russians and Ukrainians accounted for 50 percent of the population of Tashkent. The Red Army and secret police, dominated by Slavs, maintained a firm rule that crushed the Basmachi revolt and allowed 2 to 3 million Kazakhs to die in the famine of 1932–1933.

The government isolated Central Asian Moslems from their Moslem brethren across the border. Even the changes of alphabet, from Arabic to Latin (1922) and to Cyrillic (1937), promoted this isolation. By closing nearly all religious and theological schools and ending public religious instruction, the govern-

---

[13]Rakowska-Harmstone, *Russia and Nationalism in Central Asia,* p. 32.

ment tried to cripple Islam in the younger generation. Through education, modern health care, promotion of a local elite, and rising standards of living, Moscow tried to build a new secular base and maintain its centralized control. Despite hostile populations and inefficient and corrupt local regimes, it ruled Central Asia without serious opposition after crushing the Basmachi revolt.

In World War II the Germans never reached Central Asia, but they would surely have received a positive reception. Roughly half of the Turkestanis called up deserted the Red Army in World War II. Central Asian Moslems did not forgive a regime that closed 25,000 mosques, leaving only 1300 mosques functioning in the entire region by 1942, and attacked tradition, customs, and religion.

The late Stalin years and the Khrushchev years saw a different approach. The regime, having consolidated power, turned to building up a native elite whose high status and material rewards would make it loyal to Moscow. Moscow began to industrialize and modernize Central Asia. The thirteen schools with 860 students of 1913 gave way by 1950 to 3000 schools with 300,000 students. The standard of living, while low, markedly improved.

But there were limits. In 1956 a typical family of five lived in a 250-square-foot adobe house, frequently without electricity. Central Asian Moslems were excluded from the Politburo and most power-holding positions in Moscow. A Russian was nearly always the ultimate power source as Second Secretary of the Party and Deputy Chairman of the government structure. In 1960 Europeans accounted for 40 percent of Central Asian Communists and were most of the leading government functionaries, army and secret police officials, managers, and professionals. In the early 1960s Central Asia resembled a colonial society with Europeans dominating the privileged social, economic, political, and cultural positions and clustered in modern industry while the natives were largely rural and a minor part of the elite.

Under Brezhnev there was a large-scale co-optation of Central Asian elites. The calling of Geydar Aliyev to Moscow in 1978, the close relationship between Brezhnev's brother-in-law and Central Asian elites, and the large-scale corruption all underlined this new closeness. Soviet subsidies of Central Asian industry, local preferences for hiring Moslems, and more private initiatives reflected the new policy. By 1976 Central Asia produced 6 million tons of steel (0 in 1913), 40 million tons of oil (.3 million in 1913), and 114 billion watts of electricity (.01 in 1913). Central Asia produced 90 percent of all Soviet cotton. Brezhnev stressed social welfare policies, tolerance, interethnic economic equality, and a more modernized society. Only 450 mosques were still operating in the 1970s. While denied real central power, Moslem elites gained access to the administrative, economic, technological, and party sectors. By the late 1970s Moslems were the majority of the local scientific elites and made impressive educational gains. After 1968, Brezhnev increasingly used Moslems as spokesmen for the Soviet Union in Asia. He stressed the autonomous nature of their administrative status and their cultural and linguistic freedom. When Red Army troops went into Afghanistan in 1979, 40 percent (or 40,000) of the troops and hundreds of administrators were Central Asians.[14] By 1979 a rapidly growing Moslem population reached 44 million people, greater than the number of Ukrainians in the Soviet Union.

In Kazakhstan by 1990 Russians made up 38 percent of the population, as did Kazakhs. Russians dominated Alma Ata, the capital, where Russians were 59 percent of the population, Kazakhs 23 percent. Adding in Ukrainians, Germans, Jews, and Belorussians, Europeans formed 66 percent of the population of Alma Ata. Furthermore, 78 percent of the urban Kazakhs spoke Russian fluently. In other Central Asian republics, the much smaller Russian stratum still tended to represent a strong element. Russians in 1989 were 56 percent of the population of Bishkek (Kyrgyzstan), 34 percent of the population of Tashkent (Uzbekistan), 33 percent of the population of Dushanbe (Tajikistan), and 33 percent of the population of Ashkhabad (Turkmenistan).[15]

Yet a distinctive non-Sovietized Central Asia remained. Strong devotion to traditional notions remained, even while the institutions lay in ruins. The poor performance of Central Asian troops and bureaucrats in Afghanistan signified trouble. In 1989, 97 to 99 percent of all Central Asians claimed their own language as their first one. Intermarriage with non-Moslems was rare, less than 1 percent of all marriages. Less than 2 percent of Central Asian Moslems claimed Russian as their native language. Except in Kazakhstan, only 23 to 35 percent of Central Asians claimed any serious knowledge of Russian. The industrial level of the area was only 50 percent of that of the rest of the Soviet Union. Capitalism remained strong in private farm plots and a private housing sector. Low labor productivity, reluctance to use female labor, and technological backwardness plagued the area. The local Russians were overrepresented in the power elite, but few (less than 10 percent) could speak the native languages. The demographic explosion and events in Iran and Afghanistan gave the Central Asian Moslems hope that they would eventually liberate themselves from Russian tutelage. Even the local Party and government elite were of dubious loyalty, highly corrupt, and inefficient. There was a high rate of political illiteracy. The masses, though passive, were barely touched by the political system. Ethnic tensions between native and Russians remained high.

INDEPENDENT NATION STATES

With the disintegration of the Soviet Union in 1991, the Central Asian republics gained their independence. Yet with little organized resistance to Moscow in the 1980s, independence came, as in parts of Africa in the 1960s, from above and without struggle. Russian influence remained strong, although Turkey (a

---

[14]After widespread fraternization, poor performance, and significant desertion, the Central Asians were pulled out in February 1980.
[15]Mikhail Guboglo, "Demography and Language in the Capitals of the Union Republics," *Journal of Soviet Nationalities,* vol. 1, no. 4, Winter 1990–1991, pp. 27–33.

billion dollars of aid in 1992), Iran, and even the United States began to be players in the region. By 1992 all the countries had signed some trade agreements with Russia, once the focus of all activity.[16] The bulk of the population simply accepted the change, although with pleasure. There was little understanding of, or support for, Western democracy or capitalism. The old Communist elites were able to continue to use their traditional levers of power to rule. They controlled the economy, the polity, and the culture. They transformed themselves into good nationalists and Moslems to accommodate the new ethos. A strong form of "feudal-authoritarianism," replete with rampant corruption, accommodated itself to the new order. The privileged positions of Russians and the old elite have now been questioned but not successfully challenged by the rising interest in Islam and rapid building of mosques. Dire poverty, environmental degradation, poor health care, and weak industrial development have not provided a favorable environment for transition to democracy and capitalism. While some opposition parties have functioned and the old elite has searched for new bases of support, the simple fact is that in 1993 all but one of the leaders of these five states are the former first secretaries of the Communist Party. In three of the five states the presidential election had but one candidate—a familiar Soviet practice. There has been little economic reform, promoting stagnation but avoiding the chaos found in Russia and elsewhere.

In Uzbekistan the hard liners did not support Gorbachev's reforms. By 1989 local opposition groups were routinely harassed by the government. In the February 1990 Supreme Council elections the Communists dominated, with the majority of seats reserved for the Party or without any opponents. President Islam Karimov quietly supported the August 1991 coup, but after its failure, he banned the Party from politics and confiscated its property. The Party was renamed the People's Democratic Party under Karimov. He declared Uzbekistan independent in September and in December won 86 percent of the vote in a contested election.

Little has changed in Uzbekistan. The head of the government is the former head of the Communist Party and the parliament has been made up almost exclusively of former Communists. In 1993 the government sealed the borders with Tajikistan to prevent its civil war from spilling across them. The new constitution in December 1992 was adopted, Soviet-style, by a unanimous vote of the parliament. The government has refused to legally recognize Birlik, the largest opposition group. In June 1992 government goons evidently beat up one cochairman of Birlik (Abdurakhim Pulatov), and in May 1993 they beat up the other cochairman (Shokrat Ismatullaev). Demonstrations are largely prohibited and opposition groups are weak and heavily controlled by the government. The government controls the media and prevents the creation of independent newspapers. The government has also retained control over appointment of religious leaders. In 1992 there was a heavy crackdown on all oppositionist

---

[16]See Sheila Marnie and Erik Whitlock, "Central Asia and Economic Integration," *RFE/RL Research Report*, vol. 2, no. 14, April 1993, for the complexity of the interactions.

activity. A 1990 law barring insult to the dignity and honor of the president has been a bar to free speech and opposition criticism of the regime.

There has been some small progress. No longer is there an official ideology, and there has been some small tolerance for opposition and religion. Even the government creation of opposition groups may in the long run become a positive event as they may turn into legitimate groups. Uzbekistan, with 2 billion dollars worth of trade outside the CIS and as the world's eighth largest gold producer, has tried to open up to foreign trade. Overall, though, the old has remained omnipresent in Uzbekistan.

In Turkmenistan very little has changed from the Soviet period. The former Communist Party, now renamed the Democratic Party, has become the largest and only legal party. The President of Turkmenistan, elected with opposition in November 1990, is Saparmurad Niyazov, who was First Secretary of the Turkmenistan Communist Party after 1985. In June 1992 he was reelected President without opposition. His powers are almost unlimited, even including appointing local officials by decree. The deputies of the Supreme Soviet, elected in January 1990 in largely unopposed elections, are over 90 percent former Communists. The dominant Council of Elders consists almost exclusively of former Communist Party apparatchiki. There are few opposition groups, and these are not legal and are frequently harassed. With very low political consciousness and strong traditional clan elements, but large natural gas reserves (third in the world), Turkmenistan has been little changed by events elsewhere, although in 1993 it announced that by 1996 it would change its alphabet from Cyrillic to Latin and in March 1993 its president visited Washington. Some economic changes may be likely, but progress towards democracy remains highly unlikely with the old elite still firmly in power and little challenged.

In Kyrgyzstan the March 1990 elections for the Supreme Soviet were dominated by Communists, who were 95 percent of the deputies. However, they adopted a mildly reformist line and elected as President Askar Akayev, the former head of the Academy of Sciences and not the head of the Communist Party. In October 1992 Akayev won an uncontested presidential election. After the August 1991 coup Akayev moved against the Communist Party, which split into two parts. He has been the most progressive leader in Central Asia, allowing opposition parties and newspapers to operate. However, the old elite is still in place and no free elections have been held. In 1993 Kyrzystan announced that it would issue its own currency.

In Kazakhstan, where the earliest ethnic riots broke out in Alma Ata in December 1986, President Nursultan Nazarbayev has built a good image in the West. Appointed the First Secretary of the Communist Party in 1989, Nazarbayev became president in April 1990. In an unopposed election in January 1991 he won a Soviet-style 99 percent of the vote. A close ally of Gorbachev, Nazarbayev has remained quite authoritarian and refused to register opposition groups. Only three of the almost a hundred groups and parties in Kazakhstan are legal and the Socialist Party (the renamed Communist Party) has been politically dominant. The others have been frequently harassed. In January 1992 Nazarbayev declared that he would rule by decree in localities. Favoring a secular, Western-oriented regime, he has made progress only in economic areas. In June 1992 a new decree on the KGB actually gave the new secret police almost all the powers of the old KGB. A 1992 law on protecting the dignity and honor of the president allowed major punishment, including as much as six years in jail for the offense. The government has repressed nationalist groups that would try to inflame the 40 percent of the population that is Russian or the 40 percent of the population that is Kazakh.

Kazakhstan, with 60 percent of its exports going to the West and producing 4 million tons of oil, has signed a 1.5 billion dollar deal with Chevron corporation to exploit Tengiz oil. A massive new 5 billion dollar oil pipeline is also under discussion. However, economic reforms have been slow, with output declining 16 percent in 1992 and real wages declining almost 50 percent.[17]

Tajikistan, still in the thralls of a civil war, has been in far worse position. After a slow response to change in Moscow, in February 1990 Dushanbe witnessed large demonstrations that were bloodily suppressed by the government. The government then banned opposition candidates from the March 1990 Supreme Soviet elections, which were dominated by the Communists. They elected Kakhar Makhmamov, who openly backed the failed August 1991 coup, as the president. Demonstrations after the failed coup forced him out of office, and the government declared Tajikistan independent in September 1991. The new president, Kadreddin Aslonov, suspended Communist activity and froze the Party's assets. The angry Communist deputies in parliament then ousted Aslonov and elected in his place the former First Secretary of the Communist Party, Rakhomon Nabiyev, who then reinstated the Party. This led to mass popular protest that forced Nabiyev out in October 1991. In a questionable election in November 1991, Nabiyev received 58 percent of the vote and his leading opponent thirty percent. Nabiyev then rolled back changes, arresting leaders of the opposition, restoring censorship, and tightening the criminal code. New violent demonstration, including the kidnapping of nineteen members of parliament, ensued. In the spring of 1992 President Nabiyev made concessions by taking opposition members into the Cabinet. Then in May 1992 he repressed demonstrations in Dushanbe. In one incident twelve opposition protestors were shot to death during a march. This prompted the head of the National Guard to support and arm the opposition. Nabiyev then agreed to a coalition government with the opposition. At this point parts of the country refused to accept the new regime and fighting ensued that killed thousands of people in a civil war. In Dushanbe armed gangs attacked each other. In September 1992 Nabiyev was allegedly captured trying to flee the country. In his place the head of the parliament, Akbarsho Iskandrov, became acting president. In October Nabiyev followers tried to stage a coup, which was soon smashed. In November 1992 Iskandrov resigned, ending the coalition government.

[17]*RFE/RL Research Report,* vol. 2, no. 19, April 26–30, 1993.

Former Communists dominated the new conservative government in Tajikistan after November 1992. In December the new government returned to the capital Dushanbe and closed opposition newspapers. In February 1993 the government arrested key opposition leaders and in March, having largely won the civil war, banned the four leading opposition parties. In April 1993 the government charged the leading opposition candidate in the November 1992 election, Davlat Khudonazarov, with treason. The Communists had won, but resistance continued in rugged Badakhshan and among opposition groups in Dushanbe. Russian support for the government had offset Afghan support for the rebels. The long-term prognosis has to be bleak in this setting.[18]

Artificial states, deep poverty, Russian power, and weak political consciousness have driven the Central Asian states and Kazakhstan in a direction different from other new states. Here the former Communist rulers, even in the face of civil war, have largely retained power as repainted nationalists. The transition to capitalism and democracy has barely begun, and only external national symbols have proliferated. The old elites have stepped into the vacuum left by the end of the Moscow domination of the FSU. At the same time local Islamic pressures and foreign pressures from Turkey, Iran, and even Afghanistan have been playing an increasing role. While change is always possible, the likelihood of a real transition to democracy and capitalism is weak, except perhaps in Kazakhstan, with almost 60 percent of its population urban, a strong Russian element (38 percent), and great natural resources. For the other predominantly rural and more native regions, only a slow transition is likely, if any at all.

---

[18]Bess Brown, "Tajik Opposition to be Banned," *RFE/RL Research Report,* vol. 2, no. 14, April 2, 1993.

19

Emerging Nation States: Moldova and the Baltics

The Baltics and Moldova are small, peripheral newly independent states whose histories are little known to Americans and who have been major strategic prizes fought over by the greater powers.

MOLDOVA

The new state of Moldova (formerly Moldavia) is especially obscure.[1] The former Bessarabia, in this century it has twice belonged to Rumania, twice to Russia, and now is independent. Moldavia was 16 percent of Rumanian territory, less than 1 percent of Russian territory. From 1711 to 1944 Russian forces invaded Rumania twelve times, with Moldova a major bone of contention. Only from 1812 until 1918, 1940 to 1941, and then from 1944 to 1991 was Moldova under Russian control.

In 1989 Rumanians formed 65 percent of its 4 million people, with Kishinev as the capital. In the 1989 census 92 percent of Moldavians claimed Rumanian as their native language, with 54 percent claiming a good knowledge of Russian as their second language. Rumanians were a minority in the capital (49 percent), as opposed to Russians, Ukrainians, and Jews. Nearly 12 percent of Rumanians listed Russian as their native language, giving the Russian and

[1]We rely here primarily on Nicholas Dima's fine work, *From Moldavia to Moldova: The Soviet Romanian Territorial Dispute*, Eastern European Monograph #309, distributed by Columbia University Press, New York, 1991; and to a much lesser extent on Michael Bruchis, *Nations-Nationalities-People: A Study of Nationality Policy of the Communist Party in Soviet Moldavia*, Eastern European Monograph #165, distributed by Columbia University Press, New York, 1984. There has been very little written on this topic.

Russified native element a slim majority in the capital as well as in the Dniester region.[2]

Modern Rumanians are descendants of ancient Dacia, ruled by the Romans from 106 until 270. Massive Eurasian migration left Bessarabia, a continuation of Rumanian land with the Dniester, without state authority for centuries. When this migration ended around the year 1000, the Rumanians came down from the hills and mountains and settled the flat lands, including Bessarabia. Prince Bogdan founded Moldavia (Bessarabia and Bukovina), the land between the Carpathian mountains and Dniester river, in the middle of the fourteenth century. Prince Alexander the Good (1400–1432) ousted the Tatars early in the fifteenth century. Despite battles with Hungarians, Poles, and Tatars, Bessarabia achieved its heights in the late fifteenth century under Stephen the Good (1457–1504). He fortified Bessarabia against its enemies to the north (Poland), east (Tatars), and south (Turks). Russia was far away, while the Ottoman Turks were near. After the death of Stephen the Good, his son Bogdan accepted Turkish sovereignty over Bessarabia. For over 300 years the Ottoman Turks ruled Bessarabia as a vassal state.

Ultimately the expanding Russian empire challenged Turkish control over alien Christians in Europe. As early as 1711 a Russian army under Peter the Great reached Bessarabia, but the Turks stemmed the tide. In 1774 an Austrian victory over the Turks yielded them Bukovina (northern Moldavia). Russian wars with Turkey (1711, 1768, 1788) brought Russia repeatedly to the borders of Bessarabia. In 1812 the Treaty of Bucharest gave Bessarabia (eastern Moldavia) to the Russians, thereby bringing them close to the Balkans, providing a base to attack Ottoman Turkey and annex European Christians to Russia. While Russia transformed a Rumanian area into a Russian province, Rumania moved towards independence under nominal Turkish control.

In 1877 Russia went to war with Ottoman Turkey, ostensibly to free Christians under the Turkish yoke. While the Rumanians agreed to allow the Russian army free passage across Rumania, the Russians opposed the Rumanian demand for immediate independence. Russia demanded southern Bessarabia, lost in 1853 in the Treaty of Paris, as the price. The Turks soundly beat the Russians, who turned to Rumania for help. With Rumanian help the Russians gained their victory. The 1878 Treaty of San Stefano allowed Russia to reannex southern Bessarabia, and the 1878 Congress of Berlin gave all of Bessarabia to the victorious Russians.

The Russians moved to Russify Bessarabia, thereby alienating the largely Rumanian population. Russia eliminated the Rumanian language from school, government, and church. The Bessarabians, overwhelmingly rural and few in numbers, could do little to resist. As in 1991, revolution in the center in 1917 crippled state authority and allowed local autonomy and independence. By

[2]Nadia Duik and Adrian Karatnycky, *The Hidden Nations,* Morrow, New York, 1990, p. 266 and Mikhail Guboglo, "Demography and Language in the Capitals of the Union Republics," *Journal of Soviet Nationalities,* vol. 1, no. 4, Winter 1990–1991.

December 1917 Rumanian soldiers, workers, and peasants created a State Council calling for Bessarabia to be an autonomous republic within a Russian federation. The next month the State Council called for an independent republic and in March 1918 demanded integration into Rumania. In 1920 the Paris Peace Conference reaffirmed the right of Bessarabia to reintegrate with Rumania. Wilsonian notions of national self-determination, the need to create strong states in Eastern Europe, and hatred of Bolshevik Russia promoted the cause internationally.

During the interwar period the Soviet Union refused to recognize the validity of the integration of Bessarabia with Rumania. In 1918 Lenin broke diplomatic relations with Bucharest, arrested the Rumanian Ambassador to Moscow, and confiscated assets of the Rumanian government over this issue. In 1924 the Soviet Union created its own Moldavian Autonomous Soviet Socialist Republic which, though small (500,000 people), began negotiation for reintegration of Bessarabia with the Soviet Union. That same year Moscow began putting out a publication to incite the Bessarabians and instigated a failed revolt within Bessarabia. By 1934, with the rise of Nazi Germany and Soviet joining of the League of Nations, Moscow dropped its hostility and reestablished diplomatic relations with Bucharest. In August 1939 the Molotov-Ribbentrop Pact gave Moscow a free hand in Bessarabia, where Russians and Ukrainians accounted for only 23 percent of the population.

For strategic and geographic reasons, in June 1940 the Red Army occupied Bessarabia and Northern Bukovina, a territory of 20,000 square miles with 4 million people. Ukraine annexed Northern Bukovina and the Moldavian Republic took the central two-thirds of Bessarabia. During 1941 the Soviet secret police deported 100,000 Bessarabians to the Soviet Union while 13,000 Soviet citizens moved to Moldavia. The new regime imposed Soviet laws and nationalized private property. In June 1941, 300,000 Bessarabians (many of them Jews) fled to the Soviet Union. Communist rule was tenuous. The First Congress of the Moldavian Communist Party in 1941 represented only 6000 members.

The Rumanians, with German help, rapidly retook Bessarabia and Bukovina in the summer of 1941 and moved on towards Odessa in Ukraine. The Rumanians reintegrated Bessarabia within Rumania. During the war, under German pressure, they slaughtered the bulk of Bessarabian Jews who had not fled to the Soviet Union. During the war over 250,000 Rumanian soldiers died fighting for the Third Reich and another 180,000 Rumanian soldiers became POWs. In August 1944 the victorious Red Army entered Rumania unopposed, taking another 130,000 Rumanian POWs. The returning Soviet regime promptly reintegrated Bessarabia into Moldavia and Bukovina into Ukraine.

The late 1940s were very difficult times for Bessarabia. The immediate postwar years witnessed a major drought and strong resistance to the reimposition of Soviet rule. The regime deported 10 percent of all peasants for harsh resistance to collectivization of agriculture. The party carried out mass purges of institutions and reinstated terror. In 1950 Moscow sent Leonid Brezhnev to Moldavia to improve the situation. His two years there were important, for many of his later ruling team were his associates from his Moldavian days. In addition, hundreds of thousands of Russians and Ukrainians were encouraged to move to Moldavia.

During the 1950s and 1960s the regime encouraged radical social and economic changes. With a largely rural population, temperate climate, and black soil, Moldavia was a natural place to stress agricultural development. The regime especially favored wine and tobacco production. In industry the regime stressed light industry, particularly food processing, canning, and tractors. By the early 1960s growing tensions with an independent Rumania spilled over into Moldavia. Rumanians increasingly demanded the return of Moldavia. The situation became particularly tense in the 1970s. Well-educated Russians and Russified elements held many of the political, administrative, and industrial jobs. In Kishinev in 1970 Rumanians were only 37 percent of the population. In 1979 Rumanians formed 64 percent of the population of Moldavia but only 33 percent of the Communist Party. Only gradually was there a change, with an elite largely Russian and Ukrainian and masses largely Rumanian.

The latter half of the 1980s were to witness a nationalist explosion. The 1989 census showed Rumanians with 65 percent of the population, Russians and Ukrainians with 27 percent (1.2 million people). The economy was falling apart as the standard of living declined. Massive environmental degradation scarred the landscape. The hard line duo of Ivan Bodial and Simion Grosu ran the party and government. Rumanians became increasingly restive, although not eager to rejoin the repressive Rumania of Nicolae Ceauçescu.

The explosion came with Gorbachev's easing of the reins in Moscow and calling for a new liberal regime. In May 1989 local Rumanians founded the Moldavian Popular Front, which soon claimed 1 million members. The front rallied as many as 1 million people while the Moldavian Communist Party was abandoned by Moscow. During 1989 the front displayed the Rumanian flag, denounced the Molotov-Ribbentrop Pact, took the Rumanian national anthem as its own, and helped set fire to the KGB headquarters in Kishinev. Even the overthrow of Ceaucescu in December 1989 did not bring immediate enthusiasm for a reunion with Rumania as Communists clearly remained in control.

In 1990 the Popular Front gained control of two-thirds of the republic. After the failure of the August 1991 coup in Moscow, the Moldova parliament, with support of almost 80 percent of the deputies, declared Moldova independent. Given the chaos in post-Ceaucescu Rumania, the bulk of the population did not favor immediate reunification with Rumania. The only free election came in December 1992 when Mircea Snegur, former Communist Party Secretary for Agriculture, won an uncontested election.

Major problems soon threatened Moldova. A Russia unreconciled to its new diminished role soon backed the creation of an independent Dniestr Moldova Republic in the left bank region. This republic, known as Transdniestria, proclaimed its existence in September 1990 and seceded from Moldova in August 1992. A slight majority (53 percent) of its people were Russians and Ukrainians, resulting from Stalin's addition of this area to Moldavia after World War II. Units from Russian troops stationed in the region, local Republican Guards, and volunteers from Ukraine and Russia provided the breakaway republic with substantial firepower. Warfare broke out in late 1991 and lasted for over a year. More than 1000 people were killed, 5000 were wounded, and 100,000 refugees fled their homes. A Russian-brokered truce in June 1992 helped stop the fighting but did not resolve the final status of the republic. In May 1993 a meeting between Yeltsin and Snegur in Moscow ratified the special role of Moscow and its renegade Fourteenth Army that had supported the breakaway republic. Withdrawal of the army and replacement by a joint peacekeeping force was tied to recognition of the special autonomous nature of this region. Russian power in the region, a weak Moldova, and international indifference has promoted strong Russian influence in the area.

Some progress has been made towards democracy and capitalism, but the civil war and the legacy of the old era has persisted. There are some independent newspapers but most are published by the government. The regime has assisted free emigration for minorities (50 percent of all Jews emigrated from 1989 to 1992), but the minorities remain concerned. Moldova has provided a liberal citizenship law and protection of religious freedom since 1992. The government has proclaimed its devotion to democracy. Yet there has been only one election in which a former Communist apparatchik won the presidency unopposed. Significant violence and repression of human rights has evidently been commonplace in the "Transdniester Republic" populated largely by Russians and Ukrainians. The government elite is a strange grouping of former Communists and reformers. As in the Transcaucasus, real progress toward capitalism and democracy must await the final resolution of a civil war.

THE BALTICS

The fate of the Baltics has been interwoven with that of Russia since 1721. Russia has controlled them three times in this century (1900–1918, 1940–1941, 1944–1991) and Germany once (1941–1944). The demographic problem has been most acute in Latvia and Estonia. In 1989 Russians accounted for 47 percent of the population of Riga, 41 percent of the population of Tallinn. Only in Vilnius was there a native majority (51 percent). Latvians were 83 percent of the population of Latvia in 1945, 62 percent in 1959, and 52 percent in 1989—and 100,000 of those were Russified Latvians born or raised in the Soviet Union.[3]

The history of the Baltics is long and complex. The native peoples were pagan tribes that had lived in the area for 4000 years.[4] The Lithuanians and Latvians were Indo-European in origin, the Estonians Finno-Ugaritic. The fates of the two nations in the north (Estonia and Latvia) were different from that of

---

[3]Juris Dreifelds, "Immigration and Ethnicity in Latvia," and Mikhail Guboglo, "Demography and Language in the Capitals of the Union Republics," *Journal of Soviet Nationalities,* vol. 1, no. 4, Winter 1990–1991, pp. 1–81; and Nadia Duik and Adrian Karatnycky, *Rising New Nations.*

[4]For an excellent recent treatment of the subject, see John Hiden and Patrick Salmon, *The Baltic Nations and Europe,* Longmans, London, 1991.

Lithuania in the south. The northern territories were far more open to trade and conquest than the southern territories behind their massive forests. In the late twelfth century crusading German knights, having been defeated in their repeated bids to seize the Holy Land, marched eastward from their nearby territory in Central Europe and by 1201 had created a military state around the new city of Riga. In 1346 the Danes sold Estonia to the same Teutonic Order. For the last 800 years, German domination of a Baltic peasantry has endured through Swedish, Polish-Lithuanian, and Russian rule. By the sixteenth century Sweden dominated Estonia, and Lithuania and Poland divided Latvia into three parts. In 1721 an expanding Russia under Peter the Great took over Estonia and Livonia, part of Latvia. It added another part of Latvia, Courland, after the three Polish partitions from 1772 to 1795. This Russian domination of the north lasted until the end of the Tsarist empire in 1917.

In contrast, Lithuania, with vast forests, better rulers, and more military capabilities, expanded at the expense of its neighbors. Unified in 1248, Lithuania fought both the Russians and the Tatars in the east. In 1386 Lithuania formed a close alliance with Poland and accepted Christianity. In 1410 the Lithuanian-Polish Commonwealth won a decisive battle at Tannenberg against the Teutonic Germans and in 1569 united into one entity. However, the three Polish partitions from 1772 to 1795 brought an end to Lithuanian power and ensured Russian domination of Lithuania and Courland.

By the nineteenth century then, the Baltics, although a part of the Russian Empire, were divided between Catholic Lithuania, dominated by a Polonized aristocracy, and German-dominated Lutheran Latvia and Estonia.[5] German landlords dominated the Baltic peasantry, and the German bourgeoisie dominated the cities in the north. German was the language of the universities, government, and culture. Yet German control was under assault both from a Tsarist Russia that strived to Russify the region in the later part of the nineteenth century and from a resurgent nationalism of Latvians and Estonians. By 1897 Germans were only 22 percent of the population of Riga. In Lithuania, native Lithuanians, with far lower literacy rate than their northern counterparts, were outnumbered in Kovno and Vilna by Russians, Poles, and Jews.

Despite strong indigenous effort, the fate of the Baltics was settled by outside forces. The initially victorious Germans occupied Lithuania and Courland in 1915, then all of the Baltics by February 1918. After the Treaty of Brest-Litovsk confirmed German dominance, Germany sought to create puppet states. The German defeat in November 1918 opened the way to other possibilities. The Allies, still angry at Bolshevik Russia, allowed the German forces to remain in the Baltics until the end of 1919. This, together with a British naval force and Finnish volunteers in Tallinn in December 1918, mobilization of local forces, and Red Army setbacks in the drive into Poland in 1920, gave the local states a chance to organize themselves and reach peace treaties with Russia at the end of the Russian Civil War.

The interwar period opened in chaos and ended in disaster. Intitial at-

---

[5]Latvia itself was further divided among Livonia and Courland with long separate histories.

tempts at democracy ended with authoritarian dictatorships after 1926 in Lithuania and 1934 in Estonia and Latvia. The three states, despite a brief 1934 Baltic Entente, were unable to coordinate their resistance to Germany or the Soviet Union. German and British economic power vied with a resurgent Russian military power and aggression in the 1930s. By 1939 Nazi Germany had seized Klaipeda (Memel) from Lithuania and its navy dominated the Baltics. The August 1939 Molotov-Ribbentrop Pact and subsequent amendation ceded the Baltics to Moscow. A series of Russian-imposed mutual assistance pacts in the fall of 1939 were followed by outright military occupation by the Red Army in June 1940. The new regime soon deported or killed over 150,000 Balts. In June 1941 the German army rapidly overran the Baltics, setting up civilian administrations and repressing the population. In Lithuania alone over 200,000 Jews were killed. By 1944 the advancing Red Army reimposed Russian rule, followed up by more deportations and repression.

During the next forty years Soviet domination transformed the Baltics. Large-scale industrialization modernized the economies and brought in hundreds of thousands of Russian immigrants. Between 1944 and 1952 the new regime deported over 500,000 Balts, many of whom returned after 1956. The former minorities were gone, victims of extermination (Jews) or expulsion (Germans and Poles). By the 1980s the Balts had the highest standard of living in the Soviet Union, a vital culture, and increasingly nativized elites. Yet they suffered from loss of independence, massive environmental damage, and isolation from the West. With low birth rates, they were in danger in the north of becoming minorities in their own countries.

Gorbachev's reforms met an eager response in the Baltics. By December 1988 reformers dominated the government and party elite, and large scale popular fronts had sprung up. In late 1988 and the spring of 1989 the three states declared their sovereignty. Reformers swept the historic March 1989 elections. In August 1989, 2 million Balts formed a human chain to commemorate the shameful fiftieth anniversary of the Molotov-Ribbentrop Pact that had cost them their independence. In December 1989 the Lithuanian Communist Party declared itself independent of Moscow and in March 1990 the Lithuanian Supreme Soviet declared Lithuania independent.

Gorbachev tried desperately to block Baltic independence and develop the Baltics as a showcase of perestroika. By June 1990, under pressure of a Soviet economic blockade and troop movements, there was a 100-day moratorium on independence. In January 1991 Gorbachev allowed Red Army troops to attack Vilnius and Riga. In August 1991 one of the first moves of the coup plotters was to send troops rampaging through the Baltics. But the coup failed, and the three states all reasserted their independence.

Since August 1991 the three states have gone through wrenching changes. The resentment of local Russians led to restrictions on their rights to citizenship and confrontations with Moscow, which has slowed withdrawal of Russian troops. This issue, while minor in Lithuania, is significant in Latvia and Estonia, where Russians and other non-Balts constitute a large minority and even predominate in some cities. Economic problems and lack of Western support have led to a resurgence of former Communists in Lithuania. In the parliamentary elections of October 1992 their renamed party won over 50 percent of the seats, Sajudis less than 20 percent. In February 1993 that party's leader, Algirdas Brazauskas, was elected President of Lithuania. These former Communists, though, do support national independence and market reform, albeit at a slower pace and with more social welfare measures than advocates of rapid changes propose.

The long-range future seems good for these Western-oriented regimes with high levels of education and culture and close ties to the West. Russian troop withdrawals, already under way despite problems over the treatment of Russian minorities in the Baltics, should be completed in several years. The difficulties of state building, transition to capitalism, and lack of strong Western aid threaten a rocky transition in the short run.

PART FOUR

Future
Prospects

These final three chapters move in a different direction than the earlier chapters. They try to put the drive for capitalism, democracy, and nationhood in a comparative, historical, and theoretical perspective. The fifteen new states of the former Soviet Union are not the first states ever to attempt these changes. There are numerous prior cases, in Europe and elsewhere, of such attempts, successful and failed. Some attempts at democracy, such as the German Weimar Republic in the 1920s, ended in disaster and fascism. Others, such as Italy's and Japan's attempts after World War II, were relatively successful but at a high cost that has been seen in recent defeats for the dominant party. Similarly, many quests for capitalist development have failed—but then there have also been the great successes of Japan and the Four Tigers of Asia and most recently China. And dozens of new nations emerged in the Third World in the 1950s and 1960s trying to achieve successful nation building. These chapters then attempt to take the long view, put the FSU cases into perspective, and develop likely scenarios for them.

20

The Future of Democracy

In the last several years a wave of democratization has dethroned repressive and authoritarian regimes in the Third World and built the initial framework for democracy in dozens of countries.[1] With Moscow as the indisputable epicenter of this democratic earthquake, it would seem logical that democratic forms and institutions would emerge in Moscow. With the defeat of the reactionary security-military coup in August 1991 and the April 1993 referendum support for Yeltsin, this would seem well nigh inevitable. The victory of liberal democratic capitalism in the Cold War seems to many to reflect a wonderfully efficient invisible hand insuring the triumph of liberal and democratic regimes.

But is it so? This chapter analyzes what we mean by democracy, how it was achieved, democratic successes and failures, the relationship between revolution and democracy, the Russian historical experience with democracy, obstacles to the achievement of democracy, and the likely outcome in Russia and the FSU.

IMAGES OF AMERICAN DEMOCRACY: WHAT IS IT?

For Americans democracy is obviously a two-party political system, with alternation of parties in power, for the entire population. Democratic states are peaceful and have existed for centuries.

This image is largely wrong. The path to democracy has often been long

[1]It has spawned new journals, such as the *Journal of Democracy* put out by Johns Hopkins University Press, and *Demokratizatsiya: The Journal of Post-Soviet Democratization,* put out by American University as a joint project with Moscow State University.

and torturous, and violence has been a frequent companion. True, the United States, thanks to the Declaration of Independence (1776) and the Constitution with its Bill of Rights (1789), was the "first new nation," the first nation ever to begin as a democracy. Yet it took eight years from the victory at Yorktown over Cornwallis (1781) until 1789 to create a Constitution and regime to bind together the thirteen wayward colonies.[2] Then for almost two generations the country was run largely by a group of brilliant Virginia planters—Washington, Jefferson, Madison, and Monroe. Washington himself was unopposed for reelection and warned against the dangers of parties and factions in his Farewell Address. True two-party democracy developed only in the 1820s with the emergence of Andrew Jackson.[3] Even then, slavery, that "peculiar institution" so inimical to democracy, flourished in the American South for over seventy years after independence. Only the massive killing of 600,000 soldiers in the Civil War brought slavery to an end by 1865. Even then, women were not allowed to vote until 1920, Southern blacks until 1964, and 120,000 Japanese Americans were confined in labor camps for most of World War II. None of this tarnishes the basic fact of democracy or its great appeal around the world. Rather it shows that the creation of a modern democratic regime was a long, bloody, and difficult struggle. No perfect democratic regime could emerge from the brow of Thomas Jefferson, no matter how well he conceived it on paper.

IMAGES OF DEMOCRACY ABROAD

Our traditional notions of democracy break down even faster once we look at some of the twenty or twenty-five long-term democratic regimes around the world. These include Great Britain and former British white settler colonies (United States, Canada, New Zealand, and Australia), Western Europe, Japan, Israel, India, and the like.

Two-party alternation in power is often seen as the *sine qua non* for democratic regimes. Yet Japan (forty years of Liberal Democratic Party rule), India (almost forty years of Congress Party rule, with brief interruptions), Israel (twenty-nine years of Labor Party rule, from 1949 to 1977) and Italy (over forty years of Christian Democratic Party rule) showed that democratic countries may be dominated for long periods of time by one party.

Similarly, most democratic states have more than two major parties. Even in the United States Theodore Roosevelt (1912), Strom Thurmond (1948), George Wallace (1968), John Anderson (1980), and Ross Perot (1992) have made strong third-party showings. Abroad, England has three major parties, Canada numerous national and regional parties, and Israel twenty-five parties.

Americans think of democratic regimes as relatively free from crises induced by strong nondemocratic parties. But for several decades in the postwar

---

[2]Seymour Martin Lipset, *The First New Nation*, Basic Books, New York, 1959.
[3]Richard Hofstadter, *The Emergence of the Two Party System*, University of California Press, Berkeley, 1969.

era the Communist parties were strong in Italy and France. The final years of Weimar Germany saw the emergence of powerful Nazi and Communist parties.

We think of parties as secular, and regard excessive religious influence on the political process as baleful. Yet Christian Democratic Parties are common in Europe, and in Israel there are no fewer than five or six religious parties. Although parties are presumed to be national in scope, countries like Canada and Belgium have parties with strong localist and regionalist tendencies.

Americans often perceive democratic regimes as inevitable and so popular that they can never be overturned. Yet the European experience has been very different in this century. Weimar Germany (1920–1933) was overthrown by the fascists who launched the Third Reich in 1933. In Spain the weak Republic (1931–1936) was overthrown by the fascists in the civil war. Even in France, the violent end of the Third Republic in 1940 did not keep the neofascist Vichy "New Order" from being wildly popular at first.

Finally, democracies have flourished in very different environments. Kings and democracies (Spain, England, Denmark) are perfectly compatible. So too is a strong aristocracy, as in the case of England. Many different religions and creeds have proved compatible with democracy, not merely European Christianity. Hindu India, Neo-Confucian Taiwan, Singapore, and South Korea, Shinto Japan, and Jewish Israel have all either become democratic regimes or are making the transition. Democratic governments can stress strong individual rights, as in the Anglo-American example, or a strong relationship between business and government, as in Japan and the emerging Four Tigers of Asia. Democratic regimes can be associated with mass immigration (as the four British white settler colonies and Israel) or with hostility towards immigrants (Western Europe). They can be associated with a regime that emphasizes the centrality of a Constitution (United States) or with others that have no written Constitution (England and Israel).

DEFINITIONS OF DEMOCRACY

There has never been academic agreement on the essence or causes of democracy. Aristotle divided the world into monarchies, oligarchies, and democracies, which were governments of the many and poor, as the agent of the people whom they served. With the loss of belief in the divine rights of kings and state religions and the rise of a new urban middle class, new notions of democracy arose. John Locke saw representative government as lying in rational self-interest reflected in a secular social contract guaranteeing religious pluralism. Montesquieu saw checks and balances inherent in a separation of executive, legislative, and judicial powers as critical for democracy. At the time of the American Revolution, James Madison wanted to base the democratic state on male property owners and a balance of factions that would prevent tyranny.[4]

Joseph Schumpeter argued that modern democracy requires capitalism, a

---

[4]Tatu Verhanen, *The Process of Democratization,* Taylor and Francis, New York, 1989, chapter 2.

strong middle class, industrialization, and commercial agriculture.[5] Barrington Moore similarly found a strong urban bourgeoisie "an indispensable element in the growth of democracy" and thought that commercial agriculture "augur[s] best for democracy."[6] Seymour Martin Lipset found a direct correlation between increasing wealth and democracy. In *Political Man* Lipset stressed free political competition and a high level of competition as critical for democracy. He saw democracy as

> a political system which supplies regular constitutional opportunities for changing governing officials and a social mechanism which permits the largest possible part of the population to influencing majority demands by choosing among contenders for political office.[7]

Robert Dahl viewed democracy as a way for citizens to exert relatively high control over their leaders. He saw three variants of democracy: the Madisonian, which stressed the restraint of the tyranny of the majority; the populist, which emphasized political sovereignty and equality; and the polyarchical, which provided the prerequisites for social order. In *Polyarchy: Participation and Democracy* Dahl counted eight institutional prerequisites for responsive democracy: freedom to form and join organizations, free speech, the right to vote, eligibility for public office, the right of political leaders to vie for votes, the existence of alternative sources of information. Seven conditions enhanced the possibilities for polyarchy (competitive democratic system): proper historical sequences, degree of concentration in the socio-economic order, level of development, degree of inequality, subcultural cleavages, beliefs of political activists, and absence of foreign control.

Finally, Arend Lijphart defined democracy as government by freely elected representatives of the people. He differentiated the majoritarian form as represented by Westminster England's government by majority rule and the consociational form as represented by Switzerland and Belgium with inclusion of all possible elements. Majoritarian democracy is best for homogenous societies, and consensual democracy for pluralist societies.[8]

PATHS TO DEMOCRACY

The fifteen newly independent states in the FSU are attempting to make the transition to democracy from Communism. Although there is no historical precedent for this specific journey, there have been five paths to democracy for the twenty or twenty-five long-term democracies and recent Southern European and Asian converts to democracy.[9]

---

[5]Joseph Schumpeter, *Capitalism, Socialism and Democracy*, Harper and Row, New York, 1975, p. 296.
[6]Barrington Moore, *Social Origins of Dictatorship and Democracy*, Beacon Press, Boston, 1969, pp. 418, 422.
[7]Seymour Martin Lipset, *Political Man*, Doubleday, New York, 1960, p. 45.
[8]Robert Dahl, *Polyarchy: Participation and Opposition*, University Press, New Haven, 1971.
[9]There are a number of other Third World potential democratic cases, ranging from Costa Rica, Venezuela, Colombia, and Jamaica to Turkey and Nigeria. The latter two cases have seen their

The first great path has been that of democratic revolutions which lay the groundwork for democratic development.[10] The American, British, and French Revolutions swept away autocratic monarchies (England and France) or a foreign occupying power (United States). The path to democracy was far from smooth. England (1660) and France (1814) had monarchical restorations. But the stage had been set, and eventually democratic parliamentary regimes were established in France after 1870 and in England gradually in the nineteenth century. For the United States the results were more dramatic. Thus, the first path involved wars, revolutions, setbacks, and then gradual achievement of the goals of the revolution.

The second path has been through fascism. Strikingly, all the major fascist powers of the 1930s (Germany, Italy, Spain, and Portugal) and the major Asian neo-fascist, militarist power (Japan) are now democratic states. For Japan and Germany devastating defeat in war and occupation by the Allied powers set the stage for the forcible external implantation of democracy. By the early 1950s new formal democratic regimes had been created in Japan and Germany. As for Italy, democracy emerged somewhat more spontaneously after the demise of fascism in 1943 after twenty-one years of rule by Mussolini. In Spain and Portugal the fascist regimes of Francisco Franco and Antonio Salazar survived the war into the 1970s. But the deaths of the aging leaders and the strong economic and political influence of Western Europe set the stage for a dramatic transformation from fascism to democracy.

Third, there has been the colonial experience. Surely the United States and India, as well as smaller countries, such as Sri Lanka, gained their knowledge of democracy from the colonial experience. The Virginia House of Burgesses was a model for future democratic development. However, the Europeans had dozens of colonies—only a handful became truly democratic states.

Fourth, the latest model is that of rapidly modernizing states in Asia (Singapore, Taiwan, and South Korea, perhaps soon Thailand) moving from authoritarianism to protodemocratic structures. Here the rapid development of a large middle class, strong economic integration with the West, the aging or demise of the first generation of leaders, and the magnetic appeal of Western democracy all played a strong role. This process is still incomplete. Nevertheless, Taiwan, South Korea, and Singapore all have genuine multiparty elections with real possibilities that the opposition will come to power by the end of the decade.

Finally, there has been the peaceful road to democracy of Eastern Europe. Here the crucial factor was the release of the USSR's former satellite regimes by Gorbachev in 1989, allowing them to find their own road. The process remains incomplete. The old Communist regimes have all been overthrown, although substantial elements of the old elites remain in place. In some countries, such as Rumania and Albania, democracy remains very limited; in others, such as

---

republics overthrown by military coups, and Costa Rica and Jamaica are small and isolated cases. Colombia and Venezuela also have certain peculiarities.

[10]See Moore, *Social Origins of Dictatorship and Democracy.*

Hungary, the Czech Republic, and Poland, it seems more institutionalized. Still, even in Poland strong authoritarianism pervades the polity.

These roads are likely to have limited impact on the FSU. Obviously, there has been no colonial experience for the Soviet Union nor peaceful development at the hands of an alien master. But the first two have more relevance and point to some important features of development. While Communism and fascism were markedly distinct phenomena, they did share some common features, as the theorists of totalitarianism frequently reminded us.[11] They both were highly dynamic, mobilization regimes marked by a high degree of authoritarianism, one-party rule, charismatic leaders, powerful secret police, tight control of the instruments of repression, and monopolistic control of the means of communication.

The Soviet experience with Communism was too different from the German experience with fascism to yield much hope for the future. The Soviet Union lasted seventy-four years, not thirteen years. It had positive elements (victory in World War II, achievement of superpower status, massive industrialization, and modernization) as well as negative elements (purges, terror, repression). At the end, Soviet Communism collapsed with a whimper, not with the bang of the Third Reich. The absence of Western occupation, purge of the old elite, and complete defeat created a different setting.

So too is it hard to see the new Russian revolution as a continuation of earlier American, English, and French democratizing revolutions. All those revolutions were launched against premodern autocratic monarchies, at home or abroad, not mass mobilizing, postmonarchical, quite industrialized regimes. The new Russian revolution comes against a backdrop of the February and October Revolutions in 1917 and the Stalinist revolution from above of the 1930s. The lack of violence of the revolution, the foreign assistance to the new leaders of the revolution, the lack of mass participation, and the stress on economic rather than political goals all show that this is a postmodern revolution quite distant in time, goals, and methods from the revolutions from above and below so common in earlier international history.

REVOLUTIONS AND DEMOCRACY

Revolutions have often led to wars and counterrevolution, not immediate progress towards democracy. The French Revolution led to twenty years of bloody fighting, followed by monarchical restoration in 1814 and future revolutions (1830, 1848, 1871). Only in 1871, eighty-two years after the beginning of the French Revolution, did the democratic Third Republic emerge. The English revolution of the 1640s led to three civil wars, the beheading of the king in 1649, and monarchical restoration in 1660. Only in 1688, nearly forty years after the

[11]See for example Hannah Arendt, *The Origins of Totalitarianism,* Harcourt Brace Jovanovich, New York, 1973.

original revolution, did the Glorious Revolution create a constitutional monarchy. It took several centuries before modern democracy was firmly established in England.

The 1917 Russian Revolutions led to a major civil war (1918–1920) and seventy-four years of one-party Communist rule. The 1911 Chinese Revolution that overthrew the monarchy created not democracy but sixteen years of bloody localist warlord rule, followed by three civil wars that finally brought the Communists to power in 1949. The 1989 Beijing Spring was snuffed out in the massacre in Tienanmen Square. Third World revolutions, such as those in Vietnam (1954), Cuba (1959), Cambodia (1975), Nicaragua (1979), and Iran (1979), created highly authoritarian, one-party regimes, not democracies.

Revolutions in the West may have laid the long-range basis for democracy, but everywhere, in the short run, they strengthened state power, created more effective and authoritarian regimes, and promoted the power of the army and government bureaucracy. The Russian revolutions created a Soviet state that would win World War II and become a superpower, and the Chinese Revolution created the most powerful Chinese state seen in East Asia for over a century.

PREREQUISITES FOR DEMOCRACY

Why are there only twenty or thirty genuine democratic states in a world of over 200 states? Given the common desire for mass participation and genuinely democratic regimes, why has this human goal been so hard to achieve? There are economic, political, cultural, and international prerequisites for democracies. Unfortunately, Russia and the FSU today meet very few of them.

Democratic regimes are synonymous with advanced capitalist economies. The few exceptions are Israel in the 1950s, with strong Jewish commitment to the West and democratic socialism; India since 1949, with British colonial inheritance, strong dynastic rule by three generations of the Nehru family, an incredible mosaic of religions, ethnic groups, and languages; and perhaps countries such as Costa Rica. Over 150 Third World countries have produced no strong democratic regimes, while all twenty-five First World countries are democracies.

Advanced capitalist countries have produced a strong middle class and a powerful stratum of capitalist entrepreneurs with a stake in the emerging democratic system. When countries in the last two decades have made enormous strides into the First World (Spain, Portugal, Taiwan, South Korea, Singapore), they have usually moved away from one-party authoritarian rule towards a nascent democracy. A powerful economy generates a complex web of interest groups and incentives for individuals to support a system that provides real payoffs for their participation. The large, emergent middle class sees a democratic regime as the best defender of its interests.

And Russia? While these First World democratic states average per capita

GNPs of 12,000–20,000 dollars, Russia achieves only 3220, Kyrgyzstan 1550, and Tajikistan 1040.[12] One-third to one-half of the population is below a minimal poverty line in the FSU, and the middle class is small (perhaps 15 percent of the population). Consumption is rated around fifty-fifth in the world, or well into the Third World standard. Survival, not degrees of affluence, is the problem.

The FSU also lacks the strong class of entrepreneurs which Weber and Schumpeter saw as critical for economic development. Over seventy years of Communism and centuries of Tsarist centralist authoritarian rule have dried up the pool of entrepreneurship. From 1929 to 1989 state centralized planning eliminated entrepreneurs. Creating such a class anew, after the state had long derided and attacked its very existence as parasitical, will be a difficult and protracted task.

There are also important political and cultural prerequisites for democratic regime. There must be a strong concept of property rights and tolerance for individual diversity. There needs to be a "civil culture" promoted by a strong and self-confident civil society. The role of the state must be limited.

Traditionally, these political attitudes have not been instantly created. Even in the American case it took several generations for democracy to be firmly institutionalized, for the creation of a viable two-party system. Most democratic regimes in North America and Western Europe share a common European intellectual heritage. In the cases of Japan and Germany, democracy was implanted by force. Three of the Four Tigers of Asia spent decades as colonies of Japan (South Korea and Taiwan) and England (Singapore), and Hong Kong is still a British colony. In the latter cases the democratic values are still quite tentative.

Unfortunately, as we will see in two sections below, there is almost no history of Russian democracy. The political culture historically has been authoritarian, centralist, and autocratic, under both the Tsars and the Communists. Creating a new political culture is a task for generations, not decades. Property rights, human rights, individual rights—these are not popular elements of the culture. The civic culture, traditionally profoundly anti-individualist and antidemocratic, is growing only slowly toward a strong civil society based on a modernized urban and educated Russia.

Finally, there needs to be a favorable international environment for the spread of democracy. Here there are some grounds for hope. There clearly has been a "democratic contagion" as the overthrow of a repressive regime in one country has encouraged democratic forces in other countries. The Western victory in the Cold War has encouraged democratic and capitalist forces everywhere. The unification of the European community, and the rise of a United Nations now able to support democratic forces from Cambodia to Yugoslavia and Kuwait, is a positive factor. Certainly the American and European commitment to support progressive forces in the FSU is a significant factor in the evolution of democracy in Russia. So too is the relative weakness

---

[12]For 1991 statistics, see *RFE/RL Report*, vol. 2, no. 20, May 3–7, 1993.

of nondemocratic forces in the Third World and China (itself likely to change in this decade). The collapse of authoritarianism, the decline in brutality, and new criteria for defining great powers are all positive for nascent Russian democracy.[13]

THE PATH TO DEMOCRACY: AN IRREVERSIBLE PROCESS?

The democratic wave that swept across Latin America, Africa, Eastern Europe, the Soviet Union, and parts of Asia in the 1980s and the early 1990s has produced much optimism about the future of democracy in the world. But there are also serious questions as to its staying in power in the light of the previous dismal record of democratic regimes in much of the world.

The first classic wave of democratization in this century coursed through Europe during and after World War I. In the wake of that cataclysm, over a dozen European countries, from Russia (1917) and Germany (1919) to Eastern Europe, Southern Europe, and the Baltics tried democratic regimes. As Karl Bracher has reminded us,

> The trend toward democracy, with or without a monarchical superstructure, seemed unstoppable. But appearances were deceptive; only a few years later the trend was clearly reversed. The crisis of democracy was inherent in its very triumph . . . the seeds of authoritarian and dictatorial rule had already been planted in the early days of most postwar democracies.[14]

The brief Russian attempt at some form of democracy expired quickly in 1917;[15] fascist regimes came to power in Italy (1922), Portugal (1929), Germany (1933), and Spain (1936–1939); and authoritarian regimes arose in the Baltics, Balkans, and Eastern Europe in the 1930s. By 1939 only Czechoslovakia remained as a genuine democratic regime.

The next democratic wave coursed through the Third World in the 1950s and 1960s. But again, few survived for very long. Military coups in the 1960s and 1970s overthrew democratic regimes in Argentina, Brazil, Chile, Burma, Greece, Turkey, Nigeria, and Uruguay. Incumbents overturned democracy in India and the Philippines and a civil war overthrew democracy in Lebanon (1975). Myron Weiner has commented:

> The dismal record of survival of nascent democratic regimes created in much of the Third World since World War II and the fragility of those that remain

---

[13]John Lewis Gaddis, *Tectonics, History and the End of the Cold War,* Mershon Center Occasional Paper, Ohio State University, Columbus, Ohio, 1992.

[14]Karl Bracher, *The German Dictatorship,* Praeger, New York, 1970, pp. 67–68.

[15]The Provisional Government, while not democratically elected, did aspire to hold a freely elected Constituent Assembly in November 1917 and rule by its results. The October Revolution snuffed out the results of this election and democratic roots were hardly put down in any significant way in 1917.

democratic suggest that conditions or prerequisites of democracy, especially of stable democracy, have not yet been achieved in developing countries.[16]

Latin America has been a particularly interesting case, as the third tide of democratization liquidated nearly all the authoritarian and military regimes and created democratic regimes in the 1980s. Specialists have been quick to observe the staggering economic problems at home and abroad, continuing power of the military, and difficulties in consolidating power. They observe a cyclical trend in the region, with democratic waves in the 1930s and 1950s yielding to authoritarianism in the 1940s and military rule from the mid 1960s to the 1970s, and democracy again in the 1980s. The concern about the permanence of the democratic wave of the 1980s is reflected in James Malloy's observation:

> A potentially more valuable approach to the political evaluation of most of the Latin American countries should begin by accepting what by now must be surely axiomatic—that there is no unilinear tendency toward democracy or toward authoritarian rule. Rather the predominant trend is cyclical with alternating democratic and authoritarian moments. Furthermore, both tendencies are rather strong in the area.[17]

Juan Linz has studied the breakdown of democratic regimes and has concluded that the disintegration of authoritarian regimes tends to create other authoritarian regimes, not democratic regimes. He found that breakdowns resulted from the inability of democratic regimes to cope with insolvable economic, political, and social problems given the continuing imbalance of needs and resources and the role of the military. These are sobering thoughts for Russian democracy today.[18] The only solace is that Linz found that breakdowns occurred when disloyal oppositions offer themselves as solutions. What will happen in Russia is still uncertain.

THE CLASSIC DEMOCRATIC FAILURE: WEIMAR GERMANY

To paraphrase Marx, a specter is haunting Russia, the specter of Weimar Germany. And the question on many people's lips is very simple: Will the newly democratic Russia go the way of Weimar Germany and go out in a spectacular firestorm? The parallels are striking. An autocratic, powerful European empire, with weak democratic traditions (in parliamentary institutions) and strong authoritarian roots, suddenly collapses. In the unexpected after-

---

[16]Myron Weiner, "Empirical Democratic Theory," in Myron Weiner and Ergun Ozbudun, editors, *Competitive Elections in Developing Countries,* Duke University Press, Durham, North Carolina, 1987, p. 4.

[17]See James Malloy and Mitchell Seligsen, editors, *Authoritarian and Democrats: Regime Transition in Latin America,* University of Pittsburgh Press, Pittsburgh, 1987, p. 236.

[18]Juan Linz, *The Breakdown of Democratic Regimes: Crisis, Breakdown and Reequilibrium,* Johns Hopkins University Press, Baltimore and London, 1978.

math, chaos ensues and a shaky democracy is established. But the unstable regime is faced with awesome economic, political, and social tasks. Caught in a vise between traditional Right forces, reinforced by powerful, authoritarian, bureaucratic institutions, and rising populist egalitarian discontent on the Left, the nascent democratic state simply falls apart. From the ashes of the democratic disaster arises a new, revitalized, and far more threatening authoritarian regime.

There are also significant differences. Germans, quite simply, are hardly Russians. Located in the heart of Europe, Germany is inexorably an integral part of Europe, while Russia has historically been on the geographic, political, and economic periphery. The German defeat in World War I, coming as it did when German forces were still on foreign soil, was a devastating and unexpected blow to Imperial Germany and gave rise to the "stab in the back" legend that erroneously placed the blame on the liberal and socialist elements of the new democratic regimes. Russia suffered no such defeat. International forces, ranging from the Great Depression to insistent French demands on Germany in the 1920s, were quite hostile to German democracy; international forces are supportive of Russian democracy. Western aid to Russian democracy in the 1990s stands in stark contrast to the rapacious demands on German democracy after the Treaty of Versailles in 1919.

Let us now turn to the tumultuous events of the Weimar Republic. Imperial Germany, in alliance with the Austro-Hungarian Empire and Ottoman Turkish Empire, seemed to stand on the threshold of victory early in 1918. In March 1918 Russia left the war under the harsh terms of the Treaty of Brest-Litovsk, which gave Germany one-third of Russia's population and one-half of its heavy industry. This allowed the German army to transfer 1 million soldiers from the eastern to the western front. With the United States formally in the war since April 1917 but unable to undertake major operations until the fall of 1918, a "window of opportunity" opened for the Germans. In five great offensives from March until July 1918, the German army came close to victory, but in the end it failed. By July the war was lost, and in September Marshal Erich Luddendorf, aware that 4 million fresh American troops would be in France in 1919, so informed the government.

In October 1918 Prince Max of Baden, who formed a popular cabinet of Reichstag deputies, sued for peace with President Wilson. Within a month the November Revolution, highlighted by the revolt of the Kiel sailors, swept away the monarchy and Kaiser Wilhelm and created radical workers and sailors councils. Parliamentary democracy was imposed from above and approved from below. By November 8 Prince Max approved a Provisional Government under Chancellor Friedrich Ebert, a Socialist. With the army elite renouncing responsibility, the new parliamentary regime accepted the harsh terms of the Allies and an armistice was proclaimed on November 11, 1918.

The fact that the army renounced responsibility for the war and never admitted defeat, that German troops were on foreign soil at the end of the war, and that a democratic republic signed a harsh armistice and peace treaty fueled the notorious stab in the back legend. The harsh armistice terms of General

Foch, including Allied blockade of Germany, no repatriation of 800,000 German POWs (but return of Allied POWs), transfer of substantial war booty, Allied occupation of the left bank of the Rhine and three bridgeheads across the Rhine, loss of African colonies, and retirement to 1914 frontiers, aroused public opinion against the Allies and the republic that accepted such onerous terms.[19]

The new government, confirmed in elections in January 1919, faced awesome tasks. The legacy of the past included the stab in the back legend, fragile democratic traditions, powerful authoritarian institutions and views, a middle-class fear of Communism and the working class, and susceptibility to national imperialism arising from the unfulfilled aspirations of a belatedly unified (1870) and industrialized state. Under the impetus of defeat, fervent national-ism could easily turn into authoritarianism, racism, and anti-Semitism. This was reinforced by a strong popular militarism. There would be a "republic without republicans," as the major parties were antidemocratic. The conserva-tives supported monarchy, the National Liberals and Progressives opposed socialist democracy, the Catholic Center opposed an anticlerical republic, the Socialists preferred reforms to democracy, and the Communists rejected bour-geois democracy.[20]

As in Russia, the conflict between a strongly authoritarian past and fragile democratic present had awesome consequences for Weimar Germany. The heritage of almost half a century of Imperial Germany (1870–1918) included a semiautocratic monarchical state, great military power, strong heavy industry, political repression, toothless parliament, and Prussian domination. The Prus-sian state was a model of reactionary absolutism revolving around the trinity of reactionary nationalism, an idealized powerful state, and anti-Semitism. The state was validated by rapid economic growth and vast military power.[21] The legacy was devastating for Weimar Germany as a democracy. As Karl Bracher has perceived:

> The conflict between authoritarian tradition and a new democracy had a number of consequences: non-functioning parliamentary government, agita-tion for Presidential system as sort of ersatz empire and quasi-dictatorship, splintering and lack of cooperation of ideology and politically rigid parties, rise of antidemocratic movements . . . militarization of nongovernmental sector by militant groups; spread of a terrorist power philosophy . . . the radicalization of economically and socially threatened urban and rural middle classes; sus-ceptibility of bureaucracy and judiciary to hierarchial-authoritarian ideas of order; and finally the Army's suspicious attitude toward the democratic Republic.[22]

---

[19]Erich Eyck, *A History of the Weimar Republic*, translated by Harlan Hanson and Robert Wate, Atheneum, New York, 1970, chapter 1; and John McKenzie, *Weimar Germany 1918–1933*, Rowman and Littlefield, Totowa, New Jersey, 1971, chapters 1 and 2.
[20]Karl Bracher, *The German Dictatorship*, Praeger, New York, 1970, chapters 1 and 2.
[21]S. William Halperin, *Germany Tried Democracy*, W.W. Norton, New York, 1974, chapters 1 and 2.
[22]Bracher, *The German Dictatorship*, p. 46.

The 1919 constitution was deeply flawed. Endowing the President with powers of a modern monarch, the Constitution gave the President by Article 48 the right to overrule parliament and suspend civil liberties in an emergency.[23] He also, rather than parliament, could appoint the Chancellor. In the hands of the first President, a Social Democrat (Friedrich Ebert, 1919–1925), these powers were used to protect a democratic republic. But in the hands of his aged and reactionary successor (Paul von Hindenburg), the existence of the regime was endangered. Proportional representation proliferated the number of parties in the Reichstag.

The early years of the new republic (1919–1923) were chaotic and highly unstable. In February the National Assembly, meeting in Weimar, formally elected Friedrich Ebert as its first President. In July the National Assembly approved the Constitution and in August the new Weimar Republic formally began to operate.[24] Yet 1919 and 1920 were years of chaos, strikes, and revolts. Already in January 1919 a left wing Sparticist uprising was crushed and the Party leaders (Rosa Luxemburg and Karl Liebknecht) shot in the aftermath. In March 1919 a Berlin strike led to the brutal use of the Freikorps (former servicemen) to crush it and later murder more than 1000 workers. Only a pact between General Grovener, the head of the army, and President Ebert saved the shaky regime. Ebert got the military to smash leftist uprisings in return for preserving the army in its traditional form. But the January 1919 elections, which gave the Socialists 38 percent of the vote and democratic parties over 75 percent of the vote, seemed to make this bargain worthwhile.

The chaos did not subside in 1920. The 1920 Kapp putsch developed around the hostility of General Baron Walther von Luettwitz (Berlin military commander) to the government. Wolfgang Kapp (East Prussian leader of the People's Party) led the coup based on the hostility of most military and police officers to the regime. The Ehrhardt brigade, scheduled for demobilization, marched into Berlin and occupied the capital. The government fled to Dresden. But a vast strike, led by Socialists and centrists, paralyzed the government as even many civil servants opposed Kapp. Three days later Kapp fled and the putsch was over. But the ease with which the government could be ousted, and the failure of the military and police to protect it, would not soon be forgotten.[25] Just like the abortive military-security coup in Moscow in August 1991, it offered a clear warning.

Finally there was the Hitler putsch in 1923, as well as an attempted Communist uprising. In 1923, the French occupation of the Ruhr and German passive resistance, hyperinflation, and the example of Mussolini's March on Rome brought the Weimar government near collapse. In October 1923 the army smashed Communist threats in Saxony, Hamburg, and Thuringia. In November in Bavaria Adolf Hitler, with the help of General Erich Luddendorf, launched a fascist coup. As a result of amateur planning by the coup organizers

[23]Strikingly, Yeltsin in 1993 seemed to want similar power in the new Constitution.
[24]Eberhard Kolb, *The Weimar Republic*, Unwin, Hyman, London, 1988.
[25]Halperin, *Germany Tried Democracy*, chapter 12.

and coordinated countermeasures, the coup was crushed in one day and became known as the "Munich beer hall putsch." But these were ominous harbingers of things to come.[26]

The regime also needed to combat hyperinflation and the impact of the Treaty of Versailles. An adverse balance of trade, weak foreign credit, the flight of German capital, and the French occupation of the Ruhr devastated the German economy. This came on top of massive reparations and the loss of colonies and rich territories. The government decided to print money to cover a rising deficit. The result was economic ruin and hyperinflation. In January 1923 there were 7000 marks to the dollar; in the middle of November 1923, 2.5 trillion marks to the dollar.

The political climate was poisonous. Hundreds of people were killed in these tumultuous years. From 1919 to 1924 a number of important leaders were assassinated, from Foreign Minister Walter Rathenau (1922) to Matthias Erzberger (1922), leader of the armistice talks. In the June 1920 elections the democratic parties lost their majority, receiving 11 million votes compared to 14.4 million votes for the Right and Left. Ten months after approving the constitution, the Weimar parliament lost its majority support and never regained it. During Weimar there were twenty Cabinets in fourteen years, the longest lasting less than two years.[27]

Nothing so exemplified the disastrous impact of international affairs as the Treaty of Versailles and its aftermath. In May 1919 in Versailles the French Premier Georges Clemenceau, after a bitter speech, handed over one copy of the Allied draft treaty to the German Foreign Minister. Germany was given a fourteen-day deadline, with no right to discussion or negotiation. Horrified by the terms, Germany rejected the draft, only to face a new text in June. In July, with reservation, Germany accepted its fate.

The Treaty of Versailles stripped Germany of its colonies, Alsace-Lorraine, Upper Silesia, much of western Prussia, and Mermel. Under Article 231 it accepted full responsibility for the war and unspecified war debts. The Allies disarmed Germany, which was limited to a 100,000 man army without a general staff, tanks, armored cars, or airplanes, and a 15,000 man navy with no submarines or large battleships. The Kaiser and other "war criminals" were to be turned over for trial and the union of Germany and Austria was forbidden.[28]

Germany escaped military occupation (as in 1945) or massive depredation. Germany treated defeated Russia in 1918 and occupied Europe from 1939 to 1944 much more brutally.[29] Yet the Treaty of Versailles "dealt a staggering

---

[26]Bracher, *The German Dictatorship*, pp. 108–121. Hitler received an absurdly light five-year sentence, of which he spent less than one year in jail.

[27]Bracher, *The German Dictatorship*, pp. 75–79.

[28]Kolb, *The Weimar Republic*, chapter 2.

[29]At Brest-Litovsk in March 1918 Germany stripped Russia of 35 percent of its population, compared to the 10 percent Germany lost at Versailles in 1919. In World War II the Nazi "New Order" barbarized Europe and killed over 10 million people, including 6 million Jews, in the Holocaust.

blow to the German republic . . . strengthened enormously the hand of the reactionaries and provided them with a propaganda weapon of supreme and lastingeffectiveness."[30] Although neither a Carthaginian peace nor a Wilsonian peace, the Treaty of Versailles was a "heavy encumbrance for a young democracy," unwise "in visiting the consequences of defeat on those German politicians and parties which shared Wilson's ideas concerning international understanding."[31]

The Weimar republic enjoyed relative stability from 1924 to 1929. Foreign pressure eased on Germany, the economy boomed, and the polity consolidated itself. Yet even then not all was well. The most effective German leaders, Ebert (1929) and Stresemann (1929) died at this time. There were six coalition governments in five years. The 1926 election of Paul von Hindenburg, a reactionary monarchist, as President did not bode well for the future.[32]

The final years of Weimar Germany, from 1929 to 1933, were chilling. The Great Depression saw the number of unemployed workers soar from 1.3 million in 1929 to 6 million in 1933, or over 30 percent of the worker force. With this international catastrophe, power passed from the parliament to a presidential cabinet based on the military and bureaucracy. The ineffective Reichstag met for ninety-four days in 1930, forty-two days in 1931, and five days in 1932. In 1932 and 1933 the majority of votes (56 percent) went to the radical, antidemocratic Right (Nazis) and Left (Communists).

The rise of the Nazis was tied to the misery of the country and the effectiveness of Hitler in mobilizing discontent with the failed parliamentary system. The other liberal and socialist parties failed to fight for democracy and the masses were passive or hostile to democratic parties. The economic crisis panicked the middle class and peasantry, increasingly attracted to the Nazis' skillful use of propaganda, persuasion, and terror. The center largely collapsed, and from 1930 to 1933

> political life was reduced to government by emergency law, faith in democratic solutions evaporated. The resultant power vacuum offered wide openings for radicalism of the Left and even more so that of the Right.[33]

The authoritarian, aging President was maneuvered into giving the Chancellorship to Hitler in January, 1933 after two other Chancellors (von Papen, Schleicher) had failed in 1932. Hitler became Chancellor legally and, with a series of emergency laws and terror, consolidated power rapidly. The minimal resistance to the Nazis reflected the complete collapse of Weimar Germany.[34]

[30]Halperin, *Germany Tried Democracy*, p. 152.
[31]Kolb, *The Weimar Republic*, p. 33.
[32]Kolb, *The Weimar Republic*, chapter 2.
[33]Bracher, *The German Dictatorship*, chapter 4.
[34]Bracher, *The German Dictatorship*, chapter 4.

OTHER DEMOCRATIC FAILURES: SPAIN, PORTUGAL, ITALY AND FRANCE

The spectacular failure of Weimar Germany was only one of many failures of democracy in Western Europe in this century. We review the failure of the Spanish Republic (1931–1936), Portuguese Republic (1910–1926), Italian Republic (1918–1922), and the French Third Republic (1871–1940), all overthrown and replaced by fascist or neofascist regimes. Spain, Portugal, and Italy, like the FSU, were developing countries on the periphery of Europe who lacked a democratic tradition in making a democratic transition at a time of serious internal political and economic difficulties.

The fate of the Spanish Republic in the Spanish Civil War (1936–1939) represented a *cri de coeur* for devoted democrats of the 1930s. In many ways Spain bore a significant resemblance to the FSU today. The government bureaucracy, appointed under the old authoritarian regime (that of King Alfonso XIII), was largely hostile to the new regime with only a minority being committed democrats. The military, glorying in the past grandeur of the state, was reactionary, especially in the higher ranks, and thinking of possible coups. So too were the secret police and Ministry of Interior. The new democratic republic failed to purge or renew these institutions. The middle class was weak, small, and inexperienced, trapped between the large, hostile, and relatively authoritarian and socialist lower classes on one side and the unrepentant commanding elites left over from the old regime. The plethora of parties were plagued by weak and informal organization, with only the Spanish socialists constituting a strong political force. The political leaders and deputies "found themselves either swamped, or forced to extreme positions, by their more radical followers or by groups which threatened to detach their followers." As for the deputies in Parliament, they were even worse:

> The deputies were ebullient, rhetorical, inexperienced and desirous of enjoying the fruits of public office. As with the deputies of the Third and Fourth Republics in France, the overthrow of the existing ministry was a favorite indoor sport. The Prime Minister and his leading collaborators constantly had to exercise their persuasive talents to hold their parliamentary majority in line. A wide variety of motives, from the most highly principled to most capricious or sordid, could influence the deputies' votes.[35]

The Spanish Republic, like the Russian Republic, was born after a protracted political crisis in a time of increasing economic lag behind the advanced Western countries. Large segments of the population were impoverished, indifferent, or hostile to the republic. Passionate political and intellectual crosscurrents, threat of strikes, coups, and revolts were the norm.

There were substantial differences. The power of the Spanish Catholic Church far exceeded that of the Russian Orthodox Church. Most of the social

---

[35]Gabriel Jackson, *The Spanish Republic and the Civil War 1931–1939*, Princeton University Press, Princeton, 1969, pp. 489–490.

and economic legislation demanded by the Left in Spain was enacted by the Communists in the Soviet Union. The powerful landlords and the big capitalists in Spain had no counterpart in post-Communist Russia. The Left was a rising militant and fractured force in Spain, but it was a spent and disintegrating Communist element in Russia. The majority of the population in Spain was rural; in Russia it was urban. Regional problems were more important in Spain than in Russia, far more industrialized than Spain.

After the stunning defeat in the Spanish-American War of 1898, Spain continued the long-term decline that began with the loss of Latin America in the 1820s. By 1923 King Alfonso XIII, faced with rising social and economic problems, turned over power to General Primo de Rivera. By 1929 the general was forced to resign and in 1931 the desperate monarch called for a plebiscite on monarchy versus republicanism. When he lost by a small margin, the monarch yielded power peacefully and went into exile. This set the stage for the proclamation of a liberal and moderately socialist republic with the support of a narrow majority of the population. The June 1931 elections, the first real contest ever, returned a solid majority in the Cortes to the Left (250 seats), compared to the Center (100 seats) and the Right (80 seats).

From 1931 to 1933 a socialist-dominated government under Manuel Azana vainly tried to institute major reforms that only increased the fragmentation and polarization of society. The onset of the Great Depression internationally and the rise of fascism in Germany encouraged the Right to organize and fight the Left-Center alliance and the Radical Left to attack the socialists as well.[36]

In 1933 a popular shift to the right brought a major defeat to the divided Left in November. The two leading parties were the strongly Catholic CEDA and the middle class Radicals. An increasingly militant Left, spurred by rising unemployment and the cruel repression of the Left by Nazi Germany, partially supported the failed general strike and Asturias miners' uprising in 1934. The uprising was brutally repressed, and 30,000 leftist prisoners filled Spanish jails in 1935. By February 1936 the pendulum had swung back to a newly unified Left whose Popular Front won a decisive electoral victory. The new/old Prime Minister Manuel Azana promptly amnestied the 30,000 prisoners, sent right-wing generals (as Franco) out of Spain, and proposed land reform and autonomy for cities and the Basques. Amidst rising violence and strikes, the Right prepared to strike. In July 1936 General Francisco Franco led the Spanish Army in Morocco in a revolt that, combined with several uprisings in Spain, soon seized one-third of Spain. But the Republicans, holding on to Madrid and Barcelona and the more developed areas, counterattacked. It took 2.5 years and major German and Italian intervention before the ultimate triumph of fascism.[37]

The Spanish lessons? That conservative military forces (read August 1991 Russian coup) remain a serious threat to democracy. That it takes more than a

[36]Raymond Carr, *Spain 1808–1975*, Clarendon Press, Oxford, 1982, chapter 15; and Paul Preston, *The Coming of the Spanish Civil War*, Harper and Row, New York, 1978, chapters 1–3.

[37]Jackson, *The Spanish Republic and the Civil War 1931–1939*, chapters 9–13.

few elections to institutionalize democracy. That democracy is fragile at first and easily destroyed. That lack of a strong and experienced middle class and weak economic development are serious impediments to democracy.

The Portuguese experiment with democracy (1910–1926), initiated by the flight of the last Braganca monarch (whose dynasty had ruled since 1640), showed many of the same problems seen in Spain and Russia. There was a severe economic and financial crisis, replete with high inflation, large debt, and currency devaluation. There was a conservative military, hostile to democracy, which seized power bloodlessly in 1926. There were frequent violence, political instability, and serious bureaucratic problems. There was no multiparty system, but one party (Portuguese Republican Party) won all but one election. A few bosses in Lisbon dominated the party, which was ridden by factionalism and personalism.[38]

The Portuguese Republic had an astounding forty-five governments. From a monarchy in 1909, Portugal passed to civilian rule (1910–1914), military rule (World War I), renewed civil rule with strong military influence (1919–1925), military rule in 1926, and neofascism under Antonio Salazar after 1927. There were ten coup attempts between 1921 and 1926 and the officer corps by 1926 was as large as in the war. Civil violence, strikes, and insurrection were the order of the day in this immobile, stalemated system.

The causes of the failure of democracy in Portugal? Familiar ones—a strong conservative army, Rightist unity and Leftist disunity, discredited political power, excessive politicization, weakness of parliament, and the abandonment of democracy by a weak middle class. As in Russia in 1994, a weak economy in crisis, small and vacillating middle class, powerful authoritarian tradition, weak parties, strong leaders, and reactionary military spelled the doom of the regime. There are strong differences, as Portugal is far more Catholic, with strong upper classes and a more powerful military, but the combination of factors was deadly for democracy.

The Italian Republic (1918–1922) showed even more fragility as it succumbed to weak opposition after only four years of existence. The republic period continued the domination of Italian politics by the Liberal Party from the unification of Italy (1870) until the fascist ascendancy (1922). During this period the Liberal Party was not a modern party but an elite grouping of antagonistic factions competing in a world of limited suffrage. World War I represented a Pyrrhic victory for the Italians who belonged to the victorious allies. Defeated by Austro-Hungarian forces at Caporeto in 1917, the Italian army lost 600,000 dead in the war. Despite the Allied victory, the Italians found themselves on the sidelines at Versailles and their nationalist demands over Fiume spurned by their Allies.[39]

After 1918 a frustrated Italian nationalism was reinforced by economic

---

[38]Douglas Wheeler, *Republican Portugal: A Political History 1910–1926*, University of Wisconsin Press, Madison, 1978; and Howard Wiarda, *Politics in Iberia*, Harper Collins, New York, 1993.

[39]For the Italian republic, see Rene Albrecht-Carrie, *Italy From Napoleon to Mussolini*, Columbia University Press, New York, 1950, chapters 4–5; and John Adams and Paclo Barile, *The Government of Republican Italy*, Houghton Mifflin, New York, 1972, chapter 2.

problems and political alienation. The enemies of a liberal democratic state were many: the Vatican, right wing nationalists, fascists, anarchists, and Communists. Public disorder reigned as demobilized, disgruntled soldiers battled militant workers. The liberal forces were divided. Foreign policy failures delegitimized the government, which found enemies everywhere: the Right opposed their war policy, business fought their willingness to conciliate strikers, the Left opposed any bourgeois government, and the Church fought separation of church and state.

The 1918–1922 period represented an "aimless floundering and sinking into an ever deeper political morass."[40] There were five Prime Ministers in only four years. In the 1919 and 1921 elections the Socialists were the largest party, followed by the Populists. In 1921, the fascists first gained seats in the parliament. In October 1922 Mussolini led the famous March on Rome to end the governmental strike. A general strike failed and King Victor Emmanuel, refusing to sign a martial law decree, instead gave Mussolini a mandate to form a new government. By the middle 1920s fascism was strongly entrenched in Italy and fascism had destroyed democracy.

The lessons? The acts of individuals are important. A different king could easily have declared martial law and smashed the fascists. Small movements can become a serious danger to democracy. The fascists, who began as a movement in 1915 and who in 1921 received only 7 percent of the popular vote, by late 1922 had gained the post of Prime Minister. Too, the failure of the liberals and socialists to unite gravely undermined democracy.

The final example, the end of the Third Republic (1871–1940) and beginning of Vichy France (1940–1944), is rather different. For the state crumbled not from within but from without, in the wake of the stunning defeat of France by Germany in May and June 1940. Yet what is of interest to us is the way the National Assembly of the Third Republic legally transferred power to Marshall Philippe Pétain, who established an antidemocratic, highly reactionary government at the spa of Vichy in the south of France. Even more, this government enjoyed strong popular support from 1940 to 1942 and the Resistance remained relatively isolated. Vichy's support crumbled together with Germany's war fortunes. Yet even in 1966, 51 percent of all Frenchmen thought Pétain had done some good, while only 17 percent thought he did some harm. After liberation in August 1944 the Free French under de Gaulle killed 10,000 collaborators outright and opened some 160,000 cases of collaborators, indirectly showing the breadth of support for Vichy France.

What is important is how a shock to a democratic system almost seventy years old could create a veritable passion for the neofascist Vichy regime and its leader, the eighty-four-year-old hero of Verdun, Marshal Philippe Pétain. The new regime was recognized by thirty-two states, including the United States and Soviet Union. Bringing order out of chaos produced near-universal acclaim for Pétain and the "New Order."[41] In June 1940 the National Assembly

[40]Albrecht-Carrie, *Italy From Napoleon to Mussolini*, p. 131.
[41]Robert Aron, *The Vichy Regime 1940–44*, translated by Humphrey Hare, Beacon Press, Boston, 1958, chapter I.

of the Third Republic liquidated itself at Bordeaux by a 516–18 vote to transfer executive and legislative power to Pétain. In 1940 no major public voice opposed the armistice or supported de Gaulle. In 1940 the enemies of Vichy were "miniscule," in 1941 "even smaller." As Robert Paxton has concluded,

> nor was the new regime a mere cabal. I shall try to show that it enjoyed mass support and elite participation. Its programs drew less from German and Italian models than from long festering French internal conflicts.[42]

While it controlled the southern third of France from June 1940 to December 1942, the Vichy regime developed strong roots. More traditional and reactionary than fascist, Vichy France repelled most French fascists, who preferred the German-occupied Paris to French Vichy. The National Revolution of Vichy fused integral Catholicism, Napoleonic centralism, concentration of capital, and coercion. It relied on the Church and family, on the civil service elites and upper classes, and anti-Semitism. It attacked Jews, parliamentary democracy, liberals, and Communists as the source of all evil. Vichy could draw on the nearly half of the population that voted against the Popular Front in 1936 and the 20 percent who sent their children to Catholic schools. The adoration of Pétain, the legal origins of the regime, a passion for law and order, hierarchy, and expertise, strong contempt for the Third Republic, and public fear of the cost of liberation reinforced Vichy's appeal.

As late as November 1942 roughly half the French population supported Vichy. But growing German defeats, barbarism, and economic pressure on Vichy, the German occupation of Vichy late in 1942, and the massive draft of French workers for German factories in 1943 and 1944 turned the tide. As late as April 1944 Pétain drew large crowds in Paris. But German actions drove the population passively towards the Resistance, which included 2 percent of the French adult population. In June 1944 the discredited Pétain called for French neutrality in the face of Allied landings at Normandy. By August the retreating Germans put him under house arrest. Even in 1945, 96 percent of the voters rejected the old constitution of the Third Republic and most of its deputies.

Vichy France was not innocuous. The regime deported 76,000 Jews to concentration camps, sent 650,000 workers as slave laborers to Nazi Germany, fired 35,000 civil servants, imprisoned 135,000 enemies, and killed tens of thousands of its enemies. Yet this regime enjoyed broad public support for the first two and half years of its existence and went under primarily because of external forces largely beyond its control.[43] This is a sobering thought for advocates of democracy.

RUSSIAN DEMOCRACY AND REFORMISM

The history of Russian democracy is short and sad. While Western Europe was evolving more modern predemocratic structures in the eighteenth and nine-

---

[42]Robert Paxton, *Vichy France,* Alfred Knopf, New York, 1972, pp. 38, 5.
[43]Paxton, *Vichy France.*

teenth centuries, Russia remained largely immured in the trinity of orthodoxy, autocracy, and Russian nationalism. Slavery and serfdom were largely abolished in Europe in the Middle Ages, but it was not until 1862 that serfdom was abolished in Russia. As late as 1894 Tsar Nicholas II denounced as "senseless dreaming" the desire of aristocrats to turn the *zemstvo* into self-governing legislative bodies. He also proclaimed medieval Muscovy as his ideal. Only after the massive defeats in the Russo-Japanese War (1904–1905) and the 1905 Revolution was the Tsar prepared in his October Manifesto to make some tentative steps towards democracy and mass participation in government. He created the Duma, a restricted parliament elected by the population in various forms of estates. The Tsar, who increasingly tried to emasculate this potentially democratic instrument, went through four Dumas before his overthrow twelve years later. Under the autocracy, Dumas and mass participation in the political process was systematically stifled during World War I, even during a phase of mass patriotic support for the war effort. By 1917 democracy represented more of a dream than a reality.

The eight months between the February Revolution and the October Revolution represented the most democratic period thus far in Russian history. The Provisional Government was never popularly elected but it did enjoy strong public support. Yet this protodemocratic regime was not able to address the serious problems facing Russia. The Bolshevik seizure of power in the October Revolution brought the democratic interlude to a sharp halt. When the Bolsheviks won only 25 percent of the vote in the Constituent Assembly elections, Lenin ordered the dispersal of the Assembly after a brief convocation in January. The ensuing Civil War liquidated all chances for democracy, and the victorious Bolshevik Party at the end of 1920 had been "cured" of any democratic tendencies.

Democracy, then, was a fragile flower that wilted rapidly in 1917. During the Communist era (1917–1991), it would not revive. There were reformers within the Party who, while hardly democrats, wished to move the Party in a more populist direction. The sobering reality of Soviet politics is that all these reformers—Nikolai Bukharin, Georgii Malenkov, Nikita Khrushchev, and Mikhail Gorbachev—failed and were ousted from power. On the other hand, the strong authoritarian and bureaucratic centralizers—Vladimir Lenin, Joseph Stalin, and Leonid Brezhnev—were the success cases of Soviet politics, the men who triumphed and died in power.

Nikolai Bukharin was the first major reformer.[44] Originally a Left Communist in 1918, he moved across the political spectrum and led the Right Opposition in the late 1920s. He strongly opposed the Left and Stalin's desires to move rapidly to collectivization, in the face of peasant opposition, and fast industrialization. He promoted the idea of rapprochement with the peasantry and a slow rate of industrial growth that would not alienate the population. Ruling together with Stalin in the middle 1920s, Bukharin and his compatriots (Nikolai Rykov and Mikhail Tomsky) were defeated in 1929, purged from the Politburo in 1930, and shot after a trial in Moscow in 1938.

---

[44]See Stephen Cohen, *Bukharin and the Bolshevik Revolution*, W.W. Norton, New York, 1973.

Georgii Malenkov, Stalin's heir apparent after the nineteenth Party Congress, seemed a less likely reformer. Aware of dissatisfaction with Stalinism, he created a New Course abroad and domestic reformism at home after Stalin's death in 1953. The result? By February 1955 Nikita Khrushchev, rallying the military-industrial complex, mobilized enough support to oust Malenkov as leader.

Ironically, after 1956 Khrushchev donned the mantle of reform. During the stormy period of his rule, he pushed decentralizing industry, dividing the party, emptying the labor camps, taming the secret police, and reducing the size of conventional military land forces. He stressed the importance of raising the low level of consumer goods for the population. The result? In October 1964 a coup, led by Brezhnev, Kosygin, and Podgorny, uniting disparate offended bureaucratic interests, ousted Khrushchev from power.

The final case of Mikhail Gorbachev is so fresh in our minds that we need little reminder of the key events. His radical changes abroad were far more successful than his political and economic reforms at home. The result? His efforts to reform the old society failed, he resigned from power in December 1991, and the old Soviet Union disintegrated. The record, then, of democracy and reform is truly dismal.[45]

OTHER HISTORICAL CASES OF RELEVANCE

The record of Eastern Europe is, thus far, only marginally better. Democratic elections have been held throughout Eastern Europe since the end of communism in 1989. Yet the results have often been less than edifying. In Yugoslavia the end of Communist rule unleashed a Civil War killing tens of thousands of people and producing over two million refugees. In Czechoslovakia the main result of democracy has been to split the old state into two new states as of 1993. In Rumania the old Communist elite has held onto power under a new title. In Bulgaria the Communists held power until 1991 and remain powerful. In Poland the old authoritarian ways seem somehow never destroyed and the two leading parties in the 1993 elections were dominated by former Communists. In Hungary the vice chairman of the ruling New Democratic Forum (Istvan Czurka) lambasted Jews and gypsies as the true cause of Hungary's problems before his expulsion from the party. Democracy has begun, but its roots remain fragile and ever threatened.

The other relevant cases are those of the aftermath of disintegrating empires. The end of the Soviet Union in 1991 meant not only the end of Communism but the dissolution of the former Soviet empire into fifteen new states. At the end of World War I the Ottoman Turkish Empire and Austro-Hungarian Empire dissolved as well. The result? From the ashes of the Austro-Hungarian Empire arose a number of relatively unstable Eastern Euro-

---

[45]Of course, this case could be seen as a success since Boris Yeltsin succeeded Gorbachev and there are now fifteen independent states.

pean states. Only one (Czechoslovakia) was democratic, while the rest were in varying degrees authoritarian. As for Austria, it limped along until 1938 when it embraced Anschluss (union) with Nazi Germany and had a higher percentage of Nazi party members than Germany. Hungary, the other core part, underwent a brief Communist revolution in 1919, then the long authoritarian rule of Admiral Horthy in the interwar period, and emerged as a strong ally of Nazi Germany in World War II. The demise of the Ottoman Turkish Empire caused considerable bloodshed and the disappearance of its strong influence in the Mediterranean. A relatively weak but modernizing state emerged under Ataturk, one that later came under strong military influence. The demise of Tsarist Russia in February 1917 led to a Communist Soviet Union within eight months and a free, but authoritarian, Poland and Finland. Nationalism, not democracy, has been the major beneficiary of the disintegration of empires.

IS THERE ANY HOPE FOR RUSSIAN DEMOCRACY?

This chapter has been pessimistic about the short-term prospects for Russian democracy and very mixed about prospects for the longer run. There are those with decidedly greater optimism about Russian democracy. S. Frederick Starr, citing historical roots favoring democracy and civil society, the rapid growth of civil society under Brezhnev, and the swift push for democracy under Gorbachev and Yeltsin, is quite optimistic. He feels that the gains for democracy have been rapid and that the problems only reflect short-term transitional difficulties.[46]

What can give grounds for optimism? First, the transition to democracy is fraught with such "extraordinary uncertainty" and such a "high degree of indeterminacy" that accidents, hurried decisions, specific individuals, and definition of political identity can be decisive in determining success or failure.[47] There is some hope for Russia if the outcome is so indeterminate. Charles Tilly has seen many different roads to democracy "depending on different country's prior class structure, ethnic structure, economic organization, and position within the geopolitical complex of the world."[48]

Juan Linz, Giuseppe DiPalma, Guillermo O'Donnell, and Philippe Schmitter have stressed the possibility of a significant role for political actors in impacting the outcome of the struggle. They have commented on the power of individuals, will, and initiatives to be decisive factors.[49] As a Lenin was

---

[46]S. Frederick Starr, *Prospects for Stable Democracy in Russia*, Mershon Center Occasional Papers, 1992.

[47]Guillermo O'Donnell and Philippe Schmitter, *Transitions From Authoritarian Rule*, Johns Hopkins University Press, Baltimore, 1986, pp. 3, 5.

[48]Charles Tilly, "Comments," *The Transition to Democracy: Proceedings of a Workshop*, National Academy Press, Washington, D.C., 1991, p. 59.

[49]Giuseppe DiPalma, *To Craft Democracies*, University of California Press, Berkeley and Los Angeles, 1990, p. 4; and Juan Linz, "Crisis, Breakdown and Reequilibrium," in Juan Linz and Arnold Stephens, *The Breakdown of Democratic Regimes*, Johns Hopkins University Press, Baltimore, 1978, p. 44.

instrumental in making the October Revolution, so too could a Gorbachev, a Yeltsin, or some future leader be decisive. This gives real hope for the future.

Many other analysts do not agree. Giuseppe DiPalma has argued the importance of a liberal past (which Russia lacks) in shaping a democratic future. Noting that the number of democratic states as percentage of all states was the same in 1920 as in 1990, DiPalma bluntly averred that, "In sum the hard facts of trends and numbers do not speak in favor of democracy." The world has exhausted its stock of countries with economic prosperity, relative equality, strong middle classes, and neodemocratic national cultures emphasizing tolerance, diversity, and accommodation. Gradualism and accommodation have been displaced by violence, impatience, and the mob.[50] Sidney Verba, while praising the importance of education (a Russian virtue) for democracy, has seen the lack of deeply antagonist subgroups and absence of permanent minorities as essential for democracy. This does not bode well for the future.[51]

The last word belongs to the Finnish scholar Tatu Verhanen and his exhaustive study of democratization. On his four major scaies, the former Soviet Union had scores on occupational diversity (73) and knowledge distribution (70) ranking close to those of France and West Germany. But on distribution of economic resources (0) and distribution of power resources (0) the old regime was hopeless.[52] Whether Russia can create a democratic order based on its high levels of science, culture, and education is the key question.

HOPE FOR RUSSIAN DEMOCRACY: THE DEVIANT CASE OF ITALY

The numerous obstacles to Russian democracy should induce pessimism in all but the most incurable optimists. Are there any cases sufficiently deviant as to show that democracy can survive and grow in a form and ways markedly different from those characteristic of the classic democracies? Fortunately, the great success of Italian democracy (1944–1994) offers some hope.

Italian democracy offers hope for a distinctive Russian road to democracy. Democracy based on alternation of parties in power and a strong and viable opposition seems unlikely in Russia, which lacks any real parties at all in 1994. But since 1944 there has been no alternation of power in Italy, where the Christian Democratic Party has dominated every government.[53] As Joseph LaPalombara has observed, "The Italian parliamentary system is without any opposition at all."[54] An amazing 40 percent of the electorate vote for nondemocratic parties (Communist and neofascist) outside the pale, yet the system

---

[50]Joseph LaPalombara, *Democracy: Italian Style,* Yale University Press, New Haven, 1987, chapter 8.
[51]Sidney Verba, "Comments," in *The Transition to Democracy: Proceedings of a Workshop,* p. 79.
[52]Tatu Verhanen, *The Process of Democratization,* Taylor and Francis, New York, 1989, chapter 6.
[53]The dramatic 1993 revelations in Italy of the close ties between the Christian Democratic Party and the Mafia have led in 1993 to the likely downfall of the Christian Democratic dominance, just as similar events led to the defeat of the Liberal Democratic Party in Japan in 1993.
[54]See Joseph LaPalombara, *Democracy: Italian Style,* Yale University Press, New Haven, 1987, p. 23. Much of this discussion relies on this fine work.

flourishes. All the remaining eight to ten parties jockey to join shifting coalitions with the Christian Democrats.

The Italian government itself is remarkably unstable, much like the Russian government today. There have been more than fifty governments in nearly fifty years, with no government lasting more than three years. Amazingly, the government "often seems about to sink but always stays afloat."[55]

Again as in Russia, in Italy democracy arose from a lengthy and disastrous bout with a radical, antidemocratic regime (twenty-two years of fascism). The culture hardly seems very democratic with vast political differences, endless political combat, and strong and bitter ideological passions. Political scandals, venality and corruption, terrorism, the Mafia, and political alienation are the common coin of Italian politics. As LaPalombara has observed, Italy has endured

> the enduring rivalry between church and state, age-old antagonisms among the peninsula's major regions, the rise and fall of fascism and the civil war and the bitterness it left in its wake, occupation of the country by German and then Allied troops, two devastating wars and class conflict that spawned the largest nonruling Communist Party found anywhere, to say nothing of economic disasters experienced along the way.[56]

The power of the state in Italy, as in Russia, is significantly greater than in most Western countries. A powerful government disposes of over 50 percent of the GNP. Large public and semipublic bodies dominate giant industries, roads, electricity and telecommunications, banks, media, universities, science, culture, and sports. A powerful bureaucracy, riddled with endless codes and rules, seems a major political actor. The government often runs large budget deficits, which build debt and fuel inflation. The Italian judiciary, far from being independent, is highly politicized with repressive legal codes from the fascist era still in place. Its powerful Communist party and strong trade unions would seem more likely in Moscow than Washington.

There are also many differences between Italy and Russia, ranging from the level of economic development to the role of religion and integration in the European Community. However, the case of troubled, and even at times bizarre, Italian democracy in the postwar era shows that democracy can flourish in many diverse settings. This offers some genuine hope for Russia creating its own form of democracy.

POST-SOVIET REALITIES TODAY

With the rapid defection of the Baltic states, there remained twelve nominally independent post-Soviet republics. Only four of them (Russia, Ukraine, Armenia, and Kyrgyzstan) made a stab at democracy, while the other eight republics

---

[55]Frederic Spoots and Theodor Wieser, *Italy: A Different Democracy*, Cambridge University Press, Cambridge, 1986.
[56]LaPalombara, *Democracy: Italian Style*, p. 14.

(Belarus, Azerbaijan, Georgia, Kazakhstan, and the four other Central Asian republics) did not make even that effort. What are the prospects for the two largest units, especially as poverty and incessant war threaten to sink Armenian democracy, and poverty, traditionalism, and a rising Islamic tide similarly make Kyrgyzstan's prospects poor?

In Russia in 1994 much of the old authoritarian structures and attitudes survive. There is no tradition of a rule of law supporting civil liberties and limiting the power of the government. Existing laws are still highly authoritarian, although subject to revision and not currently being well enforced. Despite some surface changes, "very little fundamental change has taken place to reform the former KGB and bring it under democratic control."[57] Similarly there have been only cosmetic changes in the still-powerful Russian military and governmental bureaucracy, where the old bureaucrats remain in power. Former Communists, from Yeltsin to Khasbulatov, dominate politics. Popular political attitudes remain fiercely combative, intolerant, and intransigent towards opposition. Nearly 200 ethnic conflicts, 20 percent of them violent, roil the political waters. And Yeltsin's hard-line confrontations with the parliament in 1992 and 1993 have not reinforced respect for democracy but rather "reinforced old habits and attitudes that reek of past abuses."[58] Already by the end of 1992 only 11 percent of European Russians were satisfied with democracy and by a 59 to 18 percent margin proclaimed themselves better off under the old Communist system. Only a thin majority felt that the people should decide the future.[59] If the questions were asked today, the results would probably be even worse for democratic hopes.

The new democratic forms often seem submerged by the old authoritarianism. Capitalism is nascent and the emerging middle class small and inexperienced. Parties are weak congeries of notables and tiny groups without significant power or aspect. An analyst has recently observed:

> The plethora of parties, their inability to coordinate advocacy of opposition positions, the lack of codified platforms and coherent policies across the spectrum—all these represent the political expression of the bazaar that has taken over the market place.[60]

Yeltsin not only has failed to create his own party but in 1991 and 1992 banned the Communist Party and the National Salvation Front. His confrontation in 1992 and 1993 with the Congress of People's Deputies showed an inability to resolve legislative-executive conflicts. The failure to create real parties, to hold genuine democratic elections, to formulate a democratic consti-

---

[57]J. Michael Waller, "When Will Democrats Control the Former KGB?," *Demokratizatsiya*, vol. 1, no. 1, Summer 1992, p. 33.

[58]*Chicago Tribune* article cited in *Denver Post*, October 3, 1993.

[59]Mark Rhodes, "The FSU and the Future: Facing Uncertainty," *RFE/RL Research Report*, vol. 2, no. 24, June 11, 1993.

[60]Mark Teeter, "Russia on the Cusp," *Demokratizatsiya*, vol. 1, no. 1, Summer 1992. Here he means that without any democratic tradition politics becomes solely a bargaining process without any principles.

tution, combined with Yeltsin's increasingly authoritarian style of ruling by decree and authoritarian plenipotentiaries, does not bode well for Russian democracy. Yet Yeltsin's commitment to democracy, his success in the April 1993 referendum and September 1993 confrontation with parliament, and his attempts to build a new constitution do offer some hope.

The prospects for Russian democracy are noticeably better than prospects for Ukrainian democracy. Here there is no tradition of central government, let alone democracy. For the last 800 years Ukraine has been ruled by foreigners— Mongols, Lithuanians, Poles, or Russians. The legacy of the Empire is ethnic divisiveness between 11 million Russians and 1 million Jews and nearly 40 million Ukrainians, whose culture and intelligentsia were suppressed by Russians for centuries. The terror of Stalinist Russia will not be easily forgotten by Ukrainian nationalists, who stress independence and chauvinism far more than democracy.

The new state, with an elected parliament, president, and referendum, arose only at the end of 1991. Its leader (Leonid Kravchuk), the majority of parliament, the bureaucracy, military, and secret police, are all former Communists. Most old Soviet laws are still in effect, with few guarantees of private property or civil liberties. The economy remains socialist and centralized with minimal privatization. The proposed constitution in 1992 contained numerous infringements on the most basic civil liberties.[61]

With the old political elite and old economic system still largely in place, the prospects for Ukrainian democracy remained grim. The agenda was staggering: resolving serious disputes over borders (Crimea) and dividing up the Soviet military with Russia, managing the transition to a market economy, tamping down ethnic conflicts among Ukrainians, Russians, and Jews, partially democratizing an authoritarian state structure and integrating into Western European political and economic structures. The tasks are enormous, yet without some successes Ukrainian democracy will remain as phantasmagorical in the future as the notion of a Ukrainian state seemed for many centuries.

In other republics, especially in the Transcaucasus and Central Asia, democratic pretensions are even weaker. Only in Armenia and Kyrgyzstan were democratic forms observed. The old Communist regimes persist nearly everywhere in Central Asia. There the primary rising force is Islamic fundamentalism, fueled by a rivalry among Turkey and Iran, not democracy. Civil wars in Georgia and Azerbaijan and war between Armenia and Azerbaijan predominated in the Transcaucasus. Without resolution of these bloody conflicts, democracy has precious little chance. Economic and political structures are less developed and authoritarian pasts give little hope for future development of democracy.

The main prerequisites for democracy are lacking in the FSU. There is no history of capitalism, strong localism, competing parties, interest groups, balance of forces. There are no democratic traditions, strong economic develop-

---

[61]Gregory Stanton, "Democratization in the Ukraine: Constitutions and the Rule of Law," *Demokratizatsiya*, vol. 1, no. 1, Summer 1992, pp. 56–60.

ment, or powerful middle class to fuel such growth. Strong security concerns and ethnic conflicts reinforce the trend to authoritarian centralism. The 1991 Russian Revolution did not eliminate the old elite and social system, or induce a foreign occupation to impose a new social and political system. There is a history of authoritarian, centralized bureaucratic rule, of strong charismatic leaders and pervasive hatred and intolerance over many generations. The rule of the Tsars was replaced by that of the Communists with only an eight-month break. Without strong economic and cultural forces to lay the groundwork for democracy, without massive foreign intrusion and with huge national and ethnic problems, the results seem almost tragically preordained. However, the creation of strong localist forces in Russia in 1992 and 1993 may augur the beginning of a counterforce that could bring democracy down to the grassroots.

The strongest case can be made for a revived authoritarian centralist (but non-Communist) state or for authoritarianism with a democratic patina. Less likely but possible is a limited democracy coexisting uneasily with strong authoritarian tendencies in government. Foreign support, economic development, a well-educated and urban population, a strong middle class, and reaction against discredited Communism could promote this end. In the short run, the tradition, forces, and institutions weigh more heavily on the side of authoritarianism than of a weak and struggling democracy.

In 1992 Peter Juviler listed eight features of the democratization process: declining ethnic conflict, creation of new autonomous social classes, peaceful and unified leaders, market economy, rule of law protecting civil liberties, resolution of executive-legislative power struggles, development of broad and strong parties, and procedural legitimation. Only time will tell if there is any hope for democracy or if this is a hopeless task.[62]

---

[62]Peter Juviler, "Will Democratization Survive Freedom in the Ex-USSR?," *Demokratizatsiya*, vol. 1, no. 1, Summer 1992, p. 79.

21

The Road to Capitalism and a Free-Market Economy

For Americans, who have grown up in a wealthy, free-market, highly competitive economy, the capitalist path seems inevitable and obvious. Yet only twenty to twenty-five countries have achieved First World capitalist growth with a per capita GNP of more than 10,000 dollars. Other paths—communism, socialism, autonomous development, feudalism, stunted capitalism—have predominated elsewhere. The success stories for 700 million people are easy to enumerate: Western and Central Europe, Great Britain and its former white settler colonies (United States, Canada, Australia, and New Zealand), Japan, and Israel.[1] The other 4.9 billion people, or 85 percent of the world, are now (with the collapse of the Second World) in the Third World. The gap is huge, with First World per capita GNP averaging around 15,000 dollars and Third World per capita GNP averaging 1300 dollars. Anyone who has visited the teeming impoverished metropolises of the Third World, from Mexico City and Cairo to Bombay and Lagos, will not mistake them for London, Paris, Frankfurt, Tokyo, or New York.

The gap between rich and poor is large and widening. While in 1800 the richest nations had twice the GNP per capita of the poorest nations, by the year 2000 the gap will widen to 20:1. The richest nations have universal literacy, a life expectancy at birth of seventy-five to seventy-eight years, and population with eight to twelve years of schooling. The poorest nations (such as Malawi, Mali, Afghanistan, and Guinea) have adult literacy rates of 18 to 50 percent of the population, a life expectancy at birth of forty-two to fifty years, and population with two or less years of schooling.[2]

---

[1] The Four Tigers of Asia (Taiwan, South Korea, Singapore, and Hong Kong) are closing in on this status with rapid, dynamic capitalist economies and per capita GNP in the 5000 to 11,000-dollar range.

[2] See John Nagle, *Introduction to Comparative Politics*, Nelson Hall, Chicago, 1993, third edition, p. 316; and *Human Development, Report 1992*, pp. 127–129.

Successful capitalist development has produced dramatic results. Already in 1848 in *The Communist Manifesto* Marx and Engels, at the beginning of capitalism, could write:

> The bourgeoisie . . . has accomplished wonders far surpassing Egyptian pyramids, Roman aqueducts and Gothic cathedrals. . . . The bourgeoisie, during its rule of scarce one hundred years, has created more massive and more colossal productive force than all preceding generations together.[3]

Between 1820 and 1990, First World capitalist countries increased production seventy-fold and real per capita income fourteen-fold, doubled life expectancy, and halved the work week. With 13 percent of the world's population, they produce over 50 percent of its GNP. The top five capitalist states (United States, Japan, Germany, France, and Great Britain) have over 13 trillion dollars in nonresidential fixed capital stock and over 1 trillion dollars of international trade each year. The top three capitalist states in the late 1980s disposed of over 380 billion dollars in international reserves. The ultimate success story was the United States, whose GNP rose 450 fold from 10 billion dollars in 1820 to 4.6 trillion dollars in 1989.[4]

The FSU, with per capita GNPs ranging from 1000 to 3200 dollars, lags far behind the West. Can it transform its undeniable assets (great natural resources, a well-educated, predominantly urbanized population, a first-rate scientific elite, a strong industrial base), that allowed it to be a first-class military superpower, into an economic superpower effectively contesting in the international economic marketplace?[5] Can it take the capitalist path after centuries of autocratic Tsarist development and a seventy-four-year detour through socialism? In the Czech Republic and East Germany, socialism could be seen, in the words of an old joke, as the longest path between capitalism and capitalism. But the FSU lacked even a distant capitalist past to shed light on the present. This chapter will give a decidedly pessimistic short-run answer and modestly positive long-run answer to the question of whether there are good prospects for capitalism in the former Soviet Union.

The notion of a Russian path to capitalism calls into question what we mean by capitalism and how it can be introduced. There are many variants of capitalism, with as many "roads to capitalism" as there were once seen to be roads to socialism. Asian capitalism, with authoritarian, patriarchal, one-party regimes, neo-Confucian ideology, a powerful government role in the economy, and suppression of trade unions, seems a far cry from laissez-faire classic entrepreneurial English capitalism. The strong social welfare state of Scandinavian democratic socialism seems equally far distant from the traditions of American free enterprise. What makes them all capitalist is a strong free-market economy, characterized by integration into the world capitalist economy, stress

---

[3]Karl Marx and Friedrick Engels, *The Communist Manifesto,* Penguin, London, 1967, pp. 82–85.
[4]Angus Maddison, *Dynamic Forces in Capitalist Development,* Oxford University Press, Oxford, 1991, pp. 1–24, 110, 198–199, 286.
[5]*RFE/RL Research Report,* vol. 2, no. 20, May 3–7, 1993.

on profits and investments, consumerism, and effective protection of private property. The notion of market is not simply reserved for goods and labor services. Rather, capitalist markets exist for foreign exchange, real assets, financial assets, capital, and land. All must be in place for capitalism to function effectively.[6]

The traditional Russian rejection of capitalism under the tsars and the Communists also calls into question whether it is possible to radically implant capitalism from above. The Stalinist attempt to implant socialism from above was ultimately a massive failure, especially in the countryside. Can capitalism do better, especially when successful capitalism—though often strongly helped by the state—has generally grown more organically from below and over several generations? Can capitalism emerge in Russia, despite poor soil, full-blown like Pallas Athena from the brow of Zeus?

BAILOUT: THE MARSHALL PLAN REVISITED

Oftentimes people seek to resolve problems through the application of histori-cal precedents. In Vietnam the American government thought it was replaying Munich; in the Persian Gulf War the Bush administration thought it was replaying World War II. These historical analogies, consciously or uncon-sciously, can have a powerful impact on our thinking. For the problem of creating a thriving capitalist society in the Soviet Union, the analogy that leaps to mind for many is that of the Marshall Plan. This seems to offer a quick and rapid transition to capitalism and prosperity for the former Soviet Union. Unfortunately, as is often the case with analogies, this one is deeply flawed when applied to the FSU.

The Marshall Plan itself was a great success. Named after Secretary of State George Marshall, the plan utilized large-scale American aid to revive the moribund economies of Western Europe, which had sustained enormous damage in the war. Massive Allied bombing and the ground fighting in the last year of the war devastated Germany. England had suffered significant damage from German bombs and rockets and overstrained its fragile economy during the war. Four years of rapacious German occupation policies had looted France. The Southern European countries languished even further behind. Communist parties, which played a major role in the resistance, flourished. The United States, seeking to create strong allies, offered a massive injection of capital for its allies to foster their political stability and economic development.

The United States spent 13 billion dollars on the Marshall Plan, a sum equal to 60 to 80 billion dollars in today's terms.[7] The results were impressive. By 1952, only four years later, Western Europe had achieved its prewar economic

---

[6]Robert Campbell, *The Socialist Economies in Transition*, Indiana University Press, Bloomington, 1991, chapter 1.

[7]Charles Maier and Gunter Bischof, editors, *The Marshall Plan and Germany*, Berg Publications, New York, 1991, pp. 1–4.

level. Agriculture in 1952 surpassed 1938 by 11 percent, industry by 40 percent.[8] By the middle 1950s democracy had taken firm hold in most of Western Europe. The "German miracle" under Konrad Adenauer changed the face of Europe. By 1958 the major countries on the continent, led by France and Germany, were so self-confident and prosperous, that they formed the European Economic Community, the forerunner of today's expanded European Community. By 1960 Western Europe had become the second leading industrial center in the world.[9]

Why can't this be done for Russia, Ukraine, and Belarus at least? With over 30,000 nuclear weapons in that area, instability on the surface of 40 percent of Europe and 40 percent of Asia could have profound consequences for the world. Russia and Ukraine have a solid industrial base, excellent natural resources, a strong scientific elite, and well-educated populations. And the prospect of turning a dreaded foe into an ally should be a strong incentive.

And yet, it will not work. The United States no longer has that kind of money to lend to Russia. The Clinton administration took office in 1993 looking at a 300 billion dollar budget deficit, 100 billion dollar trade deficit, and more than four trillion dollar debt, a debt that has quadrupled in the last twelve years. The United States, which accounted for 40 to 50 percent of the world's GNP in 1945 now accounts for 22 percent. Aid for the FSU on the order of 60 to 80 billion dollars is politically inconceivable.

There is no political will or political consensus at home to undertake such massive action. In 1948 fear of Communism in Western Europe and Soviet power overcame isolationist sentiments at home; in 1994 the slow motion disintegration of the FSU seems to pose no comparable threat to the United States. By 1947 the 38 billion dollars given by the United States to Great Britain and the Soviet Union in Lend Lease during the war set a strong precedent for the Marshall Plan; in 1994, after the Cold War, there was no precedent to aid our recently formidable enemy.[10] Similarly a weak European recovery in 1947 seemed to threaten American prosperity; in 1994 a floundering former Soviet Union was irrelevant to the American economy. In 1947 the Marshall Plan could be touted as an alternative to the 1919 Treaty of Versailles that humiliated Germany and led to fascism; in 1994 there was no such precedent.[11]

Even if the West had the will, a world only slowly coming out of recession would find it hard to mobilize such resources. There is little likelihood that such a plan would work. France, Germany, and England, the major recipients of Marshal Plan funds, all had strong capitalist economies. Their problems were temporary, caused by the impact of World War II. Indeed, they were the three most powerful economies in the world after the United States. The same is not

[8]Michael Hogan, *The Marshall Plan*, Cambridge University Press, Cambridge, 1987, p. 431.
[9]Immanuel Wexler, *The Marshall Plan Revisited*, Greenwood Press, Westport, Connecticut, 1983, pp. 249–251.
[10]Henry Pelling, *Britain and the Marshall Plan*, St. Martin's Press, New York, 1988, pp. 4–7, 125. In addition, the United States loaned Great Britain almost another four billion dollars after the war.
[11]John Gimbel, *The Origins of the Marshall Plan*, Stanford University Press, Stanford, 1976, pp. 268–272.

true for the FSU, which lacks the norms, values, entrepreneurial skills, property laws, infrastructure, democratic institutions, and work ethic so essential to capitalism. There is no issue of reviving what came before; there is nothing to revive.

The kind of money it would take to revive the Soviet Union would be staggering, far beyond the capabilities of the West. For the 290 million people in the FSU would require, as we see in the forthcoming section on the East German and Israeli experience, trillions of dollars to become a competitive capitalist society.

The money would likely be wasted. The FSU lacks many fruitful projects on which the money could be spent. Billions would undoubtedly disappear into the maws of the bureaucracy, in corruption and support of featherbedding. Only a strong internal regeneration by local forces could produce the kind of Russia which could fruitfully use the money. Ironically, as has been seen in many Third World countries, too much outside money would simply create a dependency on the West and retard development.[12] Russia and the other republics lack the prerequisites to make a successful capitalist system. By contrast, the Marshall Plan could succeed because the European countries had all the basic ingredients for a successful rehabilitation of their economy. All they needed was the capital provided by the United States.

Alan Milward has further argued against exaggerating the impact of the Marshall Plan. Given the smallness of the aid (2 percent of European GNP), the strength of non-German economies, and high capital formation (double the rate of 1938 in Germany in 1948), recovery was inevitable. This argument further emphasizes the need for objective preconditions lacking in the former Soviet Union.[13]

PATHS TO SUCCESS

The successful paths to capitalism have been almost as numerous as academic theories of developments. Alexander Gerschenkron's notion of the substitution effect for states industrializing in a late historical epoch (with banks in Germany and the state in Russia substituting for entrepreneurs in Great Britain) would have clear parallels in capitalist development in states at differing levels of development.[14]

The most recent successful paths of capitalist development, epitomized by

---

[12]Egypt, Bangladesh, and India are very good examples of this. Despite tens of billions of dollars of external aid, there has been little economic development. South Vietnam, recipient of 125 billion dollars of American military and economic aid in the 1960s and early 1970s is another example. Despite strong conventional military superiority over its enemy, it succumbed very quickly to the 1975 North Vietnamese military offensive launched without aid of airplanes or a strong tank force.

[13]Alan Milward, *The Reconstruction of Western Europe 1945–51*, University of California Press, Berkeley and Los Angeles, 1984, pp. 436–480.

[14]Alexander Gerschenkron, *Economic Backwardness in Historical Perspective*, Harvard University Press, Cambridge, 1960.

peripheral capitalism in Spain and Portugal, the trade-driven neo-Confucian capitalism of the Four Tigers of Asia (Singapore, Hong Kong, South Korea, Taiwan), and the mixed economy of Israel, are all thoroughly irrelevant to the FSU. Spanish success was built around a large infusion of European capital, membership in the European Community, a powerful tourist industry, and strong cultural, political, and economic ties to Western Europe in the post-Franco era after 1975. None of this is remotely applicable to the FSU. Neither is the experience of the Four Tigers of Asia—former (and in Hong Kong's case still) colonies of England and Japan with a strong neo-Confucian orientation, relatively small in population and Chinese in ethnic origin (save for South Korea), possessing heavily trade-driven economies with strong military and political ties to the United States and England.

As for smallish Israel, massive immigration, very close military, economic, and political ties with the United States, associate membership in the European Common Market, large-scale foreign Jewish fund raising (over 2 billion dollars a year), very high educational levels, a strong government role in the economy, and first-rate universities have propelled the mixed economy into the bottom of the First World. Apart from the last three factors, the experience of the FSU is very different—the closest tie being the 600,000 Soviet Jews who emigrated to Israel in the 1970s and early 1990s.

Earlier paths also offer little hope. The Anglo-American model featured liberal individual capitalism in countries physically removed from the European continent (England was last successfully invaded in 1066, and the United States has never been successfully invaded). With a strong Protestant ethic, a powerful entrepreneurial culture, the early rise of the bourgeoisie to power, early democratic development, a strong society and a weak state, the Anglo-American model has little to offer the FSU. For the FSU inherited a realm vulnerable to foreign invasion (1709, 1812, 1853, 1915, 1941), a Russian Orthodox tradition, heavy bureaucratic authoritarianism, and a history of a strong antidemocratic state swallowing a weak society.[15]

The German experience is more congenial to the FSU. A strong autocratic polity (Imperial Germany 1870–1918, Third Reich 1933–1945), belated and hurried industrialization after 1870, powerful cartels, a significant socialist tradition before 1914, and a strong social-welfare state all have resonance further east. However, critical elements of the German experience were very different—a powerful industrial export sector (20 percent of GNP), membership in the European Community, a geographic position in the heart of Europe, a compact size, renowned work ethic, over forty years of democracy, very close ties with the United States, and a century-long history as the strongest capitalist power on the European mainland.

And the Japanese, renowned for their "economic miracle" of the postwar

---

[15]There are some key differences between the United States and Great Britain over the issues of the social-welfare state, the role of trade unionism, class structure, and immigration-emigration patterns. These all make England, though remote, still somewhat closer to the former Soviet Union than the United States.

era but now in recession? The Japanese experience too provides few clues for the FSU. Unlike Russia, Japan sustained a far-reaching and largely successful Westernization program ever since the Meiji Restoration of 1868.[16] The powerful Japanese export thrust, close integration into the world capitalist economy, the forty years of one-party-dominated democracy since World War II, few natural resources, suppression of trade unions and consumer demand, and very close ties with the West (and especially the United States) put Japan in a class by itself. So too does its minimal military spending (1 percent of GNP) and reliance on the American nuclear umbrella for protection. Only its strong government role in the economy and excellent universal educational system would seem familiar to the FSU.

PREREQUISITES FOR SUCCESS

There are many prerequisites for the success of a capitalist system. Successful capitalist countries have most, though not all, of these prerequisites. The FSU, after seventy years of socialism, has only two or three of the ten basic prerequisites for a viable capitalist system. One is the educated, literate, and industrially trained population that is an integral element of the successful capitalist system. Early Japanese success built on an unusually literate and educated population. The fact that the majority of the world's leading educational institutions are in the United States has contributed enormously to its growth.[17] The FSU, with 20 million university graduates and a powerful and broad scientific establishment, is outstanding in this area. Ever since the 1930s great resources have been devoted to training and educating the population. The success of Soviet emigrants in the United States and Israel attests to the value of this program.

Secondly, a strong natural resource base is important, though not essential, to successful capitalist development. The vast natural resource base of the United States provided an early impetus to American growth. Other countries, such as Japan, the Four Tigers of Asia, and Israel, have been able to advance without significant natural resources. The FSU is very strong in this area, with the world's greatest oil and natural gas production and second greatest gold production.

A strong, capable, and effective political system is a vital third factor to the success of the capitalist experiment. Political systems that have fostered capitalism have varied from the authoritarianism of the Second Reich of Kaiser Wilhelm's Germany, Meiji Restoration of Japan (after 1868), and the Four Tigers of Asia (1950–1993) to the one-party-dominated (Liberal Democratic Party) democratic system of Japan in the postwar era and two-party democratic system of much of the West. The key, then, is not necessarily democracy but

---

[16]Obviously the militarist interwar Japanese experience, that culminated in World War II, belongs in a different category.

[17]By various estimates, North America has 60 to 70 percent of the world's leading universities.

rather effectiveness, legitimacy, and the ability of the system to do the myriad things necessary for strong capitalist development. A strong and unified elite is necessary in this process. The Japanese and German revolutions from above at the end of the nineteenth century ruthlessly removed feudal and regionalist obstacles to development and vigorously promoted economic development.[18]

And the former Soviet republics? The likelihood of effective political authority, respected, legitimate, and efficient in carrying out vital measures to promote capitalism, is very low. Capitalism is relatively unpopular among the masses socialized for several hundred years in an anticapitalist tradition under the Tsars and then for over seventy years under the Communists. As in the Time of Troubles (1602–1613) and in 1917, all authority has evaporated with this latest Russian revolution. Richard Pipes, in a 1992 article in *Commentary*, referred to the "disintegration" and "gigantic implosion" within the country which has resulted in "a collapse of organized life" and breakdown of all order.

> [I]n the political realm, authority has either dissolved or become paralyzed. The central Soviet government had ceased functioning long before it was officially dissolved and it is far from evident that the powers which it lost have devolved upon the republican governments that have taken its place. . . . The collapse of the political system has inevitably led to a breakdown of the national economy.[19]

Yet without strong and effective political leadership, any effort to transform the old socialist economy into a new capitalist order is hopeless. Massive changes in institutions, laws, norms, and values must occur before a strong basis is laid for capitalism.

A fourth factor of great significance is work ethos. Without a strong, individualist work ethos capitalism is a very difficult proposition. We have already seen that Confucianism (Four Tigers of Asia), Shintoism (Japan), Judaism (Israel), Protestantism (England and the United States), and Catholicism (France, Italy, and Spain) can provide the impetus. The emphasis on the importance of the work ethos in Weber's famous work on the Protestant ethic carries over here. Yet, seventy years of socialism have created a population unwilling to work, often quite content to labor under the cynical slogan "They pretend to pay us and we pretend to work." The level of apathy and drunkenness, the dislike of entrepreneurs enriching themselves in Russia and elsewhere, the cynicism towards work itself is a great hindrance on the way to capitalism. For capitalism ultimately rests on the willingness of much of the population to labor hard for uncertain returns. In Russia the history is one of limited labor for certain, but modest, returns.

A fifth factor is that of an entrepreneurial culture, in which millions of people voluntarily open up new businesses and strive for success. In the United

---

[18]Unfortunately, but perhaps logically, in both cases the result was not democracy but fascism in Germany by 1933 and violent militarism in Japan in the 1930s. However, in the next turn of the wheel after the defeat of the Axis in World War II, democratic regimes were successfully fostered in both countries by occupation regimes in the late 1940s and early 1950s.
[19]Richard Pipes, "Russia's Chance," *Commentary*, January 1992, p. 28.

States nearly 1 million new businesses open each year and small businesses have provided the bulk of new jobs. Here, there is some limited hope in Russia for there has been a burgeoning of new businesses, most started by the young. But this has met strong resistance from the middle-aged and elderly population, schooled in hatred of such enterprise, and among the less educated and less capable.

A strong legal system is an essential aspect of the system. Without such a legal system, capitalism cannot flourish because risk taking becomes prohibitively expensive. In the United States defense of private property and creation of a strong legal code has been an integral part of the system from the beginning. The Constitution forms the very core of the American system, making us a government of laws and not men. Unfortunately, the FSU is very weak in this area. The Soviet Union was a government of men, a government of the Party, and not a government of laws. In a Communist system the rights of private property were severely limited. Even now to create the necessary corpus of laws and to encourage respect for private property will be the work of a generation. In the interim, its absence is a severe limitation on the creation of a capitalist system and the importation of foreign capital. The new Constitution may provide some of the answer, but undoubtedly not all of it.

A seventh key element is the existence of a good infrastructure for industrial and capitalist development. Here the record is decidedly mixed. The Soviet economy was very advanced in heavy industry, with modern techniques and massive production of industrial staples. In the 1980s Soviet research and development accounted for an impressive 18 percent of world spending.[20] However, factories were often antiquated, safety protection rare to nonexistent, road transportation poor and irregular, the banking system ineffective, and modern telecommunications weak (telephones) to unknown (fax, computers, fiberoptic cables). Creation of a modern infrastructure, especially given the massive environmental degradation that must be repaired, will be enormously expensive. At the same time, the lack of many aspects of a modern infrastructure will hamper the creation of a modern capitalist economy. It will cost hundreds of billions of dollars, if not trillions of dollars, to fully modernize the lagging infrastructure. Where the money will come from remains a mystery.

An eighth factor is popular acceptance of the free market orientation of the regime. This is not even an issue in the West, but large elements of the population of the FSU reject capitalism. Support is limited to those isolated elements of the population who hope to benefit from such a regime or who believe in it ideologically.

A ninth factor in early capitalist success has been a limitation on the size and power of trade unions. The economic justification has been the need to retain substantial profits for reinvestment to develop international competitiveness and build a capitalist culture. The American and Japanese experiences have both reinforced the notion of the importance of maintaining firm control over the trade union movement. Yet in the FSU the rights of trade unions were

[20]John Nagle, *Introduction to Comparative Politics*, Nelson Hall, Chicago, 1993, p. 303.

trumpeted and the importance of organization of the defense of the working men hailed in theory, if not in practice.

Most successful capitalist states early on restrained social welfare spending. In the United States social security was introduced only in the 1930s and Medicare and Medicaid in the 1960s. State spending on social welfare was held down to maximize the role of investment and profits in the private sector. Yet the FSU was the welfare state par excellence, with massive subsidies of consumer and food items, cradle to grave social security, subsidized rents, and free transportation. The reduction of this welfare state will be an economically necessary, but politically unpopular, first step on the road to successful capitalism.

Overall, then, the bulk of the prerequisites for capitalism are not present in Russia. They are even less present in the economically more retarded Transcaucasus and Central Asia.

RUSSIAN EXPERIENCE WITH CAPITALISM AND ECONOMIC DEVELOPMENT

The lack of Russian historical experience with capitalism presents a serious obstacle to the creation of Russian capitalism. While Western Europe was developing a vigorous capitalism and strong bourgeoisie since the early fifteenth century, Tsarist Russia, in Richard Pipes's words, lagged far behind with a bourgeoisie so "small and inconsequential" as to be "insignificant" and "missing" from the pages of history.[21] Western notions of law, private property, and personal freedom were alien to Tsarist Russia. After a brief flirtation with capitalism in the final decade under the Tsar, Russia, after a short interlude in the 1920s, eliminated capitalism for the next sixty years.

The Mongol occupation in the thirteenth century cut Russia off from the West for over 200 years and destroyed any nascent roots of mercantile capitalism.[22] After the Mongol era, the despotic and expansionist Tsars from the fifteenth to seventeenth centuries rigorously suppressed any capitalist tendencies. They claimed absolute political power and imposed royal monopolies on all profitable enterprises. The Tsars were the number one owner of mines, industry, and land. When cities like Novgorod and Pskov were conquered, the Tsars liquidated their liberties and turned them into military-administrative outposts.

Early industrialization from the seventeenth century on brought no introduction of capitalism. The Tsars turned to Western capitalists to build and operate the plants, which were run without Russian managers. Peter the Great in the early eighteenth century continued the tradition with the use of serfs as workers. In this "traditional" industrialization so alien to Western capitalism,

---

[21]Richard Pipes, *Russia Under the Old Regime*, Charles Scribner, New York, 1974, chapter 8, p. 151.
[22]See Pipes, *Russia Under the Old Regime*, chapter 8, for the ensuing discussion of the history of capitalism in Tsarist Russia.

the state owned the means of production, set the price and absorbed nearly all the output; the management was on good behavior; the working force was enserfed. Assured of bonded labor and a market, the state-appointed state-licensed enterprises had no incentive to rationalize production. In short, though there was industry under Peter, there was no industrial capitalism.[23]

When Peter III and Catherine the Great in 1762 eliminated the right of merchants to own serfs, they dealt a further blow to nascent capitalism. For peasants using serf labor would provide a potent challenge to the already weakened urban merchants, now deprived of access to cheap labor.

By the beginning of the nineteenth century Russia lagged behind the West. Her cities were small administrative outposts, not thriving commercial centers. The merchants, deeply influenced by oriental trade, wore oriental clothes and maintained an oriental style of life. Pipes has analyzed the failure of mercantile capitalism by 1800:

> The Russian merchant had no knowledge of that whole elaborate structure of commerce on which Western European wealth was built. He was usually illiterate and even if he knew how to read and write, he usually had no idea of how to keep account of books, preferring to rely on memory. . . . Risk capital, the sinew of capitalist development, was absent.[24]

Trade fairs, phased out in Western Europe after the Middle Ages, persisted as important to business until the 1880s. Russian credit transactions by barter with little money were conducted as late as 1850 as business had been conducted in the Middle Ages in Western Europe.

The situation was little better in the countryside. Rather than commercial agriculture, Russian agriculture from the sixteenth century on was built on massive enslavement of the population. Impoverished serfs formed 50 percent of the population in 1800, 38 percent in 1860. Forced to bow and kowtow to their superiors, without legally recognized personal rights, socially segregated from the rest of the population, the serfs were known as the "dark people"—a medieval element surviving into the dawning of the modern era. They were strongly anticapitalist. As for the nobles, they held their land at the sufferance of the Tsars and did not form an independent landed aristocracy on the English model. Mostly impoverished, with a few very rich families, reliant on the crown to suppress peasant revolts and give them estates, detached from the land and often living in the cities, they had no corporate spirit and could not prevent the Tsars from implementing hostile policies like the 1861 emancipation of serfs.[25]

As for the state, by 1850 it was ever more anticapitalist. The government controlled the main forces of production, preventing the emergence of an urban bourgeoisie or commercial landed aristocracy. Private wealth was a function of government favor and reward. The government played on popular hostility to

[23]Pipes, *Russia Under the Old Regime,* p. 211.
[24]Pipes, *Russia Under the Old Regime,* p. 207.
[25]Karl Wittfogel, *Oriental Despotism,* Yale University Press, New Haven, 1957, p. 278.

capitalism. The institutional prerequisites for capitalism were absent in the Russian state of 1850. Instead there was a weak, primitive, venal, nonmodernizing bureaucracy based on a closed hereditary caste, a servile judiciary, mass censorship, and a state claiming absolute power.[26] The forces of Western European capitalism, heir to the Renaissance and Enlightenment, were largely lost to Tsarist Russia.

During the last sixty years of Tsarism, some progress was made to eliminate obstacles to capitalism. The government, under severe military pressure from the West and Japan, sought rapid industrialization. In 1861 the serfs of Russia were finally freed and given some rights. In the 1880s the state pursued a relatively successful policy of rapid industrialization. After the 1905 Revolution, the October Manifesto guaranteed basic civil liberties, provided for the creation of political parties and a parliament, known as the Duma. After 1907 the Stolypin plan allowed the peasants to leave the communes and own their land in one consolidated plot. By 1915 the majority of peasants in European Russia held land in hereditary tenure.[27]

Yet all these steps, desirable as they were, were far too little and too late. From 1861 to 1907 the peasants, forced to remain on the commune, legally segregated and bound to pay high redemption dues to the landlords, were not a capitalist element. The landlords retained most meadows, forests, and most of the land. Bound to the commune, without land tenure or full civil rights, subjected to heavy taxes and periodic redistribution of the land, the peasants remained a rebellious and impoverished neofeudal mass. Only after 1907 were peasants finally allowed to be capitalist farmers, but even by 1915 almost half were still in the communes and 90 percent had failed to consolidate their plots. In 1917, as in 1905, a disgruntled peasantry enthusiastically participated in large-scale revolts against the existing order.[28]

Nor was the rapid industrialization after the 1880s capitalist. Run heavily with foreign management, money, and technology and under the control of the Russian state, the weak Russian bourgeoisie played a small role. In 1917 foreigners accounted for 33 percent of industrial investment and 50 percent of bank capital. Politically impotent, tied to the state, the weak bourgeoisie played only a small role in 1905 and was inactive after 1917.[29]

The Bolsheviks, deeply anticapitalist, routed the remaining merchants and capitalists in the Civil War. In the early 1930s they liquidated the capitalists as a class, eliminated rural kulaks, and nationalized over 97 percent of all the means of production. Only during the New Economic Program (1921–1928) retreat was some capitalism allowed, with private retail trade and a landowning peasantry selling grain on the open market. But the NEP was a brief interlude, during which the state still regulated the economy and ran large-scale industry. As with the few years of Tsarism after 1907 ended by the onset

[26]Pipes, *Russia Under the Old Regime,* chapters 10, 11.
[27]Theodore von Laue, *Why Lenin? Why Stalin?* J.B. Lippincott, Philadelphia, 1971, p. 55.
[28]von Laue, *Why Lenin? Why Stalin?* pp. 25–55.
[29]Pipes, *Russia Under the Old Regime,* chapter 8.

of war in 1914, this Soviet flirtation with aspects of capitalism was brief and ended violently sixty-five years ago with the onset of Stalinism.

RUSSIAN ATTITUDES TOWARDS CAPITALISM

Given the wide public acceptance of capitalism in the West, it perhaps comes as a shock to realize that broad segments of the Russian public do not approve of capitalism. The lack of any serious socialist or Communist party in the United States and the isolation of the United States from the European socialist experiences have conditioned Americans to see capitalism as universally approved. However, a broader look at the world scene can lead us to different conclusions. Even in capitalist Western Europe strong anticapitalist movements have recurrently been popular. Fascism, which fed off the resentment of the inequities of capitalism, triumphed in Italy in 1922, Germany in 1933, Spain in 1939, and France (after the German victory) in 1940. After World War II and the disappearance of fascism everywhere but on the Iberian peninsula, a strong anticapitalist Communist movement flourished in France and in Italy. Only in recent years has the anticapitalist banner grown less popular.

Elsewhere in the world capitalism has been seen as more of a North Atlantic phenomenon than a successful world-wide movement. Until 1991 Communist movements predominated in the Soviet Union and Eastern Europe and still dominate China, Vietnam, and North Korea in Asia.[30] In much of the Third World various forms of authoritarianism and military rule and neosocialist movements have been the norm. Only in the past few years has capitalism gained popularity in the Third World.

In this context, the strong antipathy towards capitalism in much of Russia is more understandable. In November 1992 more people were opposed to a capitalist economy than in favor of one in Russia, Ukraine, and Belarus, with the gap between opponents and supporters reaching as high as 24 percent in Belarus, 12 percent in Ukraine, and 7 percent in Russia. The great problems of creating a capitalist economy, with inflation and unemployment, have not aided matters.[31] Without any strong tradition of native capitalism, Tsarist Russia for centuries branded capitalism as a Western perversion irrelevant to the trinity of nationalism, autocracy, and orthodoxy. Even the strong industrial development of the last forty years of Tsarist Russia was done under the auspices of the state, not indigenous capitalism. As for the Soviet Union, for seventy-four years capitalism was repeatedly branded as the source of all evil in the world, as the fountainhead of racism, imperialism, and poverty. Isolated from the rest of the world for three generations until the late 1980s, Russians were inevitably influenced by incessant Soviet Communist propaganda.

It is hard to identify many elements of Russian society supportive of

---

[30]Interestingly, capitalism has become quite strong in China and is growing in Vietnam.
[31]Mark Rhodes, "The FSU and the Future: Facing Uncertainty," *RFE/RL Research Report*, vol. 2, no. 24, June 11, 1993.

capitalist development. The massive dislocation of transition from communism to capitalism will create a "generation of the desert" that will wander for forty years and, like Moses, never enter the Promised Land. For the great majority of the old order, the costs will be great and the benefits few. For the 17 million bureaucrats and government administrators associated with a command economy, the transition to capitalism will cost many their jobs and benefit only the young, well educated, and hard working. For the 2.5 million bureaucrats administering planned agriculture, the change will be simply disastrous. For the 3 million men in the Russian armed forces and the half million men in the secret police, the future is bleak in a world in which the capitalist West is no longer their enemy. For the tens of millions of blue-collar workers, ensured in the past of livelihood and security despite their work performance, the future is even bleaker if job retention depends on their tenuous ability to survive in a competitive international capitalist environment. The popular attitude of Russians is positive towards making money but negative towards a capitalist system that seems likely to produce unemployment, poverty, and marginality in a new world economy.

EASTERN EUROPEAN EXPERIENCE WITH CAPITALISM

There are no historical cases of the transformation of Communist centrally planned economies into capitalist market economies. Even the Eastern European economies, now undergoing the same process at the same time, possess serious differences from the Soviet economy. Geographically and demographically, the seven former Communist satellite regimes of Eastern Europe (Poland, Hungary, the Czech Republic, Slovakia, East Germany, Bulgaria, and Romania) have only 35 percent of the population and 6 percent of the land mass of the FSU. Only East Germany (which has now vanished into a unified Germany) and Czechoslovakia (which has divided into two states) had a high level of industrialization comparable to that of the Soviet Union. Bulgaria and Rumania were comparatively less developed. The Soviet Union voluntarily entered into central planning in 1930, but the Eastern European states did so only under Soviet prodding in the 1950s.

And yet the Eastern European experience is sufficiently close to that of the Soviet Union to merit attention. The Soviet centrally planned economy—strong central direction, minimal private sector, political monopoly of the party, extensive policy-induced economic distortions and imbalances, stress on industry, and neglect of consumer goods—was largely replicated in Eastern Europe for forty years. The Russian per capita GNP of 3200 dollars is similar to that of Czechoslovakia and Hungary. State enterprises in the Soviet Union provided 96 percent of the value added in the economy—compared to 97 percent in Czechoslovakia, 86 percent in Hungary, 82 percent in Poland, 11 percent in Great Britain, and 1 percent in the United States. Like Poland and Hungary, the Soviet Union suffered heavily in the World War II. Like most of Eastern Europe, its economic growth rate, once booming, turned flat in the 1980s with shortages, weak technical change, low quality goods, obsolete infrastructure, and heavy pollution. By the end of the 1980s the Western European countries, which had three times the per capita GNP of Eastern Europe in 1937, now had six times. Weak services, limited shopping, ubiquitous public transportation, and vast apartment blocs testified to a lack of consumerism.[32]

The future course remains dangerous in Eastern Europe as in the FSU. The old system there too has vanished but left behind many problems. As Friedrick Levcik and Zdenek Lukas recently wrote about the dismal legacy of former Czechoslovakia:

> The system has left the economy with numerous adverse features: high production costs, distorted cost and price relations, a non-convertible currency with unrealistic exchange rates, over investment in basic and heavy industries, delays in completing buildings and installations, neglect of infrastructure, environmental problems and an underdeveloped service sector.[33]

The economic problems that helped promote the disintegration of Communism in Eastern Europe and the Soviet Union within two years of each other have intensified the difficulties of transition to capitalism. These new problems of the 1980s included the enhanced efficiency of the West after the oil shocks of the 1970s, major Western technological breakthroughs in telecommunications and computer science, and increased dependence of Eastern Europe on the West through reliance on Western imports and debts owed to Western banks. Yet the past, as with the Soviet Union, is ever with us. As Pavel Dembrinski has written on the planned economy:

> Thus, even though the CPE [centrally planned economy] system as such has ceased to exist in Eastern Europe, it remains present in the form of its surviving components. These components are profoundly conditioned by their political origins, by the logic and needs of the CPE system which governed them for the previous 40 years. That is why the replacement of a Marxist creed by a liberal one is merely the beginning of the process of transition to a market economic system—it is not the process itself. Recasting the economic system involves shifting from overall economic logic based on central planning to logic based on the market, and transforming the former components of the old system to make them compatible with new rules. The process requires time.[34]

But how to construct capitalism when a collapsed state is asked to create a whole new socio-political-economic order? And how to implant "capitalism from above" when capitalism is an evolutionary, not revolutionary, creed?

---

[32]David Turnock, *Eastern Europe: An Economic and Political Geography,* Routledge, London, 1989, chapter 1; Vittorio Corbo, Fabrizio Coricelli, Jan Bossak, editors, *Reforming Central and East European Economies: Initial Results and Challenges,* World Bank, Washington, D.C., 1991, pp. 18–68; and Alan Gelb and Cheryl Grey, "The Transformation of Economies in Central and Eastern Europe: Issues, Progress and Prospects," *Policy Research Series,* no. 17, World Bank, Washington, D.C., 1991, pp. 39, 65.

[33]Friedrick Levcik and Zdenek Lukas, "Czechoslovakia: Changes in Economic Practice Lag Behind Rhetoric," in Peter Havlik, editor, *Dismantling the Command Economy in Eastern Europe,* Westview Press, Boulder, 1991, pp. 173–174.

[34]Pavel Dembrinski, *The Logic of the Planned Economy: The Seeds of the Collapse,* Oxford University Press, Oxford, 1991.

The main debate in Eastern Europe, as in the FSU, has been between the gradualists and the radicals. The gradualists, fearing social upheaval and economic chaos if changes are made too quickly, have in Hungary, Bulgaria, and Rumania developed a slow sequenced introduction of economic reform. The radicals, triumphing in Poland (and in East Germany, with rapid integration into a unified Germany), have pushed for a "big bang" approach to economic reform. As Nobel Prize winner Wassily Leontieff argued in 1990:

> A market economy is a very complicated one and it cannot function well if all its different parts are not aligned to each other properly. Replacing the four tires on a car with tires of different designs, gradually one at a time, would unbalance the vehicle and land it in a ditch. The new tires will have to be mounted all at once.[35]

They argue that slow reforms, as in the former Czechoslovakia, will become no reforms as conservatives strangle reforms with the support of a populace tiring of reform.

All economies need to achieve the proper sequencing of four difficult tasks: attaining macroeconomic stability, redefining the role of the state, liberalizing the economy, and restructuring ownership. The results so far? Some slow progress but at a high economic cost. In the Eastern European countries most involved in the transition, the economies were sliding into recession in 1989, declined 8 percent in GDP in 1990, fell another 8 percent in 1991, and fell still another 8 percent in 1992. The United Nations Commission on Europe warns of a depression in much of Eastern Europe, especially with industrial production down 17 percent in 1991 and 11 percent in 1992.[36]

Clearly, "disappointment and bitterness" have replaced the earlier "euphoria" as "hopes fade for a quick transition to a market economy. The problems Eastern Europeans now face are far more difficult than anything they could imagine two years ago."[37] World Bank studies now project that it will take the northern sector of Eastern Europe until 1996 and the Southern sector until 2000 just to regain the meager per capita GNP of 1989. Further harmed by the collapse of the Soviet Union and by less foreign investments than expected, the problems of economic backwardness, limited investment capability, and political resistance to change will require decades to overcome.[38] One observer of the transition from command to market economy has recently written, "The [re]construction of markets in Eastern Europe, however, is obstructed by nearly insurmountable difficulties; it is a nearly impossible task."[39]

---

[35]Wassily Leontif, "Some Soviet Lessons," *Challenge,* September–October 1990, p. 19.

[36]Lief Rosenberger, "Economic Transition in Eastern Europe: Paying the Price for Freedom," *Eastern Europe Quarterly,* vol. 26, no. 3, September 1992, p. 26; Corbo et al., *Reforming Central and Eastern European Economies,* pp. 18–19.

[37]Rosenberger, "Economic Transition in Eastern Europe: Paying the Price for Freedom," *Eastern Europe Quarterly,* p. 261.

[38]Gelb and Grey, "The Transformation of Economies in Central and Eastern Europe: Issues, Progress and Prospects," *Policy Research Series,* p. 7.

[39]Raymond Dietz, "From Command to Exchange Economies," in Havlik, *Dismantling the Command Economy in Eastern Europe,* p. 33.

There are first tentative signs of success in Eastern Europe by 1993. The northern three states of Eastern Europe (Hungary, Poland, and the Czech Republic) seem to have stabilized. Industrial production has stopped falling and the GDP shows signs of upturns at 82 to 84 percent of the level of 1987. Small-scale enterprises are flourishing by the thousands. Trade has been reoriented to the European Community, which now accounts for 55 percent of Polish trade and 35 to 40 percent for Hungary and the Czech Republic. Foreign investment now tops 2.5 billion dollars in Hungary and 1.5 billion dollars in the Czech Republic. Hungary and Poland have each privatized 10 percent of state enterprises, with more to come, while the Czech Republic auctioned off 31,000 enterprises. However, Rumania, Bulgaria, and Slovakia remain in the slow lane with almost 40 percent drops in GDP, slower reform moves, and little evidence of upturn.[40]

A short-term dark future and somewhat brighter long-term future for Eastern Europe does not bode well for the FSU. The lower debt and greater natural resources of the FSU are more than outweighed by a higher level of consumerism in Hungary and the Czech Republic, and likely association with the European Community by the end of the decade. These are but distant dreams for Moscow, Kiev, and Minsk, let alone for Tashkent or Dushanbe.

COSTS: MILITARY RECONVERSION OF DISTORTED ECONOMY

The FSU was a First World superpower in the sophisticated military arena, which ate up enormous resources, perhaps 25 percent of the GNP, compared to 6 percent in the United States and 1 percent in Japan. While the military-industrial complex in the United States hired 10 to 20 percent of all engineers and scientists, in the Soviet Union it absorbed 60 to 80 percent of them. This created a distorted economy, with sophisticated military goods and primitive consumer goods. The problems of reconversion are manifold.

The military-industrial sector, together with natural resources, provided over 80 percent of Russian hard currency exports. With oil production declining and a weak world commodity market for Russian natural resources, the 2 to 3 billion dollars brought in by military exports are vital to the economy.

Overly massive reduction of the Russian military would eliminate Russia as a great power. Since it is not competitive in the economic or political arena, the military sector remains the only sector in which Russia engages the attention of the world. Too massive a reduction in this sector would push Russia to the periphery of world politics and further lessen the international desire to help Russia. Military exports also buy influence in the world: Any massive reduction would also reduce the power of Russian foreign policy, as in the Middle East.

A major reduction in the size of the Russian military might be counterproductive to Russian national interest. There are genuine security threats to

---

[40]*Economist,* December 19, 1992.

Russia in the nearby unstable Middle East and parts of Asia (especially China). There is civil war in Yugoslavia and breakup in Czechoslovakia; several civil wars are brewing on the Russian periphery. The friendly intentions of newly emerging countries, such as Ukraine and Belarus, let alone the Central Asian republics, cannot be taken for granted, given past enmities and hatreds. The position of 25 million Russians abroad may need to be protected. A force of 2 to 3 million soldiers may be important inside Russia in maintaining stability in the face of economic unrest and political upheaval. The military, although likely to be reduced, remains important in maintaining order at home and security abroad.

COSTS: EAST GERMAN AND ISRAELI EXPERIENCE

The cases of Israel and East Germany may provide some clues as to the true cost of successful capitalist development. The East German case is relevant as a former Communist state being rapidly absorbed into a highly prosperous West Germany. Israel is relevant for having absorbed over 650,000 Soviet Jews who arrived from the FSU in the 1970s and early 1990s. Of course, there are problems with both cases. East Germans are not Russians and the 16 million East Germans are an order of magnitude smaller than 145 million Russians. Soviet Jews were atypical for the Soviet population. They were better educated, totally urban, and better off than the average Soviet citizen. Emigrants are more highly motivated than those left behind and often have relatives to help them in Israel. Israel, with a public sector employing 30 percent of the work force, retains socialist elements in a capitalist economy.

East Germany is a troubling warning case for those who think transition to capitalism can be anything but lengthy and extremely costly. When the Wall came down between the two Germanies in October 1990, West German Chancellor Helmut Kohl was quite optimistic about a rapid transition to capitalism and prosperity in the east in only three or four years. True, the gap was enormous, with West Germans earning almost four times as much as East Germans. Yet surely, with strong West German help, the gap could be bridged quickly. After all, East Germans were still Germans, weren't they? And didn't the free entry of East German goods in the 1980s into West Germany mean that East German goods were at or near the world standard?

By 1993 the situation looked very different. East German industry turned out to be far more antiquated and polluting than anyone had dreamed. The transition to capitalism now seemed likely to take ten to twenty years, not three or four years, despite the privatization of 11,000 enterprises for 25 billion dollars. A *New York Times* correspondent in the spring of 1993 described the former East Germany as

> a bleak landscape . . . dotted with rusting shells of ailing steel, textile and chemical plants; crisscrossed by potholed roads and smeared with competing graffiti exhorting people to combat or to join neo-Nazi movements spawned by

economic resentment. . . . Extraordinary in scope, ominous in implication, the collapse of the industrial tissue of what was East Germany now seems certain to weigh on the entire German economy, and all of Europe, for much of this decade.[41]

The old adage that "only Germans can make Stalinism work" seemed to belong to another century. Two generations of socialism produced a different mindset in the east than in the west. The entrepreneurial spirit seemed moribund, if not quite extinguished. Emigration in the 1950s of 3 million Germans to the west had drained the pond of much of its vitality. And further emigration to western Germany threatened to make economic recovery even more hopeless. Including early retirees, those engaged in make-work, and those forced to work in West Germany, 45 percent of the East German work force was unemployed. East German industrial production by 1993 dropped a staggering 70 percent from 1990 and productivity was one-third the level in West Germany. Even worse, the cost to the government became staggering: not just 100 billion dollars a year for a year or two but seemingly for the rest of the decade. In 1992 and 1993 alone the total cost was estimated at 242 billion dollars.[42] As Richard Gardner, an executive with Deutsche Bank in Berlin, declared, "Nobody imagined anything on this scale. The more we looked at the eastern part of the country, the more decrepit we realized it really was."[43] Tens of billions of dollars of private investment would be needed yearly as well. The cost of rebuilding infrastructure and starting up new plants and services could amount to 400 to 700 billion dollars by the year 2000.

The lessons for Russia seemed sobering. Projecting such a cost for Russia would mean expenditures of astronomical sums, perhaps 3 to 5 trillion dollars. Too, Russia is more backward than East Germany, and far more geographically dispersed. For the entire FSU the cost would be 10 to 15 trillion dollars. Furthermore, even with the money, the level of disruption in East Germany was awesome. What Russian government could tolerate one-third to one-half of the work force unemployed? The political consequences would be impossible.

Even worse, the money is unavailable. Western aid in the 1990s will probably total a few billion dollars, or at most a few tens of billions of dollars.[44] And, with foreign investment remaining at less than 1 billion dollars in the last three years (compared to 50 billion dollars committed to China since 1978), external sources seem hopeless. Internal sources are inadequate even to maintain the Russian budget, which runs a massive deficit of 10 to 20 percent of GNP.

The Israeli lesson seems no more hopeful. By the late 1990s Israel will probably have absorbed upwards of 1 million Soviet Jews. By the end of 1993

---

[41]*The New York Times,* March 8, 1993, p. C1.

[42]Over 70 percent of this cost went for various income schemes and not directly for investment.

[43]*New York Times,* March 8, 1993, p. C1.

[44]Much of the vast sums of Western aid reported in the press go for debt relief or ruble stabilization schemes, and do not directly invest in the FSU economy.

almost 500,000 Soviet Jews will have arrived since 1990. The Israeli government is floating a 10 billion-dollar loan (with American loan guarantees) to help pay for their absorption. In addition, the government is budgeting 2 to 4 billion dollars a year to pay for other costs. The total costs of absorbing 1 million Soviet Jews in a Westernized First World economy (but at the bottom of the First World economically) is estimated at 25 to 40 billion dollars. Here too, despite the money, one-third of Soviet immigrants are unemployed. Only 12 percent of Soviet Jewish scientists and academics have found comparable work in Israel.[45] Apartments for Soviet Jews, currently about 50 to 60 square meters, would probably be considered unacceptable in most of the West.

Extrapolating this data to Russia, we arrive at a figure of 2 to 5 trillion dollars, very close to what we found for East Germany. For all the FSU this would come to 5 to 15 trillion dollars. And this is for absorbing Soviet Jews, whose level of education (40 percent university graduates) was far higher than that of the Russian population in general (9 percent university graduates), who were almost totally urbanized (one-third of the Russian population is still rural), and whose drive to succeed and capability to function in a world economy were undoubtedly higher than that of the Russian population as a whole.

The political problems with these two groups, East Germans and Soviet Jews, were quite serious, even though they were far better situated to integrate into the world economy than most Russians or non-Russians. East Germans were vocal in large-scale demonstrations against the pace of change. No less than 40 percent of the nearly 2000 attacks on foreign migrants in Germany in 1992 occurred in the east and not the west of Germany. The far-right neo-Nazi National Party seemed to flourish particularly amidst the despair in the east. Hundreds of thousands of East Germans continued to migrate to the West. In Israel, Soviet Jews, despite their antipathy towards socialism, voted heavily in 1992 for the Labor Party out of protest against their treatment by the ruling Likud Party. The despair and bitterness at the largely negative impact of emigration and their downward social mobility fueled resentment against the ruling parties in both Germany and Israel.[46] Within the FSU this would provide the fuel for authoritarian parties of the Right and Left opposed to reform itself.

There is one sign of hope. In both cases capitalism will ultimately triumph. In East Germany the process is slow and inordinately expensive but by early in the twenty-first century East Germany should be making the transition toward

---

[45]*Jerusalem Post*, March 6, 1993. This pattern is not simply due to the limited absorption capacity of the small Israeli economy, with its population of 5 million people. In the United States conversations with social workers dealing with Soviet Jewish immigrants in Denver and Chicago reveal a similar pattern of roughly one-half of Soviet immigrants failing to find more than menial or low-paid work (average of 13,000 dollars per year), and one-sixth winding up on welfare. Some of the problem is that of age or language, but the trend is still strikingly similar.

[46]The author, who lived in Israel from October 1990 to January 1991, on several occasions heard repeated stories of despair, weariness, and even hopelessness as Soviet immigrants struggled to cope with a Westernized system and society.

a profitable, free market, capitalist economy. In Israel, the 170,000 Soviet Jews from the 1970s became a relatively comfortable, middle-class element within Israeli society in ten to twenty years. There is no reason to doubt that their equally talented and capable brethren from the 1990s will be able to do the same by early in the next century.

The problem is the interim political and economic cost where there is no big brother, no West Germany, and no Israel to spend enormous resources on their eastern relatives. For Germany and for Israel this price is 6 to 10 percent of their GNP a year for a number of years. No one can or will do this in the east for the vast bulk of the Russian and non-Russian population.

COSTS: EXPERIENCE OF EARLY CAPITALISM

Looking at the great wealth created by modern advanced capitalism, many observers have tended to forget the high cost of early capitalist development and the protracted nature of this painful experience. Modern Western capitalism built on roughly four centuries of precapitalist (largely mercantile) development that laid the basis for the industrial capitalist surge from 1820 until today. The experience of American and British capitalism of the early and middle nineteenth century seems to be so remote as to belong to another place and another time. Yet while part of the pain was caused not by capitalism but by early industrialization—a phase which Russia passed through in the 1930s— much of it was specific to capitalism. In the extraordinarily competitive international capitalist economy of the twenty-first century, a capitalist FSU would not be able to escape much of the *angst* of early capitalism.[47]

Successful early industrial capitalism is built around sacrifice, savings, hard work, and a decline in the standard of living (Kuznet's inverted U-shaped curve). Recurrent business recessions and panics, rampant exploitation of the workers, rising inequality, unemployment, and significant environmental pollution are the order of the day.

Early English capitalist development in the Industrial Revolution after 1790 produced truly shocking conditions in the first half of the nineteenth century. William Blake denounced the "dark satanic mills," and Alexis de Tocqueville in 1835 spoke of a "damp, dark labyrinth."[48] Charles Dickens drew devastating and graphic portraits of what capitalism had wrought. In *A Tale of Two Cities* Dickens declaimed:

> The darkness of it was heavy—cold, dirt, sickness, ignorance and want were the lords in waiting on the saintly presence. . . . The mill which had worked

---

[47]This can be seen today in Vietnam where workers routinely work fifty-four hours a week under terrible conditions, without vacations or the right to strike, for as little as twenty-three dollars a month.

[48]Steven Marcus, *Engels, Manchester and the English Working Class*, Random House, New York, 1974, p. 64.

them down was the mill that grinds young people old; the children had ancient faces and grave voices; and ploughed into every furrow of age and coming up afresh was a sign, Hunger. It was prevalent everywhere.[49]

The price of England's rise to industrial predominance in the world by 1850 was high. In 1850 English farm laborers, despite poorer nutrition and wages, lived longer than industrial workers. In Manchester in 1842 the average urban laborer died at seventeen while the average gentry died at thirty-eight and rural laborers in Rutland lived to thirty-eight. Horrible work conditions, dreadful housing and sanitation, terrible filth, and massive overcrowding in squalid slums next to smelling rivers and open sewers took their toll. Despite fifty years of industrial capitalism, English industrial workers in 1850 lived on the point of subsistence, little better-off than in 1800, in wretched conditions. Massive exploitation of child labor for ten to sixteen hours a day produced a child mortality rate of 50 percent in Manchester.[50]

Nor were American conditions much better. Capitalist development in the North coincided until 1860 with that "peculiar institution" of slavery (with 4 million slaves) in the South. By 1850 skilled laborers, making 250 dollars a year in New York, received less than 50 percent of what *The New York Daily Tribune* thought would provide a family subsistence level. Day laborers were making less than 200 dollars a year, when work was available. Many were reduced to scavenging for food, begging for money, and stealing. Even in the late 1880s, 40 percent of the American working class lived in poverty. Families lived in cheap tenements, singles in coal cellars and flophouses. Poor nutrition, congestion, and bad sanitation contributed to a high mortality rate. The conditions of the masses of new immigrants flooding into America's cities was appalling.[51]

Nor was suffering confined to Anglo-American capitalism of the nineteenth century. The glittering facades of high-rise buildings in Hong Kong, Seoul, and Taipei mask serious urban poverty. Three decades after the start of the "Korean miracle," workers toil fifty-six hours a week while one-third of the population lives in one room and another third in two rooms. Recurrent labor unrest and serious street violence mirror the turbulence of the harsh early phases of industrial capitalism.

Only in the "cargo cults" of remote South Pacific islands is prosperity dropped from the sky. In the blood, sweat, and tears of early capitalist development, the pain and sacrifice is all too evident. For a country like the FSU that has gone through two devastating wars (Civil War and World War II) and

[49]Charles Dickens, *A Tale of Two Cities*, Penguin Books, London, 1985, p. 61.

[50]E.P. Thompson, *The Making of the English Working Class*, Vintage Books, New York, 1966, pp. 209, 318–330; John Rule, *The Laboring Classes in Early Industrial England 1750–1850*, Longman, London and New York, 1986, pp. 145–146, chapter 3.

[51]Louis Hacker, *The Triumph of American Capitalism*, Columbia University Press, New York, 1940, p. 277; and Ira Katznelson and Aristide Zolberg, editors, *Working Class Formation*, Princeton University Press, Princeton, 1986, pp. 206–207.

Stalinism, the question remains how much people are willing to sacrifice for individual prosperity that may take two generations to achieve.

COSTS: EMIGRATION

Immigration and emigration have greatly influenced economic growth. The massive immigration of 52 million Europeans helped change the United States from a small country of 4 million people with a modest economy in 1790 to a superpower with 250 million people in 1990 in an advanced postindustrial society. Massive European immigration helped create a modern Canada of 25 million people and Australia of 16 million people. Even now, these flows of people continue: The United States takes in over 700,000 legal immigrants a year.

But emigration can deal crippling blows to the economy of a country. The forced expulsion of several hundred thousand Jews and Moslems from a newly unified Spain in 1492 helped contribute to the ultimate decline of Spain, one only temporarily alleviated by the discovery of gold and silver in the New World in the sixteenth century. The large-scale emigration of German intellectuals during the Hitler era in Germany helped both speed the loss of Germany's intellectual predominance in the world and raise that of the United States to new heights. Numbers alone are not all that matters; so too does the quality of the emigration.

What then are the prospects for emigration? The vast majority of the population of the FSU have no prospects of emigrating in a world increasingly intolerant of immigrants. The American quota of 60,000 visas a year is unlikely to grow due to intense pressures from other parts of the world. The majority of 6 million Germans, Poles, and Jews will emigrate to Germany, Poland, Israel, and the United States. Hundreds of thousands, perhaps a million, well-educated Russians and Ukrainians will emigrate to Europe and the United States in the next decade. With 3000 top Russian scientists already in the United States and more on the way, this could be a major loss to future scientific research and development.

Another form of emigration may be within the FSU, where 25 million Russians live outside of Russia and another 35 million non-Russians live outside their ethnic homelands. With surging ethnic and national sentiments in the non-Russian republics, the eventual emigration of millions of people, especially Russians, is likely, and indeed it already has begun. While the drive for "ethnic purity" resounds within newly independent states, the consequences for capitalist development are serious. Just as with the loss of Jews and other minorities and intelligentsia elements, the loss of the largely better-educated and more technologically oriented Russians will further hamper attempts to develop capitalism in these regions.

Emigration will affect critical elements that possess the skills, talents, and drive to make a major contribution to any effort to make Russia and the other republics competitive in the international marketplace. The most cosmopolitan elements are exactly the ones most likely to leave. Their loss will further set back development, with countries like the United States and Israel the likely gainers from Russia's loss.[52]

Only in Russia and the Baltics has there been any concerted drive towards capitalism and away from socialism. The other republics remain mired in the dreadful legacy of moribund central planning. Yeltsin and his government have taken Western advice and launched many programs vital to the creation of a capitalist market and dissolution of a central socialist planned economy. The Russian government has lifted most price controls, encouraged mass privatization of government enterprises, favored family farms, strived to make the ruble fully convertible, promoted various forms of markets, and tried to raise energy and fuel prices to the world market level.

The results of radical reformism have been so disastrous as to justify pessimistic conclusions about the Russian road to capitalism. By 1993 Russia was mired in a depression with GNP having fallen a stunning 40 percent from 1990 (although some of this represents the elimination of unwanted industrial and military capacity). Real income of Russians has been halved in two years and real capital investment plummeted by 40 percent. By 1993 Russia was on the verge of hyperinflation, with Russian printing presses working twenty-four hours a day, seven days a week. Western investment was minimal, foreign exports and imports were sliding sharply, interrepublic trade was in sharp decline, and the budget deficit was equal to 10 to 20 percent of GNP.[53]

The massive decline in the Russian economy reflected the enormous problems of transition from a socialist command economy to a capitalist market economy and problems associated with the end of a Stalinist economy. The Russian economy lacks real commercial banks, a fully convertible ruble, meaningful reform of agro-industry, bankruptcy legislation, serious protection of private property, and hard budgetary constraints. With near hyperinflation, runaway budget deficits, an out-of-control money supply, and soaring company debts, the short-term future remains grim.[54]

There is more hope for the middle and long run. The disintegration of European Communism has discredited any return to the old ways and produced a reluctant popular willingness to tolerate the market. Popular discontent has thus far been remarkably low. Western support for Russian capitalism, while far below Russian expectations, will be an important long-run asset. So too will be Russian human and natural resources. The collapse of the ruble, which has left Russian workers earning ten or twenty dollars a month, has had one positive effect: Russia's labor costs are now competitive with Third World

---

[52]For Israel, it has been estimated that the immigration of 1 million Russian Jews would double its scientific capabilities by adding 20,000 scientists and over 100,000 engineers. For the United States the addition of thousands of Russian scientists at elite universities will strengthen the American drive to remain internationally competitive with Asia and Europe.

[53]Keith Bush, "An Overview of the Russian Economy," *RFE/RL Research Report*, vol. 1, no. 23, June 19, 1992; *Economist*, August 8, 1992. The statistics may exaggerate the extent of the decline.

[54]Bush, "An Overview of the Russian Economy," *RFE/RL Research Report*.

countries. Overall, Yeltsin's moves, however shaky, have laid a base for long-run success. Under the conditions of a powerful, reactionary, central bureaucratic elite, a populist and egalitarian public, a small middle class (15 percent of the population), and a weak emerging entrepreneurial class, the transition to capitalism will take decades and be slow, painful, and likely incomplete.[55] And future problems—such as massive unemployment, high inflation, and state budget cuts—will even exacerbate the problem. But at least there is more long-term hope than short-term hope.

[55] Anders Aslund, editor, *The Post-Soviet Economy*, St. Martin's Press, New York, 1992, chapter 11.

22

The Perils of Nation Building

The perils of nation building in the FSU add to the crises facing the new republics. The roads to capitalism and democracy are long and arduous, perhaps even impossible. The road to nation building will also be protracted and difficult, even if the formal structures of new nation states are now in place in the former Soviet republics. The ethnic wars in Ossetia, Abkhazia, Moldova, and Nagorno-Karabakh and the civil wars in Georgia, Tajikistan, and Azerbaijan have killed tens of thousands and may foreshadow much greater future violence.

Even "advanced" democratic societies have faced great problems in nation building. American nation building was not completed until eighty-four years after the triumph at Yorktown in 1781 with the titanic four-year bloodbath that killed 600,000 soldiers in the American Civil War. Countries such as Canada (Quebec), Great Britain (Northern Ireland), and Spain (Basque and Catalonia) remain rent by massive ethnic conflicts. Dozens of ethno-nationalist conflicts, from Yugoslavia, Lebanon, and Israel to India, Sri Lanka, and Iraq, dot the world. The explosion of ethnicity in the wake of the French Revolution had profound international political implications. As Joseph Rothschild has observed

> Because most contemporary states are multiethnic and because many ethnic groups are distributed through two or more states, politicized ethnicity has become a major aspect and issue of interstate relations. . . . Politicized ethnicity in the modern world is problematic and ambivalent. It has served as a vehicle for aggression, oppression and imperialism as well as a protective vessel against these hegemonial impulses.[1]

[1]Joseph Rothschild, *Ethnopolitics,* Columbia University Press, New York, 1981, pp. 173, 256.

The rising tide of ethno-nationalist conflict has also engulfed the FSU, where fifteen embryonic nation states have replaced the world's last great multiethnic empire. Long after the disintegration of the Ottoman Turkish and Austro-Hungarian Empires in 1918, the Russian Empire endured in different guise for another three-quarters of a century under the Communist regime.

A number of factors suggest a difficult path ahead for the new nation states, who come to nationhood very late in the day. This poses serious problems for regional and international balances of power. Those countries which came to nationhood relatively early, by the fifteenth century (England and France) or even the eighteenth century (United States), faced serious difficulties in nation building. Yet their creation did not pose insuperable problems for the international order.

However, by the middle of the nineteenth century, in the wake of the Napoleonic Wars and Congress of Vienna, a relatively tight international system had been formed. The creation of Germany and Italy in the 1860s produced great tensions in the international system. Prussia created Germany only in the wake of three major wars, against Austria, Denmark, and France. The three massive wars in the seventy-five years after 1870 (Franco-Prussian War, World War I, and World War II) can be seen as a struggle over the role of a newly unified Germany in the European and international balance of power.

The integration of lesser nation states into the international political system has also been problematic. The whole Balkan problem became an epicenter for international political struggle in the decades before 1914. Two Balkan wars immediately preceded World War I. World War I started over the assassination of the Austrian Archduke Ferdinand by a Serbian nationalist in Sarajevo, a region again scarred by enormous violence. The weak and unstable newly independent countries of Eastern Europe after World War I became a major focus of international tensions in the 1930s. Hitler's road to war lay through subordination of the weaker Eastern European countries in the late 1930s, the annexation of the newly independent Czechoslovakia (1938/1939), the absorption of newly independent Austria (1938), and the attack on newly independent Poland (1939).

Nor was the record any better during and after World War II. The creation of the states of Lebanon (1943), Israel (1948), and India and Pakistan (1949) spawned massive regional violence and led to significant international intervention. The creation of Israel led to five major wars in the region (1948, 1956, 1967, 1973, 1982) and recurring cycles of violence in the region. The creation of India led to three major wars (1949, 1965, 1972) and massive communal violence between Hindus and Moslems. The creation of Lebanon (1943) later produced a fifteen-year civil war (1976–1991) that cost 150,000 lives and ended with Syrian occupation of the bulk of the country.

From 1947 to 1970 over fifty former colonies in Africa, Asia, and the Caribbean gained independence. With limited capabilities to create capitalism and democracy, often with small populations, sparse natural resources, and cultural and socio-political obstacles, conflict was endemic in the Third World. Coups, civil wars, and the bloody repression of ethnic minorities were rampant.

Nationhood in many states, especially where arbitrary colonial boundaries remain in place, has existed more on paper than in reality.[2]

In the early 1990s the Yugoslav civil war, with more than 100,000 people dead and missing, epitomized the extreme dangers of nation-state creation. The many-sided battle among Serbs, Croats, Slovenes, and Bosnian Moslems has led to massive bloodletting, "ethnic cleansing," mass murders, and brutality not seen in Europe since the Nazi atrocities of World War II. In the spring of 1994 there seemed no end in sight to the civil war over the future borders and modalities of existence of the states of Serbia, Croatia, Slovenia, and autonomous regions of Bosnia, Macedonia, Montenegro, and Kosovo.

The emergence of fifteen new nations in a crowded European and Central Asian landscape will undoubtedly be problematic. This is true both for the stronger states, such as Russia and Ukraine, and the weaker ones, such as the Central Asian and Transcaucasian states. The massive nuclear and conventional arsenals and armed forces of Russia and Ukraine (larger than those of Germany or France) represent a significant potential for disruption. Turkey, Iran, Pakistan, and Russia are competing for influence over the weak Moslem states of Central Asia and may also be drawn into conflicts in the Transcaucasus.

Most of these new states lack the major prerequisites for nationhood. Even Russia, which was a multinational empire for 600 years, has never functioned as a simple nation state. As Boris Yeltsin declared during the March 1993 constitutional crisis,

> Russian statehood is just beginning to be formed. It would be good to have a flawless constitution, absolutely verified decisions and error-free organs of power. But where can these be found, today and tomorrow?[3]

The new states have never functioned as independent nation states or have done so only for a short period of time.[4] These are not historic nations, such as Poland, which existed as nation states for centuries and then disappeared in the late eighteenth century. There has never been an independent Ukraine or Belarus, for they were nearly always parts of other empires for a millennium.

A third major problem is that of boundaries. As in the colonial experience, existing boundaries reflect maps drawn in a distant colonial center (here Moscow), not in local realities. There are over 130 boundary disputes within the FSU. Some are serious, as over the predominantly Russian Crimea, which was awarded to Ukraine in 1954, or over predominantly Armenian Nagorno-Karabakh, awarded to Azerbaijan in 1922.

Nation building usually draws on a strong ethnic core. Yet the FSU, with over 100 ethnic minorities, presents an enormously complex picture. Nearly 60 million people live outside out of their ethnic republic or autonomous region.

---

[2]See Martin Kilson, editor, *New States in the Modern World,* Harvard University Press, Cambridge, 1975.
[3]*The New York Times,* March 25, 1993.
[4]The Baltics, with their two decades of independence in the interwar period, are a major exception.

No less than 25 million Russians and 5 million Ukrainians live outside of Russia and Ukraine, with 11 million Russians in Ukraine alone. This 21 percent figure far exceeds the "magical" 7 percent line, beyond which ethnic tensions seem to be almost assured. A high level of intermarriage with Russians and significant Russification in cities outside of Russia, have created perhaps 10 to 20 million Russified non-Russians, for whom Russian is their first language, Russians are often their mates, and Moscow, not Dushanbe or Kiev, is their emotional center. Under these conditions a strong Russia will, as seen in the Baltics and Moldova, feel impelled to come to the aid of its ethnic brethren, thereby creating further problems in nation building.

NATION BUILDING

There is a substantial literature on nation building, one created in the 1950s and 1960s and renewed in the 1980s. This literature, when projected on the FSU, makes for gloomy reading.

Anthony Smith, in a recent work on the ethnic origins of nations, has demonstrated the roots of nations in the evolution of ethnic communities, with ethnicity residing in myths, memories, values, and symbols.[5] Ethnic identity resides in collective name, common myth of descent, shared history, distinctive shared culture, association with a specific territory, and sense of solidarity. While Western nation formation came early in England, France, and Spain, replete with economic integration, territorial centralization, mass education, and equality of legal rights, it came later in the nineteenth century in Eastern Europe and the Middle East—and without these revolutionary aspects. In these areas the ethnic concept of nation was much stronger than the territorial concept. This created grave difficulties given the need for ethnic homogeneity and cultural unity as critical to successful nation building. As a consequence, in most new nations "there remains a vast distance to traverse before this population can become a homogeneous nation."[6]

The nation building experience of Western Europe, as interpreted by Charles Tilly, provides little encouragement to modern attempts at nation building.[7] The massive reduction in the number of states in Western Europe, from 500 in 1500 to 25 in 1900, meant that the vast majority of protostates fell by the wayside in brutal competition. There was to be no Scotland, Savoy-Piedmont, Bohemia, Burgundy, Bavaria, Wales, Brittany, or Alsace. Most state-building efforts failed as the great majority of political units were smashed or absorbed into others. The process of state building and nation building "cost tremendously in death, suffering, loss of rights and unwilling surrender of

[5]Anthony Smith, *The Ethnic Origins of Nations,* Basil Blackwell, Oxford, 1986.
[6]Smith, *The Ethnic Origins of Nations,* p. 145.
[7]Charles Tilly, editor, *The Formation of National States in Western Europe,* Princeton University Press, Princeton, 1975. This book is exceptionally good in delineating the paths and varieties of European experiences.

land, goods or labor."[8] Only those states that grew apace with markets, capital, communications, and productivity thrived and prospered.

Factors promoting successful nation building included availability of extractible resources, a protected position in time and space, political entrepreneurship, success in war, a homogenous population, a strong coalition of centralized power and landed commercial elements, and a favorable international context. Nation states were far from inevitable in a world in which the Roman Empire, Moslem world, Imperial China, and Byzantium had not possessed a single nation state. The bulk of these conditions are not met in the FSU. The economic status of most new states is chaotic and desperate, political entrepreneurship is a scarce commodity, and the former Soviet empire has been exposed, rather than protected, in time and space. There have been successful wars but the populations are rarely homogenous, the landed commercial elements are weak to nonexistent, and the periphery (Middle East, China, Iran) is unfavorable.

Worse yet, Tilly found that progress did not depend on a modernizing elite or modernizing personality, around which so much current Western policy seems to revolve. Rather, he argued:

> We discover a world in which small groups of power-hungry men fought off numerous rivals and great popular resistance in pursuit of their own ends and inadvertently promoted formation of national states and widespread popular involvement in them.[9]

Thus, there seems relatively little that can be consciously done to promote such nation building.

The experience of the United States as the "first new nation," in Seymour Martin Lipset's felicitous phrase, is equally discouraging.[10] For the keys to American success seem to be lacking in the FSU. Lipset observed that the new United States built legitimacy and acceptance through demonstrating its effectiveness in economic development. A strong native bourgeoisie, excellent natural endowment, isolation from powerful enemies, significant government intervention in the economy, large British investment, and the Protestant ethos all promoted rapid economic growth. By contrast, as we saw in an earlier chapter, there are largely dismal economic prospects for the FSU.

Second, there were no strong military threats to the nation's existence. With weak neighbors, the state could maintain an army of 672 men in 1789. In 1837 Abraham Lincoln made the famous observation that all the armies of Europe, with all the treasure of Europe, and the generalship of another Napoleon, could not take a drink in the Ohio river. This is very remote from the FSU experience.

Third, there was no ancient tradition or strong parochialism inhibiting the creation of a new nation. Americans had a relatively homogeneous population, common language and religion, and a new society and new nation. The former

---

[8]Tilly, *The Formation of National States in Western Europe*, p. 71.
[9]Tilly, *The Formation of National States in Western Europe*, p. 635.
[10]Seymour Martin Lipset, *The First New Nation*, Basic Book, New York, 1963.

Soviet nations are often very old nations with powerful traditions and parochialism, dating from the millennium of the Russian Empire and before.

Fourth, there always was a strong American tradition of the rule of law, with each colony enjoying a charter and the rights of Englishmen. Here, instead, there was Tsarist and Communist absolutism, a powerful state rather than powerful individuals.

Fifth, there were no great gaps in the social structure of the United States. The former Soviet states do have a well-educated populace, but they also have 80 million peasants, huge physical distances, and great gaps within the population and social structure that mitigate against the integration of the polity.

Sixth, a charismatic leader (Washington) and gifted political elite (Adams, Jefferson, Madison, Franklin, Monroe) guided the transition to statehood in the United States. In the former Soviet states there are largely Communist apparatchiki with varying degrees of commitment to democracy.

Finally, despite all this, Lipset argued that the United States, in 1783 and 1861, nearly failed. Given this, what are the prospects for nationhood of regimes with far fewer of these qualities necessary for success?

Late national state building, then, came primarily in former clients and colonies with thereby diminished prospects. These states have to face a series of crises, challenges, and problems in a compressed time period. The political development literature of the 1960s created by Lucien Pye, Gabriel Almond, and their collaborators, developed the following desiderata for new states:

1. Penetration. To be resolved by establishment of a rational field administration for resource mobilization, creation of public order, and coordination of collective efforts.
2. Integration. To be resolved by establishment of allocation rules equalizing the shares of offices, benefits, resources among all culturally and/or politically distinct sectors of the national community.
3. Participation. Extension of suffrage to hitherto underprivileged strata of population. Protection of the rights of organized opposition.
4. Identity. Development of media and agencies for socialization of future citizens into the national community: schools, literary media, institutionalized rituals and symbols.
5. Legitimacy. Any effort to create loyalty to and confidence in the established structure of political institutions in the given system and to ensure regular conformity to rules and regulations issued by the agencies authorized within the system.
6. Distribution. Establishment of social services and social security measures, income equalization through progressive taxation, and transfers between poorer and richer localities.[11]

The contrast between the lengthy time available for nation building in Western Europe and the shortened time available in the Third World has created enormous difficulties and a greater possibility of failure. The outcome

[11]Stein Rokkan *et al.*, *Citizens, Elections, Parties*, McKay, New York, 1970.

remains "uncertain" with fragmentary, piecemeal nation building the result. For as Reinhard Bendix has concluded, the "instances of failure at nation building may well be more numerous in the end than those of a success."[12] Joseph Strayer, seeing nation building as a "painful process" of social and political mobilization that "promises to be an endless rounds of coups, conquests, revolutions and war" in the Third World, delineated the process in the early 1960s:

> Building a nation-state is a slow and complicated affair, and most political entities created in the past fifty years are never going to complete this process. Mere imitation will not solve their problems; institutions and beliefs must take root in native soil or they will wither. The new states that have the best chance of success are those which correspond fairly closely to old political units; those whose experience living together for many generations within a continuing political framework has given people some sense of identity; those where the political unit coincides roughly with distinct cultural areas; and those where there are indigenous institutions and habits of political thinking that can be connected to forms borrowed from outside.[13]

Lucien Pye, concurring in the "gloomy" prospects for new nations facing such a multitude of tasks, has addressed the human crisis in facing a nation-building process that is "neither autonomous in its dynamics nor free to select at random its goals." He has limned the "psychological travail" and pain of people who now have "the form but not the substance of nationhood," who live in the painful state of transitional societies, who face a

> time of personal insecurity, for millions must make frightening adjustments in their personal perspectives on life. Never has the extent of basic social change touched the lives of so many, shaking intellectual, moral and emotional foundations of their individual worlds. In addition to suffering the pain and discomfort of being torn from the old and the known, they are confronted with the most of human issues, that of individual integrity and personal identity. The logic of tragedy underlies the psychological travail of millions as they seek to adjust to the new because "they" of the new once conquered or dominated or belittled the "we" of the old.[14]

What better summary of the tragic fate facing several hundreds of millions of peoples in the FSU!

Several more recent works on nation building have some distinctive relevance. Myron Weiner (1974) has depicted a tragic process of nation building requiring national integration, territorial integration, value integration,

---

[12]Reinhard Bendix, *Nation-Building and Citizenship*, John Wiley and Sons, New York, 1964, p. 301.

[13]Joseph Strayer, "The Historical Experience of Nation Building," in Karl Deutsch and William Foltz, editors, *Nation-Building*, Atherton Press, New York, 1963, p. 25. William Foltz has similarly seen building a nation as an "exceedingly difficult and long task" which has not been completed in Latin America in over a century of independence, where the masses tend to remain subjects rather than participants. (p. 117)

[14]Lucien Pye, *Politics, Personality and Nation Building: Burma's Search For Identity*, Yale University Press, New Haven, 1966, p. 4.

elite/mass integration, and integrative behavior. The integration of minorities has often involved assimilation, population transfer, or genocide—a view too tragically fulfilled again in "ethnic cleansing" in the former Yugoslavia.[15] All of these integrations are highly problematic in most of the former Soviet states with large ethnic minorities, territorial disputes, value problems, elite arrogance towards the masses, and lack of cooperative modes of interaction. Similarly, Rupert Emerson has pointed to vanished states, such as Poland, Hungary, Bohemia, and Bulgaria, which left behind strong national precipitates on which to build a modern nation state.[16] Here too, most of the former Soviet states lack such national ancestors.

Recent work by Su-hon Lee (1988) has emphasized the retarding impact of dependent transnational development on peripheral state building of new nations.[17] For the Transcaucasus and Central Asia their peripheral position in the international capitalist system will be severely impacted by transnational structures. Even larger and more powerful Russia and Ukraine are now heavily dependent on transnational structures beyond their control. The former Soviet states are likely to be weak states, dependent, manipulated, and relatively powerless, lacking significant shares of the world market or influence in the international arena.

Thomas and Paikiusothy (1989) suggested much the same fate.[18] The historical record of state building in Africa, the Middle East, Central America, and South Asia has been highly problematic. Only in Southeast Asia are there some relative success stories in ethnically homogeneous societies. Most new states lacked societal cohesion or infrastructure strength. As Caroline Thomas concluded, these Third World states can "generally be defined by total insecurity," insecurity in borders, military might, infrastructure, and international transactions.[19] Apart from military weakness, these are all problems likely to plague the former Soviet nations. The future then does not appear bright, especially for the more peripheral and weaker new Soviet states.

NEW NATIONS CREATED FROM COLLAPSED EMPIRES

The collapse of the Soviet empire between 1989 and 1991 and the creation of fifteen new nation states is not unprecedented in modern history. In 1917 and 1918 the Austro-Hungarian Empire, Tsarist Russian Empire, and Ottoman

[15]Myron Weiner, "Political Integration and Political Development," in Frank Tachau, editor, *The Developing Nations: What Path to Modernization?* Dodd, Mead and Company, New York, 1974, pp. 63–74.

[16]Rupert Emerson, "Nationalism," in Tachau, *The Developing Nations: What Path to Modernization?* pp. 75–77.

[17]Su-hon Lee, *State-Building in the Contemporary Third World,* Westview Press, Boulder, Colorado, 1988, chapter 1.

[18]Caroline Thomas and Paikiusothy, editors, *The State and Instability in the South,* St. Martin's Press, New York, 1989.

[19]Thomas and Paikiusothy, *The State and Instability in the South,* p. 188.

Turkish Empires collapsed. From the wreckage of these empires arose a series of independent states: Poland, Czechoslovakia, Hungary, Bulgaria, Rumania, and Albania, as well as the former core states Austria and Turkey. Let us see the impact of the disintegration of these empires on the new nation states born amidst war, revolution and violence.

Like the fifteen new states, the states of Eastern Europe too lacked a lengthy national background and had been divided among several multinational empires for centuries. Both sets of protonation states were far removed from the historical experiences and nation building of Western Europe. Like the Soviet Union, Hapsburg and Austro-Hungarian rule had cut off the national development of peoples with long historical backgrounds.

The Bulgars had an empire as early as the ninth century, the Albanians the thirteenth century, and the Serbs the fourteenth century. The Greeks and Albanians had a history of over 4000 years, the Rumanians over 2300 years. The Polish Commonwealth was once one of the largest states in Europe and reached its high point in the sixteenth and seventeenth centuries before the three partitions. In this context, the Russian, Ottoman, and Hapsburg conquests cut off these nations from the Western European path. The Ottoman victory at Kosovo in 1389 helped isolate the Serbs, Bulgars, Greeks, Croats, Rumanians, Slovenians, and Albanians from Europe for 400 to 500 years, until the late nineteenth century or early twentieth century. By 1800 the Turks ruled 240,000 square miles of Europe with 9 million people. Similarly, Russian advances (together with the Hapsburg and Prussian empires) subjected the Poles late in the eighteenth century and Finland, Bessarabia, and the Baltics in the early nineteenth century. The Hapsburg Empire ruled Central Europe for several centuries.[20]

In 1800 there were no sovereign nation states in Eastern Europe, which was divided among the Hapsburg (Austro-Hungarian), Ottoman (Turkish), Russian, and Prussian empires. By 1912 there were twelve sovereign states and even more after World War I. Yet by the late 1930s Austria and Czechoslovakia had disappeared as states and German domination of the region was extensive, for "the geopolitical map of inter-war Eastern Central Europe, with its plethora of new, restored, and enlarged *soi-disant* nation-states, was not congruent with the real distribution of power in Europe."[21]

The interwar period, which started so optimistically with the creation and recognition of a dozen Eastern European states, ended in disaster. The regimes suffered from severe economic backwardness (save Czechoslovakia), significant ethnic strife, regional rivalries, and the predatory behavior of the major powers. The list of the border disputes in the region was almost endless—Poland and Czechoslovakia quarreled over Teschen; Hungary and Rumania fought over Transylvania; Bulgaria battled with Yugoslavia and Rumania over

[20]See Charles Jelavich and Barbara Jelavich, *The Establishment of the Balkan National States 1804–1920,* University of Washington Press, Seattle and London, 1977, introductory chapter and chapter 1.
[21]Joseph Rothschild, *Return to Diversity: A Political History of East Central Europe Since World War II,* Oxford University Press, New York, 1989, p. 1.

Macedonia and Southern Dobruja; Hungary and Czechoslovakia argued over Slovakia and Ruthenia. Germany wanted the return of the Pomeranian corridor and part of Silesia from Poland, while demanding the Sudetenland from Czechoslovakia and union with Austria. The Soviet Union wanted Bessarabia from Rumania and western Ukraine and western Belarus from Poland. Italy too coveted the Dalmatian coast of Yugoslavia. Within countries such as Czechoslovakia and Poland, 30 to 50 percent of the population did not belong to the dominant ethnic group. There was an effort to nationalize the cultural, political, and economic resources and drive out or restrict minority groups. The words of Joseph Rothschild may sound as relevant for the 1990s as they were for the 1930s:

> [T]he "blame" for the demise of the region's independence must be charged to its own fundamental weaknesses, the instability of its institutions, and its irresponsible governments, as well as to the active and passive faults of the Great Powers. . . . The spirit of the age was not supranational, as it had been naively predicted during the war, but ultranational.[22]

The fates of the Eastern European countries make highly relevant reading.[23] Czechoslovakia, with strong economic development, powerful military industry, compact size, mountainous and defensible borders, and democratic traditions, seemed the most promising country. However, it had 3.5 million Germans, 3 million Slovaks, and over 1 million Hungarians and Jews, constituting 50 percent of its population. It succumbed to the German demands at Munich in 1938 when no major power was willing to come to its rescue and passively accepted its demise in 1939 (as it would again in 1948 and 1968).

Poland was also one-third minorities, with almost 10 million Ukrainians, Jews, Belorussians, and Germans. Buffeted by Russia and Germany, saddled with severe economic retardation and differing histories of the partitioned areas that had belonged to Prussia, Russia, and Austria before 1918, Poland lurched through the interwar period. Popular anti-Semitism was very strong against Poland's 3 million Jews. Marshall Jozef Pilsudski, who led the independence struggle and staged a coup d'etat in 1926, was the political leader. Poland even participated in the division of Czechoslovakia in 1938, only to fall prey to the German invasion that began World War II in 1939. Joseph Rothschild has summarized the interwar period of newly independent Poland:

> Interwar Poland's faults and weaknesses were many and serious: imprudent imbalance between frontiers and institutions, alienation of ethnic minorities, rural overpopulation and industrial backwardness, political decline from original semidemocracy to Pilsudski's semidictatorship and then to his heirs' semiauthority.[24]

---

[22]Rothschild, *Return to Diversity*, pp. 8–9.
[23]The following discussions of the interwar period draws heavily on Joseph Rothschild, *East Central Europe Between the Two World Wars*, University of Washington Press, Seattle and New York, 1974.
[24]Rothschild, *East Central Europe Between the Two World Wars*, p. 72.

Hungary's fate was little better or more cheering, only more colorful. Hungary could not evade occupation or harsh treatment at the hands of the Allies. An outraged Hungary saw a Communist regime under Bela Kun that carried out a massive radical program before its demise at the hands of invading Rumanians after four months in 1919. The resulting White terror killed more than 6000 people. In the 1920 Treaty of Trianon Hungary lost two-thirds of its historic territory and one-third of its Magyar population. Hungary, like Germany, was restricted to a small army (35,000 men) with no airplanes or tanks. Under Admiral Horthy Hungary moved increasingly in an authoritarian, anti-Semitic, and profascist direction that saw its irredentism supported by Nazi Germany in return for its active participation in the invasion of Russia in 1941.

Rumania fared little better. Almost 30 percent of the population consisted of 1.4 million Hungarians, 700,000 Germans, 700,000 Jews, and 400,000 Ukrainians. In an economically backward region, the parties were weak and ethnic tensions strong. Almost half the population was illiterate and infant mortality was high. In the 1920s the leading parties discredited themselves and in the 1930s a rising tide of royalist dictatorship under King Carol prevailed. In the late 1930s the Iron Guard, a neofascist party stressing anti-Semitism, anti-Marxism, and ascetic purity, gained ascendancy. Although the army ultimately controlled the Iron Guard, the Antonescu regime brought Rumania into the war on Germany's side.

Bulgaria fared little better in the interwar period. The radical peasant policies of Prime Minister Aleksandr Stamboliskii were ended in 1923 by a military coup which literally beheaded him. Terrorism, spawned by the IMRO organization dedicated to the liberation of Macedonia, was frequent and common. Despite egalitarian policies amidst a relatively homogeneous population, Bulgaria moved to a royal dictatorship under Tsar Boris after 1935. Despite its strong relationship with Russia, Bulgaria moved into the German camp and participated in the German war effort.

Yugoslavia and Albania were little more promising. By the late 1920s the newly independent Albania came under the royal dictatorship of King Zog, who in the 1930s in turn yielded to Italian hegemony. By 1939 the Italians formally occupied Albania and extinguished its independence. As for Yugoslavia, its politics were noted for "brutality and cynicism," for "sheer incompetence and corruption" as a royal dictatorship at the end of the 1930s struggled to cope with "her major ethnic communities unreconciled, her citizens' civil liberties violated, her economic unification and development stunted and her agrarian problems only partly alleviated at the price of economic and political dependence on Germany."[25]

During World War II German dominance of the region was virtually complete, until replaced by the Russian dominance at the end of the war. Some states were passive victims (Czechoslovakia), some calculating satellites (Hungary, Rumania, and Bulgaria), some temporarily independent dependencies (Slovakia and Croatia), some resisting victims (Poland and Yugoslavia), and one

---

[25]Rothschild, *East Central Europe Between the Two World Wars*, p. 278.

a colony of Italy (Albania). Economic and political weakness, reinforced by local ethno-national rivalries, exposed the region to great power domination.[26] Hungary and Rumania participated actively in the German war effort, with Rumania suffering 500,000 casualties. Bulgaria and Czechoslovakia were relatively passive save for the Slovak independent state created under German tutelage. Poland and Yugoslavia resisted the most, with 400,000 Tito partisans battling the Germans in Yugoslavia and the Polish underground staging its uprising in Warsaw in 1944. They also suffered the most, with 1.7 million Yugoslavs killed in the bloody civil war among Serbs, Croats, and Germans and 6 million Poles killed, including 3 million Polish Jews in the Holocaust.[27]

After World War II Soviet domination replaced German domination. The new Soviet regimes in Eastern Europe were thoroughly socialized and nationalized, although never to the extent of the Soviet Union. They did not totally accept their fate. There were major revolts in East Germany (1953), Hungary (1956), Poland (1956, 1970, 1980), and Czechoslovakia (1968). Yet when the Red Army was used to crush dissent, as in Hungary in 1956 and Czechoslovakia in 1968, the outcome was predictable. By the late 1980s the local regimes, save in a few places like Hungary, had lost nearly all of their legitimacy. Once Gorbachev withdrew the threat of Red Army intervention, the transition to independent, more democratic regimes went relatively peacefully, save in Rumania and Yugoslavia. Only after 1989 did we witness the emergence of new, truly independent states.[28]

AUSTRIA AND TURKEY

The end of the Hapsburg and Ottoman Turkish empires was especially painful for the "core" states of Austria and Turkey, whose influence had greatly exceeded their size. They now had to accept painful reductions in their territory and population, as well as come to grips with their new identities. In both states the old monarchies and traditional systems were cast aside and new republics were born amidst great difficulties. Turkey, however surprisingly, made a better adjustment than Austria, which always had to come to grips with its German identity.

Austria, after almost 640 years as the center of the Hapsburg Empire, had severe problems in becoming a normal nation state.[29] The collapse of the empire in 1918 transformed Austria from the core of a significant empire of ten nations and over 50 million people to a small nation of fewer than 7 million

---

[26]Total industrial production in the region in 1938 was only 8 percent of the total production for all of Europe outside of the Soviet Union. And one-third of this came from Czechoslovakia. Underproductivity, underconsumption, underemployment, overpopulation, pervasive misery and ethnic tensions made for a vicious cycle of all embracing alienation and discontent in the region, of immobility and instability. See Rothschild, *Return to Diversity*, chapter 3.

[27]Rothschild, *Return to Diversity*, chapters 1 and 2.

[28]See Rothschild, *East Central Europe Between the Two World Wars*, chapter 1.

[29]For two useful works on Austria see Malcolm Bullock, *Austria 1918–1938: A Study in Failure*, Macmillan, London, 1939; and Elisabeth Barker, *Austria 1918–1972*, University of Miami Press, Coral Gables, Florida, 1973.

people with little importance to the world. In an earlier era Spain, the Nether-
lands, and Northern Italy had all belonged to Austria. The sudden disintegration of the empire in October 1918 and the defeat in war the following month
came as a total shock to the Austrians. There were no agreed-upon boundaries
for a core Austrian state, which lacked any autonomous economic unit or
parliamentary government. Three million Germans, who logically might have
been included in the new Austria, were soon to find themselves in Czechoslovakia. Without economic viability or political legitimacy, the new rump Austrian state faced a "terrifying array of problems, internal and external, psychological, political and economic. Weapons in their hands were few but
important."[30]

The end of World War I found the Council of State ending the monarchy
and empire, proclaiming a Republic of Austria, and supporting union with a
republican Germany. Poland, Czechoslovakia, Croatia, Hungary, and Austria
all emerged from the old Hapsburg Empire. It began, in Malcolm Bullock's
words, "surrounded by enemies, a Republic without true republicans, a democratic failure from the beginning."[31] Its former nationality minorities despised
it, its army was disbanded, the Allies blockaded it as the heir to an enemy
empire, and the local population was dubious about the whole Austrian and
democratic enterprise. By December 1918 food rations were 50 percent of the
low level of the war. Inflation was rampant and food was scarce. In the first
elections in February 1919 the Social Democrats under Karl Renner, the only
major party to support a democratic republic, narrowly triumphed. The following month the Allied blockade was lifted.

In June 1919 the Treaty of Saint Germain was signed. Its harsh terms
confirmed the loss of Bohemia and Moravia to Czechoslovakia, the loss of
Southern Tyrol to Italy, the limitation to a 30,000-man army with no air force,
the transfer of Hapsburg war equipment to the Allies, and a provision to send
2000 cows, 100 bulls, 2000 sheep, 3000 horses, and 2000 pigs to three neighbor-
ing countries. Austrians felt completely deserted in their new, small, weak
state, one encumbered by a large bureaucracy and small population and
minimal Allied aid. Austrian economic miseries continued through 1920 with
the collapse of the former empire economy, Allied restrictions, and hostilities
with most of the former constituent elements. By 1920 there were 2000 Austrian
crowns to the English pound compared to twenty-four in 1914.

By 1921 the vast majority of the population favored union with Germany
as a solution. Inflation continued with 93,000 crowns to the pound by June 1922.
By the fall of 1922 the majority of all factories were closed, the monetary system
was out of control, and the American Minister in Vienna warned visitors not to
go to Vienna. Bitter strife among the major parties paralleled this economic
catastrophe, one that occurred at the same time as Mussolini's March on Rome
in Italy. Only in October 1922, with major international economic intervention,
was disaster staved off.

---

[30]Barker, *Austria 1918–1972*, chapter 1, especially p. 12.
[31]Bullock, *Austria 1918–1938, A Democratic Failure*, p. 17.

The rest of the 1920s saw a tenuous economic and political recovery. Austria seemed to be creating its own viable path. Yet many obstacles remained. Frequent strikes and disturbances, strong popular majorities in favor of union with Germany, and growing anti-Semitism boded poorly for the future. The Christian Socialists and Social Democrats increasingly feuded and strengthened their own private armies. By the early 1930s the rise of fascism in Europe impacted Austria with its close ties to Germany, rising unemployment, and negative trade balance. By 1932 the neofascist Chancellor Engelbert Dollfuss ruled Austria. His emergency powers effectively ended the parliamentary system by 1933. Though a neofascist, he was an Austrian chauvinist who banned the Nazi party in 1933 and preferred Mussolini to Hitler. In a brief civil war in February 1934 Dollfuss smashed the Viennese army of the Social Democrats in a two-day battle that took 400 casualties. In July 1934 Dollfuss was killed in a failed coup attempt by the Nazis.

During 1934 there were over 38,000 political arrests of leftists and over 100,000 searches of houses. The new Chancellor Kurt von Schuschnigg, also pro-Mussolini, continued the suppression of parties. Italian power declined with the grave difficulties of the Ethiopian campaign. Yet even in 1936 Schuschnigg resisted German pressure to legalize the Nazi party. A weakening Italy and strengthened Germany spelt doom for Austria. In early 1938 Chancellor Schuschnigg tried to hold a plebiscite to show that most Austrians still resisted the German embrace. This was the last straw, and over 100,000 German troops invaded Austria (even after the plebiscite was called off). Hitler had now forcibly reintegrated the country of his birth.

The end of the Ottoman Empire brought a stormy period to the new Turkish state. In 1918 the victorious Allies occupied most parts of the Ottoman Empire except for part of Inner Anatolia. In February 1919 a French general rode into Constantinople and in March 1919 a new government there swore to work with the British, French, Greek, and Italian occupiers. Incensed nationalists, led by General Mustafa Kemal, demanded a liberal American protectorate instead of the Allied occupation, Greek control of Western Anatolia, and Armenian independence. When a Greek advance led to the overthrow of the Sultan, the nationalists under Kemal won control of the parliament. The 1920 Treaty of Sevres made Armenia independent, gave Eastern Thrace to Greece, the Arab lands to France and England, and divided ethnic Turkey. In 1921 and 1922 General Kemal won battles against the Greeks, who were deserted by their allies. By 1923 Kemal had mobilized the population, liberated Izmir and Istanbul (Constantinople), moved the capital to Ankara, and proclaimed a shrunken Turkish republic. He had challenged the monarchy, Islam, and the empire in the name of the republic, secular values, and nonimperialism. By creative politics, military victories, and charismatic authority, Mustafa Kemal created a new Turkish republic out of the ruins of Ottoman Turkey.[32]

This history highlights the importance of a favorable international environ-

---

[32]Irvin Schick and Ertuguil Tonak, editors, *Turkey in Transition,* Oxford University Press, New York, 1987, chapters 1–3.

ment and creative political leadership in shaping political outcomes. New rising forces can, in the space created by the national revolutions, form something dynamically new—or depressingly old and failed. The choice, as Turkey showed, is not preordained. But Austria reminds us of how near to the surface failure is in such circumstances.

RUSSIA AND THE RUSSIAN EMPIRE

The fifteen new states grew organically from the Tsarist and Soviet Empire. The Russian empire was the third greatest in time and space in the history of the world, lagging behind only the British Empire and Mongol Empire. Muscovy itself dated to 1147 and began its expansion after the decisive defeat of the Mongols in the Battle of Kulikovo in 1380. The empire then expanded exponentially for five centuries, until it ceased its growth at the time of the 1905 Revolution. At that time it lost Manchuria and the Southern Sakhalins to Japan, and in the wake of the Russian Civil War Poland, Finland, and the Baltics became independent, Bessarabia returned to Rumania, Kars to Turkey, and western Ukraine and western Belarus to the new Poland. Only during World War II was some of the Tsarist patrimony, including the Baltics, Eastern Finland, Bessarabia, and southern Sakhalins, recovered.

The Russian empire was unique in several ways. It was built not through expeditions across seas, like the British or French empires, but by traversing contiguous land masses. Movement from the core to the periphery was common, not rare, as in other empires. There was a strong push to lift the colonies to the level of the metropolis. Various groups were treated differently. Only nature and strong nations stopped expansion. Russian cadres always dominated the military and security forces. By 1914, at the end of the expansion, 77 million Russians were only 45 percent of the population. But only three other groups exceeded 5 percent of the empire's population—31 million Ukrainians (18 percent), 11 million Poles (7 percent), and 18 million diverse Moslems (11 percent).[33]

Russification occurred in various ways. For centuries there was a systematic prejudice in favor of the core Russian population. There was large-scale assimilation of borderland nationalities. Intellectual and cultural matters for the empire were centralized in Moscow and Saint Petersburg. Non-Russians were largely confined to the teeming but backward countryside. The bulk of the urban migrants were Russians.[34] There was little sense of loyalty to the Russian nation, but rather to the Russian empire, until the Napoleonic invasion of 1812. After that there was a slow growth of Russian nationalism, as distinct from

---

[33]Michael Rywkin, editor, *Russian Colonial Expansion to 1917*, Mansell Publishing Ltd., London and New York, 1988, p. xv and chapter 1.
[34]Alexander Motyl, *Will the Non-Russians Rebel?* Cornell University Press, Ithaca, New York, 1987, chapter 3.

Russian imperialism, especially under Alexander III and Nicholas II. But the state continued to grow much faster than the nation.[35]

Under the Soviet Union Russian domination continued apace, even though Marxism was hostile to any explicit claims of Russian supremacy. During the 1920s liberalization allowed promotion of language, schools, administration, and literature of non-Russian nationalities. But the 1930s witnessed a dramatic increase in Russian chauvinism and attacks on bourgeois nationalism (that is, non-Russian nationalism). Even the Tsars were brought back and glorified. This was intensified in the wake of World War II, with Stalin's proclamation of thanks to the Russian nation in the victory toast in 1945. Russian nationalism, and attendant anti-Semitism, intensified further during the final years under Stalin. Under Khrushchev there was some easing of restrictions, and promotions of Ukrainians, but the situation did not change radically. Under Brezhnev there was a gradual reversal of trends back towards Russian nationalism, one not reversed by Gorbachev, an unconscious Russian chauvinist with no experience in the nationality areas.

By 1989, 145 million Russians made up but 51 percent of the total population of the Soviet Union.[36] Yet Russian domination was far greater than these numbers would allow. On a per capita basis the Russian Republic had 47 percent more fixed assets than the norm, 66 percent more new capital investment, 78 percent less poverty, and 30 percent more retail trade. Its infant mortality rates were 60 percent below the norm (19.3 per 1000 in the Russian Republic, 58 per 1000 in Turkmenistan).[37] In 1980 Russians were 52 percent of the population of the Soviet Union but 58 percent of the working class, 68 percent of the scientific workers, 60 percent of all Communists. More than 80 percent of all books and 90 percent of all newspapers were published in Russian language. While 3 percent of Russians know a non-Russian language, 50 percent of non-Russians know Russian well. In 1990 Russians were the great majority of members of the army general staff, and the leading members of the Academy of Sciences, trade unions, Council of Ministers, and Presidential Council. No fewer than 87 percent of the ministers and heads of state committees were Russians.[38] In 1990 Russians were 51 percent of the population but 79 percent of the members of the Politburo (15 of 19).

Under these conditions Russian nationalism, as opposed to Soviet nationalism, was slow to develop. Only in 1990 was a Russian Communist Party, as distinct from the Communist Party of the Soviet Union, formed as the separation between Russia and the Soviet Union became clearer. In late 1991, with the

---

[35]Hugh Seton-Watson, "Russian Nationalism in Historical Perspective," in Robert Conquest, editor, *The Last Empire,* Stanford University Press, Stanford, 1986.

[36]Discontent by the 49 percent of the Soviet population that was not Russian was a major factor in the breakup of the Soviet Union. The desire of fourteen nationality republics for independence was important to the failure of Gorbachev's vision of a rejuvenated union.

[37]Nadia Diuk and Adrian Karatnycky, *The Hidden Nations,* William Morrow and Company, New York, 1990, pp. 49–52.

[38]Motyl, *Will the Non-Russians Rebel?* chapter 3; and Diuk and Karatnycky, *The Hidden Nations,* pp. 54–66.

breakup of the Soviet Union, the Russian republic did appear. With 6.6 million square miles, with 146 million people (85 percent Russian), with enormous territory running 2500 miles north-south and 5600 miles east-west, a Russian state had finally appeared. Furthermore, there are emerging ethnic challenges to Russian federalism from within the eighty-nine regions of Russia, especially from those dominated by non-Russians. In the fall of 1993 Yeltsin faced increasing opposition from the regions fearful of an increasingly powerful and authoritarian center.

This came in response to the creation of a number of new non-Russian states. There were great variations in the nature and response of these new states to Russian domination. Economically, Russia and the Baltics were closer to the level of a Poland or Hungary, Belarus and Ukraine to Yugoslavia, Armenia to Rumania, and Central Asia to Iran or Syria. In 1980 Russian national income per capita was more than double that of Kyrgyzstan and two and a half times that of Tajikistan. There were large and persistent gaps among nationalities with a strong dependence on the center.[39]

Nation building, especially on top of developing democracy and capitalism, promises to be a lengthy and difficult project for the fifteen new states of the former Soviet Union. Internal conflicts within these states (Tatarstan within Russia, Abkhazia and Ossetia within Georgia) further complicates the task. In the end nationhood may be easier to deliver than capitalism, but unfortunately its cargo will probably include ethnic chauvinism, discrimination against local minorities, and perhaps a few more little wars. Hopefully, they will stay limited.

---

[39]Gertrude Schroeder, "Social and Economic Aspects of the Nationality Problem," in Conquest, *The Last Empire*, pp. 300, 309.

23

Epilogue

The dramatic events of the last few years are seared forever in our collective memory—the end of the Cold War, the fall of the Berlin Wall, the dissolution of the Soviet Union, the end of Communism in Eastern Europe, the Israeli-Palestinian peace accord. Capitalism and to a lesser extent democracy have been on the march throughout the Third World, from China and Vietnam to Brazil and Argentina and numerous African countries.[1] The world has suddenly moved to fast forward, and now even the least developed countries, such as China, are making the fastest economic progress. Truly, everything seems possible as the world for the first time creates a genuinely global capitalist system, and communism, fascism, and authoritarianism are beginning to be faded memories in many areas that knew only the old horrors of torture, repression, and coercion for many decades and centuries.

And yet, a small voice whispers that this is not guaranteed, that the old authoritarianism, the old collectivism, the former national hatreds are not gone but submerged and remain alive and well. The massacres of the Yugoslav and Angolan civil wars, the little civil wars in Georgia, Tajikistan, and Moldova, and the war between Armenia and Azerbaijan over Nagorno-Karabakh show that the old is yet much with us. The great success scored by the neofascist Vladimir Zhirinovsky, the Communists, and the old-guard Agrarians in the December 1993 elections—where they won over 40 percent of the total vote—shows that the old is far from dead. And they reinforce the notion that a specter is haunting Europe, the specter of a massive civil war in the former Soviet Union that would blot out the bright and sunny prospects for the twenty-first century. The large-scale bloodshed and setting on fire of the parliament build-

---

[1] In China capitalism has made serious progress, and democracy, though repressed in 1989, may yet resurface after the demise of Deng Xiaoping.

ing in Moscow in October 1993, together with all the other civil wars on the periphery of the FSU, and the rise of authoritarianism in the majority of the FSU, seem to indicate that this is highly possible. The sight of Boris Yeltsin ordering the tanks to fire on demonstrators in Moscow and the visage of Georgian President Eduard Shevardnadze fleeing a smoking Sukhumi in October 1993 are ever on our minds. So too is the ever-worsening situation in Ukraine, where President Kravchuk clings to power with an economy and polity that smells distinctively of the old regime. This touches on the core question of this epilogue: Whither the FSU in the final years of the twentieth century?

If a major civil war erupts in the FSU, the consequences for the world would be potentially devastating. For the FSU covers 8.6 million square miles, a vast terrain occupying 40 percent of Europe and 40 percent of Asia. The enormous military arsenal still remaining on this territory ranges from over 1000 ICBMs, 6000 jet fighters, 40,000 tanks, and 27,000 nuclear weapons to massive quantities of ammunition and shells and over 4 million troops well trained in how to use this vast panoply of weapons. The last Russian Civil War (1918–1920) saw 11 million people die.

How shall we know the future course of the FSU? The history that has been stressed in seven chapters in Part Two provides part of the answer—and it is not reassuring. The Tsarist and Soviet legacies over six centuries have strongly skewed the answer in favor of imperialism, bureaucracy, centralism, and authoritarianism. They have greatly obstructed the transition to capitalism, democracy, and nation building by giving the new leaders of the fifteen republics relatively little material on which to build. There is no developed middle class, no tradition of entrepreneurship, no respect for law, no protection of private property, and no favorable economic or political ethos or history on which to draw. The harsh physical and demographic realities depicted in Part One—an unrelenting climate, weak transportation infrastructure, poor agricultural base, and vast and empty internal spaces—do not bode well for Russia. The other states have somewhat better physical structures but lack any history of independence, face serious problems of Russian and foreign interference in their internal affairs, and often have difficult ethnic problems, of both the Russian and non-Russian sorts. Dismantling the old planned economy and constructing the new order is very difficult, when capitalism and democracy are best built from below, from local indigenous forces, rather than implanted somewhat artificially from above. Under these circumstances it is, to use an old Bolshevik phrase, no accident that the majority of the new states have largely given up any hope of a rapid transition, apart from the Baltics on the fringe of Europe. Even Russia faces severe problems in making the transition.

Civil war then is a distinct possibility, as the bloody repression in Moscow in October 1993 where 400 people died showed so clearly. The lines of division could be numerous: Russia versus Ukraine, Russia versus the other republics, conservatives versus reformers, urban versus rural, minorities versus Russians inside Russia, local versus center, non-Russians versus Russians outside of Russia, new states against other new states, and all versus all within the other fourteen republics. The role of foreign intervention would be distinctly limited given the huge size of the FSU and its large population. Famine, starvation, chaos, terror, and fighting on a large scale would be likely.

Is it all hopeless? We must say no, especially in the longer run. Simply put, there is in the long run no alternative for the world or for these states, especially in the Slavic region and the Baltics. Eventually they will become at least peripherally integrated into European and international capitalism and democracy, even if in forms that may seem as removed from the Anglo-American tradition as the capitalism and democracy of Japan and the Four Tigers of Asia. These distinctive forms will be heavily skewed towards a strong social-welfare state, heavy state interference in the economy, a powerful state, and a weak judiciary. The great assets of the Slavic states—well-educated populace, strong scientific establishment, vast natural resources, burgeoning new entrepreneurial spirit among the young—will have their impact in a generation. And, quite simply, it is the lack of a reasonable alternative model that will impel at least the Slavs and the Balts towards some form of capitalism and democracy. As for the Transcaucasians, change will be slowed down by the virulent ethnic feuds and Central Asia, apart perhaps from Kazakhstan, will come in the rear.

In the end history matters and shapes the likely outcome in the FSU. Yet history is not destiny, and history itself shows numerous cases where nations have made sharp and decisive breaks with the past. Lacking many of the major prerequisites for capitalism, democracy, and nation building, and sitting on a vast powder keg inherited from the past, the FSU lurches forward unsteadily into the future. Hopefully, the forces of international capitalism, the abject failure of communism, Western aid, and the current lack of a demonstrable alternative will overcome the strong forces pulling the FSU backwards to chaos, authoritarianism, and civil war. At the very least, these forces may nudge the FSU enough in the direction of limited democracy, capitalism, and nation building to avoid the extreme outcome. The fate of the progress of the world in a more hopeful direction may seriously depend on the outcome of that struggle. In the late spring of 1994, with the Zhirinovsky phenomenon in full bloom and the old guard of Communists showing signs of rebirth, hope is still in short supply in the former Soviet Union.

BIBLIOGRAPHY

Adams, John, and Paclo Barile: *The Government of Republican Italy*, Houghton Mifflin, New York, 1972.

Adelman, Jonathan R.: *Prelude to the Cold War*, Lynne Rienner Publications, Boulder, Colorado, 1988.

————: *Revolution, Armies and War*, Lynne Rienner Publications, Boulder, Colorado, 1985.

————: *The Revolutionary Armies*, Greenwood Press, Westport, Connecticut, 1980.

———— and Cristann Gibson, editors: *Contemporary Soviet Military Affairs: The Legacy of World War II*, Unwin, Hyman, Boston, 1989.

Albrecht-Carrie, Rene: *Italy From Napoleon to Mussolini*, Columbia University Press, New York, 1950.

Alstadt, Audrey: *The Azerbaijani Turks*, Hoover Institution Press, Stanford, California, 1992.

Arendt, Hannah: *The Origin of Totalitarianism*, Harcourt, Brace, Jovanovich, New York, 1973.

Armstrong, John: *Ukrainian Nationalism*, Columbia University Press, New York, 1963.

Aron, Robert: *The Vichy Regime 1940–44*, translated by Humphrey Hare, Beacon Press, Boston, 1958.

Aslund, Anders: *Gorbachev's Struggle for Economic Reform*, Cornell University Press, Ithaca, New York, 1989.

————: *The Post-Soviet Economy*, St. Martin's Press, New York, 1992.

Avrich, Paul: *Kronstadt 1921*, Princeton University Press, Princeton, 1970.

Balzer, Harley, editor: *Five Years That Shook the World*, Westview Press, Boulder, Colorado, 1991.

Barker, Elisabeth: *Austria 1918–1972*, University of Miami Press, Coral Gables, Florida, 1973.

Barry, Donald, and Carol Barner-Barry: *Contemporary Soviet Politics*, Prentice-Hall, New York, 1987.

Bendix, Reinhard: *Nation-Building and Citizenship*, John Wiley and Sons, New York, 1964.

Bennigsen, Alexandre, and Marie Broxup: *The Islamic Threat to the Soviet State*, St. Martin's Press, New York, 1983.

Bernstein, Morris: *The Soviet Economy: Continuity and Change,* Westview Press, Boulder, Colorado, 1981.

Bialer, Seweryn: *Stalin's Successors,* Cambridge University Press, Cambridge, 1980.

————, editor: *Stalin and His Generals,* Pegasus, London, 1970.

————: *The Soviet Paradox: External Expansion, Internal Decline,* Alfred Knopf, New York, 1986.

Birman, Igor: *Personal Consumption in the USSR and USA,* St. Martin's Press, New York, 1989.

Blackwell, William, editor: *Russian Economic Development From Peter the Great to Stalin,* Franklin Watts, New York, 1974.

Bracher, Karl: *The German Dictatorship,* Praeger, New York, 1970.

Breslauer, George: *Khrushchev and Brezhnev As Leaders Building Authority in Soviet Politics,* Allen and Unwin, London, 1982.

Brinton, Crane: *Anatomy of a Revolution,* Random House, New York, 1938.

Brumberg, Abraham: *Chronicle of a Revolution,* Pantheon, New York, 1990.

Bruchis, Michael: *Nations—Nationalities—People: A Study of Nationality Policy of the Communist Party in Soviet Moldavia,* Eastern European Monograph no. 165, distributed by Columbia University Press, New York, 1984.

Brzezinski, Zbigniew: *Ideology and Power in Soviet Politics,* Praeger, New York, 1962.

Brynes, Robert, editor: *After Brezhnev: Sources of Soviet Conduct in the 1980s,* Indiana University Press, Bloomington, 1983.

Bullock, Malcolm: *Austria 1918–1938: A Study in Failure,* Macmillan, London, 1939.

Campbell, Robert: *The Socialist Economies in Transition,* Indiana University Press, Bloomington, 1991.

Carr, Raymond: *Spain 1808–1975,* Clarendon Press, Oxford, 1982.

Chamberlin, William: *The Russian Revolution,* 2 volumes, Princeton University Press, Princeton, 1987.

Chernenko, K.C.: *Speeches and Writings,* 2d edition, Pergammon, Oxford, 1984.

Chotiner, Barbara: *Khrushchev's Party Reform,* Greenwood Press, Westport, Connecticut, 1984.

Cohen, Stephen: *Bukharin and the Bolshevik Revolution,* W.W. Norton, New York, 1973.

Colton, Timothy, and Thane Gustafson, editors: *Soldiers and the Soviet States,* Princeton University Press, Princeton, 1989.

Commission on Security and Cooperation in Europe: *Human Rights and Democratization in the Newly Independent States of the Former Soviet Union,* Government Printing Office, Washington, D.C., 1993.

————: *Presidential Elections and Independence Referendums in the Baltic States, the Soviet Union and Successor States,* Government Printing Office, Washington, D.C., 1992.

————: *The Presidential Election in Azerbaijan,* Government Printing Office, Washington, D.C., 1992.

————: *Report on Georgia's Presidential Elections,* Government Printing Office, Washington, D.C., 1992.

Conquest, Robert: *The Great Terror,* Macmillan, New York, 1968.

————: *The Harvest of Sorrow,* Oxford University Press, Oxford, 1986.

————, editor: *The Last Empire,* Stanford University Press, Stanford, 1986.

————: *The Nation Killers: The Soviet Deportation of Nationalities,* Macmillan, New York, 1970.

Corbo, Vittorio, Fabrizio Coricelli, and Jan Bossak, editors: *Reforming Central and East European Economies: Initial Results and Challenges,* World Bank, Washington, D.C., 1991.

Crankshaw, Edward: *Khrushchev: A Career*, Viking, New York, 1966.

Curtis, John: *The Russian Army Under Nicholas I, 1825–1855*, Duke University Press, Durham, North Carolina, 1965.

D'Agonisto, Anthony: *Soviet Succession Struggles*, Allen and Unwin, Boston, 1988.

Dahl, Robert: *Polyarchy: Participation and Opposition*, Yale University Press, New Haven, 1971.

Dallin, Alexander: *German Rule in Russia, 1941–1944*, Macmillan, London, 1957.

Daniels, Robert: *Conscience of the Revolution*, Simon and Schuster, New York, 1969.

Davies, R.W.: *The Soviet Economy in Turmoil, 1929–1930*, Harvard University Press, Cambridge, 1989.

Dembrinski, Pavel: *The Logic of the Planned Economy: The Seeds of the Collapse*, Oxford University Press, Oxford, 1991.

d'Encausse, Helene Carrere: *The End of the Soviet Empire*, translated by Franklin Philip, Harper Collins, New York, 1993.

————: *Stalin: Order Through Terror*, Viking Press, New York, 1978.

Derbyshire, Ian: *Politics in the Soviet Union From Brezhnev to Gorbachev*, W. and R. Chambers, Cambridge, England, 1987.

Desai, Padmai: *The Soviet Economy: Problems and Prospects*, Basil Blackwell, Oxford, 1987.

de Tocqueville, Alexis: *The Old Regime and the French Revolution*, Doubleday Anchor, New York, 1955.

Deutsch, Karl, and William Foltz, editors: *Nation-Building*, Atheneum, New York, 1963.

Deutscher, Isaac: *Stalin*, Vintage, New York, 1967.

Dickens, Charles: *A Tale of Two Cities*, Penguin, London, 1985.

Dima, Nicholas: *From Moldavia to Moldova: The Soviet Romanian Territorial Dispute*, Eastern European Monograph no. 309, distributed by Columbia University Press, New York, 1991.

DiPalma, Giuseppe: *To Craft Democracies*, University of California Press, Berkeley and Los Angeles, 1990.

Diuk, Nadia, and Adrian Karatnycky: *The Hidden Nations*, William Morrow, New York, 1990.

————: *New Nations Rising*, John Wiley and Sons, New York, 1993.

Dmytryshyn, Basil: *USSR: A Concise History*, Charles Scribner's Sons, New York, 1971.

Doder, Dusko: *Shadows and Whispers: Power Politics Inside the Kremlin From Brezhnev to Gorbachev*, Random House, New York, 1986.

———— and Louise Branson: *Gorbachev: Heretic in the Kremlin*, Viking, New York, 1990.

Donnelly, Christopher, editor: *Gorbachev's Revolution*, James, Medford, England, 1989.

Dornberg, John: *Brezhnev: The Masks of Power*, Andre Deutsch, London, 1974.

Erickson, John: *The Road to Berlin*, Westview Press, Boulder, Colorado, 1983.

————: *The Road to Stalingrad*, Weidenfeld and Nicholson, London, 1975.

Eyck, Erich: *A History of the Weimar Republic*, translated by Harlan Hanson and Robert Wate, Atheneum, New York, 1970.

Fainsod, Merle: *Smolensk Under Soviet Rule*, Harvard University Press, Cambridge, 1958.

Federal Institute for East European and International Studies: *The Soviet Union 1984/85: Events, Problems, Perspectives*, Westview Press, Boulder, Colorado, 1986.

Feher, Ferenc, and Andrew Arato, editors: *Gorbachev: The Debate*, Humanities Press, Atlantic Highlands, New Jersey, 1989.

Felshman, Neil: *Gorbachev, Yeltsin and the Last Days of the Soviet Empire*, St. Martin's Press, New York, 1992.

Feshbach, Murray, and Alfred Firendly, Jr.: *Ecocide in the USSR*, Basic Books, New York, 1992.

Figes, Orlando: *Peasant Russia, Civil Russia*, Clarendon Press, Oxford, 1989.

Fitzpatrick, Sheila, editor: *Cultural Revolution in Russia, 1928–1931*, Indiana University Press, Bloomington, 1978.

Florinsky, Michael, editor: *Encyclopedia of Russia and the Soviet Union*, McGraw-Hill, New York, 1961.

Friedrich, Carl, and Zbigniew Brzezinski: *Totalitarian Dictatorship and Autocracy*, Praeger, New York, 1956.

Gaddis, John Lewis: *Tectonics, History and the End of the Cold War*, Mershon Center Occasional Paper, Ohio State University, Columbus, 1992.

Gatrell, Peter: *The Tsarist Economy, 1850–1917*, St. Martin's Press, New York, 1986.

Gelb, Alan, and Cheryl Grey: *The Transformation of Economies in Central and Eastern Europe: Issues, Progress and Prospects*, Policy Research Series no. 17, World Bank, Washington, D.C., 1991.

Gentzler, Israel: *Kronstadt 1917–1921*, Cambridge University Press, New York, 1983.

Gerschenkron, Alexander: *Economic Backwardness in Historical Perspective*, Harvard University Press, Cambridge, 1960.

Getty, J. Arch: *The Origins of the Great Purges*, Cambridge University Press, Cambridge, 1985.

Gimbel, John: *The Origins of the Marshall Plan*, Stanford University Press, Stanford, 1976.

Ginzburg, Evgeniia: *Journey Into the Whirlwind*, translated by Paul Stevenson, Harcourt, Brace and World, New York, 1967.

Glenny, Michael, and Norman Stone: *The Other Russia: The Experience of Exile*, Viking, New York, 1991.

Goldman, Marshall: *What Went Wrong With Perestroika*, W.W. Norton, New York, 1991.

Gorbachev, Mikhail: *The August Coup*, Harper Collins, New York, 1991.

Gregory, James: *Russian Land, Soviet People*, Pegasus, New York, 1968.

Gregory, Paul: *Restructuring the Soviet Economic Bureaucracy*, Cambridge University Press, Cambridge, 1990.

———: *Russian National Income, 1855–1913*, Columbia University Press, New York, 1982.

Hacker, Louis: *The Triumph of American Capitalism*, Columbia University Press, New York, 1940.

Halperin, S. William: *Germany Tried Democracy*, W.W. Norton, New York, 1974.

Hasegawa, Paul: *The February Revolution: Petrograd 1917*, University of Washington Press, Seattle, 1981.

Havlik, Peter, editor: *Dismantling the Command Economy in Eastern Europe*, Westview Press, Boulder, Colorado, 1991.

Hazen, Baruch: *Gorbachev And His Critics*, Westview Press, Boulder, Colorado, 1990.

———: *Gorbachev's Gamble—The Nineteenth All Union Party Conference*, Westview Press, Boulder, Colorado, 1990.

Hewett, Ed: *Reforming the Soviet Economy*, Brookings Institute Press, Washington, D.C., 1989.

Hiden, John, and Patrick Salmon: *The Baltic Nations and Europe*, Longmans, London, 1991.

Hogan, Michael: *The Marshall Plan*, Cambridge University Press, Cambridge, 1987.

Hofstadter, Richard: *The Emergence of the Two Party System*, University of California Press, Berkeley, 1969.

Hough, Jerry, and Merle Fainsod: *How the Soviet Union Is Governed*, Harvard University Press, Cambridge, 1979.

Human Development Report 1992, Oxford University Press, New York, 1992.

Hyland, William, and Richard Shyrock: *The Fall of Khrushchev*, Funk and Wagnalls, New York, 1968.

Inside Gorbachev's Kremlin: The Memoirs of Yegor Ligachev, translated by Catherine Fitzpatrick, Michele Berdy, Dobrochna Dyrcz-Freeman, Pantheon, New York, 1993.

Jackson, Gabriel: *The Spanish Republic and the Civil War, 1931–1939,* Princeton University Press, Princeton, 1969.

Jelavich, Charles and Barbara: *The Establishment of the Balkan Nation States 1804–1920,* University of Washington Press, Seattle and London, 1977.

Jones, Anthony, Walter Connor, and David Powell, editors: *Soviet Social Problems,* Westview Press, Boulder, Colorado, 1991.

——— and William Markoff, editors: *Perestroika and the Economy: New Thinking in Soviet Economics,* M.E. Sharpe, Armonk, New York, 1989.

Jorre, Georges: *The Soviet Union, Its Land and Its People,* John Wiley and Sons, New York, 1967.

Kahan, Arcadius: *Russian Economic History: The Nineteenth Century,* University of Chicago Press, Chicago, 1989.

Karklins, Rasma: *Ethnic Relations in the USSR,* Allen and Unwin, Boston, 1986.

Katkov, George: *The Trial of Bukharin,* Stein and Day, New York, 1969.

Katsnelson, Ira, and Aristide Zolberg, editors: *Working Class Formation,* Princeton University Press, Princeton, 1986.

Kelley, Donald, editor: *Soviet Politics in the Brezhnev Era,* Praeger, New York, 1980.

———, editor: *Soviet Politics From Brezhnev to Gorbachev,* Praeger, New York, 1987.

Kennan, George: *The Marquis de Custine and His Russia in 1839,* Princeton University Press, Princeton, 1971.

Khrushchev Remembers, translated by Strobe Talbott, Little Brown, Boston, 1974.

Khrushchev Speaks, University of Michigan Press, Ann Arbor, 1963.

Kilson, Martin, editor: *New States in the Modern World,* Harvard University Press, Cambridge, 1975.

Koenker, Diane, William Rosenberg, and Ronald Suny, editors: *State and Society in the Russian Civil War,* Indiana University Press, Bloomington, 1989.

Kolb, Eberhard: *The Weimar Republic,* Unwin, Hyman, London, 1988.

Kritsman, Lev: *Geroicheskii period russkoi revolutsii,* Gosizdat, Moscow, 1925.

Kuromiya, Hiroakia: *Stalin's Industrial Revolution,* Cambridge University Press, Cambridge, 1988.

Lang, David: *A Modern History of Soviet Georgia,* Grove Press, New York, 1962.

LaPalombara, Joseph: *Democracy: Italian Style,* Yale University Press, New Haven, 1987.

Lee, Su-hon: *State-Building in the Contemporary Third World,* Westview Press, Boulder, Colorado, 1988.

Leites, Nathan: *The Operational Code of the Politburo,* McGraw-Hill, New York, 1951.

Lewin, Moshe: *The Gorbachev Phenomenon,* University of California Press, Berkeley, 1989.

———: *Political Undercurrents in Soviet Economic Debates,* Princeton University Press, Princeton, 1974.

Lincoln, W. Bruce: *Red Victory,* Simon and Schuster, New York, 1989.

Lindblom, Charles: *Planning and Markets,* Yale University Press, New Haven, 1982.

Linden, Carl: *Khrushchev and the Soviet Leadership,* Johns Hopkins University Press, Baltimore, 1990.

Linz, Juan, and Arnold Stephens: *The Breakdown of Democratic Regimes,* Johns Hopkins University Press, Baltimore and London, 1978.

Linz, Susan, editor: *The Impact of World War II on the Soviet Union,* Rowman and Allanheld, Totowa, New Jersey, 1985.

Lipset, Seymour Martin: *The First New Nation,* Basic Books, New York, 1959.

Little, David: *Ukraine: The Legacy of Intolerance,* U.S. Institute of Peace, Washington, D.C., 1991.

Lubachenko, Ivan: *Belorussia Under Soviet Rule, 1917–1957,* University of Kentucky Press, Lexington, 1972.

Luckett, Richard: *The White Generals,* Viking Press, New York, 1971.

Macauley, Martin, editor: *Khrushchev and Khrushchevism,* Indiana University Press, Bloomington, 1987.

————, editor: *The Soviet Union After Brezhnev,* Holmes and Meier, New York, 1983.

Maddison, Angus: *Dynamic Forces in Capitalist Development,* Oxford University Press, Oxford, 1991.

Maier, Charles, and Gunter Bischof, editors: *The Marshall Plan and Germany,* Berg Publications, New York, 1991.

Malloy, James, and Mitchell Seligson, editors: *Authoritarians and Democrats: Regime Transition in Latin America,* University of Pittsburgh Press, Pittsburgh, 1987.

Mandel, David: *Petrograd Workers and the October Revolution,* St. Martin's Press, New York, 1981.

Mann, Dawn: *Paradoxes of Soviet Reform: The Nineteenth Party Conference,* Center for Strategic and International Studies, Washington, D.C., 1988.

Marcus, Steven: *Engels, Manchester and the English Working Class,* Random House, New York, 1974.

Marples, David: *Ukraine Under Perestroika,* St. Martin's Press, New York, 1991.

Marx, Karl, and Frederick Engels: *The Communist Manifesto,* Penguin, London, 1967.

Mawdsley, Evan: *The Russian Civil War,* Allen and Unwin, Boston, 1987.

Mazour, Anatole: *The First Russian Revolution 1825,* Stanford University Press, Stanford, 1944.

McKenzie, John: *Weimar Germany 1918–1933,* Rowman and Allanheld, Totowa, New Jersey, 1971.

Medvedev, Roy: *Let History Judge,* translated by Colleen Taylor, Alfred Knopf, New York, 1972.

———— and Giulietto Chiesa: *Time of Change,* translated by Michael Moore, Pantheon, New York, 1989.

———— and Zhores Medvedev: *Khrushchev: The Years in Power,* translated by Andrew Durkin, Columbia University Press, New York, 1976.

Medvedev, Zhores: *Andropov,* W.W. Norton, New York, 1984.

————: *Gorbachev,* W.W. Norton, New York, 1986.

Millar, James, editor: *Politics, Work and Daily Life in the USSR,* Cambridge University Press, Cambridge, 1987.

Milward, Alan: *The Reconstruction of Western Europe, 1945–51,* University of California Press, Berkeley and Los Angeles, 1984.

Moore, Barrington: *Social Origins of Dictatorship and Democracy,* Beacon Press, Boston, 1965.

Motyl, Alexander: *Will the Non-Russians Rebel?* Cornell University Press, Ithaca, 1991.

Murphy, Paul: *Brezhnev: Soviet Politician,* McFarland and Company, Jefferson, North Carolina, 1981.

Nagle, John: *Introduction to Comparative Politics,* Nelson Hall, Chicago, 1993.

Nogee, Joseph, editor: *Soviet Politics: Russia After Brezhnev,* Praeger, New York, 1985.

Nove, Alec: *An Economic History of the USSR,* Penguin Books, Harmondworth, England, 1969.

————: *Glasnost in Action,* Unwin, Hyman, Boston, 1989.

————: *Stalinism and After,* Allen and Unwin, London, 1979.

O'Donnell, Guillermo, and Philippe Schmitter: *Transitions From Authoritarian Rule,* Johns Hopkins University Press, Baltimore, 1986.

Pares, Bernard: *A History of Russia,* Alfred Knopf, New York, 1947.

Paxton, Robert: *Vichy France,* Alfred Knopf, New York, 1972.

Pelling, Henry: *Britain and the Marshall Plan,* St. Martin's Press, New York, 1988.

Pipes, Richard: *Russia Under the Old Regime,* Charles Scribner's Sons, New York, 1974.

Preston, Paul: *The Coming of the Spanish Civil War,* Harper and Row, New York, 1978.

Pye, Lucien: *Politics, Personality and Nation Building: Burma's Search For Identity,* Yale University Press, New Haven, 1966.

Rabinowitch, Alexander: *The Bolsheviks Come to Power: The Revolution of 1917 in Petrograd,* W.W. Norton, New York, 1978.

———: *Petrograd Bolsheviks and the July 1917 Uprising,* Indiana University Press, Bloomington, 1968.

Rakowska-Harmstone, Teresa: *Russia and Nationalism in Central Asia,* Johns Hopkins University Press, Baltimore and London, 1970.

Rokkan, Stein, *et al.: Citizens, Elections, Parties,* McKay, New York, 1970.

Rothschild, Joseph: *East Central Europe Between the Two World Wars,* University of Washington Press, Seattle and New York, 1974.

———: *Ethnopolitics,* Columbia University Press, New York, 1981.

———: *Return to Diversity: A Political History of East Central Europe Since World War II,* Oxford University Press, New York, 1989.

Rudnytsky, Ivan: *Essays in Modern Ukrainian History,* Harvard University Press, Cambridge, 1987.

Rule, John: *The Laboring Classes in Early Industrial England 1750–1850,* Longmans, London and New York, 1986.

Ryan, Michael, and Richard Prentice: *Social Trends in the Soviet Union From 1950,* St. Martin's Press, New York, 1987.

Rywkin, Michael: *Moscow's Muslim Challenge,* M.E. Sharpe, Armonk, New York, 1982.

———, editor: *Russian Colonial Expansion to 1917,* Mansell Publishing Ltd., London and New York, 1988.

Sablinsky, Walter: *The Road to Bloody Sunday,* Princeton University Press, Princeton, 1976.

Salisbury, Harrison: *The 900 Days: The Siege of Leningrad,* Harper and Row, New York, 1989.

Schapiro, Leonard, and Peter Reddaway, editors: *Lenin: The Man, The Theorist, The Leader,* Praeger, New York, 1967.

Schick, Irving, and Ertuguil Tonak, editors: *Turkey in Transition,* Oxford University Press, New York, 1987.

Schmidt-Hauer, Christian: *Gorbachev: The Path to Power,* translated by Ewald Osers and Chris Romber, Salem House, Topsfield, Massachusetts, 1986.

Schumpeter, Joseph: *Capitalism, Socialism and Democracy,* Harper and Row, New York, 1975.

Schwartz, Donald, editor: *Resolutions and Decisions of the Communist Party of the Soviet Union,* vol. 5 (*The Brezhnev Years*), University of Toronto Press, Toronto, 1982.

Shanin, Teodor: *The Awkward Class,* Cambridge University Press, Cambridge, 1972.

Shlapentokh, Vladimir: *Public and Private Life of the Soviet People,* Oxford University Press, New York, 1989.

Skocpol, Theda: *States and Social Revolutions,* Cambridge University Press, Cambridge, 1979.

Smith, Anthony: *The Ethnic Origins of Nations,* Basil Blackwell, New York, 1986.

Smith, Graham, editor: *The Nationalities Question in the Soviet Union,* Longmans, London and New York, 1990.

Solovyov, Vladimir, and Elena Klepikova: *Boris Yeltsin,* G.P. Putnam's Sons, New York, 1992.

Solzhenitsyn, Alexander: *The Gulag Archipelago,* 3 volumes, translation, Harper and Row, New York, 1974–1985.

Spoots, Frederic, and Theodor Wiesner: *Italy: A Different Democracy,* Cambridge University Press, Cambridge, 1986.

Sovetskaya voennaya entsiklopedia, Voenizdat, Moscow, 1978.

Spulber, Nicholas: *Restructuring the Soviet Economy,* University of Michigan Press, Ann Arbor, 1991.

Stalin, Joseph: *Works,* Foreign Languages Publishing House, Moscow, 1955.

Starr, S. Frederick: *Prospects for Stable Democracy in Russia,* Mershon Center Occasional Papers, Ohio State University, Columbus, 1992.

Stavrou, Theofanis, editor: *Russia Under the Last Tsar,* University of Minnesota Press, Minneapolis, 1969.

Steele, Jonathan, and Eric Abraham: *Andropov in Power,* Doubleday, Garden City, New York, 1984.

Subtelny, Orest: *Ukraine: A History,* University of Toronto Press, Toronto, 1988.

Suny, Ronald: *The Making of the Georgian Nation,* Indiana University Press, Bloomington, 1988.

Swietochowski, Tadeusz: *Russian Azerbaijan, 1905–1920,* Cambridge University Press, Cambridge, 1985.

Tachau, Frank, editor: *The Developing Nations: What Path to Modernization,* Dodd, Mead and Company, New York, 1974.

Terkel, Studs: *The Good War: An Oral History of World War II,* Pantheon, New York, 1984.

Thomas, Caroline, and Paikiusothy, editors: *The State and Instability in the South,* St. Martin's Press, New York, 1989.

Thompson, E.P.: *The Making of the English Working Class,* Vintage Books, New York, 1966.

Tilly, Charles: *The Formation of the Modern European State System,* Princeton University Press, Princeton, 1975.

The Transition to Democracy: Proceedings of a Workshop, National Academy Press, Washington, D.C., 1991.

Treadgold, Donald: *Twentieth Century Russia,* Rand McNally, Chicago, 1964.

Trotsky, Leon: *1905,* translated by Anya Bostock, Random House, New York, 1971.

Tucker, Robert: *Stalin As Revolutionary, 1879–1929: A Study in History and Personality,* W.W. Norton, New York, 1973.

————: *Stalin In Power: The Revolution From Above, 1928–1941,* W.W. Norton, New York, 1990.

Turnock, David: *Eastern Europe: An Economic and Political Geography,* Routledge, London, 1989.

Ulam, Adam: *Stalin: The Man and His Era,* Viking, New York, 1973.

Vakar, Nicholas: *Belorussia: The Making of a Nation,* Harvard University Press, Cambridge, 1956.

Verhanen, Tatu: *The Process of Democratization,* Taylor and Francis, New York, 1989.

Van Goudoever, Albert: *The Limits of DeStalinization in the Soviet Union,* translated by Frans Hijkoop, St. Martin's Press, New York, 1986.

Von Laue, Theodore: *Why Lenin? Why Stalin?* J.P. Lippincott, Philadelphia, 1974.

Walker, Christopher: *Armenia: The Survival of a Nation,* St. Martin's Press, New York, 1980.

Weiner, Myron, and Ergun Ozbudun, editors: *Competitive Elections in Developing Countries,* Duke University Press, Durham, North Carolina, 1987.

Werth, Alexander: *Russia at War, 1941–1945,* Dutton, New York, 1964.

Wexler, Immanuel: *The Marshall Plan Revisited,* Greenwood Press, Westport, Connecticut, 1983.

Wheeler, Douglas: *Republican Portugal: A Political History 1910–1926,* University of Wisconsin Press, Madison, 1978.

Wheeler, Geoffrey: *The Modern History of Soviet Central Asia,* Praeger, New York, 1964.

White, Stephen: *Gorbachev in Power,* Cambridge University Press, Cambridge, 1990.

———: *Gorbachev and After,* Cambridge University Press, Cambridge, 1992.

Wiarda, Howard: *Politics in Iberia,* Harper Collins, New York, 1993.

Wildman, Allan: *The End of the Russian Imperial Army,* Princeton University Press, Princeton, 1980.

Wittfogel, Karl: *Oriental Despotism,* Yale University Press, New Haven, 1957.

Wittlin, Tadeusz: *Commissar,* Macmillan, New York, 1970.

World Bank, OECD, IMF and the European Bank of Reconstruction and Development: *A Study of the Soviet Economy,* OECD, Washington, D.C., 1991.

Zemstov, Ilya: *Chernenko: The Last Bolshevik,* Transaction Books, New Brunswick, New Jersey, 1989.

Index